Battle Prayer
for Divine Healing
Field Manual 2

DEDICATION

I've been there. I got the call and, with my wife, rushed to the hospital in a panic. I did not know what to do to bring success, but we did enough right things so that, in my ignorance, God was able to be merciful and healed. But I've also been there when God did not heal, when His mercy was not evident. Since then I learned that God has answers and have now seen Him be our help in powerfully answered divine healing prayers.

This book is dedicated to all those who have a sudden report of bad news and need to get answers from God to get someone healed. It might be a loved one or it might be you yourself. No longer do you have to shout in your heart, "Where is my help in God?"

As Jesus is the Living Word of God, God's answer has always been the same: Ps 107:19 "Then they cry unto the Lord in their trouble, and he saveth them out of their distresses. 20 He sent his word, and healed them, and delivered them from their destructions. 21 Oh that men would praise the Lord for his *chesed*/goodness (*grace and love*), and for his wonderful works to the children of men!" God's answer is to get you to rightly divide His Word so that you can work with Him to provide a path through which He can deliver the needed divine healing. Make that path, and He will come!

This book is designed for the new believer, for anyone who has forgotten God's attitude concerning healing, or for anyone desiring to learn and keep fresh these living truths for divine healing—or any other need for that matter.

Acknowledgments

I thank the ever-faithful **Lord Jesus Christ of Nazareth**, who purchased me with His blood and now intercedes for me by the will of **Father God** and **Holy Spirit,** who dwells within me.

I also thank my wife, **Cindy**, and our children, **Christina and Jonathan**, who have been used of the Lord to show me His goodness and love. I also thank **Margie and Carroll Harlow** for being such good friends and for Margie's invaluable help in the proofing of this work.

Contents

Bible Book Abbreviations Used 9
About the Title 10
About the Use of the Author's Study Helps 11
Introduction 12

Part I: Salvation 19
    The Basic Gospel 21

Part II: Healing Teachings by John G. Lake 25
  1. God's Way of Healing 27
  2. Do You Know God's Way of Healing? 35
  3. A Sermon on Healing (Circa 1916) 39
  4. A Teaching on the Subject of Healing for the Body 42

Part III: Other Healing Teachings 49
  1. On Confidence and Washing 51
  2. On Mouth Power 59
  3. On Holiness 61
  4. On Two Ways to Power with God 69
  5. On Doubts Coming 82
  6. On Stirring Yourself Up 95
  7. On Faith 102
  8. On the New Covenant 111
  9. On the Word of God As Medicine 115
10. On the Believer's Qualifications 117
11. On the Laying On of Hands 119
12. On the Power of Agreement 121
13. On the Use of Prayer Cloths and Other Such Items 123
14. On Warrior Love 124
15. On How Your Faith Works 126
16. On Healing and Miracles 128

17. On Persistent Faith	130
18. On Continuous Prayer	132
19. On Why Some Aren't Healed	134
20. On Renewing Your Mind	143
21. On Mental Assent	158
22. On Faith Building	165
23. On Power Levels	183
24. On Warrior Techniques	185
25. On Doing Our Part	190
26. On Who Does the Healing	206
27. On Propitiation and Communion	212
A Final Prayer and Confession	226

PART IV: FAITH-BUILDING SCRIPTURES 231
  1. The Healing Scriptures 233
  2. Why Jesus Came Scriptures 311
  3. The Blood of Jesus Scriptures 359

PART V: THE MINISTER'S CONFESSION 371
  Prayers and Confessions of Preparation 373

PART VI: THE BATTLE PRAYER 417
  1. Beginning the Battle Prayer 419
  2. THE BATTLE PRAYER 427
  3. Repeating the Battle Prayer 483

PART VII: A SUMMARY 493
  Some Conclusions 495

APPENDICES 509
  Recommended Reading 510
  Glossary Contents 511
  A Glossary of Oft-Misunderstood Biblical Words 512
  Bibliography 576

  Ministry Page 577

Bible Book Abbreviations Used

For Old Testament Books

Gen	Genesis	Eccl	Ecclesiastes
Ex	Exodus	Song	Song of Solomon
Lev	Leviticus	Isa	Isaiah
Num	Numbers	Jer	Jeremiah
Deut	Deuteronomy	Lam	Lamentations
Josh	Joshua	Ezek	Ezekiel
Judg	Judges	Dan	Daniel
Ruth	Ruth	Hos	Hosea
1 Sam	1 Samuel	Joel	Joel
2 Sam	2 Samuel	Am	Amos
1 Kings	1 Kings	Ob	Obadiah
2 Kings	2 Kings	Jon	Jonah
1 Chron	1 Chronicles	Mic	Micah
2 Chron	2 Chronicles	Nah	Nahum
Ezra	Ezra	Hab	Habakkuk
Neh	Nehemiah	Zeph	Zephaniah
Esther	Esther	Hag	Haggai
Job	Job	Zech	Zechariah
Ps	Psalms	Mal	Malachi
Prov	Proverbs		

For New Testament Books

Matt	Matthew	1 Tim	1 Timothy
Mark	Mark	2 Tim	2 Timothy
Luke	Luke	Titus	Titus
John	John	Philem	Philemon
Acts	Acts	Heb	Hebrews
Rom	Romans	James	James
1 Cor	1 Corinthians	1 Pet	1 Peter
2 Cor	2 Corinthians	2 Pet	2 Peter
Gal	Galatians	1 John	1 John
Eph	Ephesians	2 John	2 John
Phil	Philippians	3 John	3 John
Col	Colossians	Jude	Jude
1 Thes	1 Thessalonians	Rev	Revelation
2 Thes	2 Thessalonians		

EXAMPLE: 2 Cor 5:17 refers to the book, 2 Corinthians and the scripture found in chapter 5, verse 17. 2 Cor 5:17-6:2 refers to the book 2 Corinthians with the passage starting at chapter 5, verse 17 and going through to chapter 6, verse 2 of that book.

About the Title

Battle Prayer: The Bible is full of military analogies and attitudes. We are told to 1 Tim 6:12 "fight the good fight of faith, *lambano*/lay hold on eternal *zoe*/life … ." That word *lambano* means to hold on and not let go as a way to fight in faith. Part of that includes for you to hold on in the face of evil circumstances on the outside, terrors on the inside and people telling you, "There is no hope in God."

We are also told in military terms: 1 Cor 15:57 "But thanks be to God, which giveth us the victory through our Lord Jesus Christ. 58 Therefore, my *agape*/beloved brethren, be ye stedfast, unmoveable, always abounding in the work of the Lord, forasmuch as ye know that your labour is not in vain in the Lord." "Victory," "stedfast," and "unmovable" are military terms. "Labour" is just that, hard work. Ephesians 6 is also full of military terms on fighting the devil with prayer and a right attitude.

So there is the attitude of the warrior in divine healing, an attitude that fights to win over God's and our enemy. You can still have victory when you do not get the instant answer in prayer, so the focus of the title is for you to enter the battle and fight. With God's help and Word, you will be steadfast and unmovable until you get the victory promised you. He will strengthen you as you exercise the love, care and courage to fight and win in the name of Jesus. This manual is designed to show you an effective way to use the name of Jesus to set captives free in a prayer battle.

Field Manual 2 (FM2): *Field Manual 1* (FM1) is a much smaller version of this same material. It consists of a few teachings on healing, the Minister's Confession and the Battle Prayer. In size, it is a quarter-page format (4.5 by 5.5 inches) and about 1/2 inch thick, so that it fits nicely into a woman's purse and can be used for ministry at hospitals. Pastors started to use the FM1, with great success, but gradually they requested more material, so they could use it for teaching and longer times of personal spiritual development. So, we added teaching sections, healing scriptures, more faith-building affirmations, and a glossary of commonly misunderstood Bible terms. All this additional material was aimed for a deeper understanding of God's healing promises and to build confidence, per 1 John 5:14 "And this is the confidence that we have in him, that, if we *aiteo*/ask any thing according to his will, he heareth us: 15 and if we know that he hear us, whatsoever we *aiteo*/ask, we know that we have the *aiteo*/petitions that we *aiteo*/desired of him." Thus, *Field Manual 2* was born.

ABOUT THE USE OF THE AUTHOR'S STUDY HELPS

Wherever a Scripture reference is underlined, any adjustments in tense, person, count or additions are italicized. This identifies what has been modified or added to the original translation's text. The original language Old or New Testament (i.e., Hebrew or Greek) words are added occasionally for emphasis in the format of *aiteo* or *aiteo*/ask.

Capitalization: Multiple scriptures after the same reference have the capitalization adjusted where there is no capitalization across verses, after commas, colons and semicolons except when the new word is either someone speaking or a quote from another part of the Bible.

Quotation Marks Around Scripture: Not used at the option of the author when in a prayer, affirmation, confession or a list of scriptures such as in the Healing Affirmations section (see prayer example below). When no quotation marks are used, any added words between or after the scriptures are in italics to the end of the paragraph, as in the example below.

Additional meanings and expansions within Scripture are in parentheses and in italics. Also inserted implications are in brackets and in italics. Occasionally the punctuation is changed to fit the content.

For Example: Heb 3:12-13 as a prayer becomes: **Father, in the name of Jesus**, work in us so that I and those I pray for Heb 3:12 take heed, *among the* brethren, lest there be in any of *us* an evil heart of unbelief (*unpersuadableness, offense or lack of confidence*), in departing from *You, Father,* the *zao*/living God. 13 But *by Your grace in us we* exhort one another daily, while it is called To day; lest any of *us* be hardened through the deceitfulness of sin [*in corrupt thoughts, words and actions in believing that God is not your friend, helper, near or that His word cannot fail, and thus living in the mind of the carnal flesh and not in the spirit by the Word of God*]. *Thank You Father. In the name of Jesus, thank You!*

HOLY SPIRIT: You will notice that there is no "the" in addressing or describing Holy Spirit where written by the author. Holy Spirit is the third person of the Godhead; Holy Spirit is His revealed name. He is not an "it" but a person. The article *the* is not in the original Greek and, unless within the particular translation used, it is not used by the author to address Him. The King James Version often translates the Greek word *pneuma* as *ghost* or *spirit*. Holy Spirit is used by the author rather than Holy Ghost, recognizing that both are the same word.

INTRODUCTION

If you are in a crisis, go straight to **The Battle Prayer**. Then read the rest of the manual later, as there is much fear-destroying, and faith-building material contained in it.

The wonder of Heaven is that it has no misery of any kind. God reigns there, and all is well. When God can find a human who agrees with Him, then that person and God bring Heaven to Earth. Jesus is that Man, and He dwells in the Christian by Holy Spirit to do the same thing today.

Bringing this to pass is the experiential, vital, or living portion of the salvation Jesus obtained for us. Healing and wholeness of every kind are included. God is eager to bring it to Earth now and not wait until the days of Revelation 21 and 22.

The scary truth is that there is not a shortage of information, but a shortage of application to doing that makes the difference. This is true "knowing," not as a student, but as a skilled workman.

John 6:38 For I (*Jesus*) came down from heaven, not to do mine own will, but the will of him that sent me.

Col 1:26 Even the mystery which hath been hid from ages and from generations, but now is made manifest to his saints: 27 to whom God would make known what is the riches of the glory of this mystery among the Gentiles; **which is Christ in you**, the hope of glory: 28 whom we preach, warning every man, and teaching every man in all wisdom; that we may present every man perfect in Christ Jesus: 29 whereunto I also labour, striving according to his working, which worketh in me mightily.

2 Cor 13:5 Examine yourselves, whether ye be in the faith; prove your own selves. Know ye not your own selves, how that **Jesus Christ is in you**, except ye be reprobates?

Philem 6 That the communication (*outworking*) of thy faith may become effectual (*bringing Heaven to Earth in power*) by the *epignosis*/acknowledging (*knowing and experiencing as a master craftsman*) of every good thing which is in you in Christ Jesus.

Heb 13:8 Jesus Christ the same yesterday, and to day, and for ever.

Every time we pray to Father God in the name of Jesus, we are engaged in a battle that started before the Fall of Adam, and will end as described in Revelation 21 and 22. We are to overcome the devil and all his works, and this is our fight. We are commanded: 1 Tim 6:12 "Fight the good fight of faith, *lambano*/lay hold (*take, seize and hold tightly*) on eternal *zoe*/life, whereunto thou art also called…"

Note: The primary purpose of this book is to provide scriptural ideas and God's Word as prayer in the assurance that these are His will, so that the one who prays may have confidence that God will hear their prayers and will do them, as they remain in faith according to: 1 John 5:14 "And this is the confidence that we have in him, that, if we *aiteo*/ask (*keep on asking*) any thing according to his will, he heareth us: 15 and if we know that he hear us, whatsoever we *aiteo*/ask (*demand, require and expect as due by covenant promise*), we know that we have the *aiteo*/petitions that we *aiteo*/desired of him."

Jesus was sent to show the real nature of Father God: Heb 1:1 "God, who at sundry times and in divers manners spake in time past unto the fathers by the prophets, 2 hath in these last days spoken unto us by his Son, whom he hath appointed heir of all things, by whom also he made the worlds; 3 who being the brightness of *the Father's* glory, and the express image of *the Father's* person, and upholding all things by the word of his power, when he had by himself purged our sins, sat down on the right hand of the Majesty on high;" *Purged* means "destroyed, dissolved and fully removed." Acts 10:43 "To him (*Jesus*) give all the prophets witness, that through his name whosoever believeth in him shall receive remission (*purging*) of sins."

Rather than focusing on gifts, impartations, anointings or a special ministry of healing, this manual emphasizes obtaining healing based on believing in the anointing in and on the Word of God. Ps 107:20 "He sent his word, and healed them, and delivered them from their destructions. 21 Oh that men would praise the Lord for his *chesed*/goodness, and for his wonderful works to the children of men!" This makes healing available to every believer. God gives us, as Christians, the same Spirit that Jesus had, and this is for the same purpose, to continue doing what Jesus started 2000 years ago.

This manual is designed to be used either at the bedside of a sick one, outside in a waiting room, or even thousands of miles away, knowing that someone is in need, or for yourself.

If you are in a hospital, you may find others also asking for prayer for their loved ones. Do what James 5:16 directs. James 5:16 "Confess your faults one to another, and pray one for another, that ye may be healed. The effectual fervent prayer of a righteous man availeth much." You can include others who are in critical condition even as you pray for the one you started with. As you sow healing, you will reap healing: Gal 6:7 "Be not deceived; God is not mocked: for whatsoever a man soweth, that shall he also reap. 8 For he that soweth to his flesh shall of the flesh reap corruption; but he that soweth to the Spirit shall of the Spirit reap *zoe/ life everlasting.* 9 And let us not be weary in well doing: for in due season we shall reap, if we faint not. 10 As we have therefore opportunity, let us do good unto all men, especially unto them who are of the household of faith." There are no free sins; Jesus suffered for each one, so blessing includes continually sowing good in order to reap good.

This is a practical field manual for doing and not just a theological discussion. Most explanations lead to application, to actually doing it. The introduction describes how to use the book. Next comes a brief discussion of salvation and a salvation prayer. The first teaching section is based on the writings of Dr. John G. Lake, a man who ministered divine healing from about 1900-1935 (more on him and his successful healing ministry later). These are followed by some of my own teachings. Next are sections of Scriptures on Healing, Why Jesus Came, and The Blood of Jesus. The Minister Confession is designed for daily use, to build your heart confidence in God through spoken repetition of His anointed Word and affirmations of Christ in you. The section called Beginning the Battle Prayer is for preparation. The Battle Prayer itself has 28 different prayers, some short and some long. Together they provide tools to minister for seconds, minutes, hours, days or weeks—as necessary. Next is a discussion on Repeated Prayer. The final section is a Glossary with working definitions of various Bible words.

The Battle Prayer for Divine Healing got its start when I began to take a very effective, short healing prayer, based on Rev. Jay Snell's prayer as recorded in our book, *The Prayer Cards,* and expand it for mind-renewing purposes in those situations when it seemed that God required longer prayer to bring results, or as I needed to stir myself up for battle to extend the Kingdom of God so that I could use shorter prayers.

I have been involved in cases in which, as I prayed, vital signs stabilized and improved, but when I stopped, the person got worse. So how do we persevere in prayer when we are tempted to stop and add the faithless phrase "if it be thy will" so that we can go on to sleep, and if the person dies, to say, "It must have been God's will" or accept defeat if the answer does not come soon enough or even if the person we are praying for stops breathing? The answer is what John Lake discovered: don't stop and don't give up, resist the devil and he will flee! This manual provides the prayers, teaching, and techniques to stay in the battle and win. Jesus paid the price for us to win, and we can ... if we are willing to stay in the battle. Faint not!

As I started to recall from the Scriptures that God's will is always to heal or save (*sozo*: "healed, made whole in every way") from any oppression of the devil, I started listing mind-renewing scriptures: John 6:38 "For I (*Jesus*) came down from heaven, not to do mine own will, but the will of him that sent me." Acts 10:38 "How God anointed Jesus of Nazareth with the Holy Ghost and with power: who went about (*random walking*) doing good, and healing all that were oppressed (*under the active dominion, reign or lordship*) of the devil; for God was with him."

Note there are several original Old and New Testament words that we put next to the translated English word to remind us of what the real word is. Usually the original language is much stronger in emphasis than our English words, either the KJV or the modern. Often, in italics, behind the word, will be alternate translations, expansions, or interpretations of the word or phrase. I suggest using *Vine's Expository Dictionaries of Old and New Testament Words* for additional study.

Bible quotations in this book are derived from the King James Version unless otherwise noted. (References are included.) They are sometimes personalized, paraphrased, or abridged to facilitate clarity and encourage individual application. We have taken the liberty of confirming them in structure, to the person and tense of their contextual application. This is often seen in the prayers and confessions throughout this book.

Speak Out Loud: So how do I use the Battle Prayer? It is used out loud and, because of the extensive Scriptures, at the same time it is also a method for me to "stir-up" myself into what God has given me though Jesus Christ, and thereby make my faith effective here on the Earth: Philem 6 "That the communication of thy faith may become effectual by the acknowledging of every good thing which is in you in Christ Jesus." Thus my confidence or faith grows as I use the Battle Prayer. 1 John 5:13 "These things have I written unto you that believe on the name of the Son of God; that ye may know that ye have eternal *zoe*/life, and that ye may believe on the name of the Son of God. 14 And this is the confidence that we have in him, that, if we *aiteo*/ask (*by demanding, expecting as due by covenant promise*) any thing according to his will, he heareth us: 15 and if we know that he hear us, whatsoever we *aiteo*/ask (*by demanding, expecting as due by covenant promise*), we know that we have the petitions that we *aiteo*/desired of him." If the situation does not allow speaking out loud, you can do it silently, but for most, it is harder to maintain concentration.

Reconciliation Ministry: The ministry for all Christians is to bring the reconciliation of Jesus into every situation. 2 Cor 5:18 "And all things are of God, who hath reconciled us to himself by Jesus Christ, and hath given to us the ministry of reconciliation; 19 to wit, that God was in Christ, reconciling the world unto himself, not imputing their trespasses unto them; and hath committed unto us the word of reconciliation." (*Reconciliation* as an accounting term means "to bring into agreement.") In this ministry, we are bringing the healing blessing of Heaven to the Earth to match God's Word accomplished in the stripes of Jesus.

2 Cor 4:6 "For God, who commanded the light to shine out of darkness, hath shined in our hearts, to give the light of the knowledge of the glory of God in the face of Jesus Christ. 7 But we have this treasure in earthen vessels, that the excellency of the *dunamis*/power (*ability*) may be of God, and not of us." Notice that this knowledge is actually power = the ability to get things done in Jesus! As Christians, the power of God is in us! So as we grow in knowledge of the truth in Jesus we reconcile the evils of this Earth to the blessings of Heaven, and people get healed in the name of Jesus. This is how we destroy the works of the devil.

Ministry for Others: The ministry of Jesus was indiscriminate in the sense that He denied no Jew healing, and if a Gentile requested it, He also healed them. Jesus is Lord of Heaven and Earth. Ps 24:1"The earth is the LORD's, and the fulness thereof; the world, and they that dwell therein." 1 Cor 10:26 "For the earth is the Lord's, and the fulness thereof." Ps 50:12 "If I (*God*) were hungry, I would not tell thee: for the world is mine, and the fulness thereof." Healing is an act of God's authority over the created Earth and over all His created beings.

God gave Adam dominion over all the Earth for His sake. A human body is made of the dust of the Earth, and healing is just setting that dust free. Jesus exercised the Father's dominion in His ministry and then gave that job to the members of the Body of Christ in the Great Commission. When you minister healing to a person, whether they are aware of it or not, or in agreement or not, you are exercising the dominion of Jesus on the Earth for the Father's sake and executing the judgment of God against the devil. When Jesus raised the dead boy in Nain, He went against the will of the mother, the boy, and the whole town. No one asked Him to raise the boy. He did it in His ministry against the devil and for people because God *agape*/loves people. Acts 10:36 "The word which God sent unto the children of Israel, preaching peace by Jesus Christ: (he is Lord of all:) 37 that word, I say, ye know, which was published throughout all Judaea, and began from Galilee, after the baptism which John preached; 38 how God anointed Jesus of Nazareth with the Holy Ghost and with power: who went about doing good, and healing all that were oppressed (*under the active dominion, reign or lordship*) of the devil; for God was with him." This is crushing the works of the devil on Earth.

That Word of God manifested by Jesus was God executing the judgment of the devil declared in Genesis. Gen 3:15 "And I will put enmity between thee (*Satan*) and the woman, and between thy seed and her seed; it shall bruise (*crush*) thy head (*lordship and power on Earth*), and thou shalt bruise his heel." God, Ps 103:3 "who forgiveth all thine iniquities; who healeth all thy diseases; ... 6 The Lord executeth righteousness and judgment for all that are oppressed." When a Christian exercises the authority in the name of Jesus against the devil, the issue is between God and the devil, and the person maimed or diseased in any way is the devil's victim to be set free. You minister healing by faith in the name of Jesus for the Father's sake. As in a good police or military rescue, the victim's faith is not really the issue.

As a Christian, a Christ-like-one, a member of the body of Christ, a new creation in Christ, I am an agent God uses to release His glory into the Earth. I make the path for Him to operate: Mark 16:20 "And they went forth, and preached everywhere, the Lord working with them, and confirming the word with signs following. Amen." The more I do, the more glory I will see. The more you do, the more glory you will see.

Jesus, by Holy Spirit, does the healing in confirming His Word. The more our words and intentions line up with Him, the more He can do through us. Eph 4:17 "This I say therefore, and testify in the Lord, that ye henceforth walk not as other Gentiles walk, in the vanity of their mind, 18 having the understanding darkened, being alienated from the *zoe*/life of God through the ignorance that is in them, because of the blindness of their heart." Friendship with *zoe*/life = healing!

Dr. John Lake (1870-1935) was unique in that not only did he have an extraordinary healing ministry of over 100,000 people healed in five years (that is 20,000 a year or 80 healed a day, and each of these had a valid diagnosis of the disorder and a valid follow-up showing that the disorder was healed) but he was also unique in that he was also able to train other people to minister divine healing. He discovered that an accurate knowledge of Scriptures released born-again people to deliver God's healing power—not by impartation, not by special gifting or anointing, but by education and practice. So once you get more accurate teaching, go lay hands on and pray for the sick in the name of Jesus. This manual is designed to give the necessary information so that you can make the difference in the life of whoever you are ministering healing to. I have proven this to be true in my own life, and the same is true for all those who have grasped the teaching.

Truth works if you work it. John 8:31 "Then said Jesus to those Jews which believed on him, If ye continue in my word, then are ye my disciples indeed; 32 And ye shall know the truth, and the truth shall make you free (*to be and do all that God has made you to be*)." James 1:22 "But be ye doers of the word, and not hearers only, deceiving your own selves." Mere study without action leads to deception.

This is not about feeling but about knowing the facts of redemption, salvation, righteousness, sanctification, adoption and *zoe*/life in spite of your feelings. 2 Cor 5:7 "For we walk by faith, not by sight." Pray to get started, and then start doing it. Use the prayer below to get going. John Lake said, "It is a fact of the human mind that you can act your way into believing quicker than you can believe your way into acting." (Blake, *The Voice of Healing*, Episode 1.) To develop your believing, study to go and do, and then don't stop until you win in Jesus.

We do the laying on of hands and the commanding, and God does the healing. Our job is to believe that God wants the person healed because He loves them and that we are His agent. The words we employ are not all that important, except for the use of the name of Jesus. What is critical is knowing that you speak for God. Use this manual to get the facts straight, and then go minister life as needed. No amount of explanation can accomplish what actually doing it will teach you. Holy Spirit is your teacher, so trust Him.

Faith is deciding God is not a liar and to praise Him for His truth. When doubts come, repeat His Word and praise Him for His truth. Nothing is greater than God, for God is greater than all that is.

Father, in the name of Jesus, get me to speak Jesus' Word more effectively so that Jesus can do more healing through me. Acts 14:3 "Long time therefore abode they speaking boldly in the Lord, which gave testimony unto the word of his grace, and granted signs and wonders to be done by their hands." Father, use this manual to grow me in the knowledge of Your grace, Yourself, Holy Spirit and Jesus Christ, to walk in *agape*/love, and to demonstrate Your *agape*/love for all men in Your great work in Jesus by the cross. Heal me of all lying vanities against You. Set me free of dreadful fear and set me into confidence in You and Your power. Thank You, Father. In the name of Jesus, thank You.

NOTE: Please notice that for any situation in which you need God's help, a small change in the wording to the prayers or commands in this manual for healing will suffice. The principles are the same. Just find the appropriate scriptures and modify the prayers as needed. For example, for financial needs, just change the wording from physical healing to financial prosperity, for all of the abundance of God for Heaven on Earth is included in the word *soteria*/salvation.

Donald C. Mann
Landenberg, Pennsylvania

PART I

SALVATION

So shall my word be that goeth forth out of my mouth: it shall not return unto me void, but it shall accomplish that which I please, and it shall prosper in the thing whereto I sent it. (Isa 55:11)

THE BASIC GOSPEL

Here is the basic Gospel: You can only be right with the God of all creation and enter His great love plan for you through Jesus Christ: John 14:6 "Jesus saith unto him, I am the way, the truth, and the *zoe*/life: no man cometh unto the Father, but by me. 7 If ye had known me, ye should have known my Father also: and from henceforth ye know him, and have seen him." If you want to know what Father God is really like, just look at Jesus.

Rom 4:24 "But for us also, to whom (*righteousness with God*) shall be imputed, if we believe on him that raised up Jesus our Lord from the dead; 25 who was delivered for our offences, and was raised again for our justification (*being made just as if you had never sinned or will sin again to right standing as a joint heir with Jesus as a son of God*)."

1 Cor 15:1 "Moreover, brethren, I declare unto you the gospel which I preached unto you, which also ye have received, and wherein ye stand; 2 by which also ye are (*being*) *sozo*/saved, if ye keep in memory what I preached unto you, unless ye have believed in vain. 3 For I delivered unto you first of all that which I also received, how that Christ died for our sins according to the scriptures; 4 and that he was buried, and that he rose again the third day according to the scriptures." And this same Jesus is now seated at the right hand of the Father.

Rom 10:8 "But what saith it? The word is nigh thee, even in thy mouth, and in thy heart: that is, the word of faith, which we preach; 9 that if thou shalt confess with thy mouth the Lord Jesus, and shalt believe in thine heart that God hath raised him from the dead, thou shalt be *sozo*/saved. 10 For with the heart man believeth unto righteousness; and with the mouth confession is made unto *soteria*/salvation. 11 For the scripture saith, Whosoever believeth on him shall not be ashamed."

A Salvation Prayer: "Lord Jesus, I believe You died for my sins, were buried and were raised by Father God on the third day for my justification according to the Scriptures. Jesus, You are Lord. I make you Lord of my life. Come rule and reign in and through me, my King. Baptize me with Your Holy Spirit and fire. Heal every part of my life. Teach me Your truth in love that I may walk to Your glory. Amen! And thank You."

And a Simpler One: "Jesus, God raised You from the dead, You are Lord. Fill me with Your Spirit to walk in love. Thank You!"

Now that you are born again by the action of God in your spirit, the next step is for you to get water baptized. Matt 28:19 "Go ye therefore, and teach all nations, baptizing them in the name of the Father, and of the Son, and of the Holy Ghost:" You also need fellowship with other believers. We recommend you find a local Christian church to join, and get water baptized there.

If you want to know what God is really like, the Bible makes it very plain. Look to Jesus. Heb 1:1 "God, who at sundry times and in divers manners spake in time past unto the fathers by the prophets, 2 hath in these last days spoken unto us by his Son, whom he hath appointed heir of all things, by whom also he made the worlds; 3 who being the brightness of his glory, and the express image of his person, and upholding all things by the word of his power, when he had by himself purged (*remitted, obliterated, destroyed*) our sins, sat down on the right hand of the Majesty on high."

So whatever your view of God, He declares that the right view has to include all that Jesus is, not His people who obviously still fail, but Jesus Himself. Seeing Jesus in the gospels is the place to begin knowing what God is really like. Everything Jesus did was Father God in action. In and through Jesus, God set things the way He wants them. When this message becomes key to your life, you will be also: Col 1:12 "giving thanks (*continually*) unto the Father, which hath made us meet (*qualified and enabled us by grace*) to be partakers of the inheritance of the saints in light: 13 who hath delivered us from the power of darkness, and hath translated us into the kingdom of his *agape*/dear Son: 14 in whom we have redemption through his blood, even the forgiveness (*remission, purging, obliteration and putting away*) of sins: 15 who is the image of the invisible God, the firstborn of every creature."

Salvation has two parts, an eternal one with God and our life here on Earth now. The earthly process of salvation is how God finishes the job of making Heaven on Earth, and this is a key to the Lord's Prayer. Matt 6:9 "After this manner therefore pray ye: Our Father which art in heaven, Hallowed be thy name. 10 Thy kingdom come. Thy will be done in earth, as it is in heaven. 11 Give us this day our daily bread. 12 And forgive us our debts, as we forgive our debtors. 13 And lead us not into temptation, but deliver us from evil: for thine is the kingdom, and the power, and the glory, for ever. Amen. 14 For if ye forgive men their trespasses, your heavenly Father will also forgive you: 15

Salvation

but if ye forgive not men their trespasses, neither will your Father forgive your trespasses."

This includes you forgiving God. Many have opinions about how the world is and ultimately blame God. Forgiving Him for our ignorance and pride is a key part of success. Then include others who have hurt you in any way. Ask God for His grace to do this in you.

When you believe God unto righteousness, God infuses your spirit by Holy Spirit with His *zoe*/life, destroying the death from the sin of Adam (and your own sin) that was in your spirit. Rom 5:16 "And not as it was by one (*Adam*) that sinned, so is the gift: for the judgment was by one (*Adam*) to condemnation [*death for all men*], but the free gift is of many offences unto justification. 17 For if by one man's (*Adam's*) offence death reigned (*to produce all the cruelty, lack, sorrow and death seen in the history of the human race*) by one; much more they which (*continually*) *lambano*/receive abundance of grace and of the gift of righteousness shall reign (*to produce the Kingdom of God for God*) in *zoe*/life by one, Jesus Christ.) 18 Therefore as by the offence of one (*Adam*) judgment (*the sentence of spiritual and physical death*) came upon all men to condemnation; even so by the righteousness of one (*Jesus*) the free gift came upon all men unto justification of *zoe*/life."

When you believed God raised Jesus from the dead and confessed Jesus as your Lord, you were made the righteousness of God in Christ Jesus, all your sins were remitted, you were sealed with Holy Spirit as a sign of ownership and authority, you received the seal of your adoption as a child of God and you entered into the great salvation of God obtained by our redemption in the blood of Jesus. Eph 1:13 "In whom (*Jesus*) ye also trusted, after that ye heard the word of truth, the gospel of your *soteria*/salvation: in whom also after that ye believed, ye were sealed with that holy Spirit of promise, 14 which is the earnest of our inheritance until the redemption (*taking over full control by God to His pleasure*) of the purchased possession, unto the praise of his glory."

Through your believing, God signed your transfer to His Kingdom forever. Now, so that He can release in you all that He has done for you by Jesus, you must major on these redemption-unto-salvation truths. The more this becomes part of you, the more you will be: Col 1:12 "giving thanks (*continually*) unto the Father, which hath made us meet (*qualified and enabled by grace*) to be partakers of the inheritance of the saints in light: 13 who hath delivered us from the power of darkness, and hath translated us into the kingdom of his *agape*/dear Son: 14 in whom we have redemption through his blood, even the *aphesis*/forgiveness (*purging, washing and removal*) of sins."

Here is a summary of the Gospel Jesus preached. Jesus, the Christ/Messiah, came to demonstrate that now is the Day of Salvation from the evil rule of Satan in the present world system. This was seen in Jesus' preaching of truth, and in the miracles of healing, dead raising, food multiplication, stopping storms and walking on water. This means God solved the problem of how God, by Jesus, through Holy Spirit, can reign on the Earth through men to bring Heaven to Earth and destroy the kingdom of darkness. This restores man to his original position as the vehicle by which God will fill the Universe with the glory of God. Man is the hope of Heaven, and Jesus did the work to make this a past completed potential. When you get born again, with indwelling Holy Spirit, you step into this awesome potential.

Men must pray and act in order for God to get the job done. Titus 2:13 "Looking for that blessed hope, and the glorious appearing of the great God and our Saviour Jesus Christ; 14 who gave himself for us, that he might redeem us from all iniquity (*wrong thinking*), and purify unto himself a peculiar people, zealous of (*doing*) good works." These "*good works*" include man-level works like prayer, alms and clothing the naked, as well as the God-level works such as healing the sick, casting out demons and raising the dead.

Stirring yourself in God to deliver healing is one such good work and gets you operating more in God's great love plan for you.

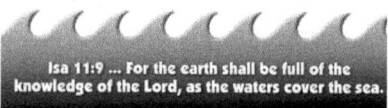

Isa 11:9 ... For the earth shall be full of the knowledge of the Lord, as the waters cover the sea.

Part II

Healing Teachings
by
John G. Lake

The thief cometh not, but for to steal, and to kill, and to destroy: I am come that they might have zoe/life, and that they might have it more abundantly. (John 10:10)

The following are the teachings of Rev. John G. Lake, who ministered from about 1900 to 1935. He established the Healing Rooms in Spokane, Washington, in 1914, where well over 100,000 healings in a 5-year period were validated. His basic healing methods were that if the initial prayer commands did not produce healing miracles, then daily repeated hearing of scripture and daily loud dominion prayer within 30 days would. He fought till he won. Since most of the words are his, my inserted words are in brackets.

~ 1 ~

GOD'S WAY OF HEALING

(Brett Wyatt, *The Fire of God*, Riley Christian Media, Spokane, WA, 2002, pp 23-24)

God's way of healing is a person, not a thing. Jesus said, "I am the way, the truth, and the *zoe*/life ..." and He has ever been revealed to His people in all ages by the covenant name, Jehovah Rophi, or, "I am the Lord that healeth thee" (John 14:6 and Ex 15:26).

The Lord Jesus Christ is still the Healer by the power of the Holy Spirit. He cannot change, for "He is the same yesterday, today, and forever," and He is still with us, for He said, "Lo, I am with you always, even unto the end of the world (Heb 13:5-8 and Matt 28:20). Because He is unchangeable, and because He is present in Spirit, just as when in the flesh, He is still the healer of His people.

Divine healing rests on Christ's Atonement. It was prophesied of Him, "Surely he hath borne our griefs (*Hebrew: infirmities*) and carried our sorrows (*Hebrew: sicknesses*), and with his stripes we are healed," and it is expressly declared that this was fulfilled in His ministry of healing, which still continues (Isa 53:4-5 and Matt 8:17).

Diseases can never be God's will. It is the devil's work consequent on sin, and it is impossible for the work of the devil ever to be the will of God. Christ came to destroy the works of the devil, and when He was on Earth, He, "healed every sickness and every disease," and all these diseases have been expressly declared to have been the "oppression of the devil" (1 John 3:8, Matt 4:23 and Acts 10:38).

[DCM: Christ came to destroy the works of the devil, not make them stronger: 1 John 3:8 "He that committeth sin is of the devil; for the devil sinneth from the beginning. For this purpose the Son of God was manifested, that he might destroy the works of the devil."

Jesus never said to anybody, "I will not heal until you learn your lesson, get free from sin, forgive, believe on Me, make restitution or you have a curse from God I cannot heal, etc." No, He healed when anyone came to Him or He found those needing His healing on the way. It did not matter. Jesus never said, "I will not heal until you get more faith or you learn some lesson God is teaching you with this sickness or disease." Jesus never said, "God is taking this person home through this disease, so I cannot heal them." The only issue He had was that people would not come to Him for healing (Matt 13:57-58). Every act of Jesus was attacking the devil in some way. The people were the victims; He the Deliverer. Isa 49:24 "Shall the prey be taken from the mighty, or the lawful captive delivered? But thus saith the LORD, Even the captives of the mighty shall be taken away, and the prey of the terrible shall be delivered: for I will contend with him that contendeth with thee, and I will save thy children." Jesus never told anyone "no" because they had sin.

The Lord still heals though His Word as we preach this truth of Jesus the Healer: Mark 16:20 "And they went forth, and preached everywhere, the Lord working with them, and confirming the word with signs following. Amen." Acts 14:3 "Long time therefore abode they (*Paul and Barnabas*) speaking boldly in the Lord, which gave testimony unto the word of his grace, and granted signs and wonders to be done by their hands." 1 Cor 2:4 "And my speech and my preaching was not with enticing words of man's wisdom, but in demonstration of the Spirit and of power: 5 that your faith should not stand in the wisdom of men, but in the power of God." Heb 2:3 "How shall we escape, if we neglect so great *soteria*/salvation; which at the first began to be spoken by the Lord, and was confirmed unto us by them that heard him; 4 God also bearing them witness, both with signs and wonders, and with divers miracles, and gifts of the Holy Ghost, according to his own will?" Gal 4:6 "And because ye are sons, God hath sent forth the Spirit of his Son into your hearts, crying, Abba, Father." As the Father used Jesus He will use you. John 14:10 "But the Father that dwelleth in me [*by Holy Spirit*], he doeth the works [*by Holy Spirit*]."

Death in all its forms is God's enemy. 1 Cor 15:26 "The last enemy that shall be destroyed is death." Rev 1:18 "I (*Jesus*) am he that *zao*/liveth, and was dead; and, behold, I am *zao*/alive for evermore, Amen; and have the keys of hell and of death." Sickness, disease, poverty, infirmity, weakness, sin are all God's enemies attacking God's creation to hurt God. You are not the end target; God is.

Since the devil cannot get to God, he attacks the Word of God, not just you, but more importantly, the Word you are holding onto: Mark 4:15 "And these are they by the way side, where the word is sown; but when they have heard, Satan cometh immediately, and taketh away the word that was sown in their hearts." Satan tried to overthrow God, and now he is attacking God's creation to get to God. Notice that Jesus gives us authority over the devil even in nature, so sickness is an even more apparent enemy of God. Luke 10:19 "Behold (*make this change your life*), I give unto you power to tread on (*break the power of*) serpents and scorpions, and over all the power of the enemy: and nothing shall by any means hurt you."

This same Jesus is inside of you by His Spirit, if you are born again. Col 1:27 "To whom God would make known what is the riches of the glory of this mystery among the Gentiles (*to all men*); which is Christ in you, the hope of glory." 2 Cor 13:5 "Examine yourselves, whether ye be in the faith; prove your own selves. Know ye not your own selves, how that Jesus Christ is in you, except ye be reprobates (*useless, impotent in your Christian faith*)?" 1 John 4:4 "Ye are of God, little children, and have overcome them: because greater is he that is in you, than he that is in the world."

Jesus wants us to demand of the Father covenant promises so Father's will can be done on Earth as it is in Heaven: John 20:21 "Then said Jesus to them again, Peace (*blessed be the confidence of effective working of anything you do like I do to bring the Kingdom of God to Earth*) be unto you: as my Father hath sent me, even so send I you." John 14:9 "Jesus saith unto him, Have I been so long time with you, and yet hast thou not known me, Philip? he that hath seen me hath seen the Father; and how sayest thou then, Shew us the Father? 10 Believest thou not that I am in the Father, and the Father in me? the words that I speak unto you I speak not of myself: but the Father that dwelleth in me, he doeth the works. 11 Believe me that I am in the Father, and the Father in me: or else believe me for the very works' sake. 12 Verily, verily, I say unto you, He that believeth on me, the works that I do shall he do also; and greater works than these shall he do; because I go unto my Father. 13 And whatsoever ye shall *aiteo*/ask (*by demanding, expecting as due by covenant promise*) in my name, that will I do, that the Father may be glorified in the Son. 14 If ye shall *aiteo*/ask (*by requiring, demanding and expecting as due by covenant promise*) any thing in my name, I will do it." We have an open ticket with God to bring His promises to Earth, including healing, by using the name of Jesus in the form of *aiteo* demands, requests, requirements, desires and commands.

Ask/*aiteo*: A*iteo* is the Greek word translated "ask" or "desire" in many New Testament scriptures related to prayer. It means to ask or demand of one in authority because the one made a promise based on requirements, and now the requirements have been met, so the one is now to give the desired promise. It also includes an intensity or focus in your desire to see the request fulfilled. For example: you are working on a task, and you promised your little daughter that you would take her for an ice cream cone or some other treat when you were done. You are now done, and your daughter *aiteo*/demands by saying, "You are finished. You said you would take me when you were done. You are done; please take me now." Or, in a legal sense, such as in a situation where you fell behind in your property taxes and, as they come to kick you out, you get the money and pay the taxes. Then you wave your paid-up receipt and *aiteo*/say, "I paid my taxes; take your people and go now!" Or you pawned an item, and now you have the money to redeem it. You *aiteo*/say, as you wave the ticket, "Here is the money; give it back, now!" Even if the pawnshop owner had a better offer for your item, he must give it back to you. *Aiteo* is not a quiet or polite word in that sense.

In this manual we base our prayer on the covenant promises of God. This is what He has said He will do. Ps 138:2 "I will worship toward thy holy temple, and praise thy name for thy *chesed*/loving-kindness and for thy truth: for thou hast magnified thy word above all thy name." His name is our access to God. We are to use His name to release His covenant promises, His Word, on the Earth. The general principle is to find a promise of God in the Scriptures and *aiteo* Him to perform it, for whatever is resisting it to *aiteo* go, and for the situation to become as you *aiteo* it— all in Jesus' name.

Those great prayer scriptures in John 14-16 all use this word *aiteo* for *ask*. Here is just one as an example: John 14:12 "Verily, verily, I say unto you, He that believeth on me, the works that I do shall he do also; and greater works than these shall he do; because I go unto my Father. 13 And whatsoever ye shall *aiteo*/ask (*require, demand and expect as due by covenant promise*) in my name, that will I do, that the Father may be glorified in the Son." As you see in this case, wherever the Greek word is *aiteo*, we usually added in a version of the phrase, *"require, demand and expect as due by covenant promise"* behind the translated word.

Notice, in a cruel example of the use of the word *aiteo*, that once King Herod made a promise, even if he did not want to keep it, he had to perform upon the *aiteo*/asking because he had made a promise. Mark 6:22 "And when the daughter of the said Herodias came in, and danced, and pleased Herod and them that sat with him, the king said unto the damsel, *Aiteo*/ask (*require, demand and expect as due by promise knowing all the requirements have been met*) of me whatsoever thou wilt, and I will give it thee. 23 And he sware unto her, Whatsoever thou shalt *aiteo*/ask (*require, demand and expect as due by promise knowing all the requirements have been met*) of me, I will give it thee, unto the half of my kingdom. 24 And she went forth, and said unto her mother, What shall I *aiteo*/ask (*require, demand and expect as due by promise knowing that all the requirements have been met*)? And she said, The head of John the Baptist. 25 And she came in straightway with haste unto the king, and *aiteo*/asked (*required, demanded and expected as due by promise knowing that all the requirements have been met*), saying, I will that thou give me by and by in a charger the head of John the Baptist. 26 And the king was exceeding sorry; yet for his oath's sake, and for their sakes which sat with him, he would not reject her. 27 And immediately the king sent an executioner, and commanded his head to be brought: and he went and beheaded him in the prison, 28 and brought his head in a charger, and gave it to the damsel: and the damsel gave it to her mother." This is the power of the word *aiteo* and how it is used.

Part of the word *aiteo* is to know the requirements for the one in authority or control to fulfill the promise have been met. All the requirements for God to fulfill any scripture promise we require of Him have been fully met in Jesus. 2 Cor 1:19 "For the Son of God, Jesus Christ, who was preached among you by us, even by me and Silvanus and Timotheus, was not yea and nay, but in him was yea. 20 For all the promises of God in him are yea, and in him Amen, unto the glory of God by us. 21 Now he which stablisheth us with you in Christ, and hath anointed us, is God; 22 who hath also sealed (*qualified and enabled*) us, and given the earnest of the Spirit in our hearts." Not only has God granted every promise in Jesus, but placed Holy Spirit, the administrator of all the power of God, inside the born-again Christian.

So a more complete Christian phrase in prayer where *aiteo* is used would be, "require, demand and expect as due by covenant promise, knowing that Jesus has fulfilled all the requirements, and there is no reason not to do it because the time of God's salvation in any form is now." Your faith is believing God will fulfill His word as you *aiteo*.

Another key in prayer is the statement by God: Isa 45:11 "Thus saith the LORD, the Holy One of Israel, and his Maker, Ask (*require*) me of things to come concerning my sons, and concerning the work of my hands command ye me." This culminates in the statements: Heb 4:14 "Seeing then that we have a great high priest, that is passed into the heavens, Jesus the Son of God, let us hold fast our profession. 15 For we have not an high priest which cannot be touched with the feeling of our infirmities; but was in all points tempted like as we are, yet without sin. 16 Let us therefore **come boldly** unto the throne of grace, that we may obtain mercy, and find grace to help in time of need." Rom 8:15 "For ye have not received the spirit of bondage again to fear; but ye have received the Spirit of adoption, whereby we cry, Abba (*Daddy*), Father." Eph 3:11 "According to the eternal purpose which he purposed in Christ Jesus our Lord: 12 in whom we have **boldness and access** with confidence by the faith of him." Heb 10:19 "Having therefore, brethren, **boldness to enter** into the holiest by the blood of Jesus, 20 by a new and *zao*/living way, which he hath consecrated for us, through the veil, that is to say, his flesh" Heb 13:6 "So that **we may boldly say**, The Lord is my helper, and I will not fear what man shall do unto me." If you want to bombard the gates of Heaven that is your choice, but you are already in the throne room!

Jesus said our joy will include many victories in His name: John 16:24 "Hitherto have ye *aiteo*/asked (*by demanding as due by covenant promise*) nothing in my name: *aiteo*/ask (*by demanding as due by covenant promise*), and ye shall receive, that your joy may be full. 25 These things have I spoken unto you in proverbs: but the time cometh, when I shall no more speak unto you in proverbs, but I shall shew you plainly of the Father. 26 At that day ye shall *aiteo*/ask (*by demanding as due by covenant promise*) in my name: and I say not unto you, that I will pray the Father for you: 27 for the Father himself *agape*/loveth you, because ye have *agape*/loved me, and have believed that I came out from God. 28 I came forth from the Father, and am come into the world: again, I leave the world, and go to the Father." The proof He will is your believing He will do it.

So we use the intensity of the word *aiteo* in intercession with the Father, in commanding the devil to release a captive or oppressed one or a sick or broken body to hear and obey and be healed, whole in the name of Jesus—knowing all the requirements have been met in Jesus. Faith is believing God will do what He said He will do.

Here is how Jesus met the requirements: Isa 53:4 "Surely he hath borne our griefs (*infirmities*), and carried our sorrows (*sicknesses*): yet we did esteem him stricken, smitten of God, and afflicted. 5 But he was wounded for our transgressions, he was bruised for our iniquities: the chastisement of our peace was upon him; and with his stripes we are healed. 6 All we like sheep have gone astray; we have turned every one to his own way; and the LORD hath laid on him the iniquity of us all. …11 He shall see of the travail of his soul, and shall be satisfied: by his knowledge shall my righteous servant justify many; for he shall *nasa*/bear their iniquities." This word *justify* in verse 11 is the basis for all the New Testament scriptures on justification: made as if you had never sinned, will ever sin again and all things healed to Father's God's standard forever, i.e., righteous. The issue for today is not that it is done, but how to speed up the timing so it is delivered now, and not at some future heavenly state for "Today is the Day of Salvation."

Notice there is a speaking to the problem in this kind of *aiteo* prayer that is a key understanding. Mark 11:22 "And Jesus answering saith unto them, Have faith in God. 23 For verily I say unto you, That whosoever shall **say unto this mountain**, Be thou removed, and be thou cast into the sea; and shall not doubt in his heart, but shall believe that those things which he saith shall come to pass; he shall have whatsoever he saith. 24 Therefore I say unto you, What things soever ye *aiteo*/desire (*require, demand and expect as due by covenant promise knowing all requirements have been met in Jesus*) when ye pray, believe that ye receive them, and ye shall have them." Our focus is for the end result, with the problem gone. So we speak to the problem, the mountain, and command it to move, fully expecting God to empower that word to the end result. We speak and then give thanks in advance.

We speak to Father God as our superior, with promises to make good, and we speak to the devil and his works, to obey as under our feet. Notice the commands in the "Our Father" (the Greek imperative or command words are bold and underlined): Matt 6:9 "After this manner therefore pray ye: Our Father which art in heaven (*meaning pay attention, wake up, hear and listen*), **Hallowed** be thy name. 10 Thy kingdom **come.** Thy will **be done** in earth, as it is in heaven. 11 **Give** us this day our daily bread. 12 And **forgive** us our debts, as we forgive our debtors. 13 And **lead** us not into temptation, but **deliver** us from evil: For thine is the kingdom, and the power, and the glory, for ever. Amen." There is no begging in this prayer, and this is how Jesus said to pray.

Notice the command here: Acts 16:17 "The same followed Paul and us, and cried, saying, These men are the servants of the most high God, which shew unto us the way of *soteria*/salvation. 18 And this did she many days. But Paul, being grieved, turned and **said to the spirit**, I command thee in the name of Jesus Christ to come out of her. And he came out the same hour." Notice it obeyed within an hour. Not quite instant, but the job got done.

And notice the attitude of Jesus as He laid His hands on this woman: Luke 13:11 "And, behold, there was a woman which had a spirit of infirmity (*sickness, disease*) eighteen years, and was bowed together, and could in no wise lift up herself. 12 And when Jesus saw her, he called her to him, and said unto her [*in judgment against the devil and his works*[, Woman, thou art loosed from thine infirmity (*sickness, disease*). 13 And he laid his hands on her: and immediately she was made straight, and glorified God. 14 And the ruler of the synagogue answered with indignation, because that Jesus had healed on the sabbath day, and said unto the people, There are six days in which men ought to work: in them therefore come and be healed, and not on the sabbath day. 15 The Lord then answered him, and said, Thou hypocrite, doth not each one of you on the sabbath loose his ox or his ass from the stall, and lead him away to watering? [*And with the attitude of a righteous shepherd*] 16 And ought not this woman, being a daughter of Abraham, whom Satan hath bound, lo, these eighteen years, be loosed from this bond on the sabbath day?" This speaking to the problem and this "ought not" attitude fits right in with the attitude of *aiteo*.

Jesus used this kind of demand/command prayer in His ministry. John G. Lake discovered that this kind of dominion attitude produced far more results than begging intercession. For a more complete treatment of this see *The Prayer Cards, OK, God, Now What?* and *The Mind Renewing Battle Prayer* by the author and, of course, the writings of John G. Lake, and the many resources of Curry Blake (www.jglm.org).

Go and Do Likewise: The people who hear and receive this word of confidence in the grace of God, "believers," will do the same miraculous works as the apostles: Mark 16:15 "And he (*Jesus*) said unto them, Go ye into all the world, and preach the gospel to every creature. 16 He that believeth and is baptized shall be *sozo*/saved; but he that believeth not shall be damned. 17 And these signs shall follow them that believe; In my name shall they cast out devils; they shall speak with new tongues; 18 they shall take up serpents; and if they drink any deadly thing, it shall not hurt them; they shall lay hands on the sick, and they shall recover. 19 So then after the Lord had spoken unto them, he was received up into heaven, and sat on the right hand of God. 20 And they went forth, and preached everywhere, the Lord working with them, and confirming the word with signs following. Amen."

Jesus still heals today as we obey Him. John 20:21 "Then said Jesus to them again, Peace be unto you: as my Father hath sent me, even so send I you." Notice, per Mark 16:15 above, the power for miracles is included in the word of His grace: Acts 20:32 "And now, brethren, I commend you to God, and to the word of his grace, which is able to build you up, and to give you an inheritance among all them which are sanctified." Acts 14:3 "Long time therefore abode they speaking boldly in the Lord, which gave testimony unto the word of his grace, and granted signs and wonders to be done by their hands."

And what is "the word of his grace"? Eph 2:4 "But God, who is rich in mercy, for his great *agape*/love wherewith he *agape*/loved us, 5 even when we were dead in sins, hath quickened us together with Christ, (**by grace ye are *sozo*/saved**;) 6 and hath raised us up together, and made us sit together in heavenly places in Christ Jesus: 7 that in the ages to come he might shew the **exceeding riches of his grace** in his kindness toward us through Christ Jesus. 8 For **by grace are ye *sozo*/saved** through faith; and that not of yourselves: it is the gift of God: 9 not of works, lest any man should boast. 10 For we are his workmanship, created in Christ Jesus unto good works, which God hath before ordained that we should walk in them." Titus 2:11 "For the **grace of God that bringeth *soteria*/salvation** hath appeared to all men." Titus 3:4 "But after that the kindness and *agape*/love of God our Saviour toward man appeared, 5 not by works of righteousness which we have done, but according to his **mercy he *sozo*/saved us**, by the washing of regeneration, and renewing of the Holy Ghost; 6 which he shed on us abundantly through Jesus Christ our Saviour; 7 that being **justified by his grace**, we should be made heirs according to the hope of eternal *zoe*/life." Notice this grace of salvation is all in the past tense!

God's desire is not only healing, but for you to walk in total divine health and prosperity: 3 John 2 "*Agape*/beloved, I wish (*pray*) above all things that thou mayest prosper and be in health, even as thy soul prospereth." Rom 8:5 "For they that are after the flesh do mind the things of the flesh; but they that are after the Spirit the things of the Spirit. 6 For to be carnally minded is death; but to be spiritually minded (*in Bible truth*) is *zoe*/life and peace." Rom 16:20 "And the God of peace shall bruise Satan under your feet shortly (*as shattered glass*). The grace of our Lord Jesus Christ be with you. Amen."]

⊢═Word=Of=God═⊢

~ 2 ~

DO YOU KNOW GOD'S WAY OF HEALING?
(Ibid, pp 59-64)

Let it be supposed that the following words are a conversation between the reader (A) and the writer (B).

A. What does this question mean? Do you really suppose that God has some special way of healing in these days of which men may know and avail themselves?
B. That is exactly my meaning and I wish very much that you should know God's Way of Healing, as I have done for many years.

A. What is the way, in your opinion?
B. You should rather ask, WHO is God's Way? For the Way is a Person, not a thing. I will answer your question in His own words. "I am the Way, and the Truth, and the Life: no one cometh unto the Father, but by Me." These words were spoken by our Lord Jesus Christ, the Eternal Son of God, who is both our Savior and our Healer (John 14:6).

A. But I always thought that these words only referred to Him as the Way of Salvation. How can you be sure that they refer to Him as the Way of Healing also?
B. Because He cannot change. He is "the same yesterday and today, yea and forever." (Heb 13:8). He said that He came to Earth not only to save us, but to heal us (Luke 4:18), and He did this when in the flesh on Earth. Being unchanged, He must be able and willing and desirous to heal now.

BATTLE PRAYER FOR DIVINE HEALING: FIELD MANUAL 2

A. But is there not this difference, namely, that He is not with us now?
B. No; for He said, "Lo, I am with you always, even unto the end of the world" and so He is with us now, in Spirit, just as much as when He was here in the flesh.

A. But did He not work these miracles of healing when on Earth merely to prove that He was the Son of God?
B. No; there was still a greater purpose than that. He healed the sick who trusted in Him in order to show us that He came to die not only for our sins, but for our sickness, and to deliver us from both. [DCM: Healing was not the proof of His divinity, as the twelve (12) and the seventy (70) also healed, as did Moses, Elijah and Elisha in the Old Testament, but healing and miracles are a proof that God sent Him and that Jesus rightly spoke the words of God in healing.]

A. Then, if that is so, the atonement which He made on the Cross must have been for our sicknesses as well as our sins. Can you prove that is a fact from the Scriptures?
B. Yes, I can, and the passages are very numerous. I need quote two only. In Isa 53:4-5, it is written of Him, "Surely He hath borne our griefs (Hebrew: infirmities), and carried our sorrows (Hebrew: sicknesses): ... and with His stripes we are healed." Then, in the Gospel according to Matthew, this passage was quoted and directly applied to the work of bodily healing, in chapter 8, 17th verse, "That it might be fulfilled which was spoken by Isaiah the prophet, saying, Himself took our infirmities, and bare our diseases." [DCM: Thus healing is absolutely part of the eternal priestly ministry of Jesus and, therefore, still within the Body of Christ, the Church, His present Body on the Earth. As a true priest, Jesus never said He would not heal until a person had no sin or that they would be healed when they stopped sinning. He never said "learn the lesson first."]

A. But do you not think that sickness is often God's will, and sent for our good, and therefore God may not wish us to be healed?
B. No, that cannot possibly be: for diseases of every kind are the devil's work and his work can never be God's will, since Christ came for the very purpose of destroying "the works of the devil" (1 John 3:8).

A. Do you mean to say that all disease is the work of Satan?
B. Yes, for if there had been no sin (which came through Satan) there would never have been any disease and Jesus never in one single instance told any person that sickness was God's work or will, but the very contrary.

Healing Teachings by John G. Lake

A. Can you prove from scripture that all forms of sickness and infirmity are the devil's work?

B. Yes, that can be done very easily. You will see in Matthew 4:23 and 9:35 that when Jesus was here in the flesh, He healed "all manner of disease and all manner of sickness among the people." Then if you will refer to Acts 10:38 you will see that the Apostle Peter declares that He (Jesus) "went about doing good and healing all that were oppressed of the devil." Notice that all whom He healed, not some, but all were suffering from Satan's evil power.

A. But does disease never come from God?

B. No, it cannot come from God, for He is pure, and disease is unclean: and it cannot come out of Heaven, for there is no disease there.

A. That is very different from the teachings which I have received all my life from ministers and in the churches. Do you really think that you are right, and that they are all wrong in this matter?

B. It is not a question as between myself and them. The only question is, "What does God's Word say?" God has said in all ages to His Church, "I am the Lord that healeth thee" (Ex 15:26), and therefore it would be wicked to say that He is the Defiler of His people. All true Christians must believe the Bible, and it is impossible to believe that good and evil, sickness and health, sin and holiness could have a common origin in God. If the Bible really taught that, it would be impossible to believe our Lord Jesus Christ when He says, "A good tree cannot bring forth evil fruit, neither can a corrupt tree bring forth good fruit" (Matt 7:18).

A. But even if I agree with all you say, is it not true that the Gifts of Healing were removed from the Church, and are not in it now?

B. No, the "Gifts of Healing" were never withdrawn, and can never be withdrawn from the true Church of God: for it is written, "the gifts and the calling of God are without repentance" (Rom 11:29). There are nine gifts of God to the Church (enumerated in 1 Cor 12:8 to 11), and all these are in the Holy Spirit. Therefore, so long as the Holy Spirit is in the Church, all the gifts must be there also. If they are not exercised, that does not prove that they do not exist, but that the faith to exercise them is lacking in God's servants. The gifts are all perfectly preserved: for the Holy Spirit, not the Church, keeps them safely.

A. What should a Christian then do when overtaken with sickness?

B. A Christian should obey God's command, and at once turn to Him. Healing is obtained from God in one of four ways, namely: **First** by the direct prayer of faith, without any aid from the officers of the Church, praying as the Centurion did in Matt 8:13; **Second,** by two faithful disciples praying in perfect agreement, in accordance with the Lord's promise in Matt 18:19; **Third,** by the anointing of the Elders and the prayer of faith, according to the instruction in James 5:14 and 15; and **Fourth,** by the laying on of the hands of them who believe, as the Lord commands in Mark 16:18 and in other places.

A. But are people healed in this way in these days?
B. Yes, in thousands of cases. I have myself laid hands upon many hundreds of thousands of persons and have seen the Lord's Power manifested in the healing of great numbers, many of whom are living witnesses in many countries, who have testified publicly before thousands, and who are prepared to testify at any time. The ministry is being exercised by devoted Christians in many parts of America, Europe, Africa and elsewhere.

A. But how shall I obtain the necessary faith to receive healing, which faith I am at present conscience I do not possess?
B. It is written "Belief cometh of hearing, and hearing by the Word of Christ" (Rom 10:17). Our meetings are held for the express purpose of teaching fully the Word of God in this matter, and I very heartily invite you to attend the meetings. All are welcome and there are no charges of any kind made, for all God's gifts are free gifts. [DCM: This entire book, especially the Minister Confessions, said daily with enthusiasm and thanksgiving will give this truth priority in your heart to increase your faith in God by His word. Thus you can more effectively obey: <u>John 8:31</u> "Then said Jesus to those Jews which believed on him, If ye continue in my word, then are ye my disciples indeed; 32 and ye shall know the truth, and the truth shall make you free." And: <u>John 15:7</u> "If ye abide in me, and my words abide in you, ye shall *aiteo*/ask *(require, demand and expect as due by covenant promise)* what ye will, and it shall be done unto you. 8 Herein is my Father glorified, that ye bear much fruit; so shall ye be my disciples."]

~ 3 ~

A SERMON ON HEALING (CIRCA 1916)
(Ibid, pp 30-32)

The wonderful record of the healings of Jesus, and of His other miracles, have always held the mind of man with a strange fascination. Until 400 A.D. healing in the church was common. Every authorized elder or minister prayed the prayer of faith that saved the sick. [DCM: Historical records show most healing and casting out of demons was performed by the laity, the average Christian, per Mark 16:17-18, as well as the leadership, per James 5:14-15.] It was only after Christianity attained her great popularity in the 4th century and was recognized by Constantine as the state religion that the power of God for healing declined [and moved to only the leadership, if at all]. Since that time the modern church has taught that the days of miracles are past, that the miracles of healing, though common to the ministry of Jesus and of the apostles in the early church, were not needed any more, because now the world has become wise, the science of medicine has been developed, etc. In fact, it is usually believed that God does not heal the sick anymore and that the ministry of healing is a thing of the past.

This we emphatically deny. Instead, we proclaim the recognized fact that Jesus is the Healer still, and that everyman [everyone] who will come to Him ... may receive the healing touch.

There are various methods of healing taught in the Scriptures.

First: In Matt 8:1 we have the story of a leper who came to Jesus and made his own plea for healing and received on the spot His healing touch. There was no intermediary. The man made his own definite request to Jesus, and Jesus instantly responded with His "I will," the answer He ever gave to the sick, and the man was healed. [In the Greek, the emphasis is much stronger so that it could be stated as: "I delight to always heal, and will always heal anytime, anywhere, or anyone; this is what I am made for, and I do."]

Second: In Matt 18:19 we read: "If two of you shall agree on earth as touching anything that they shall *aiteo*/ask (*require, demand and expect as due by covenant promise*), it shall be done for them of my Father which is in heaven." This is an agreement of two souls in faith for one object. Many are thus healed. A husband will pray for his wife, the wife for her husband, the sister for her brother, the brother for his friend, parents for a child, etc.

Third: In James 5:13-15 we have definite instructions concerning what a Christian must do when he is sick: "Is any sick among you? let him call for the elders of the church; and let them pray over him, anointing him with oil in the name of the Lord: and the prayer of faith shall *sozo*/save the sick, and the Lord shall raise him up; and if he have committed sins, they shall be forgiven him."

The Word commands him what to do. He must send for the elders. That is the thing a Christian should do. A man of the world, who does not pretend to obey God, can send for whom he likes or what he likes, but the Christian, the Christ-follower, sends for the elders of the church, who in turn are commanded to pray the prayer of FAITH. And God declares that if he does, He [the Lord] will raise the sick man up. And if the sick man has committed sins, his sins will also be forgiven [DCM: without any confession of sin].

Fourth: Jesus gave still another method of healing. After his resurrection and just before His ascension, when He was giving His parting message to His disciples, He spoke these remarkable words:

"These signs shall follow them that BELIEVE; In my name shall they cast out devils; they shall speak with new tongues ... . They shall lay their hands on the sick, and they shall recover" Mark 16:17-18. This latter method is the one I feel called of God to use in praying for the sick. As I lay my hands on people in prayer, as Jesus Himself did, I believe and expect that God will cause His blessed Holy Spirit to flow through my hands into the one who is sick and make them whole.

When a minister is ordained to the ministry, the bishop invariably lays his hands on the candidate, praying God to qualify him with the Holy Spirit for the work of the ministry. In many churches, the bishop or minister likewise lays his hands on the heads of children who are confirmed as members of the church, expecting as he prays that the Spirit of God will be imparted to the child.

The disciples received from Heaven the baptism of the Holy Spirit, as we read in the second chapter of Acts. Their whole being was filled with the Spirit of God, so much so that in Acts 19:12 we read that God wrought special miracles by the hands of Paul, so that handkerchiefs and aprons were brought to Paul that they

MIGHT TOUCH HIS BODY. Then they were carried to the sick and placed upon them, and the sick were healed thereby, and demons were cast out.

The logic of this is that Paul's person was so filled with the Spirit of God that when he took the handkerchiefs or aprons in his hands, the handkerchiefs or aprons likewise became impregnated with the power of God. And when these were laid upon the sick one, the power of God that was in them from having been in contact with Paul's person, flowed into the sick one and made him whole.

It was the possession of this vital, conscious, living power of God [*zoe*/life], through the Holy Spirit, that gave us the remarkable record of the ministry of the apostles in the New Testament. It was the possession of this power that made possible the record of the first four hundred years of Christianity, a marvel of religious history. It is the possession of this same power of the Spirit that will once again revolutionize the church of God, and instead of forms of worship, the mighty power of God will be manifested.

[DCM: John Lake said that as he healed hundreds and even thousands day after day in the name and dominion of Jesus, he wanted to know more and more this God who gave so much love and power through him (Liardon, Roberts. Compiler and editor, *John G. Lake: The Complete Collection of His Life Teachings*, New Kensington, PA 15068, Whitaker House, 1999, page 377).]

~ 4 ~

A Teaching on the Subject of Healing for the Body

(Ibid, pp. 42-47)

The WORD OF GOD, that neither World, Church, Preacher, doctor or devil can deny.

1. HEALING BY GOD, THROUGH FAITH AND PRAYER, WAS PRACTICED BY THE PATRIARCHS. "… Abraham prayed unto God: and God healed Abimelech, and his wife, and his maid-servants; and they bare children" Gen 20:17.

2. GOD MADE A COVENANT OF HEALING WITH THE CHILDREN OF ISRAEL. A covenant is an indissoluble agreement that can never be annulled. The laws of South Carolina recognized marriage as a Covenant, not a legal contract [*circa 1920*]. Therefore in that state there was no divorce. A Covenant cannot be annulled or divorced.

God tested the Nation at the Waters of Marah, and made a COVENANT with them, known as the Covenant of Jehovah Rophi: God the Healer [DCM: Or in Hebrew: *Yahweh Rapha*].

a. "IF THOU WILT DILIGENTLY HEARKEN TO THE VOICE OF THE LORD THY GOD.
b. AND WILT DO THAT WHICH IS RIGHT IN HIS SIGHT.
c. AND GIVE EAR TO HIS COMMANDMENTS.
d. AND KEEP HIS STATUTES.

I will put none of these diseases upon thee, which I have brought upon the Egyptians: for I AM THE LORD THAT HEALETH THEE" Ex 15:26.

3. DAVID REJOICED IN THE KNOWLEDGE OF THIS COVENANT.
"Bless the Lord, O my soul: and all that is within me, bless his Holy name. Bless the Lord, O my soul, and forget not all His benefits: Who forgiveth all thine iniquities; who HEALETH ALL THY DISEASES" Ps 103:1-3.

4. ISAIAH PROCLAIMED IT.
"Then the eyes of the blind shall be opened, and the ears of the deaf shall be unstopped. Then shall the lame man leap as an hart, and the tongue of the dumb sing" Isa 35:5-6. [DCM: Jesus told John the Baptist, as he languished in prison, that the signs based on this scripture were proof that Jesus was and is the One from God: Matt 11:3 "And said unto him, Art thou he that should come, or do we look for another? 4 Jesus answered and said unto them, Go and shew John again those things which ye do hear and see: 5 The blind receive their sight, and the lame walk, the lepers are cleansed, and the deaf hear, the dead are raised up, and the poor have the gospel preached to them. 6 And blessed is he, whosoever shall not be offended in me."]

5. JESUS MADE HEALING ONE OF THE PLANKS OF HIS PLATFORM.
a. "The Spirit of the Lord is upon me, because HE HATH ANOINTED ME TO PREACH THE GOSPEL TO THE POOR
b. HE HATH SENT ME TO HEAL THE BROKEN-HEARTED,
c. TO PREACH DELIVERANCE TO THE CAPTIVES
d. AND RECOVERING OF SIGHT TO THE BLIND
e. TO SET AT LIBERTY THEM THAT ARE BRUISED."
   Luke 4:18

6. JESUS MINISTERED HEALING TO THE SICK.
"And Jesus went about all Galilee, teaching in their synagogues, and preaching the gospel of the Kingdom, HEALING ALL MANNER OF SICKNESS AND ALL MANNER OF DISEASE among the people" Matt 4:23.

7. HEALING IS IN THE ATONEMENT OF CHRIST, (See Matt 8:1-17; especially verse 17.)
a. Healing of the Leper. Matt 8:1-4.
b. Healing of the Centurion's Servant. Matt 8:5-13.

c. Healing of Peter's wife's mother. Matt 8:14-15.
d. Healing of the multitude. Matt 8:16.
e. His REASON GIVEN for these healings, verse 17.
"That it might be fulfilled which was spoken by Isaiah the Prophet, saying, HIMSELF TOOK OUR INFIRMITIES AND BARE OUR SICKNESSES." [DCM: Matt 8:17 is a repeat of Isa 53:4.]

8. JESUS BESTOWED THE POWER TO HEAL UPON HIS TWELVE DISCIPLES.

"Then He called His twelve disciples together, and GAVE THEM POWER AND AUTHORITY OVER ALL DEVILS and to CURE DISEASES And he sent them to preach the Kingdom of God, and to HEAL THE SICK ... and they departed, and went through the towns, preaching the gospel, and HEALING EVERYWHERE" Luke 9: 1-2 and 6.

9. HE LIKEWISE BESTOWED POWER UPON THE SEVENTY.

"After these things the Lord appointed other seventy also, and sent them two and two before his face into every city and place, wither he himself would come. ... HEAL THE SICK that are therein, and say unto them, The Kingdom of God is come nigh unto you" Luke 10:1. [*Note: At one time there were 83 healing the sick: Jesus+12+70*].

10. AFTER JESUS' RESURRECTION, HE EXTENDED THE POWER TO ALL WHO BELIEVE.

"He (*Jesus*) said unto them, Go ye into all the world, and preach the gospel to every creature. He that believeth and is baptized shall be saved; but he that believeth not shall be damned. And THESE SIGNS SHALL FOLLOW THEM THAT BELIEVE; In my name shall they CAST OUT DEVILS; they shall speak with new tongues; they shall take up serpents; and if they drink any deadly thing; it shall not hurt them; they shall LAY HANDS ON THE SICK, AND THEY SHALL RECOVER" Mark 16:15-18.

11. AND LEST HEALING SHOULD BE LOST TO THE CHURCH, HE PERPETUATED HEALING FOREVER AS ONE THE NINE GIFTS OF THE HOLY GHOST:

"To one is given by the Spirit the word of wisdom; to another the word of knowledge by the same Spirit; to another faith by the same Spirit; to another GIFTS OF HEALING by the same Spirit; to another the WORKING OF MIRACLES; to another prophecy; to another discerning of spirits; to another divers kinds of tongues; to another the interpretation of tongues" 1 Cor 12:8-10.

12. THE CHURCH WAS COMMANDED TO PRACTICE IT.

"Is any among you afflicted? Let him pray. Is any merry? Let him sing psalms. Is any sick among you? Let him CALL FOR THE ELDERS OF THE CHURCH; AND LET THEM PRAY OVER HIM, anointing him with oil in the name of the Lord: and the PRAYER OF FAITH SHALL SAVE THE SICK, and the Lord shall raise him up; and if he hath committed sins, they shall be forgiven him. Confess your faults one to another, and pray one for another, that ye may be HEALED. The effectual fervent prayer of a righteous man availeth much" James 5:13-16.

13. THE UNCHANGEABLENESS OF GOD'S ETERNAL PURPOSE IS THEREBY DEMONSTRATED.

"Jesus Christ the same yesterday, and today and forever" Heb 13:8.

"... I am the Lord, I change not" Mal 3:6.

14. GOD ALWAYS WAS THE HEALER.

He is the Healer still, and will ever remain the Healer. Healing is for you. Jesus healed, "all that came to him." He never turned anyone away. He never said, "It is not God's will to heal you." Or that it was better for the individual to remain sick, or that they were being perfected in character through the sickness. He healed them ALL, thereby demonstrating FOREVER God's unchangeable will concerning sickness.

[DCM: If sickness were what God used to teach us lessons, then Jesus would have been born with severe birth and genetic defects and would have been the sickest man in the universe. Also Jesus would have made the disciples sick, as well as the Pharisees, the Sadducees and anyone else who needed straightening out. But the message is quite the opposite: <u>Matt 15:30</u> "And great multitudes came unto him, having with them those that were lame, blind, dumb, maimed, and many others, and cast them down at Jesus' feet; and he healed them." <u>Luke 9:11</u> "And the people, when they knew it, followed him: and he received them, and spake unto them of the kingdom of God, and healed them that had need of healing." Holy Spirit even said Jesus came to get rid of sickness as part of His main mission: <u>Matt 8:16</u> "When the even was come, they brought unto him many that were possessed with devils: and he cast out the spirits with his word, and healed all that were sick: 17 that it might be fulfilled which was spoken by Esaias the prophet, saying, Himself took our infirmities, and bare our sicknesses" (Isa 53:4). The message is clear; sickness is an enemy of God, and still through Jesus' Body, the Church, Father God wants people to help Him heal the same way Jesus did.]

Have you need of healing? Pray. Pray to God in the name of Jesus Christ to remove the disease. Command it to leave, as you would sin. Assert your divine authority and refuse to have it. Jesus purchased your freedom from sickness as He purchased your freedom from sin.

"His own self BARE our sins in His own body on the tree, that we being dead to sins, should *zao*/live unto righteousness: BY WHOSE STRIPES YE WERE HEALED" 1 Pet 2:24.

Therefore, mankind has a right to health, as he has a right to deliverance from sin. If you do not have it it's because you are being cheated out of your inheritance. It belongs to you. In the name of Jesus Christ, go after it and get it.

If your faith is weak, call for those who believe and to whom the prayer of faith and the ministry of healing have been committed.

[DCM: Rev. Lake understood that sin in the flesh of Rom 8:3 included all sickness, disease, pain, sorrow, grief or imperfection in the human body. Rom 8:3 "For what the law could not do, in that it was weak through the flesh, God sending his own Son in the likeness of sinful flesh, and for sin, condemned sin in the flesh." Rom 6:12 "Let not sin therefore reign in your mortal body, that ye should obey it in the lusts thereof." Sin cannot reign in your mortal body except in such things as sickness, drug addictions, old age, hunger, thirst and poverty. And every one of these Jesus and the apostles attacked and set people free from to demonstrate the reign of God. Sin in your mind is the source of most outward sin, from greed to murder, i.e., the crimes of man. Sin in your body makes you bow to its desires, and it rules your life in sickness and disease. Any sin left unchecked (mind or body) will kill you.

Per: 1 Thes 5:23 "And the very God of peace sanctify you wholly; and I pray God your whole spirit and soul and body be preserved blameless unto the coming of our Lord Jesus Christ." A sanctified body has no defects or disease of any kind, so casting out demons, healing and restorative miracles are establishing the righteousness of God in the fleshly body. We need sanctification of our bodies now, because when we get our glorified, heavenly body, they will not need healing. There is no need in Heaven for healing; it is needed for this life, now.

We are to cooperate with Holy Spirit to keep our bodies in divine health: Rom 8:11 "But if the Spirit of him that raised up Jesus from the dead dwell in you, he that raised up Christ from the dead shall also quicken your mortal bodies by his Spirit that dwelleth in you." Your mortal body is the one you have now; the one that returns to dust, and not the one that is resurrected, which is an immortal body. Thus this prayer fits right in: 3 John 2 "*Agape*/beloved, I wish (*pray*) above all things that thou mayest prosper and be in health, even as (*as well as*) thy soul prospereth." To the Apostle John, this was a first, above all, priority, and is the mind of Christ, as evidenced by all those He, His disciples and followers healed.

Since He is the Lord who changes not and cannot lie, He still heals those who learn to work with Him: Matt 8:16 "When the even was come, they brought unto him many that were possessed with devils: and he cast out the spirits with his word, and healed all that were sick: 17 that it might be fulfilled which was spoken by Esaias the prophet, saying, Himself took our infirmities, and bare our sicknesses." For 2 Cor 6:2 "… behold (*appreciate, understand and make this change your life*), now is the accepted time; behold, now is the day of *soteria*/salvation." This Day of Salvation will last until the Day of Judgment, so we are still in it. Let us be about our Father's business preaching peace the way Jesus did, as we have been given the SAME SPIRIT! (see Acts 10:34-38 and Gal. 4:6)

1 John 5:6 "This is he that came by water and blood, even Jesus Christ; not by water only, but by water and blood. And it is the Spirit that beareth witness, because the Spirit is truth. 7 For there are three that bear record in heaven, the Father, the Word, and the Holy Ghost: and these three are one. 8 And there are three that bear witness in earth, the spirit, and the water, and the blood: and these three agree in one. 9 If we receive the witness of men, the witness of God is greater: for this is the witness of God which he hath testified of his Son." God was in Jesus, showing how He really is. See the message! Jesus is our light!]

Isa 11:9 … For the earth shall be full of the knowledge of the Lord, as the waters cover the sea.

Part III

Other Healing Teachings

Behold, I give unto you power to tread on serpents and scorpions, and over all the power of the enemy: and nothing shall by any means hurt you. Notwithstanding in this rejoice not, that the spirits are subject unto you; but rather rejoice, because your names are written in heaven. (Luke 10:19-20)

~ 1 ~

ON CONFIDENCE AND WASHING

Any possible reasons anyone could have for God not healing anyone at anytime were fully resolved by God in His reconciliation through Jesus. The issue of current sickness or delayed healing is with man and the way we think, not God. 1 John 2:1 "My little children, these things write I unto you, that ye sin not. And if any man sin, we have an advocate with the Father, Jesus Christ the righteous: 2 and he is the propitiation for our sins: and not for ours only, but also for the sins of the whole world." 1 John 4:9 "In this was manifested the *agape*/love of God toward us, because that God sent his only begotten Son into the world, that we might *zao*/ live through him. 10 Herein is *agape*/love, not that we *agape*/loved God, but that he *agape*/loved us, and sent his Son to be the propitiation for our sins." *Propitiation* means "full payment to total removal of all issues unto total and aggressive blessing." 2 Cor 5:18 "And all things are of God, who hath reconciled us to himself by Jesus Christ, and hath given to us the ministry of reconciliation; 19 to wit, that God was in Christ, reconciling the world unto himself, not imputing their trespasses unto them; and hath committed unto us the word of reconciliation." That means the will of Heaven can come to Earth by our word.

We are reconciled to God! Reconciliation means healing of everything in Jesus. We have been given the job of convincing the world that God is not the problem. Reconciliation means that, from God's side, all in the way of His *agape*/love to us is now removed. This is the Gospel of the New Covenant in the blood of Jesus. His blood is totally sufficient forever. We deliver that reconciliation by faith in the word of God's reconciliation. 2 Cor 5:20 "Now then we are ambassadors for Christ, as though God did beseech you by us: we pray you in Christ's stead, be ye reconciled to God. 21 For he hath made him to be sin for us, who knew no sin; that we might be made the righteousness of God in him." Listen as God begs us to hear Him.

As I use the Battle Prayer, not only am I building myself in the Word of God; I am building my confidence in God to perform His Word through me because of Jesus. And I am believing and depending on Holy Spirit to use that Word to release more of His *zoe*/life in and by me, and by the washing of the water of the Word of God, to convict the worldly parts of me of sin, righteousness and judgment per John 16:8 "And when he (*Holy Spirit*) is come, he will reprove the world of sin, and of righteousness, and of judgment:" So that I might 1 John 1:7 "... walk in the light, as *Father God* is in the light, we (*Father God and I along with other believers*) have fellowship (*in eternal covenantal relationship of* chesed, racham, agape/love) one with another, and the blood of Jesus Christ his Son cleanseth us from all sin." Gal 5:25 "If we *zao*/live in the Spirit, let us also walk in the Spirit."1 John 2:5 "But whoso keepeth his word, in him verily is the *agape*/love of God perfected: hereby know we that we are in him. 6 He that saith he abideth in him ought himself also so to walk, even as he walked." John 3:19 "And this is the condemnation, that light is come into the world, and men *agape*/loved darkness rather than light, because their deeds were evil. 20 For every one that doeth evil hateth the light, neither cometh to the light (*of the word of God, Holy Spirit*), lest his deeds should be reproved. 21 But he that doeth truth cometh to the light, that his deeds may be made manifest, that they are wrought in God."

This is so that I might see all my sins and the fruits of sin (sickness, destructions, poverty and death) placed on Jesus, paid for by Jesus and totally made whole in Jesus forever 2000 years ago. Notice this forgiveness (remission, purging, obliteration and putting away) is all past tense, 2000 years ago. With the Battle Prayer on my lips I now extend the Kingdom of God, the peace of God, the reign of God, on Earth, when short prayers do not seem to do the job.

The way I should see sin is to know sin is far worse than I think it is and that Jesus has already purged me of my sins 2000 years ago at the cost of unimaginable suffering and death. It is the pride of the world that wants to say Jesus was not good enough. John 16:8 "And when he (*Holy Spirit*) is come, he will reprove the world of sin, and of righteousness, and of judgment: 9 of sin, because they believe not on me; 10 of righteousness, because I go to my Father, and ye see me no more; 11 of judgment, because the prince of this world is judged."

The first thing I want Holy Spirit to convict me of is what Father has accomplished in Jesus for me. Jesus said: John 8:23 "And he said unto them, Ye are from beneath; I am from above: ye are of this world; I am not of this world. 24 I said therefore unto you, that ye shall die in your sins: for if ye believe not that I am he, ye shall die in your sins." 1 Cor 15:17 "And if Christ be not raised, your faith is vain; ye are yet in your sins." Acts 4:12 "Neither is there *soteria*/salvation in any

OTHER HEALING TEACHINGS

other: for there is none other name under heaven given among men, whereby we must be *sozo*/saved." Luke 24:46 "And said unto them, Thus it is written, and thus it behoved Christ to suffer, and to rise from the dead the third day: 47 and that repentance and remission (*purging, obliteration, removal and putting away*) of sins should be preached in his name among all nations, beginning at Jerusalem. 48 And ye are witnesses of these things. 49 And, behold, I send the promise of my Father upon you: but tarry ye in the city of Jerusalem, until ye be endued with power (*ability*) from on high [*on the Day of Pentecost in Acts 2*]."

The next is to convict me: John 16:10 "Of righteousness, because I go to my Father, and ye see me no more." That in spite of what I see in me and others: 2 Cor 5:17 "Therefore if any man be in Christ, he is a new creature: old things are passed away; behold, all things are become new. 18 And all things are of God, who hath reconciled us to himself by Jesus Christ, and hath given to us the ministry of reconciliation; 19 to wit, that God was in Christ, reconciling the world unto himself, not imputing their trespasses unto them; and hath committed unto us the word of reconciliation. 20 Now then we are ambassadors for Christ, as though God did beseech you by us: we pray you in Christ's stead, be ye reconciled to God. 21 For he hath made him to be sin for us, who knew no sin; that we might be made the righteousness of God in him. 6:1 We then, as workers together with him, beseech you also that ye receive not the grace of God in vain. 2 (For he saith, I have heard thee in a time accepted, and in the day of *soteria*/salvation have I succoured thee: behold, now is the accepted time; behold, now is the day of *soteria*/salvation (*healing, making whole to just like Heaven on Earth.*)" Rom 4:24 "But for us also, to whom it (*righteousness*) shall be imputed, if we believe on him that raised up Jesus our Lord from the dead; 25 who was delivered for our offences, and was raised again for our justification. 5:1 Therefore being justified by faith, we have peace with God through our Lord Jesus Christ: 2 by whom also we have access by faith into this grace wherein we stand, and rejoice in hope (*joyful expectation of coming good*) of the glory of God. 3 And not only so, but we glory (*loud, thanksgiving, praise and rejoicing*) in tribulations also: knowing that tribulation worketh patience; 4 and patience, experience; and experience, hope (*joyful expectation of coming good*): 5 and hope (*joyful expectation of coming good*) maketh not ashamed; because the *agape*/love of God is shed abroad in our hearts by the Holy Ghost which is given unto us. 6 For when we were yet without strength, in due time Christ died for the ungodly. 7 For scarcely for a righteous man will one die: yet peradventure for a good man some would even dare to die. 8 But God commendeth his *agape*/love toward us, in that, while we were yet sinners, Christ died for us. 9 Much more then, being now justified by his blood, we shall be *sozo*/saved from wrath through him. 10 For if, when we were enemies, we were reconciled to God by the death of his Son, much more, being reconciled, we shall be *sozo*/saved by his *zoe*/life. 11 And not only so, but we also joy in God through our Lord Jesus Christ, by whom we have now received the atonement (*reconciliation*)." God, by Jesus, has made us worthy for Him to move in power through and by us.

The third thing Holy Spirit will convict me of is that the devil has been judged and his power broken by Jesus. John 16:11 "Of judgment, because the prince of this world is judged." Heb 2:14 "Forasmuch then as the children are partakers of flesh and blood, he also himself likewise took part of the same; that through death he might destroy him that had the power of death, that is, the devil," 1 John 3:8 "He that committeth sin is of the devil; for the devil sinneth from the beginning. For this purpose the Son of God was manifested, that he might destroy the works of the devil." Eph 4:8 "Wherefore he saith, When he ascended up on high, he led captivity (*the bondages of the devil, curses of the Law*) captive, and gave gifts unto men. 9 (Now that he ascended, what is it but that he also descended first into the lower parts of the earth? 10 He that descended is the same also that ascended up far above all heavens, that he might fill all things.)" Col 1:12 "Giving thanks (*continually*) unto the Father, which hath made us meet (*qualified and enabled by grace*) to be partakers of the inheritance of the saints in light: 13 who hath delivered us from the power of darkness, and hath translated us into the kingdom of his *agape*/dear Son: 14 in whom we have redemption through his blood, even the forgiveness (*remission, purging, putting away, and obliteration*) of sins." Col 2:13 "And you, being dead in your sins and the uncircumcision of your flesh, hath he quickened together with him, having forgiven you all trespasses; 14 blotting out the handwriting of ordinances that was against us, which was contrary to us, and took it out of the way, nailing it to his cross; 15 and having spoiled principalities and powers (*the devil and his rulers reigning in death*), he made a shew of them openly (*public humiliation*), triumphing over them in it."

We do not see all of this complete destruction of the works of the devil today, for Jesus has given us, the Church, His Body on Earth now, the job of finishing the task of destroying the works of the devil. It is like an evil king has surrendered, but his evil army of rebels do not accept that victory unless it is forced upon them. Our job is to enforce the victory of Jesus wherever we discover evil working: John 20:21 "Then said Jesus to them again, Peace be unto you: as my Father hath sent me, even so send I you." Luke 10:18 "And he said unto them, I beheld Satan as lightning fall from heaven. 19 Behold (*make this change your life*), I give unto you power (*commission, authority and the resources of heaven*) to tread on serpents and scorpions, and over all the power (*works, ability*) of the enemy: and nothing shall by any means hurt you. 20 Notwithstanding in this rejoice not, that the spirits are subject unto you; but rather rejoice, because your names are written in heaven." 2 Cor 10:3 "For though we walk in the flesh, we do not war after the flesh: 4 (for the weapons of our warfare are not carnal, but mighty through God to the pulling down of strong

Other Healing Teachings

holds;) 5 casting down imaginations, and every high thing that exalteth itself against the knowledge of God, and bringing into captivity every thought to the obedience of Christ; 6 and having in a readiness to revenge all disobedience, when your obedience is fulfilled." Healing is a judgment of God that crushes the devil's works.

Answered prayer is controlled by us and the resistance of the devil we allow. God is always willing and eager to heal as Jesus said: Luke 5:12 "And it came to pass, when he was in a certain city, behold a man full of leprosy: who seeing Jesus fell on his face, and besought him, saying, Lord, if thou wilt, thou canst make me clean. 13 And he put forth his hand, and touched him, saying, I will (*I delight to, I am always inclined to, this is what I am made for and I will gladly do it*): be thou clean. And immediately the leprosy departed from him." This aspect of God never changes: Ps 103:2 "Bless the LORD, O my soul, and forget not all his benefits: 3 who forgiveth all thine iniquities; who healeth all thy diseases." Heb 13:8 "Jesus Christ the same yesterday, and to day, and for ever." Jesus is all of God in a man.

Just like God told the Israelites to perform, implement and execute God's judgment against the people in the land of Canaan (the Amalekites, etc.), we have been told to deliver the judgment of God against the devil and set people free from his oppressions in the name of Jesus. Just like Jesus would do if He were here–which He is, in us, and in His name on our lips. Luke 10:19 "Behold (*make this change your life*), I give unto you power to tread on serpents and scorpions, and over all the power of the enemy: and nothing shall by any means hurt you."

We are specifically told to keep fighting the devil till we are able to deliver any individual, group or nation of any oppression of the devil: Eph 6:12 "For we wrestle not against flesh and blood, but against principalities, against powers, against the rulers of the darkness of this world, against spiritual wickedness in high places. 13 Wherefore take unto you the whole armour of God, that ye may be able to withstand in the evil day (*when it looks like the devil is winning or has won, and the Word of God has not yet been manifested*), and having done all, to stand (*keep at it until you win*)." James 4:7 "Submit yourselves therefore to God (*do what you have been called to do*). Resist (*actively fight, not people, but*) the devil, and he (*the devil*) will flee from you." 1 Pet 5:8 "Be sober, be vigilant; because your adversary the devil, as a roaring lion, walketh about, seeking whom he may devour: 9 whom resist (*fight*) stedfast in the faith, knowing that the same afflictions are accomplished in your brethren that are in the world." Ps 91:4 "He shall cover thee with his feathers, and under his wings shalt thou trust: his truth shall be thy shield and buckler. ... 13 Thou shalt tread upon the lion and adder: the young lion and the dragon shalt thou trample under feet."

God, who is ever near, sympathizes with need but is released by faith: the absolute assurance of things currently unseen, but promised by God, and the joyful expectation of coming good from the hand of God. Heb 11:1 "NOW FAITH is the assurance (the confirmation, the title deed) of the things [we] hope for (*as evidenced by our joyful expectation of coming good*), being the proof of things [we] do not see and the conviction of their reality [faith perceiving as real fact what is not revealed to the senses]." AMP Thus the greater our confidence/faith/courage in God (evidenced by joy, praise, and thanks), the quicker we will see the result in healing. Just as with the prayers in this manual, the issue is not so much the methods employed, but our faith in the God of the Word, who backs the methods.

Look at the confidence demonstrated in the will of God and the access to Father God of a righteous one (in this case, Jesus): John 11:41 "Then they took away the stone from the place where the dead was laid. And Jesus lifted up his eyes, and said, Father, I thank thee that thou hast heard me. 42 And I knew that thou hearest me always: but because of the people which stand by I said it, that they may believe that thou hast sent me. 43 And when he thus had spoken, he cried with a loud voice, Lazarus, come forth." Notice that Jesus used a LOUD VOICE! He did not use a typical quiet, "church" voice.

Jesus is waiting for the Church to rise and finish the work He started. Matt 22:44 "The LORD said unto my Lord, Sit thou on my right hand, till I make thine enemies thy footstool?" Heb 1:13 "But to which of the angels said he at any time, Sit on my right hand, until I make thine enemies thy footstool?"And who is Father God using to do this work? Eph 3:10 "To the intent that now unto the principalities and powers in heavenly places might be known by the church the manifold wisdom of God," Rom 16:20 "And the God of peace shall bruise Satan under your feet shortly (*as shattered glass*). The grace of our Lord Jesus Christ be with you [*to accomplish this*]. Amen." Luke 10:8 "And into whatsoever city ye enter, and they receive you, eat such things as are set before you: 9 and heal the sick that are therein, and say unto them, The kingdom of God is come nigh unto you."

Be aware that a desire to see God heal through you is Holy Spirit working to get you to do what you are made to do. Eph 2:10 "For we are his workmanship, created in Christ Jesus (*of the nature Jesus*) unto good works (*doing*), which God hath before ordained that we should walk in them." Phil 2:13 "For it is God which worketh in you both to will and to do of his good pleasure." 2 Cor 4:7 "But we have this treasure in earthen vessels, that the excellency of the *dunamis*/power (*ability*) may be of God, and not of us." Jesus lived the life of a warrior against the lies and power of the devil, and we have the same calling. It is our ignorance and lack of knowledge that destroys us. True knowledge is *zoe*/life.

As I read the Scriptures I expect, even require, Holy Spirit to convict me to operate as Jesus operated in mercy, grace and truth through faith, confidence or courage working by *agape*/love: Acts 10:36 "The word which God sent unto the children of Israel, preaching peace by Jesus Christ: (he is Lord of all:) 37 that word, I say, ye know, which was published throughout all Judaea, and began from Galilee, after the baptism which John preached; 38 how God anointed Jesus of Nazareth with the Holy Ghost and with power: who went about doing good, and healing all that were oppressed (*under the active dominion, reign or lordship*) of the devil; for God was with him." For: 1 John 4:17 "Herein is our *agape*/love made perfect, that we may have boldness in the day of judgment: because as he is, so are we in this world. 18 There is no fear in *agape*/love; but perfect *agape*/love casteth out fear: because fear hath torment. He that feareth is not made perfect in *agape*/love."

As a king is anointed, called for a purpose, and then God gives His Spirit to accomplish that calling, we have been given the same Spirit as Jesus to operate/walk as did Jesus in the loving faith, confidence, and courage in Father God by His Spirit. 2 Cor 1:21 "Now he which stablisheth us with you in Christ, and hath anointed us, is God; 22 who hath also sealed us, and given the earnest of the Spirit in our hearts." Gal 4:6 "And because ye are sons, God hath sent forth the Spirit of his Son into your hearts, crying, Abba (*Daddy*), Father."

Jesus said: Acts 1:8 "But ye shall receive *dunamis*/power (*the ability like Jesus has*) after that the Holy Ghost is come upon you: and ye shall be witnesses unto me (*showing what Father God is really like, in my name, just as I did when I was on Earth*) both *at home*, and unto the uttermost part of the earth." 2 Cor 1:19 "For the Son of God, Christ Jesus (the Messiah), Who has been preached among you by us, by myself, Silvanus, and Timothy, was not Yes and No; but in Him it is [always the divine] Yes. 20 For as many as are the promises of God, they all find their Yes [answer] in Him [Christ]. For this reason we also utter the Amen (so be it) to God through Him [in His Person and by His agency] to the glory of God (*the free reign of* zoe/*life by Holy Spirit on Earth through men*). 21 But it is God Who confirms and makes us steadfast and establishes us [in joint fellowship] with you in Christ, and has consecrated and anointed us [*for* enduing us with the gifts of the Holy Spirit]; 22 [He has also appropriated and acknowledged us as His by] putting His seal upon us and giving us His [Holy] Spirit in our hearts as the security deposit and guarantee [of the fulfillment of His promise]. AMP Rom 8:15 "For [the Spirit which] you have now received [is] not a spirit of slavery to put you once more in bondage to fear, but you have received the Spirit of adoption [the Spirit producing sonship] in [the bliss of] which we cry, Abba (*Daddy*)! Father! 16 The Spirit Himself [thus] testifies together with our own spirit, [assuring us] that we are children of God." AMP Gal 4:4 "But when the proper time had fully come, God sent His Son, born of a woman, born subject to [the regulations of] the Law, 5 to purchase the freedom of (to ransom, to redeem, to atone for) those who were subject to the Law, that we might be adopted and have sonship conferred upon us [and be recognized as God's sons]. 6 And because you [really] are [His] sons, God has sent the [Holy] Spirit of His Son into our hearts, crying, Abba (*Daddy*)!

Father!" AMP Thus with confidence we can say: 1 John 4:4 "Ye are of God, little children, and have overcome them: because greater is he that is in you, than he that is in the world."

Knowing who and what we are in Christ is part of the process of washing by the Word to make our calling more effective. Philem 6 "That the communication of thy faith may become effectual by the acknowledging of every good thing which is in you in Christ Jesus."

~ 2 ~

ON MOUTH POWER

One of the secrets of power with God is attention to the words that flow out of our mouths all day long. The more we lie (bold lies, white lies, fibs, stretching the truth, exaggeration, etc.), make excuses, blame others, or gossip, the less we believe anybody, including God. Prov 18:20 "A man's belly shall be satisfied with the fruit of his mouth; and with the increase of his lips shall he be filled. 21 Death and life are in the power of the tongue: and they that love it shall eat the fruit thereof." Eph 4:29 "Let no corrupt communication proceed out of your mouth, but that which is good to the use of edifying, that it may minister grace (*the free gift of God to live out His life in Jesus in you by His Spirit*) unto the hearers. 30 And grieve not the holy Spirit of God, whereby ye are sealed unto the day of redemption." If God has given men the power of death, life and grace by our tongues, then the issue is us and not God. In Jesus, He has done His part, and we have the authority—if we will but use it.

This is not just "church talk" but wherever we are, all the time. The more we respect the words that come out of our mouths in every part of life, the more we respect the words out of God's mouth—the Bible. So be very diligent to keep appointments and promises in personal or business relationships, or do not make them in the first place. Matt 7:12 "Therefore all things whatsoever ye would that men should do to you, do ye even so to them: for this is the law and the prophets." Luke 6:31 "And as ye would that men should do to you, do ye also to them likewise." 1 John 4:20 "If a man say, I *agape*/love God, and hateth his brother, he is a liar: for he that *agape*/loveth not his brother whom he hath seen, how can he *agape*/love God whom he hath not seen? 21 And this commandment have we from him, That he who *agape*/loveth God *agape*/love his brother also." By our actions of treating people as less than God's agents on Earth, we judge others as less than ourselves: Matt 7:1 "Judge not, that ye be not judged. 2 For with what judgment ye judge, ye shall be judged: and with what measure ye mete, it shall be measured to you again." So judge to help and set free in love.

~ 3 ~

ON HOLINESS

Do we have to be perfect before God answers our prayers? Of course not, else how could anyone get the greatest miracle of being born again or saved when they are in the worst state, that of a sinner without a covenant/testament with God? The only one perfect since the fall of Adam has been Jesus Christ. Every other person lived and died in some level of imperfection or sin. Rom 3:10 "As it is written, There is none righteous, no, not one: 11 there is none that understandeth, there is none that seeketh after God. 12 They are all gone out of the way, they are together become unprofitable; there is none that doeth good, no, not one. 13 Their throat is an open sepulchre; with their tongues they have used deceit; the poison of asps is under their lips: 14 whose mouth is full of cursing and bitterness: … 23 For all have sinned, and come short of the glory of God." God's standard for man is the glory of God, His full nature, fully operating throughout the Earth through humans. So unless God has a way for men to get that level of holiness, no one except Jesus is qualified to go to Heaven.

Our access to God is through Jesus Christ: Heb 4:14 "Seeing then that we have a great high priest, that is passed into the heavens, Jesus the Son of God, let us hold fast our profession (*confession*). 15 For we have not an high priest which cannot be touched with the feeling of our infirmities; but was in all points tempted like as we are, yet without sin. 16 Let us therefore come boldly unto the throne of grace, that we may *lambano*/obtain mercy (*not what we deserve for our imperfections, or others because of theirs, but blessed beyond measure because of Jesus*), and find (*perceive*) grace (*the free ability of God to be and do the nature of God on the Earth*) to help in time of need." Rom 3:22 "Even the righteousness of God which is by faith of Jesus Christ unto all and upon all them that believe: for there is no difference: 23 for all have sinned, and come short of the glory of God; 24 being justified freely by his grace through the redemption that is in Christ Jesus: 25 whom God hath set forth to be a propitiation (*blessing now coming as all sins have been reconciled, remitted, purged, removed and healed in Jesus unto aggressive blessing*) through faith in his blood, to declare his righteousness for the remission of sins that are past, through the forbearance of God; 26 to declare, I say, at this time his righteousness: that he might be just, and the justifier of him which believeth in Jesus. 27 Where is boasting then? It is excluded. By what law? of works? Nay: but by the law of faith." Notice faith is a law, just like gravity. Just as sure as a rock falls and a bird flies by the law of flight to overcome gravity, if you operate in the law of faith, God is allowed to move and overcome the natural laws of this world by you.

It is not our holiness that makes the difference, but trusting in the holiness of Jesus, as Peter explained when he and John healed the lame man. Acts 3:12 "And when Peter saw it, he answered unto the people, Ye men of Israel, why marvel ye at this? Or why look ye so earnestly on us, as though by our own power or holiness we had made this man to walk? … 16 And his (*Jesus'*) name through faith in his name hath made this man strong, whom ye see and know: yea, the faith which is by him hath given him this perfect soundness in the presence of you all. 17 And now, brethren, I wot that through ignorance ye did it, as did also your rulers. 18 But those things, which God before had shewed by the mouth of all his prophets, that Christ should suffer, he hath so fulfilled. 19 Repent (*in ignoring Jesus or not knowing Him as Lord and Messiah*) ye therefore, and be converted, that your sins may be blotted out (*purged, put away, remitted, forgiven and justified*), when the times of refreshing shall come from the presence of the Lord." Peter used the name of Jesus to access the holiness of Jesus to get this miracle done, as he had trust that the Lord would do it as promised. (See also Isa 28:12 for the refreshing they would not hear.)

Holiness is not just being free from sin. That makes you a dead rock, and the Earth is already full of those. Holiness means that God can move though you just as He does in Jesus in every part of your life. So you will be perfected in holiness when you are perfected in *agape*/love. 1 John 2:3 "And hereby we do know that we know him, if we keep his commandments. 4 He that saith, I know him, and keepeth not his commandments, is a liar, and the truth is not in him. 5 But whoso keepeth his word, in him verily is the *agape*/love of God perfected: hereby know we that we are in him. 6 He that saith he abideth in him ought himself also so **to walk, even as he walked.**" Eph 4:13 "Till we all come in the unity of the faith, and of the knowledge of the Son of God, unto a perfect man, unto **the measure of the stature of the fulness of Christ**: 14 that we henceforth be no more children, tossed to and fro, and carried about with every wind of doctrine, by the sleight of men, and cunning craftiness, whereby they lie in wait to deceive; 15 but speaking the truth in *agape*/love, may **grow up into him in all things**, which is the head, even Christ." Any other standard is not from God, and not the Gospel that works by faith.

This is the same standard seen in: Rom 3:23 "For all have sinned, and come short of the glory of God." As long as you know the standard is to be just like Jesus Christ, whether you think that is possible or not, you will certainly be free from trusting in your own holiness and fully dependent upon God's mercy. Rom 3:27 "Where is boasting then? It is excluded. By what law? Of works? Nay: but by the law of faith. 28 Therefore we conclude that a man is justified by faith without the deeds of the law." When we begin comparing ourselves with others instead of to Jesus or Father God or Holy Spirit, we get in trouble. 2 Cor 10:12 "For we dare not make ourselves of the number, or compare ourselves with some that commend themselves: but they measuring themselves by themselves, and comparing themselves among themselves, are not wise."

This great promise, made a reality in Jesus, is to control our lives: 2 Cor 6:18: "And will be a Father unto you, and ye shall be my sons and daughters, saith the Lord Almighty. 7:1 Having therefore these promises, dearly *agape*/beloved, let us cleanse ourselves from all filthiness of the flesh and spirit, perfecting holiness in the fear of God." We are to exercise our faith to labor with Holy Spirit to become pure in our souls before God, knowing the entire time that (until we are perfected in holiness) the blood of Jesus has already purged our sin. 1 John 1:5 "This then is the message which we have heard of him, and declare unto you, that God is light, and in him is no darkness at all. 6 If we say that we have fellowship with him, and walk in darkness, we lie, and do not the truth: 7 but if we walk in the light (*letting the Word of God expose our sins to us*), as he is in the light, we have fellowship one with another, and the blood of Jesus Christ his Son cleanseth us from all sin (*for it speaks forever*). 8 If we say that we have no sin, we deceive ourselves, and the truth is not in us. 9 If we confess our sins, he is faithful and just to forgive us our sins (*because of the work of Jesus 2000 years ago*), and to cleanse us from all unrighteousness. 10 If we say that we have not sinned, we make him a liar, and his word is not in us." Notice the standard of cleansing in verse 9: "all unrighteousness." The key to cleansing ourselves is to agree with Him that we sinned and that Jesus already purged our sins 2000 years ago. But it is always against the standard of God Himself. 1 John 2:5 "But whoso keepeth his word, in him verily is the *agape*/love of God perfected: hereby know we that we are in him. 6 He that saith he abideth in him ought himself also so to walk, even as he walked."

We are called to holiness, where God can operate as freely though us as He does Jesus. We are to do this knowing we are made righteous in Jesus, in spite of our current sinful lives/imperfections/failures, as we finish our course in the Earth. 1 Pet 1:14 "As obedient children, not fashioning yourselves according to the former lusts in your ignorance: 15 but as he which hath called you is holy, so be ye holy in all manner of conversation (*words, actions, lifestyle*); 16 because it is written, Be ye holy; for I am holy. 17 And if ye call on the Father, who without respect of persons judgeth according to every man's work, pass the time of your sojourning here in fear: 18 forasmuch as ye know that ye were not redeemed with corruptible things, as silver and gold, from your vain conversation received by tradition from your fathers (*i.e., anything in your life that leads you to believe that you can be anything less than just like Jesus*); 19 but with the precious blood of Christ, as of a lamb without blemish and without spot: 20 who verily was foreordained before the foundation of the world, but was manifest in these last times for you." Rom 6:22 "But now being made free from sin, and become servants to God, ye have your fruit unto holiness, and the end everlasting *zoe*/life. 23 For the wages of sin is death; but the gift of God is eternal *zoe*/life through Jesus Christ our Lord." 2 Cor 7:1 "Having therefore these promises, dearly *agape*/beloved, let us cleanse ourselves from all filthiness of the flesh and spirit, perfecting holiness in the fear of God." A Christian is one made complete, to grow into perfection or maturity in Jesus, to walk like Jesus. Col 2:10 "And ye are complete in him … ."

If you are going to be saved and get to Heaven, God has to do something, if you do not think and act just like Him when you arrive; else you will turn Heaven into another mess. God has a solution; put your sins under the blood of Jesus as soon as you are aware of them now. In other words, keep short accounts with God, or He will deal with your sins later. For Christians, we can clean ourselves by confession and receiving the forgiveness/remission and healing given by grace 2000 years ago, or have it done on the Day of Judgment. 1 Cor 3:11 "For other foundation can no man lay than that is laid, which is Jesus Christ. 12 Now if any man build upon this foundation gold, silver, precious stones, wood, hay, stubble; 13 every man's work shall be made manifest: for the day shall declare it, because it shall be revealed by fire; and the fire shall try every man's work of what sort it is. 14 If any man's work abide which he hath built thereupon, he shall receive a reward. 15 If any man's work shall be burned, he shall suffer loss: **but he himself shall be *sozo*/saved**; yet so as by fire. 16 Know ye not that ye are the temple of God, and that the Spirit of God dwelleth in you?"

The New Testament makes a lot more sense when you focus on verse 15. While showing up on that Day with all of our lives burned as waste/garbage, as Christians we will still pass that day into the fullness of eternal salvation. Even showing up empty-handed with no trace of gold, silver or jewel works is still a wonder worthy of God's love. He has better plans for all of us. Eph 2:10 "For we are his workmanship, created in Christ Jesus unto good works, which God hath before ordained that we should walk in them." Eph 4:1 "I therefore, the prisoner of the Lord, beseech you that ye walk worthy of the vocation wherewith ye are called."

However God is going to do it on that Day, if you are going to Heaven, then that Day will be part of the process that makes you fit to walk there. Preparation for

OTHER HEALING TEACHINGS

that Day is a continual message of the New Testament, not for whether or not you will pass it, but how pleasant will be the process. <u>1 Thes 5:4</u> "But ye, brethren, are not in darkness, that that day should overtake you as a thief. 5 Ye are all the children of light, and the children of the day: we are not of the night, nor of darkness. 6 Therefore let us not sleep, as do others; but let us watch and be sober. 7 For they that sleep sleep in the night; and they that be drunken are drunken in the night. 8 But let us, who are of the day, be sober, putting on the breastplate of faith and *agape*/love; and for an helmet, the hope of *soteria*/salvation. 9 For God hath not appointed us to wrath, but to obtain *soteria*/salvation by our Lord Jesus Christ." If these Christians were not living in darkness, He never would have said, "Wake up!"

There is a more pleasant alternative: <u>1 John 4:16</u> "And we have known and believed the *agape*/love that God hath to us. God is *agape*/love; and he that dwelleth in *agape*/love dwelleth in God, and God in him. 17 Herein is our *agape*/love made perfect, that we may have boldness in the day of judgment: because as he is, so are we in this world. 18 There is no fear in *agape*/love; but perfect *agape*/love casteth out fear: because fear hath torment. He that feareth is not made perfect in *agape*/love." Evil fear keeps us bound to less than God has made us to be. We are to overcome evil fear by walking in *agape*/love.

In 1 Cor 3:15 that word *loss* is not a pleasant experience and is a cause for "terror." <u>2 Cor 5:9</u> "Wherefore we labour, that, whether present or absent, we may be accepted of him. 10 For we must all appear before the judgment seat of Christ; that every one may receive the things done in his body, according to that he hath done, whether it be good or bad. 11 Knowing therefore the terror of the Lord, we persuade men; but we are made manifest unto God; and I trust also are made manifest in your consciences."

<u>Titus 3:3</u> "For we ourselves also were sometimes foolish, disobedient, deceived, serving divers lusts and pleasures, *zao*/living in malice and envy, hateful, and hating one another. 4 But after that the kindness and *agape*/love of God our Saviour toward man appeared, 5 not by works of righteousness which we have done, but according to his mercy he *sozo*/saved us, by the washing of regeneration, and renewing of the Holy Ghost; 6 which he shed on us abundantly through Jesus Christ our Saviour; 7 that being justified by his grace, we should be made heirs according to the hope of eternal *zoe*/life." <u>Titus 2:11</u> "For the grace of God that bringeth *soteria*/salvation hath appeared to all men, 12 teaching us that, denying ungodliness and worldly lusts, we should *zao*/live soberly, righteously, and godly, in this present world; 13 looking for that blessed hope, and the glorious appearing of the great God and our Saviour Jesus Christ; 14 who gave himself for us, that he might redeem us from all iniquity (*wrong thinking that leads to wrong actions or omissions of sin in thought, word or deed*), and purify unto himself a peculiar people, zealous of good works. 15 These things speak, and exhort, and rebuke with all

authority. Let no man despise thee." Acts 3:25 "Ye are the children of the prophets, and of the covenant which God made with our fathers, saying unto Abraham, And in thy seed shall all the kindreds of the earth be blessed. 26 Unto you first God, having raised up his Son Jesus, sent him to bless you, in turning away every one of you from his iniquities." We are to learn to be more pure as we look to pure Jesus.

Holy Spirit went to great trouble to get us the Bible, the Word of God, not as history, but what we need to be successful in God in this world now. It records His promises that He will fulfill. As proved by the life of Jesus, the issue is not His willingness; it is the lack of people who will believe Him in His Word so He can fulfill these promises. It makes sense to trust in the God who cannot lie, whose Word cannot fail, and in whom there is no evil. Num 23:19 "God is not a man, that he should lie; neither the son of man, that he should repent: hath he said, and shall he not do it? or hath he spoken, and shall he not make it good?" Heb 6:17 "Wherein God, willing more abundantly to shew unto the heirs of promise the immutability of his counsel, confirmed it by an oath: 18 that by two immutable things, in which it was impossible for God to lie, we might have a strong consolation (*encouragement*), who have fled for refuge to lay hold upon the hope set before us: 19 which hope we have as an anchor of the soul, both sure and stedfast, and which entereth into that within the veil; 20 whither the forerunner is for us entered, even Jesus, made an high priest for ever after the order of Melchisedec." Rom 3:4 "God forbid: yea, let God be true, but every man a liar; as it is written, That thou mightest be justified in thy sayings, and mightest overcome when thou art judged." Titus 1:2 "In hope of eternal *zoe*/life, which God, that cannot lie, promised before the world began; 3 but hath in due times manifested his word through preaching, which is committed unto me according to the commandment of God our Saviour," 1 John 1:5 "This then is the message which we have heard of him, and declare unto you, that God is light, and in him is no darkness at all." James 1:17 "Every good gift and every perfect gift is from above, and cometh down from the Father of lights, with whom is no variableness, neither shadow of turning." Deut 32:2 "My doctrine shall drop as the rain, my speech shall distil as the dew, as the small rain upon the tender herb, and as the showers upon the grass: 3 because I will publish the name of the LORD: ascribe ye greatness unto our God. 4 He is the Rock, his work is perfect: for all his ways are judgment: a God of truth and without iniquity, just and right is he."

As we walk in the Spirit of God by His Word, we will walk in holiness and fulfill all the requirements of the law. So right works do not make us righteous; faith in the blood of Jesus does that; but the righteous walk in holiness as they sow to themselves in righteousness. Rom 8:1 "There is therefore now no condemnation to them which are in Christ Jesus, who walk not after the flesh, but after the Spirit. 2 For the law of the Spirit of *zoe*/life in Christ Jesus hath made me free from the law of sin and death. 3 For what the law could not do, in that it was weak through the

OTHER HEALING TEACHINGS

flesh, God sending his own Son in the likeness of sinful flesh, and for sin, condemned sin in the flesh: 4 that the righteousness of the law might be fulfilled in us, who walk not after the flesh, but after the Spirit. 5 For they that are after the flesh do mind the things of the flesh; but they that are after the Spirit (*the Scriptures, especially of the new creation*) the things of the Spirit. 6 For to be carnally minded is death; but to be spiritually minded (*in and through the word of God with Holy Spirit indwelling new-creation people*) is *zoe*/life and peace (*produces Heaven on Earth*)." We have to choose if our mind is to be trained into full cooperation with the mind of Christ.

This is not about our strength, but His. We are to exercise His sovereignty, dominion and rulership of getting things done the way He wants, i.e. grace reigning through us: Rom 5:15 "But not as the offence, so also is the free gift. For if through the offence of one many be dead, much more the grace of God, and the gift by grace, which is by one man, Jesus Christ, hath abounded unto many. 16 And not as it was by one that sinned, so is the gift: for the judgment was by one to condemnation, but the free gift is of many offences unto justification. 17 For if by one man's offence death reigned (*as king as evidenced to all the evil and sadness in the world where it is not like Heaven on Earth*) by one; much more they which (*continually*) *lambano*/receive abundance of grace and of the gift of righteousness shall reign (*as kings for Jesus Christ*) in *zoe*/life by one, Jesus Christ. 18 Therefore as by the offence of one judgment came upon all men to condemnation; even so by the righteousness of one the free gift came upon all men unto justification of *zoe*/life. 19 For as by one man's disobedience many were made sinners, so by the obedience of one shall many be made righteous. 20 Moreover the law entered, that the offence might abound. But where sin abounded, grace did much more abound: 21 that as sin hath reigned (*as king through all the forms of slow and fast death, including sickness and disease*) unto death, even so might grace reign (*as king to bring Heaven on Earth by reconciling every evil, including sickness and disease to make Heaven on Earth*) through righteousness unto eternal *zoe*/life by Jesus Christ our Lord." The mission given us by God is certainly of a magnitude worthy of the terrible suffering death of His own Beloved Son, Jesus, the Christ. Jesus paid the price; we get the benefits.

Certainly wanting to see people healed and situations made holy are of God. As we grow in grace, we will see more healing as it is the word of grace which builds us up and not the letter of the Law. 2 Pet 3:18 "But grow in grace, and in the knowledge of our Lord and Saviour Jesus Christ. To him be glory both now and for ever. Amen." Titus 2:11 "For the grace of God that bringeth *soteria*/salvation hath appeared to all men." 2 Cor 3:5 "Not that we are sufficient of ourselves to think any thing as of ourselves; but our sufficiency is of God; 6 who also hath made us able ministers of the new testament; not of the letter, but of the spirit: for the letter (*preaching the Law without the indwelling Spirit to help us*) killeth, but the spirit giveth *zoe*/life. 7 But if the ministration of death, written and engraven in stones, was glorious, so that the children of Israel could not stedfastly behold the face of Moses for the glory of his countenance; which glory was to be done away (*in Jesus*)." Acts 14:3 "Long time therefore abode they (*Paul and Barnabas*) speaking boldly in the Lord, which gave testimony unto the word of his grace, and granted signs and wonders to be done by their hands." Acts 20:24 "But none of these things move me, neither count I my life dear unto myself, so that I might finish my course with joy, and the ministry, which I have received of the Lord Jesus, to testify the gospel of the grace of God. ... 32 And now, brethren, I commend you to God, and to the word of his grace, which is able to build you up, and to give you an inheritance among all them which are sanctified (*to walk like Jesus*)." Col 3:16 "Let the word of Christ dwell in you richly in all wisdom; teaching and admonishing one another in psalms and hymns and spiritual songs, singing with grace in your hearts to the Lord." Acts 26:18 "To open their eyes, and to turn them from darkness to light, and from the power of Satan unto God, that they may receive forgiveness (*remission, purging, putting away and obliteration*) of sins, and inheritance among them which are sanctified by faith that is in me." Col 1:21 "And you, that were sometime alienated and enemies in your mind by wicked works, yet now hath he reconciled 22 in the body of his flesh through death, to present you holy and unblameable and unreproveable in his sight: 23 if ye continue in the faith grounded and settled, and be not moved away from the hope of the gospel, which ye have heard, and which was preached to every creature which is under heaven; whereof I Paul am made a minister."

~ 4 ~

ON TWO WAYS TO POWER WITH GOD

Here are two ways to see God move in power as He did in Jesus:

1) One way is doing right, with no sin in your life anywhere and knowing you are doing right, your holiness of walking just like Jesus.
2) The other way is by faith in the goodness of God independent of your holiness because of your redemption in Jesus.

Let us start with a scripture we often hear quoted out of context and that thus delivers the exact opposite message than intended in this Psalm. Ps 66:18 "If I regard iniquity in my heart, the Lord will not hear me."

First, a definition: *Iniquity* is "those thoughts that are not of God that lead you to sin in any act of commission (doing) or omission (not doing)." When you keep such a thing in your heart, it is called a propensity to sin. So this verse says that God will not hear me unless I have perfect thoughts, i.e., until I think just like Him in my entire heart.

To make it clear, here is another similar rule, God's definition of wickedness: Ps 10:4 "The wicked, through the pride of his countenance, will not seek after God: God is not in all his thoughts." So if your thoughts are not always on God, then you are "wicked" by this definition. So the oft-given explanation for Psalm 66:18: if you regard non-God thoughts = iniquity, or are not thinking on God continually, you are wicked and will not get your prayers answered.

Now let us go back to Psalm 66 and put verse 18 in context: Ps 66:16 "Come and hear, all ye that fear God, and I will declare what he hath done for my soul. 17

I cried unto him with my mouth, and he was extolled with my tongue. 18 If I regard iniquity in my heart, the Lord will not hear me: 19 but verily God hath heard me; he hath attended to the voice of my prayer. 20 Blessed be God, which hath not turned away my prayer, nor his *chesed*/mercy from me."

Notice the message is the exact opposite. In spite of his imperfection, God answered his prayer anyway! This is a great example of: Hos 4:6 "My people are destroyed for lack of knowledge … ." (See also Matt 22:29, Mark 12:24, Eph 4:17 and Heb 4:2.) So all of us who are less than perfect can still get our prayers answered as we focus on the goodness of the Lord. So, as far as God is concerned, greater than iniquity, sin, fault, failure or imperfection is our desire to come to God for help! Therefore God says: Ps 40:4 "Blessed is that man that maketh the Lord his trust … ," 1 Pet 1:3 "Blessed be the God and Father of our Lord Jesus Christ, which according to his abundant mercy hath begotten us again (*born again*) unto a *zao*/lively hope by the resurrection of Jesus Christ from the dead." We can go to God with sin, expecting His mercy in Jesus. We want mercy, good we don't deserve, not justice to get what we deserve, for outside of Jesus no man is perfect in the sight of the Lord.

Holy Spirit shows the contrast of these two approaches of personal holiness or faith in the goodness of the Lord in prayer in the first letter of John. 1 John 3:18 "My little children, let us not *agape*/love [*just*] in word, neither in [*just*] tongue; but [*also*] in deed and in truth. 19 And hereby we know that we are of the truth, and shall assure our hearts before him. 20 For if our heart condemn us, God is greater than our heart, and knoweth all things. 21 *Agape*/beloved, if our heart condemn us not, then have we confidence toward God. 22 And whatsoever we *aiteo*/ask (*require, demand and expecting as due by covenant promise*) we receive of him, because we keep his commandments, and do those things that are pleasing in his sight. 23 And this is his commandment, That we should believe on the name of his Son Jesus Christ, and *agape*/love one another, as he gave us commandment. 24 And he that keepeth his commandments dwelleth in him, and he in him. And hereby we know that he abideth in us, by the Spirit which he hath given us."

The issue here is our confidence in God, not God's willingness to act. We act first, then God moves in us so that we are stronger in Him. The issue is our inner attitude, not what He has already given us. Ps 31:23 "O love the Lord, all ye his saints: for the Lord preserveth the faithful, and plentifully rewardeth the proud doer. 24 Be of good courage, and he shall strengthen your heart, all ye that hope in the Lord." Eph 2:4 "But God, who is rich in mercy, for his great *agape*/love wherewith he *agape*/loved us, 5 even when we were dead in sins, hath quickened us together with Christ, (by grace ye are *sozo*/saved;) 6 and hath raised us up together, and made us sit together in heavenly places in Christ Jesus: 7 that in the ages to come he might shew the exceeding riches of his grace in his kindness toward us

OTHER HEALING TEACHINGS

through Christ Jesus. 8 For by grace are ye *sozo*/saved through faith; and that not of yourselves: it is the gift of God: 9 not of works, lest any man should boast. 10 For we are his workmanship, created in Christ Jesus unto good works, which God hath before ordained that we should walk in them." God has solved all issues from His side with the price of Jesus, by whom He made all that is. He begs us, "Be ye reconciled to God." Stop being at war with Him and declare and make Him your friend.

First John 3:21 says if our heart condemns us not (from either deep inner knowledge of our salvation and forgiveness of sins in Jesus, or because we have been walking in total *agape* love or holiness just like Jesus), then this confidence in us allows God to move in power from Heaven to perform works in the Earth, i.e., answered prayer. Notice that the critical factor is our confidence in God, not His willingness to answer. Our confidence in God opens the door and drives the blessing. Or, as Abraham was described: Rom 4:20 "He staggered not at the promise of God through unbelief; but was strong in faith, (*by*) giving glory (*loud thanks and praise*) to God; 21 and being fully persuaded that, what he had promised, he was able also to perform." It is up to us to keep the door open. The only brass Heaven now is our lack of confidence in God and ignorance of His Word. According to this passage in 1 John, sin consciousness keeps us from confidence in God.

With sin consciousness, we major in guilt, and that makes us cowards before God, "our heart condemns us." We have confidence when "our heart condemn us not," or, as in verse 19, "assure our hearts" with truth. With sin consciousness, there is always something "missing" in our ability to believe God and take Him at His word. We know we are guilty, unworthy and in dread of justly-deserved wrath. And there is no reason for God to answer us, for such a mindset is on the flesh of the world system, and not the truth of the Gospel: Rom 8:5 "For they that are after the flesh do mind the things of the flesh; but they that are after the Spirit the things of the Spirit. 6 For to be carnally minded is death; but to be spiritually minded (*in the knowledge of the true Gospel that no man is right with God so God made all men right in Jesus*) is *zoe*/life and peace. 7 Because the carnal mind is enmity against God: for it is not subject to the law of God, neither indeed can be. 8 So then they that are in the flesh cannot please God [*for we are essentially saying that Jesus did not get the job done of dealing with and healing our rebellion and wicked works, in spite of our best intentions*]." Heb 11:6 "But without faith it is impossible to please him: for he that cometh to God must believe that he is, and that he is a rewarder of them that diligently seek him." Eph 4:17 "This I say therefore, and testify in the Lord, that ye henceforth walk not as other Gentiles walk [*based on sight of what is now, and not on what God says in His great work in Jesus*], in the vanity of their mind, 18 having the understanding darkened, being alienated (*divorced, at war, running and hating*) from the *zoe*/life of God through the ignorance that is in them, because of the blindness of their heart: 19 who being past feeling have given themselves over unto lasciviousness, to work all uncleanness with greediness (*in lack because we lust for everything and never will have enough*). 20 But ye have not so learned Christ." Col 1:21 "And you, that were sometime alienated and enemies in your mind by wicked works, yet now hath he reconciled 22 in the body of his flesh through death, to present you holy and unblameable and unreproveable in his sight." Gal 5:17 "For the flesh lusteth against the Spirit, and the Spirit against the flesh: and these are contrary the one to the other: so that ye cannot do the things that ye would (*because your born again spirit only wants to walk like Jesus*). ... 25 If we *zao*/live in the Spirit, let us also walk in the Spirit." To pay for sin required the blood of Jesus, but our healing required a terrible suffering in His body. By them, He obtained Holy Spirit to dwell in us now, while we still sin. Our salvation is about the purity of Jesus, not ours, for He gives us His purity, and by faith we receive His righteousness.

Thus we look to Holy Spirit in the Word of God and believe God that we are right with Him through Jesus Christ, or we walk in the delusion that anything we can do (or not do) is worthy of God even looking at us. First John 3:21 is the confidence we have when we have been walking in *agape*/love. So the only time we think we qualify for that is:

a) We are ignorant of our real, not just-like-Jesus, walk,

b) We are walking just like Jesus in the full glory of God, or

c) We have renewed our mind into our redemption by the blood of Jesus, and our righteousness is based on Jesus and not ourselves.

In the same chapter, just before this comment on prayer, Holy Spirit says: 1 John 2:6 "He that saith he abideth in him (*Jesus*) ought himself also so to walk, even as he walked." 1 John 3:6 "Whosoever abideth in him sinneth not: whosoever sinneth hath not seen him, neither known him. 7 Little children, let no man deceive you: he that doeth righteousness is righteous, even as he is righteous. 8 He that committeth sin is of the devil; for the devil sinneth from the beginning. For this purpose the Son of God was manifested, that he might destroy the works of the devil." So instead of thinking you are not sinning, agree early with God and know that you are forgiven and healed in Jesus 2000 years ago. The issue is not our sin or imperfections, but our trust in His work of redemption by the cross.

But notice the sin Holy Spirit is talking about in verse 23. 1 John 3:23 "And this is his commandment, That we should believe on the name of his Son Jesus Christ, and *agape*/love one another, as he gave us commandment." So not believing in the effectiveness of the name of Jesus to get acts of *agape*/love for ourselves and others is the sin of concern here. Agree that Jesus died for any unbelief and get your healing.

First John 3:20 is clear, even if our heart condemns us, **GOD DOES NOT!** God is greater than any misdirected, immature, carnal-minded, flesh-driven, faithless, prideful, ignorant, un-renewed Christian heart. Rom 8:32 "He that spared not his own Son, but delivered him up for us all, how shall he not with him also freely give us all things? 33 Who shall lay any thing to the charge of God's elect? It is God that justifieth. 34 Who is he that condemneth? It is Christ that died, yea rather, that is risen again, who is even at the right hand of God, who also maketh intercession for us. 35 Who shall separate us from the *agape*/love of Christ? shall tribulation, or distress, or persecution, or famine, or nakedness, or peril, or sword?"

But self-righteousness can keep us from operating in the grace of God in Jesus! Gal 2:21 "I do not frustrate the grace of God: for if righteousness come by the law, then Christ is dead in vain." Gal 5:4 "Christ is become of no effect unto you, whosoever of you are justified by the law; ye are fallen from grace." Rom 10:2 "For I bear them record that they have a zeal of God, but not according to knowledge. 3 For they being ignorant of God's righteousness, and going about to establish their own righteousness, have not submitted themselves unto the righteousness of God. 4 For Christ is the end of the law for righteousness to every one that believeth." You don't fall from grace by sinning; you fall from grace by not believing that your sins are purged, remitted, redeemed, forgiven and healed in Jesus 2000 years ago, and your total healing was paid for in His body.

A real issue is our self-condemnation. Rom 5:16 "And not as it was by one that sinned, so is the gift: for the judgment was by one (*Adam*) to condemnation, but the free gift is of many offences unto justification (*made without sin through faith in Jesus Christ*)." In self-condemnation you know you are not perfect before God and therefore you are not right with Him because it is about you and not Jesus. Self-righteousness is thus our efforts to cover over our self-condemnation. Titus 3:10 "A man that is an heretick [*in walking in the mind of the flesh in self-righteousness, and not acknowledging the truth that all fall short of the glory of God and we are all justified only by faith in the redeeming and propitiating blood of Jesus,*] after the first and second admonition reject; 11 knowing that he that is such is subverted (*blinded by the devil and unable to receive the* agape/love *of the truth in the Gospel of Jesus Christ*), and sinneth, being condemned of himself."

Note: we are not to cut such people off in our heart. Instead, we are to walk in *agape*/love toward them and get them healed with grace and truth: Gal 6:1 "Brethren, if a man be overtaken in a fault, ye which are spiritual, restore such an one in the spirit of meekness; considering thyself, lest thou also be tempted. 2 Bear ye one another's burdens, and so fulfil the law of Christ." Jude 20 "But ye, *agape*/beloved, building up yourselves on your most holy faith, praying in the Holy Ghost, 21 keep yourselves in the *agape*/love of God, looking for the mercy of our Lord Jesus Christ unto eternal *zoe*/life. 22 And of some have compassion, making a difference: 23 and others *sozo*/save with fear, pulling them out of the fire; hating even the garment spotted by the flesh. 24 Now unto him that is able to keep you from falling, and to present you faultless before the presence of his glory with exceeding joy, 25 to the only wise God our Saviour, be glory and majesty, dominion and power, both now and ever. Amen."

Here is a definition of the level of righteousness Holy Spirit is talking about: 2 Cor 5:21 "For he (*Father God*) hath made him (*Jesus*) to be sin for us, who knew no sin; that we might be made the righteousness of God in him (*Jesus*)." There is no higher level of righteousness than what Father God has in Jesus, The Righteous One. And in Jesus we are made that righteousness of God IN JESUS!

Notice the opposite of condemnation is justification or being made righteousness. 2 Cor 3:9 "For if the ministration of condemnation be glory (*as seen in the face of Moses which faded away over time*), much more doth the ministration of righteousness exceed in glory (*in the face of Jesus which still glows to this day*)." Yes, there is a glory in speaking the law (do right or die, God will not hear you if you regard iniquity in your heart), but that glory, the nature of God released into the Earth from the Law, is nothing compared to the glory of righteousness in Jesus. 2 Cor 3:10 "For even that which was made glorious (*the Law through Moses*) had no glory in this respect (*compared to grace and truth through Jesus*), by reason of the glory that excelleth (*in the grace that justifies us to righteousness*). 11 For if that which is done away (*the Law*) was glorious (*it did release the blessings and miracles of God as seen in the Old Testament*), much more that which remaineth (*being made righteous/justified to zoe/life by faith in Jesus Christ*) is glorious (*the true glory of God, His* agape/love *and nature moving in the Earth in power*)." Rom 5:18 "Therefore as by the offence of one judgment came upon all men to condemnation; even so by the righteousness of one the free gift came upon all men unto justification of *zoe*/life."

Here is a summation of what God did in Jesus, and a warning not to ignore it: Acts 13:37 "But he, whom God raised again, saw no corruption. 38 Be it known unto you therefore, men and brethren, that through this man (*Jesus*) is preached unto you the forgiveness (*remission, purging, putting away and obliteration*) of sins: 39 and by him all that believe are justified from all things, from which ye could not be justified by the law of Moses. 40 Beware therefore, lest that come upon you, which is spoken of in the prophets; 41 behold, ye despisers, and wonder, and perish: for I work a work in your days, a work which ye shall in no wise believe, though a man declare it unto you." More grace and truth means more power!

And this truth of the grace of God is a stumbling block for many, including many Christians, as the following was written to Christians: 1 Pet 2:6 "Wherefore also it is contained in the scripture, Behold, I lay in Sion a chief corner stone, elect, precious: and he that believeth on him shall not be confounded. 7 Unto you therefore which believe he is precious: but unto them [*Jews and those Christians like the Galatians who focus on the Law rather than grace for being right and therefore blessed of God*] which be disobedient, the stone which the builders disallowed, the same is made the head of the corner, 8 and a stone of stumbling, and a rock of offence, even to them which stumble at the word, being disobedient: whereunto also they were

Other Healing Teachings

appointed. 9 But ye are a chosen generation, a royal priesthood, an holy nation, a peculiar people; that ye should shew forth the praises of him who hath called you out of darkness into his marvellous light: 10 which in time past were not a people, but are now the people of God: which had not obtained mercy, but now have obtained mercy." 1 Cor 1:23 "But we preach Christ crucified, unto the Jews a stumblingblock, and unto the Greeks foolishness; 24 but unto them which are called, both Jews and Greeks, Christ the power of God, and the wisdom of God." Rom 10:4 "For Christ is the end of the law for righteousness to every one that believeth." How foolish to think that any level of our right works brings us up to the level of God! Yet, in Jesus, we are brought to that very level: Eph 2:6 "And hath raised us up together, and made us sit together in heavenly places in Christ Jesus: 7 that in the ages to come he might shew the exceeding riches of his grace in his kindness toward us through Christ Jesus. 8 For by grace are ye *sozo*/saved through faith; and that not of yourselves: it is the gift of God: 9 not of works, lest any man should boast." The only cure for sin before God is the blood of Jesus shed 2000 years ago.

When we focus on the glory, the nature of God demonstrated and released in Jesus to make us the righteousness of God in Him, we are changed so that glory now flows though us as it does in Jesus. 2 Cor 3:17 "Now the Lord is that Spirit: and where the Spirit of the Lord is, there is liberty (*to be all God wants us to be*). 18 But we all, with open face beholding as in a glass (*mirror*) the glory of the Lord, are changed into the same image from glory to glory, even as by the Spirit of the Lord." This is the work of Holy Spirit in us now, to get us to really look and see Jesus: Heb 12:2 "Looking unto Jesus the author and finisher of our faith; who for the joy that was set before him endured the cross, despising the shame, and is set down at the right hand of the throne of God. 3 For consider him that endured such contradiction of sinners against himself, lest ye be wearied and faint in your minds." Notice this is a mind, attitude, information or soul problem, and not a fact problem.

Once John has made it clear that the problem is us and the way we think, our minds and hearts, and not God, he then tells us how to get answers to prayer. 1 John 5:9 "If we receive the witness of men, the witness of God is greater: for this is the witness of God which he hath testified of his Son. 10 He that believeth on the Son of God hath the witness in himself: he that believeth not God hath made him (*God*) a liar; because he believeth not the record that God gave of his Son. 11 And this is the record, that God hath given to us eternal *zoe*/life [*by the righteousness of Jesus the free gift came upon all men unto justification of* zoe/*life*], and this *zoe*/life is in his Son. 12 He that hath the Son hath *zoe*/life; and he that hath not the Son of God hath not *zoe*/life. [*A true Christian is one who has* zoe/*life by Holy Spirit dwelling in them*] 13 These things have I written unto you that believe on the name of the Son of God; that ye may know that ye have eternal *zoe*/life, and that ye may believe on the name of the Son of God. 14 And (*because of this knowing*) this is the confidence that we have in him, that, if we (*keep*) *aiteo*/ask*ing* (*requiring, demanding and expecting as due by covenant promise*) any thing according to his will, he heareth us: 15 and if we know that he hear us, whatsoever we *aiteo*/ask (*require, demand and expecting as due by covenant promise*) we know that we have the petitions that we *aiteo*/desired of him. 16 If any man see his brother sin a sin which is not unto death, he shall *aiteo*/ask (*require, demand and expecting as due by covenant promise*), and he shall give him *zoe*/life for them that sin not unto death. There is a sin unto death: I do not say that he shall pray for it. 17 All unrighteousness is sin: and there is a sin not unto death [*as with Ananias and Sapphira in Acts 5:1-10*]." While all sin is of the devil and leads to death, some sin leads to immediate death with little time for repentance.

Notice before John shows us we are falling short of the glory of God by defining our sin, he makes sure we know our sins have already been remitted, purged, washed, destroyed in Jesus: 1 John 2:1 "My little children, these things write I unto you, that ye sin not. And if any man sin, we have an advocate with the Father, Jesus Christ the righteous: 2 and he is the propitiation for our sins: and not for ours only, but also for the sins of the whole world." Now, according to 1 John 5:14, we can now have confidence in the blood of Jesus and get our prayers answered based on this confidence. Or a simpler version: You have the *zoe*/life of God by Jesus to do good, get confidence in God through Jesus and walk in *agape*/love by setting others free by grace, or get more truth of the Gospel in you so you can walk in more love power.

So two ways to get answered prayer are:

1) Holiness or perfection in God, or
2) Faith in the blood of Jesus and trust in God's goodness.

Thus Peter said after one notable miracle: Acts 3:12 "And when Peter saw it, he answered unto the people, Ye men of Israel, why marvel ye at this? or why look ye so earnestly on us, as though by our own power or holiness we had made this man to walk? ... 16 And his name (*Jesus*) through faith in his name hath made this man strong, whom ye see and know: yea, the faith which is by him hath given him this perfect soundness in the presence of you all."

If you already see it, then you do not need to have faith for it. Faith is about things unseen in the current world, but seen in your mind's eye as coming true. This thing called faith is that which God makes substance, reality, in the near or far future out of the absolute assurance of things unseen on the Earth of God's Word, and this assurance, confidence and persuasion, in the love and the honesty of God produces the joyful expectation of coming good, per Heb 11:1. And what is this core faith we are to have? Acts 24:24 "And after certain days, when Felix came with his wife Drusilla, which was a Jewess, he sent for Paul, and heard him concerning the faith in Christ. 25 And as he reasoned of righteousness, temperance, and judgment to come ..." Rom 4:5 "But to him that worketh not, but believeth on him that justifieth the ungodly, his faith is counted for righteousness. 6 Even as David also describeth the blessedness of the man, unto whom God imputeth righteousness without works, 7 saying, Blessed are they whose iniquities are forgiven, and whose sins are covered. 8 Blessed is the man to whom the Lord will not impute sin."

Eph 3:11 "According to the eternal purpose which he purposed in Christ Jesus our Lord: 12 in whom we have boldness and access with confidence by the faith of him."

Phil 3:9 "And be found in him, not having mine own righteousness, which is of the law, but that which is through the faith of Christ, the righteousness which is of God by faith."

Col 2:6 "As ye have therefore received Christ Jesus the Lord, so walk ye in him: 7 rooted and built up in him, and stablished in the faith, as ye have been taught, abounding therein with thanksgiving. 8 Beware lest any man spoil you through philosophy and vain deceit, after the tradition of men, after the rudiments of the world, and not after Christ. 9 For in him dwelleth all the fulness of the Godhead bodily. 10 And ye are complete in him, which is the head of all principality and power: 11 in whom also ye are circumcised with the circumcision made without hands, in putting off the body of the sins of the flesh by the circumcision of Christ: 12 buried with him in baptism, wherein also ye are risen with him through the faith of the operation of God, who hath raised him from the dead. 13 And you, being dead in your sins and the uncircumcision of your flesh, hath he quickened together with him, having forgiven you all trespasses; 14 blotting out the handwriting of ordinances that was against us, which was contrary to us, and took it out of the way, nailing it to his cross; 15 and having spoiled principalities and powers, he made a shew of them openly, triumphing over them in it." Notice Col 2:6 commands us to walk in Jesus so the world cannot tell the difference between us and Jesus, as Father God in the flesh. That is the standard set by God and made possible in Jesus, and we cannot offer the excuse that we can never meet it.

Heb 10:38 "Now the just shall *zao*/live by faith: but if any man draw back, my soul shall have no pleasure in him. 39 But we are not of them who draw back unto perdition; but of them that believe to the *sozo*/saving of the soul (*heart, mind, will and emotions*)."

Heb 11:11 "Through faith also Sara herself received strength to conceive seed, and was delivered of a child when she was past age, because she judged him faithful who had promised. 12 Therefore sprang there even of one, and him as good as dead, so many as the stars of the sky in multitude, and as the sand which is by the sea shore innumerable."

Heb 12:2 "Looking unto Jesus the author and finisher of our faith; who for the joy that was set before him endured the cross, despising the shame, and is set down at the right hand of the throne of God. 3 For consider him that endured such contradiction of sinners against himself, lest ye be wearied and faint in your minds."

1 Pet 1:21 "Who by him do believe in God, that raised him up from the dead, and gave him glory; that your faith and hope might be in God. 22 Seeing ye have purified your souls in obeying the truth through the Spirit unto unfeigned *phileo*/love of the brethren, see that ye *agape*/love one another with a pure heart fervently: 23 being born again, not of corruptible seed, but of incorruptible, by the word of God, which *zao*/liveth and abideth for ever. 24 For all flesh is as grass, and all the glory of man as the flower of grass. The grass withereth, and the flower thereof falleth away: 25 but the word of the Lord endureth for ever. And this is the word which by the gospel is preached unto you" and by which you are born again.

Rev 1:5 "And from Jesus Christ, who is the faithful witness, and the first begotten of the dead, and the prince of the kings of the earth. Unto him that *agape*/loved us, and washed us from our sins in his own blood, 6 and hath made us kings and priests unto God and his Father; to him be glory and dominion for ever and ever. Amen. ... 17 And when I saw him, I fell at his feet as dead. And he laid his right hand upon me, saying unto me, Fear not; I am the first and the last: 18 I am he that *zao*/liveth, and was dead; and, behold (*make this change your life*), I am *zao*/alive for evermore, Amen; and have the keys of hell and of death."

Luke 24:46 "And (*Jesus*) said unto them, Thus it is written, and thus it behoved Christ to suffer, and to rise from the dead the third day: 47 and that repentance and remission (*purging, removal, obliteration, washing, separating and freeing*) of sins should be preached in his name among all nations, beginning at Jerusalem."

Acts 10:36 "The word which God sent unto the children of Israel, preaching peace by Jesus Christ: (he is Lord of all:) 37 that word, I say, ye know, which was published throughout all Judaea, and began from Galilee, after the baptism which John preached; 38 how God anointed Jesus of Nazareth with the Holy Ghost and with power: who went about doing good, and healing all that were oppressed (*under the active dominion, reign and lordship*) of the devil; for God was with him. 39 And we are witnesses of all things which he did both in the land of the Jews, and in Jerusalem; whom they slew and hanged on a tree: 40 him God raised up the third day, and shewed him openly; 41 not to all the people, but unto witnesses chosen before of God, even to us, who did eat and drink with him after he rose from the dead. 42 And he commanded us to preach unto the people, and to testify that it is he which was ordained of God to be the Judge of quick and dead. 43 To him give all the prophets witness, that through his name whosoever believeth in him shall receive remission (*obliteration*) of sins."

Acts 20:21 "Testifying both to the Jews, and also to the Greeks, repentance toward God, and faith toward our Lord Jesus Christ."

Other Healing Teachings

Rom 5:1 "Therefore being justified by faith, we have peace with God through our Lord Jesus Christ: 2 by whom also we have access by faith into this grace wherein we stand, and rejoice in hope of the glory of God."

Gal 2:16 "Knowing that a man is not justified by the works of the law, but by the faith of Jesus Christ, even we have believed in Jesus Christ, that we might be justified by the faith of Christ, and not by the works of the law: for by the works of the law shall no flesh be justified. … 21 I do not frustrate the grace of God: for if righteousness come by the law, then Christ is dead in vain."

Let us see this faith in operation. Peter had denied Christ not many months before and knew he had nothing to offer God, but: Acts 3:6 "Then Peter said, Silver and gold have I none; but such as I have give I thee: In the name of Jesus Christ of Nazareth rise up and walk." The more we know "such as I have," the more we will be able to get in better agreement with God and see more answered prayer.

But it takes work: John 15:7 "If ye abide (*continue, tarry in pleasure or expecting good and enjoying it, comfortable*) in me, and my words abide (*continue, tarry in pleasure or expecting good and enjoying it, comfortable*) in you, ye shall *aiteo*/ask (*require, demand and expecting as due by covenant promise*) what ye will, and it shall be done unto you. 8 Herein is my Father glorified, that ye bear much fruit; so shall ye be my disciples." John 8:31 "Then said Jesus to those Jews which believed on him, If ye continue in my word, then are ye my disciples indeed; 32 and ye shall know the truth, and the truth shall make you free [*so you can set yourself and others free*]."

So until we walk like Jesus, I recommend trusting in the finished work of Jesus by the cross rather than our own holiness, but still labor with Holy Spirit to walk as He walked. That trusting will actually release more of Jesus in your life. If you find yourself depending on your own holiness as to why God will answer prayer, just ask Holy Spirit to show you where you are not walking just as He walked. Phil 3:8 "Yea doubtless, and I count all things but loss for the excellency of the knowledge of Christ Jesus my Lord: for whom I have suffered the loss of all things, and do count them but dung, that I may win Christ, 9 and be found in him, not having mine own righteousness, which is of the law [*as I do more holiness in Jesus*], but that which is through the faith of Christ, the righteousness which is of God by faith: 10 that I may know him, and the power of his resurrection, and the fellowship of his sufferings, being made conformable unto his death; 11 if by any means I might attain unto the resurrection of the dead. 12 Not as though I had already attained, either were already perfect: but I follow after, if that I may apprehend that for which also I am apprehended of Christ Jesus. 13 Brethren, I count not myself to have apprehended: but this one thing I do, forgetting those things which are behind, and reaching forth unto those things which are before, 14 I press toward the mark for the prize of the high calling of God in Christ Jesus. 15 Let us therefore, as many as be perfect, be thus minded: and if in any thing ye be otherwise minded, God shall reveal even this unto you."

What is more, we have been commanded to cooperate with God. If I have a bag with red, green, and white rocks, the rocks are set apart from all other rocks because they are in a bag. If I pour out the rocks and separate the red from the green and white, the red are now separated from the other rocks that were in the bag. This is the meaning of sanctification, being set apart. So the rocks in the bag are sanctified from all other rocks on the earth, and when I poured them out and set apart the red rocks, and the red rocks were thus sanctified from the other rocks in the bag and from all other rocks in the earth. If I now say, no one else can use the red rocks but me, the red rocks are sanctified and set apart only for my use or made holy unto me. That is what holy means, set apart for exclusive use. So when the Bible says we are sanctified in Jesus, we are set apart from all other men in Christ. When the Bible says we are holy, this means we are dedicated for the exclusive use of God through Christ. Growth in Christ is the process by which we actually see ourselves set apart from other men and into Christ, and holiness is when God actually can move in us as He wants. This is the essence of the New Covenant. Heb 8:10 "For this is the covenant that I will make with the house of Israel after those days, saith the Lord; I will put my laws into their mind, and write them in their hearts: and I will be to them a God, and they shall be to me a people: 11 and they shall not teach every man his neighbour, and every man his brother, saying, Know the Lord: for all shall know me, from the least to the greatest. 12 For I will be merciful to their unrighteousness, and their sins and their iniquities will I remember no more." Because of Jesus, sin is no longer an issue between God and you.

The New Covenant does not depend on your righteousness or freedom from sin, but on Jesus and His freedom from sin. In the Gospel of Jesus, you are now a temple of God, a place where God dwells in the Earth so He can produce Heaven on Earth through you. 2 Cor 6:16 "And what agreement hath the temple of God with idols? for ye are the temple of the *zao*/living God; as God hath said, I will dwell in them, and walk in them; and I will be their God, and they shall be my people." Actually producing Heaven on Earth through you, by you and God working together, is God's New Testament definition of holiness. He does not inhabit our sin, but God does inhabit our spirit by Holy Spirit. 1 Cor 3:16 "Know ye not that ye are the temple of God, and that the Spirit of God dwelleth in you?" He dwells in us because of His grace toward us in Jesus when we got born-again in the new creation, and not our holiness.

God tells us: Rom 6:22 "But now being made free from sin, and become servants (*slaves*) to God, ye have your fruit unto holiness (*God working through*

OTHER HEALING TEACHINGS

you to manifest Heaven on Earth because you know you are made the righteousness of God in Christ Jesus, and not based on your current level of purity in walking just like Jesus), and the end everlasting *zoe*/life. 23 For the wages of sin is death; but the gift of God is eternal *zoe*/life through Jesus Christ our Lord." You releasing *zoe*/life by grace is holiness God commands.

While we diligently work by faith to get as pure as Jesus is pure, we are to *lambano* continually the abundance of grace and the permanent gift of righteousness to deliver the *zoe* life of God, as needed. That means we hold on to the legal right to the use of the name of Jesus and expect His *zoe* life to flow in healing power, as we *aiteo* in the name of Jesus against the devil and for the one in need. This is how we reign for Jesus to deliver His *zoe* life while we still sin now.

Holy Spirit says it this way: Rom 5:17 "For if by one man's offence death reigned (*as king in the sickness, death, poverty and lack of Hell on Earth*) by one; much more they which (*continually*) *lambano*/receive abundance of grace and of the [*permanent*] gift of righteousness shall reign (*right now as a king in the healing, abundance and prosperity of Heaven on Earth*) in *zoe*/life by one, Jesus Christ.) ... 21 that as sin hath reigned unto death (*as king in the sickness, death, poverty and lack of Hell on Earth*), even so might grace reign (*right now as king in the healing, life, abundance and prosperity of Heaven on Earth*) through [*the permanent gift*] righteousness unto eternal *zoe*/life by Jesus Christ our Lord."

It is not about our holiness but our knowing that we are made the righteousness of God in Jesus by our faith: 1 Cor 1:30 "But of him (*Father God*) are ye in Christ Jesus, who of God is made unto us wisdom, and righteousness, and sanctification, and redemption."

And the wonder of the ages is that our faith in the work of Jesus, combined with the power of the name of Jesus, produces the reign of the Kingdom of God. Acts 3:12 "And when Peter saw it, he answered ... [*it was not*] by our own power or holiness we had made this man to walk? ... 16 [*but by*] his (*Jesus'*) name through faith in his name hath made this man strong, whom ye see and know: yea, the faith which is by him (*Jesus*) hath given him this perfect soundness (*healing to walking and leaping*) in the presence of you all."

Once you have some of these basics facts in your mind, then start to exercise the dominion or Kingdom of Jesus, as a king for Jesus, by *aiteo*ing the devil to get out of that situation in the name of Jesus and calling those things that be not as if they are, just like Jesus did. And if it already is, then you give thanks, praise and joy before you see it! This is how the imperfect Christian can walk in the power of the perfect Jesus.

~ 5 ~

ON DOUBTS COMING

A key promise in God is that the devil will attack and resist the Word of God you believe. Matt 13:18 "Hear ye therefore the parable of the sower. 19 When any one heareth the word of the kingdom, and understandeth it not, then cometh the wicked one, and catcheth away that which was sown in his heart. This is he which received seed by the way side. 20 But he that received the seed into stony places, the same is he that heareth the word, and anon with joy receiveth it; 21 yet hath he not root in himself, but dureth for a while: **for when tribulation or persecution ariseth because of the word, by and by he is offended**. 22 He also that received seed among the thorns is he that heareth the word; and the care of this world, and the deceitfulness of riches, choke the word, and he becometh unfruitful. 23 But he that received seed into the good ground is he that heareth the word, and understandeth it; which also beareth fruit, and bringeth forth, some an hundredfold, some sixty, some thirty."

According to verse 19 the devil steals what we do not understand. No belief means no attack. If we have some understanding then the devil challenges the truth of that word with attacks that attempt to cause us to be offended in God and believe that He is not trustworthy in His Word, but a liar. Matt 13:21 "Yet hath he not root in himself, but dureth for a while: for when tribulation or persecution ariseth **because of the word**, by and by he is **offended**." This is the territory of doubting and fainting, and all must pass through it. We are promised harassing fear and evil circumstances before the answer comes.

Other Healing Teachings

Next, the devil attacks by keeping you "busy" so you have little time for the things of God or for God Himself. Finally, the successful one *lambano*/receives the word and keeps it against all attacks to success. Luke 8:15 "But that on the good ground are they, which in an honest and good heart, having heard the word, keep it (*continually seize and grip it through offenses, doubts, resistance, trials, temptations and worldly distractions*), and bring forth fruit with patience (*consistency and faithfulness*)." Mark 4:20 "And these are they which are sown on good ground; such as hear the word, and *lambano*/receive it, and bring forth fruit, some thirtyfold, some sixty, and some an hundred."

This process is a promise, a warning, and a description of how we are to overcome to the end that God is glorified in His people: John 15:5 "I am the vine, ye are the branches: he that abideth in me, and I in him, the same bringeth forth much fruit: for without me ye can do nothing. 6 If a man abide not in me, he is cast forth as a branch, and is withered; and men gather them, and cast them into the fire, and they are burned. 7 If ye abide in me, and my words abide in you, ye shall *aiteo*/ask (*require, demand and expect as due by covenant promise*) what ye will, and it shall be done unto you. 8 Herein is my Father glorified, that ye bear much fruit; so shall ye be my disciples." Abiding in Him means simply knowing you are in Him and *agape*/loved by grace. The issue is how well we abide in Jesus in knowing His *zoe*/life is still in us, in spite of our sins.

So do not think attacks, offenses and fear-storms are unusual; this is a secret of God's Kingdom. Your faith will be tried in this process of believing God in His Word while the devil is in the world. The Word of God does nothing until you start to believe it in the face of present conditions that say it is wonderful, but there is no way in the natural for this to happen: 1 Pet 1:6 "Wherein ye greatly rejoice, though now for a season, if need be, ye are in heaviness through manifold temptations: 7 that the trial of your faith, being much more precious than of gold that perisheth, though it be tried with fire, might be found unto praise and honour and glory at the appearing of Jesus Christ: 8 whom having not seen, ye *agape*/love; in whom, though now ye see him not, yet believing, ye rejoice with joy unspeakable and full of glory: 9 receiving the end of your faith, even the *soteria*/salvation of your souls." Notice one of the ways to *agape*/love God is to *lambano* with joy crying, "I will see it yet" until you win and produce fruit. Notice in verse 6 you are admonished to greatly/continuously rejoice (excited, loud yelling, arm waving, jumping and dancing) while your feelings are in "heaviness" or depression. This is a major change for those trained to follow only their feelings.

One of the primary ways the devil attacks the Word you are believing, "*lambano*ing," is to assail you with actual circumstances that conflict with the Word and/or doubts. These doubts can come with great pressure and include thoughts such as: "Who do you think you are to heal the sick?" "God will not answer you." "This will never work." "It is taking too long." "You are not worthy." "They/you have too much sin." "You/They will die." Or "Even God cannot heal or do that." The list goes on and on.

Doubting thoughts are not the problem, but fainting or stopping is. Ps 27:13 "I had fainted, unless I had believed to see the goodness of the Lord in the land of the living." Many mocked Jesus to get Him to doubt. We all have doubts and often with great intensity. The problem is allowing them to stay as they exalt themselves against the knowledge of God to get us to not believe Him and to faint or stop in our believing efforts of right confession, *aiteo*/commanding, thanksgiving, praise and rejoicing. 2 Cor 10:3 "For though we walk in the flesh, we do not war after the flesh: 4 (for the weapons of our warfare are not carnal, but mighty through God to the pulling down of strong holds;) 5 casting down imaginations, and every high thing that exalteth itself against the knowledge of God, and bringing into captivity every thought to the obedience of Christ." All successful people control their thoughts!

Doubting is not about the thoughts; it is about entertaining them or being offended by them so that we no longer do the necessary good works. As you *aiteo*/ask to get the sick healed, or any other aspect of God's salvation into the Earth, the devil would not attack you with doubts if you were not doing him any harm. He is happy to have you lost in carnal, fleshly pursuits. Instead of lonely and terrifying doubts, the devil through others will actually encourage you to stay in sin. It really does not matter to him which they are, just as long as you do not do the works of faith. In this case, the intensity of the doubts is almost a backhanded compliment. You are hurting him, and he wants you to stop. So keep swinging that sword of the Word of God, keep praying/ *aiteo*/asking and thanking and praising! We are to respond to these doubts and twisted truths the same way Jesus did, with the Word of God. James 1:21 "Wherefore lay apart all filthiness and superfluity of naughtiness, and *lambano*/receive with meekness the engrafted word, which is able to *sozo*/save your souls (*heart, mind, will and emotions*). 22 But be ye doers of the word, and not hearers only, deceiving your own selves." The failure to *aiteo*, give thanks, praise and rejoice will keep you deceived!

Also keep your attitudes right: Phil 4:4 "Rejoice in the Lord alway: and again I say, Rejoice (*excited, loud yelling, shouting, arm waving, jumping and dancing*). 5 Let your moderation be known unto all men. The Lord is at hand. 6 Be careful for nothing; but in every thing by prayer and supplication with thanksgiving (*excited, loud yelling words of thanks and praise with arm waving, jumping and dancing*) let your requests (*aiteo*/demands) be made known unto God. 7 And the peace of God, which passeth all understanding, shall keep your hearts and minds through Christ Jesus. 8 Finally, brethren, whatsoever things are true, whatsoever things are honest, whatsoever things are just, whatsoever things are pure, whatsoever things are lovely, whatsoever things are of good report; if there be any virtue, and if there be any praise, think on these things. 9 Those things, which ye have both learned, and received, and heard, and seen in me, do: and the God of peace shall be with you." The salvation of God is simply His Word, settled in Heaven, now manifested on Earth.

This is exactly what God told Joshua. When He told Joshua to have courage, He was saying to have faith in God. And yes, it will require you to do this in the face of impossible situations and while your mind is plagued with negative thoughts and people's accusations and mockery night and day. Study and meditate on the Word of God, especially His promises. As Jesus told the devil, "It is written ..." (Luke 4:1-14 and Matt 4:1-11). So open your mouth and speak truth, God's promises, as needed.

To meditate in the Old Testament means to "chew as a cow chews its cud." It is not emptying your mind, as in Eastern meditation. Instead, it is keeping it filled with God's Word. This is not a speed contest, but a deep diving or a hard-rock mining contest. Start with one or two key scriptures. Work the Word, study, ponder and keep it in your mind all day and night to make your way successful. Put the particular verses you have chosen on index cards to help in memorization and in reminding you to speak them out loud, and make them into songs and chants. Josh 1:5 "There shall not any man be able to stand before thee all the days of thy life: as I was with Moses, so I will be with thee: I will not fail thee, nor forsake thee. 6 **Be strong and of a good courage** (*in* aiteo, *confession, thanksgiving, praise and rejoicing*)**:** for unto this people shalt thou divide for an inheritance the land, which I sware unto their fathers to give them. 7 **Only be thou strong and very courageous**, that thou mayest observe to do according to all the law, which Moses my servant commanded thee: turn not from it to the right hand or to the left, that thou mayest prosper whithersoever thou goest. 8 This book of the law shall not depart out of thy mouth; **but thou shalt meditate (***chew with your mouth***) therein day and night**, that thou mayest observe to do according to all that is written therein: for then thou shalt make thy way prosperous, and then thou shalt have good success. 9 Have not I commanded thee? **Be strong and of a good courage** (*in* aiteo, *confession, thanksgiving, praise and rejoicing*)**; be not afraid, neither be thou dismayed**: for the LORD thy God is with thee whithersoever thou goest."

Jesus described doubting as that which you let get into your heart that gets you to stop believing and to stop doing those things to bring His Word to pass. Matt 21:21 "Jesus answered and said unto them, Verily I say unto you, If ye have faith, and doubt not, ye shall not only do this which is done to the fig tree, but also if ye shall say unto this mountain, Be thou removed, and be thou cast into the sea; it shall be done. 22 And all things, whatsoever ye shall *aiteo*/ask (*require, demand*

and expect as due by covenant promise) in prayer, believing, ye shall receive." Mark 11:20 "And in the morning, as they passed by, they saw the fig tree dried up from the roots. 21 And Peter calling to remembrance saith unto him, Master, behold, the fig tree which thou cursedst is withered away. 22 And Jesus answering saith unto them, Have faith in God (*or operate in faith like God does*). 23 For verily I say unto you, That whosoever shall say unto this mountain, Be thou removed, and be thou cast into the sea; and shall not doubt in his heart, but shall believe that those things which he saith shall come to pass; he shall have whatsoever he saith. 24 Therefore I say unto you, What things soever ye *aiteo*/desire (*require, demand and expect as due by covenant promise*) when ye pray, believe that ye receive them, and ye shall have them. [*And to show how to overcome the real faith killer of not walking in forgiveness.*] 25 And when ye stand praying, forgive, if ye have ought against any: that your Father also which is in heaven may forgive you your trespasses. 26 But if ye do not forgive, neither will your Father which is in heaven forgive your trespasses."

Jesus made it clear that getting miracles done is not dependent upon the amount of *agape*/love you walk in. This is stated in Matt 7: 21-23 and, of course, when referring to a loveless, mountain-moving faith in 1 Cor 13:1-3. Many have said, "Lord, Lord," and worked mighty miracles without actually knowing the God of *Agape*/Love. They did understand the legal position of Jesus as Lord and the power of His name to release the *zoe*/life of God. And much like a crooked, or less-than-perfect policeman, even though he may be crooked, that does not change the power of the badge he wears. The name of Jesus, as Lord, is our badge. Healing, in that sense, is far more mechanical or legal.

The problem comes when we believe that healing or miracles are dependent upon our holiness or righteousness. That becomes a limitation not from God. If it were true that healing depends upon our holiness, the only miracles in the Bible would have been those of Jesus, and this is absolutely not the case. Any weakening of the standard of God Himself is un-holiness. Until you are just like Jesus in your entire walk, you have un-holiness in your life. If you are going to focus on perfection or holiness then none of the disciples from the gospels onward would qualify. The more you walk in *agape*/love the more you can fulfill the purpose for which God saved us, to reflect Himself into the Earth just like Jesus does, and the less of your life that will burn on the Day of Judgment as wood, hay and stubble (see 1 Cor 3:10-16).

God loves all mankind, and to walk in any offense or unforgiveness means that you have an area where you and God disagree. As we hold unforgiveness, we are calling ourselves greater than God, and thus it is a form of idolatry, covetousness and evil lust. This is also described as a lack of fellowship, partnership, agreement, communion or relationship, for God sends His rain on the just and the unjust alike. Rom 5:6 "For when we were yet without strength, in due time Christ died for the ungodly." No one Jesus healed was worthy of healing, and it is no different today. The problem is in us. So in the same way a police badge gives authority independent of the policeman, it is not our holiness, but the name of Jesus and faith in that name that can release God's love even though you are not perfect in your Christ-like walk.

As a policeman fires his gun, when you keep speaking *aiteo* commands against the devil, just like the bullets from a gun do their job when properly aimed, so will your *aiteo* thoughts, words, looks or touch. That is why healing and being healed are of grace and not our holiness. Acts 3:12 "And when Peter saw it, he answered unto the people, Ye men of Israel, why marvel ye at this? or why look ye so earnestly on us, as though by our own power or holiness we had made this man to walk? … 16 And his name (*Jesus*) through faith in his name hath made this man strong, whom ye see and know: yea, the faith which is by him hath given him this perfect soundness in the presence of you all."

Healing is about Jesus' holiness, not ours. In any healing battle you can focus only on Jesus as Lord, and for extra punch and personal benefit, God's love for people, and get people healed. Imperfection is not a limitation. This is the miracle of Christ in you, the hope of glory. Keep in the fight and do not stop because of doubt. Use the Battle Prayer to stir yourself up into abundant grace and the gift of righteousness, and command life in the name of Jesus.

Here Jesus describes doubting as beginning to look at the problems or the chaos around you more than looking to God: Matt 14:28 "And Peter answered him and said, Lord, if it be thou, bid me come unto thee on the water. 29 And he said, Come. And when Peter was come down out of the ship, he walked on the water, to go to Jesus. 30 But when he saw the wind boisterous, he was afraid; and beginning to sink, he cried, saying, Lord, *sozo*/save me. 31 And immediately Jesus stretched forth his hand, and caught him, and said unto him, O thou of little faith, wherefore didst thou doubt?" Notice that Peter did not sink like a stone but, starting to fear and thus losing his confidence in God, he began to sink. So he was still in power or ability, just not enough to keep him fully on top of the situation.

In the Old Testament, we trusted in the God who was with us, but not in us. In the New Testament, new creation, God dwells within us, and we are a new kind of creature. We abide and defeat the doubts by continually confessing our status in Jesus in the New Creation with thanksgiving, praise and joy. We renew our minds to truth by staying in the word of Christ (the New Testament) with thanksgiving, praise and joy, not as feelings, but as actions reflecting the power, *agape*/love, the mind of Christ in us, mercy, acceptance, grace and truth of Jesus.

While we find much about salvation in the Old Testament, you won't find much of this "Christ in you" there. Eph 3:2 "If ye have heard of the dispensation of the grace of God which is given me to you-ward: 3 how that by revelation he made known unto me the mystery; (as I wrote afore in few words, 4 whereby, when ye read, ye may understand my knowledge in the mystery of Christ) 5 **which in other ages was not made known unto the sons of men,** as it is now revealed unto his holy apostles and prophets by the Spirit; 6 that the Gentiles should be fellowheirs, and of the same body, and **partakers of his promise in Christ by the gospel**: 7 whereof I was made a minister, according to the gift of the grace of God given unto me by the effectual working of his power." Col 1:25 "Whereof I am made a minister, according to the dispensation of God which is given to me for you, to fulfil the word of God; 26 even the mystery which hath **been hid from ages and from generations**, but now is made manifest to his saints: 27 to whom God would make known what is the riches of the glory of this mystery among the Gentiles; **which is Christ in you, the hope of glory**: 28 whom we preach, warning every man, and teaching every man in all wisdom; that we may present every man perfect in Christ Jesus: 29 whereunto I also labour, striving according to his working, which worketh in me mightily." 1 Cor 2:7 "But we speak the wisdom of God in a mystery, **even the hidden wisdom**, which God ordained before the world unto our glory: 8 which none of the princes of this world knew: for had they known it, they would not have crucified the Lord of glory." Gal 1:3 "Grace be to you and peace from God the Father, and from our Lord Jesus Christ, 4 who gave himself for our sins, that he might deliver us from this present evil world, according to the will of God and our Father: 5 to whom be glory for ever and ever. Amen." Gal 4:4 "But when the fulness of the time was come, God sent forth his Son, made of a woman, made under the law, 5 to redeem them that were under the law, that **we might receive the adoption of sons**. 6 And because ye are sons, **God hath sent forth the Spirit of his Son into your hearts**, crying, Abba, Father. 7 Wherefore thou art no more a servant, but a son; and if a son, then an heir of God through Christ." 1 Pet 1:9 "Receiving the end of your faith, even the *soteria*/salvation of your souls. 10 Of which *soteria*/salvation the prophets have inquired and searched diligently, who prophesied **of the grace that should come unto you**: 11 searching what, or what manner of time the Spirit of Christ which was in them did signify, when it testified beforehand the sufferings of Christ, and the glory that should follow. 12 Unto whom it was revealed, that not unto themselves, but unto us they did minister the things, which are now reported unto you by them that have preached the gospel unto you with the Holy Ghost sent down from heaven; which things the angels desire to look into. 13 Wherefore gird up the loins of your mind, be sober, and hope to the end for the grace that is to be brought unto you at the revelation of Jesus Christ." Rom 16:25 "Now to him that is of power to stablish you according to my gospel, and the preaching of Jesus Christ, according to the revelation of the mystery, **which was kept secret since the world began,** 26 but now is made manifest, and by the scriptures of the prophets, according to the commandment of the everlasting God, made known (*now*) to all

OTHER HEALING TEACHINGS

nations for the obedience of faith: 27 to God only wise, be glory through Jesus Christ for ever. Amen." This is the New Testament revelation of Christ in us.

If you become shaken in your confidence, tired, offended or bitter, get your heart re-aligned with God. Read the Scriptures, study and research the teachings, make the confessions and thanksgivings with your mouth, and get back in the battle by praying the Battle Prayer. This is the work of patience, consistency, and faithfulness when it is no fun. In this way we "keep," guard, renew and *sozo*/save, heal our souls. Jesus said: Luke 21:19 "In your patience (*constant and faithful exuberant thanks, praise and joy to God*) possess (*keep under righteous control*) ye your souls (*heart, mind, will, and emotions*)." Luke 8:15 "But that on the good ground are they, which in an honest and good heart, having heard the word, keep it, and bring forth fruit with patience (*consistency, faithfulness*)." Gratefully rejoice always!

When you find yourself under attack by doubts, here is an ancient prayer: **Ps 61:1** "Hear my cry, O God; attend unto my prayer. 2 From the end of the earth will I cry unto thee, when my heart is overwhelmed: lead me to the rock that is higher than I. 3 For thou hast been a shelter for me, and a strong tower from the enemy. 4 I will abide in thy tabernacle for ever: I will trust in the covert of thy wings. Selah. 5 For thou, O God, hast heard my vows: thou hast given me the heritage of those that fear thy name. 6 Thou wilt prolong the king's life: and his years as many generations. 7 He shall abide before God for ever: O prepare *chesed*/mercy and truth, which may preserve him. 8 So will I sing praise unto thy name for ever, that I may daily perform my vows." Notice that the daily habit of thanksgiving, praise and prayer, especially for those in government, is one of your attack weapons and your defense against doubts (see 1 Tim 2).

This controlled, sound mind attitude is expressed this way: James 1:2 "My brethren, count it all joy when ye fall into divers temptations (*trials, devil attacks and tests, as promised in the parable of the sower—Matt 13, Mark 4 and Luke 8*); 3 knowing this, that the trying of your faith worketh patience (*practiced consistency and faithfulness*). 4 But let patience (*consistency, faithfulness*) have her perfect work, that ye may be perfect and entire, wanting nothing. 5 If any of you lack wisdom, let him *aiteo*/ask (*keep on requiring, demanding and expecting as due by convent promise, knowing all requirements have been met in Jesus*) of God, that giveth to all men liberally, and upbraideth not; and it shall be given him. 6 But let him *aiteo*/ask in faith (*requiring, demanding and expecting as due by convent promise, knowing all requirements have been met in Jesus*) nothing wavering. For he that wavereth is like a wave of the sea driven with the wind and tossed. 7 For let not that man think that he shall receive any thing of the Lord. 8 A double minded man is unstable in all his ways." Heb 10:36 "For ye have need of patience (*consistency, faithfulness*), that, after ye have done the will of God, ye might receive the promise. 37 For yet a little while, and he that shall come will come, and will not tarry. 38 Now the just shall *zao*/live (*see the power of*

God in the Earth) by faith: but if any man draw back [*from faith battles*], my soul shall have no pleasure in him. 39 But we are not of them who draw back unto perdition (*letting death rule in any situation*); but of them that believe to the *sozo*/saving of the soul (*to operate fully in the heart, mind, will and emotions as Jesus would*)." Thanksgiving clears the heart-crud from a hardening or hardened heart.

Testing the Spirits: Another method to defeat doubts from the devil is to discover their source. Those that are not of God, refute them. We are going to be doing physical things, according to the Word of God and having an impact on the spiritual world that can be seen in the physical world. We are told: 2 Cor 10:3 "For though we walk in the flesh (*physical world in physical bodies*), we do not war after the flesh: 4 (for the weapons of our warfare are not carnal, but mighty through God to the pulling down of strong holds;) 5 casting down imaginations, and every high thing that exalteth itself against the knowledge of God, and bringing into captivity every thought to the obedience of Christ." Notice the battleground of this spiritual battle is in our minds. The requirement is to determine the source of every thought and measure them against whether or not Jesus would think or keep thinking on them. This is a way to make captive "every thought to the obedience of Christ."

Besides having the entire Bible in your heart, we are told also to deal directly with the spiritual realm to validate our thoughts by challenging the source of every thought. 1 John 4:1 "*Agape*/beloved, believe not every spirit, but try the spirits whether they are of God: because many false prophets are gone out into the world. 2 Hereby know ye the Spirit of God: Every spirit that confesseth that Jesus Christ is come in the flesh is of God: 3 and every spirit that confesseth not that Jesus Christ is come in the flesh is not of God: and this is that spirit of antichrist, whereof ye have heard that it should come; and even now already is it in the world."

This command is from God and is one of the 1,050 or so New Testament commands for a successful Christian life. The *beloved* in verse 1 includes the Christian people to whom John was writing. A definition for *prophet* is "one who speaks for a spirit." A false prophet is one who does not speak for God, but for the devil/spirit of antichrist/spirit of error. John is warning them that error starts with accepting apparent truth in our thoughts, leading to more and more vocal or outward deception, so that the evil spirits can speak freely through Christians. The same result is even worse among men in general. A hallmark of our time is deceiving spirits that deceive even the elect. Mark 13:22 "For false Christs and false prophets shall rise, and shall shew signs and wonders, to seduce, if it were possible, even the elect." Matt 16:23 "But he (*Jesus*) turned, and said unto Peter, Get thee behind me, Satan: thou art an offence unto me: for thou savourest not the things that be of God, but those that be of men." Luke 9:53 "And they did not receive him, because his face was as though he would go to Jerusalem. 54 And when his disciples James and

Other Healing Teachings

John saw this, they said, Lord, wilt thou that we command fire to come down from heaven, and consume them, even as Elias did? 55 But he turned, and rebuked them, and said, Ye know not what manner of spirit ye are of." Wow! They were deceived even as they talked with Jesus!

There are several specific examples of Christians being deceived in the New Testament. We know the dramatic events related in Galatians when Peter no longer thought in the mind of Christ (see Gal 2:11-16) and was publicly rebuked by Paul. The conclusion of that passage is the heart of the mighty work of God in Jesus: Gal 2:21 "I do not frustrate the grace of God: for if righteousness come by the law, then Christ is dead in vain." Peter was in great deception in this case, not to mention the entire church in Galatia: Gal 3:1 "O foolish Galatians, who hath bewitched you, that ye should not obey the truth, before whose eyes Jesus Christ hath been evidently set forth, crucified among you?" Concerning other Christians lost in deception, Paul wrote: 1 Tim 1:19 "Holding faith, and a good conscience; which some having put away concerning faith have made shipwreck: 20 of whom is Hymenaeus and Alexander; whom I have delivered unto Satan, that they may learn not to blaspheme."

Just as Satan deceived Adam and Eve and the Galatians with false arguments and doubts that essentially attacked the integrity and honesty of God and the work of Jesus Christ by the cross, the devil is still at it. Here is a source of antichrist and error deception: 1 John 2:15 "*Agape*/love not the world, neither the things that are in the world. If any man *agape*/love the world, the *agape*/love of the Father is not (*operative*) in him. 16 For all that is in the world, the lust of the flesh, and the lust of the eyes, and the pride of *bios*/life, is not of the Father, but is of the world. 17 And the world passeth away, and the lust thereof: but he that doeth the will of God abideth for ever." In this command, Holy Spirit is telling us Christians to continually validate what and who we are really loving in our desires, words and actions.

This passage, in 1 John 4:1-3, tells us that many of our thoughts are from other spirits, God's and the devil's, and we are to talk directly to the source of our thoughts to discover their source. We are to command them to confess that "Jesus Christ is come in the flesh"–an exact formula. If the thought is of God, then God will be pleased with your obedience to His Word. After all, this is His command on how to avoid and refute deception and doubts, and Holy Spirit will gladly respond, and devils/lying/antichrist/error spirits will not.

One way to perform the truths expressed in 1 John 4:1-3 is when you are aware of any thoughts (especially decisions, scriptural interpretations or assessments of people and situations). *Confess* means to agree that it is true by repeating it back. Then, in your mind, or out loud, command the source of the thought to confess "Jesus Christ is come in the flesh." This usually means confess back to your mind, but if you see angels/spiritual beings that appear in the flesh, follow the same procedure. This is a command, and you are a child of God, and you should expect to hear the exact wording back. If you do not hear the confession "Jesus Christ is or has come in the flesh," in reply and rather quickly, then it is not of God. In that case, command it to go in the name of Jesus, and ask the Lord to get truth into your life in that area. If you hear the exact wording being repeated back to you, then the thought is of God, as in verse 4:2. In that case, thank Father God for confirming His Word, and respond appropriately to what you have heard. If you want to know the will of God, this is a method He has given. Like many things of the Spirit in God, you will become more proficient the more you do this.

What follows is a simple sequence upon being aware of a thought. First ask or think, "Lord is that you?" Then wait for a yes or no in your mind. Then whatever you hear (silence is usually the same as a "no"), command that spirit to confess that Jesus Christ is come in the flesh, in the name of Jesus, right then. If you hear, "Jesus Christ is come in the flesh," as in accordance with 1 John 4:2, that is Holy Spirit. If not, command it to go immediately in the name of Jesus, and ignore the thought. Then quote a refuting scripture against the thought, and ask the Lord to teach you His ways in that particular area.

Jesus said: John 10:27 "My sheep hear my voice, and I know them, and they follow me." First of all, the word for *sheep* in this scripture means a mature ewe or female sheep, not a lamb. Christian maturity is not measured by how long you have been a Christian, but by how much you are like Jesus in your current walk. While healings and miracles are included, even immature Christians work miracles as seen in Mark 16 and 1 Cor 12. If you are mature in Christ, then: 1 John 2:5 "But whoso keepeth his word, in him verily is the *agape*/love of God perfected: hereby know we that we are in him. 6 He that saith he abideth in him ought himself also so to walk, even as he walked." Until we walk in this maturity of perfected *agape*/love, to the measure of the fullness of Christ, and grow into Him in all things per Eph 4:13-15, we need to obey 1 John 4:1-3.

The person with a Christ-like mind, operating, not in the spirit of fear or unbelief, but in the spirit of power, *agape*/love and a sound mind wants to know this is God speaking, and that he or she is walking in the light of truth by Holy Spirit and not a deceiving angel of light. This is no different than the verification processes used in a bank for cashing a check, or in the military upon receipt of orders of any kind. In both cases, identification and validation are required. This is a war, and you need to know who is talking to you. Here is the "doing truth" attitude we should have in this process: John 3:20 "For every one that doeth evil hateth the light, neither cometh to the light, lest his deeds should be reproved. 21 But he that doeth truth cometh to the light, that his deeds may be made manifest, that they are wrought in God." Eph 5:10 "Proving what is acceptable unto the Lord. 11 And have no fellowship with the unfruitful works of darkness, but rather reprove them. 12

OTHER HEALING TEACHINGS

For it is a shame even to speak of those things which are done of them in secret. 13 But all things that are reproved are made manifest by the light: for whatsoever doth make manifest is light. 14 Wherefore he saith, Awake thou that sleepest, and arise from the dead, and Christ shall give thee light. 15 See then that ye walk circumspectly, not as fools, but as wise, 16 redeeming the time, because the days are evil. 17 Wherefore be ye not unwise, but understanding what the will of the Lord is." 1 Thes 5:18 "In every thing give thanks: for this is the will of God in Christ Jesus concerning you. 19 Quench not the Spirit. 20 Despise not prophesyings. 21 Prove all things; hold fast that which is good. 22 Abstain from all appearance of evil. 23 And the very God of peace sanctify you wholly; and I pray God your whole spirit and soul and body be preserved blameless unto the coming of our Lord Jesus Christ." Luke 16:13 "No servant can serve two masters: for either he will hate the one, and *agape*/love the other; or else he will hold to the one, and despise the other. Ye cannot serve God and mammon. ... 15 And he said unto them, Ye are they which justify yourselves before men; but God knoweth your hearts: for that which is highly esteemed among men is abomination in the sight of God."

This manual is designed as a self-contained tool, along with the Battle Prayer, to get you going in time of crisis, teaching you and helping build your confidence; and it contains many scriptures you can study and then release or deliver more *zoe*/life to a hurting world. John 10:10 "The thief cometh not, but for to steal, and to kill, and to destroy: I am come that they might have *zoe*/life, and that they might have it more abundantly." 1 John 5:13 "These things have I written unto you that believe on the name of the Son of God; that ye may know that ye have eternal *zoe*/life, and that ye may believe on the name of the Son of God." And this knowledge should change the kinds of prayers you pray and the results you see: 1 John 5:14 "And this is the confidence that we have in him, that, if we *aiteo*/ask (*keep on demanding and require*) any thing according to his will, he heareth us: 15 and if we know that he hear us, whatsoever we *aiteo*/ask, we know that we have the petitions that we *aiteo*/desired of him. 16 If any man see his brother sin a sin which is not unto death, he shall *aiteo*/ask (*demand, require*), and he (*Father God*) shall give him *zoe*/life for them that sin not unto death. There is a sin unto death (*see Acts 5*): I do not say that he shall pray for it. 17 All unrighteousness (*that which is not just like Jesus Christ in thought, word or deed*) is sin: and there is a sin not unto death."

Therefore God has given us, the Church, the Body of Christ, the hands and feet of Jesus on Earth, the job of implementing the *agape*/love reconciliation God did in Jesus, by getting others healed and having our righteous prayers answered. The word *salvation* includes total healing and restoration to the best of God. 2 Cor 5:14 "For the *agape*/love of Christ constraineth us; because we thus judge, that if one died for all, then were all dead: 15 and that he died for all, that they which *zao*/live should not henceforth *zao*/live unto themselves, but unto him which died for them, and rose again. 16 Wherefore henceforth know we no man after the flesh: yea, though we have known Christ after the flesh, yet now henceforth know we him no more. 17 Therefore if any man be in Christ, he is a new creature: old things are passed away; behold, all things are become new. 18 And all things are of God, who hath reconciled us to himself by Jesus Christ, and hath given to us the ministry of reconciliation; 19 to wit, that God was in Christ, reconciling the world unto himself, not imputing their trespasses unto them; and hath committed unto us the word of reconciliation. 20 Now then we are ambassadors for Christ, as though God did beseech you by us: we pray you in Christ's stead, be ye reconciled to God. 21 For he hath made him to be sin for us, who knew no sin; that we might be made the righteousness of God in him. 6:1 We then, as workers together with him, beseech you also that ye receive not the grace of God in vain. 2 (For he saith, I have heard thee in a time accepted, and in the day of *soteria*/salvation have I succoured thee: behold (*appreciate, understand and make this change your life*), now is the accepted time; behold, now is the day of *soteria*/salvation.)"

As I continue proclaiming and *aiteo*/praying the Scriptures, I am getting them more into me, to convert myself (writing them in my heart and in my mind), so that I may operate as Father God desires: <u>James 1:21</u> "Wherefore lay apart all filthiness and superfluity of naughtiness, and *lambano*/receive with meekness the engrafted word, which is able to *sozo*/save your souls (*mind, will, emotions, and hearts, to match your Christian/born-again spirit and Holy Spirit who dwells within you*). 22 But be ye doers of the word, and not hearers only, deceiving your own selves." Of course reading, reading out loud, thanksgiving, praise, rejoicing, praying *aiteo*/commanding and healing the sick are all acts of "doing" our faith. To stop "doing" is to walk in doubt. To walk in obedience and faith is to start doing. As John Lake said, "You can pray and pray, but if you do not start doing, you pray yourself into unbelief." (Blake, *Writings from Africa*, p 99.) Resist those doubts, knowing the answers will come by putting the Word of God in your mouth, and start doing, and you will see God move. He is waiting on us.

~ 6 ~

ON STIRRING YOURSELF UP

As I read aloud the Scriptures in this manual and in the Battle Prayer itself, I am stirring myself up to believe the love of God and the knowledge that, as Jesus is inside me by the gift of Holy Spirit, He wants to manifest His finished work even more than I do. Jesus paid for our healing at a great price. We are simply the delivery agents and enforcers of what He has already done. 2 Tim 1:6 "Wherefore I put thee in remembrance that thou stir up the gift of God, which is in thee by the putting on of my hands. 7 For God hath not given us the spirit of fear; but of power (*ability*), and of *agape*/love, and of a sound mind." All that is needed is in me. As I renew my mind to agree with God on healing and keep myself stirred-up or agitated, I see healing.

Words related to *stir or stirred-up* include encouraged, excited, committed, confident, determined, enthusiastic, shouting, exhorting, giving a pep-talk, comforting, and strengthening myself in God, and being strong in the Lord and in the power of His might. Isa 42:12 "Let them give glory unto the LORD, and declare his praise in the islands. 13 The LORD shall go forth as a mighty man, he shall stir up jealousy (*intense desire to destroy his enemies*) like a man of war: he shall cry, yea, roar; he shall prevail against his enemies." Being an imitator of God means we stir ourselves up also!

Notice God stirring Himself up is related to our praise. If God does it, I know that so must I: Ps 35:23 "Stir up thyself, and awake to my judgment, even unto my cause, my God and my Lord. 24 Judge me (*for deliverance*), O LORD my God, according to thy righteousness; and let them not rejoice over me. 25 Let them not say in their hearts, Ah, so would we have it: let them not say, We have swallowed him up. 26 Let them be ashamed and brought to confusion together that rejoice at mine hurt: let them be clothed with shame and dishonour that magnify themselves against me. 27 Let them shout for joy, and be glad, that favour my righteous cause: yea, let them say continually, Let the LORD be magnified, which hath pleasure in the prosperity of his servant. 28 And my tongue shall speak of thy righteousness and of thy praise all the day long." Let's shout "The Lord be magnified!"

Again God says to stir ourselves up. 2 Pet 1:12 "Wherefore I will not be negligent to put you always in remembrance of these things, though ye know them, and be established in the present truth. 13 Yea, I think it meet, as long as I am in this tabernacle, to stir you up by putting you in remembrance." 1 Pet 4:10 "As every man hath received the gift [*Holy Spirit*], even so minister [*in enthusiasm*] the same one to another, as good stewards of the manifold grace of God." And notice how related this is to speaking: Eph 4:29 "Let no corrupt communication proceed out of your mouth, but that which is good to the use of edifying, that it may minister grace unto the hearers. 30 And grieve not the holy Spirit of God, whereby ye are sealed unto the day of redemption. 31 Let all bitterness, and wrath, and anger, and clamour, and evil speaking, be put away from you, with all malice: 32 and be ye kind one to another, tenderhearted, forgiving one another, even as God for Christ's sake hath forgiven you." So get firm and rejoice: dance, shout, clap your hands, confess the Scriptures, praise and stir yourself up into confidence in God. Be strong in the Lord and the power of His might!

Holy Spirit fully declares: 1 Cor 2:4 "And my speech and my preaching was not with enticing words of man's wisdom, but in demonstration of the Spirit and of *dunamis*/power: 5 that your faith should not stand in the wisdom of men, but in the *dunamis*/power of God." While many have struggled to get the Gospel truth out, it is fair to say that, for the most part, in the Western world at least, preaching has emphasized more the wisdom of men and not the power of God. In general, Western Christian churches are not places where people go to get healed of blindness, arthritis, cancer or any other infirmity. Yet Jesus said, prophesied, this is what believers would do. In the 2nd and 3rd worlds, many do go to the Christian churches, of a variety of denominations, and there are healed in the name of Jesus.

A renewed mind must deal with the fact that we are to grow up into Jesus in "all" respects, and that includes healing and signs and wonders in the name of Jesus. Eph 4:13 "Till we all come in the unity of the faith, and of the knowledge of the Son of God, unto a perfect, mature man, unto the measure of the stature of the fulness of Christ: 14 that we henceforth be no more children, tossed to and fro, and carried about with every wind of doctrine, by the sleight of men, and cunning craftiness, whereby they lie in wait to deceive; 15 but speaking the truth in *agape/love*, may grow up into him in all things, which is the head, even Christ." Jesus

OTHER HEALING TEACHINGS

healed, and so must those who are like Him. This is clear, according to 1 Pet 2:24 "… by his stripes ye were healed."

Jesus is ever the Healer, for He cannot change His nature: Heb 13:8 "Jesus Christ the same yesterday, and to day, and for ever." We have the same Spirit as Jesus had. Gal 4:6 "And because ye are sons, God hath sent forth the Spirit of his Son into your hearts, crying, Abba, Father." Therefore our inner desire is to walk just like Jesus walked, because He is in us. It takes much training in soul corruption to continue to deny this core nature of a Christian, the Christ in you.

Based on the historical records (and the Bible is one of the supreme, historically-validated, ancient documents), ancient Judaism and early Christianity are steeped in the miraculous power of God demonstrated through less-than-perfect men and women. Not the least of these was Peter, who, for years, was a central figure for God, and then, in Galatians, denied the core of the work of Jesus. It is not our purpose to provide the scriptural evidence for healing. I simply offer that the word *Christian*, "a Christ-like one," says it all.

The Ministry Confessions in this book contain numerous references to the fact that each believer is to readily minister healing per Mark 16:17-18. Other ancient texts of the first three hundred years of Christianity support that it was the laymen, and not just the leaders, who were known for miracles, thus living out Mark 16:17-18. A renewed mind with the purpose of operating in the *agape*/love of God includes this healing ability from God, as one is stirred up in Him.

The Anglican Church studied the powerful events reported in South Africa under the ministry of Dr. John G. Lake around 1912, concluded that it was biblical and started a healing ministry within that church that continues today (the Emmanuel Society and The Order of Saint Luke). *The Healing Reawakening* by Francis MacNutt (Chosen Books, Grand Rapids MI, 2006) states that today in Africa a church that cannot deliver healing in the name of Jesus loses attendance. Thus, the Catholic Church is now operating in such miracles on that continent. For more details on this, please visit www.jglm.org, the official website of John G. Lake Ministries. Immersion into this material is a way to stir yourself up in God.

The Ministry Confessions contain appropriate scripture confessions for healing, assuming that Mark 16:17-18 is the expected behavior for every Christian, and not just a special few. The issue is to align your soul with grace and truth, to release grace and truth.

One way to describe how healing, or any other activity, releases the *zoe*/life of God into a situation is to imagine an irrigation pump. First, there is a source of water. This is the healing *zoe* in the Word of God and in your spirit with Holy Spirit. Faith is both the hose and the pump. The valve for water to flow through is your heart, single-minded on healing in compassion and/or in the power of the name of Jesus. Put the hose to the water, turn on the pump, open the valve and you can pump life. We are the hose, the pump and the valve is our soul, and the *zoe* travels by faith through our soul to the one in need. Soul agreement with God in compassion, authority, righteousness and judgment is the pump pressure. Together, as co-laborers, man and God heal people of the devil's oppressions with God's *zoe*/life.

The fuel for this operation is authority in the name of Jesus, compassion, righteousness and judgment to make people free rising up within you. And, just as you need a spark plug and ignition system to start an engine, the "stirring up" is our ignition system, to light the fires that burns in our souls. That "stirring up" process aligns our hearts and our minds (opens the valve) with God and His *agape*/love so He can flow readily though us. With a heart firmly entrenched in the Word of God (a hose connected to the lake), the valve open and the pump running, we release the *zoe* of God to heal, just as Jesus did, with our words and/or hands.

Jesus is our example, and we see that He walked in great confidence in Father God and freely delivered *zoe*/life, God's resurrection power. John 11:33 "When Jesus therefore saw her weeping, and the Jews also weeping which came with her, he groaned (*snorted as a war horse ready to go to battle, a sign of stirring himself up*) in the spirit, and was troubled (*stirred, agitated in himself*)." This was equivalent to Jesus stirring Himself up as the "pump" to push out the *zoe* of God.

Here we see Him continuing in this "stirring-up." Notice, first, they knew that God heard Him and that Jesus could deliver the *zoe*/life of God at will. John 11:37 "And some of them said, Could not this man, which opened the eyes of the blind, have caused that even this man should not have died? 38 Jesus therefore again groaning (*stirred-up to change something, agitated in an aggressive manner*) in himself cometh to the grave. It was a cave, and a stone lay upon it."

Notice the confidence Jesus had with God: John 11:39 "Jesus said, Take ye away the stone. Martha, the sister of him that was dead, saith unto him, Lord, by this time he stinketh: for he hath been dead four days. 40 Jesus saith unto her, Said I not unto thee, that, if thou wouldest believe, thou shouldest see the glory of God? 41 Then they took away the stone from the place where the dead was laid. And Jesus lifted up his eyes, and said, **Father, I thank thee that thou hast heard me. 42 And I knew that thou hearest me always:** but because of the people which stand by I said it, that they may believe that thou hast sent me. 43 And when he thus had spoken, he cried with a loud voice (*strong and direct*), Lazarus, come forth. 44 And he that was dead came forth, bound hand and foot with graveclothes: and his face was bound about with a napkin. Jesus saith unto them, Loose him, and let him go." Notice the glory of God includes raising the dead. God's glory is seen in tangible acts of His power.

Jesus was not quiet or subdued throughout this entire process. So a quiet church is not always the stirred-up attitude necessary to raising the dead or getting the power of God moving through you.

OTHER HEALING TEACHINGS

Jesus was agitated, stirred up to fix a wrong, and had confidence that God heard Him. Our confidence in God is one of the paths for God to be able to answer our *aiteo* (asking, requiring, demanding, expecting and desiring) Him to move in power. 1 John 5:13 "These things have I written unto you that believe on the name of the Son of God; that ye may know that ye have eternal *zoe*/life, and that ye may believe on the name of the Son of God. 14 And this is the confidence that we have in him, that, if we *aiteo*/ask (*and keep on* aiteo/*asking*) any thing according to his will, he heareth us: 15 and if we know that he hear us, whatsoever we *aiteo*/ask (*require, demand and expect as due by covenant promise*), we know that we have the petitions that we *aiteo*/desired of him. 16 If any man see his brother sin a sin which is not unto death, he shall *aiteo*/ask, and he shall give him *zoe*/life for them ... ." The issue is our "knowing" Father God heard us to obey us in our request. (Right hearing means you hear and you obey what you have heard. Answered prayer means God heard and obeyed your *aiteo* demands per His covenant promises.)

Confidence expressed in our mouth and our actions is the valve. For this to be successful, our subconscious (or heart) needs to cooperate with our intentions and attitude to deliver healing. Right affirmations are one of God's ways to build these right attitudes. Thanksgiving, praise, gladness, enthusiasm, agitation, invigoration, and being stirred up are all parts of the pump to empower the *zoe*/life to flow where it is needed. We focus on the power of the death, resurrection and glorification of Jesus seated beside the Father, and not the bad situation.

This does not mean just outward invigoration but can be an attitude of the heart so that on the outside you are calm, but on the inside a raging furnace of God's *agape*/love to release His *zoe*/life into the Earth for people and/or indignation against the devil. Rev 1:13 "And in the midst of the seven candlesticks one like unto the Son of man, clothed with a garment down to the foot, and girt about the paps with a golden girdle. 14 His head and his hairs were white like wool, as white as snow; and **his eyes were as a flame of fire**; 15 and his feet like unto fine brass, as if they burned in a furnace; and his voice as the sound of many *roaring* waters." You can have the fire of Jesus burning in your heart to release the *zoe*/of God. 1 John 4:17 "... because as he is, so are we in this world." Constant repetition is needed to stir yourself into this.

I have observed, for myself and others, that when ministering *zoe*/life I need to take a few moments to stir myself up to start or to maintain the enthusiasm of Holy Spirit. Often this is done with a few moments of praise or speaking in tongues, walking and clapping and shouting. To get the "pump" going may require much longer if you are in a "cold start." Even during periods of long ministry to many people, the effective minister will regularly stop ministering and take a few moments to get refreshed and stirred up again into God's enthusiasm. This is when ministering to large groups of people on a one-by-one basis. As a normal course of your life, if you stay stirred up into God's *agape*/love all day you can be ready to minister in a moment's notice, as you stop to let compassion build to release His *zoe* anytime, anywhere.

If you become distracted by what others think or how inadequate you are, put your mind back on the Lord who came to destroy the works of the devil and left us with the job of finishing the work. Fear of man is a snare, and with continued use of the Minister Confessions you will renew your mind to be a useful co-laborer with God and overcome any fear of man. Since healing and being healed are by grace, you will never be worthy, so start praising God for His strength instead.

The people of Israel were asked to cross the Jordan River and kill giants. Most of them lived a "bad report," and they died in the desert. Ps 78:41 "Yea, they turned back and tempted God, and limited the Holy One of Israel." A bad attitude in mere men stopped God. We may have Holy Spirit dwelling within us, but He is still limited by our soul's enthusiasm and confidence. 2 Tim 1:6 "Wherefore I put thee in remembrance that thou stir up the gift of God, which is in thee by the putting on of my hands. 7 For God hath not given us the spirit of fear; but of *dunamis*/power (*ability*), and of *agape*/love, and of a sound mind (*to think and act just like Jesus would*)." Notice we may have the gift and power of Holy Spirit, but until we get our thinking and our emotions lined up, He cannot come out and exercise that *dunamis* power and *agape* love and get us into right Jesus-thinking in the mind of Christ in the Scriptures.

One of the goals is that this affirmation becomes, not theory, but a reality, and you are deeply conscious of the ever-present Christ in your life for every situation and event on His terms, not just yours. Gal 2:19 "For I through the law am dead to the law, that I might *zao*/live unto God. 20 I (*have been*) crucified with Christ: nevertheless I *zao*/live; yet not I, but Christ *zao*/liveth in me: and the life which I now *zao*/live in the flesh I *zao*/live by the faith of the Son of God, who *agape*/loved me, and gave himself for me. 21 I do not frustrate the grace of God: for if righteousness come by the law, then Christ is dead in vain." Walking in this is walking in the confidence that Jesus had.

Make your faith effective in demonstrating the supernatural power of God as Jesus did. 2 Cor 13:5 "Examine yourselves, whether ye be in the faith; prove your own selves. Know ye not your own selves, how that Jesus Christ is in you, except ye be reprobates (*useless, like garbage, ineffective*)?" Philem 6 "That the communication of thy faith may become effectual by the acknowledging of every good thing which is in you in Christ Jesus." 1 Cor 2:5 "That your faith should not stand in the wisdom of men, but in the power of God." Right stirring up changes your focus toward God and off of yourself.

You can take almost any section of the Minister Confessions and use it to "stir yourself up into God" into enthusiasm, with loud words, bold confessions, shout-

OTHER HEALING TEACHINGS

ing, clapping, dancing, walking, running, prancing, smiling, singing, jumping, arm waving, and yelling. Fullness of joy is not quite or sad but, rather, full of life, praise and thanksgiving. So delivering the healing of God is part of being like Jesus in fullness of joy. Ps 16:11 "… in thy presence is fulness of joy … ."

With the Ministry Confession we can keep our heart in the Word of God as they contain many scriptures on divine healing. With our attaching strong positive emotion to the right thoughts and actions to deliver healing, we prepare our heart to cooperate, and not fight us, as we *aiteo* for ourselves or others. Our faith (confidence, courage) opens the heart valve to deliver the *zoe*/life that God so longs to deliver through each of us in the Body of Christ. As we focus on the completeness of the body and blood propitiation of Jesus and the power and love of His resurrection, we now operate from Jesus seated with the Father, and not in the pain and fear of any present evil situation.

If you do not see the results you need in one hour, repeat 3 to 20 times per hour, each hour, until you do. This is about results and not just saying, "Well, I prayed; let's see what God will do." You are the determining factor, not God. Luke 10:19 "Behold (*appreciate, understand and make this change your life*), I give unto **YOU** power (*commission and ability*) to tread on serpents and scorpions, and over all the power of the enemy: and nothing shall by any means hurt you. 20 Notwithstanding in this rejoice not, that the spirits are subject unto you; but rather rejoice, because your names are written in heaven." *Tread* includes many steps of dominion until subdued. What you tolerate you force God to tolerate until you will tolerate it no longer, until you get stirred up into His attitude toward any work of the devil, and your heart cry becomes: "Out, in the name of Jesus!"

The secret, as learned by Dr. Lake, is to stir yourself up in God and stay that way so your spirit is running your soul, and not the other way around. With a renewed mind, your soul will cooperate in this. Smith Wigglesworth said, "If the spirit is not moving, I move the spirit." And Dr. Lake said, "It is a law of the human mind that one can act themselves into believing quicker than they can believe themselves into acting" (Blake, *The Voice of Healing*, Episode 2, for both quotes.)

~ 7 ~
ON FAITH

The world is currently in great need, yet there seems to be little of God's promises in action. But need does not move God or allow Him to move in goodness on the Earth. God honors faith in Him, not need. Heb 11:1 "Now faith is the substance of things hoped for, the evidence of things not seen. … 6 But without faith it is impossible to please him: for he that cometh to God must believe that he is, and that he is a rewarder of them that diligently seek him." (Diligence = Focused, Continuous Effort). So, to see God move, we need to operate in faith in Him, per His Word, as He has declared His Word is even greater than His name. Ps 138:2 "I will worship toward thy holy temple, and praise thy name for thy *chesed*/lovingkindness and for thy truth: for thou hast magnified thy word above all thy name." John 17:17 "… thy truth: thy word is truth." To operate in truth means to operate in the Word of God. Faith is before you see it done, not after.

There are various levels of faith in God. Rom 12:6 "Having then gifts differing according to the grace that is given to us, whether prophecy, let us prophesy according to the **proportion of faith**." That Greek word translated *proportion* is the combination of two words: *piece* or portion, and *word*. The issue is us, not God, for all of God is in or behind His Word in Jesus. So the level of faith is what proportion of it you are really operating in. Holy Spirit gives; we use what proportion we have faith for, whether full or partial.

Your greatest gift and the gift of the ages is Holy Spirit. Gal 3:13 "Christ hath redeemed us from the curse of the law, being made a curse for us: for it is written, Cursed is every one that hangeth on a tree: 14 that the blessing of Abraham might come on the Gentiles through Jesus Christ; that we might receive the promise of the Spirit through faith." Holy Spirit is all the gifts and the ability of God. He needs God's words to act on. You can operate by faith in the gifts, or by faith in the Giver of the gifts; it is up to you. I see more results as I expect Holy Spirit to provide whatever is needed. The key is to give Holy Spirit the words of God He can use to get the job done.

Jesus is the living Word of God. John 1:1 "In the beginning was the Word, and the Word was with God, and the Word was God. 2 The same was in the beginning with God. 3 All things were made by him; and without him was not any thing made that was made. 4 In him was *zoe*/life; and the *zoe*/life was the light of men." Rev 19:13 "… and his name is called The Word of God." The Bible, the written Word of God, is our only physical connection to God. As we read the Word of God, we can hear the words of God in our mind, or if we speak it out loud, we can hear the Word of God in our ears. Jesus is that Word made flesh, so we can see the way God really is and how He wants to act in a man. 1 John 1:1 "That which was from the beginning, which we have heard, which we have seen with our eyes, which we have looked upon, and our hands have handled, of the Word of *zoe*/life; 2 (for the *zoe*/life was manifested, and we have seen it, and bear witness, and shew unto you that eternal *zoe*/life, which was with the Father, and was manifested unto us;) 3 that which we have seen and heard declare we unto you, that ye also may have fellowship with us: and truly our fellowship is with the Father, and with his Son Jesus Christ. 4 And these things write we unto you, that your joy may be full." John 1:14 "And the Word [*of God, per God's promise*] was made flesh, and dwelt among us, (and we beheld his glory, the glory as of the only begotten of the Father,) full of grace and truth."

For many, in the days when Jesus walked the earth, just coming to Him was sufficient faith in God. Or Jesus (or one of the disciples, the 12 or the 70) coming upon people in need was sufficient faith in God. Just someone asking you to pray, or you deciding to pray is sufficient faith in God. You and Holy Spirit agreeing to get the glory of God in a situation are sufficient for filling the Earth with the glory of God. This is part of our purpose, as it has always been for God's people. Num 14:21 "But as truly as I live, all the earth shall be filled with the glory of the LORD." Thank God He has a plan, and we are part of it!

Faith calls those things of God that are not as if they are. Rom 4:16 "Therefore it (*righteousness*) is of faith, that it might be by grace; to the end the promise might be sure to all the seed; not to that only which is of the law, but to that also which is of the faith of Abraham; who is the father of us all, 17 (as it is written, I have made thee a father of many nations,) before him whom he believed, **even God, who quickeneth the dead, and calleth those things which be not as though they were.** 18 Who against hope believed in hope, that he might become the father of many nations; according to that which was spoken, So shall thy seed be. 19 And being not weak in faith, he considered not [*the facts of*] his own body now dead, when he was about an hundred years old, neither yet the deadness of Sara's womb [*who was 90 years old and, for some 70 years, had produced no children--a long record of failure*]: 20 **he staggered not at the promise of God through unbelief (***unpersuadableness***); but was strong in faith, giving glory (***thanksgiving and praise***) to God;** 21 and being fully persuaded that, what he had promised, he was able also to perform [*in spite of the present facts*]. 22 And therefore it was imputed to him for righteousness." It is always right to believe God in spite of the circumstances and to proclaim His Word over it rather than accept any evil report and give up by agreeing that is the way it will be. Proclaiming God's Word gives Holy Spirit what He needs to move, create or change in the situation to God's will. Truth by faith can trump evil facts.

When you have proclaimed, spoken boldly, God's Word over that situation, keep thinking God's Word on it until you speak again: Phil 4:6 "Be careful for nothing; but in every thing by prayer and supplication with thanksgiving let your requests (*aiteo/demands*) be made known unto God. 7 And the peace of God, which passeth all understanding, shall keep your hearts and minds through Christ Jesus. 8 Finally, brethren, whatsoever things are true, whatsoever things are honest, whatsoever things are just, whatsoever things are pure, whatsoever things are lovely, whatsoever things are of good report; if there be any virtue, and if there be any praise, think on these things."

What is so special about words? Hear Holy Spirit, as He encourages us to use right words. Heb 11:3 "Through faith we understand that the worlds were framed by the word of God, so that things which are seen were not made of things which do appear." Notice that the things of substance in the Universe were made from words, things which, like the wind, exist but do not have a direct "appearance" or are visible. Thus words, good or bad, are a way to connect with the spirit world. Right words in the mouth of a human are what Holy Spirit uses to create what we see of God's goodness.

Jesus often referred to faith and the Word of God as seeds. When a gardener buys a packet of seeds, there is a picture of what he will get on the package. This is what the gardener is hoping for. All the time he plants and keeps the garden, in the gardener's mind's eye there is a vision of what he will get. He sees the seed, and does not ponder the seed, but what it will produce. Once planted, he leaves the seed to grow. He does spend time making sure the conditions for the seed to grow are right in soil, water, sun and nutriments. The gardener is always looking at or for the finished result. He even starts lining up how he will use the produce, even before he plants the seeds. If it is beans, he is planning how to pick, freeze, cook, eat, give away or sell the resulting beans.

Any gardener knows that he must prepare the soil to accept the seed, else the seed will not produce abundance. No gardener or farmer expects much produce, if the soil is not prepared. This soil preparation (i.e., renewing your mind) is usually much harder than just planting the seed. But the farmer/gardener knows it must be done so he can sell, give away or eat those beans pictured on the seed packet. This is faith in the power of the seed process.

In the parable of the sower and the seed (Mark 4, Luke 8 and Matt 13), the Word of God is called a seed. In Eph 5, the Word of God is called water; in Eph 6 the Word of God is called a sword; in Heb 4, the Word of God is called a sharp sword that nothing can hide from; in Phil 2, the Word of God is called the Word of *zoe*/life; and in John 1:1-3 and 1 John 1:1-2, we see that Jesus is the Word of *zoe*/life. (Eph 5:26 "That he might sanctify and cleanse it with the washing of water by the word (*continual saying*)," Eph 6:17 "And take the helmet of *soteria*/salvation [*to protect your thoughts*], and the sword of the Spirit, which is the word of God (*to proclaim the word of God over that situation*)." Heb 4:12 "For the word of God is quick, and powerful, and sharper than any twoedged sword, piercing even to the dividing asunder of soul and spirit, and of the joints and marrow, and is a discerner of the thoughts and intents of the heart. 13 Neither is there any creature that is not manifest in his sight: but all things are naked and opened unto the eyes of him with whom we have to do." Phil 2:16 "Holding forth the *logos*/word (*saying*) of *zoe*/life ..." 1 John 1:1 "That which was from the beginning, which we have heard, which we have seen with our eyes, which we have looked upon, and our hands have handled, of the Word of *zoe*/life; 2 (for the *zoe*/life was manifested, and we have seen it, and bear witness, and shew unto you that eternal *zoe*/life, which was with the Father, and was manifested unto us.)" John 1:1 "In the beginning was the Word, and the Word was with God, and the Word was God. 2 The same was in the beginning with God. 3 All things were made by him; and without him was not any thing made that was made. 4 In him was *zoe*/life; and the *zoe*/life was the light of men."

Putting this together: You plant a seed of the Word of God to believe God to bring it to pass, knowing the devil is resisting the life because he attacks that Word. You water it by speaking the Word of God. You put *zoe*/life into it by speaking/saying the Word of God, and you fight off enemies of that Word by speaking the Word of God, knowing none can hide. You bring Jesus to the scene with the Word of God in the name of Jesus, and you keep a vision of that Word of God fulfilled in your mind. The *logos* Word, the written, thought or spoken word, becomes *rhema*, a *zao*/living word, as you do it. God's Word only works for you as you use it as a tool. It is a learn-and-keep-it-strong-by-doing-it tool. At a minimum you read the Word of God and speak it over the situation, with the final result you want to accomplish in mind. Your believing God in joy to do per His Word is the evidence of faith. Your continued believing by continually giving God glory is the substance that does it.

Many times we see Jesus asking what the person wanted, yet He did not ask what was needed when He raised Lazarus (see John 11) or the widow's son in Nain (see Luke 7:11-16). If He did not see the problem, He asked so He knew what He was defeating. He did not need faith in the victim; He did need to know what was needed. In this way, He built a vision of the finished work in His mind. You do not need a medical diagnosis, just a name to call it and a result you desire. "That thing causing _____" is sufficient. You have authority to defeat it, as if Jesus were present in the flesh, and command the healing Jesus earned by suffering with His stripes to come forth. Luke 10:19 "Behold (*make this change the way you live your life*), I give unto you power (*commission, authority and the resources of heaven*) to tread on serpents and scorpions, and over all the power (*ability, works*) of the enemy: and nothing shall by any means hurt you."(Notice that Jesus spoke the words of Luke 10:19 to the 70 and, perhaps, a larger crowd, and not just the 12 apostles.) Matt 28:18 "And Jesus came and spake unto them, saying, All power is given unto me in heaven and in earth. 19 Go ye therefore, and teach all nations, baptizing them in the name of the Father, and of the Son, and of the Holy Ghost: 20 teaching them to **observe all things** whatsoever I have commanded you: and, lo, I am with you alway, even unto the end of the world. Amen." John 20:21 "Then said Jesus to them again, Peace be unto you: as my Father hath sent me, even so send I you." Like Jesus, you speak, lay hands, and then trust God to do the works.

We follow the same process we are to use to renew our mind. Rom 13:10 "*Agape*/love worketh no ill to his neighbour: therefore *agape*/love is the fulfilling of the law. 11 And that, knowing the time, that now it is high time to awake out of sleep: for now is our *soteria*/salvation nearer than when we believed. 12 The night is far spent, the day is at hand: let us therefore cast off the works of darkness, and let us put on the armour of light. 13 Let us walk honestly, as in the day; not in rioting and drunkenness, not in chambering and wantonness, not in strife and envying. 14 But put ye on the Lord Jesus Christ, and make not provision for the flesh, to fulfil the lusts thereof." "Put on Jesus" means to change your self-image and actions.

This mind-renewing process also prepares our "heart-soul soil" to accept and then *lambano*/hold on to or keep the Word to produce fruit, per the Parable of the Sower. Luke 8:11 "Now the parable is this: The seed is the word of God. 12 Those by the way side are they that hear; then cometh the devil, and taketh away the word out of their hearts, lest they should believe and be *sozo*/saved. 13 They on the rock are they, which, when they hear, receive the word with joy; and these have no root, which for a while believe, and in time of temptation fall away. 14 And that which fell among thorns are they, which, when they have heard, go forth, and are choked with cares and riches and pleasures of this *bios*/life, and bring no fruit to perfection. 15 But that on the good ground are they, which in an honest and good heart, having heard the word, keep (*hold onto*) it (*through attack, resistance, delay, distraction and prosperity*) and bring forth fruit with patience (*faithfulness, reliability and consistency*)." We do not deny the symptoms; we deny their right to remain.

OTHER HEALING TEACHINGS

Here is a process based on Rom 13, Eph 4 and Col 3. YOU see the problem and call it what it is, a work of the devil and not a work of the God of *agape*/love. YOU stir yourself up in battle, knowing that every second evil operates is a limitation on the Kingdom of God and must be removed so that the salvation/total healing of God may come. YOU know that Jesus paid for it with the suffering in His body and that God has united us with Himself in the New Covenant in the blood of Jesus, and that God hates this evil more than you and paid the price of His very own Son to get it healed, when Jesus took the stripes and when God raised Him (Jesus) from the dead. YOU put on the armor of the righteousness of God in Christ Jesus, knowing this is not about you, but the holiness of Jesus through faith in His name. YOU determine your walk by your words and actions, as you speak to cast off the demons in the situation, by naming them and commanding them to go in the name of Jesus, and then YOU put on the salvation of God by commanding healing in the name of Jesus. Next YOU rejoice that it is already done in Jesus. YOU show tenacious, *agape*/love by keeping at it until you see the healing already done or manifested. YOU use this process for any unrighteousness, either for sin in yourself or others, or sickness, or any other work that is not like Heaven on Earth.

The healing in Jesus was done 2000 years ago; the devil is still resisting it until a human commands God's Word to come to pass. And just as for Lazarus, command that life to come forth in the finished Word for that situation. So to the cripple you say, "Walk," and to the dead you say "Rise," all in the name of Jesus. After all, this is God's goal for the church: Eph 4:13 "Till we all come in the unity of the faith, and of the knowledge of the Son of God, unto a perfect man, unto the measure of the stature of the fulness of Christ: 14 that we henceforth be no more children, tossed to and fro, and carried about with every wind of doctrine, by the sleight of men, and cunning craftiness, whereby they lie in wait to deceive; 15 but speaking the truth in *agape*/love, may grow up into him in all things, which is the head, even Christ." Phil 2:5 "Let this mind be in you, which was also in Christ Jesus." 1 Cor 2:12 "Now we have received, not the spirit of the world, but the spirit which is of God; that we might know the things that are freely given to us of God. ... 16 For who hath known the mind of the Lord, that he may instruct him? But we have the mind of Christ." 2 Tim 1:7 "For God hath not given us the spirit of fear; but of *dunamis*/power, and of *agape*/love, and of a sound mind." And that sound mind operates just like Jesus in any situation.

So call your problem defeated by God's Word, and counter every evil report with God's Word. Look at every detail of the situation and believe God to overcome each step and for the full finished work per His Word. 1 Pet 2:24 "Who his own self bare our sins in his own body on the tree, that we, being dead to sins, should *zao*/live unto righteousness: by whose stripes ye were healed. 25 For ye were as sheep going astray; but are now returned unto the Shepherd and Bishop of your souls." Rom 8:5

"For they that are after the flesh (*governed by evil circumstances, evil reports and ignorance of God's ways/Word*) do mind the things of the flesh; but they that are after the Spirit the things of the Spirit (*governed by the promises of God to make every situation like Heaven on Earth*). 6 For to be carnally minded is death (*the evil circumstances and evil reports rule or reign as king*); but to be spiritually minded (*per the promises of God to make Heaven on Earth through you*) is zoe/life and peace (*Heaven on Earth and every work of your hands blessed*). 7 Because the carnal mind is enmity (*is at war*) against God: for it is not subject to the law of God, neither indeed can be. 8 So then they that are in the flesh (*governed by evil reports and circumstances that conflict with the Word of God and ignorant of God's ways, Word and the gift of righteousness in Jesus*) cannot please God [*because the carnal mind is saying the situation governs, that God is not relevant and the work of Jesus is not sufficient to make it right*]. 9 But ye are not in the flesh, but in the Spirit, if so be that the Spirit of God dwell in you. Now if any man have not the Spirit of Christ, he is none of his. 10 And if Christ be in you, the body is dead because of sin; but the Spirit is zoe/life because of righteousness. 11 But if the Spirit of him that raised up Jesus from the dead dwell in you, he that raised up Christ from the dead shall also quicken your mortal bodies by his Spirit that dwelleth in you. 12 Therefore, brethren, we are debtors, not to the flesh, to zao/live after the flesh. 13 For if ye zao/live after the flesh, ye shall die: but if ye through the Spirit do mortify the deeds of the body, ye shall zao/live. 14 For as many as are led by the Spirit of God (*operating through the Word of God, just like Jesus would*), they are the sons of God. 15 For ye have not received the spirit of bondage again to fear; but ye have received the Spirit of adoption, whereby we cry, Abba (*Daddy*), Father." As you "tune in" and cooperate with your born-again spirit in a renewed mind, you operate in Holy Spirit power and set people free of the oppressions of the devil. Tools like this manual can help in that right programming into the Christ mind.

Give glory to God by praising Him before you see the answer, just as Abraham did (see Rom 4:20). Faith does not deny the problem; it denies the right for it to remain in the salvation of Jesus. You apply God's Word, and God produces the results against the devil, as you *lambano*, hold on to, the grace of salvation and the gift of righteousness, per Rom 5:17, and *aiteo* command for and in Jesus.

Your faith is in God empowering His Word, not your faith. You and your faith can fail. God's Word is unstoppable and cannot die, God cannot lie, and God cannot fail. Trust in Him, not you. Ask Him to strengthen you in the battle and keep you there. As you hold on to Him in His Word, you will see His love finally released to move in answer. Spend time in praise to keep your heart right. Psalms 3, 18, 19, 23, 47, 48, 62, 66, 91, 93, 97-105 and 139 are favorites, or all one hundred fifty (150). And do dance, shout, sing, clap and play instruments to God.

This is not about getting God to move; it is more about us doing those things in us that allow Him to move. The problem is not God; it is us. John 8:29 "And he

Other Healing Teachings

that sent me is with me: the Father hath not left me alone; for I do always those things that please him." This means Jesus operated by faith per Heb 11:6, just like we have to. Heb 11:6 "But without faith it is impossible to please him: for he that cometh to God must believe that he is, and that he is a rewarder of them that diligently seek him." Jesus completed His mission as a man, and not as God, to show us how to do our mission in life. He was tempted as a man, because men can be tempted to sin, but God cannot be tempted to do evil. Heb 4:15 "For we have not an high priest which cannot be touched with the feeling of our infirmities; but was in all points tempted like as we are, yet without sin." James 1:13 "Let no man say when he is tempted, I am tempted of God: for God cannot be tempted with evil, neither tempteth he any man." So Jesus had to walk just like we do, when it comes to healing or any other benefit of God, by faith, and then see it come to pass. Jesus healed and went to the cross, believing God by the Bible, all by faith.

Jesus said, of the Spirit He died to send to us on the Day of Pentecost: John 7:38 "He that believeth on me, as the scripture hath said, out of his belly shall flow rivers of *zao*/living water. 39 (But this spake he of the Spirit, which they that believe on him should receive: for the Holy Ghost was not yet given; because that Jesus was not yet glorified.)" See Acts 2:33 and 3:13.

If you have Holy Spirit, the river is there. If all you have is a trickle, the more the trickle flows, eventually the larger the hole and the more you get. This does not happen by accident. 1 Cor 15:10 "But by the grace of God I am what I am: and his grace which was bestowed upon me was not in vain; but I laboured more abundantly than they all: yet not I, but the grace of God which was with me."

This manual is a tool to labor with. Heb 4:9 "There remaineth therefore a rest to the people of God. 10 For he that is entered into his rest, he also hath ceased from his own works, as God did from his. 11 Let us labour therefore to enter into that rest, lest any man fall after the same example of unbelief. 12 For the word of God is quick, and powerful, and sharper than any twoedged sword, piercing even to the dividing asunder of soul and spirit, and of the joints and marrow, and is a discerner of the thoughts and intents of the heart. 13 Neither is there any creature that is not manifest in his sight: but all things are naked and opened unto the eyes of him with whom we have to do." Make the Word work on you. Start with one scripture. Meditate on it, sing it, and preach it to yourself in order to renew your mind.

These scriptures describe right attitudes that God blesses in prayer/asking: Luke 11:5 "And He said to them, Which of you who has a friend will go to him at midnight and will say to him, Friend, lend me three loaves [of bread], 6 for a friend of mine who is on a journey has just come, and I have nothing to put before him; 7 and he from within will answer, Do not disturb me; the door is now closed, and my children are with me in bed; I cannot get up and supply you [with anything]? 8 I tell you, although he will not get up and supply him anything because he is his friend, **yet because of his shameless persistence and insistence** he will get up and give him as much as he needs. 9 So I say to you, *Aiteo*/ask (*by requiring, demanding and expecting as due by covenant promise*) and keep on *aiteo*/asking and it shall be given you; seek and keep on seeking and you shall find; knock and keep on knocking and the door shall be opened to you. 10 For everyone who *aiteo*/asks and keeps on *aiteo*/asking (*requiring, demanding and expecting as due by covenant promise*) receives; and he who seeks and keeps on seeking finds; and to him who knocks and keeps on knocking, the door shall be opened. 11 What father among you, if his son *aiteo*/asks (*by requiring, demanding as due by covenant promise*) for a loaf of bread, will give him a stone; or if he *aiteo*/asks (*by requiring, expecting as due by covenant promise*) for a fish, will instead of a fish give him a serpent? 12 Or if he *aiteo*/asks (*by demanding as due by covenant promise*) for an egg, will give him a scorpion? 13 If you then, evil as you are, know how to give good gifts [gifts that are to their advantage] to your children, how much more will your heavenly Father give the Holy Spirit [*and other good things*] to those who *aiteo*/ask (*by demanding as due by covenant promise*) and continue to *aiteo*/ask Him!" AMP Isa 45:11 "Thus saith the Lord, the Holy One of Israel, and his Maker, Ask (*require*) me of things to come concerning my sons, and concerning the work of my hands command ye me."

Our faith is in God to perform His promises, His Word, but faith without action is dead, stillborn, does not produce the Kingdom of God. James 2:26 "For as the body without the spirit is dead, so faith without works is dead also." We have to do works of faith, often against impossible situations and feelings, but we must control our minds and obey God, else we become deceived that the situations are greater than God. James 1:22 "But be ye doers of the word, and not hearers only, deceiving your own selves."

Faith actions include *aiteo* commands, thanksgiving, praise and joy before you see the answer—even if it is delayed. Keep repeating with mind-renewing in the appropriate scriptures. And anytime you hear a fearful thought or word or get fearful over the result, go and obey: Phil 4:4 "Rejoice in the Lord alway: and again I say, Rejoice. 5 Let your moderation be known unto all men. The Lord is at hand [*in power*]. 6 Be careful (*anxious, fearful, terrorized, in dread, hopeless*) for nothing; but in every thing by prayer and supplication with thanksgiving let your *aiteo*/requests be made known unto God. 7 And the peace of God, which passeth all understanding, shall keep your hearts and minds through Christ Jesus. 8 Finally, brethren, whatsoever things are **true**, whatsoever things are **honest**, whatsoever things are **just**, whatsoever things are **pure**, whatsoever things are **lovely**, whatsoever things are of **good report**; if there be any **virtue**, and if there be any **praise**, think on these things. 9 Those things, which ye have both learned, and received, and heard, and seen in me, do: and the God of peace shall be with you [*in power*]."

~ 8 ~

ON THE NEW COVENANT

By the New Testament in the blood of Jesus, Father God will remember our sins no more. This agreement was made in the blood of Jesus Christ. Matt 26:28 "For this is my blood of the new testament, which is shed for many for the remission (*cancellation, removal*) of sins." Mark 14:24 "And he said unto them, This is my blood of the new testament, which is shed for many." Heb 8:6 "But now hath he obtained a more excellent ministry, by how much also he is the mediator of a better covenant, which was established upon better promises. 7 For if that first covenant (*Moses'*) had been faultless, then should no place have been sought for the second. 8 For finding fault with them, he saith, Behold, the days come, saith the Lord, when I will make **a new covenant** with the house of Israel and with the house of Judah: 9 not according to the covenant that I made with their fathers in the day when I took them by the hand to lead them out of the land of Egypt; because they continued not in my covenant, and I regarded them not, saith the Lord. 10 For this is the covenant that I will make with the house of Israel after those days, saith the Lord; I will put my laws into their mind, and write them in their hearts: and I will be to them a God, and they shall be to me a people: 11 and they shall not teach every man his neighbour, and every man his brother, saying, Know the Lord: for all shall know me, from the least to the greatest. 12 **For I will be merciful to their unrighteousness, and their sins and their iniquities will I remember no more.** 13 In that he saith, A new covenant, he hath made the first (*Moses'*) old. Now that which decayeth and waxeth old (*Moses'*) is ready to vanish away." Heb 10:12 "But this man (*Jesus*), after he had offered one sacrifice for sins for ever, sat down on the right hand of God; 13 from henceforth expecting till his enemies be made his footstool. 14 For by one offering he hath perfected for ever them that are sanctified. 15 Whereof the Holy Ghost also is a witness to us: for after that he had said before, 16 **This is the covenant** that I will make with them after those days, saith the Lord, I will put my laws into their hearts, and in their minds will I write them; 17 **and their sins and iniquities will I remember no more.** 18 Now where remission (*removal, cancellation, purging, and reconciliation by the blood of Jesus*) of these (*sins and iniquities of the entire human race from Adam to the last person's sin*) is, there is no more offering for sin." The only cure for sin before God has been applied 2000 years ago in the blood of Jesus for the sins of Adam to the last human alive. 1 John 2:2 "And he is the propitiation for our sins: and not for ours only, but also for the sins of the whole world."

Without knowledge of this New Covenant versus the covenant of Moses, much of the New Testament scriptures make little sense. If the law of sin and death was sufficient (you must do right to be right with God or else you die, are cursed, the devil has the right to oppress you) then Jesus would never have needed to come because that law is in the law of Moses. But Jesus came to implement a New Covenant between God and man. Acts 10:36 "The word which God sent unto the children of Israel, preaching peace by Jesus Christ: (he is Lord of all:) 37 that word, I say, ye know, which was published throughout all Judaea, and began from Galilee, after the baptism which John preached; 38 how God anointed Jesus of Nazareth with the Holy Ghost and with power: who went about doing good, and healing all that were oppressed (*under the active dominion, reign or lordship*) of the devil; for God was with him." Every miracle of Jesus was a declaration by God, through Jesus, that He is not at war with man. He is our Friend, not our enemy and never has been an enemy! But the consequence of sin had to be paid for, and God did it in and by Jesus. God has no other solution than Jesus!

The New Testament in the blood of Jesus is greater than the covenant of Moses. Acts 13:37 "But he, whom God raised again, saw no corruption. 38 Be it known unto you therefore, men and brethren, that through this man is preached unto you the forgiveness (*remission, purging, putting away and obliteration*) of sins: 39 and by him all that believe are justified from all things, from which ye could not be justified by the law of Moses." Rom 10:3 "For they (*those who focus only on the requirements of the law to be right with God*) being ignorant (*blinded*) of God's righteousness, and going about to establish their own righteousness (*based on works*), have not submitted themselves unto the righteousness of God. 4 For Christ is the end of the law for righteousness to every one that believeth (*has faith in the effectiveness of the blood and work of Jesus*)." 1 John 2:1 "My little children, these things write I unto you, that ye sin not. And if any man sin, we have an advocate with the Father, Jesus Christ the righteous: 2 and he is the propitiation for our sins: and not for ours only, but also for the sins of the whole world." 1 John 3:4 "Whosoever committeth sin transgresseth also the law: for sin is the transgression of the law. 5 And ye know that he was manifested to take away (*remit, purge, remove, wash away and obliterate*) our sins; and in him is no sin."

In the New Covenant, we are placed into Jesus: 1 Cor 1:30 "But of him are ye in Christ Jesus, who of God is made unto us wisdom, and righteousness, and sanctifica-

Other Healing Teachings

tion, and redemption." 2 Cor 1:21 "Now he which stablisheth us with you in Christ, and hath anointed us, is God; 22 who hath also sealed us, and given the earnest of the Spirit in our hearts." 2 Cor 5:17 "Therefore if any man be in Christ, he is a new creature: old things are passed away; behold (*make this change your life*), all things are become new." Gal 6:15 "For in Christ Jesus neither circumcision availeth anything, nor uncircumcision, but a new creature." Eph 2:13 "But now in Christ Jesus ye who sometimes were far off are made nigh by the blood of Christ. 14 For he is our peace, who hath made both one, and hath broken down the middle wall of partition between us; 15 having abolished in his flesh the enmity, even the law of commandments contained in ordinances; for to make in himself of twain one new man, so making peace; 16 and that he might reconcile both unto God in one body by the cross, having slain the enmity thereby: 17 and came and preached peace to you which were afar off, and to them that were nigh. 18 For through him we both have access by one Spirit unto the Father."

In Him we are made like a perfect baby, complete in every aspect and fully equipped to grow into Him in all respects. Col 2:9 "For in him dwelleth all the fulness of the Godhead bodily. 10 And **ye are complete in him**, which is the head of all principality and power: 11 in whom also ye are circumcised with the circumcision made without hands, in putting off the body of the sins of the flesh by the circumcision of Christ: 12 buried with him in baptism, wherein also ye are risen with him through the faith of the operation of God, who hath raised him from the dead. 13 And you, being dead in your sins and the uncircumcision of your flesh, hath he quickened together with him, **having forgiven you all trespasses**; 14 blotting out the handwriting of ordinances that was against us, which was contrary to us, and took it out of the way, nailing it to his cross; 15 **and having spoiled principalities and powers**, he made a shew of them openly, triumphing over them in it."

You may remember your sins, your neighbor may remember your sins, your family, spouse or friends may remember your sins, and the devil, for sure, remembers your sins, but in Jesus God does not. So my sins or those of the one I am ministering to are not admissible in the court of the Great King and Judge, God Almighty. This is what it means that our sins are remitted, forgiven, purged, redeemed, justified, put away, washed away and reconciled in the blood of Jesus and the righteousness of God in Jesus imputed or counted to us, as we believe God raised Jesus from the dead, after bearing our sins on the cross. As I recall that our sins are under the blood of Jesus 2000 years ago, I glorify His work by His Mighty Arm, Jesus of Nazareth, and also bring Him into "remembrance" to allow Him to perform His promises: Isa 43:25 "I, even I, am he that blotteth out thy transgressions for mine own sake, and will not remember thy sins. 26 Put me in remembrance: let us plead together: declare thou, that thou mayest be justified." Jer 1:12 "Then said the Lord to me, You have seen well, for I am alert and active, watching over My word to perform it." AMP

The New Covenant in the blood of Jesus is the declaration by God that all our sins are remitted, purged and put away in Jesus, and we now have all the benefits of God's wonderful salvation available to us in Jesus. Heb 10:16 "This is **the covenant** that I will make with them after those days, saith the Lord, I will put my laws into their hearts, and in their minds will I write them; 17 **and their sins and iniquities will I remember no more.**"

And in this life we are not guaranteed that we will accept His writing of His laws into our hearts and minds. We must cooperate with the process. 2 Cor 6:1 "We then, as workers together with him, beseech you also that ye receive not the grace of God in vain. 2 (For he saith, I have heard thee in a time accepted, and in the day of *soteria*/salvation have I succoured thee: behold, now is the accepted time; behold, now is the day of *soteria*/salvation.)" Part of this process is to obey: Philem 6 "That the communication of thy faith may become effectual by the acknowledging of every good thing which is in you in Christ Jesus." And thus we must know: 1 Cor 1:30 "But of him (*Father God*) are ye in Christ Jesus, who of God is made unto us wisdom, and righteousness, and sanctification, and redemption: 31 that, according as it is written, He that glorieth, let him glory in the Lord." 2 Cor 1:20 "For all the promises of God in him (*Jesus*) are yea, and in him Amen, unto the glory of God by us. 21 Now he which stablisheth us ... in Christ, and hath anointed us, is God; 22 who hath also sealed us, and given the earnest of the Spirit in our hearts." 2 Cor 5:20 "Now then we are ambassadors for Christ, as though God did beseech you by us: we pray you in Christ's stead, be ye reconciled to God. 21 For he (*Father God*) hath made him (*Jesus*) to be sin for us, who knew no sin; that we might be made the righteousness of God in him (*Jesus*)."

This New Testament/New Covenant is so wonderful, awesome and comprehensive, that few appreciate it fully. But rely on any aspect of it and you will allow God to fulfill it in you now. Heb 8:10 "For this is the covenant that I will make with the house of Israel after those days, saith the Lord; I will put my laws into their mind, and write them in their hearts: and I will be to them a God, and they shall be to me a people: 11 and they shall not teach every man his neighbour, and every man his brother, saying, Know the Lord: for all shall know me, from the least to the greatest. 12 For I will be merciful to their unrighteousness, and their sins and their iniquities will I remember no more."

The key is to write the Word on your heart and mind now, before the Last Day, when God finishes the job. So be diligent to write the Word of God in the Scriptures on your mind and heart now, so you can build gold, silver and jewels in this life that will survive and be rewards for you on the Last Day (see 1 Cor 3:1-16). Getting others healed in the name of Jesus is one such right, New Covenant work.

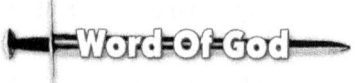

~ 9 ~
ON THE WORD OF GOD AS MEDICINE

As I use this manual, I am continually looking at the Word of God. If I read it aloud for myself, my ministry target, or those around me, I am also delivering the healing that is within the Word of God. Prov 4:20 "My son, attend to my words; incline thine ear unto my sayings. 21 Let them not depart from thine eyes; keep them in the midst of thine heart. 22 For they are life unto those that find them, and health to all their flesh. 23 Keep thy heart with all diligence; for out of it are the issues of life."

As I read and repeat the Battle Prayer, I am helping myself (and my listeners) to "attend to" and "incline" my ear, while I "keep them in my eyes" and renew my mind, so my heart can get adjusted to courage in God's love by the blood of Jesus by His Word. The Word of God has power and life when properly taken and applied. Note, this is not casual reading, but intense effort to "attend to" and "incline" unto the Word to "hear" unto glad obedience.

God works through men to perform His promises. We work with God to write His laws on our hearts and minds in this life, to release God's awesome ability contained in His words. Heb 8:10 "For this is the covenant that I will make with the house of Israel after those days, saith the Lord; I will put my laws into their mind, and write them in their hearts: and I will be to them a God, and they shall be to me a people: 11 and they shall not teach every man his neighbour, and every man his brother, saying, Know the Lord: for all shall know me, from the least to the greatest. 12 For I will be merciful to their unrighteousness, and their sins and their iniquities will I remember no more."

We are also commanded: James 1:21 "Wherefore lay apart all filthiness and superfluity of naughtiness, and *lambano*/receive with meekness the engrafted word, which is able to *sozo*/save your souls. 22 But be ye doers of the word, and not hearers only, deceiving your own selves." Writing God's Word on our heart and mind so we now live them is part of the process of saving our souls, and it is our job in this life.

We "incline" by going to the Scriptures multiple times a day, just as if taking medicine, believing that as we work with the Word, God is renewing our minds and giving *zoe* life to our bodies as a medicine for health and strength. Do it, just like medicine, 3 to 12 times a day for at least 5 minutes each time, the more time the better. And between times you "attend" by staying in the Word and imagining yourself doing or living that Word, and then looking for opportunities to actually do that Word as you go about your day.

For example, when you read a verse that says, "Praise the Lord," you stop and take a few minutes to praise the Lord, preferably out loud and with great vigor (which is included in the meaning of the word praise).

Thus I am cooperating with Holy Spirit, as He writes His laws into my heart and mind, per the New Covenant. As I keep myself in the Word and faith, He is doing it. 1 Tim 4:13 "Till I come, give attendance to (*public*) reading, to exhortation, to doctrine." 2 Tim 2:15 "Study to shew thyself approved unto God, a workman (*not a student, ever learning, but one who uses the Word of God to get the results of God into the Earth*) that needeth not to be ashamed, rightly dividing the word of truth [*to produce the* zoe/*life of God in any situation*]." 2 Tim 3:15 "And that from a child thou hast known the holy scriptures, which are able to make thee wise unto *soteria*/salvation through faith which is in Christ Jesus. 16 All scripture is given by inspiration of God, and is profitable for doctrine, for reproof, for correction, for instruction in righteousness: 17 that the man of God may be perfect (*fully mature, complete*), throughly furnished unto all good works."

The promise of Proverbs 4 is that the Word of God can be a medicine, if we do it right. It is *zoe* life to those who find it as a treasure of great price. So keep in the Word, trusting Holy Spirit for supernatural health, wealth, wisdom and understanding. And if you are in a faith battle, it is your only valid answer, for the Word of God is your armor, sword and shield. 1 Tim 6:12 "Fight the good fight of faith, *lambano*/lay hold on eternal *zoe*/life, whereunto thou art also called ... ." The same way you renew your mind for a faith battle is the same way you take the Word of God as a medicine—diligently and continuously.

━┝═Word═Of═God═┥━

~ 10 ~

ON THE BELIEVER'S QUALIFICATIONS

The only qualification needed to minister healing is to be a believer: <u>Mark 16:15</u> "And He (*Jesus*) said to them, Go into all the world and preach and publish openly the good news (the Gospel) to every creature [of the whole human race]. 16 **He who believes** [who adheres to and trusts in and relies on the Gospel and Him Whom it sets forth] and is baptized will be *sozo*/saved [from the penalty of *earthly and* eternal death]; but he who does not believe [who does not adhere to and trust in and rely on the Gospel and Him Whom it sets forth] will be condemned. 17 And **these attesting signs will accompany those who believe:** in My name they will drive out demons; they will speak in new languages; 18 they will pick up serpents; and [even] if they drink anything deadly, it will not hurt them; **they will lay their hands on the sick, and they will get well.** 19 So then the Lord Jesus, after He had spoken to them, was taken up into heaven and He sat down at the right hand of God [Ps 110:1]. 20 And they went out and preached everywhere, while the Lord kept working with them and confirming the message by the attesting signs and miracles that closely accompanied [it]. Amen (so be it)" AMP

This passage has been demonstrated, not just in Acts, but also throughout Christian history, to be abundantly true. For example, in the ministry of John Wesley, who started the Methodist movement in the 1700's, there are over 240 recorded cases of healing (and one was for his horse, Hank). And yet Rev. Wesley did not preach healing as a specific emphasis. In the 1940's Rev. Jack Coe was sued in a Florida court for practicing medicine without a license. There was irrefutable proof of the numerous powerful and dramatic healings in the name of Jesus in Rev. Coe's ministry. The conclusion of the court was that no license was needed for "Christian healing" in the name of Jesus (Liardon, Roberts, *God's Generals*, Vol. 8 Jack Coe, Tulsa, Oklahoma, Albury Publications: 1996). Thank God He has made a way for Christian divine healing in America. The healing word can go forth freely.

Here the qualification is based on Jesus and not our holiness. Since we heal by grace and receive by grace, it is all about the work of Jesus and not us. Our job is to know throughout our whole being what Jesus accomplished and can do through us. Col 1:12 "Giving thanks (*continually*) unto the Father, which hath made us meet (*qualified by grace*) to be partakers of the inheritance of the saints in light: 13 who hath delivered us from the power of darkness, and hath translated us into the kingdom of his *agape*/dear Son: 14 in whom we have redemption through his blood, even the forgiveness (*remission, removal and putting away*) of sins." As you understand this qualification by the body and blood of Jesus and the grace of God more and more, you, too, will continually be giving thanks with joy, more and more.

The only other qualification is to be willing to believe in the power of the name of Jesus and use it. Mark 9:38 "And John answered him, saying, Master, we saw one casting out devils in thy name, and he followeth not us: and we forbad him, because he followeth not us. 39 But Jesus said, Forbid him not: for there is no man which shall do a miracle in my name, that can lightly speak evil of me."

Here, one who was not a follower of Jesus but believed in that name as the access to God's goodness was working miracles. Jesus did not rebuke him, but His disciples tried to stop the man. Thus, anyone, Christian or not, can use the name of Jesus to do miracles in the name of Jesus.

Notice, God was glad to do the miracles, as it is Holy Spirit who does the miracles at the direction of Father God. Today Jesus is the Administrator of Holy Spirit, and Jesus does the miracles by Holy Spirit for Father God.

So the two qualifications to be a healing agent of God are to either be a believing Christian or to believe in the name of Jesus. As all healing is by grace, there is no mention here of sin on the part of the worker or of the one being healed.

~ 11 ~
ON THE LAYING ON OF HANDS

Several healing methods may work for different people; we will describe here the most effective we have seen. We see laying on of hands or touching for healing as a specific action and not just the typical holding or touching showing love. For the specific act of ministering healing, if possible, let everyone stop touching the person until the laying on of hands is complete. Or let the others put their hands on the minister (as he places his hands on the sick person) to help deliver life through the minister.

We see more effective results with not holding hands or touching while you command/*aiteo* before you lay on hands. First *aiteo*/command and then touch, proclaiming, "Receive, in the name of Jesus." (Alternate words include: "Freedom," "Life," "Be Healed," etc.)

Here it is as if you are "pushing" or "driving" all the power of God into the person/situation in that one word. But do not push or shove the person as you touch with your hands, but keep touching/holding for a few moments (up to about two minutes). You may feel the *zoe*/life flowing. Let go when it "feels right."

If you see any manifestation such as shaking or falling down, just keep going. Most of the time you will not feel anything, but you or the person (but not necessarily both) may experience electricity, shaking, heat, sweating, falling down, weakness, numbness, shouts, or tingling. These feelings are fine, but we are moved by faith, not feelings. If "feelings" come, fine; if not, that's fine also. While the biblical record does record some feelings, the majority of the text does not.

For healing, the Bible shows touching the person's hands most often. As often it is natural to grasp another's hand, grasp and then *aiteo* healing (or *aiteo* and then grasp) commanding LIFE in Jesus' name. Others minister by having all lay hands on the person, but this requires touching some other part than the hands, and you need to be wise.

When possible, same sex grasping or holding hands is best. Other generally accepted forms of opposite-sex touching are not wrong, but be wise as if among snakes. Give no cause for offense. For example, all women touching parts of a woman have less issues than men touching other parts, even the back, head, shoulders, or legs of a woman. When possible, you can have a woman lay her hands first and then the man lay his hand on the woman's hand. Be wise, gentle and act with love.

What we have in Jesus is eternal *zoe* life. That is what we impart or release in any healing situation, to bring the glory of God. 1 John 5:11 "And this is the record, that God hath given to us eternal *zoe*/life, and this *zoe*/life is in his Son. 12 He that hath the Son hath *zoe*/life; and he that hath not the Son of God hath not *zoe*/life. 13 These things have I written unto you that believe on the name of the Son of God; that ye may know that ye have eternal *zoe*/life, and that ye may believe on the name of the Son of God." We use the name of Jesus to release *zoe*/life by Holy Spirit.

There are several ways to impart or release the *zoe* life with Holy Spirit with or in the name of Jesus:
1. Touching—usually by hands, but feet or other body parts and clothing also
2. Using objects with *zoe* life stored in them—"prayer cloths," letters and other items
3. Verbal prayer or command or decree (present with the person, some distance away or over the telephone or radio)
4. Looking with the eyes and/or pointing with the hand (often with verbal commands)
5. Your shadow passing over the sick
6. Thoughts
7. As the word of grace in Jesus is preached
8. An e-mail and/or touching the computer screen.

The laying on of hands is the most common method mentioned in the New Testament and the method we use most often, but if you are ministering healing to someone thousands of miles away, it is still Holy Spirit *zoe*/life that will produce the glory of God.

~ 12 ~

ON THE POWER OF AGREEMENT

The Battle Prayer, unlike the laying on of hands, does not require your immediate presence with the one you are praying for or ministering to. Prayer with others in agreement is wonderful: Matt 18:19 "Again I say unto you, That if two of you shall agree on earth as touching any thing that they shall *aiteo*/ask (*demand, expect as due by covenant promise*), it shall be done for them of my Father which is in heaven." Holy Spirit (or *Ghost* as both are the same Greek word) is here on the Earth. Acts 2:32 "This Jesus hath God raised up, whereof we all are witnesses. 33 Therefore being by the right hand of God exalted, and having received of the Father the promise of the Holy Ghost (*Spirit*), he hath shed forth this, which ye now see and hear." Rom 5:5 "And hope maketh not ashamed; because the *agape*/love of God is shed abroad in our hearts by the Holy Ghost (*Spirit*) which is given unto us." 1 John 3:24 "… And hereby we know that he abideth in us, by the Spirit (*Ghost*) which he hath given us."

If Holy Spirit and you are in agreement, then those are the two necessary on Earth. Here is an example of just one person and Holy Spirit, showing this is all that is necessary. Acts 9:17 "And Ananias went his way, and entered into the house; and putting his hands on him said, Brother Saul, the Lord, [even] Jesus, that appeared unto thee in the way as thou camest, hath sent me, that thou mightest receive thy sight, and be filled with the Holy Ghost. 18 And immediately there fell from his eyes as it had been scales: and he received sight forthwith, and arose, and was baptized." Holy Spirit and I make two; He is here on the Earth, and so am I. When we agree in the name of Jesus, Father directs Holy Spirit by Jesus to do the work.

When Holy Spirit and I agree, I start thinking like Him. And, remember, He changes not! Mark 10:27 "And Jesus looking upon them saith, With men it is impossible, but not with God: for with God all things are possible." Matt 21:22 "And all things, whatsoever ye shall *aiteo*/ask (*by demanding, expecting as due by covenant promise*) in prayer, believing, ye shall receive." Rom 8:31 "What shall we then say to these things? If God be for us, who can be against us? 32 He that spared not his own Son, but delivered him up for us all, how shall he not with him also freely give us all things?" All things include those things impossible to man. So when we are looking at the Goliath of sickness, plague, pestilence, famine or other impossibilities, God will back His covenant as we attack in the name of Jesus. We are Jesus' feet on the Earth to be about His business.

~ 13 ~

ON THE USE OF PRAYER CLOTHS AND OTHER SUCH ITEMS

Others have used this prayer successfully as part of a process of praying over cloths, papers or other items to be sent to the one who is sick, per Acts 19:11 "And God wrought special miracles by the hands of Paul: 12 so that from his body were brought unto the sick handkerchiefs or aprons, and the diseases departed from them, and the evil spirits went out of them." Note, it does not say that Paul prayed over these items, just that he laid hands on them, or they took them from his body. We know of one cloth that brought 10 healings.

If you want to pray over cloths, you can add, "**Father, in the name of Jesus,** put Your Spirit in this cloth, per Acts 19:12, to heal _____'s body and cast out demons as needed. I impregnate this cloth, in the name of Jesus, with the *zoe*/life of God so that whoever comes near this cloth will be healed, saved, delivered and have demons cast out of them. *Zoe*/life, fill this cloth, in the name of Jesus. Thank You, Father. In the name of Jesus, thank You." Note: there was no oil, just Paul's touching with hands or wearing the cloths. For other methods, here is a rule: Matt 9:29 "… According to your faith be it unto you."

Rejoice: More importantly: Psalm 40:16 "Let all those that seek thee rejoice and be glad in thee: let such as love thy salvation say continually, The LORD be magnified." So I say, "Lord be magnified," Rev 7:10 "… saying, *soteria*/salvation to our God which sitteth upon the throne, and unto the Lamb. 12 Saying, Amen: Blessing, and glory, and wisdom, and thanksgiving, and honour, and power, and might, [be] unto our God for ever and ever. Amen."

~ 14 ~

ON WARRIOR LOVE

God appears to have changed the rules when John the Baptist came along. No longer would the knowledge of God be spread with the military might of Israel, but it still takes work. Jesus said: Luke 16:16 "The law and the prophets were until John: since that time the kingdom of God is preached, and every man presseth into it." As the kingdom is within you, there lies a battle. And Father will help: Luke 12:32 "… it is your Father's good pleasure to give you the kingdom."

We use good works, prayer and boldness in spreading the *agape*/love of God. While not often considered a fighting scripture, actually doing this can be real combat. Prov 3:5 "Trust in the LORD with all thine heart; and lean not unto thine own understanding. 6 In all thy ways acknowledge him, and he shall direct thy paths." Trust is total reliance, such as leaning against a wall or hanging by a rope made by entwining stands of truth and *agape* love, i.e. God, into every part of your life and acknowledging He is there and His goodness is providing any goodness you have. Trusting can be a battle, as Paul said: Phil 3:13 "Brethren, I count not myself to have apprehended: but this one thing I do, forgetting those things which are behind, and reaching forth unto those things which are before, 14 I press toward the mark for the prize of the high calling of God in Christ Jesus." There is an attitude of the undefeatable fighter in the Spirit of God. He will never give up, nor will you, as you operate in the mind of Christ. 1 Tim 6:12 "Fight the good fight of faith, *lambano*/lay hold on eternal *zoe*/life, whereunto thou art also called … ." This is "warrior" talk.

The Spirit of *Agape*/Love, Holy Spirit in us, teaches us to *agape*/love like this: 1 Cor 13:4 "*Agape*/charity suffereth long, and is kind; *agape*/charity envieth not; *agape*/charity vaunteth not itself, is not puffed up, 5 doth not behave itself unseemly, seeketh not her

OTHER HEALING TEACHINGS

own, is not easily provoked, thinketh no evil; 6 rejoiceth not in iniquity, but rejoiceth in the truth; **7 beareth all things, believeth all things, hopeth all things, endureth all things. 8** *Agape*/**charity never faileth … .**" There is tenacity in *agape*/love that will keep fighting till the victory is won. 1 Thes 4:9 "But as touching *phileo*/brotherly love ye need not that I write unto you: for ye yourselves are taught of God to *agape*/love one another."

Those thoughts to pray or help others are from Father God. As we obey, His *agape*/love flows to bring the Kingdom of God to Earth. Holy Spirit teaches us to *agape*/love per 1 Cor 13, not some lesser way. He also uses means (works of praise, charity and effective prayer). Much of 1 John also shows that the issue now is not your legal status as a son of God but your actual walk in cooperation with Holy Spirit by the new creation in Jesus. We are to know we have eternal *zoe* life and walk in *agape* love. Thus sin stops you, as it limits your thinking to yourself, not your sonship in God.

This tenacity, I-will-not-give-up attitude, is based on what the one loved needs, no matter what the price: John 3:16 "For God so *agape*/loved the world, that he gave his only begotten Son, that whosoever believeth in him should not perish, but have everlasting *zoe*/life. 17 For God sent not his Son into the world to condemn the world; but that the world through him might be *sozo*/saved." This is included in: 1 John 3:8 "He that committeth sin is of the devil; for the devil sinneth from the beginning. For this purpose the Son of God was manifested, that he might destroy the works of the devil."

John 3:16 emphasizes the *agape*/love of God in the price paid. 1 John 3:8 emphasizes the war we are in. And, again, God paid the price so we could walk in His victory over the devil. As we live for Him, we will pay the price in prayer and patience/persistence to set others free for Him, as we cooperate with the Spirit of *agape*/love and grace within us. 1 Cor 15:10 "But by the grace of God I am what I am: and his grace which was bestowed upon me was not in vain; but I laboured more abundantly than they all: yet not I, but the grace of God which was with me." 2 Cor 5:14 "For the *agape*/love of Christ constraineth us; because we thus judge, that if one died for all, then were all dead: 15 and that he died for all, that they which *zao*/live should not henceforth *zao*/live unto themselves, but unto him which died for them, and rose again." 1 Cor 15:55 "O death, where is thy sting? O grave, where is thy victory? 56 The sting of death is sin; and the strength of sin is the law. 57 But thanks be to God, which giveth us the victory through our Lord Jesus Christ. 58 Therefore, my *agape*/beloved brethren, be ye stedfast, unmoveable, always abounding in the work of the Lord, forasmuch as ye know that your labour is not in vain in the Lord." *Steadfast* means to keep at it till you overcome! Faint not; don't give up!

~ 15 ~

ON HOW YOUR FAITH WORKS

John G. Lake learned (and it is demonstrated by many, including Curry Blake, in our time [www.jglm.org]) that if God did not give a miracle today, He will give healing and a miracle tomorrow–every day. Rev. Lake practiced that if someone came every day for 30 days for battle prayer, somewhere in that time of 30 days they would see the manifestation of God's healing power to blast the work of the devil right out of their life. Some even came daily for 75 to 90 days. They and Rev. Lake would not give up until the victory was won. This is godly tenacity. The results from God were dramatic and powerful against every kind of sickness, disease, infirmity, deformity, accident, damage and problem. Dr. Lake's results were well documented and verified by many, many former skeptics. He had 100,000 healed over a period of 5 years, that is about 80 a day!

Another thing John Lake learned was that you do not have to expect the victim of Satan to have faith for their healing. If they did, they would not need you to fight or pray for them. They would have already set themselves free. So you have the faith, whether they like it or agree with you. You destroy, through the mighty power of God, the works of the devil in the name of Jesus wherever you find them. Rom 12:12 "… continuing instant in prayer … ."

Look at how Jesus destroyed a fine funeral in Nain by raising a dead boy, without anyone asking Him to do it. Luke 7:11 "And it came to pass the day after, that he went into a city called Nain; and many of his disciples went with him, and much people. 12 Now when he came nigh to the gate of the city, behold, there was a dead man carried out, the only son of his mother, and she was a widow: and much people of the city was with her. 13 And when the Lord saw her, he had compassion

OTHER HEALING TEACHINGS

on her, and said unto her, Weep not. 14 And he came and touched the bier: and they that bare him stood still. And he said, Young man, I say unto thee, Arise. 15 And he that was dead sat up, and began to speak. And he delivered him to his mother. 16 And there came a fear on all: and they glorified God, saying, That a great prophet is risen up among us; and, That God hath visited his people." This is wandering around and doing good and healing those oppressed (*under the active rule and lordship*) of the devil, per Acts 10:38.

Nor did a certain young woman or her owners want the profitable and powerful spirit of divination cast out of her, but Holy Spirit did it anyway, at the agitation and command of Paul: <u>Acts 16:16</u> "And it came to pass, as we went to prayer, a certain damsel possessed with a spirit of divination met us, which brought her masters much gain by soothsaying: 17 the same followed Paul and us, and cried, saying, These men are the servants of the most high God, which shew unto us the way of *soteria*/salvation. 18 And this did she many days. But Paul, being grieved, turned and said to the spirit, I command thee in the name of Jesus Christ to come out of her. And he came out the same hour." See also the lame man of Acts 3 and 4. Jesus did not need a reason to heal, other than a need. His disciples practiced the same.

God has always looked for those who will work with Him. <u>Isa 59:16</u> "And he saw that there was no man, and wondered that there was no intercessor: therefore his arm brought salvation unto him; and his righteousness, it sustained him. 17 For he put on righteousness as a breastplate, and an helmet of salvation upon his head; and he put on the garments of vengeance for clothing, and was clad with zeal as a cloak." <u>Isa 50:2</u> "Wherefore, when I came, was there no man? when I called, was there none to answer? Is my hand shortened at all, that it cannot redeem? or have I no power to deliver? behold, at my rebuke I dry up the sea, I make the rivers a wilderness: their fish stinketh, because there is no water, and dieth for thirst. 3 I clothe the heavens with blackness, and I make sackcloth their covering." <u>2 Chron 16:9</u> "For the eyes of the LORD run to and fro throughout the whole earth, to shew himself strong in the behalf of them whose heart is perfect toward him … ."

You be the one God is looking for, the intercessor, the messenger He can trust to go around doing good, healing all who are oppressed of the devil, for Father God is with you, in Holy Spirit and power, to do just this. Loud thanks and praise starts the ball rolling.

~ 16 ~

ON HEALING AND MIRACLES

Healing is a process over time. While not trying to make a rigid definition, miracles are usually instantaneous to within 48 to 72 hours. I give God the glory for any answered prayer. I especially enjoy giving Him glory for those "impossible" answers, but all acts of righteousness and all answered prayer are acts of war against the kingdoms of this world and serve to extend the Kingdom of our God. Luke 10:17 "And the seventy returned again with joy, saying, Lord, even the devils are subject unto us through thy name. 18 And he said unto them, I beheld Satan as lightning fall from heaven. 19 Behold (*make this change your life*), I give unto you power (*authority*) to tread on serpents and scorpions, and over all the power (*ability*) of the enemy: and nothing shall by any means hurt you. 20 Notwithstanding in this rejoice not, that the spirits are subject unto you; but rather rejoice, because your names are written in heaven."

We have what we need: Jesus' authority and Holy Spirit power over all the works of the devil. All of Heaven will back us, as we exercise the authority of God in the name of Jesus for us to tread, stomp, and crush any work of the devil. We are to focus continually on the fact that we are made the righteousness of God in Jesus and His total victory, as we are now seated in Jesus beside the Father.

One of the ways we understand divine healing to work is that we, as a co-worker with God, blast with Holy Spirit power to break the power of the devil over a situation and command him to go, and then we let the healing work of Jesus manifest. It may be quick (a miracle), or slower (a healing), but as we stay persistent, we will see the desired result manifested. A good attitude for healing is this: "I may not see it yet, but I have it. It is not a matter of 'if,' but 'when.' Thank You, Father, in the name of Jesus, it is done." Then obey Phil 4:6-9 to stay in faith.

Faith actions include *aiteo* commands, thanksgiving, praise and joy before you see the answer, even if it is delayed. Keep repeating with mind-renewing in the appropriate Scriptures. And anytime you hear a fearful thought or word, or get fearful over the result, go and obey: Phil 4:4 "Rejoice in the Lord alway: and again I say, Rejoice. 5 Let your moderation be known unto all men. The Lord is at hand [*in power*]. 6 Be careful (*anxious, fearful, terrorized, in dread, hopeless*) for nothing; but in every thing by prayer and supplication with thanksgiving let your *aiteo*/requests be made known unto God [*by proclaiming His promises and* aiteo/*asking, by requiring, demanding and expecting as due by covenant promise His answer unto joyful thanksgiving, for I* lambano/*receive it, knowing I will possess it*]. 7 And the peace of God, which passeth all understanding, shall keep your hearts and minds through Christ Jesus. 8 Finally, brethren, whatsoever things are **true**, whatsoever things are **honest**, whatsoever things are **just**, whatsoever things are **pure**, whatsoever things are **lovely**, whatsoever things are of **good report**; if there be any **virtue**, and if there be any **praise**, think on these things. 9 Those things, which ye have both learned, and received, and heard, and seen in me, do: and the God of peace shall be with you [*in power to victory over any oppression, reign or lordship of the devil and operate in you, as you think rightly in the dominion, triumph,* agape *love, compassion and mind of Christ*]."

Operating in the mind of Christ will keep you looking at what is possible with God, by His promises, in confidence, and not at the natural world impossibilities of the situation. Or, said simpler: look not on what cannot be, but on what can be in Jesus. The more you think and act like Jesus on healing, the more you will see of God's healing power in healing and miracles.

Keep doing faith actions until you get the promised result. Faint not!

~ 17 ~

ON PERSISTENT FAITH

Jesus described faith as persistence that does not give up. He also warned that giving up or fainting is a major temptation in prayer. Luke 18:1 "And he spake a parable unto them to this end, that men ought always to pray, and not to faint; 2 saying, There was in a city a judge, which feared not God, neither regarded man: 3 and there was a widow in that city; and she came unto him, saying, Avenge me of mine adversary. 4 And he would not for a while: but afterward he said within himself, Though I fear not God, nor regard man; 5 yet because this widow troubleth me, I will avenge her, lest by her continual coming she weary me. 6 And the Lord said, Hear what the unjust judge saith. 7 And shall not God avenge his own elect, which cry day and night unto him, though he bear long with them? 8 I tell you that he will avenge them speedily. Nevertheless when the Son of man cometh, shall he find faith on the earth?" Note: no specific time for how long we need to pray is given except when the need continues to exist.

There are many lessons in this passage. Here are a few of them. First, in verse 7, Jesus asks will He find this kind of faith when He returns. So this is important to Him. Next, notice, in verse 6, how often He expects prayer on a subject: night and day. This could be all day and night continuously or at least twice a day, once in daylight and once in the nighttime. Here is a related scripture: Ps 55:16 "As for me, I will call upon God; and the LORD shall save me. 17 Evening, and morning, and at noon, will I pray, and cry aloud: and he shall hear my voice." Also notice that this was a legal issue, much like the covenant promises, so the woman was appealing on the basis of law and not whim. Here is a lesson: know the scriptures you are basing your prayer on.

OTHER HEALING TEACHINGS

Per this story, for whatever reasons, God cannot answer some prayers right away; but He still hears and expects you to keep praying earnestly until the answer comes. You have to decide if you will hang in there for 1 minute, 1 hour, 1 day, 1 week, 1 month, 1 year, 10 years, 30 years or longer. But this scripture says your part is to keep praying as much as the woman did–day and night—till the answer comes. Work to get your mind off the dread and fear "if God does not heal," and into the persuaded assurance that He has promised, He is able, He *agape*/loves the sick person and you, and He will do it. Fear not and be not afraid. Deut 31:6 "Be strong (*in His strength for you*) and of a good courage (*in your heart, with bold words and thanksgiving, praise and joy*), fear not (*by considering only failure, but look at the victory*), nor be afraid (*or harassed by the evil power*) of them: for the Lord thy God, he it is that doth go with thee; he will not fail thee, nor forsake thee."

Jesus also warns that God is not unjust. He is good, but He is righteous in taking time to answer. Also notice the judge ... , "he feared not God nor man." This is a good description of the devil, so, ultimately, in prayer, you are fighting the devil either directly or through the lies of the devil people believe, hope or operate in. Your prayers are not fighting God; they are helping Him do what He needs to do. If you quit your part, He may not have enough to get the job done. Jesus demonstrated that sickness and devils go out relatively quickly, but even He did not live long enough to see all the people be converted to Him. God allows time for people to repent, even when we want it fast. He gives humans time to choose to obey Him, so keep at your prayer for them.

Above all, Jesus said, this persistence is the type of faith He is looking for. Heb 10:38 "Now the just shall *zao*/live by faith: but if any man draw back, my soul shall have no pleasure in him. 39 But we are not of them who draw back unto perdition (*ruin, loss*); but of them that believe to the *sozo*/saving of the soul." So key attributes of faith are to base your prayer on the Scriptures and to keep at it, knowing that fainting is a major temptation. Thus we all need daily encouragement.

Heb 3:10 "(Wherefore I was grieved with that generation (*who escaped out of Egypt with Moses yet died in the desert while God was in their midst in daily signs and wonders*), and said, They do alway err in their heart; and they have not known my ways. 11 So I sware in my wrath, They shall not enter into my rest.) 12 Take heed, brethren (*fellow new-creation/born-again Christians with indwelling Holy Spirit*), lest there be in any of you an evil heart of unbelief, in departing from the *zao*/living God. 13 **But exhort one another daily**, while it is called To day; lest any of you be hardened through the deceitfulness of sin. 14 For we are made partakers of Christ, if we hold the beginning of our confidence stedfast unto the end." Note: holding onto confidence by continual repetition of Gospel benefits with profession, confession, affirmation, *aiteo*, and exuberant thanksgiving, praise and joy against challenging circumstances is our job. The Minister Confession section of this book is designed to help in this.

⊢─Word-Of-God─

~ 18 ~

ON CONTINUOUS PRAYER

One practice of continuous prayer is dedicating time alone for extended periods. Another is in teams, where one prays out loud continuously, each one for an hour or two and then switches off. A variation is for the one to pray 1 to 5 minutes every 15 minutes, or for 5 to 15 minutes every hour. So pray non-stop or at regular intervals by one, by groups or in teams. Another is united prayer, where a group all prays the same thing at the same time, as they did in Acts 4. Or one leads and the others agree with the leader. This manual fits all these methods of prayer. NOTE: If your subject dies, plan on raising them from the dead commanding: "Live now, in Jesus' name." Faint not!

Many take the statement by Jesus in Matt 6:7 as meaning that we should pray only once, in spite of all the clear commands for multiple prayer until the answer comes. Matt 6:7 "But when ye pray, use not vain repetitions, as the heathen do: for they think that they shall be heard for their much speaking. 8 Be not ye therefore like unto them: for your Father knoweth what things ye have need of, before ye *aiteo*/ask him. 9 After this manner therefore pray ye: Our Father which art in heaven, Hallowed be thy name."

Remember, Jesus commanded, in Luke 18, for day and night prayer. In the Garden of Gethsemane, He prayed the exact same thing three times. This was repetition, but it was not "vain." It took three times for Jesus to resolve the issue. During that same time, Jesus also told the disciples to pray for 1 hour to not enter into temptation. This term or idea, "not enter into temptation," is included in the "Our Father." The "Our Father" takes about 15 seconds to pray, or you could do it 4 times in a minute, or 240 times in an hour. Few think that this is what Jesus

OTHER HEALING TEACHINGS

meant, but had the disciples done that, it might have kept them from falling asleep.

The key in Matt 6:7 is "vain repetitions." *Vain* means useless, usually with lots of visibility, but not effective. Biblically, *vain* refers to thoughts, words or actions that will not stand on the Day of Judgment. And more importantly, they will not create the path to allow God to move in the immediate situation. The opposite of vanity in this case is knowing that God hears you and cares.

Instead, we are to pray with *aiteo* commands, knowing God will hear and obey those commands (the biblical word, *hear*, in Matt 6:7, means "to hear and obey gladly"). Matt 6:8 "Be not ye therefore like unto them: for your Father knoweth what things ye have need of, before ye *aiteo*/ask him." Instead, you are to *aiteo*, knowing each time you do you are providing more for God to be able to move. Additionally, Jesus tells us to *aiteo*/ask and keep on asking in Matt 7:7-11, Luke 11:9 and John 16:24. This is readily seen in the Amplified Bible where the present continuous tense is accurately translated. John 16:24 "Up to this time you have not *aiteo*/asked (*required, demanded and expected as due by covenant promise*) a [single] thing in My Name [as presenting all that I AM]; but now *aiteo*/ask and keep on *aiteo*/asking (*by requiring, demanding and expecting as due by covenant promise*) and you will receive, so that your joy (gladness, delight) may be full and complete." AMP

This understanding of prayer does not negate the "one time" prayer, but obviously fits with the habits of the early disciples. Here is how "Jesus-trained people" dealt with one problem. Acts 12:5 "Peter therefore was kept in prison: but prayer was made without ceasing of the church unto God for him."

If you need an answer, and you pray with *aiteo*, and it does not appear to be complete, go into continuous prayer in obedience, until that unjust judge, the devil, let's go, and God triumphs through you, as you labor in prayer. 1 Cor 15:57 "But thanks be to God, which giveth us the victory through our Lord Jesus Christ. 58 Therefore, my *agape*/beloved brethren, be ye stedfast, unmoveable, always abounding in the work of the Lord, forasmuch as ye know that your labour is not in vain in the Lord." This is what Dr. Lake learned as a secret to victory in healing.

So yes, we all love the "one-prayer" healing victory, but if you do not get it, keep in continuous prayer until complete freedom comes. If life and death are on the line, then continuous prayer is a clear directive. (See also Part VI-3: Repeating the Battle Prayer.)

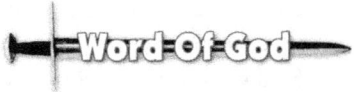

~ 19 ~

ON WHY SOME AREN'T HEALED

Each case of sickness or need is unique, but here are some important guidelines. First, if no one ministers healing, or the person in need does not tell you of the problem, or they do not come to you, or they do not go to God, the minister does not pray long or often enough, or they do not have their own faith as they pray for themselves, the person will probably not be healed by God. God requires that faith in Him be exercised by someone for Him to move on the Earth. So, whatever else is going on, it is not God that is hindering the healing.

The general principle of God is that it is not a lack of anointing or a lack His power. The Christian has Holy Spirit dwelling in them and sealed in them until the Day of Redemption, so Holy Spirit is not the problem. Holy Spirit is a person, so if you have Him, you have all of Him, and He is the power of God. He is the answer, as He will teach us all things concerning Jesus. 1 John 2:27 "But the anointing which ye have received of him abideth in you, and ye need not that any man teach you: but as the same anointing teacheth you of all things, and is truth, and is no lie, and even as it hath taught you, ye shall abide in him." Eph 1:13 "In whom (Jesus) ye also trusted, after that ye heard the word of truth, the gospel of your *soteria*/salvation: in whom also after that ye believed, ye were sealed with that holy Spirit of promise, 14 which is the earnest of our inheritance until the redemption of the purchased possession, unto the praise of his glory." Eph 4:30 "... holy Spirit of God, whereby ye are sealed unto the day of redemption."

So the issue is not more power or more anointing, but it is, as it always has been, a lack of cooperating with God in His Word, in His knowledge that does not govern our lives sufficiently. Hos 4:6 "My people are destroyed for lack of knowledge ... ."

OTHER HEALING TEACHINGS

Destroyed includes political, governmental, economic, geographical, weather wise, physical, mental and physical, i.e., every effect of the curse of the Law. So right information and understanding leads to a different way of viewing the world, and results in matching thinking and behaviors, and this is the answer to getting more of any healing. It is an education, motivation and confidence problem in us, and not God.

The anointing, all the power of God, in Holy Spirit, is here to teach us these things, and His primary tool, above all others, is the Word of God. John 15:26 "But when the Comforter is come, whom I will send unto you from the Father, even the Spirit of truth, which proceedeth from the Father, he shall testify of me." John 14:16 "And I will pray the Father, and he shall give you another Comforter, that he may abide with you for ever 17 Even the Spirit of truth; whom the world cannot receive, because it seeth him not, neither knoweth him: but ye know him; for he dwelleth with you, and shall be in you." John 16:13 "Howbeit when he, the Spirit of truth, is come, he will guide you into all truth: for he shall not speak of himself; but whatsoever he shall hear, that shall he speak: and he will shew you things to come. 14 He shall glorify me: for he shall receive of mine, and shall shew it unto you. 15 All things that the Father hath are mine: therefore said I, that he shall take of mine, and shall shew it unto you." 2 Pet 1:20 "Knowing this first, that no prophecy of the scripture is of any private interpretation. 21 For the prophecy came not in old time by the will of man: but holy men of God spake as they were moved by the Holy Ghost." 2 Tim 3:15 "… the holy scriptures, which are able to make thee wise unto *soteria*/salvation (*including healing*) through faith which is in Christ Jesus. 16 All scripture is given by inspiration of God, and is profitable for doctrine, for reproof, for correction, for instruction in righteousness: 17 that the man of God may be perfect, throughly furnished unto all good works." So the answer is in more truth, more believing the Scriptures and not more anointing. As Moses and Samson proved, if you agree with what God wants done, if even for the wrong reasons, the power is there.

Sickness, or any disease, is nothing more than sin or iniquity reigning in a body for evil. It calls the shots and determines if the person lives or dies, or if they can have peace and prosperity. Sin and the effects of sin, the curse of the Law, have a cure from God. Prov 16:6 "By *chesed*/mercy and truth iniquity (*sin and the effects of sin, the curse, including all manner of disease and limitation*) is purged: and by the fear of the Lord men depart from evil." Fearing the Lord means obeying Him and doing things His way, knowing that any other way leads to death and destruction in fast or slow forms. Prov 14:12 "There is a way which seemeth right unto a man, but the end thereof are the ways of death." Sickness is a slow form of death, and disease adds torment to the process.

Cooperating with Holy Spirit is the answer. John 16:8 "And when he (*Comforter, Encourager and Holy Spirit*) is come, he will reprove the world of sin, and of righteousness, and of judgment: 9 of sin, because they believe not on me (*for remission of sin, salvation or healing*); 10 of righteousness, because I go to my Father, and ye see me no more (*making us the righteousness of God by the new birth and totally blessed*); 11 of judgment, because the prince of this world (*Satan, the devil*) is judged (*against*)." Satan is the enforcer of the law of sin and death, and he is the source of the disease and why it remains, not God. We Christians have been given the job of enforcing the salvation of Jesus, God's judgment against the devil, on the devil and destroying his works, and all of Heaven is behind us to do our job. Luke 10:19 "Behold (*hear and make this change your view of life*), I give unto you power (*authority, the right, the commission and the ability of Heaven*) to tread on serpents and scorpions, and over all the power of the enemy (*Satan*): and nothing shall by any means hurt you. 20 Notwithstanding in this rejoice not, that the spirits are subject unto you; but rather rejoice, because your names are written in heaven."

This is what Holy Spirit said through Peter and James: 1 Pet 5:6 "Humble yourselves therefore under the mighty hand of God, that he may exalt you in due time: 7 casting all your care upon him; for he careth for you. 8 Be sober, be vigilant; because your adversary the devil, as a roaring lion, walketh about, seeking whom he may devour: 9 whom resist stedfast in the faith, knowing that the same afflictions are accomplished in your brethren that are in the world." James 4:7 "Submit yourselves therefore to God. Resist the devil, and he will flee from you." So the issue is how we obey God, and how we relate to the devil, and not a problem of God "withholding" His power. We hold the power, and we are to attack and destroy the works of the devil with that power, knowing it is the will of God to do so. Acts 10:38 "How God anointed Jesus of Nazareth with the Holy Ghost and with power: who went about doing good, and healing all that were oppressed (*under the active dominion, reign or lordship*) of the devil; for God was with him."

If you are in Jesus, i.e., a Christian, then you have the same anointing, in the same Holy Spirit of power, sealed to you unto the Day of Redemption. 2 Cor 1:21 "Now he which stablisheth us with you in Christ, and hath anointed us, is God; 22 who hath also sealed us, and given the earnest of the Spirit in our hearts."

Proverbs 16:6 says that by *chesed*/mercy and truth we are set free from the effects of sin (that includes sickness) so that healing and prosperity can come. While not exact, the best Greek word for the Hebrew word *chesed* is translated as grace. So by grace and truth people are healed. This is exactly what Jesus came to do. John 1:14 "And the Word was made flesh, and dwelt among us, (and we beheld his glory, the glory as of the only begotten of the Father,) full of grace and truth. 15 John bare witness of him, and cried, saying, This was he of whom I spake, He that cometh after me is preferred before me: for he was before me. 16 And of his fulness have all we received, and grace for grace. 17 For the law was given by Moses, but grace and truth came by Jesus Christ. 18 No man hath seen God at any time;

OTHER HEALING TEACHINGS

the only begotten Son, which is in the bosom of the Father, he hath declared him (*showed us exactly how Father God is, by every word and action Jesus did*)."

So yes, the law and obedience to the law, just as it did for Moses, can get and keep you healed, but with Jesus it is knowing that of Him we receive *chesed* or grace to overcome our lack of right knowledge of and obedience to the law and, as Jesus amply demonstrated, get people healed. Jesus and His work is so far beyond Moses that Moses and the Law is insignificant when compared to Jesus and His works. That is the wonder of the New Testament: Col 1:27 "To whom God would make known what is the riches of the glory of this mystery among the Gentiles; which is Christ in you, the hope of glory." That glory includes healing sickness and raising the dead. John 11:40 "Jesus saith unto her (*Martha, concerning the dead Lazarus*), Said I not unto thee, that, if thou wouldest believe, thou shouldest see the glory of God?" Thus the answer is information that transforms the minister's attitude about the devil in order to get healing. Remember healing is a process; miracles are acts of power that are instant—an hour up to about 3 days.

A wrong attitude about God, healing and the devil is called unbelief; or, by breaking down the meaning of the word *unbelief* itself, obedience to a different word than God's. That different, twisted, corrupt, deceiving or evil word controls how you think, speak and act. So healing comes by obeying the right word of God, and Jesus is the living Word of God, so He is our example. Per Mark 16, believers (those who obey the Word of God, as revealed in the Scriptures and especially in the life of Jesus and the New Testament) will lay hands on the sick, and they will recover. When the disciples could not cast out a demon, first Jesus showed the will of God by healing the boy. Matt 17:19 "Then came the disciples to Jesus apart, and said, Why could not we cast him out? 20 And Jesus said unto them, Because of your unbelief: for verily I say unto you, If ye have faith as a grain of mustard seed, ye shall say unto this mountain, Remove hence to yonder place; and it shall remove; and nothing shall be impossible unto you. 21 Howbeit this kind (*of unbelief*) goeth not out but by prayer and fasting."

The Greek word for *belief* is the verb form of the noun *faith*. Jewish prayer was mostly praying the Scriptures back to God for Him to perform. So pray for God to reveal Himself to you in the Scriptures, especially His *agape*/love for you and all men. You can add fasting to your prayer and, with this manual as a guide, let the Word of God wash out unbelief or faithlessness, and then act with thanks, praise, joy, faith, courage, *agape*/love, persistence, persuadableness and confidence in God as you minister. Feelings will come later, if at all. Information means you act on facts and not feelings.

Notice, in the case where the disciples could not heal, Jesus answered by telling them to look at even bigger tasks and not to get fixated on the relatively smaller problem at hand. Most would believe moving an entire mountain is bigger than casting out a demon. As part of an answer to grow their faith, Jesus gave them a technically impossible example. Major changes would be necessary for a tree to walk down the road and then to grow in water. Luke 17:5 "And the apostles said unto the Lord, Increase our faith. 6 And the Lord said, If ye had faith as a grain of mustard seed, ye might say unto this sycamine tree, Be thou plucked up by the root, and be thou planted in the sea; and it should obey you."

Again Jesus switched from a relatively small task to a major one. He said even the smallest amount of faith can do the impossible, as you speak to the problem. This makes even raising the dead a smaller challenge. Get your eyes on the awesome power of God released by even a tiny amount of faith that will not give up, and off of the speck of demon power keeping someone sick. Speak to the problem, tell it what to do, and get that person healed in the name of Jesus. Faint not!

The problem is not sin, as no one until after Jesus was crucified could have their sins remitted. So Moses, Elijah, the 12 apostles, and the 70 Jesus chose and sent out all had sin, yet they all healed sick people. And certainly no one Jesus healed of the oppressions of the devil was perfect (see Acts 10:38). So sin or imperfection is not the problem. But as we sin, we enliven the flesh, and that keeps us in fear, and limits our ability to believe God to get ourselves or others healed. This is why Jesus said: John 8:31 "Then said Jesus to those Jews which believed on him, If ye continue in my word, then are ye my disciples indeed; 32 and ye shall know the truth, and the truth shall make you free." John 15:7 "If ye abide in me, and my words abide in you, ye shall *aiteo*/ask (*by demanding, expecting as due by covenant promise*) what ye will, and it shall be done unto you."

Another reason people are not healed is that the minister is focused on law and not grace and/or faith, per Rom 5:17 and Gal 3:5. Rom 5:17 "For if by one man's offence death reigned *as king* by one; much more they (*Christians*) which (*continually*) **lambano**/receive (*hold on to no matter what the*) abundance of grace and of the gift of righteousness shall reign (*as kings for Jesus*) in *zoe*/life by one, Jesus Christ.)" 2 Cor 5:21 "For he (*Father God*) hath made him (*Jesus*) to be sin for us, who knew no sin; that we might be made the righteousness of God in him." Gal 3:2 "This only would I learn of you, Received ye the Spirit by the works of the law, or by the hearing of faith? 3 Are ye so foolish? having begun in the Spirit, are ye now made perfect by the flesh? 4 Have ye suffered so many things in vain? if it be yet in vain. 5 He therefore that ministereth to you the Spirit, and worketh miracles among you, doeth he it by the works of the law, or by the hearing of faith?" Both healing and being healed are by grace and faith in the work of Jesus by the cross.

Lambano is a Greek word that means to hold on to like a man would hold on to a life preserver when overboard in a raging sea. It is often translated "receive" in the KJV. Here it means to receive, as if you were a football player trying to catch a ball in the middle of a group of strong defenders. You catch it, and the defenders try to knock and grab the ball from your hand. Another meaning is to carry a very heavy item, like a very heavy bucket and carry it no matter how far or difficult the ground you must traverse. We *lambano* the Word of God by keeping it in our mind and mouth, in spite of the present situation, until we have the results. As we *lambano* the grace of God and the gift of righteousness in Jesus, we will implement the reign of God in power to operate like Jesus did. That is ultimate being right! To reign means your words have power, and things happen the way you say. God will flow in your words, as you learn to obey these scriptures.

Jesus said another reason for unbelief in a minister is the traditions we hold that make the Word of God of no effect. Mark 7:13 "Making the word of God of none effect through your tradition, which ye have delivered: and many such like things do ye." Gal 5:4 "Christ is become of no effect unto you, whosoever of you are justified by the law; ye are fallen from grace." The opposite of grace is works, guilt and condemnation. Either by official church doctrine or folklore that contradicts or lessens the Word of God's grace, many do not know the truth unto right action. The basic answer is to challenge any idea you have for why God will not heal and search the Scriptures for why He will heal anyway. Jesus came to show exactly how Father God is. Repeatedly the Scriptures say, "He healed them all." This is God's will, done by God's right-thinking man. There are many concepts in the New Testament that we do not understand today and that need to be brought back to better understand. For more on this subject, I recommend the excellent material of Curry Blake (www.jglm.org) and ours at www.CovenantPeaceMinistries.com.

In a similar passage of scripture, God shows that His Word is powerful; but not everyone makes use of that power. What God has said He will do He will do. What He has said we must do we must do. Heb 4:11 "Let us labour therefore to enter into that rest, lest any man fall after the same example of unbelief. 12 For the word of God is quick, and powerful, and sharper than any twoedged sword, piercing even to the dividing asunder of soul and spirit, and of the joints and marrow, and is a discerner of the thoughts and intents of the heart. 13 Neither is there any creature that is not manifest in his sight: but all things are naked and opened unto the eyes of him with whom we have to do." Notice this takes labor, not a magic wand. Gifts can be imparted or developed, but no one can impart to or anoint you to use them. You alone have the power and responsibility to keep yourself in a renewed mind. It takes diligent work.

The men who put Jesus on the cross had the entire Old Testament memorized, and yet they killed the One sent to help them, the answer to centuries of prayer and belief. To prevent the same problem from occurring again, we must work with Holy Spirit to learn the Scriptures. Pray Eph 1:16-23 often. A simple but time-consuming method, which leads to great freedom, is to read every scripture reference in a given book, including this one, and read the two Bible chapters before it and the two following it to see for yourself if what is being said fits the scripture. (Yes, that is 5 chapters for each reference.) If it does not fit, put that explanation aside, but stay with the Scriptures. Acts 17:11 "These were more noble than those in Thessalonica, in that they received the word with all readiness of mind, and searched the (*Old Testament*) scriptures daily, whether those things were so. 12 Therefore many of them believed; also of honourable women which were Greeks, and of men, not a few." Too often we read books or accept statements that are not true without confirming with the Scriptures. Verse 12 above says that this is how the people came to belief, and we all should do likewise. (Please send me anything you wish to challenge in the book, and I will be happy to work to improve my explanations. The first test is always, "What do the Scriptures say?")

We are our own limitations: One message of Jesus was this: Matt 9:29 "... saying, According to your faith be it unto you." So if you believe you have to wear a certain red shirt to minister healing, you will have to wear that red shirt (or carry that special Bible, or use that oil, fast, or whatever). But your example is Jesus, not someone else.

John Lake indicated that ministries that minister/pray only once (as in a prayer line/single visit) typically see 1 to 3 healed per each 10 to 15 prayed for. That was how Dr. Lake developed his basic plan of 30 days, and he saw a lot more results. Since we can act our way to believing quicker than believing our way to acting, John Lake demonstrated that persistent daily ministry over 30 days got most people healed, including those "last chancers" whom medical science had given up to die. Some kept coming back for 60 to 91 days, whatever it took. So one reason people are not healed is really two reasons:
1. We don't act in faith, and
2. We don't keep at it with perseverance to win, to overcome, to set the person free from the devil and his works.

Another reason some are not healed, as related by John Lake, is that the minister has let him- or herself grow cold in the process. 2 Tim 1:6 "Wherefore I put thee in remembrance that thou stir up the gift of God, which is in thee by the putting on of my hands. 7 For God hath not given us the spirit of fear; but of *dunamis*/power, and of *agape*/love, and of a sound mind." Here we are told to stir ourselves up to access the spirit of power, stirring ourselves up in God. Speaking in tongues is specifically listed as one way we can do this. 1 Cor 14:4 "He that speaketh in an unknown tongue edifieth himself ... ." Jude 20 "But ye, *agape*/beloved, building up yourselves on your most holy faith, praying in the Holy Ghost, 21 keep yourselves in the *agape*/love of God, looking for the mercy of our Lord Jesus Christ unto eternal *zoe*/life."

Notice Timothy had Holy Spirit, who is *dunamis*/power, *agape*/love and the mind of Christ, yet Timothy had to stir himself up in God to release that *dunamis*/power and *agape*/love and operate in the mind of Christ. They were there, but inaccessible or limited, until he got his attitude right in his soul. You stir yourself up in spirit and soul much like a coach in a locker room with affirmations, confessions, proclamations, preaching, thanksgiving, praise and joy, with the Word of God in Christ. The Psalms and tongues are great tools to use for this.

Pray in tongues loud, hard and fast, aiming at the problem for about 2 hours, and then command healing in tongues or your own language. When you get experienced in this, it may only take a moment or two to focus on God and His *agape/love*, as your spirit and soul are already stirred up in Holy Spirit.

John Lake also said that one reason for prayer failure was not obeying Jesus in persevering prayer. You are not attacking God, but you are attacking the devil. God is not the problem. If it takes you months or years, then it takes you months or years. After telling the disciples to not faint at the delay of the answer, but to keep praying day and night against the unjust judge, the devil, Jesus went on to ask: Luke 18:8 "... Nevertheless when the Son of man cometh, shall he find faith on the earth?" It may be like a stubborn spot. It does not seem to move, but you keep at it, until it does go. The more you get free of the fear of failure and the dreadful consequences of the evil in the situation, and, consequently, more persuaded that God has spoken, He cannot lie, He *agape*/loves the sick person and you, He paid the awful price of Jesus to get this healing and He will do it ... , the more you persuade yourself of this, the more *zoe*/life you will push by trust in God each time you minister. *Zoe* is life.

Jesus never said, "I will not heal until you get more faith, or you learn some lesson God is teaching you with this sickness or disease." Jesus never said, "God is taking this person home with this disease, so I cannot heal them." Don't let the devil tell you God is working some lesson by the delay in a healing. The only delay lesson Jesus gave was when the disciples could not cast out a demon, and He healed the boy right away. See also Matt 17:14-20; Mark 9:14-29; Luke 9:37-43.

You attack and win, or keep attacking and keep fighting till you do win. Hear Holy Spirit's exhortation to Timothy: 1 Tim 6:11 "But thou, O man (*or woman*) of God, flee these things (*of agape/loving worldly lust and power*); and follow after righteousness, godliness, faith, *agape*/love, patience, meekness. 12 Fight (*labor reverently and strive to win*) the good fight (*contention and battle*) of faith, *lambano*/lay hold on eternal *zoe*/life, whereunto thou art also called, and hast professed a good profession before many witnesses. 13 I give thee charge in the sight of God, who quickeneth all things, and before Christ Jesus, who before Pontius Pilate witnessed a good confession; 14 that thou keep this commandment (*to fight and win*) without spot, unrebukeable, until the appearing of our Lord Jesus Christ."

He is telling us that faith is a fight, and we are to *lambano* what we have, the abundance of grace, the gift of righteousness, indwelling Holy Spirit of *dunamis/power*, *agape*/love and the sound mind of Christ and the *zoe*/life of God to deliver to others in prayer and laying on of hands to set them free from the oppressions of the devil, as an under-king for Jesus. If Holy Spirit had to exhort Timothy to do certain things and adjust his attitude, the issue is not God, but the Christian. Holy Spirit was limited by what Timothy did (or did not do by not stirring himself up in God).

This attitude of the *agape*/love warrior will be built as you use this entire manual as part of your ministry and see your faith, your believing, your power in *zoe*/life grow, and, consequently, more of God's compassion delivered. Matt 14:14 "And Jesus went forth, and saw a great multitude, and was moved with compassion toward them, and he healed their sick." Let this mind be in you, knowing we are His body to do the same. Heb 13:8 "Jesus Christ the same yesterday, and to day, and for ever." Acts 14:3 "Long time therefore abode they (*Paul and Barnabas*) speaking boldly in the Lord, which gave testimony unto the word of his grace, and granted signs and wonders to be done by their hands."

God's New Testament answer is to focus on the totality of the victory of Jesus over sin and death with us in Him by faith in His blood, and not the apparent power of evil in the present condition. Rom 5:17 "For if by one man's offence death reigned (*as a cruel and relentless king*) by one; much more they which (*continually*) *lambano*/receive abundance of grace and of the gift of righteousness (*of God in Christ Jesus independent of your own right acts*) shall reign (*to bring the Kingdom of God by their thoughts, words and actions*) in *zoe*/life by one, Jesus Christ.)" The healing blessing is by grace and not works. So labor with and in that grace to victory.

Another reason for unanswered *aiteo* in healing is to be doubled minded, of multiple opinions, on the matter. James 1:5 "If any of you lack wisdom (*what to do for success in temptations and trials*), let him *aiteo*/ask (*keep requiring, demanding and expecting as due by covenant promise*) of God, that giveth to all men liberally, and upbraideth not; and it shall be given him. 6 But let him *aiteo*/ask (*expect, require and demand as due by covenant promise*) in faith (*as evidenced by glad joy and thanksgiving in advance of seeing the answer*), nothing wavering. For he that wavereth is like a wave of the sea driven with the wind and tossed. 7 For let not that man think that he shall receive any thing of the Lord. 8 A double minded man is unstable in all his ways."

Getting rid of false opinions, attitudes or beliefs is all part of renewing the mind into the glorious Gospel. This entire manual is designed to help in that purpose. Since no labor in the Lord is in vain, then keep in *aiteo* and other faith works, knowing that each time you minister, *zoe* is flowing, and eventually you will do enough. Expect that as you renew your mind and keep yourself stirred up into the dominion of Jesus, the *agape* love of God and His compassion, more *zoe* will be released and thus results will be faster and more complete. Faint not!

~ 20 ~

ON RENEWING YOUR MIND

The secret to strong faith and power, as a Christian, is how well you renew and keep renewed your mind or your soul into the Gospel of Jesus Christ. As a new creation in Christ Jesus, we are now to: Eph 4:23 "... be renewed in the spirit of your mind; 24 and that ye put on (*as a new skin and self concept*), the new man, which after God is created in righteousness and true holiness." Eph 4:7 "But unto every one of us is given grace according to the measure of the gift of Christ." How much more grace is there? The issue is believing in the new creation or new man and not the old creation, old man, carnal mind, or fleshly trained mind or heart. We are learning to operate and grow in knowledge in what we already are. Eph 5:8 "For ye were sometimes darkness, but now are ye light in the Lord: walk as children of light." Rom 13:13 "Let us walk honestly, as in the day; not in rioting and drunkenness, not in chambering and wantonness, not in strife and envying. 14 But put ye on the Lord Jesus Christ (*as your self-concept, your self-identity and your mode of thought and action*), and make not provision for the [*mind of the*] flesh, to fulfil the lusts thereof."

So how do you renew your mind? You start with the basics, per the Scriptures: Eph 4:20 "But ye have not so learned Christ; 21 if so be that ye have heard him, and have been taught by him, as the truth is in Jesus: 22 that ye put off concerning the former conversation the old man, which is corrupt according to the deceitful lusts; 23 and be renewed in the spirit of your mind; 24 and that ye put on the new man, which after God is created in righteousness and true holiness."

You acknowledge that your true, born-again nature is just like Father God's in Jesus in righteousness and true holiness. That is who and what you are. Your true new nature or spirit only does the will of God gladly, and it never sins. This same message is found in Rom 6 and Rom 13:10-14, where it ends with Rom 13:14 "But put ye on the Lord Jesus Christ, and make not provision for the flesh, to fulfil the lusts thereof." Then, again, in Col 3:10 "And have put on the new man, which is renewed in knowledge after the image of him that created him." Notice you are to focus your mind on the real you, the born-again-in-spirit man, and not your fleshly, un-renewed soul.

So, when you find yourself in sin, call it what it is, something Jesus had to die for, thank Father you are already forgiven of and already healed of it, cast out the devils associated with it, proclaim your true nature in Christ, and command that healing to manifest in the name of Jesus. Then go make whatever earthly restitution or reconciliation needed. If you find yourself in fear or worry, call it sin and confess that God did not give you that: 2 Tim 1:7 "For God hath not given us the spirit of fear; but of power, and of *agape*/love, and of a sound mind."

Then ask the Lord to convict you of any presumption or pride and to set you free as a son. Then command your soul to walk as a son in Jesus, put Scripture in your mouth to clean out your heart, and go do acts of *agape*/love. Deal with every sin the same way. This is how you renew your mind and stop calling God a liar in the new birth. Note: See the Glossary under The Wrath of God for a ten-step description of this process. It is the root of renewing your soul (heart, mind, will and emotions).

This also builds in your mind God's goal for you: Eph 4:13 "Till we all come in the unity of the faith, and of the knowledge of the Son of God, unto a perfect man, unto the measure of the stature of the fulness of Christ: 14 that we henceforth be no more children, tossed to and fro, and carried about with every wind of doctrine, by the sleight of men, and cunning craftiness, whereby they lie in wait to deceive; 15 but speaking the truth in *agape*/love, may grow up into him in all things, which is the head, even Christ."

For you to stop sinning, the primary answer of God is for you to renew your mind into your new-creation self-identity with glad cooperation with the mind of Christ within you: 1 Cor 2:16 "For who hath known the mind of the Lord, that he may instruct him? But we have the mind of Christ." John 16:13 "Howbeit when he, the Spirit of truth, is come, he will guide you into all truth: for he shall not speak of himself; but whatsoever he shall hear, that shall he speak: and he will shew you things to come. 14 He shall glorify me: for he shall receive of mine, and shall shew it unto you." John 15:26 "But when the Comforter is come, whom I will send unto you from the Father, even the Spirit of truth, which proceedeth from the Father, he shall testify of me:" 1 Cor 3:16 "Know ye not that ye are the temple of God, and that the Spirit of God dwelleth in you?"

OTHER HEALING TEACHINGS

The issue is not if God is speaking or not; it is if we can hear Him to obey Him. On the Day of Judgment we will not be able to point to God and say that He failed us. Instead, we will see all the times we missed Him just as men and women did when Jesus walked the Earth in the flesh. That still applies to us as much just as it did in the days of Jesus or the apostles. We cannot afford the price of a hardened heart toward God. Matt 13:15 "For this people's heart is waxed gross, and their ears are dull of hearing, and their eyes they have closed; lest at any time they should see with their eyes, and hear with their ears, and should understand with their heart, and should be converted, and I should heal them." Notice God holds them accountable for their hard heart. Thus we have a major part in the process.

Modern science is shedding some light on the mechanics of the benefits of obedience to God and His ways. While there has been debate for centuries that still continues, the Bible makes clear that the parts of the inner man include: spirit, soul, mind, emotions, will, heart, and conscious. This scripture tells us that the main parts of man are the spirit, soul and body: 1 Thes 5:23 "And the very God of peace sanctify you wholly; and I pray God your whole *pneuma*/spirit and *psuche*/soul and body be preserved blameless unto the coming of our Lord Jesus Christ." And here we learn that the spirit and the soul are very closely related, but different. Heb 4:12 "For the word of God is quick, and powerful, and sharper than any twoedged sword, piercing even to the dividing asunder of *psuche*/soul and *pneuma*/spirit, and of the joints and marrow, and is a discerner (*inspector, appraiser, judge, evaluator* of the thoughts and intents of the *kardia*/heart."

For practical purposes, the spirit is the real you, what is made brand new in the new creation in Christ Jesus, when Holy Spirit makes you the righteousness of God in Christ Jesus unto the *zoe*/life of Father God. The body is the physical body. Both the spirit and the body belong to God in the new creation: 1 Cor 6:19 "What? know ye not that your body is the temple of the Holy Ghost which is in you, which ye have of God, and ye are not your own? 20 For ye are bought with a price: therefore glorify God in your body, and in your spirit, which are God's." Eph 1:12 "That we should be to the praise of his glory, who first trusted in Christ. 13 In whom ye also trusted, after that ye heard the word of truth, the gospel of your *soteria*/salvation: in whom also after that ye believed, ye were sealed with that holy Spirit of promise, 14 which is the earnest of our inheritance until the redemption of the purchased possession, unto the praise of his glory." The new creation is Holy Spirit indwelling a person.

The purpose of your life on Earth right now is to save or renew your soul to as much like God's as possible before you leave. James 1:21 "Wherefore lay apart all filthiness and superfluity of naughtiness, and *lambano*/receive with meekness the engrafted word, which is able to *sozo*/save your *psuche*/souls." 1 Pet 1:9 "Receiving the end of your faith, even the *soteria*/salvation of your *psuche*/souls."

From the biblical perspective, the spirit, the real you, is thought to be located near the heart or *solar plexus* region. The mind is that which is located in the cranium or brain. The mind makes decisions and receives thoughts and intentions. The soul is thought to be separate from the real you and yet communicates with your spirit: Ps 116:3 "The sorrows of death compassed me, and the pains of hell gat hold upon me: I found trouble and sorrow. 4 Then called I upon the name of the LORD; O LORD, I beseech thee, deliver my *nepesh*/soul. 5 Gracious is the LORD, and righteous; yea, our God is merciful. 6 The LORD preserveth the simple: I was brought low, and he helped me. 7 Return unto thy rest, O my *nepesh*/soul; for the LORD hath dealt bountifully with thee. 8 For thou hast delivered my *nepesh*/soul from death, mine eyes from tears, and my feet from falling."

Man is to purify, operate and manage his soul and heart toward God. Deut 6:5 "And thou shalt love the LORD thy God with all thine *lebab*/heart, and with all thy *nepesh*/soul, and with all thy *meod*/might (*excited, positive, right attitude and enthusiasm*)." Prov 2:9 "Then shalt thou understand righteousness, and judgment, and equity; yea, every good path. 10 When wisdom entereth into thine *leb*/heart, and knowledge is pleasant unto thy *nepesh*/soul." This is a reprogramming or complete re-learning process. Rom 12:2 "And be not conformed to this world: but be ye transformed (*into an effective new creation man*) by the renewing of your mind, that ye may prove what is that good, and acceptable, and perfect, will of God."

Jesus repeated and re-affirmed this distinction of the heart, soul and mind in the Gospels: Matt 22:37 and: Mark 12:29 "And Jesus answered him, The first of all the commandments is, Hear, O Israel; The Lord our God is one Lord: 30 and thou shalt *agape*/love the Lord thy God with all thy *kardia*/heart, and with all thy *psuche*/soul, and with all thy *dianoia*/mind (*imagination, understanding and pondering*), and with all thy *ischus*/strength (*power, ability, money*): this is the first commandment. 31 And the second is like, namely this, Thou shalt *agape*/love thy neighbour as thyself. There is none other commandment greater than these."

Modern culture has a slightly different view. To modern society, man is composed of two parts: body and soul. The self, the part that you think of as yourself, by thinking in your brain behind your eyes, this is called the cognitive or conscious mind and is thought to be housed in the cerebral cortex, which is the top part of the brain. The part of the brain under the cerebral cortex and the neural ganglia throughout the rest of the body houses the unconscious mind. Modern science has not yet defined the spirit and often calls it the soul or the heart or emotion.

Rather than debate the details, Jesus said the issues of life are found in the heart and evidenced by what comes out of your mouth and your actions. Matt 15:16 "And Jesus said, Are ye also yet without understanding? 17 Do not ye yet understand, that whatsoever entereth in at the mouth goeth into the belly, and is cast out into the draught? 18 But those things which proceed out of the mouth come forth from the heart; and they defile the man. 19 For out of the heart proceed evil thoughts, murders, adulteries, fornications, thefts, false witness, blasphemies: 20 these are the things which defile a man: but to eat with unwashen hands defileth not a man." Matt 12:34 "O generation of vipers, how can ye, being evil, speak good things? for out of the abundance of the heart the mouth speaketh. 35 A good man out of the good treasure of the heart bringeth forth good things: and an evil man out of the evil treasure bringeth forth evil things. 36 But I say unto you, That every idle (*useless to God*) word that men shall speak, they shall give account thereof in the day of judgment. 37 For by thy words thou shalt be justified, and by thy words thou shalt be condemned." So the measure of your heart condition is how many of your words will extend the Kingdom of God to survive that Day.

Or, as Solomon said: Prov 4:23 "Keep thy heart with all diligence; for out of it are the issues of life. 24 Put away from thee a froward mouth, and perverse lips put far from thee." Modern science would call the mind of the heart the neural ganglia around the heart, and it is included in the mental processes by which we operate every day. Or, for a simpler definition: the heart is the subconscious mind. Recent findings not only concur with Solomon and Jesus, but say that controlling the subconscious mind is the secret to faith in God as well as success in every aspect of life, including health and longevity. Managing the heart is a key learning or remedial reprogramming process.

This is just as James said: James 1:5 "If any of you lack wisdom, let him *aiteo*/ask (*keep requiring, demanding and expecting as due by covenant promise*) of God, that giveth to all men liberally, and upbraideth not; and it shall be given him. 6 But let him *aiteo*/ask (*require, demand and expect as due by covenant promise*) in faith (*as evidenced by glad joy and thanksgiving in advance of seeing the answer*), nothing wavering. For he that wavereth is like a wave of the sea driven with the wind and tossed. 7 For let not that man think that he shall receive any thing of the Lord. 8 **A double minded man** is unstable in all his ways." James 4:7 "Submit yourselves therefore to God. Resist the devil, and he will flee from you. 8 Draw nigh to God, and he will draw nigh to you. Cleanse your hands, ye sinners; and **purify your hearts, ye double minded**."

The heart, the inner you, and the mind, your thinking you, in this scripture, are related. It is as if the corrupt heart with godly and ungodly beliefs or attitudes results in a double mind and thus makes you unstable in your convictions. Thus the heart is in the territory of the unconscious mind that manifests itself in your cognitive mind and behaviors. Here we see that a double mind not only is faithless, but the working territory of the devil. In this case, a single-minded heart is submitted to God and fights the devil, not men, no matter what the situation (except the military and police). In the new birth, the spirit is recreated, not reprogrammed. The heart and the mind require reprogramming and continual maintenance.

We are going to explore this just enough to understand how to control what our hearts operate in, and how to produce more of God's desired results in our own lives and in the lives of others. Modern science has learned that we operate mostly by the sub or unconscious mind, and it is the seat of long-term or permanent memory and our automatic responses. The cognitive mind has short-term memory of 3 to 5 days at best. Decisions made by only the conscious or cogitative mind, such as a resolution to lose weight in the New Year, are usually ineffective. Physical fitness business experts will tell you that more than 75% of new gym memberships go unused after only a few months. The Bible would call this a double mind, and until you get single-minded, you will not fulfill the promise of a physical fitness program.

The process, as currently defined by modern science, works this way: All information your body perceives through senses or even your thoughts is stored permanently in your subconscious. The subconscious mind, or heart, has the long-term memories. For recall, memories with emotion are recovered or given priority over memories with no or little emotion. Your subconscious mind operates independently of your cognitive mind and sends thoughts to the cognitive mind to reinforce old habit patterns, when any new thought pattern or event is introduced or experienced. The subconscious always tries to keep your life stable against the "normal" of your past. So if your past did not include physical fitness, then that is your normal past, and your subconscious will work to keep you out of the gym. It does this by sending you "second thoughts" after your mind has given you "first" or logical or will-driven thoughts to go there. Additionally, as the cogitative mind only has short-term memory, you simply forget your resolution or do not have your subconscious trained to give you supporting thoughts to overcome the resistance, temptations and scheduling to keep on a fitness program. So, while you had good intentions, you did not have a heart prepared to make this an "issue of life."

All thoughts are electrical patterns or impulses that travel along the neurons of the body's nervous system, especially in the brain. The more you think a thought, the more the brain, with apparent infinite capacity, builds a neural pathway to make that thought easier to be remembered. To build this pathway requires 4 days to start (if you use daily repetition 15 to 120 minutes a day) to build and reinforce the thought, habit, attitude, belief, or prejudice. Then, after continued repetition, it takes about 21 days from the start to complete the neural pathway for that thought. Now the thought, attitude or belief is readily available as a neural connection whenever the situation fits for the subconscious to recall. If you also add in strong emotion, the subconscious will give it priority over other thoughts and beliefs.

In order to reduce the priority of the old thoughts that may conflict with the new thought or belief, it takes a minimum of 90 days of repetition with strong emotion to remove or subdue the old thought process. Apparently this process of 4 days to start, 21 days to build, and 90 days to subdue can take longer, but not less.

OTHER HEALING TEACHINGS

If it does take less, it means that you already have supporting thoughts and beliefs to the new thoughts, and the old thoughts are not in direct conflict with the new.

During the period of 90 days, as you are trying to replace an old limiting thought with a new, more powerful thought and emotion, you will have your subconscious fight your new thought with "double-mindedness" until the 90 days are complete. Since the memories never go away, if you drift back into the old way of thinking, you will now cause the old thought to "rise" and, thus, increase your double-mindedness and perhaps go back to your "old" ways. This double-mindedness or "second-mindedness" is also the source of our "conscious."

If you are trying to improve your life with God's truth and good things, the source of these conflicting thoughts or voices are:

a) Your corrupted subconscious (or heart memories) anywhere it is not like Jesus. Your corrupted, stained conscious (the voice of the subconscious) trying to keep you in your past, **ungodly** normal.
b) Your pure subconscious (or heart memories) anywhere it is like Jesus. Your **godly** conscious (the voice of the subconscious) trying to keep you in your past, **godly** normal.
c) Your own cognitive mind "reasoning" or "understandings."

d) Your born-again, new-creation, like-Jesus spirit in thoughts to persuade and stir your subconscious and conscious mind to support the **godly** thoughts and attitudes.
e) Holy Spirit and God's angels in thoughts to persuade and stir your subconscious and conscious mind to support the **godly** thoughts and attitudes.
f) The devil and/or demons in thoughts to persuade and stir your subconscious and conscious mind to support the **ungodly** thoughts and attitudes.

This list shows the types or sources of thoughts you "hear" inside your head. To that, may be added people and things (anything around you, from television to people's words, to the wind in your hair) you perceive with your senses and which vie for your attention and approval.

The devil keeps us in bondage by our thoughts or strongholds of lies in our subconscious with its long-term memory. 2 Cor 10:3 "For though we walk in the flesh, we do not war after the flesh: 4 (for the weapons of our warfare are not carnal, but mighty through God to the pulling down of strong holds;) 5 casting down imaginations, and every high thing that exalteth itself against the knowledge of God, and bringing into captivity every thought to the obedience of Christ." 2 Tim 2:24 "And the servant of the Lord must not strive; but be gentle unto all men, apt to teach, patient, 25 in meekness instructing those that oppose themselves; if God peradventure will give them repentance to the acknowledging of the truth; 26 and that they may recover themselves out of the snare of the devil, who are taken captive by him at his will." Notice repetition is needed to win the heart to truth.

So the devil gets us to add strong emotion to thoughts, attitudes and desires contrary to God's *agape*/love and truth. They get built or written into our hearts as our "normal," and, thus, when the devil repeats them to us in our thoughts or through others, we agree, and do not go through the 90-day process to replace and subdue them. If we are well trained in his deceptions, we will actually spread and reinforce these lies to others and attack those who are operating in more of God's truth than we are. So all the devil has to do is to whisper that thought; we hear it, accept it, and reinforce it and, thus, keep ourselves in bondage. But even if the devil does not attack us, our self-normalizing-to-the-past subconscious will also attack us to keep us from operating in these new thoughts and attitudes for at least 90 days, if we positively attack the old limiting beliefs with diligence. In either case we are in a battle of thoughts.

Our souls are built to be warriors for God to bring Heaven to Earth. We see this in this command: Gen 1:28 "And God blessed them, and God said unto them, Be fruitful, and multiply, and replenish the earth, and subdue it: and have dominion over the fish of the sea, and over the fowl of the air, and over every living thing that moveth upon the earth." *Subdue* means "to fight tough battles against opposition and fight until you win." *Dominion* means "once it is subdued, keep it that way." Again, it is a battle or war message.

So we are made to go into a situation that is not like Heaven on Earth, but with a vision in our heart of what it should look like, fight while it is still wrong and then make it right. Your subconscious is designed to keep a vision, self-image, memory in your mind and not lose it in spite of conflicting evidence. Else you would stop subduing and let Hell remain and not bring Heaven to Earth. This feature works really great if you start with a perfect heart, but if, at any time, your heart gets corrupted, your subconscious or heart will want to stay in that past corruption until you renew your mind to the image or vision God has for you.

Thus Jesus could look at a situation, not accept the present condition and heal all who came to Him in the way Father God would want. At the same time, the religious leaders fought over healing on the Sabbath (as if Jesus were an ordinary man with special "powers," and not from Father God, who was doing the miracles through His cooperating human, Jesus) because that was their heart-normal. They refused to see God in what Jesus was doing. They used the healing on the Sabbath to "prove" that He was not from God.

Notice, in 2 Tim 2:24-25, it takes repetition of goodness and right attitude by the teacher before the victim of lies can set themselves free. This is what Jesus also said: John 8:31 "Then said Jesus to those Jews which believed on him, If ye continue in my word (*keep in high positive attitude of praise, joy and thanksgiving with much repetition*), then are ye my disciples indeed; 32 and ye shall *epignosis*/know the truth, and the truth shall make you free."

Until you receive the love of the truth, you will stay in bondage to death in some way: 2 Thes 2:9 "Even him, whose coming is after the working of Satan with all power and signs and lying wonders, 10 and with all deceivableness of unrighteousness in them that perish (*death working fast or slow*); because they *lambano*/received not the *agape*/love of the truth, that they might be *sozo*/saved." Devil-fed deception is why we cannot hear God to do *agape*.

The Bible describes the process of letting the heart get corrupted again (failure to maintain right dominion of grace and truth in our hearts): 2 Pet 2:20 "For if after they have escaped the pollutions of the world through the knowledge of the Lord and Saviour Jesus Christ, they are again entangled therein, and overcome, the latter end is worse with them than the beginning. 21 For it had been better for them not to have known the way of righteousness, than, after they have known it, to turn from the holy commandment delivered unto them. 22 But it is happened unto them according to the true proverb, The dog is turned to his own vomit again; and the sow that was washed to her wallowing in the mire." Or as in the books of Hebrews and Galatians, they were going back to the temple, the law, to get forgiveness/remission of sins and, thus, denying the work of Jesus by the cross.

Information in the memory can also have emotion attached to it. The emotion can be either positive or negative. The stronger the emotion, the greater the priority given by the subconscious mind or heart to recalling the thought, habit, belief or attitude. Negative emotions like fear and anger cause the subconscious to tell you to avoid that situation, and positive ones such as acceptance, thanksgiving, joy, pleasure or happiness will lead you to repeat those situations. The key is the emotion's type and strength in the memory.

Concerning the fitness program, as the cognitive mind only operates by short-term memory, you soon "forget" those New Year's weight loss resolutions, and go back to your old lifestyle, unless you can add strong positive emotion and repetition to your memories and thought patterns so you feel "good." But these emotions must be positive and not negative, if you want to stay in the gym and gladly live the life of "no pain, no gain, therefore I am in pain to gain."

The subconscious cannot tell the difference between what your 5 senses detect, your thinking conclusions, what you read and see or what you imagine or visualize. To the subconscious, or heart, they are all the same, real and perfectly valid. So if you read about the joys of mountain climbing often enough, with strong positive emotions, you will find yourself desiring to climb mountains. If, every time you think about or hear about mountain climbing, you add fear, cold, discomfort, etc., the less you will want to climb mountains, and you will discourage others from doing the same. All this is powered by your subconscious the way you trained it, by adding emotion, positive or negative, to information stored in the subconscious. If you have no previous negative thoughts about mountain climbing or your fitness, then in 21 days you can become a committed mountain climber. If you have had past negative experiences and now want to climb again, it will take 90 days of much positive affirmation before you are again single-minded on gladly climbing.

In the same way, your subconscious cannot tell the difference between real feelings and "faking-it" emotion. If you act like you are excited and thankful every time you read about mountains, you can subdue old fears and give the new thinking priority in 90 days. This is also how to train your heart or subconscious mind in anything. Even if you do not, at the time, like it, if you repeat the thoughts and add positive "faking-it" emotions for at least ninety 90 days your subconscious will store it as memories with strong positive emotions and, thus, give it priority in recall and "second thoughts" that encourage and do not hinder mountain climbing. You are now controlling your "mind." For example, in healing, do not let the evil in a situation harass you in potential failure, but ignore that and focus on the greatness of God to heal.

The result is for at least 90 days you will experience numerous, continual and strong negative "second thoughts" against mountain climbing while you build new and strong positive-emotion thoughts about mountain climbing. These second thoughts or double-mindedness are from the past-normalizing feature of the subconscious. With a corrupt conscious, the devil does not have to do much to keep you in bondage.

Faith in God works the same way. Your subconscious mind or heart helps or hinders your logical, mental affirmations to believe and obey God. So the keys to single-minded devotion to God is to listen to the words out of your mouth to test what is like Jesus or not, and if you find any difference, go on a focused 90-day program of scripture affirmation and confession, with much repetition and strong positive emotion, to re-program or renew your mind to operate in and with the mind of Christ within you.

Note: one of the main reasons Israel lost the promised blessing was failure to obey God with gladness. Deut 28:47 "Because thou servedst not the LORD thy God with joyfulness, and with gladness of heart, for the abundance of all things; 48 therefore shalt thou serve thine enemies which the LORD shall send against thee, in hunger, and in thirst, and in nakedness, and in want of all things: and he shall put a yoke of iron upon thy neck, until he have destroyed thee." Learning the rules without gladness will cost you the blessing.

The people of Israel got this way by failing to give God thanks for all His benefits. That is, they let other thoughts of labor and hardness in God, lack of generosity and evil fear with unforgiveness take priority in their subconscious, or hearts, over

OTHER HEALING TEACHINGS

gladness and thanksgiving in serving God, and appreciation for His prosperity and abundance in all things. This is described here: Rom 1:19 "Because that which may be known of God is manifest in them; for God hath shewed it unto them. 20 For the invisible things of him from the creation of the world are clearly seen, being understood by the things that are made, even his eternal power and Godhead; so that they are without excuse: 21 because that, when they knew God, they glorified him not as God, neither were thankful; but became vain in their imaginations, and their foolish heart was darkened. 22 Professing themselves to be wise, they became fools." Notice: not keeping an "attitude of gratitude" toward God in verse 21 actually caused their minds to become dark (cooperating with the devil and not God) and cost them dearly. In Hebrews 2-6, this attitude is also described and applied to Christians.

Thus, to make their way successful God gave a steady diet of constant and glad repetition and fighting of evil fear with faith or courage, based on the promises of God: Josh 1:5 "There shall not any man be able to stand before thee all the days of thy life: as I was with Moses, so I will be with thee: I will not fail thee, nor forsake thee. 6 Be strong and of a good courage: for unto this people shalt thou divide for an inheritance the land, which I sware unto their fathers to give them. 7 Only be thou strong and very courageous, that thou mayest observe to do according to all the law, which Moses my servant commanded thee: turn not from it to the right hand or to the left, that thou mayest prosper whithersoever thou goest. 8 This book of the law shall not depart out of thy mouth; but thou shalt meditate therein day and night, that thou mayest observe to do according to all that is written therein: for then thou shalt make thy way prosperous, and then thou shalt have good success. 9 Have not I commanded thee? Be strong and of a good courage; be not afraid, neither be thou dismayed: for the LORD thy God is with thee whithersoever thou goest." Notice that a big enemy would be evil fear of man, and it would take lots of "whole life" focus and repetition to win over that fear.

By obeying God's command, Joshua was able to operate in power even greater than Moses, when he stopped the sun to remain in battle. Josh 10:12 "Then spake Joshua to the LORD in the day when the LORD delivered up the Amorites before the children of Israel, and he said in the sight of Israel, Sun, stand thou still upon Gibeon; and thou, Moon, in the valley of Ajalon. 13 And the sun stood still, and the moon stayed, until the people had avenged themselves upon their enemies. Is not this written in the book of Jasher? So the sun stood still in the midst of heaven, and hasted not to go down about a whole day." Notice how Joshua used *aiteo* in commanding the sun by the Lord.

These are the benefits of the mind-renewing program of God in the Old Testament. Here are New Testament versions: Phil 4:4 "Rejoice in the Lord alway: and again I say, Rejoice. 5 Let your moderation be known unto all men. The Lord is at hand. 6 Be careful (*anxious*) for nothing; but in every thing by prayer and supplication with thanksgiving let your requests (*aiteo, demands*) be made known unto God. 7 And the peace of God, which passeth all understanding, shall keep your hearts and minds through Christ Jesus. 8 Finally, brethren, whatsoever things are **true**, whatsoever things are **honest**, whatsoever things are **just**, whatsoever things are **pure**, whatsoever things are **lovely**, whatsoever things are of **good report**; if there be any **virtue**, and if there be any **praise**, think on these things." Eph 5:17 "Wherefore be ye not unwise, but understanding what the will of the Lord is. 18 And be not drunk with wine, wherein is excess; but be filled with the Spirit; 19 speaking to yourselves in psalms and hymns and spiritual songs, singing and making melody in your heart to the Lord; 20 giving thanks always for all things unto God and the Father in the name of our Lord Jesus Christ; 21 submitting yourselves one to another in the fear of God." Col 3:14 "And above all these things put on *agape*/charity, which is the bond of perfectness. 15 And let the peace of God rule in your hearts, to the which also ye are called in one body; and be ye thankful. 16 Let the word of Christ dwell in you richly in all wisdom; teaching and admonishing one another in psalms and hymns and spiritual songs, singing with grace in your hearts to the Lord. 17 And whatsoever ye do in word or deed, do all in the name of the Lord Jesus, giving thanks to God and the Father by him." This is the ultimate positive attitude program.

So, we see, the paths of power with God have never changed. Had we obeyed even these New Testament commands, for most of us, our lives would be dramatically different. But God has even more in store. Modern science has also discovered that the secret to overcoming great trails to bring a vision or dream to pass, whether it is in sports or finance or anything else, is the self-image a person has. A positive self-image is defined by your belief that you can do anything or overcome any obstacle no matter how great the challenge. This is what defines the "one who overcomes."

God has given us the ultimate self-image correction in His command for us to renew our minds. We are to continually keep in remembrance that Christ is in us and we are re-made in the image of God to do what Jesus would do here and now. Col 3:1 "If ye then be risen with Christ, seek those things which are above, where Christ sitteth on the right hand of God. 2 Set your affection on things above, not on things on the earth. 3 For ye are dead, and your *zoe*/life is hid with Christ in God. ... 10 And have put on the new man, which is renewed in knowledge after the image of him that created him: 11 where there is neither Greek nor Jew, circumcision nor uncircumcision, Barbarian, Scythian, bond nor free: but Christ is all, and in all." Eph 4:20 "But ye have not so learned Christ; 21 if so be that ye have heard him, and have been taught by him, as the truth is in Jesus: 22 that ye put off concerning the former conversation the old man, which is corrupt according to the deceitful lusts;

23 and be renewed in the spirit of your mind; 24 and that ye put on the new man, which after God is created in righteousness and true holiness." Rom 13:13 "Let us walk honestly, as in the day; not in rioting and drunkenness, not in chambering and wantonness, not in strife and envying. 14 But put ye on the Lord Jesus Christ, and make not provision for the flesh, to fulfil the lusts thereof." Phil 4:13 "I can do all things through Christ which strengtheneth me."

When we become born again into the new creation we are made ... Eph 4:24 "... after God ... created in righteousness and true holiness." All of this wonder in the spirit is made effective or translated into the world by a renewed soul or limited by an un-renewed soul. We Christians are to control this as we "save our souls." James 1:21 "Wherefore lay apart all filthiness and superfluity of naughtiness, and *lambano*/receive with meekness the engrafted word, which is able to *sozo*/save your souls. 22 But be ye doers of the word, and not hearers only, deceiving your own selves." Rom 6:17 "But God be thanked, that ye were the servants of sin, but ye have obeyed from the heart that form of doctrine which was delivered you. 18 Being then made free from sin, ye became the servants of righteousness." This is not just learning, but doing to excellence. This is a read and also do Gospel.

You start to make this effective by knowing and thanking God for what He has done for you in Christ Jesus. Philem 6 "That the communication of thy faith may become effectual by the acknowledging of every good thing which is in you in Christ Jesus." Since we are made new into His image, we have all the parts in our new being, we are complete in Him, so we can grow into Him in maturity. Heb 6:1 "Therefore leaving the principles of the doctrine of Christ, let us go on unto perfection (*maturity*) ... ." 2 Cor 13:9 "For we are glad, when we are weak, and ye are strong: and this also we wish, even your perfection (*maturity*)." Eph 4:12 "For the perfecting (*maturation*) of the saints, for the work of the ministry, for the edifying of the body of Christ: 13 till we all come in the unity of the faith, and of the knowledge of the Son of God, unto a perfect, mature man, unto the measure of the stature of the fulness of Christ: 14 that we henceforth be no more children, tossed to and fro, and carried about with every wind of doctrine, by the sleight of men, and cunning craftiness, whereby they lie in wait to deceive; 15 but speaking the truth in *agape*/love, may grow up into him in all things, which is the head, even Christ: 10 therefore I write these things being absent, lest being present I should use sharpness, according to the power which the Lord hath given me to edification and not to destruction."

So, we see, the process is to continually, with frequent and glad repetition, persuade our subconscious or our hearts with many 90-day plans, calling sin as that which Jesus already died for and (if need be), faking positive emotions of thanksgiving, praise, joy and gladness in God's wonderful promises and the work of His Mighty Arm, Jesus, our Savior and Lord. This is the purpose of the Minster Confessions. Thus, we are talking a lifestyle change, starting with our first 90-day program and then continuing to keep ourselves pure.

The "faking it" is only because you are fighting strongholds in your heart that need to be torn down in 90-day programs. When your heart is pure and single-minded in God and His truth, you will find yourself living in thanksgiving, praise and joy in the power of: Col 1:12 "Giving thanks (*continually*) unto the Father, which hath made us meet (*qualified and enabled by grace*) to be partakers of the inheritance of the saints in light: 13 who hath delivered us from the power of darkness, and hath translated us into the kingdom of his *agape*/dear Son: 14 in whom we have redemption through his blood, even the forgiveness (*remission, purging, putting away and obliteration*) of sins: 15 who is the image of the invisible God, the firstborn of every creature: 16 For by him were all things created, that are in heaven, and that are in earth, visible and invisible, whether they be thrones, or dominions, or principalities, or powers: all things were created by him, and for him: 17 and he is before all things, and by him all things consist. 18 And he is the head of the body, the church: who is the beginning, the firstborn from the dead; that in all things he might have the preeminence. 19 For it pleased the Father that in him should all fulness dwell; 20 and, having made peace through the blood of his cross, by him to reconcile all things unto himself; by him, I say, whether they be things in earth, or things in heaven." This is the proper response to our propitiation in Christ.

Modern science has discovered another truth from God. If you continually think negative, biblically bad thoughts and speak negative words, you are building and strengthening these neural pathways in your brain. The neural pathways for evil thoughts are different than those for good, pleasant thoughts. These evil-thought neural pathways actually secrete damaging materials into your blood stream, and, over time, weaken your body. God said it this way: Ps 34:12 "What man is he that desireth life, and loveth many days, that he may see good? 13 Keep thy tongue from evil, and thy lips from speaking guile. 14 Depart from evil, and do good; seek peace, and pursue it." This verse is repeated again in 1 Pet 3:10-11, and an even stronger version in Phil 4:1-13. How you think determines your life, prosperity and how long you will live.

Take a tape recorder or tell your kids (or spouse) to see if your words are what Jesus would say, as a measure of the true status of your heart. Note: We have another book, *OK, God, Now What?* that goes into this process in more detail.

Every day, all day long, when you are awake and when you are asleep, the process of your subconscious receiving and storing information goes on. By how we react, what we say and do, and what we allow, we are adding new priority beliefs, attitudes and thoughts, strengthening existing ones and occasionally building new ones, and, in controlled environments, subduing old ones. This happens whether you actively participate or not. So the command to "bring every thought captive to the obedience of Christ" is not a casual idea but critical to your success in working with the mind of Christ within the born-again Christian. If you do not do it, others are placing and reinforcing thoughts,

OTHER HEALING TEACHINGS

attitudes and beliefs that may not match God's Word. But you are accountable for the results.

The devout first-century Jewish life consisted of prayer 7 times a day and focused on asking God to perform His covenant promises for the nation first and then the individual. There was prayer, scripture quotations and songs upon rising, then at 9 AM, Noon, 3 PM, dinner time, upon going to bed and then the worshiper rose at midnight to read, quote and sing scripture. This fits with: Ps 119:164 "Seven times a day do I praise thee because of thy righteous judgments." Ps 119:62 "At midnight I will rise to give thanks unto thee because of thy righteous judgments."

Thus, the good observant Jew spent 3 to 6 hours a day staying renewed in the mind and building right attitudes and beliefs. Jesus and all the first believers were such observant Jews, and practiced the same, if not more, time in prayer. After the Day of Pentecost, to this schedule was added praying in tongues. With muttering or under your breath tongues, this can be done almost all day as you do other tasks, and then include other times of louder speaking and singing in tongues (1 Cor 12 and 14). This regular schedule of 3 to 6 hours and the use of tongues is the idea behind the Christian command: 1 Thes 5:16 "Rejoice evermore. 17 Pray without ceasing. 18 In every thing give thanks: for this is the will of God in Christ Jesus concerning you. 19 Quench not the Spirit. 20 Despise not prophesyings. 21 Prove all things; hold fast that which is good. 22 Abstain from all appearance of evil. 23 And the very God of peace sanctify you wholly; and I pray God your whole spirit and soul and body be preserved blameless unto the coming of our Lord Jesus Christ." You get verse 23 when you do verses 16 through 22.

The Minister Confessions in this manual are for daily use to renew your mind into these truths in Christ, especially for healing. One way to use them is to read through them completely at least once a day. Then go back and add (if need be, fake) glad emotions for your favorite sections. Aim for 1 to 2 hours per day for at least 90 to 180 days. Is 1 to 2 hours every day enough? That is a bare minimum, and depending on how many old thoughts and false belief networks you have to replace and subdue and the culture you live in, the process may take much longer than 90 or even 180 days. If the 3 to 6 hours of Jewish prayer per day are a standard, then that is the minimum required to keep your heart right **after** you have gotten it purified. 1 Tim 1:5 "Now the end of the commandment is *agape*/charity out of a pure heart, and of a good conscience, and of faith unfeigned: 6 from which some having swerved have turned aside unto vain jangling." Failure to establish and subdue a clean heart and then maintain righteous dominion gives room for much "vain jangling." Note: for immediate results, "cramming" for several days can work. This manual is designed so you can actually do the "cramming" process as you pray in the intensity of a crises or severe need. You are heart multi-tasking for the immediate need, and then building transformation as you continue with a regular program.

~ 21 ~

ON MENTAL ASSENT

The great mystery of God is that His divine secrets are in plain sight within the words of the Scriptures. It is not a matter of knowing what the Scriptures say; that is nothing more than mental assent. What we need, rather, is having the Word of God transcend mere head recognition to connect our head and heart to our spirit, where Holy Spirit dwells, by renewing our self-concept in our soul (heart, mind, will and emotions). He changes not, so your thinking has to! When you do it and agree without thinking like Jesus did, the living Word of God is now part of you.

It is a glory-to-glory process. In that area where you act as Jesus would, your mind is now renewed, at least for a while. We are told to renew our minds by acknowledging what and who we are in Christ. We could call this mind re-programming or renewing (See Rom 6, 12 and 13, Eph 4, Col 3, Philem 6 and 2 Pet 1:1-15). Your mind is where it starts. Then the rest of your soul gets converted or re-programmed to the truth. Right Bible training requires Holy Spirit to enlighten you so you see not just the Scriptures, but also the God behind the Scriptures and His *agape*/love, grace and power. A critical step is to make the Bible your final authority. Repetition of truth with passion drives it into your heart and your life. You use your cognitive mind acceptance of Scripture to make the decision to start re-programming your subconscious mind.

Memorized Scripture is like the bones of a skeleton or the framework of a house. They are there always as reference and leverage, but bones without living flesh are dead, and a house framework without walls and a roof provides no comfort in a storm. But you do need the framework. The basic assumption of the New Testament is that the reader has the first 5 books of the Bible memorized and

OTHER HEALING TEACHINGS

most of the rest of the Old Testament. To the believers of old, theirs was an oral culture. Remember there was no New Testament until well after the letters to the churches were written. So everything of importance was memorized and used as a reference for all future decisions. For the new non-Jewish Christian, that meant the Old Testament.

The Pharisees had the entire Old Testament memorized and still missed God by looking for rules and not God Himself. Matt 22:29 "Jesus answered and said unto them, Ye do err, not knowing the scriptures, nor the power of God." John 5:39 "Search the scriptures; for in them ye think ye have eternal *zoe*/life: and they are they which testify of me. 40 And ye will not come to me, that ye might have *zoe*/life. 41 I receive not honour from men. 42 But I know you, that ye have not the *agape*/love of God in you. [*They were not* agape/*loving their neighbors as themselves as a way to* agape/*love God*]. 43 I am come in my Father's name, and ye receive me not: if another shall come in his own name, him ye will receive. 44 How can ye believe, which receive honour one of another, and seek not the honour that cometh from God only?" Luke 11:42 "But woe unto you, Pharisees! for ye tithe mint and rue and all manner of herbs, and pass over judgment and the *agape*/love of God: these ought ye to have done, and not to leave the other undone." Matt 23:23 "Woe unto you, scribes and Pharisees, hypocrites! for ye pay tithe of mint and anise and cummin, and have omitted the weightier matters of the law, judgment, mercy, and faith: these ought ye to have done, and not to leave the other undone." They had the rules, but did not walk in *agape*/love. 1 Tim 1:5 "Now the end of the commandment is *agape*/charity out of a pure heart, and of a good conscience, and of faith unfeigned: 6 from which some having swerved have turned aside unto vain jangling." 1 Tim 5:15 "For some are already turned aside after Satan."

Mental assent agrees that the Word of God is true, even beautiful, but at best, it ignores the commands or considers them irrelevant. Mental assent says that Jesus still heals but then cannot get anyone healed. Or that God answers prayer and then trusts in man and not God. Jesus described it this way: Matt 22:29 "Jesus answered and said unto them, Ye do err, not knowing (*considering as vital and critical in how you run your life or advise others, and have proved it true in your own life*) the scriptures, nor the *dunamis*/power of God."

Mental assent is when we substitute academic knowledge of the Scriptures for lives that are the living Word of God, in which we do the things of God, just as Jesus would. In this mental assent state, religious observance is more important than actually walking in the *agape*/love of God. James 1:27 "Pure religion and undefiled before God and the Father is this, to visit the fatherless and widows in their affliction, and to keep himself unspotted from the world." Remaining unstained by the world includes: 2 Cor 10:5 "Casting down imaginations, and every high thing that exalteth itself against the knowledge of God, and bringing into captivity every thought to the obedience of Christ."

The solution to mental assent is to attack any hardness of heart i.e., attitudes, beliefs, and thoughts that do not match God's Word. Rom 2:4 "Or despisest thou the riches of his goodness and forbearance and longsuffering; not knowing that the goodness of God leadeth thee to repentance? 5 But after thy hardness and impenitent heart treasurest up unto thyself wrath against the day of wrath and revelation of the righteous judgment of God; 6 who will render to every man according to his deeds." Notice the way back includes thankfulness for God's goodness that you are still alive.

A hardened heart comes about as you fill or defend your subconscious mind with beliefs, emotions, attitudes and prejudices that do not match the mind of Christ. God's rules are that if you will not think and do right, you reap what you sow. He takes credit for this process of heart hardening. Mark 16:14 "Afterward he (*Jesus*) appeared unto the eleven as they sat at meat, and upbraided them with their unbelief and hardness of heart, because they believed not them which had seen him after he was risen." Matt 13:14 "And in them is fulfilled the prophecy of Esaias, which saith, By hearing ye shall hear, and shall not understand; and seeing ye shall see, and shall not perceive: 15 for this people's heart is waxed gross, and their ears are dull of hearing, and their eyes they have closed; lest at any time they should see with their eyes, and hear with their ears, and should understand with their heart, and should be converted, and I should heal them. 16 But blessed are your eyes, for they see: and your ears, for they hear."

Unforgiveness or offense is a form of hate. God does not hate people, His creations, but identified Himself with fallen man in Jesus. When we hold unforgiveness toward other people, each one of them is specially loved by God. Father sent Jesus to suffer and die for each one, and when Jesus rose from the dead, He raised them and us with Jesus. That is the status of all men to God. God is not at enmity with man, yet unforgiveness is. When we hold unforgiveness, much less resentment, bitterness or murder, we hold ourselves as a greater god than God Himself, who will not hold the sins of those people against them, but held their sins against Jesus instead. Father had Jesus pay for them. Eph 2:3 "Among whom also we all had our conversation in times past in the lusts of our flesh, fulfilling the desires of the flesh and of the mind; and were by nature the children of wrath, even as others. 4 But God, who is rich in mercy, for his great *agape*/love wherewith he *agape*/loved us, 5 even when we were dead in sins, hath quickened us together with Christ, (by grace ye are *sozo*/saved;) 6 and hath raised us up together, and made us sit together in heavenly places in Christ Jesus: 7 that in the ages to come he might shew the exceeding riches of his grace in his kindness toward us through Christ Jesus. 8 For by grace are ye *sozo*/saved through faith; and that not of yourselves:

Other Healing Teachings

it is the gift of God: 9 not of works, lest any man should boast." By faith we enter into this great work.

These people whom God raised up with Jesus, whether they have believed the Gospel or not, are reconciled to God. He is not at war with anyone, but in unforgiveness we are, as we stand as accusers of those whom God has called *agape*/loved. Unforgiveness in any form is not reconciliation. 2 Cor 5:18 "And all things are of God, who hath reconciled us to himself by Jesus Christ, and hath given to us the ministry of reconciliation; 19 to wit, that God was in Christ, reconciling the world unto himself, not imputing their trespasses unto them; and hath committed unto us the word of reconciliation." So we deny our calling as we remain in unforgiveness. As we justify our sin, we close our heart and deny the Gospel. God calls this a hard heart, and the fruit of it is called mental assent, when the Word is true, but it is not life.

In order for you to be unforgiving, you must harbor resentment, offense and separation in your heart. That is a way of thinking. If you will not change your way of thinking, your unforgiveness can spread to all who offend you in the slightest way. You have to repent and clean your heart to remove the attitude of unforgiveness. God states: Matt 6:14 "For if ye forgive men their trespasses, your heavenly Father will also forgive you: 15 But if ye forgive not men their trespasses, neither will your Father forgive your trespasses." You choose what blessing of God you will walk in, not God.

The Bible word used for *forgiveness* does not mean remittance, but, instead, fellowship healing. As long as you remain in unforgiveness, in that area you and God are not in agreement, and your heart is hard against the ways of God. If you stay that way, you will write that offense on your heart, and left alone, it will grow into bitterness. Bitterness is a hard heart and not *agape*/love. In other areas, you and God can work in agreement. God knows we are not perfect, yet He still answers your prayers. Jesus gave us His holiness to enable us to receive answered prayer in spite of our sins, bitterness and hardness of heart. That is why He says: Rom 5:17 "… much more they which (*continually*) *lambano*/receive abundance of grace and of the gift of righteousness shall reign in *zoe*/life by one, Jesus Christ."

Here, by holding onto the gift of righteousness in Jesus, we can still reign for God, and deliver His *zoe*/life to get people healed. This is how we overcome the evil one, who knows your sin in unforgiveness and will oppress you with guilt, to hinder your confidence in God. The simple way to deal with this is to keep short accounts with God, restoring fellowship with confession of sin, and believing in the work of Jesus by the cross for your own past remission and current forgiveness of sin, and for healing for the one in need, whether it be yourself or others. We are always responsible to clean our own hearts in cooperation with God and His Word. As long as you disagree with God in a particular area or action, *zoe*/life is limited or does not flow at all. Thus we limit what God can do.

As we hold on to that offense and rehearse it in our minds and talk about it to others, we start the 4-day process of building a brain neural connection. Stay at it for 21 days, and it becomes a permanent memory, with a godless, demonic, devilish, negative emotion assigned to it. Keep at it for 90 days, and you now subdue *agape/love* and forgiveness thoughts from God and become expert at defending your sinful unforgiveness, and, if not already there, start to enter into bitterness. Now whatever that person does "fits" with your evil attitudes of unforgiveness, and you reconfirm and harden the evilness and separation of that person in your heart. Your mind is now set on the flesh and at war with God. In your offended or hardened state, the people you refuse to forgive are not victims of demonic deception, but your enemies. And all this time you are sowing to the flesh to reap the corruption of the flesh for yourself. Mental assent keeps you thinking you are *agape*/loving, but you are not. This is a core message of 1 John. As you continue in the carnal, flesh mind, your ability to believe God in other areas gets covered over with mental assent, self-deception, and less and less prayer or, at the very least, little answered prayer.

Mental assent is described this way: James 1:21 "Wherefore lay apart all filthiness and superfluity of naughtiness, and *lambano*/receive with meekness the engrafted word, which is able to *sozo*/save your souls. 22 But be ye doers of the word, and not hearers only, deceiving your own selves." The judgment of God is that you reap what evil you sow, unless and until you apply His grace in Jesus to the situation.

The opposite of thinking like God is not some neutral ground. Prov 14:12 "There is a way which seemeth right unto a man, but the end thereof are the ways of death." Here is Jesus' comment on not thinking like Him. Mark 8:33 "But when he had turned about and looked on his disciples, he rebuked Peter, saying, Get thee behind me, Satan: for thou savourest not the things that be of God, but the things that be of men." Luke 4:8 "And Jesus answered and said unto him, Get thee behind me, Satan: for it is written, Thou shalt worship the Lord thy God, and him only shalt thou serve." Thinking like a "normal" man is thinking like the devil.

Holy Spirit said through James in: James 3:14 "But if ye have bitter envying and strife in your hearts [*which is the sin of those who put Jesus on the cross*], glory not, and lie not against the truth. 15 This wisdom descendeth not from above, but is earthly, sensual, devilish (*demonic, like Cain, who killed Abel, a constant accusation against others unto death*). 16 For where envying and strife is, there is confusion and every evil work. 17 But the wisdom that is from above is first pure, then peaceable, gentle, and easy to be intreated, full of mercy and good fruits, without partiality, and without hypocrisy. 18 And the fruit of righteousness is sown in peace of them that make peace."

That peace includes what Jesus did: Acts 10:36 "The word which God sent unto the children of Israel, preaching peace by Jesus Christ: (he is Lord of all:) 37

OTHER HEALING TEACHINGS

that word, I say, ye know, which was published throughout all Judaea, and began from Galilee, after the baptism which John preached; 38 how God anointed Jesus of Nazareth with the Holy Ghost and with power: who went about doing good, and healing all that were oppressed (*active dominion, rulership and lordship*) of the devil [*as a judgment against the devil*]; for God was with him." Jesus demonstrated the word of reconciliation with His life. John the Baptist preached repentance from sin, but no one Jesus healed was required to confess their sin. Jesus just healed them in peace.

Concerning anyone's sins, we are commanded: Acts 10:42 "And he (*Father God*) commanded us to preach unto the people, and to testify that it is he (*Jesus*) which was ordained of God to be the Judge of quick and dead [*with the same effectiveness as Jesus did when He judged against the devil in everyone He healed or had healed through His followers*]. 43 To him give all the prophets witness, that through his name whosoever believeth in him shall receive remission (*purging, removal, obliteration and putting away*) of sins."

Notice hardness of heart and unbelief are closely related. So the cure is the same: Rom 10:17 "So then faith cometh by hearing, and hearing by the word of God (*in the Gospel of Christ in you, that God reigns through men because of Jesus*)." Heb 4:11 "Let us labour therefore to enter into that rest, lest any man fall after the same example of unbelief (*bitterness, unpersuadableness*). 12 For the word of God is quick, and powerful, and sharper than any twoedged sword, piercing even to the dividing asunder of soul and spirit, and of the joints and marrow, and is a discerner of the thoughts and intents of the heart. 13 Neither is there any creature that is not manifest in his sight: but all things are naked and opened unto the eyes of him with whom we have to do."

The Jews of the desert under Moses had hardness of heart toward the Egyptians and distrusted God, so they had hardness of heart, unforgiveness and bitterness toward God. At every problem, they murmured and complained against God. Heb 3:15 "While it is said, To day if ye will hear his voice, harden not your hearts, as in the provocation. 16 For some, when they had heard, did provoke: howbeit not all that came out of Egypt by Moses. 17 But with whom was he grieved forty years? was it not with them that had sinned, whose carcases fell in the wilderness? 18 And to whom sware he that they should not enter into his rest, but to them that believed not [*could not be persuaded of God's ability, truth, inability to lie, love, care and power*] ? 19 So we see that they could not enter in because of unbelief (*unpersuadableness*)." The fruit of this was that they died in the desert while the God of all salvation, love, creation and blessing was right there with them!

Recognize that if you do not walk like Jesus, then you are not perfected in *agape*/love and have hardness in your hearts, and, thus, evil fear somewhere in your beliefs, attitudes and preconceptions. 2 Tim 1:6 "Wherefore I put thee in remembrance that thou stir up the gift of God, which is in thee by the putting on of my hands. 7 For God hath not given us the spirit of fear; but of power, and of *agape/love*, and of a sound mind." If you are not constantly stirring yourself up, you may still be constantly staying asleep!

So confess this lack of keeping yourself stirred up and encouraged in God by His Word as a sin Jesus already died for and healed you of, put on the new man in Christ Jesus, pray Psalm 119 and Eph 1:16-23 often, and actively renew your mind, as described in the above section, and confess the Minister Confessions often out loud with glad passion, thanksgiving and joy (faking it, if necessary).

As you work through and keep yourself free of mental assent, by renewing your mind into the Gospel, you will be denying the devil the right to harass you with fear of failure, and will become strong in the persuaded assurance that God is good and that He is good toward you, and you will see the goodness of the Lord in the land of the living. Phil 2:5 "Let this mind be in you, which was also in Christ Jesus."

Your measuring stick should be this: Col 1:12 "... giving thanks (*constantly*) unto the Father, which hath made us meet (*qualified and enabled by grace*) to be partakers of the inheritance of the saints in light: 13 who hath delivered us from the power of darkness, and hath translated us into the kingdom of his *agape*/dear Son: 14 in whom we have redemption through his blood, even the *aphesis*/forgiveness (*remission, purging, and putting away*) of sins: 15 who is the image of the invisible God, the firstborn of every creature."

When you reach this level, with heart-felt and not-just-faking-it, but continual faith behavior spontaneously throughout the day, you will have mental assent on the run! You will start to become proficient at seeing what God has said in the Bible as greater than what evil now is or could be, and in working with God to manifest God's Word in that situation in spirit and in truth. You will become proficient at seeing, not what is or is threatened, but what can be in Jesus. Then the manifestation of healing will be greater than your profession. This is seeing Jesus clearly. Now you and God are working together to manifest His *zoe* life into this world.

The stirring up process in the cognitive mind may temporarily push down or overwhelm mental assent so you can build the path for healing to come on a specific occasion/battle. But until your sub-conscious/heart is reprogrammed/renewed in a 90-day effort you can fall back in 3-5 days into mental assent. The cure is to renew your mind in continual 90-day programs and then keep it renewed so you are always ready, "in season or out." (2 Tim 4:2) So the goal of God for us is a lifestyle of mind renewal and not just for specific events.

~ 22 ~

ON FAITH BUILDING

The first element of faith building is to follow: Rom 10:17 "So then faith cometh by hearing, and hearing by the word of God (*in the Gospel of Christ in you, that God reigns through men because of Jesus*)." This kind of hearing is with our ears and our heart unto obedience in right doing. Until you make the commitment to start doing the Word of God, it will do you little good. You may treat it as academic material to pass a Sunday school test, debate for hours, or even get a divinity degree, but until you start actually discovering how to do it, knowing you are working with the God of the Universe in the process, you will not build faith. This "hearing" means to hear unto obedience. Until you decide to enter into battle, win over the devil, and get God's healing delivered to a person in need, you can debate forever. Until you start to learn by doing and until your testimony lines up with Scriptures, you will never "know" what God is talking about. We are to define our lives by the Scriptures and not define the Scriptures by our experience (except where they line up with the Scriptures). God cannot lie, and He cannot fail when He has a way to work.

God has spoken His will in healing in Isaiah 53 and in the gospels. The issue is not the will of God; it is our operating in faith in God by His Word to bring His will to Earth. He has given us His Word. The written Scriptures are greater than the power of His name, so there can be no doubt as to what His will is: Ps 138:1 "I will praise thee with my whole heart: before the gods will I sing praise unto thee. 2 I will worship toward thy holy temple, and praise thy name for thy *chesed/* lovingkindness and for thy truth: for thou hast magnified thy word above all thy name." Prov 22:19 "That thy trust may be in the LORD, I have made known to thee this day, even to thee. 20 Have not I written to thee excellent things in counsels and knowledge, 21 that I might make thee know the certainty of the words of truth; that thou mightest answer the words of truth to them that send unto thee?" 2 Pet 1:19 "We have also a more sure word of prophecy (*in the Old Testament Scriptures than the experience of Peter, James and John on the mount, when Jesus was transfigured, i.e., their experiences*); whereunto ye do well that ye take heed, as unto a light that shineth in a dark place, until the day dawn, and the day star arise in your hearts: 20 knowing this first, that no prophecy of the scripture is of any private interpretation. 21 For the prophecy (*the Scriptures*) came not in old time by the will of man: but holy men of God spake as they were moved by the Holy Ghost." Settle it in your heart that the Word of God is first.

Any difference between you and a promise of God is a lie or lies from the devil that you have believed, or a demon active in some way. Deal with the lies with grace and truth, in renewing the mind, and command the devil and his works to go in the name of Jesus, and healing will come. God is not the problem, and the devil is not the problem. We are the problem. God is no respecter of persons. So whether you are new in the Lord or an "old" saint, you meet God's requirements, and you will see God's promises fulfilled, including healing, when you minister to others or seek healing for yourself.

The main cry of the unbelieving against the Word of God is this: Mark 15:29 "And they that passed by railed on him, wagging their heads, and saying, Ah, thou that destroyest the temple, and buildest it in three days, 30 *sozo*/save thyself, and come down from the cross. 31 Likewise also the chief priests mocking said among themselves with the scribes, He *sozo*/saved others; himself he cannot *sozo*/save. 32 Let Christ the King of Israel descend now from the cross, that we may see and believe. And they that were crucified with him reviled him." Here the physical evidence totally ignored the Word of God and the power of God. The minds of the people were accepting the evil harassment of dreadful fear and were full of worldly power and present circumstances and the confidence that God could not change any of them. They were sincerely wrong!

The cry of the believing, or those in faith with God, is like this: John 16:16 "A little while, and ye shall not see me (*Jesus*): and again, a little while, and ye shall see me, because I go to the Father." Jesus had total confidence in God and in His Word. That is the voice of believing God. This is being fully persuaded that God cannot lie and that He can and will do what He said He will do. Plus, you know His will toward you in a particular situation based on His Scriptures. This is confidence in God: not allowing distrust, controlling your thoughts by not allowing doubt and fear to rule, but holding firm in the promises of God and knowing that He has heard you and He will do what He said.

This manual is some 90% scripture for a purpose. As I speak out loud the words of this book, I am not only obeying 1 Tim 4:13 "Till I come, give attendance to *public* reading, to exhortation, to doctrine." I am also putting the Word of God in my ears so I can "hear" it to obey it. One can describe this process as continually persuading yourself that God is able and will do what He has promised, per Rom 4:21 "And being fully persuaded that, what he had promised, he was able also to perform."

So as I re-program my heart and my mind with the Word of God, I more readily agree with Holy Spirit to do the works of God. And this increases my belief in Jesus as Healer. John 6:28 "Then said they unto him, What shall we do, that we might work the works of God? 29 Jesus answered and said unto them, This is the work of God, that ye believe (*have faith*) on him (*Jesus*) whom he (*God*) hath sent." Our believing God is evidenced by our joy and thanksgiving before we see the manifestation of His promise.

So, how do we work with Holy Spirit to do the works of God? Gal 3:2 "This only would I learn of you, Received ye the Spirit by the works of the law, or by the hearing of faith? 3 Are ye so foolish? having begun in the Spirit, are ye now made perfect by the flesh (*your own right works*) 4 Have ye suffered so many things in vain? if it be yet in vain. 5 He therefore that ministereth to you the Spirit, and worketh miracles among you, doeth he it by the works of the law, or by the hearing of faith?" Miracles are not about our holiness, but Jesus' holiness!

And what is the message of faith we are to hear? Gal 2:16 "Knowing that a man is not justified by the works of the law, but by the faith of Jesus Christ, even we have believed in Jesus Christ, that we might be justified by the faith of Christ, and not by the works of the law: for by the works of the law shall no flesh be justified. … 19 For I through the law am dead to the law, that I might *zao*/live unto God. 20 I am crucified with Christ: nevertheless I *zao*/live [*in spite of my current imperfection or sin*]; yet not I, but Christ *zao*/liveth in me: and the life which I now *zao*/live in the flesh I *zao*/live by the faith of the Son of God, who *agape*/loved me, and gave himself for me. 21 I do not frustrate the grace of God: for if righteousness come by the law, then Christ is dead in vain."

An important principle for increasing our faith is found in: Philem 6 "That the communication of thy faith may become effectual (*in* agape *and miracles*) by the acknowledging of every good thing which is in you in Christ Jesus."

Throughout this manual are many confessions of what God has done in Jesus for us and, specifically, for us as born-again Christians. As we confess, agree that it is true in spite of our failures, this makes our faith more effective on Earth. For example, consider: 2 Cor 13:5 "Examine yourselves, whether ye be in the faith; prove your own selves. Know ye not your own selves, how that Jesus Christ is in you, except ye be reprobates (*useless, worthy of garbage, a shame and impotent*)?" And: 2 Cor 3:18 "But we all, with open face beholding as in a glass (*mirror*) the glory of the Lord (*of seeing Jesus manifesting Himself though us*), are changed into the same image from glory to glory, even as by the Spirit of the Lord." And: 2 Pet 1:8 "For if these things (*of godliness and the divine nature*) be in you, and abound, they make you that ye shall neither be barren nor unfruitful in the knowledge of our Lord Jesus Christ. 9 But he that lacketh these things (*of godliness and the divine nature*) is blind, and cannot see afar off, and hath forgotten that he was purged from his old sins. 10 Wherefore the rather, brethren, give diligence to make your calling and election sure (*to walk as an agent of God, seeing more answered prayer*): for if ye do these things, ye shall never fall."

So we need to remember: Rev 1:5 "And from Jesus Christ, who is the faithful witness, and the first begotten of the dead, and the prince of the kings of the earth. Unto him that *agape*/loved us, and washed us from our sins in his own blood, 6 and hath made us kings and priests unto God and his Father; to him be glory and dominion for ever and ever. Amen." Heb 1:3 "Who being the brightness of (*Father God's*) glory, and the express image of his person, and upholding all things by the word of his power, when he (*Jesus*) had by himself purged our sins, sat down on the right hand of the Majesty on high." 1 Pet 2:24 "Who his own self bare our sins in his own body on the tree, that we, being dead to sins, should *zao*/live unto righteousness: by whose stripes ye were healed (*physical and spiritual wholeness*). 25 For ye were as sheep going astray; but are now returned unto the Shepherd and Bishop of your souls."

Notice, if Jesus did not purge our sins 2000 years ago by the cross, He is not ever going to do it again. So settle it that you were purged, redeemed, reconciled, made whole and forgiven 2000 years ago for all your sins—past, present and future. Two thousand years ago every sin you would ever commit was all in the future. Keeping this in mind constantly is a key to successful Christian growth in the divine nature of God. 2 Pet 1:8 "For if these things be in you, and abound, they make you that ye shall neither be barren nor unfruitful in the knowledge of our Lord Jesus Christ. 9 But he that lacketh these things is blind, and cannot see afar off, and hath forgotten that he was purged from his old sins." Heb 10:12 "But this man, after he had offered **one sacrifice for sins for ever**, sat down on the right hand of God; 13 from henceforth expecting till his enemies be made his footstool. 14 For by one offering he hath perfected for ever them that are sanctified. 15 Whereof the Holy Ghost also is a witness to us: for after that he had said before, 16 This is the covenant that I will make with them after those days, saith the Lord, I will put my laws into their hearts, and in their minds will I write them; 17 and their sins and iniquities will I remember no more. 18 **Now where remission of these (*sins and iniquities*) is, there is no more offering for sin.**" Settle it in your heart: Jesus got the job done!

This forgiveness is related to healing: James 5:15 "And the prayer of faith shall *sozo*/save the sick, and the Lord shall raise him up; and if he have committed sins

OTHER HEALING TEACHINGS

(*those un-confessed*), they shall be forgiven him (*communion or friendship with God restored, for the issue is not that the Christian sins, but if he will confess them to God and receive his own healing for any curses of sin such as sickness, disease, or lack*)." Luke 5:22 "But when Jesus perceived their thoughts, he answering said unto them, What reason ye in your hearts? 23 Whether is easier, to say, Thy sins be forgiven thee; or to say, Rise up and walk? 24 But that ye may know that the Son of man hath power upon earth to forgive sins, (he said unto the sick of the palsy,) I say unto thee, Arise, and take up thy couch, and go into thine house. 25 And immediately he rose up before them, and took up that whereon he lay, and departed to his own house, glorifying God."

To build our faith more, to get strong in faith, we need to learn and do more faith works. Biblical faith is believing God to perform or manifest in the Earth per His Word. Here is a biblical description of faith. Heb 11:1 "Now faith is the substance of things hoped for, the evidence of things not seen." And again: Heb 11:1 "NOW FAITH is the assurance (the confirmation, the title deed) of the things [we] hope for, being the proof of things [we] do not see and the conviction of their reality [faith perceiving as real fact what is not revealed to the senses]." AMP The essence of faith is believing God to make manifest what we do not yet see, per His promise. The legal title deed of that event, and the substance that makes it manifest is your believing God to do as He said, as evidenced in glad thanksgiving.

The definition of hope is a key in this description. The original word for hope is much stronger than in modern usage. In modern usage, hope is a vague desire for some good to come your way. The original Old and New Testament words for hope are much stronger. There the meaning of *hope* is "the joyful expectation of a coming good or an exciting general wellbeing." If you are not in joy, you are not it biblical hope. And joy signifies an explosion of human activity in thanksgiving, praise and triumph, as displayed in jumping, shouting, dancing, prancing, arm waving, clapping, yelling, loud singing, and playing musical instruments. So faith is more concrete or specific than hope, which can mean someday, but hope is included in faith. In faith, you are in present tense active, visible and audible demonstration of joy for a specific thing hoped for, and you believe you will have it by the promise of God in His Word. You call it as if it is, and it will be, as you become joyful. Hope is general; faith is more specific.

So a more expanded description of faith is this: Heb 11:1 "NOW FAITH is the (*absolute*) assurance (*of confidence in God performing His word*) (the confirmation, the title deed) of the things [we] hope for (*with joyous thanksgiving, praise, dancing, jumping and shouting for already having what we have* aiteo/*asked for, and this loud and joyous praise, confessions of truth and proclamations of what will be even though as yet unseen*) being the proof of things [we] do not *yet* see and the conviction of their reality (*to be manifest as defined by the promise of God's Word*) [faith perceiving as real fact what is not *yet* revealed to the senses (*words combined with and in His spirit, to produce the physical things of this universe*)]." Faith is not mental agreement, except as demonstrated in your physical body by your mouth and your actions. Mental asset is reading the Word of God but not believing it, as demonstrated by biblical faith. Our believing is what allows God to manifest His promises in the Earth. We are the limit, not God. The evidence of Bible faith is in your words and your joy about coming good. 2 Cor 4:13 "… we also believe, and therefore speak."

Thus, the Bible proclaims that strong faith exhibits this joyous behavior, in spite of the fact that right now it does not look as if it can, or is going to, happen. Rom 4:16 "Therefore it is of faith, that it might be by grace; to the end the promise might be sure to all the seed; not to that only which is of the law, but to that also which is of the faith of Abraham; who is the father of us all, 17 (as it is written, I have made thee a father of many nations,) before him whom he believed, **even God, who quickeneth the dead, and calleth those things which be not as though they were.** 18 Who against (*or beyond*) hope believed in hope, that he might become the father of many nations; according to that which was spoken, So shall thy seed be. 19 And being not weak in faith, he considered not his own body now dead, when he was about an hundred years old, neither yet the deadness of Sara's womb: 20 he staggered not at the promise of God through unbelief; **but was strong in faith, giving glory** (*thanksgiving, praise and rejoicing*) **to God;** 21 and being fully persuaded that, what he had promised, he was able also to perform. 22 And therefore it was imputed to him for righteousness. 23 Now it was not written for his sake alone, that it was imputed to him; 24 but for us also, to whom it (*righteousness*) shall be imputed, if we believe on him that raised up Jesus our Lord from the dead; 25 who was delivered for our offences, and was raised again for our justification." This is resting in God's Word.

Notice that weak faith looks more at the impossibilities of the situation and not at God and His strength. Strong faith is here defined as faith that looks at the impossibilities of the situation, believes God is able to overcome them and will do it, and thus gives glory (or praise, per the original Greek) to God. Thus, strong faith rejoices that God can do the impossible and this good, hoped-for thing will come, because God, who cannot lie, calls it as is, although we do not yet see it. So you give God joyous thanksgiving and praise, as if you already had it, per His scripture promise, until you do have it, and then you give Him more joyous praise because you now have it. Rom 4:19 "He (*Abraham*) did not weaken in faith when he considered the [utter] impotence of his own body, which was as good as dead because he was about a hundred years old, or [when he considered] the barrenness of Sarah's [deadened] womb. [Gen 17:17; 18:11] 20 No unbelief or distrust made him waver … concerning the promise of God, but he grew strong and was empowered by faith **as he gave praise and glory to God**, 21 fully satisfied

Other Healing Teachings

and assured that God was able and mighty to keep His word and to do what He had promised. 22 That is why his faith was credited to him as righteousness (right standing with God)."AMP

Notice that in Rom 4:20 Abraham grew strong as he looked at the impossible situation and praised/glorified God anyway, based on the Word of God. Notice the many scriptures that say our joy releases God's strength through us into the situation. Neh 8:10 "… for the joy of the LORD is your strength." Ps 28:7 "The LORD is my strength and my shield; my heart trusted in him, and I am helped: therefore my heart greatly rejoiceth; and with my song will I praise him. 8 The LORD is their strength, and he is the saving strength of his anointed." Ps 149:2 "Let Israel rejoice in him that made him: let the children of Zion be joyful in their King. 3 Let them praise his name in the dance: let them sing praises unto him with the timbrel and harp. 4 For the LORD taketh pleasure in his people: he will beautify the meek with salvation." Isa 61:10 "I will greatly rejoice in the LORD, my soul shall be joyful in my God; for he hath clothed me with the garments of salvation, he hath covered me with the robe of righteousness, as a bridegroom decketh himself with ornaments, and as a bride adorneth herself with her jewels. 11 For as the earth bringeth forth her bud, and as the garden causeth the things that are sown in it to spring forth; so the Lord GOD will cause righteousness and praise to spring forth before all the nations." Eph 6:10 "Finally, my brethren, be strong in the Lord, and in the power of his might." 1 Pet 1:3 "Blessed be the God and Father of our Lord Jesus Christ, which according to his abundant mercy hath begotten us again unto a *zao*/lively hope by the resurrection of Jesus Christ from the dead, 4 to an inheritance incorruptible, and undefiled, and that fadeth not away, reserved in heaven for you, 5 who are kept by the power of God through faith unto *soteria*/salvation ready to be revealed in the last time. 6 **Wherein ye greatly rejoice**, though now for a season, if need be, ye are in heaviness through manifold temptations: 7 that the trial of your faith, being much more precious than of gold that perisheth, though it be tried with fire, might be found unto praise and honour and glory at the appearing of Jesus Christ: 8 whom having not seen, ye *agape*/love; in whom, though now ye see him not, **yet believing, ye rejoice** with joy unspeakable (*incoherent shouts*) and full of glory: 9 receiving the end of your faith, even the *soteria*/salvation of your souls (*heart, mind, will and emotions unto operating just like Jesus*)." James 1:2 "My brethren, count it all joy when ye fall into divers temptations; 3 knowing this, that the trying of your faith worketh patience. 4 But let patience have her perfect work, that ye may be perfect and entire, wanting nothing." 1 Thes 5:16 "Rejoice evermore. 17 Pray without ceasing. 18 In every thing give thanks: for this is the will of God in Christ Jesus concerning you." Rom 12:12 "Rejoicing in hope; patient in tribulation; continuing instant in prayer." Phil 4:4 "Rejoice in the Lord alway: and again I say, Rejoice. 5 Let your moderation be known unto all men. The Lord is at hand.

6 Be careful (*anxious or fearful*) for nothing; but in every thing by prayer and supplication with thanksgiving let your *aiteo*/requests (*demands*) be made known unto God. 7 And the peace of God, which passeth all understanding, shall keep your hearts and minds through Christ Jesus. 8 Finally, brethren, whatsoever things are true, whatsoever things are honest, whatsoever things are just, whatsoever things are pure, whatsoever things are lovely, whatsoever things are of good report; if there be any virtue, and if there be any praise, think on these things. 9 Those things, which ye have both learned, and received, and heard, and seen in me, do: and the God of peace (*who gives victory over all the works of the devil in the name of Jesus*) shall be with you." Make your faith stronger by joy before the answer comes, per His written Word which is all "yea and amen" in Jesus.

So a simple definition of strong faith is bold declarations of a Bible promise, as if it has already come to pass, in glad thanksgiving and rejoicing, in advance of the manifestation, as you keep rigid control on your thoughts and the words that come forth from your mouth: Ps 27:6 "And now shall mine head be lifted up above mine enemies round about me: therefore will I offer in his tabernacle sacrifices of joy; I will sing, yea, I will sing praises unto the LORD. 7 Hear, O LORD, when I cry with my voice: have mercy also upon me, and answer me. 8 When thou saidst, Seek ye my face; my heart said unto thee, Thy face, LORD, will I seek." Ps 107:22 "And let them sacrifice the sacrifices of thanksgiving, and declare his works with rejoicing." Ps 116:17 "I will offer to thee the sacrifice of thanksgiving, and will call upon the name of the LORD." Heb 13:15 "By him therefore let us offer the sacrifice of praise (*thanksgiving*) to God continually, that is, the fruit of our lips giving thanks to his (Jesus') name (*as you aiteo the promises*)."

Note: the "sacrifice" part is when you do it when the answer is not yet there, and rejoicing as if you already had it, even while you suffer in heaviness. Look not at the situation, but at the Word of God, as Lord. Whose report will you believe, as evidenced by confessions, thanksgiving, praise and joy?

Jesus said it this way: Mark 11:22 "And Jesus answering saith unto them, Have faith in God. 23 For verily I say unto you, That whosoever shall say unto this mountain, Be thou removed, and be thou cast into the sea; and shall not doubt in his heart, but shall believe that those things which he saith shall come to pass; he shall have whatsoever he saith. 24 Therefore I say unto you, What things soever ye *aiteo*/desire (*require, demand and expect as due by covenant promise*), when ye pray, believe that ye *lambano*/receive them, and ye shall have (*possess*) them."

The Greek word for faith, *pistis*, is the noun form of the verb translated as *believe*. Both words are related to obedience. So you exercise faith by obeying, or keeping your heart, mind and mouth in obedience to the words, the promises of God, by rejoicing and giving glory to God until you see the answer manifested, knowing: Heb 11:6 "But without faith it is impossible to please him (*Father God*):

OTHER HEALING TEACHINGS

for he that cometh to God must believe that he is, and that he is a rewarder of them that diligently seek him." This diligent part means to continue on with effort, faithfulness and consistency. For example, Abram agreed with God, when God changed his name to Abraham, which means Father of Many Nations or Multitudes (see Gen 17:5). So Abraham carried that name a year before he saw his promised son Isaac.

Remember Bible faith is believing God to perform His Word in spite of what now looks impossible and/or improbable. And that faith is evidenced by what comes out of your mouth. 2 Cor 4:13 "We having the same spirit of faith, according as it is written, I believed, and therefore have I spoken; we also believe, and therefore speak." All the promises of God are part of His salvation, and His salvation is primarily released by our mouths. Rom 10:10 "For with the heart man believeth unto righteousness; and with the mouth confession is made unto *soteria*/salvation." So agree with your mouth out loud that the promise of God is true and you will yet have it, and you are now operating in faith. Ps 142:5 "I cried unto thee, O LORD: I said, Thou art my refuge and my portion in the land of the living." Ps 27:13 "I had fainted, unless I had believed to see the goodness of the LORD in the land of the living. 14 Wait (*entwine*) on the LORD: be of good courage, and he shall strengthen thine heart: wait (*entwine*), I say, on the LORD." We do the good courage part, and God does the strength/power part. Good courage looks a lot like thanksgiving, rejoicing, and praise, done with passion and intensity, faking it, if need be.

This does take a concentrated effort. Heb 6:11 "And we desire that every one of you do shew the same **diligence** to the full assurance of hope unto the end: 12 that ye **be not slothful**, but followers of them who through faith and patience (*consistency*) inherit the promises. 13 For when God made promise to Abraham, because he could swear by no greater, he sware by himself, 14 saying, Surely blessing I will bless thee, and multiplying I will multiply thee. 15 And so, after he had patiently endured, he obtained the promise. 16 For men verily swear by the greater: and an oath for confirmation is to them an end of all strife. 17 Wherein God, willing more abundantly to shew unto the heirs of promise the immutability of his counsel, confirmed it by an oath: 18 that by two immutable things, (*His promise and His covenant oath*) in which it was impossible for God to lie, we might have a strong consolation, who have fled for refuge to lay hold upon the hope set before us: 19 which hope we have as an anchor of the soul (*heart, mind, will and emotions*), both sure and stedfast, and which entereth into that within the veil; 20 whither the forerunner is for us entered, even Jesus, made an high priest for ever after the order of Melchisedec."

Faith or courage is not promised to be easy. Here is part of God's definition of being blessed: Deut 28:7 "The LORD shall cause thine enemies that rise up against thee to be smitten before thy face: they shall come out against thee one way, and flee before thee seven ways." So to be blessed does not mean to have no problems or enemies. Remember, we are sent to make the world a better place, which means we have evil enemies that will resist and attack us, whether we attack them or not. Instead, to be blessed means that we will defeat them as they come against our face–eyeball-to-eyeball, breath-to-breath, as we *aiteo*. The power to do this is expressed over and over again in Hebrews 11 as "by faith." Therefore: Heb 10:38 "Now the just shall *zao*/live by faith: but if any man draw back, my soul shall have no pleasure in him. 39 But we are not of them who draw back unto perdition (*death stays in charge*); but of them that believe to the *sozo*/saving of the soul (*heart, mind, will and emotions to operating just like Jesus*)." 2 Tim 1:6 "Wherefore I put thee in remembrance that thou stir up the gift of God, which is in thee by the putting on of my hands. 7 For God hath not given us the spirit of fear; but of *dunamis*/power (*ability*), and of *agape*/love, and of a sound mind." James 4:7 "Submit yourselves therefore to God. Resist the devil, and he will flee from you. 8 Draw nigh to God, and he will draw nigh to you. Cleanse your hands, ye sinners; and purify your hearts, ye double minded." Eph 6:10 "Finally, my brethren, be strong in the Lord, and in the power of his might. 11 Put on the whole armour of God, that ye may be able to stand against the wiles of the devil. 12 For we wrestle not against flesh and blood, but against principalities, against powers, against the rulers of the darkness of this world, against spiritual wickedness in high places. 13 Wherefore take unto you the whole armour of God, that ye may be able to withstand in the evil day, and having done all, to stand." Staying in the Word until it is more real than circumstances is part of the mind-renewing process, as described earlier.

Jesus addressed building faith with the disciples in three major events:

a) The cursing of the fig tree,

b) Their failure to cast out a demon, and

c) When they asked Him specifically to increase their faith.

In all cases, the issue was never God, but, rather, the knowledge, mental attitude and beliefs of the disciples.

Mark 11:12 "And on the morrow, when they were come from Bethany, he was hungry: 13 and seeing a fig tree afar off having leaves, he came, if haply he might find any thing thereon: and when he came to it, he found nothing but leaves; for the time of figs was not yet. 14 And Jesus answered and said unto it, No man eat fruit of thee hereafter for ever. And his disciples heard it. ... 20 And in the morning, as they passed by, they saw the fig tree dried up from the roots. 21 And Peter calling to remembrance saith unto him, Master, behold, the fig tree which thou cursedst is withered away. 22 And Jesus answering saith unto them, Have faith in God. 23 For verily I say unto you, That whosoever shall say unto this mountain, Be thou removed, and be thou cast into the sea; and shall not doubt in his heart, but shall believe that those things which he saith shall come to pass; he shall have whatsoever he saith. 24 Therefore I say unto you, What things soever ye *aiteo*/

OTHER HEALING TEACHINGS

desire (*require, demand and expect as due by covenant promise of God*), when ye pray, believe that ye *lambano*/receive them, and ye shall have them. 25 And when ye stand praying, forgive, if ye have ought against any: that your Father also which is in heaven may forgive you your trespasses. 26 But if ye do not forgive, neither will your Father which is in heaven forgive your trespasses."

There are several things here. First, notice in verse 14 that Jesus went close to the tree to look for fruit, and then shouted at the tree, loud enough for the disciples to hear Him way back on the road. Faith is not necessarily quiet.

Then Jesus addressed how to have faith in verse 22, which could also be translated as "have the faith of God" or "operate in the faith of God" or "use the same faith God uses, and you do it too." Jesus fully expected the disciples in their un-born-again state to operate in faith just like He did. He saw no limitations in them; they were their own limitations.

Then, in verse 24, He tells them that He expected the prayer process to use requirements or demands of God based on His *chesed* covenant promises. In verse 23, Jesus says to speak to the problem, not to others about how bad it is, but to speak directly to it, as if it were a person, for it to go and do as needed to get the situation right, per God's covenant promises. This is also an *aiteo*-type command.

Then, in verse 23, also He tells them to believe those things which they say shall come to pass, which includes imagination or visualization of the finished work the way you want it. They are to believe that they already have it, if they do speak to it in an *aiteo* command.

The last major issue here is unforgiveness or offense toward anybody. Jesus warned that God will treat you the way you treat others (similar to what He described in the "Our Father"). So, if you want to not be offended in God, make sure you deal with offense or unforgiveness in your own heart. This includes any unforgiveness you may have toward God for any past event in which God did not answer your prayer the way you wanted. Per the Parable of the Sower and the Seed, Jesus warns that the first attack of the devil is to get us offended in some way, preferably at God and then other people.

So building faith includes dealing with unforgiveness. The best measure I know of this would be: if you can say anything negative about another person without going into prayer to get them healed and blessed, you have an unforgiveness or offense problem. Make your confession to God simple and quick, and ask Him to deal with you over it, as you minister healing to others. Being healed or ministering healing are both acts of grace, and this is not about your perfection or holiness, but Jesus' holiness released by His name, to manifest a Bible promise. Unforgiveness, by itself, will not stop you from healing or being healed.

This story is also found in: Matt 21:20 "And when the disciples saw it, they marvelled, saying, How soon is the fig tree withered away! 21 Jesus answered and said unto them, Verily I say unto you, If ye have faith, and doubt not, ye shall not only do this which is done to the fig tree, but also if ye shall say unto this mountain, Be thou removed, and be thou cast into the sea; it shall be done. 22 And all things, whatsoever ye shall *aiteo*/ask in prayer, believing, ye shall *lambano*/receive."

Notice that in this story Jesus goes from a dead fig tree to moving a mountain as the object of faith. He goes from the relatively small and unimportant to the relatively large and important. This is about creative imagination or visualization, where you imagine it done before it is done. He said for them to understand they could operate in the faith that God operated in. As you *aiteo* the mountain, per God's covenant promises, it will obey what you say. Imagine it happening as you speak. Since it is God's faith you are operating in, Father God will then direct Holy Spirit to do it. Since, for us, God has already said His promises are yea (absolutely I want them done), and amen (so be it, I will do it), then the issue is us and not God. This also fits with the great command of God: Mark 12:29 "And Jesus answered him, The first of all the commandments is, Hear, O Israel; The Lord our God is one Lord: 30 and thou shalt *agape*/love the Lord thy God with all thy *kardia*/heart, and with all thy *psuche*/soul, and with all thy *dianoia*/mind (*imagination, understanding and pondering*), and with all thy *ischus*/strength (*power, ability, money*): this is the first commandment. 31 And the second is like, namely this, Thou shalt *agape*/love thy neighbour as thyself. There is none other commandment greater than these."

From Romans 4, with Abraham, we learn that strong faith looks at the situation, in spite of all the impossibilities and proclaims, through rejoicing, that you already have the answer from God, per His Word, knowing that your thanksgiving, praise and rejoicing builds strength in you and is used of God to defeat the works of the devil through you. Weak faith may not rejoice at all, but it still works as you hang on to (*lambano*) the Word of God. Matt 17:20 "And Jesus said unto them, (*on why they could not cast out a demon*), Because of your unbelief: for verily I say unto you, If ye have faith as a grain of (*the tiny*) mustard seed, ye shall say unto this mountain, Remove hence to yonder place; and it shall remove; and nothing shall be impossible unto you." Strong faith or tiny faith, the issue is to keep at it until you see the answer (with or without feelings). Be relentless against anxiety and dreadful fear of any kind, and any past offense, but count on God.

The main characteristic of a mustard seed is that it does not let its tiny size, as a starting place, stop it. It keeps at it, focusing on the end result of becoming a large tree and not how small it is right now. Every day it does the same thing over and over again, growing day and night faithfully, until it reaches its goal. So, in the same manner as Elijah prayed/praised/affirmed 3 times to raise a dead boy or 8 times to bring rain, we are to keep speaking to the situation the promise of God over it until we see the work done.

Small, mustard seed faith means much saying without fail. Speak to the situation, call it what it is, *aiteo* it to get right, per God's Word, and then proclaim God's

OTHER HEALING TEACHINGS

promise over it until you have it. Faith follows a blueprint. The blueprint of the mustard seed makes a large tree. The believing internal visualization of the manifested Word of God is the blueprint for the mountain moving. God speaks the end from the beginning while it is not yet there. This is where God-faith starts. This is like weight training: keep at it, and the muscles will get stronger. If you stop, doubt (faint, fail to act or fear), go back and start again, and this time keep at it longer. Then keep going to the weight room to maintain that gain. If you stop going to the gym, you lose strength. So stay in the gym of the *agape*/love of God. Every day you are doing something. Yes, it requires a change in priority to get the benefits of God to do what He requires. No pain in the gym, no gain and no strength. It is your call. You determine the result.

Note the attitude of the mustard seed in the *agape*/love of God. It never gives up. 1 Cor 13:7 "[Agape/*love*] beareth all things, believeth all things, hopeth all things, endureth all things. 8 *Agape*/ charity never faileth." And neither does the mustard seed. Get your eyes off the dreadful fear potential in the situation, and onto the *agape*/ love of God that paid Jesus for healing of all men in His physical, spiritual and soul suffering, and God wants that healing released now. So keep in *aiteo* against the devil, and in praise to God in Jesus.

Note, in the next verse: Matt 17:21 "Howbeit this kind goeth not out but by prayer and fasting." This word *kind* is not about the demons, but the unbelief that gives up and focuses on the situation, and not the promise of God. Jewish prayer focuses on praying the Scriptures. So fasting with scripture-based prayer is a way to get rid of unbelief and, thus, build faith/believing. Fasting is a form of afflicting your soul (heart, mind, will and emotions) to right or godly thinking. When you are in unbelief or despair, your soul is in need of "saving." James 1:21 "Wherefore lay apart all filthiness and superfluity of naughtiness, and *lambano*/receive with meekness the engrafted word, which is able to *sozo*/save your souls (*heart, mind, will and emotions*)."

In this same story, Jesus says: Matt 17:20 "And Jesus said unto them, Because of your unbelief: for verily I say unto you, If ye have faith as a grain of mustard seed, ye shall say unto this mountain, Remove hence to yonder place; and it shall remove; and nothing shall be impossible unto you." The size of the start does not matter!

This is similar to what Jesus said when the disciples asked Him how to build their faith. Luke 17:5 "And the apostles said unto the Lord, Increase our faith. 6 And the Lord said, If ye had faith as a grain of mustard seed, ye might say unto this sycamine (*mulberry*) tree, Be thou plucked up by the root, and be thou planted in the sea; and it should obey you." So see what can happen, not what cannot. Visualize the end from the beginning and *aiteo* it to get that way.

In these cases Jesus says to get your mind off a small faith target, and get it on a much larger one. If you are standing next to a mountain or a tree, and you start to get your believing up to the level of moving the mountain or seeing that tree get its roots out of the ground and start walking to the sea, that sounds a whole lot larger than killing a fig tree, casting out a demon or healing a maimed body. To call it done before you see it, use imagination. For those with a background in science, the challenge of a tree starting to walk and then changing its biochemistry to live in water is even greater than moving a physical mountain. The point is to look at a bigger faith problem first before or while you tackle the smaller ones.

One way to do this would be: whatever seems like a large problem to you, consider either your past faith and God's goodness successes, your God-testimony, or consider the worst that can happen, and get solid in your confidence that God can handle the worst or biggest through you, and then the dreadful fear of the present situation will not cause you to get offended in God and fail to act in faith.

One example of this was David, as he prepared to charge Goliath. 1 Sam 17:34 "And David said unto Saul, Thy servant kept his father's sheep, and there came a lion, and a bear, and took a lamb out of the flock: 35 And I went out after him, and smote him, and delivered it out of his mouth: and when he arose against me, I caught him by his beard, and smote him, and slew him. 36 Thy servant slew both the lion and the bear: and this uncircumcised Philistine shall be as one of them, seeing he hath defied the armies of the living God. 37 David said moreover, The LORD that delivered me out of the paw of the lion, and out of the paw of the bear, he will deliver me out of the hand of this Philistine. And Saul said unto David, Go, and the LORD be with thee." This is an example of David stirring himself up in spirit. David was recalling how, when he was younger and weaker, he had God's help to kill the lion and the bear.

Another example would be Abraham, who took Isaac to the mountain in obedience, believing God to raise the boy from the dead if necessary. Abraham got his heart ready for the bigger challenge, rebuilding a burned and dead body, rather than focusing on what he actually got, a ram caught in a thicket. Heb 11:17 "By faith Abraham, when he was tried (Gen 22), offered up Isaac: and he that had received the promises offered up his only begotten son, 18 of whom it was said, That in Isaac shall thy seed be called: 19 accounting that God was able to raise him up, even from the dead; from whence also he received him in a figure." This is putting God's ability in the vision of your mind's eye to believing His promise and that no problem will stop that promise.

In all these cases where lack of faith is the issue, Jesus responded by telling the disciples to get their minds ready for bigger things, and then the present, smaller one would be easier. Gird your mind for battle.

Still on the subject of building faith, Jesus then spoke about sense of purpose, calling, faithfulness, endurance, and godly humility. Luke 17:7 "But which of you, having a servant plowing or feeding cattle, will say unto him by and by, when he is come from the field, Go and sit down to meat? 8 And will not rather say unto him, Make ready wherewith I may sup, and gird thyself, and serve me, till I have eaten and drunken; and afterward thou shalt eat and drink? 9 Doth he thank that servant because he did the things that were commanded him? I trow not. 10 So likewise ye, when ye shall have done all those things which are commanded you, say, We are unprofitable servants: we have done that which was our duty to do."

So Jesus, in part, is saying, If you move physical mountains or trees, heal the sick, multiply food, or stop the sun and moon for a day, as Joshua did, you are just doing what you are made for. Even if you did it perfectly all the time, you have not added to God; you have only accomplished that for which you were made. Eph 2:8 "For by grace are ye *sozo*/saved through faith; and that not of yourselves: it is the gift of God: 9 not of works, lest any man should boast. 10 For we are his workmanship, created in Christ Jesus unto good works, which God hath before ordained that we should walk in them." So whatever the faith challenge, it is really you lining up with the mind of Christ to operate in the faith-work already created for you in Jesus.

So, we see several ways to build faith:

- First, you must hear the Word of God of Christ in you, the hope of glory.
- Then, you believe God enough to put the words of the promises of God in your mouth, in spite of the evils of the situation, to *aiteo*.
- Next, you refuse to look at the impossibilities or the dreadful fear of the situation, and, instead, give God joyous thanksgiving, praise and triumph, calling those things that be not as if they were, knowing God is able, will do it and cannot lie.
- Persuade yourself by His Bible's truths.
- Build your heart-confidence in God: that He already paid for it in Jesus; that all your sins were healed in Jesus 2000 years ago; and that Christ is in you to do it.
- The last step is: like the mustard seed, keep at it until you see the answer. Trust that each time you minster *zoe*/life flows for "no labor in the Lord is in vain."

Notice what Jesus said: John 5:26 "For as the Father hath *zoe*/life in himself; so hath he given to the Son to have *zoe*/life in himself; 27 and hath given him authority (*commission and resources*) to execute judgment also, because he is the Son of man." This is the kind of judgment we saw Jesus deliver: Ps 103:6 "The LORD executeth righteousness and judgment for all that are oppressed." Acts 10:38 "How God anointed Jesus of Nazareth with the Holy Ghost and with power: who went about doing good, and healing all that were oppressed (*under the active dominion, reign or lordship*) of the devil; for God was with him." And each Christian has the same calling.

Jesus delivered Acts 10:38 because He said He had *zoe*/life and authority to execute the plan of God in judgment against the devil, to set people free. Now you see why Jesus said: Matt 28:18 "And Jesus came and spake unto them, saying, All power is given unto me in heaven and in earth. 19 Go ye therefore, and teach all nations, baptizing them in the name of the Father, and of the Son, and of the Holy Ghost: 20 teaching them to observe all things whatsoever I have commanded you: and, lo, I am with you alway, even unto the end of the world. Amen."

Jesus has given Christians the authority to execute the plan of God, just as Jesus did, and then Holy Spirit shows we have the same *zoe*/life and the use of Jesus' name to do the same thing Jesus did. 1 John 5:11 "And this is the record, that God hath given to us eternal *zoe*/life, and this *zoe*/life is in his Son. 12 He that hath the Son hath *zoe*/life; and he that hath not the Son of God hath not *zoe*/life. 13 These things have I written unto you that believe on the name of the Son of God; that ye may know that ye have eternal *zoe*/life, and that ye may believe on the name of the Son of God (*to manifest the Bible promises of God on the Earth*)."

Here is how we are to use this confidence (faith, courage, believing, assurance, certainty, and knowing) so that we have *zoe*/life and the authority to use the name of Jesus to manifest the will of God: 1 John 5:14 "And this is the confidence that we have in him, that, if we (*keep on*) *aiteo*/asking (*requiring, demanding and expecting as due by covenant promise*) any thing according to his will, he heareth us: 15 and if we know that he hear us, whatsoever we *aiteo*/ask (*require, demand and expect as due by covenant promise*), we know that we have the *aiteo*/petitions that we *aiteo*/desired (*require, demand and expect as due by covenant promise*) of him. 16 If any man see his brother sin a sin which is not unto death, he shall *aiteo*/ask (*require, demand and expect as due by covenant promise*), and he shall give him *zoe*/life for them (*just like He did with Jesus*) ... ."

Commanding the devil to go, the disorder to stop being, the healing to be, and the person to be whole are all such *aiteo* commands. This is all about your confidence that you are *aiteo*ing the will of God and that God hears you, not some reason why God will not move. Father God has given us His *zoe*/life, Jesus' authority, the name of Jesus, grace, truth, mercy, Holy Spirit, righteousness, peace and abundant *agape*/love. You are the key, not God. Holy Spirit will teach you, but we must do the doing, the believing.

Do not forget, Adam was created to multiply, be fruitful, subdue and establish dominion for God. These are all characteristics of a warrior king. If you think your purpose is to enjoy life and be blessed for your own benefit and lack of troubles, you are missing the story of Luke 17:7-10. Our job is to make Heaven on Earth now, not to run to Heaven as a hiding place. Heb 10:12 "But this man, after he had offered one sacrifice for sins for ever, sat down on the right hand of God; 13 from henceforth expecting till his enemies be made his footstool." Rom 16:20 "And the God of peace shall bruise Satan under your feet shortly. The grace of our Lord Jesus Christ be with you [*to know, be and do this*]. Amen." Let us be about our Father's business.

Peace is not to be without trouble; it is to win by bringing the will of God into any situation. This is our job, being a peacemaker unto reconciliation. Lose sight of this and have a different life purpose, and you will find it difficult to say: Luke 17:10 "So likewise ye, when ye shall have done all those things which are commanded you, say, We are unprofitable servants: we have done that which was our duty to do." To Jesus, this was a core attitude of His ministry, and He tells us plainly here it is to be ours, as a key to effective faith. The great news is this: by His great redemption in His blood, we have the tools and the legal conditions to make this happen for Him. As you renew your mind with the tools in this book, you can keep a loved one alive and get them healed in the name of Jesus. Let us labor with the grace and truth of God to deliver His *agape*/love through healing.

The final step in building faith is to obey the scripture: Rom 5:16 "And not as it was by one that sinned, so is the gift: for the judgment was by one to condemnation, but the free gift is of many offences unto justification. 17 For if by one man's offence death reigned by one; much more they which (*continually*) *lambano*/receive abundance of grace and of the [*permanent*] gift of righteousness shall reign in *zoe*/life by one, Jesus Christ.) 18 Therefore as by the offence of one judgment came upon all men to condemnation; even so by the righteousness of one the free gift came upon all men unto justification of *zoe*/life. 19 For as by one man's disobedience many were made sinners, so by the obedience of one shall many be made righteous. 20 Moreover the law entered, that the offence might abound. But where sin abounded, grace did much more abound: 21 that as sin hath reigned unto death, even so might grace reign through righteousness unto eternal *zoe*/life by Jesus Christ our Lord."

Every answered prayer and *aiteo*/demand is an act of war against the kingdom of darkness, and builds and enforces the reign or Kingdom of God. We will reign, exercise the right wisdom and power of God in Jesus, based on how well we *lambano*/hold on to, never let go of, the abundant grace of God, the gift of God to know, will, be and do whatever is needed, and the gift of being made the righteousness of God in Christ Jesus. It is not about you!

We have to *lambano* these in the face of conflicting situations, vivid and harsh physical realities, emotions, thoughts, our own sins and failures, the sins and failures of others, our corrupt consciences, and bodily weaknesses. How well we hold on to this, that we have all the resources of God and the ability of God to make Heaven on Earth by using the name of Jesus, will determine how well we reign for

Him—not because of us or our holiness, but because of Jesus and His holiness and Lordship, because God *agape*/loves people and wants His *agape*/love manifested to and in them.

As we know this, we will gladly execute the reign of God on the Earth, execute the judgment written against the devil, and set people free of all oppressions of the devil. Get strong in the Word of Christ, of our redemption and of our salvation in the New Testament. You do this by renewing your mind. For this the Minister Confession said daily is powerful.

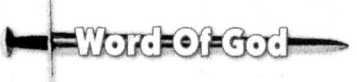

~ 23 ~

ON POWER LEVELS

Dr. Lake graduated hundreds of what he called Divine Healing Technicians (DHTs), and many physicians converted to the ministry to do more healing than was possible with medicine. This training included the same scriptures that are in this book and also personally working with Dr. Lake. So it was a combination of learning and doing. As the modern church has proved, mere learning or mental assent does not usually produce the works of God. We must enter into the process of ministering to the sick with results, to "know" as God requires.

DHT graduation consisted of going to a terminally ill patient and ministering until that person was healed. Dr. Lake demonstrated that continued prayer fit this scripture: 1 Cor 15:58 "Therefore, my *agape*/beloved brethren, be ye stedfast, unmoveable, always abounding in the work of the Lord, forasmuch as ye know that your labour is not in vain in the Lord." Wanting people healed is of God, and diligently seeking God His way for healing is a true labor in the Lord. So whether you get seen or unseen results, all has benefit. It is faith in God that pushes the power.

It is as if there is a certain amount of power or *zoe*/life necessary to get a job done. Even Jesus had to pray twice in one recorded case: Mark 8:23 "And he took the blind man by the hand, and led him out of the town; and when he had spit on his eyes, and put his hands upon him, he asked him if he saw ought. 24 And he looked up, and said, I see men as trees, walking. 25 After that he put his hands again upon his eyes, and made him look up: and he was restored, and saw every man clearly." Jesus did not say, "Oops!" He just ministered again! So if you see no result or the job is not finished, minister again. Like Jesus, ask if the person feels or can move better or is fully healed. If not, minister again, and again, until you win and the work of the devil leaves by the authority of the name of Jesus.

We are told to minister like Elijah. James 5:17 "Elias was a man subject to like passions as we are, and he prayed earnestly that it might not rain: and it rained not on the earth by the space of three years and six months. 18 And he prayed again, and the heaven gave rain, and the earth brought forth her fruit." This references 1 Kings 18:42-45 where Elijah prayed 8 times (1 + 7) to get rain. While not explicitly stated after the first time, it appears after each time he prayed he sent his servant to look for the cloud. So each time, Elijah prayed/affirmed as if it was the last time. He did this 8 times, and we are told to pray like him. The mustard seed may be small, but it does not give up until it produces a large tree. So "prayed again" means to pray until the job is done, not just once. Faint not; keep at it!

It is as if a problem takes 100 units of *zoe*/power and, as no labor in the Lord is in vain, you may deposit a tenth of a unit, 1 or 5 or 25 or all 100 units in any given session. But until all 100 units are deposited, the job is not done. So you minister one time, giving 100 units, or 100 times, giving 1 unit. If you minister 500 units on a 100-unit job, it may just go faster, or other things in the person may also be healed. The problem is not God; it is us and how stirred up and determined in God, in judgment against the devil, we are. Jesus showed how to walk in His fullness, and we are to grow into Him, per Ephesians 4, but along the way we grow in knowledge and in the amount of *zoe*/life, power we operate in. Each time we minister we push more *zoe*/life.

Since the Word of God is a seed, as you first minister, you deposit the Word of God, and then you strengthen it to produce. The seed is called the word of reconciliation, to make what is written in Heaven a reality on Earth. The seed is perfect, indestructible and of God, and it will produce the results needed. Any delay in achieving results is not a seed problem. As you minister *zoe*/life each time, you strengthen that seed and it grows. The rate of growth is dependent upon the amount of *zoe*/life deposited. Either way, per 1 Cor 15:58, "no labor in the Lord is in vain," so faint not.

Thus, Dr. Lake would say to come for 30- to 60-minute sessions every day for 30 days, and people would get markedly better or fully healed. Some got healed on the first day, some on the thirtieth, and some took as many as 91 days or more, but he did not stop until victory came. In more recent times, Curry Blake (www.jglm.org) has trained thousands and set up similar Divine Healing Rooms, to great effect. What seems to be true is that the more you get the word of grace and truth in you and the more you minister healing, the less time it takes i.e., the more *zoe*/life or power you operate in each time you minister.

You do your part, knowing God will do His. Faint not!

~ 24 ~

ON WARRIOR TECHNIQUES

If you can only *aiteo* for 15 minutes or an hour, or 15 days, the devil knows this and will try to outlast you. So go with the attitude that you will not stop. This is not about trying, but getting the work done.

Praying in the Spirit builds you up, and in a spiritual battle you need to stay spiritually built up. Keep in shape with 1 to 3 hours of hard, loud and fast speaking in tongues every day, and/or preach to yourself any sections of this manual. As you pray in tongues, you build yourself up in faith: Jude 20 "But ye, *agape*/beloved, building up yourselves on your most holy faith, praying in the Holy Ghost, 21 keep yourselves in the *agape*/love of God, looking for the mercy of our Lord Jesus Christ unto eternal *zoe*/life." There can be no doubt that this builds you up on your faith in God in His word of *agape*/love.

Then go and preach to yourself one of the teaching or confession sections to get the Word of God in you and build your confidence in Him. This is preaching, not reading out loud. Preach to get through to yourself what you are saying. Notice that all of this is a "stirring-up" process. Shouting focuses you and brings up the fight in you to win. This is more about attitude, boldness and confidence than anything else. Just like a boxer hits to win, preach, *aiteo*, and pray to win! Keep your eyes on what God can do through you. He is Almighty God, nothing is impossible for Him!

Also, one of our weapons is thanksgiving and praise. The Battle Prayer has praise and prayer breaks. Use them; they work. Take any section or verse of scriptures and make them into songs, chants, or shouts.

First, if you do not pray in tongues, diligently seek the Lord for the gifts, including tongues, per 1 Cor 12:31 and 14:1, and, in the meantime, pray at least the

Psalms daily, as they are spirit and *zoe*/life. Another alternative is to proclaim the Scriptures over the situation, which is how the Battle Prayer is already structured.

One approach that has proven successful (and this is how Dr. Lake trained his Divine Technicians in their graduation test to heal a terminally ill person) is to use dominion or commanding prayer for a period, say 1 to 2 hours, and then break and pray in tongues loud, hard and fast for another period, say 10 minutes to 2 hours, then go back to dominion commands. This cycle is repeated until victory comes. In the case of Dr. Lake, many times it was reported that others could hear the ministers' loud voices and shouts down the street. It seemed that the more successful were also the loudest. Who said life and death battles are quiet?

Using this approach, you may be able to sleep for 2 to 4 hours at a time and continue for 6 weeks or more. With Dr. Lake's students, if the patient died, they used the same technique to raise them from the dead. In those days (and in many foreign countries today), the dead were not whisked away immediately, so they had more time, 1 to 5 days. If you are in a hospital situation, you may have to ask permission for time to work. Include that in your prayer.

A variation is to pray 1 or 2 of the Battle Prayers, say No. 1 for battle and No. 28 for thanksgiving. Then, if the sick person is not fully healed, pray in tongues loud, hard and fast for 5 to 60 minutes. The amount of time is up to you. Then minister to the sick again (praying and/or laying hands on them). Repeat this 5 to 15 times. If they are still not fully healed, then go back and get more Scripture in you, Read out loud the Minister Confession; read any of the scripture sets; then minister again. Add in thanksgiving and praise. Mix and match any of the techniques, as appropriate, until you get the full job done. Notice the pattern: pray in tongues, then get the Word of God in you, with praise and thanksgiving, then minister again. If you do not pray in tongues, do the pattern without tongues.

Concerning fasting, Jesus showed that this was to be a normal Christian practice. Matt 9:15 "And Jesus said unto them, Can the children of the bridechamber mourn, as long as the bridegroom is with them? but the days will come, when the bridegroom shall be taken from them, and then shall they fast." The basic style is addressed in Matt 6:16-18. A typical practice is to skip 2 meals a week or even 2 whole days, but there are many variations. Use the time you would normally eat to give thanks, praise, pray and hear from God, all with scripture (see Proverbs 1-8 and Ephesians 1). Reading scripture out loud in groups or with a recording, while fasting, is very powerful.

But God has a deeper fast that produces even greater results. Isa 58:6 "Is not this the fast that I have chosen? to loose the bands of wickedness, to undo the heavy burdens, and to let the oppressed go free, and that ye break every yoke? ... 9 Then shalt thou call, and the LORD shall answer; thou shalt cry, and he shall say, Here I am. If thou take away from the midst of thee the yoke, the putting forth of the finger, and speaking vanity; 10 and if thou draw out thy soul to the hungry, and satisfy the afflicted soul; then shall thy light rise in obscurity, and thy darkness be as the noonday: 11 and the LORD shall guide thee continually, and satisfy thy soul in drought, and make fat thy bones: and thou shalt be like a watered garden, and like a spring of water, whose waters fail not. 12 And they that shall be of thee shall build the old waste places: thou shalt raise up the foundations of many generations; and thou shalt be called, The repairer of the breach, The restorer of paths to dwell in." These promises are for those who set the oppressed of the devil free in healing. The reference to not pointing the finger means if you see sin or error, you get *zoe* life for that person to heal them, and don't just accuse them. Instead, give up your unforgiveness and fault finding, and bless that person (see Matt 7:1-7, Rom 12:14-21, Matt 5:44-48, Luke 6:27-36 and Eph 4:29-32). This is the fast of Isaiah 58 and what God blesses.

IS THE DEVIL ALWAYS INVOLVED?

The following scripture shows that he is: Acts 10:38 "How God anointed Jesus of Nazareth with the Holy Ghost and with power: who went about doing good, and healing all that were oppressed (*under the active dominion, reign or lordship*) of the devil; for God was with him." Thus, every healing was a judgment against the devil. How the devil is involved can be different. If you get someone who has just broken an arm, if there are no other complications, the devil has not had much time to work. Commands for the body to be healed should be sufficient. But if pain starts, he is there. If infection or other issues come up, he is there. Jesus said it this way: John 10:10 "The thief cometh not, but for to steal, and to kill, and to destroy: I am come that they might have *zoe*/life, and that they might have it more abundantly." If what you see happening fits stealing, killing or destroying, then the devil is there, and we are charged to get rid of his works by making him obey us. Luke 10:19 "Behold (*make this change your view of life and go do it*), I give unto you power (*authority, commission and ability*) to tread on serpents and scorpions, and over all the power (*ability*) of the enemy: and nothing shall by any means hurt you. 20 Notwithstanding in this rejoice not, that the spirits are subject unto you; but rather rejoice, because your names are written in heaven." He gave us this authority, commission and the resources of Heaven to use; so we must use them.

Jesus made a point of describing the following situation as a work of the devil: Luke 13:10 "And he was teaching in one of the synagogues on the sabbath. 11 And, behold, there was a woman which had a spirit of infirmity (*sickness, disease*) eighteen years, and was bowed together, and could in no wise lift up herself. 12 And when Jesus saw her, he called her to him, and said unto her, Woman, thou art loosed from thine infirmity. 13 And he laid his hands on her: and immediately she was made straight, and glorified God. 14 And the ruler of the synagogue answered with indignation, because that Jesus had healed on the sabbath day, and said unto the people, There are six days in which men ought to work: in them therefore come and be healed, and not on the sabbath day. 15 The Lord then answered him, and said, Thou hypocrite, doth not each one of you on the sabbath loose his ox or his ass from the stall, and lead him away to watering? 16 And ought not this woman, being a daughter of Abraham, whom Satan hath bound, lo, these eighteen years, be loosed from this bond on the sabbath day?" If you doubt this, ask the Lord to persuade you (see 1 John 3:8).

Look at the way Jesus sent out the twelve and the seventy. If the demons are not directly involved, authority over them still heals their effects. Matt 10:1 "And when he had called unto him his twelve disciples, he gave them *exousia*/power (*authority, commission and ability*) against unclean spirits, to cast them out, and to heal all manner of sickness and all manner of disease. ... 7 And as ye go, preach, saying, The kingdom of heaven is at hand. 8 Heal the sick, cleanse the lepers, raise the dead, cast out devils: freely ye have received, freely give." Here Jesus gives specific power over unclean spirits, to cast them out, and also power to heal all sicknesses and diseases.

Mark 6:7 "And he called unto him the twelve, and began to send them forth by two and two; and gave them *exousia*/power (*authority, commission and ability*) over unclean spirits. ... 12 And they went out, and preached that men should repent. 13 And they cast out many devils, and anointed with oil many that were sick, and healed them." Here the authority over unclean spirits results in both casting out demons and healings.

Luke 9:1 "Then he called his twelve disciples together, and gave them *dunamis*/power (*ability*) and *exousia*/authority over all devils (*demons*), and to cure diseases. ... 6 And they departed, and went through the towns, preaching the gospel, and healing every where." Here authority over unclean spirits and curing diseases results in what is described as healings. Based on this detail in Luke, implicit in the authority is the *dunamis*/power to enforce that authority.

In all three versions, Jesus gave authority over unclean spirits and the fruit was demons cast out, people healed and the dead raised. So it would appear that this authority over unclean spirits can either cast out demons or their work (all kinds of sickness, all kinds of diseases, leprosy, direct demon afflictions or death) and, thus, sick people are healed. Not once did Jesus ever say to ask God to stop inflicting someone with a sickness or for them to ask God to heal. Rather, it was the reverse; they were healing for Jesus, and, therefore, for God. As seen in Job, the devil causes evil, and God heals. As Jesus said: John 10:10 "The thief cometh not, but for to steal, and to kill, and to destroy: I am come that they might have *zoe*/life, and that they might have it more abundantly."

When Jesus sent out the 70, this was again repeated. Luke 10:1 "After these things the Lord appointed other seventy also, and sent them two and two before

OTHER HEALING TEACHINGS

his face into every city and place, whither he himself would come. ... 9 And heal the sick that are therein, and say unto them, The kingdom of God is come nigh unto you. ... 17 And the seventy returned again with joy, saying, Lord, even the devils (*demons*) are subject unto us through thy name. 18 And he said unto them, I beheld Satan as lightning fall from heaven. 19 Behold (*make this change your life*), I give unto you *exousia*/power (*authority, commission and ability*) to tread on (*crush, destroy*) serpents and scorpions, and over all the *dunamis*/power (*ability*) of the enemy: and nothing shall by any means hurt you. 20 Notwithstanding in this rejoice not, that the spirits are subject unto you; but rather rejoice, because your names are written in heaven." As an agent of Heaven, you have all the resources of Heaven to get the job done.

Here the authority to heal the sick results in demons being cast out. So casting out demons and healings of all kind are the fruit of authority over demons or unclean spirits. In Luke 10:19, Jesus attributes all deadly evil in nature (poisonous and irritating snakes, spiders and scorpions) and, by inference, every evil work in the Earth, to the work of demon spirits. The answer to curing these evil works is to exercise authority by treading upon these spiritual beings in the name of Jesus, knowing you have authority, commission and all the resources of Heaven to back you. This treading can be one stomp of the foot or many stomps of the feet, in the same or in multiple situations, but the result is the lessening of demonic ability to hurt and kill people, and healing and restoration to wholeness from their evil effects.

Here we are told that our battle, our assigned task and war, is not against people, but the devil and his works: Eph 6:12 "For we wrestle not against flesh and blood, but against principalities, against powers, against the rulers of the darkness of this world, against spiritual wickedness in high places." James 4:7 "Submit yourselves therefore to God. Resist (*fight*) the devil, and he will flee from you."

These reiterate the summary of Jesus' ministry: Acts 10:38 "How God anointed Jesus of Nazareth with the Holy Ghost and with power: who went about doing good, and healing all that were oppressed (*under the active dominion, reign or lordship*) of the devil; for God was with him." Every act Jesus did was, in some way, an act of war against the devil and his works. This is God's definition of how we are to make peace and demonstrate or bring to pass peace, getting rid of the devil and his works. Since the devil is the enemy, and, yes, evil, what is not in Heaven cannot happen without the devil. We are sent by God to heal what the enemy does, to be God's peacemakers. Per the Great Commission, present day believers are to do and teach others to do what Jesus taught the first believers to do. If they healed, so should we.

~ 25 ~

ON DOING OUR PART

We have been given a job, and the Lord will not take our job from us. <u>Rom 11:29</u> "For the gifts and calling of God are without repentance." He will help you, but we have to do our job or calling. We are to exercise His authority on His behalf. So commanding healing, like the work of a police officer, is part of our job description. We are to lay hands on the sick, and we are to cast out devils. Everything else can be style. We can ask and require God to strengthen and enforce it; but we take responsibility and do our work, with Holy Spirit.

Look at Moses: <u>Ex 14:13</u> "And Moses said unto the people, Fear ye not, stand still, and see the salvation of the Lord, which he will shew to you to day: for the Egyptians whom ye have seen to day, ye shall see them again no more for ever. 14 The Lord shall fight for you, and ye shall hold your peace. 15 And the Lord said unto Moses, Wherefore criest thou unto me? speak unto the children of Israel, that they go forward: 16 but lift thou up thy rod, and stretch out thine hand over the sea, and divide it: and the children of Israel shall go on dry ground through the midst of the sea. ... 21 And Moses stretched out his hand over the sea; and the Lord caused the sea to go back by a strong east wind all that night, and made the sea dry land, and the waters were divided. 22 And the children of Israel went into the midst of the sea upon the dry ground: and the waters were a wall unto them on their right hand, and on their left."

Notice, between verses 14 and 15, Moses said God would fight for them, but God said, "Moses, you have to do something. I will fight, as you do your part in Me." Moses had to divide the sea with his hand and his rod, and then God

Other Healing Teachings

moved. Jesus said we have to *aiteo*/ask; we have to lay hands on sick people; then He can move. God fights for us and through us as His normal mode. The armies of Israel had to engage the enemy, soldier against soldier, sword against sword. God fought through them, to give them victory, but they had to engage and swing their swords. Even though each individual soldier had to face death at the hands of giants, God said: Ps 44:3 "We have heard with our ears, O God, our fathers have told us, what work thou didst in their days, in the times of old. 2 How thou didst drive out the heathen with thy hand, and plantedst them; how thou didst afflict the people, and cast them out. 3 For they got not the land in possession by their own sword, neither did their own arm save them: but thy right hand, and thine arm, and the light of thy countenance, because thou hadst a favour unto them." As each Israeli soldier swung his sword, God provided the strength in the midst of the battle, to cut down giants.

It is still the same way. We have to do our part. Eph 3:20 "Now unto him that is able to do exceeding abundantly above all that we *aiteo*/ask (*by demanding, expecting as due by covenant promise*) or think, according to the power that worketh in us, 21 unto him be glory in the church by Christ Jesus throughout all ages, world without end. Amen." As no labor in the Lord is in vain, keep at it, and you will see victory as a function of how much power you operate in. This book will help you increase in that *zoe*/life power. We are God's voice and His hands. Remember, this is a learn–and-then-go-do program.

Part of that learning is this: in spite of all you see that looks contrary, *lambano*/hold on to (as if your life depends upon it) the grace of God and the gift of righteousness in Jesus. This will determine how much we effectively reign/deliver the *agape*/love of God to others in healing or any other power of God. Rom 5:14 "Nevertheless death reigned (*as king, determining how death will work in poverty, famine, sickness and disease etc., to keep or enforce Hell on Earth*) from Adam to Moses, even over them that had not sinned after the similitude of Adam's transgression, who is the figure of him that was to come. 15 But not as the offence, so also is the free gift. For if through the offence of one many be dead, much more the grace of God, and the gift by grace, which is by one man, Jesus Christ, hath abounded unto many. 16 And not as it was by one that sinned, so is the gift: for the judgment was by one to condemnation, but the **free gift is of many offences unto justification.** 17 For if by one man's offence death reigned (*as king, determining what judgments will stand of death, such as sickness*) by one; much more they which (*continually*) **lambano/receive** abundance of **grace and** of the **gift of righteousness** shall reign (*as a king for Jesus doing the works of Jesus on the Earth in His place*) in *zoe*/life by one, Jesus Christ.) 18 Therefore as by the offence of one judgment came upon all men to condemnation; even so by the righteousness of one the free gift came upon all men unto justification (*just as if you had never sinned, or will ever sin again, to a full-status adopted son of*

God, where there is no divorce, being un-born again or loss of adoption to the level) of *zoe/* life. 19 For as by one man's disobedience many were made sinners, so by the obedience of one shall many be made righteous (*the right standing of God in Jesus with Himself*). 20 Moreover the law entered, that the offence might abound. But where sin abounded, grace did much more abound: 21 that as sin hath reigned (*as king enforcing death and misery wherever and however it can*) unto death (*by any form, fast or slow*), even so might grace reign (*as a king, for Jesus to do the works of Jesus to bring Heaven to Earth*) through righteousness (*this same right standing as Jesus has with God, as a free gift by believing in the blood of Jesus by faith and not by how well we obey God's laws or our own holiness*) unto eternal *zoe/life* (*that does everything from God's wisdom to raising the dead*) by Jesus Christ our Lord." Power is in knowing freely given grace and righteousness. Works you earn; grace is free, by faith.

We have two ways to release the power of God:
- By our own holiness of walking just like Jesus, as any other standard falls short of the mark and is sin; and
- By *lambano*ing the abundant grace of God and the gift of righteousness in Jesus.

Both rest on our confidence in God and not the level of power we have, for we have been given Holy Spirit, who is the power of God. Once you have Holy Spirit, there is not any other source to go to. You already have all the power there is. So any shortage of power is not in God, nor the devil, who must flee and cannot stop the power of God, but in our ability to release that saving power, to His glory. We are the gateway of power of and for God.

God will heal because He loves people. It is not about you, but God loving people just like He did with Jesus. With Holy Spirit in you, He is ready to heal right then. Get your eyes on how much God loves people and His love is the reason for healing, and you will see more of God's power delivered through you. Ps 103:3 "Who forgiveth all thine iniquities; who healeth all thy diseases; ... 6 The LORD executeth righteousness and judgment for all that are oppressed." Ps 72:4 "He shall judge the poor of the people, he shall save the children of the needy, and shall break in pieces the oppressor." Through Jesus, God has separated your lack of holiness from His desire to love. He does not focus on what He is going to remove out of your life; He focuses on what He has made you in Jesus. God is good; God is *agape/* love. This is not about you, but Him. Focus on His love for people and His power, and He can heal through you because of Jesus. You are just the gateway of power.

The devil wants you to be sin and failure conscious. Our ability to deliver the power of God, in spite of our sin-awareness, will depend on how well we *lambano/* receive the gift of righteousness to *zoe/*life by the indwelling of Holy Spirit. Jesus dwells in us by His Spirit, the same Spirit of glory and *zoe/*life that raised Him

OTHER HEALING TEACHINGS

from the dead and healed Him from taking upon Himself every sin of all mankind. Rom 4:24 "But for us also, to whom it shall be imputed (*righteousness*), if we believe on him that raised up Jesus our Lord from the dead; 25 who was delivered for our offences (*sins, failures*), and was raised again for (*to complete*) our justification (*when we were fully justified*)." So healing, or any grace of God, is just a manifestation of the fact that the sins of all mankind are forgiven/purged in the blood of Jesus and healed in the great work of God. The more we gladly magnify in our hearts the power and effectiveness of the work of Jesus, the Mighty Arm of God, the more we will effectively deliver the *zoe*/life of God to any situation, including healing, that we participate in.

Notice again the message that how well we *lambano* the gift of God, the more effectively we access the power of God in that gift. 1 Pet 4:8 "And above all things have fervent *agape*/charity among yourselves: for *agape*/charity shall cover the multitude of sins. ... 10 As every man **hath *lambano*/received the gift, even so minister the same** one to another, as good stewards of the manifold grace of God. 11 If any man speak, let him speak as the oracles (*prophet, preacher*) of God; if any man minister, let him do **it as of the (*totally unlimited*) ability which God giveth**: that God in all things may be glorified through Jesus Christ, to whom be praise and dominion for ever and ever. Amen." The name *Jesus* means: God's salvation now.

Our ability to work with Holy Spirit with gifts, or the Word of God in general, depends on how well we believe in the unseen results promised by God. Rom 12:6 "Having then gifts differing according to the grace that is given to us, whether prophecy, let us prophesy according to the proportion of faith." Notice we prophecy according to our faith, not according to what God has given, as we have been given grace to the measure of Christ. (Eph 4:7)

The power of the prophecy is up to the prophet, not God. But all the gifts come from Holy Spirit, so the level of the gift is not limited by God, but us, as Holy Spirit has/is all the power of God. 1 Cor 12:4 "Now there are diversities of gifts, but the same Spirit." You can operate by gift from Holy Spirit or by Holy Spirit, who has all the gifts. The best gift is the one needed for the situation. Since it is all by grace and not works, we have access to whatever is needed. Rom 3:24 "Being justified freely by his grace through the redemption that is in Christ Jesus:" Eph 4:7 "For unto every one of us is given grace according to the measure of the gift of Christ." Eph 1:19 "And what is the exceeding greatness of his power to us-ward who believe, according to the working of his mighty power, 20 which he wrought in Christ, when he raised him from the dead, and set him at his own right hand in the heavenly places."

2 Cor 6:1 "We then, as workers together with him, beseech you also that ye *lambano*/receive not the grace of God in vain (*this gift of righteousness in Jesus and salvation, where all the promises of God are yea and amen*). 2 (For he saith, I have heard

thee in a time accepted, and in the day of *soteria*/salvation have I succoured thee: behold, now is the accepted time; behold, now is the day of *soteria*/salvation.)" Again the message is: it is up to us to *lambano* the grace of God, and it takes work in building this faith in Jesus into yourself. 1 Cor 15:10 "But by the grace of God I am what I am: and his grace which was bestowed upon me was not in vain; but I laboured more abundantly than they all: yet not I, but the grace of God which was with me." Notice Paul was actively involved in the process.

Thus, we are to major on the messages of the New Testament letters, as this is where the grace of God is revealed. Col 1:25 "Whereof I (*Paul*) am made a minister, according to the dispensation of God which is given to me for you, to fulfil the word of God; 26 even the mystery which hath been hid from ages and from generations, but now is made manifest to his saints: 27 to whom God would make known what is the riches of the glory of this mystery among the Gentiles; **which is Christ in you, the hope of glory** (*the free reign of Holy Spirit in every part of life*): 28 whom we preach, warning every man, and teaching every man in all wisdom; that we may present every man perfect, *mature* in Christ Jesus (*in the spiritual standing of Christ before God and the right outworked life/walk by walking in the spirit*): 29 whereunto I also labour, striving according to his working, which worketh in me mightily." Eph 3:4 "Whereby, when ye read, ye may understand my knowledge in the mystery of Christ) 5 which in other ages was not made known unto the sons of men, **as it is now revealed** unto his holy apostles and prophets by the Spirit;" You will not find this detailed in the Old Testament. It is what Jesus came to bring.

Notice again it takes our diligence in knowing our sins are purged 2000 years ago to use the promises of God by faith to deliver the divine nature of God to the Earth. 2 Pet 1:2 "Grace (*the free ability of God to do and be the will of God in any situation*) and peace (*calm assurance that in any situation you deliver the zoe/life power of God to establish the Kingdom of God and shatter the devil and all his works in the name of Jesus, just as Jesus would do*) be multiplied unto you through the *epignosis*/knowledge of God, and of Jesus our Lord, 3 according as his divine power hath given unto us all things that pertain unto *zoe*/life and godliness, through the *epignosis*/ knowledge of him that hath called us to glory and virtue: 4 whereby are given unto us exceeding great and precious promises: that by these ye might be partakers of the divine nature, having escaped the corruption that is in the world through lust (*by the new birth*). 5 And beside this, **giving all diligence**, add to your faith virtue; and to virtue knowledge; 6 and to knowledge temperance; and to temperance patience; and to patience godliness; 7 and to godliness brotherly kindness; and to brotherly kindness *agape*/charity. 8 For if these things be in you, and abound, they make you that ye shall neither be barren nor unfruitful in the knowledge of our Lord Jesus Christ. 9 But he that lacketh these things is blind, and cannot see afar off, and hath forgotten that he was purged from his old sins. 10 Wherefore the rather,

OTHER HEALING TEACHINGS

brethren, **give diligence** to make your calling and election sure: for if ye do these things, ye shall never fall (*in producing the* zoe/*life of God in any situation you decide to fight in*)." We can fight in situations in which we find ourselves under dreadful fear pressure, or go, by *agape*/love, and find others in dreadful fear pressure of current evil conditions, and set them free. Both release the glory of God into the Earth, and, thus, build the Kingdom of God. God is *agape*/love, and as we are perfected in *agape*/love, we overcome all fear.

God's answer to everything is Holy Spirit and you working together with the Word of God to deliver zoe/life and make the Kingdom, the reign of God, effective. As you work with the grace of God, Holy Spirit, to accomplish this He will actually make the way more effective for you, as you work harder/diligently in these things. 2 Pet 1:11 "For so an entrance shall be ministered unto you abundantly into the everlasting kingdom of our Lord and Saviour Jesus Christ."

Holy Spirit says we can never tire of being reminded of these things. 2 Pet 1:12 "Wherefore I will not be negligent **to put you always in remembrance of these things**, though ye know them, and be established in the present truth (*of the Gospel of Jesus Christ*). 13 Yea, I think it meet, as long as I am in this tabernacle, to stir you up by putting you in remembrance." Heb 3:13 "But exhort one another (*daily in the grace of God and the gift of righteousness through the mighty and great work of God in Jesus*), while it is called To day (*the Day of Salvation in Jesus*); lest any of you be hardened through the deceitfulness of sin (*to not believing in the purging of our sins by the blood of Jesus and the gift of Holy Spirit dwelling in us, so that Jesus dwells in us by His Spirit for us to deliver the salvation of God in any situation, in the name of Jesus*). 14 For we are made partakers of Christ (*in our earthly walk to deliver* zoe/*life power into any situation*), if we hold the beginning of our confidence stedfast unto the end." This is not about Heaven, except the process of bringing Heaven to Earth. In Heaven the power and glory of God are freely flowing, with no sin, sickness, poverty or death. Our goal is to bring this to the Earth in each situation we find ourselves in or put ourselves in by *agape*/love. We can help bring the answer to: Matt 6:9 "… Our Father which art in heaven, Hallowed be thy name. 10 Thy kingdom come. Thy will be done in earth, as it is in heaven …."

It goes right back to how much we obey this scripture: Philem 6 "That the communication (*the outworked life*) of thy faith may become effectual (*potent in seeing the glory of God manifested in every situation you decide to fight in*) by the acknowledging of every good thing which is in you in Christ Jesus." Rom 5:17 "For if by one man's offence death reigned (*as king*) by one; much more they which (*continually*) lambano/receive abundance of grace and of the gift of righteousness shall reign (*as kings for Jesus*) in zoe/life by one, Jesus Christ.) 18 Therefore as by the offence of one judgment came upon all men to condemnation; even so by the righteousness of one the free gift came upon all men unto justification of zoe/life. 19 For as by one man's disobedience many were made sinners, so by the obedience of one shall many be made righteous. 20 Moreover the law entered, that the offence might abound. But where sin abounded, grace did much more abound: 21 that as sin hath reigned (*as king*) unto death (*in every slow and fast form possible*), even so might grace reign (*as a king for Jesus*) through righteousness unto eternal zoe/life (*total right wholeness of the peace of God*) by Jesus Christ our Lord." Heb 4:9 "There remaineth therefore a rest to the people of God. 10 For he that is entered into his rest, he also hath ceased from his own works, as God did from his. 11 Let us labour (*to* lambano *the grace of God and gift of righteousness in Jesus*) therefore to enter into that rest (*where God does His works through us*), lest any man fall after the same example of unbelief (*not believing by rejoicing that the impossible is possible through God*). 12 For the word of God is quick, and powerful, and sharper than any twoedged sword, piercing even to the dividing asunder of soul and spirit, and of the joints and marrow, and is a discerner of the thoughts and intents of the heart. 13 Neither is there any creature that is not manifest in his sight: but all things are naked and opened unto the eyes of him with whom we have to do. 14 Seeing then that we have a great high priest, that is passed into the heavens, Jesus the Son of God, let us hold fast our profession (*confession*). 15 For we have not an high priest which cannot be touched with the feeling of our infirmities; but was in all points tempted like as we are, yet without sin. 16 Let us therefore come boldly unto the throne of grace, that we may *lambano*/obtain [*hold on to in faith*] mercy (*the compassion actions that bring Heaven to Earth*, and find grace (*whatever gift is needed for the situation by indwelling Holy Spirit*) to help in time of need."

We have God in us! Lord Jesus, get me to cooperate with You. Thank You!

Our part includes reckoning the Word of God to be true in spite of the circumstances we see. This is walking in the Spirit versus the flesh. Gal 5:17 "For the flesh (*a mind governed only by the present circumstances*) lusteth (*intense passion*) against the Spirit (*a mind set on God's truth proclaiming that the evil circumstances have no right to be there because of the mighty work of Jesus*), and the Spirit against the flesh: and these are contrary the one to the other: so that ye cannot do the things that ye would (*because your born-again nature/spirit believes God in His Word and wants your mind to agree with God to change every evil situation into Heaven on Earth*)." Rom 8:5 "For they that are after the flesh (*minds governed by circumstances and not God's ways*) do mind the things of the flesh (*accepting every evil report as the way it will be, and there is no hope in God*); but they that are after the Spirit (*the Word of God*) the things of the Spirit (*the ways of God to bring* zoe/life *into every evil situation to God's glory, i.e. Heaven on Earth*). 6 For to be carnally minded (*governed only by what now is and without faith in God*) is death; but to be spiritually minded (*knowing God's Word is true and evil situations can change by calling those things that are not as if they are in the name of Jesus*) is zoe/life and peace. 7 Because the carnal mind (*set on only the evil circumstances*) is enmity against God: for it is not subject to the law of God, neither indeed can be. 8 So then they that are in the flesh (*governed only by the evil circumstances*) cannot please God. 9 But ye are not in the flesh, but in the Spirit (*you have Holy Spirit zoe/life available to heal every situation*), if so be that the Spirit of God dwell in you. Now if any man have not the Spirit of Christ, he is none of his. 10 And if Christ be in you, the body is dead because of sin; but the Spirit is *zoe*/life because of righteousness." So Father, get me to know what I am in Jesus so I cooperate with You. In the name of Jesus, thank You!

Our digging into the truth of God's Word in the face of evidence that says the contrary is what grows/matures us into Jesus. That evidence can be our own sin, the sin of others, sickness that seems to stay or problems in our own body or life that refuse to move. We can quote scripture without believing it. We can tell others what God says without it being our heart belief. But the longer and more frequently you quote it, sing it, speak it, shout it and meditate on it, you do drive it into your heart. The more you apply His truth to situations; you drive it into your heart. The more you go to God and work with Holy Spirit to break the hardness in your heart till His truth is your life, the deeper you drive it in. This entire book is designed to help drive His truth, grace and *agape*/love into our hearts. John 8:31 "Then said Jesus to those Jews which believed on him, If ye continue in my word, then are ye my disciples indeed; 32 and ye shall *ginosko*/know (*be aware of, perceive and understand*) the truth, and the truth shall make you free." John 8:47 "He that is of God heareth God's words (*to confident obedience, persuaded*): ye therefore hear them not (*to confident obedience, persuaded*), because ye are not [*coming from the direction or attitude*] of God." Col 3:1 "If ye then be risen with Christ, seek those things which are above, where Christ sitteth on the right hand of God. 2 Set your affection on things above, not on things on the earth. 3 For ye are dead, and your *zoe*/life is hid with Christ in God." Change your position to see well. Change to His position to see properly. Father, get me to see what You see! Thank You, in Jesus' name!

As our speaking matches up with our believing truth, God can move. It is because we know we are speaking for Him. Our faith is in God to perform His Word, and we keep believing, in persuaded confidence, His Word in spite of any present unhappy condition. Jer 1:12 "Then said the Lord unto me, You have seen well, for I will hasten (*am watching over*) My word to perform it." This is the Word on our lips and in our heart. John 1:12 "But as many as *lambano*/received him, to them gave he power (*authority*) to become the sons of God, even to them that believe on his name: 13 which were born, not of blood, nor of the will of the flesh, nor of the will of man, but of God." God chose you and re-created you, and is in you. He is with you and for you right now.

Now that we are born again and give God the glory for what that means, we implement that born-again status as we *lambano* the grace of God and the gift of righteousness, knowing: Rom 8:29 "For whom he did foreknow, he also did predestinate to be conformed to the image of his Son, that he might be the firstborn among many brethren. 30 Moreover whom he did predestinate, them he also called: and whom he called, them he also justified: and whom he justified, them he also glorified. 31 What shall we then say to these things? If God be for us, who can be against us? 32 He that spared not his own Son, but delivered him up for us all, how shall he not with him also freely give us all things? 33 Who shall lay any thing to the charge of God's elect? It is God that justifieth."

A child of 6 can lay hands on a cancer victim and, in the name of Jesus, command healing in a loud voice, and in 30 minutes watch the cancer fall off that face. Ever let this challenge you. It is not in all the details you know, but in the details of God in grace and truth you focus on in the situation. This is the heart of a believing child.

As an adult, at some point, you have got to make a decision you are going to believe God and be confident in Him to perform His Word, no matter what. You can act like it, refusing to be afraid, while feeling afraid. This is equal to courage, until you do walk in it freely. You must decide to stand and exert the authority God has given and make the devil leave, knowing God will back you up. Keep at it, and one day it will be a natural action, as part of who and what you are, an effective child of God who works by and with Holy Spirit in the name of Jesus. Mark 1:15 "And (*Jesus*) saying, The time is fulfilled, and the kingdom of God is at hand: repent ye, and believe the gospel." Luke 17:20 "And when he was demanded of the Pharisees, when the kingdom of God should come, he answered them and said, The kingdom of God cometh not with observation: 21 neither shall they say, Lo here! or, lo there! for, behold, the kingdom of God is within you." Luke 12:31 "But rather seek ye the kingdom of God; and all these things shall be added unto you. 32 Fear not, little flock; for it is your Father's good pleasure to give you the kingdom." Really believing the Gospel may be the greatest work we ever do.

The simple Gospel message means you no longer go anywhere else for purging of sins. Luke 24:46 "... Thus it is written, and thus it behoved Christ to suffer, and to rise from the dead the third day: 47 and that repentance and *unto/into* remission of sins should be preached in his name among all nations ... ." Repent for thinking that the Law or its sacrifices can save or prosper you. All eleven of the disciples and all the new converts after the Day of Pentecost knew they had denied and failed the Christ, yet within a few days they were working miracles, knowing how remitted their sins were. That is what awaits us as we *lambano* God. 2 Cor 6:1 "We then, as workers together with *God*, beseech you also that ye *lambano*/receive not the grace of God in vain." John 1:16 "And of his (*Jesus'*) fulness have all we *lambano*/received, and grace for grace. 17 For the law (*how to live in holiness*) was given by Moses, but grace and truth (*Christ in you the hope of glory by faith independent of your right works or sins*) came by Jesus Christ."

OTHER HEALING TEACHINGS

All of this is part of the process of renewing our minds. We are to work with Holy Spirit to renew our minds into the reality of what Father God has done for us in Jesus. Eph 4:17 "This I say therefore, and testify in the Lord, that ye henceforth walk not as other Gentiles walk, in the vanity of their mind, 18 having the understanding darkened, being alienated from the *zoe*/life of God through the ignorance that is in them, because of the blindness of their heart: 19 who being past feeling have given themselves over unto lasciviousness, to work all uncleanness with greediness. 20 But ye have not so learned Christ; 21 if so be that ye have heard him, and have been taught by him, as the truth is in Jesus: 22 that ye put off concerning the former conversation the old man, which is corrupt according to the deceitful lusts; 23 and be renewed in the spirit of your mind; 24 and that ye put on the new man, which after God is created in righteousness and true holiness." We do the putting off of the old (sin, fear and lust–driven self) and put on the new man made like Jesus. This is most effective when done with thankful intensity. The putting off can be rather short while you major on the praise, thanksgiving and rejoicing of the "putting on" the new man in Jesus.

So our true born-again nature is to walk like Jesus in every way. We are required to recognize when we are not walking like Jesus, cast off the bonds of the devil, and re-establish in our hearts that our true born-again nature is just like Jesus in every way. Rom 13:14 "But put ye on the Lord Jesus Christ, and make not provision for the flesh, to fulfil the lusts thereof." Walk in the new man you are. Eph 5:8 "For ye were sometimes darkness, but now are ye light in the Lord: walk as children of light." Start acting like Jesus would.

The work in Jesus is complete, and God is waiting on us to make the next move. As we move in His direction, He gives more grace for us to keep moving toward Him. James 4:6 "But he giveth more grace. Wherefore he saith, God resisteth the proud, but giveth grace unto the humble. 7 Submit yourselves therefore to God. Resist the devil, and he will flee from you. 8 Draw nigh to God, and he will draw nigh to you. Cleanse your hands, ye sinners; and purify your hearts, ye double minded. 9 Be afflicted, and mourn, and weep: let your laughter be turned to mourning, and your joy to heaviness. 10 Humble yourselves in the sight of the Lord, and he shall lift you up."

God has already spoken in Jesus. He (God) is not the limitation. Heb 1:1 "God, who at sundry times and in divers manners spake in time past unto the fathers by the prophets, 2 hath in these last days spoken unto us by his Son, whom he hath appointed heir of all things, by whom also he made the worlds; 3 who being the brightness of his glory, and the express image of his person, and upholding all things by the word of his power, when he had by himself purged our sins, sat down on the right hand of the Majesty on high." How Jesus healed in the gospels is the same as what He will do for and through us.

Any limitation we may have is in our confidence in the fact that God hears us. 1 John 5:9 "If we receive the witness of men, the witness of God is greater: for this is the witness of God which he hath testified of his Son. 10 He that believeth on the Son of God hath the witness in himself: he that believeth not God hath made him a liar; because he believeth not the record that God gave of his Son. 11 And this is the record, that God hath given to us eternal *zoe*/life, and this *zoe*/life is in his Son. 12 He that hath the Son hath *zoe*/life; and he that hath not the Son of God hath not *zoe*/life. 13 These things have I written unto you that believe on the name of the Son of God; that ye may know that ye have eternal *zoe*/life, and that ye may believe on the name of the Son of God. 14 And this is **the confidence** that we have in him, that, if we *aiteo*/ask any thing according to his will, he heareth us: 15 and **if we know that he hear us**, whatsoever we *aiteo*/ask, **we know that we have** the petitions that we *aiteo*/desired of him. [*We are to use this power in this way:*] 16 If any man see his brother sin a sin which is not unto death [*this includes sickness, lack, etc.*], he shall *aiteo*/ask, and he shall give him *zoe*/life for them ... ."

The healing results we get depends on what we believe at the moment we exercise the healing ministry. Ignore other people, the past or the future, and focus on the now like a child confident in God, believing that God will do it as you command for Him without fear or dread. Focus on the fact that God is greater than the evil of the situation, He hates the evil in that situation, He already gave Jesus as a price for the healing, He is able, He will do it, He *agape*/loves the sick person, and He will move as you *aiteo* His truth—whether it is in the laying on of hands or speaking the word over a phone or writing it in a letter or email. At that moment, you must be like Abraham: Rom 4:18 "Who against hope (*wanting it to be,*) believed (*that he would have it anyway in spite of all the hindrances*) in hope, that he might become the father of many nations; according to that which was spoken, So shall thy seed be. 19 And being not weak in faith, he considered not his own body now dead, when he was about an hundred years old, neither yet the deadness of Sara's womb: 20 he staggered not at the promise of God through unbelief (*unpersuadableness*); but was strong in faith, giving glory (*thanks, praise and joy*) to God; 21 and being fully persuaded that, what he had promised, he was able also to perform." You will get the result you are believing for. The more you believe God for right now, the more you will see it "right now" (in a minute, an hour or up to 3 days).

The issue is this: if you are persuaded, mind renewed, that at that moment God can fully heal, make whole, deliver, etc., based on His promise right then, it will happen right then because you *aiteo*/demanded it of Him. If you believe that it will be by degree, then it will be by degree. It is determined by how persuaded in God you are. That is the purpose of all the teaching and scriptures in this manual, to get and keep you persuaded into God's simple truth for right now.

The pre-written prayers in this manual are to give you a starting place. The exact words do not matter. Just express what you are believing for at that moment. This is what Jesus referred to when He said: Matt 7:22 "Many will say to me in that day, Lord, Lord, have we not prophesied in thy name? and in thy name have cast out devils? and in thy name done many *dunamis*/wonderful (*God's power*) works? 23 And then will I profess unto them, I never knew you: depart from me, ye that work iniquity." This is far more mechanical than many teach.

Notice, they did powerful signs, but they did not have a right relationship with Jesus. They could exercise the power of God by the name of Jesus, but did not also seek after the *agape*/love of God, and yet the person they ministered to received the power of God anyway. Acts 3:12 "And when Peter saw it, he answered unto the people, Ye men of Israel, why marvel ye at this? or why look ye so earnestly on us, as though by our own power or holiness we had made this man to walk? ... 16 And his name through faith in his name hath made this man strong, whom ye see and know: yea, the faith which is by him hath given him this perfect soundness in the presence of you all."

Look at the faith attitude of Jesus: John 8:29 "And he that sent me is with me: the Father hath not left me alone; for I do always those things that please him." Jesus knew that every act He did that was recorded in the Bible was pleasing to God, including healing the sick and raising the dead. And it takes faith to please God. Heb 11:6 "But without faith it is impossible to please him: for he that cometh to God must believe that he is, and that he is a rewarder of them that diligently seek him."

The result was God did the miracles through Jesus, the Son of Man. John 5:19 "Then answered Jesus and said unto them, Verily, verily, I say unto you, The Son can do nothing of himself, but what he seeth the Father do: for what things soever he doeth, these also doeth the Son likewise." John 14:10 "Believest thou not that I am in the Father, and the Father in me? the words that I speak unto you I speak not of myself: but the Father that dwelleth in me, he doeth the works." Jesus kept the ability and willingness of Father God in His mind over the present evil condition.

We see Jesus in operation at the grave of Lazarus: John 11:41 "Then they took away the stone from the place where the dead was laid. And Jesus lifted up his eyes, and said, **Father, I thank thee that thou hast heard me. 42 And I knew that thou hearest me always**: but because of the people which stand by I said it, that they may believe that thou hast sent me. 43 And when he thus had spoken, he cried with a loud voice, Lazarus, come forth." Notice Jesus knew Father God heard Him always and so, other than shouting (which focuses and gets the fight, or intensity, up in your heart), His confidence was in the fact that His command was pleasing to Father God, and Lazarus would come forth by God's power. We need the same confidence of being fully persuaded that God is able to and will do what we *aiteo* because we speak for Him and He hears us.

Our greatest limitation is believing we are not worthy or somehow out of sync with God in healing. To overcome this, you must work to know you are justified by faith in the resurrection and the blood of Jesus. Rom 5:1 "Therefore being justified by faith, we have peace with God through our Lord Jesus Christ: 2 by whom also we have access by faith into this grace wherein we stand, and rejoice in hope of the glory of God. ... 15 But not as the offence, so also is the free gift. For if through the offence of one many be dead, much more the grace of God, and the gift by grace, which is by one man, Jesus Christ, hath abounded unto many. 16 And not as it was by one that sinned, so is the gift: for the judgment was by one to condemnation, but the free gift is of many offences unto justification. 17 For if by one man's offence death reigned [*as a king for hell*] by one; much more they which (*continually*) lambano/receive abundance of grace and of the (*free*) gift of righteousness shall reign [*as kings for Heaven*] in zoe/life by one, Jesus Christ.) 18 Therefore as by the offence of one judgment came upon all men to condemnation; even so by the righteousness of one the free gift came upon all men unto justification of zoe/life. 19 For as by one man's disobedience many were made sinners, so by the obedience of one shall many be made righteous. 20 Moreover the law entered, that the offence might abound. But where sin abounded, grace did much more abound: 21 that as sin hath reigned [*as king*] unto death, even so might grace reign [*as a king for Jesus*] through righteousness unto eternal zoe/life by Jesus Christ our Lord." Col 1:12 "Giving thanks (*continually*) unto the Father, which hath made us meet (*qualified*) to be partakers of the inheritance of the saints in light."

Rom 5:17 makes it clear that it depends on how well you *lambano*/hold on to, no matter what, God's new creation free gift of righteousness unto *zoe*/life and grace in peace with God unto *soteria*/salvation (we are saved by grace through faith). God has done His part; now we have to be fully persuaded and stay that way. Others can help, but you must work in the Gospel to let Holy Spirit convince you from the Scriptures and not let the grace of God go to waste in your life. 2 Cor 5:20 "Now then we are ambassadors for Christ, as though God did beseech you by us: we pray you in Christ's stead, be ye reconciled to God. 21 For he hath made him to be sin for us, who knew no sin; that we might be made the righteousness of God in him. 6:1 We then, as workers together with him, beseech you also that ye receive not the grace of God in vain. 2 (For he saith, I have heard thee in a time accepted, and in the day of *soteria*/salvation have I succoured thee: behold (*make this change your life*), now is the accepted time; behold, now is the day of *soteria*/salvation.)" *Lambano* is another way of saying to renew your mind into the truth of the Gospel of our salvation by grace in Jesus.

Power for healing is not about your holiness or how well you know Jesus. It is what you are really believing at that moment. Dr. Lake said there are two parts: faith and power, with faith as the more important. Power determines how much

Other Healing Teachings

zoe/life is released; faith releases and pushes it. If you can believe God (Father, Son or Spirit) is able and will do it right then, then He will move through you right then. Father God paid the beyond-measure greater price of Jesus for this healing 2000 years ago, but He is limited to what you believe in the moment. Right teaching will get rid of the doctrines that limit your believing. The pre-written prayers in this manual will keep your mind focused on the key issues, as you war, especially in crisis.

If the need is urgent and you do not see the results you need, you have two immediate choices:
- Keep praying and release what *zoe*/life you can to keep the one you are ministering to alive and eventually get them healed, and/or
- While in the battle build your believing by getting yourself more fully persuaded, as did Abraham, to *lambano* the abundance of grace and the gift of righteousness of God in Christ. Know the promises and our redemption in the blood of Jesus and our adoption to remove every doubt you have as to why God will not do it, so He is fully able in your heart to do it, and then minister again, with *aiteo*, for the devil to go and the healing to come.

Either way is to operate in agreement with Holy Spirit. This manual is designed so you can do both at once, when you must have results. Confidence simply means to refuse to let dreadful fear rule. You may be harassed with multiple levels of fear, but you only focus on the stripes He took, the blood Jesus shed to pay for healing, Jesus' resurrection and glorification, and His *agape*/love.

The third choice is to start now and become proficient in believing God for healing now. Per various videos I have seen (some of them on YouTube.com), Todd White started by praying for 6 to 8 people every day for about 3 months before he saw his first immediate answer. That was some 500 apparent failures (often people may get healed days or months later, but he did not see it). Each day Todd studied the Scriptures and kept renewing his mind, along with regular fasting and prayer. Todd now sees 30 to hundreds healed every day. When Curry Blake started his active ministry in around 1995, he got about 50% of the people healed, using his more forceful style, and, by several weeks was at 75% or so. He now reports that he operates at better than 95% of full healings. The difference came when Curry got Dr. Lake's teaching and then continued with practice and scripture study. Roger Sapp started by believing for healing, using the same techniques his Methodist group employed for renewing minds. This included much scripture memorization and repetition. Rev. Sapp reports that he started to see healing results within 3 years, and he now operates full-time in healing. For all three of these men, if they do not see immediate prayer results, they keep at it as long as others will let them. In none of them was there a special healing anointing, gifting or touch, just obedience to the practice defined in the Scriptures–"labor to enter in." This requires continually mixing the Word of God with faith.

Battle Prayer for Divine Healing: Field Manual 2

These other methods were available to the Jews before the Day of Pentecost, but unique to after that Day of Pentecost is the free use of the gift of tongues. So another way to increase the Holy Spirit power we operate in is to speak in tongues. 1 Cor 14:4 "He that speaketh in an unknown tongue edifieth himself … ." Notice this implies either making your spirit stronger and more intense, your soul more accommodating to Holy Spirit in your heart, your soul more able to listen in glad agreement when Holy Spirit speaks, or some combination of all three. For soul work, this means the leverage point, fulcrum or portal, is with the Scriptures already in your heart (subconscious mind) or currently controlling your mind (cognitive mind).

That word *"edifieth,"* and, thus, the benefits of using the gift of tongues includes:
- Strengthening against pressure to break or give up,
- Increase in power, energy, capacity and ability,
- Ability to resist and win,
- Ability to exhort and encourage others,
- Ability to carry others,
- Ability to overcome, remove or destroy,
- Ability to have patience until things do make sense,
- Ability to endure longer than your enemy to victory,
- Build your life in God's direction and plan for you,
- Clearing out any hindrances in your soul (right purging),
- Ability to understand and keep the Word of God better,
- Ability to believe God and His promises in a greater way, and
- Ability to keep yourself in the agape love of God better.

Since power is about intensity, then the more intense your tongues (loud, hard and fast) the more effective you will be in building power and confidence in God. Many recommend a believer spend at least 2 hours a day in hard, fast and loud tongues, to remain strong in Spirit. While 4 or more hours is better, this may take some practice, so work up to it gradually.

When we are speaking in tongues, Holy Spirit is speaking through us in perfect prayer to God, for what needs to be done by God's priorities. This will not stop doubts, temptations, tests and trials, but over time with diligence, it will change how you respond to them.

As to your doubts, seek the Lord to show you where you are blocked. Get His wisdom in you. For sure, the answer is in Jesus. 1 Cor 1:30 "But of him are ye in Christ Jesus, who of God is made unto us wisdom, and righteousness, and sanctification, and redemption." Col 2:2 "That their hearts might be comforted (*strengthened and encouraged into right thinking and action*), being knit together in *agape*/love, and unto all riches of the full assurance of understanding, to the acknowledgement of the mystery of God, and of the Father, and of Christ; 3 in whom are hid all the treasures of wisdom and knowledge." Heb 12:2 "Looking (*with a steady gaze where everything*

OTHER HEALING TEACHINGS

else pales in comparison and, thus, commands your whole attention) unto Jesus the author and finisher of our faith; who for the joy that was set before him endured the cross, despising the shame, and is set down at the right hand of the throne of God." We heal or are healed by grace, a gift of love. Speak to that mountain in *aiteo*.

Look to Jesus in the Scriptures, especially the gospels. See yourself acting as Jesus would. Do not look at the faith (if any) of the people He ministered to. Only look to Jesus. He is your example. Jesus recognized faith, but He was not limited by its absence or presence. 2 Cor 3:17 "Now the Lord is that Spirit: and where the Spirit of the Lord is, there is liberty [*for God to bring Heaven on Earth through you*]. 18 But we all, with open face beholding as in a glass (*mirror*) the glory of the Lord [*resident in you and coming out through you to release Heaven into Earth in any situation*], are changed into the same image [*of Jesus in you, the realized hope of glory*] from glory to glory, even as by the Spirit of the Lord." 2 Cor 4:6 "For God, who commanded the light to shine out of darkness, hath shined in our hearts, to give the light of the knowledge of the glory of God in the face of Jesus Christ. 7 But we have this treasure in earthen vessels, that the excellency of the *dunamis*/power may be of God, and not of us." Eph 4:13 "Till we all come in the unity of the faith, and of the knowledge of the Son of God, unto a perfect man, unto the measure of the stature of the fulness of Christ: 14 that we henceforth be no more children, tossed to and fro, and carried about with every wind of doctrine, by the sleight of men, and cunning craftiness, whereby they lie in wait to deceive; 15 but speaking the truth in *agape*/love, may grow up into him in all things, which is the head, even Christ." Col 2:6 "As ye have therefore received Christ Jesus the Lord, so walk ye in him." It is up to us to *lambano* Christ in us.

We must continually pray: Eph 1:18 "The eyes of your understanding being enlightened; that ye may know what is the hope of his calling, and what the riches of the glory of his inheritance in the saints, 19 and what is the exceeding greatness of his *dunamis*/power to us-ward who believe, according to the working of his mighty *dunamis*/power, 20 which he wrought in Christ, when he raised him from the dead, and set him at his own right hand in the heavenly places, 21 far above all principality, and power, and might, and dominion, and every name that is named, not only in this world, but also in that which is to come: 22 and hath put all things under his feet, and gave him to be the head over all things to the church, 23 which is his body, the fulness of him that filleth all in all."

~ 26 ~

ON WHO DOES THE HEALING

Jesus made it clear that, in His ministry prior to the cross, He did not do the healings and other such works; His Father did them. John 14:8 "Philip saith unto him, Lord, shew us the Father, and it sufficeth us. 9 Jesus saith unto him, Have I been so long time with you, and yet hast thou not known me, Philip? he that hath seen me hath seen the Father; and how sayest thou then, Shew us the Father? 10 Believest thou not that I am in the Father, and the Father in me? the words that I speak unto you I speak not of myself: but the Father that dwelleth in me, he doeth the works. 11 Believe me that I am in the Father, and the Father in me: or else believe me for the very works' sake."

John 5:17 "But Jesus answered them, My Father worketh hitherto, and I work. 18 Therefore the Jews sought the more to kill him, because he not only had broken the sabbath, but said also that God was his Father, making himself equal with God. 19 Then answered Jesus and said unto them, Verily, verily, I say unto you, The Son can do nothing of himself, but what he seeth the Father do: for what things soever he doeth, these also doeth the Son likewise. 20 For the Father *agape/loveth* the Son, and sheweth him all things that himself doeth: and he will shew him greater works than these, that ye may marvel. 21 For as the Father raiseth up the dead, and quickeneth them; even so the Son quickeneth whom he will. 22 For the Father judgeth no man, but hath committed all judgment (*including against the devil in healing, deliverance, signs and wonders*) unto the Son." Acts 2:22 "Ye men of Israel, hear these words; Jesus of Nazareth, a man approved of God among you by miracles and wonders and signs, which God did by him in the midst of you, as ye yourselves also know."

OTHER HEALING TEACHINGS

When the woman with the issue of blood touched Jesus' garment, Jesus, other than as a right-thinking vessel of God, did not participate in the healing. Father God approved her faith and healed her by His vessel of Holy Spirit, Jesus. He [Jesus] felt the *dunamis* power or virtue go out, but He did not know about it until after the fact had been done by Father God. Mark 5:27 "When she had heard of Jesus, came in the press behind, and touched his garment. 28 For she said, If I may touch but his clothes, I shall be whole. 29 And straightway the fountain of her blood was dried up; and she felt in her body that she was healed of that plague. 30 And Jesus, immediately knowing in himself that *dunamis*/virtue had gone out of him, turned him about in the press, and said, Who touched my clothes? 31 And his disciples said unto him, Thou seest the multitude thronging thee, and sayest thou, Who touched me? 32 And he looked round about to see her that had done this thing."

Part of the language of God is the miracles He does to confirm His Word. Heb 1:1 "God, who at sundry times and in divers manners spake in time past unto the fathers by the prophets, 2 hath in these last days spoken unto us by his Son, whom he hath appointed heir of all things, by whom also he made the worlds."

Heb 2:3 "How shall we escape, if we neglect so great *soteria*/salvation; which at the first began to be spoken by the Lord, and was confirmed unto us by them that heard him; 4 God also bearing them witness, both with signs and wonders, and with divers miracles, and gifts of the Holy Ghost, according to his own will?"

Jesus told the leper that His purpose and delight was to heal people: Matt 8:2 "And, behold, there came a leper and worshipped him, saying, Lord, if thou wilt, thou canst make me clean. 3 And Jesus put forth his hand, and touched him, saying, I will; be thou clean. And immediately his leprosy was cleansed." The Greek in this passage is very emphatic. When Jesus said, "I will" a more accurate translation would be, "Yes, I delight to do it. This is why I came, this is what I do, and I live to do this." In this, He was the agent of God, knowing God's will, and eager and glad to deliver God's will. This is His attitude and His desire, and He changes not. Heb 13:8 "Jesus Christ the same yesterday, and to day, and for ever."

Now Jesus, from His exalted position at the right hand of the Father, has been glorified and, as the Administrator of Holy Spirit, does the healing though those who will use His name. John 14:12 "Verily, verily, I say unto you, He that believeth on me, the works that I do shall he do also; and greater works than these shall he do; because I go unto my Father. 13 And whatsoever ye shall *aiteo*/ask (*require, demand and expect as due by covenant promise*) in my name, that will I do, that the Father may be glorified in the Son. 14 If ye shall *aiteo*/ask (*require, demand and expect as due by covenant promise*) any thing in my name, I will do it."

When we get others healed in the name Jesus, it is Jesus who does the healing by Holy Spirit from the Father. God (Father, Son and Spirit) does the healing through you. Jesus is working through us, as members of His Body, and we cooperate with Him to deliver the healing He already obtained. Acts 4:29 "And now, Lord (*Father God*), behold their threatenings: and grant unto thy servants, that with all boldness they may speak thy word, 30 by stretching forth thine hand to heal; and that signs and wonders may be done by the name of thy holy child Jesus." Acts 14:3 "Long time therefore abode they speaking boldly in the Lord, which gave testimony unto the word of his grace, and granted signs and wonders to be done by their hands." James 5:15 "And the prayer of faith shall *sozo*/save the sick, and the Lord shall raise him up; and if he have committed sins, they shall be forgiven him." Acts 9:34 "And Peter said to him, Aeneas, Jesus Christ (the Messiah) [now] makes you whole. Get up and make your bed! And immediately [Aeneas] stood up." AMP Mark 16:19 "So then after the Lord had spoken unto them, he was received up into heaven, and sat on the right hand of God. 20 And they went forth, and preached everywhere, the Lord working with them, and confirming the word with signs following. Amen."

It is the name of Jesus that gives us access to God to both call on and deliver His power, as needed. Just like Father God needed a man, Jesus, to deliver His healing, Jesus now needs us, His Body on Earth, to do our part. Acts 3:12 "And when Peter saw it, he answered unto the people, Ye men of Israel, why marvel ye at this? or why look ye so earnestly on us, as though by our own power or holiness we had made this man to walk? 13 The God of Abraham, and of Isaac, and of Jacob, the God of our fathers, hath glorified his Son Jesus; whom ye delivered up, and denied him in the presence of Pilate, when he was determined to let him go. 14 But ye denied the Holy One and the Just, and desired a murderer to be granted unto you; 15 and killed the Prince of *zoe*/life, whom God hath raised from the dead; whereof we are witnesses. 16 And his name through faith in his name hath made this man strong, whom ye see and know: yea, the faith which is by him hath given him this perfect soundness in the presence of you all." Acts 4:9 "If we this day be examined of the good deed done to the impotent man, by what means he is made whole; 10 be it known unto you all, and to all the people of Israel, that by the name of Jesus Christ of Nazareth, whom ye crucified, whom God raised from the dead, even by him doth this man stand here before you whole. 11 This is the stone which was set at nought of you builders, which is become the head of the corner. 12 Neither is there *soteria*/salvation in any other: for there is none other name under heaven given among men, whereby we must be *sozo*/saved (*made whole, healed, delivered, rescued, set free and unbound*)."

Using the name of Jesus and knowing Jesus are two different things, but using the name of Jesus as the Lord Almighty and having faith in that name, independent of your personal relationship with Him, is the basis of divine healing in our age. Matt 7:22 "Many will say to me in that day, Lord, Lord, have we not prophesied

Other Healing Teachings

in thy name? and in thy name have cast out devils? and in thy name done many wonderful works? 23 And then will I profess unto them, I never knew you: depart from me, ye that work iniquity." So, once again, healing and miracles are not part of holiness, per Acts 3:12, or how well you know Jesus.

It is the name of Jesus and faith in His name that release Holy Spirit to heal. Mark 9:38 "And John answered him, saying, Master, we saw one casting out devils in thy name, and he followeth not us: and we forbad him, because he followeth not us. 39 But Jesus said, Forbid him not: for there is no man which shall do a miracle in my name, that can lightly speak evil of me. 40 For he that is not against us is on our part." Luke 9:49 "And John answered and said, Master, we saw one casting out devils in thy name; and we forbad him, because he followeth not with us. 50 And Jesus said unto him, Forbid him not: for he that is not against us is for us." This one had learned how to use the name of Jesus, even though he was definitely not one of Jesus' recognized disciples. One conclusion is that healing, signs and wonders may not be a sign of one's holiness but, rather, the ability of one to believe in the power of the name of Jesus.

1 John 5:12 "He that hath the Son hath *zoe*/life; and he that hath not the Son of God hath not *zoe*/life. 13 These things have I written unto you that believe on the name of the Son of God; that ye may know that ye have eternal *zoe*/life, and that ye may believe on the name of the Son of God." Here God specifically requests us to use the name of Jesus. 1 John 5:14 "And this is the confidence that we have in him, that, if we *aiteo*/ask (*require, demand and expect as due*) any thing according to his will (*which includes all His covenant promises*), he heareth us: 15 and if we know that he hear us, whatsoever we *aiteo*/ask (*require, demand and expect as due by covenant promise*), we know that we have the petitions that we desired of him."

God gave His name as His presence, awareness and point of power to Israel. They had the name before they built the temple and wanted the name to be in the temple. 1 Kings 8:27 "But will God indeed dwell on the earth? behold, the heaven and heaven of heavens cannot contain thee; how much less this house that I have builded? 28 Yet have thou respect unto the prayer of thy servant (*Solomon*), and to his supplication, O LORD my God, to hearken unto the cry and to the prayer, which thy servant prayeth before thee to day: 29 that thine eyes may be open toward this house night and day, even toward the place of which thou hast said, My name shall be there: that thou mayest hearken unto the prayer which thy servant shall make toward this place. 30 And hearken thou to the supplication of thy servant, and of thy people Israel, when they shall pray toward this place: and hear thou in heaven thy dwelling place: and when thou hearest, forgive."

The temple in Jerusalem became the place where a believer could know that God, by His name, dwelt and would answer prayer. Ps 118:11 "They compassed me about; yea, they compassed me about: but in the name of the LORD I will destroy them." Ps 124:8 "Our help is in the name of the Lord, who made heaven and earth." Prov 18:10 "The name of the Lord is a strong tower: the righteous runneth into it, and is safe."

Now we Christians, individually and corporately, are the dwelling place of God. 1 Cor 3:16 "Know ye not that ye are the temple of God, and that the Spirit of God dwelleth in you?" 2 Tim 1:14 "That good thing which was committed unto thee keep by the Holy Ghost which dwelleth in us." Rom 8:11 "But if the Spirit of him that raised up Jesus from the dead dwell in you, he that raised up Christ from the dead shall also quicken your [*current*] mortal bodies by his Spirit that dwelleth in you." Eph 1:13 "In whom ye also trusted, after that ye heard the word of truth, the gospel of your *soteria*/salvation: in whom also after that ye believed, ye were sealed with that holy Spirit of promise." Eph 4:30 "And grieve not the holy Spirit of God, whereby ye are sealed unto the day of redemption."

So wherever a Christian is, Holy Spirit is, and we release Him by using the name of the Lord Jesus, who was declared Lord and Christ by Father God when He sent His Spirit on the Day of Pentecost. Acts 2:21 "And it shall come to pass, that whosoever shall call on the name of the Lord shall be *sozo*/saved. 22 Ye men of Israel, hear these words; Jesus of Nazareth, a man approved of God among you by miracles and wonders and signs, which God did by him in the midst of you, as ye yourselves also know: 23 him, being delivered by the determinate counsel and foreknowledge of God, ye have taken, and by wicked hands have crucified and slain: 24 whom God hath raised up, having loosed the pains of death: because it was not possible that he should be holden of it. ... 33 Therefore being by the right hand of God exalted, and having received of the Father the promise of the Holy Ghost, he hath shed forth this, which ye now see and hear. 34 For David is not ascended into the heavens: but he saith himself, The Lord said unto my Lord, Sit thou on my right hand, 35 until I make thy foes thy footstool. 36 Therefore let all the house of Israel know assuredly, that God hath made that same Jesus, whom ye have crucified, both Lord and Christ." So calling on the name of Jesus is the same as calling on the name of the Lord. John 15:7 "If ye abide in me, and my words abide in you, ye shall *aiteo*/ask (*require, demand and expect as due by covenant promise*) what ye will, and it shall be done unto you. 8 Herein is my Father glorified, that ye bear much fruit; so shall ye be my disciples." So we use the name of Jesus to access healing. It becomes our point of faith. In that name, we speak, lay hands on the sick or give prayer cloths, and Father God does the healing.

We each have our part to play, but Jesus did not say, "Pray and see what happens." Instead He said: Matt 10:8 "Heal the sick, cleanse the lepers, raise the dead, cast out devils: freely ye have received, freely give." Luke 9:2 "And he sent them to preach the kingdom of God, and to heal the sick." Luke 10:8 "And into whatsoever city ye enter, and they receive you, eat such things as are set before you: 9 and heal the sick that are therein, and say unto them, The kingdom of God is come nigh unto you." *Lambano*/keep confidence in God.

The message is clear; we have our part to play. God has limited Himself to man working with God as co-laborers to produce the results of God in the Earth in this, the Day of Salvation. Here Holy Spirit describes Philip as the one doing the miracles. Acts 8:5 "Then Philip went down to the city of Samaria, and preached Christ unto them. 6 And the people with one accord gave heed unto those things which Philip spake, hearing and seeing the miracles which he did." So it is using the name of Jesus and having faith in that name that is our part. We think, speak and lay hands on the sick, and Jesus, as Administrator of Holy Spirit, assures the works are done through the Father by Holy Spirit.

We are to exert the authority He has given against the devil and get the job done. Luke 10:19 "Behold (*appreciate, understand and make this change your life*), I give (*have given*) unto you power (*authority, commission, ability and the resources of Heaven*) to tread on serpents and scorpions, and over all the power (*ability and works*) of the enemy: and nothing shall by any means hurt you. 20 Notwithstanding in this rejoice not, that the spirits are subject unto you; but rather rejoice, because your names are written in heaven." Matt 28:18 "And Jesus came and spake unto them, saying, All power is given unto me in heaven and in earth. 19 Go ye therefore, and teach all nations, baptizing them in the name of the Father, and of the Son, and of the Holy Ghost: 20 teaching them to observe all things whatsoever I have commanded you: and, lo, I am with you alway, even unto the end of the world. Amen." Mark 16:13 "And they went and told it unto the residue: neither believed they them. 14 Afterward he appeared unto the eleven as they sat at meat, and upbraided them with their unbelief and hardness of heart, because they believed not them which had seen him after he was risen. 15 And he said unto them, Go ye into all the world, and preach the gospel to every creature. 16 He that believeth and is baptized shall be *sozo*/saved; but he that believeth not shall be damned. 17 And these signs shall follow them that believe; In my name shall they cast out devils; they shall speak with new tongues; 18 they shall take up serpents; and if they drink any deadly thing, it shall not hurt them; they shall lay hands on the sick, and they shall recover. 19 So then after the Lord had spoken unto them, he was received up into heaven, and sat on the right hand of God. 20 And they went forth, and preached everywhere, the Lord working with them, and confirming the word with signs following. Amen."

~ 27 ~

ON PROPITIATION AND COMMUNION

The great work of God was Jesus' propitiation through the cross. God did not even start creating the Earth until He had already resolved sin and the curse of sin. His plan was that Jesus was to die and resolve all sin and the effects of sin by redemption through His blood and it was decided before the foundation of the Earth was ever laid.

2 Tim 1:8 "… but be thou partaker of the afflictions of the gospel according to the power of God; 9 who hath *sozo*/saved us, and called us with an holy calling, not according to our works, but according to his own purpose and grace, which was given us in Christ Jesus before the world began, 10 but is now made manifest by the appearing of our Saviour Jesus Christ, who hath abolished death, and hath brought *zoe*/life and immortality to light through the gospel."

1 Pet 1:18 "Forasmuch as ye know that ye were not redeemed with corruptible things, as silver and gold, from your vain conversation received by tradition from your fathers; 19 but with the precious blood of Christ, as of a lamb without blemish and without spot: 20 who verily was foreordained before the foundation of the world, but was manifest in these last times for you."

Col 1:12 "Giving thanks (*continually*) unto the Father, which hath made us meet (*qualified and enabled by grace*) to be partakers of the inheritance of the saints in light: 13 who hath delivered us from the power of darkness, and hath translated us into the kingdom of his *agape*/dear Son: 14 in whom we have redemption through his blood, even the forgiveness (*remission, purging, putting away, and obliteration*) of sins: … 20 and, having made peace through the blood of his cross, by him to reconcile all things unto himself; by him, I say, whether they be things in earth, or things

OTHER HEALING TEACHINGS

in heaven. 21 And you, that were sometime alienated and enemies in your mind by wicked works, yet now hath he reconciled."

We are redeemed by Jesus' blood from the power of the devil and reconciled into His kingdom of *agape*/love. This is the great work of the Mighty Arm of God, Jesus. We are redeemed by His blood from the power of the devil. Redemption from sin and from the curse of sin and healing or salvation are just opposite sides of the same coin.

This is described in Isaiah 53. This chapter is referenced in the New Testament many times as the key act of the Mighty Arm of God for both sin and healing. Here are a few instances: John 12:37 "But though he had done so many miracles before them, yet they believed not on him: 38 that the saying of Esaias the prophet might be fulfilled, which he spake, Lord, who hath believed our report? and to whom hath the arm of the Lord been revealed (*Isa 53:1*)" Acts 8:30 "And Philip ran thither to him (*the Ethiopian eunuch*), and heard him read the prophet Esaias, and said, Understandest thou what thou readest? 31 And he said, How can I, except some man should guide me? And he desired Philip that he would come up and sit with him. 32 The place of the scripture which he read was this, He was led as a sheep to the slaughter; and like a lamb dumb before his shearer, so opened he not his mouth: 33 in his humiliation his judgment was taken away: and who shall declare his generation? for his life is taken from the earth (*Isa 53:7*). 34 And the eunuch answered Philip, and said, I pray thee, of whom speaketh the prophet this? of himself, or of some other man? 35 Then Philip opened his mouth, and began at the same scripture, and preached unto him Jesus." 1 Pet 2:21 "For even hereunto were ye called: because Christ also suffered for us, leaving us an example, that ye should follow his steps: 22 who did no sin, neither was guile found in his mouth: 23 who, when he was reviled, reviled not again; when he suffered, he threatened not; but committed himself to him that judgeth righteously: 24 who his own self bare our sins in his own body on the tree, that we, being dead to sins, should *zao*/live unto righteousness: by whose stripes ye were healed. 25 For ye were as sheep going astray; but are now returned unto the Shepherd and Bishop of your souls (*Isa 53:5-7*)." Matt 8:14 "And when Jesus was come into Peter's house, he saw his wife's mother laid, and sick of a fever. 15 And he touched her hand, and the fever left her: and she arose, and ministered unto them. 16 When the even was come, they brought unto him many that were possessed with devils: and he cast out the spirits with his word, and healed all that were sick: 17 that it might be fulfilled which was spoken by Esaias the prophet, saying, Himself *lambano*/took our infirmities, and bare (*completely*) our sicknesses (*Isa 53:4*)."

In particular, Matt 8:17 shows a more complete translation of Isa 53:4 "Surely he hath *nasa*/borne our griefs (*infirmities*), and *cabal*/carried our sorrows (*sicknesses*): yet we did esteem him stricken, smitten of God, and afflicted." This is concerning infirmities (the inability to operate with power in this physical world) and sicknesses (any and every disease of any kind). Jesus took/bore for us death operating in any form, slow or fast.

While Isaiah 53 uses two different Hebrew words *borne* (*nasa*) and *carried* (*cabal*), both mean to take, carry or bear so that the requirement is now fully carried, contained and removed with nothing left out. It is thus applied in Matt 8:14-17 as specific to physical healing. These same words are used for sin and iniquity in Isa 53:11 "He shall see of the travail of his soul, and shall be satisfied: by his knowledge shall my righteous servant justify many; for he shall *cabal*/**bear** their iniquities. 12 Therefore will I divide him a portion with the great, and he shall divide the spoil with the strong; because he hath poured out his soul unto death: and he was numbered with the transgressors; and he *nasa*/**bare** the sin of many, and made intercession for the transgressors."

Thus Jesus bore and carried our infirmities, sicknesses, sin, transgression, iniquities, and curse all in the same mighty work, so there is no requirement from God for any human to ever bear them again. Jesus bore what we deserve, and we receive mercy, not justice. He took our curse upon Himself.

Heb 9:26 "For then must he often have suffered since the foundation of the world: but now once in the end of the world hath he appeared to put away sin by the sacrifice of himself. 27 And as it is appointed unto men once to die, but after this the judgment: 28 so Christ was once offered to bear the sins of many; and unto them that look for him shall he appear the second time without sin unto *soteria/salvation*."

Heb 10:12 "But this man, after he had offered one sacrifice for sins for ever, sat down on the right hand of God; 13 from henceforth expecting till his enemies be made his footstool. 14 For by one offering he hath perfected for ever them that are sanctified. 15 Whereof the Holy Ghost also is a witness to us: for after that he had said before, 16 This is the covenant that I will make with them after those days, saith the Lord, I will put my laws into their hearts, and in their minds will I write them; 17 and their sins and iniquities will I remember no more. 18 Now where remission (*obliteration, removal and putting away*) of these (*sins and iniquities*) is, there is no more offering for sin."

Matt 26:27 "And he took the cup, and gave thanks, and gave it to them, saying, Drink ye all of it; 28 for this is my blood of the new testament (*covenant*), which is shed for many for the remission (*purging, removal*) of sins."

Acts 13:38 "Be it known unto you therefore, men and brethren, that through this man is preached unto you the forgiveness (*remission, obliteration, removal and putting away*) of sins: 39 and by him all that believe are justified from all things, from which ye could not be justified by the law of Moses."

Other Healing Teachings

As far as God is concerned, forgiveness of sin and physical healing were accomplished in the great work of His Mighty Arm, Jesus, the Christ of God, who cut the New Covenant with His own body and blood. **Isa 53:1** "Who hath believed our report? and to whom is the arm of the Lord revealed? 2 For he shall grow up before him as a tender plant, and as a root out of a dry ground: he hath no form nor comeliness; and when we shall see him, there is no beauty that we should desire him. 3 He is despised and rejected of men; a man of sorrows, and acquainted with grief: and we hid as it were our faces from him; he was despised, and we esteemed him not. 4 Surely he hath *cabal*/borne our griefs (*infirmities*), and *nasa*/carried our sorrows, (*sicknesses*): yet we did esteem him stricken, smitten of God, and afflicted. 5 But he was wounded for our transgressions (*willful sin acts*), he was bruised for our iniquities (*sin thoughts, actions and the curse due*): the chastisement of our peace (*poverty, impotency and misery due for sin*) was upon him; and with his stripes (*tearing, cutting or breaking of His body*) we are *physically* healed. 6 All we like sheep have gone astray; we have turned every one to his own way; and the Lord hath laid on him the iniquity of us all. 7 He was oppressed, and he was afflicted, yet he opened not his mouth: he is brought as a lamb to the slaughter, and as a sheep before her shearers is dumb, so he openeth not his mouth. 8 He was taken from prison and from judgment: and who shall declare his generation? for he was cut off out of the land of the living: for the transgression of my people was he stricken. 9 And he made his grave with the wicked, and with the rich in his death; because he had done no violence, neither was any deceit in his mouth. 10 Yet it pleased the Lord to bruise him; he hath put him to grief (*sickness*): when thou shalt make his soul an offering for sin, he shall see his seed, he shall prolong his days, and the pleasure of the Lord shall prosper in his hand. 11 He shall see of the travail of his soul, and shall be satisfied: by his knowledge shall my righteous servant justify many; for he shall *cabal*/bear their iniquities. 12 Therefore will I divide him a portion with the great, and he shall divide the spoil with the strong; because he hath poured out his soul unto death: and he was numbered with the transgressors; and he *nasa*/bare the sin of many, and made intercession for the transgressors."

This is the propitiation of Jesus, not just the atonement, which is a covering of sin, but remission, a total removal of sin unto blessing in propitiation.

This dual connection of sin and sickness is seen again in: **James 5:15** "And the prayer of faith shall *sozo*/save the sick, and the Lord shall raise him up; and if he have committed sins, they shall be forgiven him." Notice the sin forgiveness is the result of praying for healing. So even though there is no confession of sin, the one prayed for is forgiven anyway. See also Matt 9:4-8 in the healing of the man with palsy.

We understand that the bruises and wounds (lacerations or stripes) Jesus received in the crucifixion included the initial binding, followed by the beatings, the lashing at the whipping post, the crown of thorns, the stumbling and falling as He carried the cross, the nails in His hands and feet, the ripping of His back, hands and feet every time He lifted Himself up to breath when nailed to the cross, and the final spear in His side.

Knowing that sin, sickness and a lack of prosperity (peace) were all healed by Jesus is summarized in Isa 53:5 as part of the New Covenant. Isa 49:8 "Thus saith the Lord, In an acceptable time have I heard thee, and in a day of salvation have I helped thee: and I will preserve thee, and give thee for a covenant of the people, to establish the earth, to cause to inherit the desolate heritages."

This is also seen in a messianic prophecy: Isa 57:18 "I have seen his ways, and will heal him: I will lead him also, and restore comforts unto him and to his mourners. 19 I create the fruit of the lips; Peace, peace to him that is far off, and to him that is near, saith the Lord; and I will heal him."

While many emphasize eternal rewards, here is what Holy Spirit says this time on Earth is right now: 2 Cor 5:20 "Now then we are ambassadors for Christ, as though God did beseech you by us: we pray you in Christ's stead, be ye reconciled to God. 21 For he hath made him to be sin for us, who knew no sin; that we might be made the righteousness of God in him. 6:1 We then, as workers together with him, beseech you also that ye receive not the grace of God in vain. 2 (For he saith, I have heard thee in a time accepted, and in the day of *soteria*/salvation have I succoured thee: behold, now is the accepted time; behold, now is the day of *soteria*/salvation.)"

Notice the warning of 2 Cor 6:1: it is possible to be born again in this Day of Salvation and yet not walk in the fullness of our salvation. *Vain* means "useless, ineffective, will not survive the Day of Judgment." 2 Cor 6:1 "We then, as workers together with him, beseech you also that ye receive not the grace of God in vain." This means you have to make a choice.

This we are to remember or judge properly when we take communion or the Lord's Supper. 1 Cor 11:24 "And when he had given thanks, he brake it, and said, Take, eat: this is my body, which is broken (*Greek: lacerated*) for you: this do in remembrance of me. 25 After the same manner also he took the cup, when he had supped, saying, This cup is the new testament (*covenant*) in my blood: this do ye, as oft as ye drink it, in remembrance of me. 26 For as often as ye eat this bread, and drink this cup, ye do shew the Lord's death till he come."

Jesus took the stripes and has risen, men can be born again, and now is the Day of the Salvation of God. All of God's benefits are by faith, You believe for them to be manifested based on His Word. You call it done before it is.

The punishment for failure to rightly judge your sins, sicknesses, infirmities, poverty, failures and penalties was all carried and paid for by Jesus in His body and blood 2000 years ago, and that's what it means to take the bread and wine unworthily. We do this in these ways:

Other Healing Teachings

- Not remembering the Lord in this meal,
- Not doing it at all; or
- Not doing it properly to acknowledge or show all Jesus accomplished with the terrible price of the cross with His body and blood.

Heb 10:29 "Of how much sorer punishment, suppose ye, shall he be thought worthy, who hath trodden under foot the Son of God, and hath counted the blood of the covenant, wherewith he was sanctified, an unholy thing, and hath done despite unto the Spirit of grace? 30 For we know him that hath said, Vengeance belongeth unto me, I will recompense, saith the Lord. And again, The Lord shall judge his people."

Heb 2:1 "Therefore we ought to give the more earnest heed to the things which we have heard, lest at any time we should let them slip. 2 For if the word spoken by angels was stedfast, and every transgression and disobedience received a just recompence of reward; 3 how shall we escape, if we neglect so great *soteria*/salvation; which at the first began to be spoken by the Lord, and was confirmed unto us by them that heard him; 4 God also bearing them witness, both with signs and wonders, and with divers miracles, and gifts of the Holy Ghost, according to his own will?"

You may not get the destruction of Jerusalem, but you will get the fruit of any of your wicked ways you do not put under the body and blood of Jesus.

Gal 6:7 "Be not deceived; God is not mocked: for whatsoever a man soweth, that shall he also reap. 8 For he that soweth to his flesh shall of the flesh reap corruption; but he that soweth to the Spirit shall of the Spirit reap *zoe*/life everlasting. 9 And let us not be weary in well doing: for in due season we shall reap, if we faint not. 10 As we have therefore opportunity, let us do good unto all men, especially unto them who are of the household of faith."

If the birth, death, resurrection and glorification of Jesus is the great work of God to man, ignoring it or failing to appreciate and use it is the great insult of man to God. There is no other path to God left for you until you repent and return to Jesus as your total salvation, once for all time. This is what we are to repent of in the Gospel of Jesus Christ

The punishment for failure to apply the methods God has prescribed with the right attitude of heart is that we are judged with the world that has no God, no covenant and no hope, and are, thus, left with the penalties of our sins and failures. Eph 2:12 "That at that time ye were without Christ, being aliens from the commonwealth of Israel, and strangers from the covenants of promise, having no hope, and without God in the world [*or life as a mere man without the God of Israel in power*]."

We do not judge the validity of God's promises by our inability to bring them to Earth, and we do not define the Word of God by our experience. Rather, we define our experience by the Word of God.

Heb 6:18 "That by two immutable things (*the promise in Gen 12:1-2, and the oath of the same in Gen 22:15-18*), in which it was **impossible for God to lie**, we might have a strong consolation, who have fled for refuge to lay hold upon the hope set before us: 19 which hope we have as an anchor of the soul, both sure and stedfast, and which entereth into that within the veil; 20 whither the forerunner is for us entered, even Jesus, made an high priest for ever after the order of Melchisedec."

Note: Jesus was able to take His blood to Heaven and to exercise His current High Priest ministry because of the promise to Abraham.

Titus 1:1 "Paul, a servant of God, and an apostle of Jesus Christ, according to the faith of God's elect, and the acknowledging of the truth which is after godliness; 2 in hope of eternal *zoe*/life, which **God, that cannot lie**, promised before the world began."

The path of life in God's great salvation is described in the Scriptures. 2 Tim 3:15 "And that from a child thou hast known the holy scriptures, which are able to make thee wise unto *soteria*/salvation through faith which is in Christ Jesus. 16 All scripture is given by inspiration of God, and is profitable for doctrine, for reproof, for correction, for instruction in righteousness: 17 that the man of God may be perfect, throughly furnished unto all good works."

"Wise unto *soteria*/salvation" means knowing how to apply the facts of salvation to bring the promises from Heaven to Earth.

Eph 1:3 "Blessed be the God and Father of our Lord Jesus Christ, who hath blessed us with all spiritual blessings (*or has spoken every good thing that it is possible to say/promise/proclaim*) in heavenly places in Christ: 4 according as he hath chosen us in him before the foundation of the world, that we should be holy and without blame before him in *agape*/love: 5 having predestinated us unto the adoption of children by Jesus Christ to himself, according to the good pleasure of his will, 6 to the praise of the glory of his grace, wherein he hath made us accepted in the *agape*/beloved. 7 In whom we have redemption through his blood, the forgiveness (*remission, purging, putting away and obliteration*) of sins, according to the riches of his grace; 8 wherein he hath abounded toward us in all wisdom and prudence."

Therefore Jesus said: Matt 6:8 "Be not ye therefore like unto them: for your Father knoweth what things ye have need of, before ye *aiteo*/ask him (*require, demand and expect as due by covenant promise of God*). 9 After this manner therefore pray ye: Our Father which art in heaven, Hallowed be thy name. 10 Thy kingdom come. Thy will be done in earth, as it is in heaven. 11 Give us this day our daily bread. 12 And forgive us our debts, as we forgive our debtors. 13 And lead us not into temptation, but deliver us from evil (*or the evil one*): for thine is the kingdom, and the power, and the glory, for ever. Amen. 14 For if ye forgive men their trespasses, your heavenly Father will also forgive you: 15 but if ye forgive not men their trespasses, neither will your Father forgive your trespasses."

OTHER HEALING TEACHINGS

The promise is that Christians should be healthier and live longer than the un-born again. This is the legal side of redemption. The vital side is using the Scriptures to make this a reality in our lives today.

If we are not seeing the blessings, the problem is not God, and it is not the devil. It is us. It is an education and application problem.

2 Cor 4:3 "But if our gospel be hid, it is hid to them that are lost (*have death working in them is some way, fast or slow*): 4 in whom the god of this world hath blinded (*deceived*) the minds of them which believe not, lest the light of the glorious gospel of Christ, who is the image of God, should shine unto them. 5 For we preach not ourselves, but Christ Jesus the Lord; and ourselves your servants for Jesus' sake."

Many apply this scripture to only those not born again, and it does apply to them, but in the context of verse five, it is also for those born again in the new creation but not fully matured into Christ in His full prosperity.

So the problem is not God, and it is not the devil, for the devil is doing what he does. It is with the Christian, who in either ignorance or deception (remember evil means to twist or corrupt so you cannot tell the difference) is not believing the grace and truth, to walking in God's grace, truth and *agape*/love by His Word.

1 John 1:5 "This then is the message which we have heard of him, and declare unto you, that God is light, and in him is no darkness at all. 6 If we say that we have fellowship with him (*communing, partnering or relating where you are walking, thinking and judging alike*), and walk in darkness, we lie, and do not the truth." 1 Cor 1:10 "Now I beseech you, brethren, by the name of our Lord Jesus Christ, that ye all speak the same thing, and that there be no divisions among you; but that ye be perfectly joined together in the same mind and in the same judgment [*as Holy Spirit*]."

Part of the message of Paul in First and Second Corinthians, and in most of His other letters, indeed in most of the other letters of the New Testament, is that the born again are not fulfilling all God has required of them in the benefits and calling of the new birth.

Eph 5:8 "For ye were sometimes darkness, but now are ye light in the Lord: walk as children of light: 9 (for the fruit of the Spirit is in all goodness and righteousness and truth.)"

Our union with God through the new birth is solid and permanent, but our fellowship, communion, partnership or co-laboring depends on our current thoughts and walk.

Even before Jesus died and rose from the dead, Jesus said healing was part of the bread for the children of God, including deliverance from the effects of evil spirits. How much greater is this for you, if you are a child of God under the New Covenant, and such are you, if you are born again. Whenever Jesus healed anyone, it was God declaring He hates sickness, disease and death in any form, to destroy it.

Mark 7:25 "For a certain woman, whose young daughter had an unclean spirit, heard of him, and came and fell at his feet: 26 the woman was a Greek, a Syrophenician by nation; and she besought him that he would cast forth the devil out of her daughter. 27 But Jesus said unto her, Let the children first be filled: for it is not meet to take the children's bread, and to cast it unto the dogs. 28 And she answered and said unto him, Yes, Lord: yet the dogs under the table eat of the children's crumbs. 29 And he said unto her, For this saying go thy way; the devil is gone out of thy daughter. 30 And when she was come to her house, she found the devil gone out, and her daughter laid upon the bed."

Holy Spirit reaffirmed that every healing and act of God Jesus did was freeing people of oppressions of the devil, i.e., were part of "the children's bread." Acts 10:38 "How God anointed Jesus of Nazareth with the Holy Ghost and with power: who went about doing good, and healing all that were oppressed (*under the active dominion, reign or lordship*) of the devil; for God was with him."

So how do you get this bread? Hear to obedience Jesus' answer: Matt 4:4 "But he answered and said, It is written, Man shall not *zao*/live by bread alone, but by every word (*that you do*) that proceedeth out of the mouth of God."

Failure to operate the instruction manual properly does not mean the instruction manual is wrong. The fault is not with God, but with man. Failure to mix the Word of God with faith such that you obey it has always been the issue for man. The devil will tell you the problem is God, but God says the problem is with man. Heb 4:1 "Let us therefore fear, lest, a promise being left us of entering into his rest, any of you should seem to come short of it. 2 For unto us was the gospel preached, as well as unto them: but the word preached did not profit them, not being mixed with faith in them that heard it."

This is not about your eternal salvation when you get born again. That is settled by grace because of Jesus. Your effectiveness in bringing the Kingdom of God to Earth is based on your effective faith in the more-than-sufficient blood of Jesus.

Judging your circumstances as God's fault or that the Bible is irrelevant or of not enough power will not lead to His blessing. As Jesus said to those who were not effectively believing God: Matt 22:29 "Jesus answered and said unto them, Ye do err, not knowing the scriptures, nor the power of God."

These are all the attitudes of darkness. Eph 5:11 "And have no fellowship with the unfruitful works of darkness, but rather reprove them. 12 For it is a shame even to speak of those things which are done of them in secret. 13 But all things that are reproved are made manifest by the light: for whatsoever doth make manifest is light. 14 Wherefore he saith, Awake thou that sleepest, and arise from the dead, and Christ shall give thee light. 15 See then that ye walk circumspectly, not as fools, but as wise, 16 redeeming the time, because the days are evil."

OTHER HEALING TEACHINGS

This has always been God's judgment, as proved by Israel, who for failure to follow the Lord's ways in gladness, was destroyed. Deut 28:47 "Because thou servedst not the LORD thy God with joyfulness, and with gladness of heart, for the abundance of all things; 48 therefore shalt thou serve thine enemies which the LORD shall send against thee, in hunger, and in thirst, and in nakedness, and in want of all things: and he shall put a yoke of iron upon thy neck, until he have destroyed thee."

Verses 1-14 of Deuteronomy 28 describes the blessing for joyful and glad obedience and details some of the terrible penalties for failure, the Law's curse, in verses 15-68. Here is a New Testament command on how to renew our mind to walk in this gladness to success with God. Eph 5:17 "Wherefore be ye not unwise, but understanding what the will of the Lord is. 18 And be not drunk with wine, wherein is excess; but be (*continuously being*) filled with the Spirit; 19 speaking to yourselves in psalms and hymns and spiritual songs, singing and making melody in your heart to the Lord; 20 (*continually*) giving thanks always for all things unto God and the Father in the name of our Lord Jesus Christ; 21 submitting yourselves one to another in the fear of God."

This same principle or way of God for failure to use what God has given to subdue and establish dominion over the devil is applied to those who do not use or take the Lord's Supper properly. 1 Cor 11:27 "Wherefore whosoever shall eat this bread, and drink this cup of the Lord, unworthily, shall be guilty of the body and blood of the Lord. 28 But let a man examine himself, and so let him eat of that bread, and drink of that cup. 29 For he that eateth and drinketh unworthily, eateth and drinketh damnation to himself, not discerning the Lord's body. 30 For this cause many are weak and sickly among you, and many sleep. 31 For if we would judge ourselves, we should not be judged. 32 But when we are judged, we are chastened of the Lord, that we should not be condemned with the world."

Notice, per verse 30, the effect is that you have the same health and life-span as people in the world who do not know Christ, i.e., you live as a "mere man." Proof you are doing it right includes divine health, prosperity and long life. 3 John 2 "*Agape*/beloved, I wish (*pray*) above all things that thou mayest prosper and be in health, even as thy soul prospereth. 3 For I rejoiced greatly, when the brethren came and testified of the truth that is in thee, even as thou walkest in the truth."

Or because we do not apply the grace of God in faith to our present situation, we live just as the world does: like a people who have not the real God or His covenant promises, driven by dreadful fear and a god who cannot and will not help. Or we live like one who sees no spiritual value in the death and resurrection of Jesus, to the level God has revealed in the Scriptures. Verse 29 does not mean you curse, damn yourself, as if that is something new, it means that you do not push back the death that is all around us with the *zoe*/life of God released in communion. Failure to push back (until you walk just like Jesus walks) means your evil sowing reaps its evil fruit, and the attacks of the devil are not defeated. God does not have to actively judge us by sending the devil, but just like Job, without our properly judging the body and blood of Jesus, He has no way to stop the devil when the devil comes to tempt us. The best He can do is to mitigate what the devil does, as He did with Job. Thus we limit God.

The issue has never been the will of God for healing. The issue is will we learn of the truth, the right information, and make it part of our lives in true knowledge. Hos 4:6 "My people are destroyed for lack of knowledge: because thou hast rejected knowledge, I will also reject thee, that thou shalt be no priest to me: seeing thou hast forgotten the law of thy God, I will also forget thy children."

Failure to appreciate and apply God's great work in Jesus is included in "lack of knowledge," and it means you live a life as if the work of Jesus had never been done, and you will surely eat the fruit of any wicked seeds you have sown. Gal 6:7 "Be not deceived; God is not mocked: for whatsoever a man soweth, that shall he also reap. 8 For he that soweth to his flesh shall of the flesh reap corruption; but he that soweth to the Spirit shall of the Spirit reap *zoe*/life everlasting. 9 And let us not be weary in well doing: for in due season we shall reap, if we faint not. 10 As we have therefore opportunity, let us do good unto all men, especially unto them who are of the household of faith."

This is all changed by judging your sins, miseries, wicked thoughts, defeats and failures, as being all carried and healed in Jesus, through the actions remembered by the Lord's Supper. Rom 8:2 "For the law of the Spirit of *zoe*/life in Christ Jesus hath made me free from the law of sin and death. 3 For what the law could not do, in that it was weak through the flesh, God sending his own Son in the likeness of sinful flesh, and for sin, condemned sin in the flesh: 4 that the righteousness of the law might be fulfilled in us, who walk not after the flesh, but after the Spirit."

Taking communion or the Lord's Supper rightly, per the Word of God, is a right work of the Spirit–the Gospel of Christ in Jesus.

So healing for the Christian is found in the Lord's Supper and in James 5. James 5:13 "Is any among you afflicted? let him pray. Is any merry? let him sing psalms. 14 Is any sick among you? let him call for the elders of the church; and let them pray over him, anointing him with oil in the name of the Lord: 15 and the prayer of faith shall *sozo*/save the sick, and the Lord shall raise him up; and if he have committed sins, they shall be forgiven him. 16 Confess your faults one to another, and pray one for another, that ye may be *iaomai*/healed (*physically*). The effectual fervent prayer of a righteous man availeth much. 17 Elias was a man subject to like passions as we are, and he prayed earnestly that it might not rain: and it rained not on the earth by the space of three years and six months. 18 And he prayed again (*for a total of 8 times*), and the heaven gave rain, and the earth brought forth her fruit. 19 Brethren, if any of you do err from the truth, and one convert him; 20 let him know,

OTHER HEALING TEACHINGS

that he which converteth the sinner from the error of his way shall *sozo*/save a soul from death, and shall hide a multitude of sins."

The correct response is to show the Lord's death properly in the Lord's Supper and to acknowledge who and what you are now in Christ: Eph 2:13 "But now in Christ Jesus ye who sometimes were far off are made nigh by the blood of Christ. 14 For he is our peace, who hath made both one, and hath broken down the middle wall of partition between us; 15 having abolished in his flesh the enmity, even the law of commandments contained in ordinances; for to make in himself of twain one new man, so making peace (*Isa 53:5*); 16 and that he might reconcile both unto God in one body by the cross, having slain the enmity thereby: 17 and came and preached peace to you which were afar off, and to them that were nigh (*Isa 57:18-19*). 18 For through him we both have access by one Spirit unto the Father. 19 Now therefore ye are no more strangers and foreigners, but fellowcitizens with the saints, and of the household of God; 20 and are built upon the foundation of the apostles and prophets, Jesus Christ himself being the chief corner stone; 21 in whom all the building fitly framed together groweth unto an holy temple in the Lord: 22 in whom ye also are builded together for an habitation of God through the Spirit."

We obtain the benefits by faith in the work of God in Jesus. Here is a prayer to apply these awesome realities during the Lord's Supper or Communion.

A Communion Prayer: Lord Jesus, by Your stripes I was healed 2000 years ago. (*Call to mind any sicknesses, miseries, fears or failures you are aware of and confess them to Him.*) As I eat this bread, I acknowledge all my infirmities and sicknesses were healed by Your stripes 2000 years ago. And, just as sure as this bread is going into my body, Your healing is restoring me right now in every way. Body, be whole, in the name of Jesus, NOW!

Lord Jesus, by Your stripes and Your blood, I am redeemed and my sins are remitted 2000 years ago. (*Call to mind any sins you are aware of and confess them to Him.*) As I drink this wine/juice, I acknowledge Your blood redeemed me from all sin and failure, and my sins were purged 2000 years ago in Your death. And just as sure as this drink is going into my body, I receive that forgiveness now. I am redeemed from the curse of the Law, I am made Your righteousness, Holy Spirit dwells in me, and I am in Your Kingdom of *Agape*/love. Lord Jesus, I judge that Your death paid for everything, and Your resurrection healed everything, so I thank You now for forgiveness, health, right thinking and prosperity in You. My life, be whole in the name of Jesus, NOW!

Lord Jesus, by Your stripes, Your blood, Your resurrection and Your glorification, I proclaim Your life in every part of my life to Your glory, in the name of Jesus, NOW! By You, Lord Jesus, I am now walking in Your Kingdom in righteousness, peace and joy, in Your Holy Spirit of power, *agape*/love and a sound mind. Father, in the name of Jesus, thank You for Your *agape*/love and covenant in Jesus. Thank You!

Please contact us at www.CovenantPeaceMinistries.com for a printable copy of this communion prayer.

A FINAL PRAYER AND CONFESSION

Father, in the name of Jesus, the Baptizer with Holy Spirit and fire, give abundant manifestations of Your Spirit, including words of wisdom, knowledge, faith, healings, working of miracles, prophecy, discerning of spirits, diverse kinds of tongues, interpretation of tongues, dead raising, creative restorations, wholeness and special miracles and works. Stir me that I <u>1 Cor 12:31</u> ... covet earnestly *unto effective faith* the best gifts: *and walk by Your Spirit in the* more excellent way *of* agape/love. *So that I* <u>1 Cor 14:1</u> follow after *agape*/charity, and desire spiritual gifts, but rather that *I* may prophesy *to the edification of the church and devote myself to prayer and the ministry of the Word in the unity of the Spirit and in the bond of peace. Father, teach me to walk in the glad assurance that I have the same Spirit You gave Jesus, so that I gladly confess* <u>2 Cor 13:5</u> *knowing* ... that Jesus Christ is in *me, as by Your grace I am not reprobate* (*useless in my faith in You, Father God*), *but I am proclaiming:* <u>Luke 4:18</u> The Spirit of the Lord is upon me, because he hath anointed me to preach the gospel to the poor; he hath sent me to heal the brokenhearted, to preach deliverance to the captives, and recovering of sight to the blind, to set at liberty them that are bruised, 19 to preach the acceptable year of the Lord. <u>2 Cor 6:2</u> (For he saith, I have heard thee in a time accepted, and in the day of *soteria*/salvation have I succoured thee: behold, now is the accepted time; behold, now is the day of *soteria*/salvation.) <u>Acts 10:38</u> How *that You, Father* God, *anoint us in* Jesus of Nazareth with the Holy Ghost and with power: *so we go* about doing good, and healing all that *are* oppressed (*under the active reign and lordship*) of the devil; for *You, Father* God, *are* with *us in* Him [*just like Your are with Jesus*]. <u>1 John 4:17</u> Herein is our *agape*/love made perfect, that we may have boldness in the day of judgment: because as he is, so are we in this world. *For* <u>1 John 4:4</u> ye are of God, little children, and have overcome them: because greater is he that is in you, than he that is in the world. *And to know that*

Gal 4:3 even so we, when we were children, were in bondage under the elements of the world: 4 but when the fulness of the time was come, *You, Father* God, sent forth *Your* Son, made of a woman, made under the law, 5 to redeem them that were under the law, that we might receive the adoption of sons. 6 And because *we* are sons, *You, Father* God, hath sent forth the Spirit of *Your* Son into *our* hearts, crying, Abba (*Daddy*), Father. 7 Wherefore *I am* no more a servant, but a son; and if a son, then an heir of *You, Father* God, through Christ. *Father, reveal the glory of Your inheritance in us that* Phil 3:14 *we* press toward the mark for the prize of the high calling of *You, Father* God, in Christ Jesus *so that we walk in Your total remission in Jesus that we might agape/love You totally. For Jesus said:* John 17:22 And the glory which thou gavest me I have given them; that they may be one, even as we are one: 23 I in them, and thou in me, that they may be made perfect in one; and that the world may know that thou hast sent me, and hast *agape*/loved them, as thou hast *agape*/loved me. Rom 15:6 That *we* may with one mind and one mouth glorify God, even *You*, the Father of our Lord Jesus Christ. 7 Wherefore receive *we* one another, as Christ also received us to the glory of God. 1 Cor 10:31 Whether therefore *we* eat, or drink, or whatsoever *we* do, *we* do all to the glory of God. *Father, give us Your Spirit of wisdom and revelation in the knowledge of You, that we might behold Your glory in the face of Jesus in us, that we might be changed.* 2 Cor 3:17 Now the Lord is that Spirit: and where the Spirit of the Lord is, there is liberty. 18 But we all, with open face beholding as in a glass (*mirror*) the glory of the Lord, are changed into the same image from glory to glory, even as by the Spirit of the Lord. *And that we* 2 Cor 4:5 … preach not ourselves, but Christ Jesus the Lord; and ourselves *as* servants for Jesus' sake. 6 For God, who commanded the light to shine out of darkness, hath shined in our hearts, to give the light of the knowledge of the glory of God in the face of Jesus Christ. 7 But we have this treasure in earthen vessels, that the excellency of the power may be of God, and not of us. *Father, in the name of Jesus, give me Your Spirit of wisdom and revelation in the knowledge of You, with the eyes of my understanding being enlightened, so that I* Eph 6:10 finally, *as one of the* brethren, *am* strong in the Lord, and in the power of his might. *That I* 11 put on the whole armour of God, that *I* may be able to stand against the wiles of the devil. *Knowing* 12 for we wrestle not against flesh and blood, but against principalities, against powers, against the rulers of the darkness of this world, against spiritual wickedness in high places. 13 Wherefore *I* take unto *myself* the whole armour of God, that *I* may be able to withstand in the evil day, and having done all, to stand. *So that I resist the devil, knowing he will flee from me as I* 14 stand therefore, having *my* loins girt about with truth, and having on the breastplate of righteousness; 15 and *my* feet shod with the preparation of the gospel of peace; 16 above all, taking the shield of faith, wherewith *I* shall be able to quench all the fiery darts of the wicked. 17 And take the helmet of *soteria*/salvation, and the sword of the Spirit, which is the word of God: *so that I am* 18 praying always with

OTHER HEALING TEACHINGS

all prayer and supplication in the Spirit, and watching thereunto with all perseverance and supplication for all saints; 19 and for *all preachers*, that utterance may be given unto *them*, that *we* may open *our mouths* boldly, to make known the mystery of the gospel, 20 … that therein *we* may speak boldly, as *we* ought to speak. 2 Thes 1:11 Wherefore *I pray* that *You, Father*, our God, would count *me* worthy of this calling, and fulfil all the good pleasure of *Your* goodness, and the work of faith with power: 12 that the name of our Lord Jesus Christ may be glorified in *me*, and *me* in him, according to the grace of our God and the Lord Jesus Christ. *Thank You, Father. In the name of Jesus Christ, thank You!*

Father, You have shown Yourself as He who raises the dead. When the widow's son died, Your prophet Elijah called on You: 1 Kings 17:20 "And he cried unto the Lord, and said, O Lord my God, hast thou also brought evil upon the widow with whom I sojourn, by slaying her son?" And Your resounding answer was NO! And then You commanded one who thinks like You to pray until that boy was raised. Father, in the name of Jesus, You know where I am, what I have done, what You can do through me, and that You have made me one of Your own through Jesus Christ, my Lord. Make me one whom You can think and fight through to heal the sick, raise the dead, cleanse the lepers, cast out devils and proclaim and deliver freedom to the lawful and unlawful prisoners of any kind. I want to be one whom You can work with and through. Be my strength, my courage, my help, my wisdom and my *agape*/love in Your work. Just as when the man of God, Elijah, demanded of the widow, whom You had commanded to house and feed him, her last water and last food. As she faced her fears and put her eyes on You and Your supply, she gave Elijah her last, and they were all fed as You promised for a whole year. In the same way, teach me to face my fears of lack and not enough so that I look to You rather than the situation. And when I start to sink, as I look at circumstances, just as Peter did, as he walked on the water with Jesus, send me Your living Word that picks me up and gets me back on and in You. I proclaim my testimony is: Ps 107:20 "He sent his word, and healed them, and delivered them from their destructions. 21 Oh *and I* praise the Lord for his goodness, and for his wonderful works to the children of men! 22 And *I* sacrifice the sacrifices of thanksgiving, and declare his works with rejoicing." Heb 13:15 "By *Jesus Christ I* therefore … offer the sacrifice of praise to *You, Father* God, continually, that is, the fruit of *my* lips giving thanks to *Your* name. 16 *And I* do good and *do* communicate (*in good and generous works and deliver Your salvation to all those in need, especially those in need of healing*), *I* forget not: for with such sacrifices *I know You, Father God, are* well pleased." Father, Your anointing abides on me and teaches me to walk like Jesus. For 1 John 2:27 "… the anointing which *I* have received of *You, Father*, abideth in *me*, and *I* need not that any man teach *me, so I look to You teaching me through Your Word and Your teachers for me*: but as the same anointing teacheth *me* of all things, and is truth, and is no lie, and even as it hath taught *me to renew my mind, I* shall abide in *You as I walk in You, knowing:"* 1 Cor 1:21 "Now he, which stablisheth us ... in Christ, and hath anointed us, is *You, Father* God; 22 who hath also sealed us, and given the earnest of the Spirit in our hearts." And *I* 1 John 3:1 "behold, what manner of *agape/*love *You,* the Father, hath bestowed upon us, that we should be called the sons of *You, Father* God: therefore the world knoweth us not, because it knew *Jesus* not. 2 *As the agape/*beloved, now are we the sons of *You, Father* God, and it doth not yet appear what we shall be: but we know that, when *Jesus* shall appear, we shall be like him; for we shall see him as he is. 3 And every man that hath this hope in him purifieth himself, even as he is pure." *So, Father, as I work out my own salvation in fear and trembling to purify myself by Your grace, knowing:* Gal 2:19 "For I through the law am dead to the law, that I might *zao/*live unto *You, Father* God, *just as Jesus died for me*: 20 I am crucified with Christ: nevertheless I *zao/*live; yet not I, but Christ *zao/*liveth in me: and the life which I now *zao/*live in the flesh I *zao/*live by the faith of the Son of God, who *agape/*loved me, and gave himself for me. 21 I do not frustrate the grace of *You, Father* God: for if righteousness come by the law, then Christ is dead in vain." Father, in the name of Jesus, Deut 31:6 "*I am* strong (*in Your strength for me*) and of a good courage (*in my heart*), I fear not (*by considering only failure*), nor *am I* afraid (*or allow myself to be harassed by the evil power*) of *any evil situation or people*: for *You, Father,* the LORD *my* God, *You* it is that *do* go with *me, You* will not fail *me*, nor forsake *me*." In the name of Jesus I take authority over and command all fear to leave me now, and I command my inner man to rise up and think the thoughts of God and His goodness toward me. Father, by Your grace 2 Cor 10:3 "for though *I* walk in the flesh, *I* do not war after the flesh: 4 (For the weapons of *my* warfare are not carnal, but mighty through *You, Father* God, to the pulling down of strong holds;) 5 casting down imaginations, and every high thing that exalteth itself against the knowledge of *You, Father* God, and bringing into captivity *my* every thought to the obedience of Christ." To stop all evil thoughts and only allow myself to Phil 4:4 "rejoice in the Lord alway: and again I say, Rejoice. 5 *I let my* moderation be known unto all men. *For I am continually knowing the* Lord is at hand. 6 *I am* careful for nothing; but in every thing by prayer and supplication with thanksgiving *I let my aiteo* requests be made known unto God. 7 And the peace of God, which passeth all understanding, shall keep *my heart* and *mind* through Christ Jesus. 8 Finally, *as one of the* brethren *in the Lord,* whatsoever things are **true**, whatsoever things are **honest**, whatsoever things are **just**, whatsoever things are **pure**, whatsoever things are **lovely**, whatsoever things are of **good report**; if there be any **virtue**, and if there be any **praise**, *I* only think on these things. 9 Those things, which *I* have both learned, and received, and heard, and seen in *Jesus and of God's goodness in the Scriptures I* do: and the God of peace [*to victory over any oppression, reign or lordship of the devil*] shall be with *and operate in me,*" and released by me, as I control my mind to think like You, my Father God.

OTHER HEALING TEACHINGS

So when I am harassed with dreadful fear, I fill my mind with confidence in You, Father, and Your goodness toward me. For as I am saved by Your grace, Father God, through faith, and I am made Your righteousness in Jesus to be an imitator of You in Jesus. Praise You, Father, that You get me to cooperate more and more with Holy Spirit to *zao*/live the *zoe*/life of Jesus in me to Your good pleasure. Thank You, Father, in the name of Jesus. Hallelujah! Jesus is Lord! Jesus, You are mighty, awesome and wonderful! Glory to You, O, Lord Jesus!

Isa 11:9 ... For the earth shall be full of the knowledge of the Lord, as the waters cover the sea.

Part IV

Faith-Building Scriptures

... The holy scriptures, which are able to make thee wise unto soteria/salvation (healing) through faith which is in Christ Jesus. All scripture is given by inspiration of God, and is profitable for doctrine, for reproof, for correction, for instruction in righteousness: That the man or woman of God may be perfect, thoroughly furnished unto all good [healing] works.
(2 Tim 3:15-17)

~ 1 ~

THE HEALING SCRIPTURES

Father, Jehovah Rophi, the Healing God, our Healer, in the name of Jesus Christ, teach me Your ways concerning healing. Give me, those I pray for, and all those given me Your spirit of wisdom and revelation in the knowledge of You with the eyes of our understanding being enlightened unto repentance, conversion, healing, strengthening the brethren and zealously doing good works by faith in *agape*/love, to Your glory. Cause us to know what You have accomplished in the new creation, the new birth, as You made us Your righteousness in Jesus, and that in Jesus we were/are healed by His stripes, and to fight the good fight of faith to destroy every effect of the law of sin and death by believing and using the name of Jesus righteously to Your glory. Father, in the name of Jesus, perform Your Word in us: Jer 33:6 Behold, I will bring it health and cure, and I will cure them, and will reveal unto them the abundance of peace and truth. 7 And I will cause the captivity of Judah and the captivity of Israel to return, and will build them, as at the first. 8 And I will cleanse them from all their iniquity, whereby they have sinned against me; and I will pardon all their iniquities, whereby they have sinned, and whereby they have transgressed against me. 9 And it shall be to me a name of joy, a praise and an honour before all the nations of the earth, which shall hear all the good that I do unto them: and they shall fear and tremble for all the goodness and for all the prosperity that I procure unto it. 10 Thus saith the LORD; Again there shall be heard in this place, which ye say shall be desolate without man and without beast, even in the cities of Judah, and in the streets of Jerusalem, that are desolate, without man, and without inhabitant, and without beast, 11 the voice of joy, and the voice of gladness, the voice of the bridegroom, and the voice of the bride, the voice of

BATTLE PRAYER FOR DIVINE HEALING: FIELD MANUAL 2

them that shall say, Praise the LORD of hosts: for the LORD is good; for his *chesed/ mercy endureth for ever: and of them that shall bring the sacrifice of praise into the house of the LORD. For I will cause to return the captivity of the land, as at the first (in Eden),* saith the LORD. *Father, get us to soften our hearts to You so that we know we are Yours, and that each one of us knows, by Jesus, we are a* 1 Tim 6:11 ... *man (or woman) of God, so that we flee all vanities;* and follow after righteousness, godliness, faith, *agape/love,* patience, meekness. *And that we, in faith that works by* agape/love, 12 fight the good fight of faith, *lambano/*lay hold on eternal *zoe/*life, whereunto *we are* also called ... . *Thank You, Father, in the name of Jesus Christ, Your Word made flesh, thank You! Build Your Word in us!*

Rom 8:2 For the law of the Spirit of *zoe/*life in Christ Jesus hath made me free from the law of sin and death. 3 For what the law could not do, in that it was weak through the flesh, God sending his own Son in the likeness of sinful flesh, and for sin, condemned sin in the flesh.

Rom 6:1 Knowing this, that our old man is crucified with him, that the body of sin might be destroyed, that henceforth we should not serve sin (a*ny disease/maiming/addiction is a cruel slave master*).

1 Pet 4:1 Forasmuch then as Christ hath suffered for us in the flesh, arm yourselves likewise with the same mind: for he that hath suffered in the flesh hath ceased from sin; 2 that he no longer should *zao/*live the rest of his time in the flesh to the lusts of men, but to the will of God.

Isa 52:1 Awake, awake; put on thy strength, O Zion; put on thy beautiful garments, O Jerusalem, the holy city: for henceforth there shall no more come into thee the uncircumcised and the unclean. 2 Shake thyself from the dust; arise, and sit down, O Jerusalem: loose thyself from the bands of thy neck, O captive daughter of Zion. 3 For thus saith the LORD, Ye have sold yourselves for nought; and ye shall be redeemed without money. 4 For thus saith the Lord GOD, My people went down aforetime into Egypt to sojourn there; and the Assyrian oppressed them without cause. 5 Now therefore, what have I here, saith the LORD, that my people is taken away for nought? they that rule over them make them to howl, saith the LORD; and my name continually every day is blasphemed. 6 Therefore my people shall know my name: therefore they shall know in that day that I am he that doth speak: behold, it is I. 7 How beautiful upon the mountains are the feet of him that bringeth good tidings, that publisheth peace; that bringeth good tidings of good, that publisheth salvation; that saith unto Zion, Thy God reigneth! 8 Thy watchmen shall lift up the voice; with the voice together shall they sing: for they shall see eye to eye, when the LORD shall bring again Zion. 9 Break forth into joy, sing together, ye waste places of Jerusalem: for the LORD hath comforted his people, he hath redeemed Jerusalem. 10 The LORD hath made bare his holy arm in the eyes of all the nations; and all the ends of the earth shall see the salvation of our God. 11 Depart ye, depart ye, go ye out from thence, touch no unclean thing; go ye out of the midst of her; be ye clean, that bear the vessels of the LORD. 12 For ye shall not go out with haste, nor go by flight: for the LORD will go before you; and the God of Israel will be your rearward. 13 Behold, my servant shall deal prudently, he shall be exalted and extolled, and be very high. 14 As many were astonied at thee; his visage was so marred more than any man, and his form more than the sons of men: 15 so shall he sprinkle many nations; the kings shall shut their mouths at him: for that which had not been told them shall they see; and that which they had not heard shall they consider.

Isa 53:1 Who hath believed our report? and to whom is the arm of the LORD revealed? 2 For he shall grow up before him as a tender plant, and as a root out of a dry ground: he hath no form nor comeliness; and when we shall see him, there is no beauty that we should desire him. 3 He is despised and rejected of men; a man of sorrows, and acquainted with grief: and we hid as it were our faces from him; he was despised, and we esteemed him not. 4 Surely he hath *cabal*/borne our griefs (*infirmities*), and *nasa*/carried our sorrows (*sickness*): yet we did esteem him stricken, smitten of God, and afflicted (Matt 8:17). 5 But he was wounded for our transgressions, he was bruised for our iniquities: the chastisement of our peace was upon him; and with his stripes we are healed. 6 All we like sheep have gone astray; we have turned every one to his own way; and the LORD hath laid on him the iniquity of us all. 7 He was oppressed, and he was afflicted, yet he opened not his mouth: he is brought as a lamb to the slaughter, and as a sheep before her shearers is dumb, so he openeth not his mouth. 8 He was taken from prison and from judgment: and who shall declare his generation? for he was cut off out of the land of the living: for the transgression of my people was he stricken. 9 And he made his grave with the wicked, and with the rich in his death; because he had done no violence, neither was any deceit in his mouth. 10 Yet it pleased the LORD to bruise him; he hath put him to grief: when thou shalt make his soul an offering for sin, he shall see his seed, he shall prolong his days, and the pleasure of the LORD shall prosper in his hand. 11 He shall see of the travail of his soul, and shall be satisfied: by his knowledge shall my righteous servant justify many; for he shall *cabal*/bear their iniquities. 12 Therefore will I divide him a portion with the great, and he shall divide the spoil with the strong; because he hath poured out his soul unto death: and he was numbered with the transgressors; and he *nasa*/bare the sin of many, and made intercession for the transgressors.

Battle Prayer for Divine Healing: Field Manual 2

1 Pet 2:24 *Jesus*, who his own self bare our sins in his own body on the tree, that we, being dead to sins, should *zao*/live unto righteousness: by whose stripes ye were healed. For ye were as sheep going astray; but are now returned unto the Shepherd and Bishop of your souls.

John 1:10 He was in the world, and the world was made by him, and the world knew him not. 11 He came unto his own, and his own received him not. 12 But as many as received him, to them gave he power to become the sons of God, even to them that believe on his name: 13 which were born, not of blood, nor of the will of the flesh, nor of the will of man, but of God. 14 And the Word was made flesh, and dwelt among us, (and we beheld his glory, the glory as of the only begotten of the Father,) full of grace and truth. 15 John bare witness of him, and cried, saying, This was he of whom I spake, He that cometh after me is preferred before me: for he was before me. 16 And of his fulness have all we received, and grace for grace. 17 For the law was given by Moses, but grace and truth came by Jesus Christ. 18 No man hath seen God at any time; the only begotten Son, which is in the bosom of the Father, he hath declared him.

Heb 1:1 God, who at sundry times and in divers manners spake in time past unto the fathers by the prophets, 2 hath in these last days spoken unto us by his Son, whom he hath appointed heir of all things, by whom also he made the worlds; 3 who being the brightness of his glory, and the express image of his person, and upholding all things by the word of his power, when he had by himself purged our sins, sat down on the right hand of the Majesty on high; 4 being made so much better than the angels, as he hath by inheritance obtained a more excellent name than they.

Heb 2:1 Therefore we ought to give the more earnest heed to the things which we have heard, lest at any time we should let them slip. 2 For if the word spoken by angels was stedfast, and every transgression and disobedience received a just recompence of reward; 3 how shall we escape, if we neglect so great *soteria*/salvation; which at the first began to be spoken by the Lord, and was confirmed unto us by them that heard him; 4 God also bearing them witness, both with signs and wonders, and with divers miracles, and gifts of the Holy Ghost, according to his own will?

Acts 19:11 And God wrought special miracles by the hands of Paul: 12 so that from his body were brought unto the sick handkerchiefs or aprons, and the diseases departed from them, and the evil spirits went out of them.

Rom 2:4 Or despisest thou the riches of his goodness and forbearance and longsuffering; not knowing that the goodness of God leadeth thee to repentance?

Rom 8:11 But if the Spirit of him that raised up Jesus from the dead dwell in you, he that raised up Christ from the dead shall also quicken your mortal bodies by his Spirit that dwelleth in you. 12 Therefore, brethren, we are debtors, not to the flesh, to *zao*/live after the flesh. 13 For if ye *zao*/live after the flesh, ye shall die: but if ye through the Spirit do mortify the deeds of the body, ye shall *zao*/live.

Rom 6:1 What shall we say then? Shall we continue in sin (*any thought, word or action that releases the kingdom of darkness in the curse of the law of sin and death, including sickness, disease or poverty*), that grace may abound? 2 God forbid. How shall we, that are dead to sin, *zao*/live any longer therein? 3 **Know ye not**, that so many of us as were baptized into Jesus Christ were baptized into his death? 4 Therefore we are buried with him by baptism into death: that like as Christ was raised up from the dead by the glory of the Father, even so we also should walk in newness of *zoe*/life. 5 For if we have been planted together in the likeness of his death, we shall be also in the likeness of his resurrection: 6 **knowing this**, that our old man is crucified with him, that the body of sin might be destroyed, that henceforth we should not serve sin. 7 For he that is dead is freed from sin. 8 Now if we be dead with Christ, we believe that we shall also *zao*/live with him: 9 **knowing that** Christ being raised from the dead dieth no more; death hath no more dominion over him. 10 For in that he died, he died unto sin once: but in that he *zao*/liveth, he *zao*/liveth unto God. 11 **Likewise reckon** ye also yourselves to be dead indeed unto sin, but *zao*/alive unto God through Jesus Christ our Lord. 12 Let not sin (*or any curse: sickness, poverty or lack*) therefore reign in your mortal body, that ye should obey it in the lusts thereof. 13 Neither yield ye your members as instruments of unrighteousness unto sin: but yield yourselves unto God, as those that are *zao*/alive from the dead, and your members as instruments of righteousness unto God. 14 For sin shall not have dominion over you (*in repeated sins and continual curses*): for ye are not under the law, but under grace. 15 What then? shall we sin, because we are not under the law, but under grace? God forbid. 16 **Know ye not,** that to whom ye yield yourselves servants to obey, his servants ye are to whom ye obey; whether of sin unto death, or of obedience unto righteousness? 17 But God be thanked, that ye were the servants of sin, but ye have obeyed from the heart that form of doctrine which was delivered you. 18 **Being then made free from sin**, ye became the servants of righteousness. 19 I speak after the manner of men because of the infirmity of your flesh: for as ye have yielded your members servants to uncleanness and to iniquity unto iniquity; even so now yield your members servants to righteousness unto holiness.

BATTLE PRAYER FOR DIVINE HEALING: FIELD MANUAL 2

Rom 13:10 *Agape*/love worketh no ill to his neighbour: therefore *agape*/love is the fulfilling of the law. 11 And that, knowing the time, that now it is high time to awake out of sleep: for now is our *soteria*/salvation nearer than when we believed. 12 The night is far spent, the day is at hand: let us therefore cast off the works of darkness, and let us put on the armour of light. 13 Let us walk honestly, as in the day; not in rioting and drunkenness, not in chambering and wantonness, not in strife and envying. 14 But put ye on the Lord Jesus Christ, and make not provision for the flesh, to fulfil the lusts thereof.

Eph 1:16 (*I, Paul*) cease not to give thanks for you, making mention of you in my prayers; 17 that the God of our Lord Jesus Christ, the Father of glory, may give unto you the spirit of wisdom and revelation in the knowledge of him: 18 the eyes of your understanding being enlightened; that ye may know what is the hope of his calling, and what the riches of the glory of his inheritance in the saints, 19 and what is the exceeding greatness of his power to us-ward who believe, according to the working of his mighty power, 20 which he wrought in Christ, when he raised him from the dead, and set him at his own right hand in the heavenly places, 21 far above all principality, and power, and might, and dominion, and every name that is named, not only in this world, but also in that which is to come: 22 and hath put all things under his feet, and gave him to be the head over all things to the church, 23 which is his body, the fulness of him that filleth all in all.

Eph 3:14 For this cause I bow my knees unto the Father of our Lord Jesus Christ, 15 of whom the whole family in heaven and earth is named, 16 that he would grant you, according to the riches of his glory, to be strengthened with might by his Spirit in the inner man; 17 that Christ may dwell in your hearts by faith; that ye, being rooted and grounded in *agape*/love, 18 may be able to comprehend with all saints what is the breadth, and length, and depth, and height; 19 and to know the *agape*/love of Christ, which passeth knowledge, that ye might be filled with all the fulness of God. 20 Now unto him that is able to do exceeding abundantly above all that we *aiteo*/ask (*demand, expect as due by covenant promise*) or think, according to the power that worketh in us, 21 unto him be glory in the church by Christ Jesus throughout all ages, world without end. Amen.

Eph 4:17 This I say therefore, and testify in the Lord, that ye henceforth walk not as other Gentiles walk, in the vanity of their mind, 18 having the understanding darkened, being alienated from the *zoe*/life of God through the ignorance that is in them, because of the blindness of their heart: 19 who being past feeling have given themselves over unto lasciviousness, to work all uncleanness with greediness. 20 But ye have not so learned Christ; 21 if so be that ye have heard him, and have been taught by him, as the truth is in Jesus: 22 that ye put off concerning the former conversation the old man, which is corrupt according to the deceitful lusts; 23 and be renewed in the spirit of your mind; 24 and that ye put on the new man, which after God is created in righteousness and true holiness. 25 Wherefore putting away lying, speak every man truth with his neighbour: for we are members one of another. 26 Be ye angry, and sin not: let not the sun go down upon your wrath: 27 neither give place to the devil.

Col 3:9 Lie not one to another, seeing that ye have put off the old man with his deeds; 10 and have put on the new man, which is renewed in knowledge after the image of him that created him: 11 where there is neither Greek nor Jew, circumcision nor uncircumcision, Barbarian, Scythian, bond nor free: but Christ is all, and in all. 12 Put on therefore, as the elect of God, holy and *agape*/beloved, bowels of mercies, kindness, humbleness of mind, meekness, longsuffering; 13 forbearing one another, and forgiving one another, if any man have a quarrel against any: even as Christ forgave you, so also do ye. 14 And above all these things put on *agape*/charity, which is the bond of perfectness. 15 And let the peace of God rule in your hearts, to the which also ye are called in one body; and be ye thankful. 16 Let the word of Christ dwell in you richly in all wisdom; teaching and admonishing one another in psalms and hymns and spiritual songs, singing with grace in your hearts to the Lord. 17 And whatsoever ye do in word or deed, do all in the name of the Lord Jesus, giving thanks to God and the Father by him.

2 Cor 4:10 Always bearing about in the body the dying of the Lord Jesus, that the *zoe*/life also of Jesus might be made manifest in our body. 11 For we which *zao*/live are always delivered unto death for Jesus' sake, that the *zoe*/life also of Jesus might be made manifest in our mortal flesh. 12 So then death worketh in us, but *zoe*/life in you.

2 Cor 1:9 But we had the sentence of death in ourselves, that we should not trust in ourselves, but in God which raiseth the dead: 10 who delivered us from so great a death, and doth deliver: in whom we trust that he will yet deliver us.

Matt 6:7 "But when ye pray, use not vain repetitions, as the heathen do: for they think that they shall be heard for their much speaking (*as if it takes much effort for Him to hear you*). 8 Be not ye therefore like unto them: for your Father knoweth what things ye have need of, before ye *aiteo*/ask (*require, demand and expect as due by covenant promise of*) him. 9 After this manner therefore pray ye: Our Father which art in heaven, Hallowed be thy name. 10 Thy kingdom come. Thy will be done in earth, as it is in heaven. 11 Give us this day our daily bread.

12 And forgive us our debts, as we forgive our debtors. 13 And lead us not into temptation, but deliver us from evil: For thine is the kingdom, and the power, and the glory, for ever. Amen.

Deut 11:21 That your days may be multiplied, and the days of your children, in the land which the LORD sware unto your fathers to give them, as the days of heaven upon the earth.

Deut 7:15 And the LORD will take away from thee all sickness, and will put none of the evil diseases of Egypt, which thou knowest, upon thee; but will lay them upon all them that hate thee.

Rom 8:32 He that spared not his own Son, but delivered him up for us all, how shall he not with him also freely give us all things?

Matt 7:7 *Aiteo*/ask (*and keep asking by demanding as due by covenant promise*), and it shall be given you; seek (*and keep seeking*), and ye shall find; knock (*and keep knocking*), and it shall be opened unto you: 8 for every one that *aiteo*/asketh (*by demanding, expecting as due by covenant promise*) receiveth; and he that seeketh findeth; and to him that knocketh it shall be opened. 9 Or what man is there of you, whom if his son *aiteo*/ask (*by demanding as due by covenant promise*) bread, will he give him a stone? 10 Or if he *aiteo*/ask (*by demanding as due by covenant promise*) a fish, will he give him a serpent? 11 If ye then, being evil, know how to give good gifts unto your children, how much more shall your Father which is in heaven give good things to them that *aiteo*/ask him (*by demanding as due by covenant promise*)?

Matt 7:7 Keep on *aiteo*/asking and it will be given you; keep on seeking and you will find; keep on knocking [reverently] and [the door] will be opened to you. 8 For everyone who keeps on *aiteo*/asking (*requiring, demanding and expecting as due by covenant promise*) receives; and he who keeps on seeking finds; and to him who keeps on knocking, [the door] will be opened. AMP

Isa 45:11 Thus saith the LORD, the Holy One of Israel, and his Maker, Ask (*require*) me of things to come concerning my sons, and concerning the work of my hands command ye me.

Luke 11:13 If ye then, being evil, know how to give good gifts unto your children: how much more shall your heavenly Father give the Holy Spirit to them that *aiteo*/ask him (*as due by covenant promise*)?

The Healing Scriptures

Ps 34:19 Many are the afflictions of the righteous: but the Lord delivereth him out of them all.

Jer 30:17 For I will restore health unto thee, and I will heal thee of thy wounds, saith the Lord; because they called thee an Outcast, saying, This is Zion, whom no man seeketh after.

Jer 33:6 Behold, I will bring it health and cure, and I will cure them, and will reveal unto them the abundance of peace and truth. 7 And I will cause the captivity of Judah and the captivity of Israel to return, and will build them, as at the first. 8 And I will cleanse them from all their iniquity, whereby they have sinned against me; and I will pardon all their iniquities, whereby they have sinned, and whereby they have transgressed against me.

Heb 10:12 But this man (*Jesus*), after he had offered one sacrifice for sins for ever, sat down on the right hand of God; 13 from henceforth expecting till his enemies be made his footstool. 14 For by one offering he hath perfected for ever them that are sanctified. 15 Whereof the Holy Ghost also is a witness to us: for after that he had said before, 16 this is the covenant that I will make with them after those days, saith the Lord, I will put my laws into their hearts, and in their minds will I write them; 17 and their sins and iniquities will I remember no more. 18 Now where remission of these is, there is no more offering for sin. 19 Having therefore, brethren, boldness to enter into the holiest by the blood of Jesus, 20 by a new and *zao*/living way, which he hath consecrated for us, through the veil, that is to say, his flesh; 21 and having an high priest over the house of God; 22 let us draw near with a true heart in full assurance of faith, having our hearts sprinkled from an evil conscience, and our bodies washed with pure water. 23 Let us hold fast the profession of our faith without wavering; (for he is faithful that promised;) 24 and let us consider one another to provoke unto *agape*/love and to good works: 25 not forsaking the assembling of ourselves together, as the manner of some is; but exhorting one another: and so much the more, as ye see the day approaching.

Nah 1:7 The Lord is good, a strong hold in the day of trouble; and he knoweth them that trust in him. 8 But with an overrunning flood he will make an utter end of the place thereof, and darkness shall pursue his enemies. 9 What do ye imagine against the Lord? he will make an utter end: affliction shall not rise up the second time.

Ps 2:12 Kiss the Son, lest he be angry, and ye perish from the way, when his wrath is kindled but a little. Blessed are all they that put their trust in him.

BATTLE PRAYER FOR DIVINE HEALING: FIELD MANUAL 2

Ps 34:6 This poor man cried, and the LORD heard him, and saved him out of all his troubles. 7 The angel of the LORD encampeth round about them that fear him, and delivereth them. 8 O taste and see that the LORD is good: blessed is the man that trusteth in him. 9 O fear the LORD, ye his saints: for there is no want to them that fear him. 10 The young lions do lack, and suffer hunger: but they that seek the LORD shall not want any good thing.

Ps 118:7 The LORD taketh my part with them that help me: therefore shall I see my desire upon them that hate me. 8 It is better to trust in the LORD than to put confidence in man. 9 It is better to trust in the LORD than to put confidence in princes.

Jer 17:7 Blessed is the man that trusteth in the LORD, and whose hope the LORD is. 8 For he shall be as a tree planted by the waters, and that spreadeth out her roots by the river, and shall not see when heat cometh, but her leaf shall be green; and shall not be careful in the year of drought, neither shall cease from yielding fruit.

Rom 15:12 And again, Esaias saith, There shall be a root of Jesse, and he that shall rise to reign over the Gentiles; in him shall the Gentiles trust. 13 Now the God of hope fill you with all joy and peace in believing, that ye may abound in hope, through the power of the Holy Ghost.

Isa 58:8 Then shall thy light break forth as the morning, and thine health shall spring forth speedily: and thy righteousness shall go before thee; the glory of the LORD shall be thy rearward.

Jer 17:14 Heal me, O LORD, and I shall be healed; save me, and I shall be saved: for thou art my praise.

3 John 2 *Agape*/beloved, I wish (*pray*) above all things that thou mayest prosper and be in health, even as thy soul prospereth.

1 John 3:8 He that committeth sin is of the devil; for the devil sinneth from the beginning. For this purpose the Son of God was manifested, that he might destroy the works of the devil.

1 John 4:4 Ye are of God, little children, and have overcome them: because greater is he that is in you, than he that is in the world.

1 John 4:9 In this was manifested the *agape*/love of God toward us, because that God sent his only begotten Son into the world, that we might *zao*/live through him.

10 Herein is *agape*/love, not that we *agape*/loved God, but that he *agape*/loved us, and sent his Son to be the propitiation for our sins.

1 John 4:15 Whosoever shall confess that Jesus is the Son of God, God dwelleth in him, and he in God. 16 And we have known and believed the *agape*/love that God hath to us. God is *agape*/love; and he that dwelleth in *agape*/love dwelleth in God, and God in him. 17 Herein is our *agape*/love made perfect, that we may have boldness in the day of judgment: because as he is, so are we in this world. 18 There is no fear in *agape*/love; but perfect *agape*/love casteth out fear: because fear hath torment. He that feareth is not made perfect in *agape*/love. 19 We *agape*/love him, because he first *agape*/loved us.

1 John 5:4 For whatsoever is born of God overcometh the world: and this is the victory that overcometh the world, even our faith. 5 Who is he that overcometh the world, but he that believeth that Jesus is the Son of God?

1 John 5:11 And this is the record, that God hath given to us eternal *zoe*/life, and this *zoe*/life is in his Son. 12 He that hath the Son hath *zoe*/life; and he that hath not the Son of God hath not *zoe*/life. 13 These things have I written unto you that believe on the name of the Son of God; that ye may know that ye have eternal *zoe*/life, and that ye may believe on the name of the Son of God. 14 And this is the confidence that we have in him, that, if we *aiteo*/ask any thing according to his will, he heareth us: 15 and if we know that he hear us, whatsoever we *aiteo*/ask (*by demanding, expecting as due by covenant promise*), we know that we have the *aiteo*/petitions that we *aiteo*/desired of him. 16 If any man see his brother sin a sin which is not unto death, he shall *aiteo*/ask (*by demanding, expecting as due by covenant promise*), and he shall give him *zoe*/life for them that sin not unto death. There is a sin unto death: I do not say that he shall pray for it. 17 All unrighteousness is sin: and there is a sin not unto death.

John 10:10 The thief cometh not, but for to steal, and to kill, and to destroy: I am come that they might have *zoe*/life, and that they might have it more abundantly.

Isa 54:17 No weapon that is formed against thee shall prosper; and every tongue that shall rise against thee in judgment thou shalt condemn. This is the heritage of the servants of the LORD, and their righteousness is of me, saith the LORD.

Isa 41:10 Fear thou not; for I am with thee: be not dismayed; for I am thy God: I will strengthen thee; yea, I will help thee; yea, I will uphold thee with the right hand of my righteousness. 11 Behold, all they that were incensed against thee shall be ashamed and confounded: they shall be as nothing; and they that strive with thee shall perish. 12 Thou shalt seek them, and shalt not find them, even them that contended with thee: they that war against thee shall be as nothing, and as a thing of nought. 13 For I the LORD thy God will hold thy right hand, saying unto thee, Fear not; I will help thee. 14 Fear not, thou worm Jacob, and ye men of Israel; I will help thee, saith the LORD, and thy redeemer, the Holy One of Israel. 15 Behold, I will make thee a new sharp threshing instrument having teeth: thou shalt thresh the mountains, and beat them small, and shalt make the hills as chaff.

1 Cor 6:15 Know ye not that your bodies are the members of Christ? shall I then take the members of Christ, and make them the members of an harlot? God forbid. 16 What? know ye not that he which is joined to an harlot is one body? for two, saith he, shall be one flesh. 17 But he that is joined unto the Lord is one spirit.

2 Cor 6:16 And what agreement hath the temple of God with idols? for ye are the temple of the *zao*/living God; as God hath said, I will dwell in them, and walk in them; and I will be their God, and they shall be my people.

1 John 4:17 Herein is our *agape*/love made perfect, that we may have boldness in the day of judgment: because as he is, so are we in this world. 18 There is no fear in *agape*/love; but perfect *agape*/love casteth out fear: because fear hath torment. He that feareth is not made perfect in *agape*/love.

Heb 2:14 Forasmuch then as the children are partakers of flesh and blood, he also himself likewise took part of the same; that through death he might destroy him that had the power of death, that is, the devil; 15 and deliver them who through fear of death were all their lifetime subject to bondage. 16 For verily he took not on him the nature of angels; but he took on him the seed of Abraham. 17 Wherefore in all things it behoved him to be made like unto his brethren, that he might be a merciful and faithful high priest in things pertaining to God, to make reconciliation for the sins of the people. 18 For in that he himself hath suffered being tempted, he is able to succour them that are tempted.

2 Tim 1:7 For God hath not given us the spirit of fear; but of power, and of *agape*/love, and of a sound mind.

Rom 8:15 For ye have not received the spirit of bondage again to fear; but ye have received the Spirit of adoption, whereby we cry, Abba (*Daddy*), Father. 16 The Spirit itself beareth witness with our spirit, that we are the children of God: 17 And if children, then heirs; heirs of God, and joint-heirs with Christ; if so be that we suffer with him, that we may be also glorified together.

2 Pet 1:2 Grace and peace be multiplied unto you through the knowledge of God, and of Jesus our Lord, 3 according as his divine power hath given unto us all things that pertain unto *zoe*/life and godliness, through the knowledge of him that hath called us to glory and virtue.

1 Cor 1:9 God is faithful, by whom ye were called unto the fellowship of his Son Jesus Christ our Lord.

Rom 5:17 For if by one man's offence death reigned by one; much more they which (*continually*) *lambano*/receive abundance of grace and of the gift of righteousness shall reign in *zoe*/life by one, Jesus Christ.

Rom 5:17 For if because of one man's trespass (lapse, offense) death reigned through that one, much more surely will those who *lambano*/receive [God's] overflowing grace (unmerited favor) and the free gift of righteousness [putting them into right standing with Himself *and made holy, unblameable and unreproveable*] reign as kings in *zoe*/life through the one Man Jesus Christ (the Messiah, the Anointed One). 18 Well then, as one man's trespass [one man's false step and falling away led] to condemnation for all men, so one Man's act of righteousness [leads] to acquittal and right standing with God and *zoe*/life for all men. 19 For just as by one man's disobedience (failing to hear, heedlessness, and carelessness) the many were constituted sinners, so by one Man's obedience the many will be constituted righteous (made acceptable to God, brought into right standing with Him, *holy, unblameable and unreproveable*). 20 But then Law came in, [only] to expand and increase the trespass [making it more apparent and exciting opposition]. But where sin increased and abounded, grace (God's unmerited favor) has surpassed it and increased the more and superabounded, 21 so that, [just] as sin has reigned in death, [so] grace (His unearned and undeserved favor) might reign also through righteousness (right standing with God *and made holy, unblameable and unreproveable*) which issues in eternal *zoe*/life through Jesus Christ (the Messiah, the Anointed One) our Lord. AMP

Col 1:13 Who hath delivered us from the power of darkness, and hath translated us into the kingdom of his *agape*/dear Son: 14 in whom we have redemption through his blood, even the forgiveness (*remission, purging, putting away and obliteration*) of sins.

Battle Prayer for Divine Healing: Field Manual 2

Prov 3:7 Be not wise in thine own eyes: fear the Lord, and depart from evil. 8 It shall be health to thy navel, and marrow to thy bones.

Ps 30:2 O Lord my God, I cried unto thee, and thou hast healed me.

Ps 34:6 This poor man cried, and the Lord heard him, and saved him out of all his troubles.

Ps 107:19 Then they cry unto the Lord in their trouble, and he saveth them out of their distresses. 20 He sent his word, and healed them, and delivered them from their destructions.

John 1:1 In the beginning was the Word, and the Word was with God, and the Word was God. 2 The same was in the beginning with God. 3 All things were made by him; and without him was not any thing made that was made.

John 1:14 And the Word was made flesh, and dwelt among us, (and we beheld his glory, the glory as of the only begotten of the Father,) full of grace and truth.

Luke 10:8 And into whatsoever city ye enter, and they receive you, eat such things as are set before you: 9 And heal the sick that are therein, and say unto them, The kingdom of God is come nigh unto you. ... 17 And the seventy returned again with joy, saying, Lord, even the devils are subject unto us through thy name. ... 19 Behold (*make this change your life*), I give unto you power (*commission, ability and the resources of Heaven*) to tread on serpents and scorpions, and over all the power (*ability, works*) of the enemy: and nothing shall by any means hurt you. 20 Notwithstanding in this rejoice not, that the spirits are subject unto you; but rather rejoice, because your names are written in heaven.

Luke 10:23 And he turned him unto his disciples, and said privately, Blessed are the eyes which see the things that ye see: 24 for I tell you, that many prophets and kings have desired to see those things which ye see, and have not seen them; and to hear those things which ye hear, and have not heard them.

Matt 10:1 And when he had called unto him his twelve disciples, he gave them power against unclean spirits, to cast them out, and to heal all manner of sickness and all manner of disease. ... 7 And as ye go, preach, saying, The kingdom of heaven is at hand. 8 Heal the sick, cleanse the lepers, raise the dead, cast out devils: freely ye have *lambano*/received, freely give.

The Healing Scriptures

Acts 3:6 Then Peter said, Silver and gold have I none; but such as I have give I thee: In the name of Jesus Christ of Nazareth rise up and walk. 7 And he took him by the right hand, and lifted him up: and immediately his feet and ankle bones received strength. 8 And he leaping up stood, and walked, and entered with them into the temple, walking, and leaping, and praising God. 9 And all the people saw him walking and praising God: ... 12 And when Peter saw it, he answered unto the people, Ye men of Israel, why marvel ye at this? or why look ye so earnestly on us, as though by our own power or holiness we had made this man to walk? 13 The God of Abraham, and of Isaac, and of Jacob, the God of our fathers, hath glorified his Son Jesus; whom ye delivered up, and denied him in the presence of Pilate, when he was determined to let him go. 14 But ye denied the Holy One and the Just, and desired a murderer to be granted unto you; 15 and killed the Prince of *zoe*/life, whom God hath raised from the dead; whereof we are witnesses. 16 And his name through faith in his name hath made this man strong, whom ye see and know: yea, the faith which is by him hath given him this perfect soundness in the presence of you all.

Acts 4:9 If we this day be examined of the good deed done to the impotent man, by what means he is made whole; 10 be it known unto you all, and to all the people of Israel, that by the name of Jesus Christ of Nazareth, whom ye crucified, whom God raised from the dead, even by him doth this man stand here before you whole.

Acts 4:29 And now, Lord, behold their threatenings: and grant unto thy servants, that with all boldness they may speak thy word, 30 by stretching forth thine hand to heal; and that signs and wonders may be done by the name of thy holy child Jesus. 31 And when they had prayed, the place was shaken where they were assembled together; and they were all filled with the Holy Ghost, and they spake the word of God with boldness.

Acts 5:12 And by the hands of the apostles were many signs and wonders wrought among the people; (and they were all with one accord in Solomon's porch. 13 And of the rest durst no man join himself to them: but the people magnified them. 14 And believers were the more added to the Lord, multitudes both of men and women.) 15 Insomuch that they brought forth the sick into the streets, and laid them on beds and couches, that at the least the shadow of Peter passing by might overshadow some of them. 16 There came also a multitude out of the cities round about unto Jerusalem, bringing sick folks, and them which were vexed with unclean spirits: and they were healed every one.

2 Cor 1:19 For the Son of God, Jesus Christ, who was preached among you by us, even by me and Silvanus and Timotheus, was not yea and nay, but in him was yea. 20 For all the promises of God in him are yea, and in him Amen, unto the glory of God by us.

Ps 35:27 Let them shout for joy, and be glad, that favour my righteous cause: yea, let them say continually, Let the Lord be magnified, which hath pleasure in the prosperity of his servant. 28 And my tongue shall speak of thy righteousness and of thy praise all the day long.

2 Cor 4:13 We having the same spirit of faith, according as it is written, I believed, and therefore have I spoken; we also believe, and therefore speak.

Rom 10:6 But the righteousness which is of faith speaketh on this wise, Say not in thine heart, Who shall ascend into heaven? (that is, to bring Christ down from above:) 7 Or, Who shall descend into the deep? (that is, to bring up Christ again from the dead.) 8 But what saith it? The word is nigh thee, even in thy mouth, and in thy heart: that is, the word of faith, which we preach; 9 that if thou shalt confess with thy mouth the Lord Jesus, and shalt believe in thine heart that God hath raised him from the dead, thou shalt be *sozo*/saved. 10 For with the heart man believeth unto righteousness; and with the mouth confession is made unto *soteria*/salvation. 11 For the scripture saith, Whosoever believeth on him shall not be ashamed. 12 For there is no difference between the Jew and the Greek: for the same Lord over all is rich unto all that call upon him. 13 For whosoever shall call upon the name of the Lord shall be *sozo*/saved (*healed, unbound, and made whole and prosperous in all of God's goodness–the peace of God in Jesus Christ*).

Josh 1:6 Be strong and of a good courage: for unto this people shalt thou divide for an inheritance the land, which I sware unto their fathers to give them. 7 Only be thou strong and very courageous, that thou mayest observe to do according to all the law, which Moses my servant commanded thee: turn not from it to the right hand or to the left, that thou mayest prosper whithersoever thou goest. 8 This book of the law shall not depart out of thy mouth; but thou shalt meditate therein day and night, that thou mayest observe to do according to all that is written therein: for then thou shalt make thy way prosperous, and then thou shalt have good success. 9 Have not I commanded thee? Be strong and of a good courage; be not afraid, neither be thou dismayed: for the Lord thy God is with thee whithersoever thou goest.

The Healing Scriptures

Isa 57:18 I have seen his ways, and will heal him: I will lead him also, and restore comforts unto him and to his mourners. 19 I create the fruit of the lips; Peace, peace to him that is far off, and to him that is near, saith the LORD; and I will heal him.

Jer 29:11 For I know the thoughts that I think toward you, saith the LORD, thoughts of peace, and not of evil, to give you an expected end. 12 Then shall ye call upon me, and ye shall go and pray unto me, and I will hearken unto you.

Luke 12:32 Fear not, little flock; for it is your Father's good pleasure to give you the kingdom.

Prov 4:7 Wisdom is the principal thing; therefore get wisdom: and with all thy getting get understanding. 8 Exalt her, and she shall promote thee: she shall bring thee to honour, when thou dost embrace her. 9 She shall give to thine head an ornament of grace: a crown of glory shall she deliver to thee. 10 Hear, O my son, and receive my sayings; and the years of thy life shall be many.

Prov 4:20 My son, attend to my words; incline thine ear unto my sayings. 21 Let them not depart from thine eyes; keep them in the midst of thine heart. 22 For they are life unto those that find them, and health to all their flesh. 23 Keep thy heart with all diligence; for out of it are the issues of life. 24 Put away from thee a froward mouth, and perverse lips put far from thee. 25 Let thine eyes look right on, and let thine eyelids look straight before thee. 26 Ponder the path of thy feet, and let all thy ways be established. 27 Turn not to the right hand nor to the left: remove thy foot from evil.

Prov 22:20 Have not I written to thee excellent things in counsels and knowledge, 21 that I might make thee know the certainty of the words of truth; that thou mightest answer the words of truth to them that send unto thee?

Isa 35:3 Strengthen ye the weak hands, and confirm the feeble knees [Heb 12:12]. 4 say to them that are of a fearful heart, Be strong, fear not: behold, your God will come with vengeance, even God with a recompence; he will come and save you. 5 Then the eyes of the blind shall be opened, and the ears of the deaf shall be unstopped. 6 Then shall the lame man leap as an hart and the tongue of the dumb sing: for in the wilderness shall waters break out, and streams in the desert.

2 Cor 5:18 And all things are of God, who hath reconciled us to himself by Jesus Christ, and hath given to us the ministry of reconciliation; 19 to wit,

that God was in Christ, reconciling the world unto himself, not imputing their trespasses unto them; and hath committed unto us the word of reconciliation. 20 Now then we are ambassadors for Christ, as though God did beseech you by us: we pray you in Christ's stead, be ye reconciled to God. 21 For he hath made him to be sin for us, who knew no sin; that we might be made the righteousness of God in him. 6:1 We then, as workers together with him, beseech you also that ye receive not the grace of God in vain. 2 (For he saith, I have heard thee in a time accepted, and in the day of *soteria*/salvation have I succoured thee: behold (*make this change your life*), now is the accepted time; behold, now is the day of *soteria*/salvation.)

Heb 13:20 Now may the God of peace [Who is the Author and the Giver of peace], Who brought again from among the dead our Lord Jesus, that great Shepherd of the sheep, by the blood [that sealed, ratified] the everlasting agreement (covenant, testament) [*Gen 15:18;* Isa 55:3; 63:11; Ezek 37:26; Zech 9:11], 21 strengthen (complete, perfect) and make you what you ought to be and equip you with everything good that you may carry out His will; [while He Himself] works in you and accomplishes that which is pleasing in His sight, through Jesus Christ (the Messiah); to Whom be the glory forever and ever (to the ages of the ages). Amen (so be it). AMP

Gen 12:1 Now the Lord had said unto Abram, Get thee out of thy country, and from thy kindred, and from thy father's house, unto a land that I will shew thee: 2 and I will make of thee a great nation, and I will bless thee, and make thy name great; and thou shalt be a blessing: 3 and I will bless them that bless thee, and curse him that curseth thee: and in thee shall all families of the earth be blessed.

Matt 8:16 When the even was come, they brought unto him many that were possessed with devils: and he cast out the spirits with his word, and healed all that were sick: 17 that it might be fulfilled which was spoken by Esaias the prophet, saying, Himself *lambano*/took our infirmities, and bare our sicknesses.

Isa 53:4 Surely he hath *cabal*/borne (*lambano, took*) our griefs (*infirmities*), and *nasa*/carried (*to completion*) our sorrows (*sicknesses*): yet we did esteem him stricken, smitten of God, and afflicted. 5 But he was wounded for our transgressions, he was bruised for our iniquities: the chastisement of our peace was upon him; and with his stripes we are healed.

Heb 13:6 So we take comfort and are encouraged and confidently and boldly say, The Lord is my Helper; I will not be seized with alarm [I will not fear or dread or be terrified]. What can man do to me? [Ps 27:1; 118:6.] 8 Jesus Christ (the Messiah) is [always] the same, yesterday, today, [yes] and forever (to the ages). AMP

Ps 119:47 And I will delight myself in thy commandments, which I have loved. 48 My hands also will I lift up unto thy commandments, which I have loved; and I will meditate in thy statutes. 49 Remember the word unto thy servant, upon which thou hast caused me to hope. 50 This is my comfort in my affliction: for thy word hath quickened me.

Rom 8:9 But ye are not in the flesh, but in the Spirit, if so be that the Spirit of God dwell in you. Now if any man have not the Spirit of Christ, he is none of his. 10 And if Christ be in you, the body is dead because of sin; but the Spirit is *zoe*/life because of righteousness. 11 But if the Spirit of him that raised up Jesus from the dead dwell in you, he that raised up Christ from the dead shall also quicken your (*current*) mortal bodies by his Spirit that dwelleth in you.

Rom 10:16 But they have not all obeyed the gospel. For Esaias saith, Lord, who hath believed our report? 17 So then faith cometh by hearing, and hearing by the word of God [*in the Gospel of Jesus Christ*].

John 8:31 Then said Jesus to those Jews which believed on him, If ye continue in my word, then are ye my disciples indeed; 32 and ye shall know the truth, and the truth shall make you free.

Jer 23:29 Is not my word like as a fire? saith the LORD; and like a hammer that breaketh the rock in pieces?

2 Tim 3:15 ... the holy scriptures, which are able to make thee wise unto *soteria*/salvation through faith which is in Christ Jesus. 16 All scripture is given by inspiration of God, and is profitable for doctrine, for reproof, for correction, for instruction in righteousness: 17 that the man of God may be perfect, throughly furnished unto all good works.

John 14:12 Verily, verily, I say unto you, He that believeth on me, the works that I do shall he do also; and greater works than these shall he do; because I go unto my Father. 13 And whatsoever ye shall *aiteo*/ask (*by requiring, demanding and expecting as due by covenant promise*) in my name, that will I do, that the Father may be glorified in the Son. 14 If ye shall *aiteo*/ask (*by requiring, demanding and expecting as due by covenant promise*) any thing in my name, I will do it.

John 6:29 Jesus answered and said unto them, This is the work of God, that ye believe on him whom he hath sent.

Acts 16:31 And they said, Believe on the Lord Jesus Christ, and thou shalt be *sozo*/saved, and thy house.

1 John 3:22 And whatsoever we *aiteo*/ask (*by requiring, demanding and expecting as due by covenant promise*), we receive of him, because we keep his commandments, and do those things that are pleasing in his sight. 23 And this is his commandment, That we should believe on the name of his Son Jesus Christ, and *agape*/love one another, as he gave us commandment.

1 John 5:13 These things have I written unto you that believe on the name of the Son of God; that ye may know that ye have eternal *zoe*/life, and that ye may believe on the name of the Son of God. 14 And this is the confidence that we have in him, that, if we *aiteo*/ask (*by requiring, demanding as due by covenant promise*) any thing according to his will, he heareth us: 15 and if we know that he hear us, whatsoever we *aiteo*/ask (*by demanding as due by covenant promise*), we know that we have the *aiteo*/petitions that we *aiteo*/desired of him.

John 15:7 If ye abide in me, and my words abide in you, ye shall *aiteo*/ask (*by requiring, demanding and expecting as due by covenant promise*) what ye will, and it shall be done unto you. 8 Herein is my Father glorified, that ye bear much fruit; so shall ye be my disciples.

Eph 4:23 And be renewed in the spirit of your mind; 24 and that ye put on the new man, which after God is created in righteousness and true holiness.

Ex 15:26 And said, If thou wilt diligently hearken to the voice of the LORD thy God, and wilt do that which is right in his sight, and wilt give ear to his commandments, and keep all his statutes, I will put (*permit*) none of these diseases upon thee, which I have brought upon the Egyptians: for I am the LORD that healeth thee (*Jehovah Rophi*).

2 Cor 5:20 Now then we are ambassadors for Christ, as though God did beseech you by us: we pray you in Christ's stead, be ye reconciled to God. 21 For he hath made him to be sin for us, who knew no sin; that we might be made the righteousness of God in him (*Christ Jesus*).

Ex 23:25 And ye shall serve the LORD your God, and he shall bless thy bread, and thy water; and I will take sickness away from the midst of thee. 26 There shall nothing cast (*miscarry*) their young, nor be barren, in thy land: the number of thy days I will fulfil.

Job 5:17 Behold, happy is the man whom God correcteth: therefore despise not thou the chastening of the Almighty: 18 for he maketh sore, and bindeth up: he woundeth, and his hands make whole. 19 He shall deliver thee in six troubles: yea, in seven there shall no evil touch thee. 20 In famine he shall redeem thee from death: and in war from the power of the sword. 21 Thou shalt be hid from the scourge of the tongue: neither shalt thou be afraid of destruction when it cometh. 22 At destruction and famine thou shalt laugh: neither shalt thou be afraid of the beasts of the earth. 23 For thou shalt be in league with the stones of the field: and the beasts of the field shall be at peace with thee. 24 And thou shalt know that thy tabernacle shall be in peace; and thou shalt visit thy habitation, and shalt not sin. 25 Thou shalt know also that thy seed shall be great, and thine offspring as the grass of the earth. 26 Thou shalt come to thy grave in a full age, like as a shock of corn cometh in his season. 27 Lo this, we have searched it, so it is; hear it, and know thou it for thy good.

Ps 41:3 The LORD will strengthen him upon the bed of languishing: thou wilt make all his bed in his sickness.

Ps 147:3 He healeth the broken in heart, and bindeth up their wounds.

Jer 33:6 Behold, I will bring it health and cure, and I will cure them, and will reveal unto them the abundance of peace and truth. 7 And I will cause the captivity of Judah and the captivity of Israel to return, and will build them, as at the first. 8 And I will cleanse them from all their iniquity, whereby they have sinned against me; and I will pardon all their iniquities, whereby they have sinned, and whereby they have transgressed against me. 9 And it shall be to me a name of joy, a praise and an honour before all the nations of the earth, which shall hear all the good that I do unto them: and they shall fear and tremble for all the goodness and for all the prosperity that I procure unto it.

Luke 4:17 And there was delivered unto him the book of the prophet Esaias. And when he had opened the book, he found the place where it was written, 18 The Spirit of the Lord is upon me, because he hath anointed me to preach the gospel to the poor; he hath sent me to heal the brokenhearted, to preach deliverance to the captives, and recovering of sight to the blind, to set at liberty them that are bruised, 19 to preach the acceptable year of the Lord. 20 And he closed the book, and he gave it again to the minister, and sat down. And the eyes of all them that were in the synagogue were fastened on him. 21 And he began to say unto them, This day is this scripture fulfilled in your ears.

Isa 49:8 Thus saith the Lord, In an acceptable time have I heard thee, and in a day of salvation have I helped thee: and I will preserve thee, and give thee for a covenant of the people, to establish the earth, to cause to inherit the desolate heritages; 9 that thou mayest say to the prisoners, Go forth; to them that are in darkness, Shew yourselves. They shall feed in the ways, and their pastures shall be in all high places. 10 They shall not hunger nor thirst; neither shall the heat nor sun smite them: for he that hath *racham*/mercy on them shall lead them, even by the springs of water shall he guide them. 11 And I will make all my mountains a way, and my highways shall be exalted. ... 29 And kings shall be thy nursing fathers, and their queens thy nursing mothers: they shall bow down to thee with their face toward the earth, and lick up the dust of thy feet; and thou shalt know that I am the Lord: for they shall not be ashamed that wait for me. 24 Shall the prey be taken from the mighty, or the lawful captive delivered? 25 But thus saith the Lord, Even the captives of the mighty shall be taken away, and the prey of the terrible shall be delivered: for I will contend with him that contendeth with thee, and I will save thy children.

2 Cor 6:1 We then, as workers together with him, beseech you also that ye receive not the grace of God in vain. 2 (For he saith, I have heard thee in a time accepted, and in the day of *soteria*/salvation have I succoured thee: behold, now is the accepted time; behold, now is the day of *soteria*/salvation.)

Acts 28:8 And it came to pass, that the father of Publius lay sick of a fever and of a bloody flux: to whom Paul entered in, and prayed, and laid his hands on him, and healed him. 9 So when this was done, others also, which had diseases in the island, came, and were healed.

Eph 5:18 And do not get drunk with wine, for that is debauchery; but ever be filled and stimulated with the [Holy] Spirit [Prov 23:20]. 19 Speak out to one another in psalms and hymns and spiritual songs, offering praise with voices [and instruments] and making melody with all your heart to the Lord, 20 at all times and for everything giving thanks in the name of our Lord Jesus Christ to God the Father. AMP

Prov 24:16 For a righteous man falls seven times and rises again, but the wicked are overthrown by calamity [Job 5:19; Ps 34:19; 37:24; Mic 7:8]. AMP

The Healing Scriptures

Ps 10:4 The wicked, through the pride of his countenance, will not seek after God: God is not in all his thoughts.

2 Cor 10:2 But I beseech you, that I may not be bold when I am present with that confidence, wherewith I think to be bold against some, which think of us as if we walked according to the flesh. 3 For though we walk in the flesh, we do not war after the flesh: 4 (for the weapons of our warfare are not carnal, but mighty through God to the pulling down of strong holds;) 5 casting down imaginations, and every high thing that exalteth itself against the knowledge of God, and bringing into captivity every thought to the obedience of Christ.

2 Cor 5:13 For whether we be beside ourselves, it is to God: or whether we be sober, it is for your cause. 14 For the *agape*/love of Christ constraineth us; because we thus judge, that if one died for all, then were all dead: 15 and that he died for all, that they which *zao*/live should not henceforth *zao*/live unto themselves, but unto him which died for them, and rose again. 16 Wherefore henceforth know we no man after the flesh: yea, though we have known Christ after the flesh, yet now henceforth know we him no more. 17 Therefore if any man be in Christ, he is a new creature: old things are passed away; behold, all things are become new. 18 And all things are of God, who hath reconciled us to himself by Jesus Christ, and hath given to us the ministry of reconciliation; 19 to wit, that God was in Christ, reconciling the world unto himself, not imputing their trespasses unto them; and hath committed unto us the word of reconciliation. 20 Now then we are ambassadors for Christ, as though God did beseech you by us: we pray you in Christ's stead, be ye reconciled to God. 21 For he hath made him to be sin for us, who knew no sin; that we might be made the righteousness of God in him.

2 Cor 4:17 For our light affliction, which is but for a moment, worketh for us a far more exceeding and eternal weight of glory; 18 while we look not at the things which are seen, but at the things which are not seen: for the things which are seen are temporal; but the things which are not seen are eternal.

Gen 20:17 So Abraham prayed unto God: and God healed Abimelech, and his wife, and his maidservants; and they bare children.

Acts 10:38 How God anointed Jesus of Nazareth with the Holy Ghost and with power: who went about doing good, and healing all that were oppressed (*under the active dominion, reign or lordship*) of the devil (*in judgment against the devil*); for God was with him.

BATTLE PRAYER FOR DIVINE HEALING: FIELD MANUAL 2

Acts 14:3 Long time therefore abode they (*Paul and Barnabas*) speaking boldly in the Lord, which gave testimony unto the word of his grace, and granted signs and wonders to be done by their hands.

Ps 9:9 The LORD also will be a refuge for the oppressed, a refuge in times of trouble. 10 And they that know thy name will put their trust in thee: for thou, LORD, hast not forsaken them that seek thee.

Ps 103:1 Bless the LORD, O my soul: and all that is within me, bless his holy name. 2 Bless the LORD, O my soul, and forget not all his benefits: 3 who forgiveth all thine iniquities; who healeth all thy diseases; 4 who redeemeth thy life from destruction; who crowneth thee with *chesed*/lovingkindness and *racham*/tender mercies; 5 who satisfieth thy mouth with good things; so that thy youth is renewed like the eagle's. 6 The LORD executeth righteousness and judgment for all that are oppressed.

Ps 84:11 For the LORD God is a sun and shield: the LORD will give grace and glory: no good thing will he withhold from them that walk uprightly. 12 O LORD of hosts, blessed is the man that trusteth in thee.

Ps 146:5 Happy is he that hath the God of Jacob for his help, whose hope is in the LORD his God: 6 which made heaven, and earth, the sea, and all that therein is: which keepeth truth for ever: 7 which executeth judgment for the oppressed: which giveth food to the hungry. The LORD looseth the prisoners: 8 the LORD openeth the eyes of the blind: the LORD raiseth them that are bowed down: the LORD loveth the righteous: 9 the LORD preserveth the strangers; he relieveth the fatherless and widow: but the way of the wicked he turneth upside down. 10 The LORD shall reign for ever, even thy God, O Zion, unto all generations. Praise ye the LORD.

1 Kings 8:55 And he (*Solomon*) stood, and blessed all the congregation of Israel with a loud voice, saying, 56 Blessed be the LORD, that hath given rest unto his people Israel, according to all that he promised: there hath not failed one word of all his good promise, which he promised by the hand of Moses his servant.

Ps 118:16 The right hand of the LORD is exalted: the right hand of the LORD doeth valiantly. 17 I shall not die, but live, and declare the works of the LORD. 18 The LORD hath chastened me sore: but he hath not given me over unto death. 19 Open to me the gates of righteousness: I will go into them, and I will praise the LORD: 20 this gate of the LORD, into which the righteous shall enter. 21 I will praise thee: for thou hast heard me, and art become my salvation.

The Healing Scriptures

Hos 6:1 Come, and let us return unto the Lord: for he hath torn, and he will heal us; he hath smitten, and he will bind us up. 2 After two days will he revive us: in the third day he will raise us up, and we shall live in his sight.

Isa 29:18 And in that day shall the deaf hear the words of the book, and the eyes of the blind shall see out of obscurity, and out of darkness. 19 The meek also shall increase their joy in the Lord, and the poor among men shall rejoice in the Holy One of Israel. 20 For the terrible one is brought to nought, and the scorner is consumed, and all that watch for iniquity are cut off.

Isa 35:4 Say to them that are of a fearful heart, Be strong, fear not: behold, your God will come with vengeance, even God with a recompence; he will come and save you. 5 Then the eyes of the blind shall be opened, and the ears of the deaf shall be unstopped. 6 Then shall the lame man leap as an hart, and the tongue of the dumb sing: for in the wilderness shall waters break out, and streams in the desert. 7 And the parched ground shall become a pool, and the thirsty land springs of water: in the habitation of dragons, where each lay, shall be grass with reeds and rushes. 8 And an highway shall be there, and a way, and it shall be called The way of holiness; the unclean shall not pass over it; but it shall be for those: the wayfaring men, though fools, shall not err therein. 9 No lion shall be there, nor any ravenous beast shall go up thereon, it shall not be found there; but the redeemed shall walk there: 10 and the ransomed of the Lord shall return, and come to Zion with songs and everlasting joy upon their heads: they shall obtain joy and gladness, and sorrow and sighing shall flee away.

Jer 1:12 Then said the Lord unto me, Thou hast well seen: for I will hasten my word to perform it.

Jer 1:12 Then said the Lord to me, You have seen well, for I am alert and active, watching over My word to perform it. AMP

Ezek 12:28 Therefore say unto them, Thus saith the Lord God; There shall none of my words be prolonged any more, but the word which I have spoken shall be done, saith the Lord God.

Isa 43:25 I, even I, am he that blotteth out thy transgressions for mine own sake, and will not remember thy sins. 26 Put me in remembrance: let us plead together: declare thou, that thou mayest be justified.

Rom 3:21 But now the righteousness of God without the law is manifested, being witnessed by the law and the prophets; 22 even the righteousness of God which is by faith of Jesus Christ unto all and upon all them that believe: for there is no difference: 23 for all have sinned, and come short of the glory of God; 24 being justified freely by his grace through the redemption that is in Christ Jesus: 25 whom God hath set forth to be a propitiation through faith in his blood, to declare his righteousness for the remission of sins that are past, through the forbearance of God; 26 to declare, I say, at this time his righteousness: that he might be just, and the justifier of him which believeth in Jesus.

Joel 3:10 Beat your plowshares into swords, and your pruninghooks into spears: let the weak say, I am strong.

Ps 18:31 For who is God save the Lord? or who is a rock save our God? 32 It is God that girdeth me with strength, and maketh my way perfect. 33 He maketh my feet like hinds' feet, and setteth me upon my high places. 34 He teacheth my hands to war, so that a bow of steel is broken by mine arms. 35 Thou hast also given me the shield of thy salvation: and thy right hand hath holden me up, and thy gentleness hath made me great. 36 Thou hast enlarged my steps under me, that my feet did not slip. 37 I have pursued mine enemies, and overtaken them: neither did I turn again till they were consumed. 38 I have wounded them that they were not able to rise: they are fallen under my feet. 39 For thou hast girded me with strength unto the battle: thou hast subdued under me those that rose up against me. 40 Thou hast also given me the necks of mine enemies; that I might destroy them that hate me. 41 They cried, but there was none to save them: even unto the Lord, but he answered them not. 42 Then did I beat them small as the dust before the wind: I did cast them out as the dirt in the streets.

Eph 6:10 Finally, my brethren, be strong in the Lord, and in the power of his might. 11 Put on the whole armour of God, that ye may be able to stand against the wiles of the devil. 12 For we wrestle not against flesh and blood, but against principalities, against powers, against the rulers of the darkness of this world, against spiritual wickedness in high places. 13 Wherefore take unto you the whole armour of God, that ye may be able to withstand in the evil day, and having done all, to stand. 14 Stand therefore, having your loins girt about with truth, and having on the breastplate of righteousness; 15 and your feet shod with the preparation of the gospel of peace; 16 above all, taking the shield of faith, wherewith ye shall be able to quench all the fiery darts of the wicked. 17 And take the helmet of *soteria/* salvation, and the sword of the Spirit, which is the word of God: 18 praying always with all prayer and supplication in the Spirit, and watching thereunto with all perseverance and supplication for all saints;19 and for me, that utterance may be given unto me, that I may open my mouth boldly, to make known the mystery of the gospel, 20 for which I am an ambassador in bonds: that therein I may speak boldly, as I ought to speak.

Matt 8:2 And, behold, there came a leper and worshipped him, saying, Lord, if thou wilt, thou canst make me clean. 3 And Jesus put forth his hand, and touched him, saying, I will (*for this is what I am and long to do with delight*); be thou clean. And immediately his leprosy was cleansed. 4 And Jesus saith unto him, See thou tell no man; but go thy way, shew thyself to the priest, and offer the gift that Moses commanded, for a testimony unto them.

5 And when Jesus was entered into Capernaum, there came unto him a centurion, beseeching him, 6 and saying, Lord, my servant lieth at home sick of the palsy, grievously tormented. 7 And Jesus saith unto him, I will come and heal him. 8 The centurion answered and said, Lord, I am not worthy that thou shouldest come under my roof: but speak the word only, and my servant shall be healed. 9 For I am a man under authority, having soldiers under me: and I say to this man, Go, and he goeth; and to another, Come, and he cometh; and to my servant, Do this, and he doeth it. 10 When Jesus heard it, he marvelled, and said to them that followed, Verily I say unto you, I have not found so great faith, no, not in Israel. 11 And I say unto you, That many shall come from the east and west, and shall sit down with Abraham, and Isaac, and Jacob, in the kingdom of heaven. 12 But the children of the kingdom shall be cast out into outer darkness: there shall be weeping and gnashing of teeth. 13 And Jesus said unto the centurion, Go thy way; and as thou hast believed, so be it done unto thee. And his servant was healed in the selfsame hour.

14 And when Jesus was come into Peter's house, he saw his wife's mother laid, and sick of a fever. 15 And he touched her hand, and the fever left her: and she arose, and ministered unto them.

16 When the even was come, they brought unto him many that were possessed with devils: and he cast out the spirits with his word, and healed all that were sick: 17 that it might be fulfilled which was spoken by Esaias the prophet, saying, Himself *lambano*/took our infirmities, and bare our sicknesses.

Matt 9:18 While he spake these things unto them, behold, there came a certain ruler, and worshipped him, saying, My daughter is even now dead: but come and lay thy hand upon her, and she shall *zao*/live. 19 And Jesus arose, and followed him, and so did his disciples.

20 And, behold, a woman, which was diseased with an issue of blood twelve years, came behind him, and touched the hem of his garment: 21 for she said within herself, If I may but touch his garment, I shall be whole. 22 But Jesus turned him about, and when he saw her, he said, Daughter, be of good comfort; thy faith hath made thee whole. And the woman was made whole from that hour.

23 And when Jesus came into the ruler's house, and saw the minstrels and the people making a noise, 24 he said unto them, Give place: for the maid is not dead, but sleepeth. And they laughed him to scorn. 25 But when the people were put forth, he went in, and took her by the hand, and the maid arose. 26 And the fame hereof went abroad into all that land.

27 And when Jesus departed thence, two blind men followed him, crying, and saying, Thou Son of David, have mercy on us. 28 And when he was come into the house, the blind men came to him: and Jesus saith unto them, Believe ye that I am able to do this? They said unto him, Yea, Lord. 29 Then touched he their eyes, saying, According to your faith be it unto you. 30 And their eyes were opened; and Jesus straitly charged them, saying, See that no man know it. 31 But they, when they were departed, spread abroad his fame in all that country.

32 As they went out, behold, they brought to him a dumb man possessed with a devil. 33 And when the devil was cast out, the dumb spake: and the multitudes marvelled, saying, It was never so seen in Israel.

34 But the Pharisees said, He casteth out devils through the prince of the devils.

35 And Jesus went about all the cities and villages, teaching in their synagogues, and preaching the gospel of the kingdom, and healing every sickness and every disease among the people. 36 But when he saw the multitudes, he was moved with compassion on them, because they fainted, and were scattered abroad, as sheep having no shepherd. 37 Then saith he unto his disciples, The harvest truly is plenteous, but the labourers are few; 38 pray ye therefore the Lord of the harvest, that he will send forth labourers into his harvest.

Matt 18:18 Truly I tell you, whatever you forbid and declare to be improper and unlawful on earth must be what is already forbidden in heaven, and whatever you permit and declare proper and lawful on earth must be what is already permitted in heaven. 19 Again I tell you, if two of you on earth agree (harmonize together, make a symphony together) about whatever [anything and everything] they may *aiteo*/ask (*require, demand and expect as due by covenant promise*), it will come to pass and be done for them by My Father in heaven. 20 For wherever two or three are gathered (drawn together as My followers) in (into) My name, there I AM in the midst of them. [Ex 3:14] AMP

Ex 3:14 And God said unto Moses, I AM THAT I AM: and he said, Thus shalt thou say unto the children of Israel, I AM hath sent me unto you.

Matt 21:21 Jesus answered and said unto them, Verily I say unto you, If ye have faith, and doubt not, ye shall not only do this which is done to the fig tree, but also if ye shall say unto this mountain, Be thou removed, and be thou cast into the sea; it shall be done. 22 And all things, whatsoever ye shall *aiteo*/ask (*demand, require and expect as due by covenant promise*) in prayer, believing, ye shall receive.

Matt 11:12 And from the days of John the Baptist until the present time, the kingdom of heaven has endured violent assault, and violent men seize it by force [as a precious prize—a share in the heavenly kingdom is sought with most ardent zeal and intense exertion]. AMP

Mark 9:23 Jesus said unto him, If thou canst believe, all things are possible to him that believeth.

Mark 10:27 And Jesus looking upon them saith, With men it is impossible, but not with God: for with God all things are possible.

Mark 11:22 And Jesus answering saith unto them, Have faith in God. 23 For verily I say unto you, That whosoever shall say unto this mountain, Be thou removed, and be thou cast into the sea; and shall not doubt in his heart, but shall believe that those things which he saith shall come to pass; he shall have whatsoever he saith. 24 Therefore I say unto you, What things soever ye *aiteo*/desire (*demand, require and expect as due by covenant promise of God*), when ye pray, believe that ye receive them, and ye shall have them. 25 And when ye stand praying, forgive, if ye have ought against any: that your Father also which is in heaven may forgive you your trespasses. 26 But if ye do not forgive, neither will your Father which is in heaven forgive your trespasses.

Mark 16:14 Afterward he appeared unto the eleven as they sat at meat, and upbraided them with their unbelief and hardness of heart, because they believed not them which had seen him after he was risen. 15 And he said unto them, Go ye into all the world, and preach the gospel to every creature. 16 He that believeth and is baptized shall be *sozo*/saved; but he that believeth not shall be damned. 17 And these signs shall follow them that believe; In my name shall they cast out devils; they shall speak with new tongues; 18 they shall take up serpents; and if they drink any deadly thing, it shall not hurt them; they shall lay hands on the sick, and they shall recover. 19 So then after the Lord had spoken unto them, he was received up into heaven, and sat on the right hand of God. 20 And they went forth, and preached everywhere, the Lord working with them, and confirming the word with signs following. Amen.

John 10:10 The thief cometh not, but for to steal, and to kill, and to destroy: I am come that they might have *zoe*/life, and that they might have it more abundantly. 11 I am the good shepherd: the good shepherd giveth his *psuche*/life (*soul*) for the sheep.

Gen 18:14 Is any thing too hard for the Lord? At the time appointed I will return unto thee, according to the time of life, and Sarah shall have a son.

Rom 4:16 Therefore it (*righteousness*) is of faith, that it might be by grace; to the end the promise might be sure to all the seed; not to that only which is of the law, but to that also which is of the faith of Abraham; who is the father of us all, 17 (as it is written, I have made thee a father of many nations,) before him whom he believed, even God, who quickeneth the dead, and calleth those things which be not as though they were. 18 Who against hope believed in hope, that he might become the father of many nations; according to that which was spoken, So shall thy seed be. 19 And being not weak in faith, he considered not his own body now dead, when he was about an hundred years old, neither yet the deadness of Sara's womb: 20 he staggered not at the promise of God through unbelief; but was strong in faith, giving glory to God; 21 and being fully persuaded that, what he had promised, he was able also to perform. 22 And therefore it was imputed to him for righteousness. 23 Now it was not written for his sake alone, that it was imputed to him; 24 but for us also, to whom it shall be imputed, if we believe on him that raised up Jesus our Lord from the dead; 25 who was delivered for our offences, and was raised again for our justification (*when we were justified*). 5:1 Therefore being justified by faith, we have peace with God through our Lord Jesus Christ: 2 by whom also we have access by faith into this grace wherein we stand, and rejoice in hope of the glory of God. ... 5 And hope maketh not ashamed; because the *agape/* love of God is shed abroad in our hearts by the Holy Ghost which is given unto us. 6 For when we were yet without strength, in due time Christ died for the ungodly.

Rom 8:1 There is therefore now no condemnation to them which are in Christ Jesus, who walk not after the flesh, but after the Spirit. 2 For the law of the Spirit of *zoe*/life in Christ Jesus hath made me free from the law of sin and death. 3 For what the law could not do, in that it was weak through the flesh, God sending his own Son in the likeness of sinful flesh, and for sin, condemned sin in the flesh: 4 that the righteousness of the law might be fulfilled in us, who walk not after the flesh, but after the Spirit.

2 Cor 4:13 We having the same spirit of faith, according as it is written, I believed, and therefore have I spoken; we also believe, and therefore speak; 18 while we look not at the things which are seen, but at the things which are not seen: for the things which are seen are temporal; but the things which are not seen are eternal.

Ps 17:6 I have called upon thee, for thou wilt hear me, O God: incline thine ear unto me, and hear my speech. 7 Shew thy marvellous *chesed*/lovingkindness, O thou that savest by thy right hand them which put their trust in thee from those that rise up against them. 8 Keep me as the apple of the eye, hide me under the shadow of thy wings, 9 From the wicked that oppress me, from my deadly enemies, who compass me about.

Heb 11:1 NOW FAITH is the assurance (the confirmation, the title deed) of the things [we] hope for, being the proof of things [we] do not see and the conviction of their reality [faith perceiving as real fact what is not revealed to the senses]. 2 For by [faith—trust and holy fervor born of faith *in God*] the men of old had divine testimony borne to them and obtained a good report. AMP

Isa 45:11 Thus saith the LORD, the Holy One of Israel, and his Maker, Ask (*require*) me of things to come concerning my sons, and concerning the work of my hands command ye me.

Isa 55:11 So shall my word be that goeth forth out of my mouth: it shall not return unto me void, but it shall accomplish that which I please, and it shall prosper in the thing whereto I sent it.

Rom 10:8 But what saith it? The word is nigh thee, even in thy mouth, and in thy heart: that is, the word of faith, which we preach; 9 that if thou shalt confess with thy mouth the Lord Jesus, and shalt believe in thine heart that God hath raised him from the dead, thou shalt be *sozo*/saved. 10 For with the heart man believeth unto righteousness; and with the mouth confession is made unto *soteria*/salvation. 11 For the scripture saith, Whosoever believeth on him shall not be ashamed. 12 For there is no difference between the Jew and the Greek: for the same Lord over all is rich unto all that call upon him. 13 For whosoever shall call upon the name of the Lord shall be *sozo*/saved. 14 How then shall they call on him in whom they have not believed? and how shall they believe in him of whom they have not heard? and how shall they hear without a preacher? 15 And how shall they preach, except they be sent? as it is written, How beautiful are the feet of them that preach the gospel of peace, and bring glad tidings of good things! 16 But they have not all obeyed the gospel. For Esaias saith, Lord, who hath believed our report? 17 So then faith cometh by hearing, and hearing by the word of God.

Gal 3:12 And the law is not of faith: but, The man that doeth them shall *zao*/live in them. 13 Christ hath redeemed us from the curse of the law, being made a curse for us: for it is written, Cursed is every one that hangeth on a tree: 14 that the blessing of Abraham might come on the Gentiles through Jesus Christ; that we might receive the promise of the Spirit through faith.

Gal 3:26 For ye are all the children of God by faith in Christ Jesus.

Phil 1:5 For your fellowship in the gospel from the first day until now; 6 being confident of this very thing, that he which hath begun a good work in you will perform it until the day of Jesus Christ.

Phil 2:13 For it is God which worketh in you both to will and to do of his good pleasure.

Luke 12:27 Consider the lilies how they grow: they toil not, they spin not; and yet I say unto you, that Solomon in all his glory was not arrayed like one of these. 28 If then God so clothe the grass, which is to day in the field, and to morrow is cast into the oven; how much more will he clothe you, O ye of little faith? 29 And seek not ye what ye shall eat, or what ye shall drink, neither be ye of doubtful mind. 30 For all these things do the nations of the world seek after: and your Father knoweth that ye have need of these things. 31 But rather seek ye the kingdom of God; and all these things shall be added unto you. 32 Fear not, little flock; for it is your Father's good pleasure to give you the kingdom. 33 Sell that ye have, and give alms; provide yourselves bags which wax not old, a treasure in the heavens that faileth not, where no thief approacheth, neither moth corrupteth. 34 For where your treasure is, there will your heart be also.

Phil 4:6 Do not fret or have any anxiety about anything, but in every circumstance and in everything, by prayer and petition (definite requests), with thanksgiving, continue to make your wants (*aiteo requirements*) known to God. 7 And God's peace [shall be yours, that tranquil state of a soul assured of its *soteria/salvation* through Christ, and so fearing nothing from God and being content with its earthly lot of whatever sort that is, that peace] which transcends all understanding shall garrison and mount guard over your hearts and minds in Christ Jesus. 8 For the rest, brethren, whatever is true, whatever is worthy of reverence and is honorable and seemly, whatever is just, whatever is pure, whatever is lovely and lovable, whatever is kind and winsome and gracious, if there is any virtue and excellence, if there is anything worthy of praise, think on and weigh and take account of these things [fix your minds on them]. AMP

2 Tim 1:7 For God hath not given us the spirit of fear; but of power (*ability*), and of *agape*/love, and of a sound mind [*that thinks like Jesus*].

The Healing Scriptures

<u>Heb 13:8</u> Jesus Christ the same yesterday, and to day, and for ever.

<u>Phil 4:13</u> I can do all things through Christ which strengtheneth me. ... 19 But my God shall supply all your need (*aiteo, requirements and demands*) according to his riches in glory by Christ Jesus.

<u>Heb 10:22</u> Let us draw near with a true heart in full assurance of faith, having our hearts sprinkled from an evil conscience, and our bodies washed with pure water. 23 Let us hold fast the profession of our faith without wavering; (for he is faithful that promised.)

<u>Heb 10:35</u> Cast not away therefore your confidence, which hath great recompence of reward. 36 For ye have need of patience, that, after ye have done the will of God, ye might receive the promise.

<u>Heb 13:20</u> Now the God of peace, that brought again from the dead our Lord Jesus, that great shepherd of the sheep, through the blood of the everlasting covenant, 21 make you perfect in every good work to do his will, working in you that which is wellpleasing in his sight, through Jesus Christ; to whom be glory for ever and ever. Amen.

<u>Job 2:7</u> So went Satan forth from the presence of the Lord, and smote Job with sore boils from the sole of his foot unto his crown.

<u>Job 33:23</u> If there be a messenger with him, an interpreter, one among a thousand, to shew unto man his uprightness: 24 then he is gracious unto him, and saith, Deliver him from going down to the pit: I have found a ransom. 25 His flesh shall be fresher than a child's: he shall return to the days of his youth: 26 he shall pray unto God, and he will be favourable unto him: and he shall see his face with joy: for he will render unto man his righteousness.

<u>Job 42:4</u> Hear, I (*Job*) beseech thee, and I will speak: I will demand of thee, and declare thou unto me. 5 I have heard of thee by the hearing of the ear: but now mine eye seeth thee. 6 Wherefore I abhor myself, and repent in dust and ashes. 7 And it was so, that after the Lord had spoken these words unto Job, the Lord said to Eliphaz the Temanite, My wrath is kindled against thee, and against thy two friends: for ye have not spoken of me the thing that is right, as my servant Job hath. 8 Therefore take unto you now seven bullocks and seven rams, and go to my servant Job, and offer up for yourselves a burnt offering; and my servant Job shall pray for you: for him will I accept: lest I deal with you after your folly, in that ye

have not spoken of me the thing which is right, like my servant Job. 9 So Eliphaz the Temanite and Bildad the Shuhite and Zophar the Naamathite went, and did according as the Lord commanded them: the Lord also accepted Job. 10 And the Lord turned the captivity of Job, when he prayed for his friends: also the Lord gave Job twice as much as he had before.

1 Tim 2:5 For there is one God, and one mediator between God and men, the man Christ Jesus; 6 who gave himself a ransom for all, to be testified in due time.

Mark 10:45 For even the Son of man came not to be ministered unto, but to minister, and to give his *psuche*/life (*soul*) a ransom for many.

Jer 31:10 Hear the word of the Lord, O ye nations, and declare it in the isles afar off, and say, He that scattered Israel will gather him, and keep him, as a shepherd doth his flock. 11 For the Lord hath redeemed Jacob, and ransomed him from the hand of him that was stronger than he.

Col 1:12 Giving thanks (*continually*) unto the Father, which hath made us meet (*qualified by grace*) to be partakers of the inheritance of the saints in light: 13 who hath delivered us from the power of darkness, and hath translated us into the kingdom of his *agape*/dear Son: 14 in whom we have redemption through his blood, even the forgiveness (*remission, purging, putting away and obliteration*) of sins.

Luke 22:31 And the Lord said, Simon, Simon, behold, Satan hath desired to have you, that he may sift you as wheat: 32 but I have prayed for thee, that thy faith fail not: and when thou art converted, strengthen thy brethren.

James 4:7 Submit yourselves therefore to God. Resist the devil, and he will flee from you.

1 Pet 5:8 Be sober, be vigilant; because your adversary the devil, as a roaring lion, walketh about, seeking whom he may devour: 9 whom resist stedfast in the faith, knowing that the same afflictions are accomplished in your brethren that are in the world.

Rev 12:11 And they overcame him (*Satan*) by the blood of the Lamb, and by the word of their testimony; and they *agape*/loved not their lives unto the death.

Rev 5:13 And every creature which is in heaven, and on the earth, and under the earth, and such as are in the sea, and all that are in them, heard I saying, Blessing, and honour, and glory, and power, be unto him that sitteth upon the throne, and unto the Lamb for ever and ever. 14 And the four beasts said, Amen. And the four and twenty elders fell down and worshipped him that *zao*/liveth for ever and ever.

Father, in the name of Jesus, give us Your Spirit of wisdom and revelation in the knowledge of You with the eyes of our understanding being enlightened unto repentance, conversion, healing, strengthening the brethren and zealously doing good works, by faith in *agape*/love, to Your glory, by Your Spirit, so that we righteously use communion to set and keep ourselves and others walking in Your total salvation in Jesus. Father, work in us both to will and to do of Your good pleasure concerning the Lord's Supper and teach us Your Word: 1 Cor 11:17 Now in this that I declare unto you I praise you not, that ye come together not for the better, but for the worse. 18 For first of all, when ye come together in the church, I hear that there be divisions among you; and I partly believe it. 19 For there must be also heresies among you, that they which are approved may be made manifest among you. 20 When ye come together therefore into one place, this is not to eat the Lord's supper. 21 For in eating every one taketh before other his own supper: and one is hungry, and another is drunken. 22 What? have ye not houses to eat and to drink in? or despise ye the church (*assembly*) of God, and shame them that have not? What shall I say to you? shall I praise you in this? I praise you not.

23 For I have received of the Lord that which also I delivered unto you, That the Lord Jesus the same night in which he was betrayed took bread: 24 and when he had given thanks, he brake it, and said, Take, eat: this is my body, which is broken for you: this do in remembrance of me. 25 After the same manner also he took the cup, when he had supped, saying, This cup is the new testament in my blood: this do ye, as oft as ye drink it, in remembrance of me. 26 For as often as ye eat this bread, and drink this cup, ye do shew the Lord's death till he come.

27 Wherefore whosoever shall eat this bread, and drink this cup of the Lord, unworthily, shall be guilty of the body and blood of the Lord. 28 But let a man examine himself, and so let him eat of that bread, and drink of that cup. 29 For he that eateth and drinketh unworthily, eateth and drinketh damnation to himself, not discerning the Lord's body. 30 For this cause many are weak and sickly among you, and many sleep. 31 For if we would judge ourselves, we should not be judged. 32 But when we are judged, we are chastened of the Lord, that we should not be condemned with the world. 33 Wherefore, my brethren, when ye come together to eat, tarry one for another. 34 And if any man hunger, let him eat at home; that ye come not together unto condemnation. And the rest will I set in order when I come. *Thank You and praise You, Our Father, the God of All Comfort. In the name of Jesus, thank You, Abba Father, thank You. Thank You that You had the body of Jesus broken for us that*

we might be healed by His stripes, and that through His blood You purged our sins forever by the New Covenant of His blood. Thank You for the Gospel of grace in Jesus Christ. Thank You, Father. In the name of Jesus, thank You.

Praise You, Abba Father, You sent Jesus to wage war on the works of the devil: of sin, sickness, disease, poverty and impotency. In the name of Jesus, give us Your Spirit of wisdom and revelation in the knowledge of You in the power of our words and that authority given in the name of Jesus Christ in these scriptures:

<u>1 John 3:8</u> He that committeth sin is of the devil; for the devil sinneth from the beginning. For this purpose the Son of God was manifested, that he might destroy the works of the devil.

<u>Isa 61:1</u> The Spirit of the Lord God is upon me; because the Lord hath anointed me to preach good tidings unto the meek; he hath sent me to bind up the brokenhearted, to proclaim liberty to the captives, and the opening of the prison to them that are bound; 2 to proclaim the acceptable year of the Lord, and the day of vengeance of our God; to comfort all that mourn.

<u>Luke 4:18</u> The Spirit of the Lord is upon me, because he hath anointed me to preach the gospel to the poor; he hath sent me to heal the brokenhearted, to preach deliverance to the captives, and recovering of sight to the blind, to set at liberty them that are bruised, 19 to preach the acceptable year of the Lord. 20 And he closed the book, and he gave it again to the minister, and sat down. And the eyes of all them that were in the synagogue were fastened on him. 21 And he began to say unto them, This day is this scripture fulfilled in your ears.

<u>Acts 10:38</u> How God anointed Jesus of Nazareth with the Holy Ghost and with power: who went about doing good, and healing all that were oppressed (*under the active dominion, reign or lordship*) of the devil (*in active judgment against the devil*); for God was with him.

<u>Prov 29:2</u> When the righteous are in authority, the people rejoice: but when the wicked beareth rule, the people mourn.

<u>Matt 8:8</u> The centurion answered and said, Lord, I am not worthy that thou shouldest come under my roof: but speak the word only, and my servant shall be healed. 9 For I am a man under authority, having soldiers under me: and I say to this man, Go, and he goeth; and to another, Come, and he cometh; and to my servant, Do this, and he doeth it. 10 When Jesus heard it, he marvelled, and said to

The Healing Scriptures

them that followed, Verily I say unto you, I have not found so great faith, no, not in Israel. 11 And I say unto you, That many shall come from the east and west, and shall sit down with Abraham, and Isaac, and Jacob, in the kingdom of heaven. 12 But the children of the kingdom shall be cast out into outer darkness: there shall be weeping and gnashing of teeth. 13 And Jesus said unto the centurion, Go thy way; and as thou hast believed, so be it done unto thee. And his servant was healed in the selfsame hour.

Luke 7:8 For I also am a man set under authority, having under me soldiers, and I say unto one, Go, and he goeth; and to another, Come, and he cometh; and to my servant, Do this, and he doeth it. 9 When Jesus heard these things, he marvelled at him, and turned him about, and said unto the people that followed him, I say unto you, I have not found so great faith, no, not in Israel. 10 And they that were sent, returning to the house, found the servant whole that had been sick.

Luke 9:1 Then he called his twelve disciples together, and gave them power and authority over all devils, and to cure diseases. 2 And he sent them to preach the kingdom of God, and to heal the sick.

John 5:26 For as the Father hath *zoe*/life in himself; so hath he given to the Son to have *zoe*/life in himself; 27 and hath given him authority to execute judgment also, because he is the Son of man.

Ps 103:1 Bless the LORD, O my soul: and all that is within me, bless his holy name. 2 Bless the LORD, O my soul, and forget not all his benefits: 3 who forgiveth all thine iniquities; who healeth all thy diseases; 4 who redeemeth thy life from destruction; who crowneth thee with *chesed*/lovingkindness and *racham*/tender mercies; 5 who satisfieth thy mouth with good things; so that thy youth is renewed like the eagle's. 6 The LORD executeth righteousness and judgment for all that are oppressed. 7 He made known his ways unto Moses, his acts unto the children of Israel. 8 The LORD is merciful and gracious, slow to anger, and plenteous in *chesed*/mercy.

Acts 3:12 And when Peter saw it, he answered unto the people, Ye men of Israel, why marvel ye at this? or why look ye so earnestly on us, as though by our own power or holiness we had made this man to walk? 13 The God of Abraham, and of Isaac, and of Jacob, the God of our fathers, hath glorified his Son Jesus; whom ye delivered up, and denied him in the presence of Pilate, when he was determined to let him go. 14 But ye denied the Holy One and the Just, and desired a murderer to be granted unto you; 15 and killed the Prince of *zoe*/life, whom God hath raised from the dead; whereof we are witnesses. 16 And his name through faith in his name hath made this man strong, whom ye see and know: yea, the faith which is by him hath given him this perfect soundness in the presence of you all.

Acts 4:10 Be it known unto you all, and to all the people of Israel, that by the name of Jesus Christ of Nazareth, whom ye crucified, whom God raised from the dead, even by him doth this man stand here before you whole. 11 This is the stone which was set at nought of you builders, which is become the head of the corner. 12 Neither is there *soteria*/salvation in any other: for there is none other name under heaven given among men, whereby we must be *sozo*/saved (*healed, made whole and prosperous in every part of life*).

John 1:12 But as many as *lambano*/received him, to them gave he power to become the sons of God, even to them that believe on his name: 13 which were born, not of blood, nor of the will of the flesh, nor of the will of man, but of God. 14 And the Word was made flesh, and dwelt among us, (and we beheld his glory, the glory as of the only begotten of the Father,) full of grace and truth.

Luke 1:76 And thou, child, shalt be called the prophet of the Highest: for thou shalt go before the face of the Lord to prepare his ways; 77 to give knowledge of *soteria*/salvation unto his people by the remission of their sins, 78 through the tender mercy of our God; whereby the dayspring from on high hath visited us, 79 to give light to them that sit in darkness and in the shadow of death, to guide our feet into the way of peace.

Phil 2:15 That ye may be blameless and harmless, the sons of God, without rebuke, in the midst of a crooked and perverse nation, among whom ye shine as lights in the world; 16 holding forth the word of *zoe*/life; that I may rejoice in the day of Christ, that I have not run in vain, neither laboured in vain.

Matt 10:7 And as ye go, preach, saying, The kingdom of heaven is at hand. 8 Heal the sick, cleanse the lepers, raise the dead, cast out devils: freely ye have *lambano*/received, freely give.

1 Cor 15:24 Then cometh the end, when he shall have delivered up the kingdom to God, even the Father; when he shall have put down all rule and all authority and power. 25 For he must reign, till he hath put all enemies under his feet.

Titus 2:11 For the grace of God that bringeth *soteria*/salvation hath appeared to all men, 12 teaching us that, denying ungodliness and worldly lusts, we should *zao*/live soberly, righteously, and godly, in this present world; 13 looking for that blessed hope, and the glorious appearing of the great God and our Saviour Jesus Christ; 14 who gave himself for us, that he might redeem us from all iniquity, and purify unto himself a peculiar people, zealous of good works. 15 These things speak, and exhort, and rebuke with all authority. Let no man despise thee.

Matt 28:18 And Jesus came and spake unto them, saying, All power is given unto me in heaven and in earth. 19 Go ye therefore, and teach all nations, baptizing them in the name of the Father, and of the Son, and of the Holy Ghost: 20 teaching them to observe all things whatsoever I have commanded you: and, lo, I am with you alway, even unto the end of the world. Amen.

Mark 16:15 And he said unto them, Go ye into all the world, and preach the gospel to every creature. 16 He that believeth and is baptized shall be *sozo*/saved; but he that believeth not shall be damned. 17 And these signs shall follow them that believe; In my name shall they cast out devils; they shall speak with new tongues; 18 they shall take up serpents; and if they drink any deadly thing, it shall not hurt them; they shall lay hands on the sick, and they shall recover. 19 So then after the Lord had spoken unto them, he was received up into heaven, and sat on the right hand of God. 20 And they went forth, and preached everywhere, the Lord working with them, and confirming the word with signs following. Amen.

Thank You, Father, in the name of Jesus. You declared war on the devil in the Garden, sent Jesus to Earth to destroy the devil's works and told us to put Satan under our feet in the name of Jesus Christ to Your glory. Rom 14:11 For it is written, As I *zao*/live, saith the Lord, every knee shall bow to me, and every tongue shall confess to God. Isa 45:22 Look unto me, and be ye saved (*made whole*), all the ends of the earth: for I am God, and there is none else. 23 I have sworn by myself, the word is gone out of my mouth in righteousness, and shall not return, That unto me every knee shall bow, every tongue shall swear. 24 Surely, shall one say, in the LORD have I righteousness and strength: even to him shall men come; and all that are incensed against him shall be ashamed. 25 In the LORD shall all the seed of Israel be justified, and shall glory. Phil 2:10 That at the name of Jesus every knee should bow, of things in heaven, and things in earth, and things under the earth. *Thank You, Father, that You use us to execute the judgment written on Satan by using the name of Jesus to cast out every sickness, disease and oppression in everyone in whom the devil has done his works. Thank You, Father God.* Abba, *thank You!*

The Lord still heals though His people as we preach this truth of Jesus the Healer: Mark 16:20 And they went forth, and preached everywhere, the Lord working with them, and confirming the word with signs following. Amen. Acts 14:3 Long time therefore abode they (*Paul and Barnabas*) speaking boldly in the Lord, which gave testimony unto the word of his grace, and granted signs and wonders to be done by their hands. Acts 20:32 And now, brethren, I commend you to God, and to the word of his grace, which is able to build you up, and to give you an inheritance among all them which are sanctified. 1 Cor 2:4 And my speech and my preaching was not with enticing words of man's wisdom, but in demonstration of the Spirit and of power: 5 that your faith should not stand in the wisdom of men, but in the power of God. Rom 15:19 Through mighty signs and wonders, by the power of the Spirit of God; so that from Jerusalem, and round about unto Illyricum, I have fully preached the gospel of Christ. Rom 15:19 [Even as my preaching has been accompanied] with the power of signs and wonders, [and all of it] by the power of the Holy Spirit. [The result is] that starting from Jerusalem and as far round as Illyricum, I have fully preached the Gospel [faithfully executing, accomplishing, carrying out to the full the good news] of Christ (the Messiah) in its entirety. AMP Heb 2:3 How shall we escape, if we neglect so great *soteria*/salvation; which at the first began to be spoken by the Lord, and was confirmed unto us by them that heard him; 4 God also bearing them witness, both with signs and wonders, and with divers miracles, and gifts of the Holy Ghost, according to his own will? Gal 4:6 And because ye are sons, God hath sent forth the Spirit of his Son into your hearts, crying, Abba (*Daddy*), Father. 2 Tim 1:7 For God hath not given us the spirit of fear; but of *dunamis*/power, and of *agape*/love, and of a sound mind.

1 Cor 12:4 Now there are diversities of gifts, but the same Spirit. 5 And there are differences of administrations, but the same Lord. 6 And there are diversities of operations, but it is the same God which worketh all in all. 7 But the manifestation of the Spirit is given to every man to profit withal. 8 For to one is given by the Spirit the word of wisdom; to another the word of knowledge by the same Spirit; 9 to another faith by the same Spirit; to another the gifts of healing by the same Spirit; 10 to another the working of miracles; to another prophecy; to another discerning of spirits; to another divers kinds of tongues; to another the interpretation of tongues: 11 but all these worketh that one and the selfsame Spirit, dividing to every man severally as he will. 12 For as the body is one, and hath many members, and all the members of that one body, being many, are one body: so also is Christ. 1 Cor 12:31 But covet earnestly the best gifts: and yet shew I unto you a more excellent way. 1 Cor 14:1 Follow after *agape*/charity, and desire spiritual gifts, but rather that ye may prophesy.

As the Father used Jesus, He will use you. Death, in all its forms, is God's enemy. Sickness, disease, poverty, infirmity, weakness, sin are all God's enemies attacking God's creation to hurt God. You are not the target; God is. Satan tried to overthrow God, and now He is attacking God's creation to get at God. To build the Kingdom of God, Jesus said: <u>Luke 10:19</u> Behold (*make this change your life*), I give unto you power (*authority, commission and the resources of Heaven*) to tread on serpents and scorpions, and over all the power (*ability*) of the enemy: and nothing shall by any means hurt you. <u>Col 1:27</u> To whom God would make known what is the riches of the glory of this mystery among the Gentiles, *and all men*; which is Christ in you, the hope of glory. <u>1 John 4:4</u> Ye are of God, little children, and have overcome them: because greater is he that is in you, than he that is in the world. <u>John 20:21</u> Then said Jesus to them again, Peace be unto you: as my Father hath sent me, even so send I you. <u>John 14:9</u> Jesus saith unto him, Have I been so long time with you, and yet hast thou not known me, Philip? he that hath seen me hath seen the Father; and how sayest thou then, Shew us the Father? 10 Believest thou not that I am in the Father, and the Father in me? the words that I speak unto you I speak not of myself: but the Father that dwelleth in me, he doeth the works. 11 Believe me that I am in the Father, and the Father in me: or else believe me for the very works' sake. 12 Verily, verily, I say unto you, He that believeth on me, the works that I do shall he do also; and greater works than these shall he do; because I go unto my Father. 13 And whatsoever ye shall *aiteo*/ask (*by demanding as due by covenant promise*) in my name, that will I do, that the Father may be glorified in the Son. 14 If ye shall *aiteo*/ask (*demand as due by covenant promise*) any thing in my name, I will do it. <u>John 16:24</u> Hitherto have ye asked (*by demanding as due by covenant promise*) nothing in my name: *aiteo*/ask (*by demanding, requiring and expecting as due by covenant promise*), and ye shall receive, that your joy may be full. 25 These things have I spoken unto you in proverbs: but the time cometh, when I shall no more speak unto you in proverbs, but I shall shew you plainly of the Father. 26 At that day ye shall *aiteo*/ask (*by demanding as due by covenant promise*) in my name: and I say not unto you, that I will pray the Father for you: 27 for the Father himself *agape*/loveth you, because ye have *agape*/loved me, and have believed that I came out from God. 28 I came forth from the Father, and am come into the world: again, I leave the world, and go to the Father.

<u>Acts 8:6</u> And the people with one accord gave heed unto those things which Philip spake, hearing and seeing the miracles which he did. 7 For unclean spirits, crying with loud voice, came out of many that were possessed with them: and many taken with palsies, and that were lame, were healed.

<u>Acts 9:33</u> And there he found a certain man named Aeneas, which had kept his bed eight years, and was sick of the palsy. 34 And Peter said unto him, Aeneas, Jesus Christ maketh thee whole: arise, and make thy bed. And he arose immediately.

Col 1:12 Giving thanks (*continually*) unto the Father, which hath made us meet (*qualified and enabled by grace*) to be partakers of the inheritance of the saints in light: 13 who hath delivered us from the power of darkness, and hath translated us into the kingdom of his *agape*/dear Son: 14 in whom we have redemption through his blood, even the forgiveness (*remission, purging, putting away and obliteration*) of sins.

Rom 8:29 For whom he did foreknow, he also did predestinate to be conformed to the image of his Son, that he might be the firstborn among many brethren. 30 Moreover whom he did predestinate, them he also called: and whom he called, them he also justified: and whom he justified, them he also glorified.

2 Cor 5:5 Now he that hath wrought us for the selfsame thing is God, who also hath given unto us the earnest of the Spirit.

2 Cor 5:5 Now He Who has fashioned us [preparing and making us fit] for this very thing is God, Who also has given us the [Holy] Spirit as a guarantee [of the fulfillment of His promise]. 6 So then, we are always full of good and hopeful and confident courage; we know that while we are at home in the body, we are abroad from the home with the Lord [that is promised us]. 7 For we walk by faith [we regulate our lives and conduct ourselves by our conviction or belief respecting man's relationship to God and divine things, with trust and holy fervor; thus we walk] not by sight or appearance (*or feelings*). AMP

Titus 2:14 *Jesus*, Who gave himself for us, that he might redeem us from all iniquity, and purify unto himself a peculiar people, zealous of good works.

Rev 22:14 Blessed are they that do his commandments, that they may have right to the tree of *zoe*/life, and may enter in through the gates into the city.

Rev 1:17 And when I saw him (*Jesus*), I fell at his feet as dead. And he laid his right hand upon me, saying unto me, Fear not; I am the first and the last: 18 I am he that *zao*/liveth, and was dead; and, behold (*make this change your life*), I am *zao*/alive for evermore, Amen; and have the keys of hell and of death.

Eph 2:8 For by grace are ye *sozo*/saved through faith; and that not of yourselves: it is the gift of God: 9 not of works, lest any man should boast. 10 For we are his workmanship, created in Christ Jesus unto good works, which God hath before ordained that we should walk in them. 11 Wherefore remember, that ye being in time past Gentiles in the flesh, who are called Uncircumcision by that which is called the Circumcision in the flesh made by hands; 12 that at that time ye were without Christ, being aliens from the commonwealth of Israel, and strangers from the covenants of promise, having no hope, and without God in the world: 13 but now in Christ Jesus ye who sometimes were far off are made nigh by the blood of Christ. 14 For he is our peace, who hath made both one, and hath broken down the middle wall of partition between us; 15 having abolished in his flesh the enmity, even the law of commandments contained in ordinances; for to make in himself of twain one new man, so making peace; 16 and that he might reconcile both unto God in one body by the cross, having slain the enmity thereby: 17 and came and preached peace to you which were afar off, and to them that were nigh. 18 For through him we both have access by one Spirit unto the Father. 19 Now therefore ye are no more strangers and foreigners, but fellowcitizens with the saints, and of the household of God; 20 and are built upon the foundation of the apostles and prophets, Jesus Christ himself being the chief corner stone; 21 in whom all the building fitly framed together groweth unto an holy temple in the Lord: 22 in whom ye also are builded together for an habitation of God through the Spirit.

John 20:6 Then cometh Simon Peter following him, and went into the sepulchre, and seeth the linen clothes lie [*like an Egyptian mummy or shell, except empty, with no body*], 7 and the napkin, that was about his head, not lying with the linen clothes, but wrapped together in a place by itself. 8 Then went in also that other disciple, which came first to the sepulchre, and he saw, and believed. 9 For as yet they knew not the scripture, that he must rise again from the dead. 10 Then the disciples went away again unto their own home. 11 But Mary stood without at the sepulchre weeping: and as she wept, she stooped down, and looked into the sepulchre, 12 and seeth two angels in white sitting, the one at the head, and the other at the feet, where the body of Jesus had lain [*as if they were the cherubim on the mercy seat of the ark of covenant*]. 13 And they say unto her, Woman, why weepest thou? She saith unto them, Because they have taken away my Lord, and I know not where they have laid him. 14 And when she had thus said, she turned herself back, and saw Jesus standing, and knew not that it was Jesus.

Rom 5:18 Therefore as by the offence of one judgment came upon all men to condemnation; even so by the righteousness of one the free gift came upon all men unto justification of *zoe*/life. 19 For as by one man's disobedience many were made sinners, so by the obedience of one shall many be made righteous. 20 Moreover the law entered, that the offence might abound. But where sin abounded, grace did much more abound: 21 that as sin hath reigned unto death, even so might grace reign through righteousness unto eternal *zoe*/life by Jesus Christ our Lord.

Rom 6:14 For sin shall not have dominion over you: for ye are not under the law, but under grace.

Eph 1:2 Grace be to you, and peace, from God our Father, and from the Lord Jesus Christ. 3 Blessed be the God and Father of our Lord Jesus Christ, who hath blessed us with all spiritual blessings in heavenly places in Christ: 4 according as he hath chosen us in him before the foundation of the world, that we should be holy and without blame before him in *agape*/love: 5 having predestinated us unto the adoption of children by Jesus Christ to himself, according to the good pleasure of his will, 6 to the praise of the glory of his grace, wherein he hath made us accepted in the *agape*/beloved. 7 In whom we have redemption through his blood, the forgiveness (*remission, purging, putting away and obliteration*) of sins, according to the riches of his grace; 8 wherein he hath abounded toward us in all wisdom and prudence; 9 having made known unto us the mystery of his will, according to his good pleasure which he hath purposed in himself.

Eph 2:1 And you hath he quickened, who were dead in trespasses and sins; 2 wherein in time past ye walked according to the course of this world, according to the prince of the power of the air, the spirit that now worketh in the children of disobedience: 3 among whom also we all had our conversation in times past in the lusts of our flesh, fulfilling the desires of the flesh and of the mind; and were by nature the children of wrath, even as others. 4 But God, who is rich in mercy, for his great *agape*/love wherewith he *agape*/loved us, 5 even when we were dead in sins, hath quickened us together with Christ, (by grace ye are *sozo*/saved;) 6 and hath raised us up together, and made us sit together in heavenly places in Christ Jesus: 7 that in the ages to come he might shew the exceeding riches of his grace in his kindness toward us through Christ Jesus.

John 1:14 And the Word was made flesh, and dwelt among us, (and we beheld his glory, the glory as of the only begotten of the Father,) full of grace and truth. … 16 And of his fulness have all we *lambano*/received, and grace for grace. 17 For the law was given by Moses, but grace and truth came by Jesus Christ.

Acts 14:3 Long time therefore abode they (*Paul and Barnabas*) speaking boldly in the Lord, which gave testimony unto the word of his grace, and granted signs and wonders to be done by their hands.

1 Cor 2:4 And my speech and my preaching was not with enticing words of man's wisdom, but in demonstration of the Spirit and of power: 5 that your faith should not stand in the wisdom of men, but in the power of God.

The Healing Scriptures

<u>2 Cor 5:20</u> Now then we are ambassadors for Christ, as though God did beseech you by us: we pray you in Christ's stead, be ye reconciled to God. 21 For he hath made him to be sin for us, who knew no sin; that we might be made the righteousness of God in him. 6:1 We then, as workers together with him, beseech you also that ye receive not the grace of God in vain. 2 (For he saith, I have heard thee in a time accepted, and in the day of *soteria*/salvation have I succoured thee: behold, now is the accepted time; behold, now is the day of *soteria*/salvation.)

<u>Heb 1:1</u> God, who at sundry times and in divers manners spake in time past unto the fathers by the prophets, 2 hath in these last days spoken unto us by his Son, whom he hath appointed heir of all things, by whom also he made the worlds; 3 who being the brightness of his glory, and the express image of his person, and upholding all things by the word of his power, when he had by himself purged our sins, sat down on the right hand of the Majesty on high.

<u>Num 21:4</u> And they journeyed from mount Hor by the way of the Red sea, to compass the land of Edom: and the soul of the people was much discouraged because of the way. 5 And the people spake against God, and against Moses, Wherefore have ye brought us up out of Egypt to die in the wilderness? for there is no bread, neither is there any water; and our soul loatheth this light bread. 6 And the LORD sent fiery serpents among the people, and they bit the people; and much people of Israel died. 7 Therefore the people came to Moses, and said, We have sinned, for we have spoken against the LORD, and against thee; pray unto the LORD, that he take away the serpents from us. And Moses prayed for the people. 8 And the LORD said unto Moses, Make thee a fiery serpent, and set it upon a pole: and it shall come to pass, that every one that is bitten, when he looketh upon it, shall live. 9 And Moses made a serpent of brass, and put it upon a pole, and it came to pass, that if a serpent had bitten any man, when he beheld the serpent of brass, he lived.

<u>Deut 21:22</u> And if a man have committed a sin worthy of death, and he be to be put to death, and thou hang him on a tree: 23 his body shall not remain all night upon the tree, but thou shalt in any wise bury him that day; (for he that is hanged is accursed of God;) that thy land be not defiled, which the LORD thy God giveth thee for an inheritance.

<u>John 3:14</u> And as Moses lifted up the serpent in the wilderness, even so must the Son of man be lifted up: 15 that whosoever believeth in him should not perish, but have eternal *zoe*/life. 16 For God so *agape*/loved the world, that he gave his only begotten Son, that whosoever believeth in him should not perish, but have everlasting *zoe*/life. 17 For God sent not his Son into the world to condemn the world;

but that the world through him might be *sozo*/saved. 18 He that believeth on him is not condemned: but he that believeth not is condemned already, because he hath not believed in the name of the only begotten Son of God.

John 8:28 Then said Jesus unto them, When ye have lifted up the Son of man, then shall ye know that I am he, and that I do nothing of myself; but as my Father hath taught me, I speak these things. 29 And he that sent me is with me: the Father hath not left me alone; for I do always those things that please him.

John 12:31 Now is the judgment of this world: now shall the prince of this world be cast out. 32 And I, if I be lifted up from the earth, will draw all men unto me.

Luke 10:18 And he said unto them, I beheld Satan as lightning fall from heaven. 19 Behold (*make this change your life*), I give unto you power (*authority, commission and resources*) to tread on serpents and scorpions, and over all the power of the enemy: and nothing shall by any means hurt you.

Mark 9:38 And John answered him, saying, Master, we saw one casting out devils in thy name, and he followeth not us: and we forbad him, because he followeth not us. 39 But Jesus said, Forbid him not: for there is no man which shall do a miracle in my name, that can lightly speak evil of me. 40 For he that is not against us is on our part.

Num 12:13 And Moses cried unto the LORD, saying, Heal her now, O God, I beseech thee.

Acts 20:9 And there sat in a window a certain young man named Eutychus, being fallen into a deep sleep: and as Paul was long preaching, he sunk down with sleep, and fell down from the third loft, and was taken up dead. 10 And Paul went down, and fell on him, and embracing him said, Trouble not yourselves; for his *psuche*/life is in him. 11 When he therefore was come up again, and had broken bread, and eaten, and talked a long while, even till break of day, so he departed. 12 And they brought the young man *zao*/alive, and were not a little comforted.

Ps 6:2 O LORD, rebuke me not in thine anger, neither chasten me in thy hot displeasure. 2 Have mercy upon me, O LORD; for I am weak: O LORD, heal me; for my bones are vexed. … 9 The LORD hath heard my supplication; the LORD will receive my prayer. 10 Let all mine enemies be ashamed and sore vexed: let them return and be ashamed suddenly.

The Healing Scriptures

Ps 43:44 Then will I go unto the altar of God, unto God my exceeding joy: yea, upon the harp will I praise thee, O God my God. 5 Why art thou cast down, O my soul? and why art thou disquieted within me? hope in God: for I shall yet praise him, who is the health of my countenance, and my God.

Isa 53:5 But he was wounded for our transgressions, he was bruised for our iniquities: the chastisement of our peace was upon him; and with his stripes we are healed.

Mal 4:2 But unto you that fear my name shall the Sun of righteousness arise with healing in his wings (*prayer shawl ends*); and ye shall go forth, and grow up as calves of the stall.

2 Kings 4:25 So she went and came unto the man of God (*Elisha*) to mount Carmel. And it came to pass, when the man of God saw her afar off, that he said to Gehazi his servant, Behold, yonder is that Shunammite: 26 Run now, I pray thee, to meet her, and say unto her, Is it well with thee? is it well with thy husband? is it well with the child? And she answered, It is well. 27 And when she came to the man of God to the hill, she caught him by the feet: but Gehazi came near to thrust her away. And the man of God said, Let her alone; for her soul is vexed within her: and the Lord hath hid it from me, and hath not told me. 28 Then she said, Did I desire a son of my lord? did I not say, Do not deceive me? 29 Then he said to Gehazi, Gird up thy loins, and take my staff in thine hand, and go thy way: if thou meet any man, salute him not; and if any salute thee, answer him not again: and lay my staff upon the face of the child. 30 And the mother of the child said, As the Lord liveth, and as thy soul liveth, I will not leave thee. And he arose, and followed her. 31 And Gehazi passed on before them, and laid the staff upon the face of the child; but there was neither voice, nor hearing. Wherefore he went again to meet him, and told him, saying, The child is not awaked. 32 And when Elisha was come into the house, behold, the child was dead, and laid upon his bed. 33 He went in therefore, and shut the door upon them twain, and prayed unto the Lord. 34 And he went up, and lay upon the child, and put his mouth upon his mouth, and his eyes upon his eyes, and his hands upon his hands: and he stretched himself upon the child; and the flesh of the child waxed warm. 35 Then he returned, and walked in the house to and fro; and went up, and stretched himself upon him: and the child sneezed seven times, and the child opened his eyes. 36 And he called Gehazi, and said, Call this Shunammite. So he called her. And when she was come in unto him, he said, Take up thy son.

Battle Prayer for Divine Healing: Field Manual 2

1 Kings 18:42 ... And Elijah went up to the top of Carmel; and he cast himself down upon the earth, and put his face between his knees, 43 and said to his servant, Go up now, look toward the sea. And he went up, and looked, and said, There is nothing. And he said, Go again seven times. 44 And it came to pass at the seventh time, that he said, Behold, there ariseth a little cloud out of the sea, like a man's hand. And he said, Go up, say unto Ahab, Prepare thy chariot, and get thee down, that the rain stop thee not.

James 5:17 Elias (*Elijah*) was a man subject to like passions as we are, and he prayed earnestly that it might not rain: and it rained not on the earth by the space of three years and six months. 18 And he prayed again, and the heaven gave rain, and the earth brought forth her fruit. [*Notice "prayed again" plus the first time would be 8 times in 1 Kings 18:43-44.*]

Deut 28:59 Then the LORD will make thy plagues wonderful, and the plagues of thy seed, even great plagues, and of long continuance, and sore sicknesses, and of long continuance. 60 Moreover he will bring upon thee all the diseases of Egypt, which thou wast afraid of; and they shall cleave unto thee. 61 Also every sickness, and every plague, which is not written in the book of this law, them will the LORD bring upon thee, until thou be destroyed. [*Curses of the Law removed in Jesus per Gal 3:13*]

Gal 3:9 So then they which be of faith are blessed with faithful Abraham. 10 For as many as are of the works of the law are under the curse: for it is written, Cursed is every one that continueth not in all things which are written in the book of the law to do them. 11 But that no man is justified by the law in the sight of God, it is evident: for, The just shall *zao*/live by faith. 12 And the law is not of faith: but, The man that doeth them shall *zao*/live in them. 13 Christ hath redeemed us from the curse of the law, being made a curse for us: for it is written, Cursed is every one that hangeth on a tree: 14 that the blessing of Abraham might come on the Gentiles through Jesus Christ; that we might receive the promise of the Spirit through faith.

Matt 8:17 ... That it might be fulfilled which was spoken by Esaias the prophet, saying, Himself *lambano*/took our infirmities, and bare (*to completion*) our sicknesses.

Job 5:17 Behold, happy is the man whom God correcteth: therefore despise not thou the chastening of the Almighty: 18 for he maketh sore, and bindeth up: he woundeth, and his hands make whole. 19 He shall deliver thee in six troubles: yea, in seven there shall no evil touch thee. 20 In famine he shall redeem thee from death: and in war from the power of the sword. 21 Thou shalt be hid from the scourge of the tongue: neither shalt thou be afraid of destruction when it cometh. 22 At destruction and famine thou shalt laugh: neither shalt thou be afraid of the beasts of the earth. 23 For thou shalt be in league with the stones of the field: and the beasts of the field shall be at peace with thee. 24 And thou shalt know that thy tabernacle shall be in peace; and thou shalt visit thy habitation, and shalt not sin. 25 Thou shalt know also that thy seed shall be great, and thine offspring as the grass of the earth. 26 Thou shalt come to thy grave in a full age, like as a shock of corn cometh in, in his season.

1 Kings 8:27 But will God indeed dwell on the earth? behold, the heaven and heaven of heavens cannot contain thee; how much less this house that I have builded? 28 Yet have thou respect unto the prayer of thy servant (*Solomon*), and to his supplication, O Lord my God, to hearken unto the cry and to the prayer, which thy servant prayeth before thee to day: 29 that thine eyes may be open toward this house night and day, even toward the place of which thou hast said, My name shall be there: that thou mayest hearken unto the prayer which thy servant shall make toward this place. 30 And hearken thou to the supplication of thy servant, and of thy people Israel, when they shall pray toward this place: and hear thou in heaven thy dwelling place: and when thou hearest, forgive.

1 Kings 17:17 And it came to pass after these things, that the son of the woman, the mistress of the house, fell sick; and his sickness was so sore, that there was no breath left in him. 18 And she said unto Elijah, What have I to do with thee, O thou man of God? art thou come unto me to call my sin to remembrance, and to slay my son? 19 And he said unto her, Give me thy son. And he took him out of her bosom, and carried him up into a loft, where he abode, and laid him upon his own bed. 20 And he cried unto the Lord, and said, O Lord my God, hast thou also brought evil upon the widow with whom I sojourn, by slaying her son? 21 And he stretched himself upon the child three times, and cried unto the Lord, and said, O Lord my God, I pray thee, let this child's soul come into him again. 22 And the Lord heard the voice of Elijah; and the soul of the child came into him again, and he revived. 23 And Elijah took the child, and brought him down out of the chamber into the house, and delivered him unto his mother: and Elijah said, See, thy son liveth. 24 And the woman said to Elijah, Now by this I know that thou art a man of God, and that the word of the Lord in thy mouth is truth.

Luke 7:11 And it came to pass the day after, that he went into a city called Nain; and many of his disciples went with him, and much people. 12 Now when he came nigh to the gate of the city, behold, there was a dead man carried out, the only son of his mother, and she was a widow: and much people of the city was with her. 13 And when the Lord saw her, he had compassion on her, and said unto her, Weep not. 14 And he came and touched the bier: and they that bare him stood still. And he said, Young man, I say unto thee, Arise. 15 And he that was dead sat up, and began to speak. And he delivered him to his mother. 16 And there came a fear on all: and they glorified God, saying, That a great prophet is risen up among us; and, That God hath visited his people.

Acts 9:36 Now there was at Joppa a certain disciple named Tabitha, which by interpretation is called Dorcas: this woman was full of good works and almsdeeds which she did. 37 And it came to pass in those days, that she was sick, and died: whom when they had washed, they laid her in an upper chamber. 38 And forasmuch as Lydda was nigh to Joppa, and the disciples had heard that Peter was there, they sent unto him two men, desiring him that he would not delay to come to them. 39 Then Peter arose and went with them. When he was come, they brought him into the upper chamber: and all the widows stood by him weeping, and shewing the coats and garments which Dorcas made, while she was with them. 40 But Peter put them all forth, and kneeled down, and prayed; and turning him to the body said, Tabitha, arise. And she opened her eyes: and when she saw Peter, she sat up. 41 And he gave her his hand, and lifted her up, and when he had called the saints and widows, presented her alive. 42 And it was known throughout all Joppa; and many believed in the Lord.

Ezek 33:11 Say unto them, As I live, saith the Lord GOD, I have no pleasure in the death of the wicked; but that the wicked turn from his way and live: turn ye, turn ye from your evil ways; for why will ye die, O house of Israel?

John 4:46 So Jesus came again into Cana of Galilee, where he made the water wine. And there was a certain nobleman, whose son was sick at Capernaum. 47 When he heard that Jesus was come out of Judaea into Galilee, he went unto him, and besought him that he would come down, and heal his son: for he was at the point of death. 48 Then said Jesus unto him, Except ye see signs and wonders, ye will not believe. 49 The nobleman saith unto him, Sir, come down ere my child die. 50 Jesus saith unto him, Go thy way; thy son *zao*/liveth. And the man believed the word that Jesus had spoken unto him, and he went his way. 51 And as he was now going down, his servants met him, and told him, saying, Thy son *zao*/liveth. 52 Then inquired he of them the hour when he began to amend. And they said unto him, Yesterday at the seventh hour the fever left him. 53 So the father knew that it was at the same hour, in the which Jesus said unto him, Thy son *zao*/liveth: and himself believed, and his whole house.

The Healing Scriptures

54 This is again the second miracle that Jesus did, when he was come out of Judaea into Galilee.

Mark 1:23 And there was in their synagogue a man with an unclean spirit; and he cried out, 24 Saying, Let us alone; what have we to do with thee, thou Jesus of Nazareth? art thou come to destroy (*ruin, loss of all well-being, no life*) us? I know thee who thou art, the Holy One of God. 25 And Jesus rebuked him, saying, Hold thy peace, and come out of him. 26 And when the unclean spirit had torn him, and cried with a loud voice, he came out of him. 27 And they were all amazed, insomuch that they questioned among themselves, saying, What thing is this? what new doctrine is this? for with authority commandeth he even the unclean spirits, and they do obey him. ... 29 And forthwith, when they were come out of the synagogue, they entered into the house of Simon and Andrew, with James and John. 30 But Simon's wife's mother lay sick of a fever, and anon they tell him of her. 31 And he came and took her by the hand, and lifted her up; and immediately the fever left her, and she ministered unto them.

32 And at even, when the sun did set, they brought unto him all that were diseased, and them that were possessed with devils. 33 And all the city was gathered together at the door. 34 And he healed many that were sick of divers diseases, and cast out many devils; and suffered not the devils to speak, because they knew him.

Luke 4:33 And in the synagogue there was a man, which had a spirit of an unclean devil, and cried out with a loud voice, 34 saying, Let us alone; what have we to do with thee, thou Jesus of Nazareth? art thou come to destroy (*ruin, loss of all well-being, no life*) us? I know thee who thou art; the Holy One of God. 35 And Jesus rebuked him, saying, Hold thy peace, and come out of him. And when the devil had thrown him in the midst, he came out of him, and hurt him not. 36 And they were all amazed, and spake among themselves, saying, What a word is this! for with authority and power he commandeth the unclean spirits, and they come out. 37 And the fame of him went out into every place of the country round about.

38 And he arose out of the synagogue, and entered into Simon's house. And Simon's wife's mother was taken with a great fever; and they besought him for her. 39 And he stood over her, and rebuked the fever; and it left her: and immediately she arose and ministered unto them.

40 Now when the sun was setting, all they that had any sick with divers diseases brought them unto him; and he laid his hands on every one of them, and healed them. 41 And devils also came out of many, crying out, and saying, Thou art Christ the Son of God. And he rebuking them suffered them not to speak: for they knew that he was Christ.

Matt 8:14 And when Jesus was come into Peter's house, he saw his wife's mother laid, and sick of a fever. 15 And he touched her hand, and the fever left her: and she arose, and ministered unto them.

16 When the even was come, they brought unto him many that were possessed with devils: and he cast out the spirits with his word, and healed all that were sick: 17 that it might be fulfilled which was spoken by Esaias the prophet, saying, Himself *lambano*/took our infirmities, and bare (*to completion*) our sicknesses.

Matt 4:23 And Jesus went about all Galilee, teaching in their synagogues, and preaching the gospel of the kingdom, and healing all manner of sickness and all manner of disease among the people. 24 And his fame went throughout all Syria: and they brought unto him all sick people that were taken with divers diseases and torments, and those which were possessed with devils, and those which were lunatick, and those that had the palsy; and he healed them.

Matt 8:2 And, behold, there came a leper and worshipped him, saying, Lord, if thou wilt, thou canst make me clean. 3 And Jesus put forth his hand, and touched him, saying, I will (*gladly*); be thou clean. And immediately his leprosy was cleansed. 4 And Jesus saith unto him, See thou tell no man; but go thy way, shew thyself to the priest, and offer the gift that Moses commanded, for a testimony unto them.

5 And when Jesus was entered into Capernaum, there came unto him a centurion, beseeching him, 6 and saying, Lord, my servant lieth at home sick of the palsy, grievously tormented. 7 And Jesus saith unto him, I will come and heal him. 8 The centurion answered and said, Lord, I am not worthy that thou shouldest come under my roof: but speak the word only, and my servant shall be healed. 9 For I am a man under authority, having soldiers under me: and I say to this man, Go, and he goeth; and to another, Come, and he cometh; and to my servant, Do this, and he doeth it. 10 When Jesus heard it, he marvelled, and said to them that followed, Verily I say unto you, I have not found so great faith, no, not in Israel. 11 And I say unto you, That many shall come from the east and west, and shall sit down with Abraham, and Isaac, and Jacob, in the kingdom of heaven. 12 But the children of the kingdom shall be cast out into outer darkness: there shall be weeping and gnashing of teeth. 13 And Jesus said unto the centurion, Go thy way; and as thou hast believed, so be it done unto thee. And his servant was healed in the selfsame hour.

Mark 1:39 And he preached in their synagogues throughout all Galilee, and cast out devils. 40 And there came a leper to him, beseeching him, and kneeling down to him, and saying unto him, If thou wilt, thou canst make me clean. 41 And Jesus, moved with compassion, put forth his hand, and touched him, and saith unto him, I will (*gladly*); be thou clean. 42 And as soon as he had spoken, immediately the leprosy departed from him, and he was cleansed. 43 And he straitly charged him, and forthwith sent him away; 44 and saith unto him, See thou say nothing to any man: but go thy way, shew thyself to the priest, and offer for thy cleansing those things which Moses commanded, for a testimony unto them.

Luke 5:12 And it came to pass, when he was in a certain city, behold a man full of leprosy: who seeing Jesus fell on his face, and besought him, saying, Lord, if thou wilt, thou canst make me clean. 13 And he put forth his hand, and touched him, saying, I will (*gladly for this I am and do*): be thou clean. And immediately the leprosy departed from him. 14 And he charged him to tell no man: but go, and shew thyself to the priest, and offer for thy cleansing, according as Moses commanded, for a testimony unto them. 15 But so much the more went there a fame abroad of him: and great multitudes came together to hear, and to be healed by him of their infirmities. 16 And he withdrew himself into the wilderness, and prayed.

17 And it came to pass on a certain day, as he was teaching, that there were Pharisees and doctors of the law sitting by, which were come out of every town of Galilee, and Judaea, and Jerusalem: and the power of the Lord was present to heal them. 18 And, behold, men brought in a bed a man which was taken with a palsy: and they sought means to bring him in, and to lay him before him. 19 And when they could not find by what way they might bring him in because of the multitude, they went upon the housetop, and let him down through the tiling with his couch into the midst before Jesus. 20 And when he saw their faith, he said unto him, Man, thy sins are forgiven thee. 21 And the scribes and the Pharisees began to reason, saying, Who is this which speaketh blasphemies? Who can forgive sins, but God alone? 22 But when Jesus perceived their thoughts, he answering said unto them, What reason ye in your hearts? 23 Whether is easier, to say, Thy sins be forgiven thee; or to say, Rise up and walk? 24 But that ye may know that the Son of man hath power upon earth to forgive sins, (he said unto the sick of the palsy,) I say unto thee, Arise, and take up thy couch, and go into thine house. 25 And immediately he rose up before them, and took up that whereon he lay, and departed to his own house, glorifying God. 26 And they were all amazed, and they glorified God, and were filled with fear, saying, We have seen strange things to day.

Matt 9:2 And, behold, they brought to him a man sick of the palsy, lying on a bed: and Jesus seeing their faith said unto the sick of the palsy; Son, be of good cheer; thy sins be forgiven thee. 3 And, behold, certain of the scribes said within themselves, This man blasphemeth. 4 And Jesus knowing their thoughts said, Wherefore think ye evil in your hearts? 5 For whether is easier, to say, Thy sins be forgiven thee; or to say, Arise, and walk? 6 But that ye may know that the Son of man hath power on earth to forgive sins, (then saith he to the sick of the palsy,) Arise, take up thy bed, and go unto thine house. 7 And he arose, and departed to his house. 8 But when the multitudes saw it, they marvelled, and glorified God, which had given such power unto men.

Mark 2:2 And straightway many were gathered together, insomuch that there was no room to receive them, no, not so much as about the door: and he preached the word unto them. 3 And they come unto him, bringing one sick of the palsy, which was borne of four. 4 And when they could not come nigh unto him for the press, they uncovered the roof where he was: and when they had broken it up, they let down the bed wherein the sick of the palsy lay. 5 When Jesus saw their faith, he said unto the sick of the palsy, Son, thy sins be forgiven thee. 6 But there were certain of the scribes sitting there, and reasoning in their hearts, 7 Why doth this man thus speak blasphemies? who can forgive sins but God only? 8 And immediately when Jesus perceived in his spirit that they so reasoned within themselves, he said unto them, Why reason ye these things in your hearts? 9 Whether is it easier to say to the sick of the palsy, Thy sins be forgiven thee; or to say, Arise, and take up thy bed, and walk? 10 But that ye may know that the Son of man hath power on earth to forgive sins, (he saith to the sick of the palsy,) 11 I say unto thee, Arise, and take up thy bed, and go thy way into thine house. 12 And immediately he arose, took up the bed, and went forth before them all; insomuch that they were all amazed, and glorified God, saying, We never saw it on this fashion.

2 Chron 30:18 For a multitude of the people, even many of Ephraim, and Manasseh, Issachar, and Zebulun, had not cleansed themselves, yet did they eat the passover otherwise than it was written. But Hezekiah prayed for them, saying, The good LORD pardon every one 19 that prepareth his heart to seek God, the LORD God of his fathers, though he be not cleansed according to the purification of the sanctuary. 20 And the LORD hearkened to Hezekiah, and healed the people.

James 5:14 Is any sick among you? let him call for the elders of the church; and let them pray over him, anointing him with oil in the name of the Lord: 15 and the prayer of faith shall *sozo*/save the sick, and the Lord shall raise him up; and if he have committed sins, they shall be forgiven him. 16 Confess your faults one to another, and pray one for another, that ye may be *iaomai*/healed (*physically cured*). The effectual fervent prayer of a righteous man availeth much.

John 5:2 Now there is at Jerusalem by the sheep market a pool, which is called in the Hebrew tongue Bethesda, having five porches. 3 In these lay a great multitude of impotent folk, of blind, halt, withered, waiting for the moving of the water.

4 For an angel went down at a certain season into the pool, and troubled the water: whosoever then first after the troubling of the water stepped in was made whole of whatsoever disease he had. 5 And a certain man was there, which had an infirmity thirty and eight years. 6 When Jesus saw him lie, and knew that he had been now a long time in that case, he saith unto him, Wilt thou be made whole? 7 The impotent man answered him, Sir, I have no man, when the water is troubled, to put me into the pool: but while I am coming, another steppeth down before me. 8 Jesus saith unto him, Rise, take up thy bed, and walk. ... 14 Afterward Jesus findeth him in the temple, and said unto him, Behold, thou art made whole: sin no more, lest a worse thing come unto thee. 15 The man departed, and told the Jews that it was Jesus, which had made him whole.

<u>Matt 12:10</u> And, behold, there was a man which had his hand withered. And they asked him, saying, Is it lawful to heal on the sabbath days? that they might accuse him. 11 And he said unto them, What man shall there be among you, that shall have one sheep, and if it fall into a pit on the sabbath day, will he not lay hold on it, and lift it out? 12 How much then is a man better than a sheep? Wherefore it is lawful to do well on the sabbath days. 13 Then saith he to the man, Stretch forth thine hand. And he stretched it forth; and it was restored whole, like as the other.

<u>Mark 3:1</u> And he entered again into the synagogue; and there was a man there which had a withered hand. 2 And they watched him, whether he would heal him on the sabbath day; that they might accuse him. 3 And he saith unto the man which had the withered hand, Stand forth. 4 And he saith unto them, Is it lawful to do good on the sabbath days, or to do evil? To *sozo*/save life, or to kill? But they held their peace. 5 And when he had looked round about on them with anger, being grieved for the hardness of their hearts, he saith unto the man, Stretch forth thine hand. And he stretched it out: and his hand was restored whole as the other.

<u>Luke 6:6</u> And it came to pass also on another sabbath, that he entered into the synagogue and taught: and there was a man whose right hand was withered. 7 And the scribes and Pharisees watched him, whether he would heal on the sabbath day; that they might find an accusation against him. 8 But he knew their thoughts, and said to the man which had the withered hand, Rise up, and stand forth in the midst. And he arose and stood forth. 9 Then said Jesus unto them, I will ask you one thing; Is it lawful on the sabbath days to do good, or to do evil? to *sozo*/save life, or to destroy it? 10 And looking round about upon them all, he said unto the man, Stretch forth thy hand. And he did so: and his hand was restored whole as the other.

Mark 3:9 And he spake to his disciples, that a small ship should wait on him because of the multitude, lest they should throng him. 10 For he had healed many; insomuch that they pressed upon him for to touch him, as many as had plagues. 11 And unclean spirits, when they saw him, fell down before him, and cried, saying, Thou art the Son of God. 12 And he straitly charged them that they should not make him known. 13 And he goeth up into a mountain, and calleth unto him whom he would: and they came unto him. 14 And he ordained twelve, that they should be with him, and that he might send them forth to preach, 15 and to have power to heal sicknesses, and to cast out devils.

Luke 6:17 And he came down with them, and stood in the plain, and the company of his disciples, and a great multitude of people out of all Judaea and Jerusalem, and from the sea coast of Tyre and Sidon, which came to hear him, and to be healed of their diseases; 18 and they that were vexed with unclean spirits: and they were healed. 19 And the whole multitude sought to touch him: for there went *dunamis*/virtue (*power, ability*) out of him, and healed them all.

Luke 7:20 When the men were come unto him, they said, John Baptist hath sent us unto thee, saying, Art thou he that should come? or look we for another? 21 And in that same hour he cured many of their infirmities and plagues, and of evil spirits; and unto many that were blind he gave sight. 22 Then Jesus answering said unto them, Go your way, and tell John what things ye have seen and heard; how that the blind see, the lame walk, the lepers are cleansed, the deaf hear, the dead are raised, to the poor the gospel is preached. 23 And blessed is he, whosoever shall not be offended in me.

Matt 11:2 Now when John had heard in the prison the works of Christ, he sent two of his disciples, 3 and said unto him, Art thou he that should come, or do we look for another? 4 Jesus answered and said unto them, Go and shew John again those things which ye do hear and see: 5 the blind receive their sight, and the lame walk, the lepers are cleansed, and the deaf hear, the dead are raised up, and the poor have the gospel preached to them. 6 And blessed is he, whosoever shall not be offended in me.

Matt 11:20 Then began he to upbraid the cities wherein most of his *dunamis*/mighty works were done, because they repented not.

Luke 8:1 And it came to pass afterward, that he went throughout every city and village, preaching and shewing the glad tidings of the kingdom of God: and the twelve were with him, 2 and certain women, which had been healed of evil spirits and infirmities, Mary called Magdalene, out of whom went seven devils.

Matt 8:25 And his disciples came to him, and awoke him, saying, Lord, *sozo/* save us: we perish. 26 And he saith unto them, Why are ye fearful, O ye of little faith? Then he arose, and rebuked the winds and the sea; and there was a great calm. 27 But the men marvelled, saying, What manner of man is this, that even the winds and the sea obey him! 28 And when he was come to the other side into the country of the Gergesenes, there met him two possessed with devils, coming out of the tombs, exceeding fierce, so that no man might pass by that way. 29 And, behold, they cried out, saying, What have we to do with thee, Jesus, thou Son of God? art thou come hither to torment (*cause pain by judgment*) us before the time? 30 And there was a good way off from them an herd of many swine feeding. 31 So the devils besought him, saying, If thou cast us out, suffer us to go away into the herd of swine. 32 And he said unto them, Go. And when they were come out, they went into the herd of swine: and, behold, the whole herd of swine ran violently down a steep place into the sea, and perished in the waters. 33 And they that kept them fled, and went their ways into the city, and told every thing, and what was befallen to the possessed of the devils. [*Due to different reporters different numbers are given.*]

Mark 5:2 And when he was come out of the ship, immediately there met him out of the tombs a man with an unclean spirit, 3 who had his dwelling among the tombs; and no man could bind him, no, not with chains: 4 because that he had been often bound with fetters and chains, and the chains had been plucked asunder by him, and the fetters broken in pieces: neither could any man tame him. 5 And always, night and day, he was in the mountains, and in the tombs, crying, and cutting himself with stones. 6 But when he saw Jesus afar off, he ran and worshipped him, 7 and cried with a loud voice, and said, What have I to do with thee, Jesus, thou Son of the most high God? I adjure thee by God, that thou torment (*cause pain by judgment*) me not. 8 For he said unto him, Come out of the man, thou unclean spirit. 9 And he asked him, What is thy name? And he answered, saying, My name is Legion: for we are many. 10 And he besought him much that he would not send them away out of the country. 11 Now there was there nigh unto the mountains a great herd of swine feeding. 12 And all the devils besought him, saying, Send us into the swine, that we may enter into them. 13 And forthwith Jesus gave them leave. And the unclean spirits went out, and entered into the swine: and the herd ran violently down a steep place into the sea, (they were about two thousand;) and were choked in the sea.

Luke 8:26 And they arrived at the country of the Gadarenes, which is over against Galilee. 27 And when he went forth to land, there met him out of the city a certain man, which had devils long time, and ware no clothes, neither abode in any house, but in the tombs. 28 When he saw Jesus, he cried out, and fell down before him, and with a loud voice said, What have I to do with thee, Jesus, thou Son of God most high? I beseech thee, torment (*cause pain by judgment*) me not. 29 (For he had commanded the unclean spirit to come out of the man. For oftentimes it had caught him: and he was kept bound with chains and in fetters; and he brake the bands, and was driven of the devil into the wilderness.) 30 And Jesus asked him, saying, What is thy name? And he said, Legion: because many devils were entered into him. 31 And they besought him that he would not command them to go out into the deep. 32 And there was there an herd of many swine feeding on the mountain: and they besought him that he would suffer them to enter into them. And he suffered them. 33 Then went the devils out of the man, and entered into the swine: and the herd ran violently down a steep place into the lake, and were choked.

Luke 8:41 And, behold, there came a man named Jairus, and he was a ruler of the synagogue: and he fell down at Jesus' feet, and besought him that he would come into his house: 42 for he had one only daughter, about twelve years of age, and she lay a dying. But as he went the people thronged him. 43 And a woman having an issue of blood twelve years, which had spent all her living upon physicians, neither could be healed of any, 44 came behind him, and touched the border of his garment: and immediately her issue of blood stanched. 45 And Jesus said, Who touched me? When all denied, Peter and they that were with him said, Master, the multitude throng thee and press thee, and sayest thou, Who touched me? 46 And Jesus said, Somebody hath touched me: for I perceive that *dunamis*/virtue (*power*) is gone out of me. 47 And when the woman saw that she was not hid, she came trembling, and falling down before him, she declared unto him before all the people for what cause she had touched him and how she was healed immediately. 48 And he said unto her, Daughter, be of good comfort: thy faith hath made thee whole; go in peace. 49 While he yet spake, there cometh one from the ruler of the synagogue's house, saying to him, Thy daughter is dead; trouble not the Master. 50 But when Jesus heard it, he answered him, saying, Fear not: believe only, and she shall be made *sozo*/whole. 51 And when he came into the house, he suffered no man to go in, save Peter, and James, and John, and the father and the mother of the maiden. 52 And all wept, and bewailed her: but he said, Weep not; she is not dead, but sleepeth. 53 And they laughed him to scorn, knowing that she was dead. 54 And he put them all out, and took her by the hand, and called, saying, Maid, arise. 55 And her spirit came again, and she arose straightway: and he commanded to give her meat. 56 And her parents were astonished: but he charged them that they should tell no man what was done.

Mark 5:22 And, behold, there cometh one of the rulers of the synagogue, Jairus by name; and when he saw him, he fell at his feet, 23 and besought him greatly, saying, My little daughter lieth at the point of death: I pray thee, come and lay thy hands on her, that she may be healed; and she shall *zao*/live. 24 And Jesus went with him; and much people followed him, and thronged him. 25 And a certain woman, which had an issue of blood twelve years, 26 and had suffered many things of many physicians, and had spent all that she had, and was nothing bettered, but rather grew worse, 27 when she had heard of Jesus, came in the press behind, and touched his garment. 28 For she said, If I may touch but his clothes, I shall be *sozo*/whole. 29 And straightway the fountain of her blood was dried up; and she felt in her body that she was healed of that plague. 30 And Jesus, immediately knowing in himself that *dunamis*/virtue (*power, ability*) had gone out of him, turned him about in the press, and said, Who touched my clothes? 31 And his disciples said unto him, Thou seest the multitude thronging thee, and sayest thou, Who touched me? 32 And he looked round about to see her that had done this thing. 33 But the woman fearing and trembling, knowing what was done in her, came and fell down before him, and told him all the truth. 34 And he said unto her, Daughter, thy faith hath made thee *sozo*/whole; go in peace, and be whole of thy plague. 35 While he yet spake, there came from the ruler of the synagogue's house certain which said, Thy daughter is dead: why troublest thou the Master any further? 36 As soon as Jesus heard the word that was spoken, he saith unto the ruler of the synagogue, Be not afraid, only believe. 37 And he suffered no man to follow him, save Peter, and James, and John the brother of James. 38 And he cometh to the house of the ruler of the synagogue, and seeth the tumult, and them that wept and wailed greatly. 39 And when he was come in, he saith unto them, Why make ye this ado, and weep? the damsel is not dead, but sleepeth. 40 And they laughed him to scorn. But when he had put them all out, he taketh the father and the mother of the damsel, and them that were with him, and entereth in where the damsel was lying. 41 And he took the damsel by the hand, and said unto her, Talitha cumi; which is, being interpreted, Damsel, I say unto thee, arise. 42 And straightway the damsel arose, and walked; for she was of the age of twelve years. And they were astonished with a great astonishment. 43 And he charged them straitly that no man should know it; and commanded that something should be given her to eat.

Matt 9:18 While he spake these things unto them, behold, there came a certain ruler, and worshipped him, saying, My daughter is even now dead: but come and lay thy hand upon her, and she shall *zao*/live. 19 And Jesus arose, and followed him, and so did his disciples. 20 And, behold, a woman, which was diseased with an issue of blood twelve years, came behind him, and touched the hem of his garment: 21 for she said within herself, If I may but touch his garment, I shall be *sozo*/whole. 22 But Jesus turned him about, and when he saw her, he said, Daughter, be of good comfort; thy faith hath made thee *sozo*/whole. And the woman was made *sozo*/whole from that hour. 23 And when Jesus came into the ruler's house, and saw the minstrels and the people making a noise, 24 he said unto them, Give place: for the maid is not dead, but sleepeth. And they laughed him to scorn. 25 But when the people were put forth, he went in, and took her by the hand, and the maid arose. 26 And the fame hereof went abroad into all that land. 27 And when Jesus departed thence, two blind men followed him, crying, and saying, Thou Son of David, have mercy on us. 28 And when he was come into the house, the blind men came to him: and Jesus saith unto them, Believe ye that I am able to do this? They said unto him, Yea, Lord. 29 Then touched he their eyes, saying, According to your faith be it unto you. 30 And their eyes were opened; and Jesus straitly charged them, saying, See that no man know it. 31 But they, when they were departed, spread abroad his fame in all that country. 32 As they went out, behold, they brought to him a dumb man possessed with a devil. 33 And when the devil was cast out, the dumb spake: and the multitudes marvelled, saying, It was never so seen in Israel. 34 But the Pharisees said, He casteth out devils through the prince of the devils. 35 And Jesus went about all the cities and villages, teaching in their synagogues, and preaching the gospel of the kingdom, and healing every sickness and every disease among the people. 36 But when he saw the multitudes, he was moved with compassion on them, because they fainted, and were scattered abroad, as sheep having no shepherd. 37 Then saith he unto his disciples, The harvest truly is plenteous, but the labourers are few; 38 pray ye therefore the Lord of the harvest, that he will send forth labourers into his harvest.

Matt 10:1 And when he had called unto him his twelve disciples, he gave them power against unclean spirits, to cast them out, and to heal all manner of sickness and all manner of disease. 7 And as ye go, preach, saying, The kingdom of heaven is at hand. 8 Heal the sick, cleanse the lepers, raise the dead, cast out devils: freely ye have received, freely give.

Matt 13:54 And when he was come into his own country, he taught them in their synagogue, insomuch that they were astonished, and said, Whence hath this man this wisdom, and these mighty works? 55 Is not this the carpenter's son? is not his mother called Mary? and his brethren, James, and Joses, and Simon, and Judas? 56 And his sisters, are they not all with us? Whence then hath this man all these things? 57 And they were offended in him. But Jesus said unto them, A prophet is not without honour, save in his own country, and in his own house. 58 And he did not many mighty works there because of their unbelief [*so they did not bring many to Him for healing*].

Mark 6:1 And he went out from thence, and came into his own country; and his disciples follow him. 2 And when the sabbath day was come, he began to teach in the synagogue: and many hearing him were astonished, saying, From whence hath this man these things? and what wisdom is this which is given unto him, that even such mighty works are wrought by his hands? 3 Is not this the carpenter, the son of Mary, the brother of James, and Joses, and of Juda, and Simon? and are not his sisters here with us? And they were offended at him. 4 But Jesus said unto them, A prophet is not without honour, but in his own country, and among his own kin, and in his own house. 5 And he could there do no mighty work, save that he laid his hands upon a few sick folk, and healed them. 6 And he marvelled because of their unbelief (*so they brought few to Him*). And he went round about the villages, teaching.

Luke 9:1 Then he called his twelve disciples together, and gave them power and authority over all devils, and to cure diseases. 2 And he sent them to preach the kingdom of God, and to heal the sick. ... 6 And they departed, and went through the towns, preaching the gospel, and healing every where. ... 10 And the apostles, when they were returned, told him all that they had done. And he took them, and went aside privately into a desert place belonging to the city called Bethsaida. 11 And the people, when they knew it, followed him: and he received them, and spake unto them of the kingdom of God, and healed them that had need of healing.

Mark 6:7 And he called unto him the twelve, and began to send them forth by two and two; and gave them power over unclean spirits; ... 12 And they went out, and preached that men should repent. 13 And they cast out many devils, and anointed with oil many that were sick, and healed them.

Matt 14:14 And Jesus went forth, and saw a great multitude, and was moved with compassion toward them, and he healed their sick.

Matt 14:35 And when the men of that place had knowledge of him, they sent out into all that country round about, and brought unto him all that were diseased; 36 and besought him that they might only touch the hem of his garment: and as many as touched were made *diasozo*/perfectly whole.

Battle Prayer for Divine Healing: Field Manual 2

John 6:1 After these things Jesus went over the sea of Galilee, which is the sea of Tiberias. 2 And a great multitude followed him, because they saw his miracles which he did on them that were diseased.

Mark 6:54 And when they were come out of the ship, straightway they (*of Gennesaret*) knew him, 55 and ran through that whole region round about, and began to carry about in beds those that were sick, where they heard he was. 56 And whithersoever he entered, into villages, or cities, or country, they laid the sick in the streets, and besought him that they might touch if it were but the border of his garment: and as many as touched him were made *sozo*/whole.

Mark 7:25 For a certain woman, whose young daughter had an unclean spirit, heard of him, and came and fell at his feet: 26 the woman was a Greek, a Syrophenician by nation; and she besought him that he would cast forth the devil out of her daughter. 27 But Jesus said unto her, Let the children first be filled: for it is not meet to take the children's bread, and to cast it unto the dogs. 28 And she answered and said unto him, Yes, Lord: yet the dogs under the table eat of the children's crumbs. 29 And he said unto her, For this saying go thy way; the devil is gone out of thy daughter. 30 And when she was come to her house, she found the devil gone out, and her daughter laid upon the bed. 31 And again, departing from the coasts of Tyre and Sidon, he came unto the sea of Galilee, through the midst of the coasts of Decapolis. 32 And they bring unto him one that was deaf, and had an impediment in his speech; and they beseech him to put his hand upon him. 33 And he took him aside from the multitude, and put his fingers into his ears, and he spit, and touched his tongue; 34 and looking up to heaven, he sighed (*agitated or prayed inaudibly*), and saith unto him, Ephphatha, that is, Be opened. 35 And straightway his ears were opened, and the string of his tongue was loosed, and he spake plain. 36 And he charged them that they should tell no man: but the more he charged them, so much the more a great deal they published it; 37 and were beyond measure astonished, saying, He hath done all things well: he maketh both the deaf to hear, and the dumb to speak.

Matt 15:22 And, behold, a woman of Canaan came out of the same coasts, and cried unto him, saying, Have mercy on me, O Lord, thou Son of David; my daughter is grievously vexed with a devil. 23 But he answered her not a word. And his disciples came and besought him, saying, Send her away; for she crieth after us. 24 But he answered and said, I am not sent but unto the lost sheep of the house of Israel. 25 Then came she and worshipped him, saying, Lord, help me. 26 But he answered and said, It is not meet to take the children's bread, and to cast it to dogs. 27 And she said, Truth, Lord: yet the dogs eat of the crumbs which fall from their masters' table. 28 Then Jesus answered and said unto her, O woman, great is thy faith: be it unto thee even as thou wilt. And her daughter was made *iaomai*/whole (*cured*) from that very hour. 29 And Jesus departed from thence, and came nigh unto the sea of Galilee; and went up into a mountain, and sat down there. 30 And great multitudes came unto him, having with them those that were lame, blind, dumb, maimed, and many others, and cast them down at Jesus' feet; and he healed them: 31 insomuch that the multitude wondered, when they saw the dumb to speak, the maimed to be *hugies*/whole (*sound*), the lame to walk, and the blind to see: and they glorified the God of Israel.

Mark 8:22 And he cometh to Bethsaida; and they bring a blind man unto him, and besought him to touch him. 23 And he took the blind man by the hand, and led him out of the town; and when he had spit on his eyes, and put his hands upon him, he asked him if he saw ought. 24 And he looked up, and said, I see men as trees, walking. 25 After that he put his hands again upon his eyes, and made him look up: and he was restored, and saw every man clearly.

Mark 9:14 And when he came to his disciples, he saw a great multitude about them, and the scribes questioning with them. 15 And straightway all the people, when they beheld him, were greatly amazed, and running to him saluted him. 16 And he asked the scribes, What question ye with them? 17 And one of the multitude answered and said, Master, I have brought unto thee my son, which hath a dumb spirit; 18 and wheresoever he taketh him, he teareth him: and he foameth, and gnasheth with his teeth, and pineth away: and I spake to thy disciples that they should cast him out; and they could not. 19 He answereth him, and saith, O faithless generation, how long shall I be with you? how long shall I suffer you? bring him unto me. 20 And they brought him unto him: and when he saw him, straightway the spirit tare him; and he fell on the ground, and wallowed foaming. 21 And he asked his father, How long is it ago since this came unto him? And he said, Of a child. 22 And ofttimes it hath cast him into the fire, and into the waters, to destroy him: but if thou canst do any thing, have compassion on us, and help us. 23 Jesus said unto him, If thou canst believe, all things are possible to him that believeth. 24 And straightway the father of the child cried out, and said with tears, Lord, I believe; help thou mine unbelief. 25 When Jesus saw that the people came running together, he rebuked the foul spirit, saying unto him, Thou dumb and deaf spirit, I charge thee, come out of him, and enter no more into him. 26 And the spirit cried, and rent him sore, and came out of him: and he was as one dead; insomuch that many said, He is dead. 27 But Jesus took him by the hand, and lifted him up; and he arose. 28 And when he was come into the house, his disciples asked him privately, Why could not we cast him out? 29 And he said unto them, This kind (*of unbelief*) can come forth by nothing, but by prayer and fasting.

Matt 17:14 And when they were come to the multitude, there came to him a certain man, kneeling down to him, and saying, 15 Lord, have mercy on my son: for he is lunatick, and sore vexed: for ofttimes he falleth into the fire, and oft into the water. 16 and I brought him to thy disciples, and they could not cure him. 17 Then Jesus answered and said, O faithless and perverse generation, how long shall I be with you? how long shall I suffer you? bring him hither to me. 18 And Jesus rebuked the devil; and he departed out of him: and the child was cured from that very hour. 19 Then came the disciples to Jesus apart, and said, Why could not we cast him out? 20 And Jesus said unto them, Because of your unbelief: for verily I say unto you, If ye have faith as a grain of mustard seed, ye shall say unto this mountain, Remove hence to yonder place; and it shall remove; and nothing shall be impossible unto you. 21 Howbeit this kind (*of unbelief*) goeth not out but by prayer and fasting.

Luke 9:37 And it came to pass, that on the next day, when they were come down from the hill, much people met him. 38 And, behold, a man of the company cried out, saying, Master, I beseech thee, look upon my son: for he is mine only child. 39 And, lo, a spirit taketh him, and he suddenly crieth out; and it teareth him that he foameth again, and bruising him hardly departeth from him. 40 And I besought thy disciples to cast him out; and they could not. 41 And Jesus answering said, O faithless and perverse generation, how long shall I be with you, and suffer you? Bring thy son hither. 42 And as he was yet a coming, the devil threw him down, and tare him. And Jesus rebuked the unclean spirit, and healed the child, and delivered him again to his father. 43 And they were all amazed at the mighty power of God. But while they wondered every one at all things which Jesus did, he said unto his disciples, 44 Let these sayings sink down into your ears: for the Son of man shall be delivered into the hands of men. 45 But they understood not this saying, and it was hid from them, that they perceived it not: and they feared to ask him of that saying.

Luke 9:49 And John answered and said, Master, we saw one casting out devils in thy name; and we forbad him, because he followeth not with us. 50 And Jesus said unto him, Forbid him not: for he that is not against us is for us.

Mark 9:38 And John answered him, saying, Master, we saw one casting out devils in thy name, and he followeth not us: and we forbad him, because he followeth not us. 39 But Jesus said, Forbid him not: for there is no man which shall do a miracle in my name, that can lightly speak evil of me. 40 For he that is not against us is on our part.

Matt 18:18 Verily I say unto you, Whatsoever ye shall bind on earth shall be bound in heaven: and whatsoever ye shall loose on earth shall be loosed in heaven. 19 Again I say unto you, That if two of you shall agree on earth as touching any thing that they shall *aiteo*/ask (*require, demand and expect as due by covenant promise*), it shall be done for them of my Father which is in heaven. 20 For where two or three are gathered together in my name, there am I in the midst of them.

Luke 10:1 After these things the Lord appointed other seventy also, and sent them two and two before his face into every city and place, whither he himself would come. ... 8 And into whatsoever city ye enter, and they receive you, eat such things as are set before you: 9 and heal the sick that are therein, and say unto them, The kingdom of God is come nigh unto you. ... 17 And the seventy returned again with joy, saying, Lord, even the devils are subject unto us through thy name. 18 And he said unto them, I beheld Satan as lightning fall from heaven. 19 Behold, I give unto you power (*authority, commission and the resources of Heaven*) to tread on serpents and scorpions, and over all the power (*ability*) of the enemy: and nothing shall by any means hurt you. 20 Notwithstanding in this rejoice not, that the spirits are subject unto you; but rather rejoice, because your names are written in heaven. 21 In that hour Jesus rejoiced in spirit, and said, I thank thee, O Father, Lord of heaven and earth, that thou hast hid these things from the wise and prudent, and hast revealed them unto babes: even so, Father; for so it seemed good in thy sight. 22 All things are delivered to me of my Father: and no man knoweth who the Son is, but the Father; and who the Father is, but the Son, and he to whom the Son will reveal him.

Luke 11:14 And he was casting out a devil, and it was dumb. And it came to pass, when the devil was gone out, the dumb spake; and the people wondered. ... 20 But if I with the finger of God cast out devils, no doubt the kingdom of God is come upon you.

Ex 15:26 ... for I am the LORD that healeth thee (*Jehovah Rophi*).

Ex 23:25 And ye shall serve the LORD your God, and he shall bless thy bread, and thy water; and I will take sickness away from the midst of thee. 26 There shall nothing cast (*miscarry*) their young, nor be barren, in thy land: the number of thy days I will fulfil.

Battle Prayer for Divine Healing: Field Manual 2

Ps 103:1 Bless the LORD, O my soul: and all that is within me, bless his holy name. 2 Bless the LORD, O my soul, and forget not all his benefits: 3 who forgiveth all thine iniquities; who healeth all thy diseases; 4 who redeemeth thy life from destruction; who crowneth thee with *chesed*/lovingkindness and *racham*/tender mercies; 5 who satisfieth thy mouth with good things; so that thy youth is renewed like the eagle's. 6 The LORD executeth righteousness and judgment for all that are oppressed.

Matt 12:22 Then was brought unto him one possessed with a devil, blind, and dumb: and he healed him, insomuch that the blind and dumb both spake and saw. 23 And all the people were amazed, and said, Is not this the son of David? ... 28 But if I cast out devils by the Spirit of God, then the kingdom of God is come unto you.

Luke 13:10 And he was teaching in one of the synagogues on the sabbath. 11 And, behold, there was a woman which had a spirit of infirmity (*sickness, disease*) eighteen years, and was bowed together, and could in no wise lift up herself. 12 And when Jesus saw her, he called her to him, and said unto her, Woman, thou art loosed from thine infirmity (*sickness, disease*). 13 And he laid his hands on her: and immediately she was made straight, and glorified God. 14 And the ruler of the synagogue answered with indignation, because that Jesus had healed on the sabbath day, and said unto the people, There are six days in which men ought to work: in them therefore come and be healed, and not on the sabbath day. 15 The Lord then answered him, and said, Thou hypocrite, doth not each one of you on the sabbath loose his ox or his ass from the stall, and lead him away to watering? 16 And ought not this woman, being a daughter of Abraham, whom Satan hath bound, lo, these eighteen years, be loosed from this bond on the sabbath day? 17 And when he had said these things, all his adversaries were ashamed: and all the people rejoiced for all the glorious things that were done by him.

John 9:1 And as Jesus passed by, he saw a man which was blind from his birth. 2 And his disciples asked him, saying, Master, who did sin, this man, or his parents, that he was born blind? 3 Jesus answered, Neither hath this man sinned, nor his parents: but that the works of God should be made manifest in him. 4 I must work the works of him that sent me, while it is day: the night cometh, when no man can work. 5 As long as I am in the world, I am the light of the world. 6 When he had thus spoken, he spat on the ground, and made clay of the spittle, and he anointed the eyes of the blind man with the clay, 7 and said unto him, Go, wash in the pool of Siloam, (which is by interpretation, Sent.) He went his way therefore, and washed, and came seeing.

John 11:1 Now a certain man was sick, named Lazarus, of Bethany, the town of Mary and her sister Martha. 2 (It was that Mary which anointed the Lord with ointment, and wiped his feet with her hair, whose brother Lazarus was sick.) 3 Therefore his sisters sent unto him, saying, Lord, behold, he whom thou *phileo*/lovest is sick. 4 When Jesus heard that, he said, This sickness is not unto death, but for the glory of God, that the Son of God might be glorified thereby. 5 Now Jesus loved Martha, and her sister, and Lazarus. 6 When he had heard therefore that he was sick, he abode two days still in the same place where he was. 7 Then after that saith he to his disciples, Let us go into Judaea again. 8 His disciples say unto him, Master, the Jews of late sought to stone thee; and goest thou thither again? 9 Jesus answered, Are there not twelve hours in the day? If any man walk in the day, he stumbleth not, because he seeth the light of this world. 10 But if a man walk in the night, he stumbleth, because there is no light in him. 11 These things said he: and after that he saith unto them, Our friend Lazarus sleepeth; but I go, that I may awake him out of sleep. 12 Then said his disciples, Lord, if he sleep, he shall do well. 13 Howbeit Jesus spake of his death: but they thought that he had spoken of taking of rest in sleep. 14 Then said Jesus unto them plainly, Lazarus is dead. 15 And I am glad for your sakes that I was not there, to the intent ye may believe; nevertheless let us go unto him. 16 Then said Thomas, which is called Didymus, unto his fellowdisciples, Let us also go, that we may die with him.

17 Then when Jesus came, he found that he had lain in the grave four days already. 18 Now Bethany was nigh unto Jerusalem, about fifteen furlongs off: 19 and many of the Jews came to Martha and Mary, to comfort them concerning their brother. 20 Then Martha, as soon as she heard that Jesus was coming, went and met him: but Mary sat still in the house. 21 Then said Martha unto Jesus, Lord, if thou hadst been here, my brother had not died. 22 But I know, that even now, whatsoever thou wilt ask of God, God will give it thee. 23 Jesus saith unto her, Thy brother shall rise again. 24 Martha saith unto him, I know that he shall rise again in the resurrection at the last day. 25 Jesus said unto her, I am the resurrection, and the *zoe*/life: he that believeth in me, though he were dead, yet shall he *zao*/live: 26 and whosoever *zao*/liveth and believeth in me shall never die. Believest thou this? 27 She saith unto him, Yea, Lord: I believe that thou art the Christ, the Son of God, which should come into the world. 28 And when she had so said, she went her way, and called Mary her sister secretly, saying, The Master is come, and calleth for thee. 29 As soon as she heard that, she arose quickly, and came unto him. 30 Now Jesus was not yet come into the town, but was in that place where Martha met him. 31 The Jews then which were with her in the house, and comforted her, when they saw Mary, that she rose up hastily and went out, followed her, saying, She goeth unto the grave to weep there. 32

Then when Mary was come where Jesus was, and saw him, she fell down at his feet, saying unto him, Lord, if thou hadst been here, my brother had not died.

33 When Jesus therefore saw her weeping, and the Jews also weeping which came with her, he groaned in the spirit (*like a war horse' battle snort*), and was troubled (*agitated, stirred-up*), 34 and said, Where have ye laid him? They said unto him, Lord, come and see. 35 Jesus wept. 36 Then said the Jews, Behold how he *phileo*/loved him! 37 And some of them said, Could not this man, which opened the eyes of the blind, have caused that even this man should not have died? 38 Jesus therefore again groaning in himself cometh to the grave. It was a cave, and a stone lay upon it. 39 Jesus said, Take ye away the stone. Martha, the sister of him that was dead, saith unto him, Lord, by this time he stinketh: for he hath been dead four days. 40 Jesus saith unto her, Said I not unto thee, that, if thou wouldest believe, thou shouldest see the glory of God? 41 Then they took away the stone from the place where the dead was laid. And Jesus lifted up his eyes, and said, Father, I thank thee that thou hast heard me. 42 And I knew that thou hearest me always: but because of the people which stand by I said it, that they may believe that thou hast sent me. 43 And when he thus had spoken, he cried with a loud voice, Lazarus, come forth. 44 And he that was dead came forth, bound hand and foot with graveclothes: and his face was bound about with a napkin. Jesus saith unto them, Loose him, and let him go. 45 Then many of the Jews which came to Mary, and had seen the things which Jesus did, believed on him.

<u>Luke 17:12</u> And as he entered into a certain village, there met him ten men that were lepers, which stood afar off: 13 and they lifted up their voices, and said, Jesus, Master, have mercy on us. 14 And when he saw them, he said unto them, Go shew yourselves unto the priests. And it came to pass, that, as they went, they were cleansed. 15 And one of them, when he saw that he was healed, turned back, and with a loud voice glorified God, 16 and fell down on his face at his feet, giving him thanks: and he was a Samaritan. 17 And Jesus answering said, Were there not ten cleansed? but where are the nine? 18 There are not found that returned to give glory to God, save this stranger. 19 And he said unto him, Arise, go thy way: thy faith hath made thee *sozo*/whole.

<u>Matt 20:30</u> And, behold, two blind men sitting by the way side, when they heard that Jesus passed by, cried out, saying, Have mercy on us, O Lord, thou Son of David. 31 And the multitude rebuked them, because they should hold their peace: but they cried the more, saying, Have mercy on us, O Lord, thou Son of David. 32 And Jesus stood still, and called them, and said, What will ye that I shall do unto you? 33 They say unto him, Lord, that our eyes may be opened. 34

The Healing Scriptures

So Jesus had compassion on them, and touched their eyes: and immediately their eyes received sight, and they followed him.

Mark 10:46 And they came to Jericho: and as he went out of Jericho with his disciples and a great number of people, blind Bartimaeus, the son of Timaeus, sat by the highway side begging. 47 And when he heard that it was Jesus of Nazareth, he began to cry out, and say, Jesus, thou Son of David, have mercy on me. 48 And many charged him that he should hold his peace: but he cried the more a great deal, Thou Son of David, have mercy on me. 49 And Jesus stood still, and commanded him to be called. And they call the blind man, saying unto him, Be of good comfort, rise; he calleth thee. 50 And he, casting away his garment, rose, and came to Jesus. 51 And Jesus answered and said unto him, What wilt thou that I should do unto thee? The blind man said unto him, Lord, that I might receive my sight. 52 And Jesus said unto him, Go thy way; thy faith hath made thee *sozo*/whole. And immediately he received his sight, and followed Jesus in the way.

Luke 18:35 And it came to pass, that as he was come nigh unto Jericho, a certain blind man sat by the way side begging: 36 and hearing the multitude pass by, he asked what it meant. 37 And they told him, that Jesus of Nazareth passeth by. 38 And he cried, saying, Jesus, thou Son of David, have mercy on me. 39 And they which went before rebuked him, that he should hold his peace: but he cried so much the more, Thou Son of David, have mercy on me. 40 And Jesus stood, and commanded him to be brought unto him: and when he was come near, he asked him, 41 saying, What wilt thou that I shall do unto thee? And he said, Lord, that I may receive my sight. 42 And Jesus said unto him, Receive thy sight: thy faith hath *sozo*/saved thee. 43 And immediately he received his sight, and followed him, glorifying God: and all the people, when they saw it, gave praise unto God. [*Due to different reporters different numbers are given.*]

Matt 21:10 And when he was come into Jerusalem, all the city was moved, saying, Who is this? 11 And the multitude said, This is Jesus the prophet of Nazareth of Galilee. 12 And Jesus went into the temple of God, and cast out all them that sold and bought in the temple, and overthrew the tables of the moneychangers, and the seats of them that sold doves, 13 and said unto them, It is written, My house shall be called the house of prayer; but ye have made it a den of thieves. 14 And the blind and the lame came to him in the temple; and he healed them.

John 12:37 But though he had done so many miracles before them, yet they believed not on him: 38 that the saying of Esaias (*Isaiah*) the prophet might be fulfilled, which he spake, Lord, who hath believed our report? and to whom hath the arm of the Lord been revealed? 39 Therefore they could not believe, because that Esaias said again, 40 He hath blinded their eyes, and hardened their heart; that they should not see with their eyes, nor understand with their heart, and be converted, and I should heal them. 41 These things said Esaias, when he saw his glory, and spake of him. 42 Nevertheless among the chief rulers also many believed on him; but because of the Pharisees they did not confess him, lest they should be put out of the synagogue: 43 For they *agape*/loved the praise of men more than the praise of God. 44 Jesus cried and said, He that believeth on me, believeth not on me, but on him that sent me. 45 And he that seeth me seeth him that sent me. 46 I am come a light into the world, that whosoever believeth on me should not abide in darkness. 47 And if any man hear my words, and believe not, I judge him not: for I came not to judge the world, but to *sozo*/save the world. 48 He that rejecteth me, and receiveth not my words, hath one that judgeth him: the word that I have spoken, the same shall judge him in the last day. 49 For I have not spoken of myself; but the Father which sent me, he gave me a commandment, what I should say, and what I should speak. 50 And I know that his commandment is *zoe*/life everlasting: whatsoever I speak therefore, even as the Father said unto me, so I speak.

Matt 21:18 Now in the morning as he returned into the city, he hungered. 19 And when he saw a fig tree in the way, he came to it, and found nothing thereon, but leaves only, and said unto it, Let no fruit grow on thee henceforward for ever. And presently the fig tree withered away. 20 And when the disciples saw it, they marvelled, saying, How soon is the fig tree withered away! 21 Jesus answered and said unto them, Verily I say unto you, If ye have faith, and doubt not, ye shall not only do this which is done to the fig tree, but also if ye shall say unto this mountain, Be thou removed, and be thou cast into the sea; it shall be done. 22 And all things, whatsoever ye shall *aiteo*/ask (*require, demand and expect as due by covenant promise*) in prayer, believing, ye shall receive.

Mark 11:13 And seeing a fig tree afar off having leaves, he came, if haply he might find any thing thereon: and when he came to it, he found nothing but leaves; for the time of figs was not yet. 14 And Jesus answered and said unto it, No man eat fruit of thee hereafter for ever. And his disciples heard it. ... 19 And when even was come, he went out of the city. 20 And in the morning, as they passed by, they saw the fig tree dried up from the roots. 21 And Peter calling to remembrance saith unto him, Master, behold, the fig tree which thou cursedst is withered away. 22 And Jesus answering saith unto them, Have faith in God (*or the faith of God, or think like God in faith*). 23 For verily I say unto you, That whosoever shall say unto this mountain, Be thou removed, and be thou cast into the sea; and shall not doubt in his heart, but shall believe that those things which he saith shall come to pass; he shall have whatsoever he saith. 24 Therefore I say unto you, What things soever ye *aiteo*/desire (*demand, require and expect as due by covenant promise*), when ye pray, believe that ye receive them, and ye shall have them. 25 And when ye stand praying, forgive, if ye have ought against any: that your Father also which is in heaven may forgive you your trespasses. 26 But if ye do not forgive, neither will your Father which is in heaven forgive your trespasses.

Luke 22:48 But Jesus said unto him, Judas, betrayest thou the Son of man with a kiss? 49 When they which were about him saw what would follow, they said unto him, Lord, shall we smite with the sword? 50 And one of them smote the servant of the high priest (*Malchus, John 18:10*), and cut off his right ear. 51 And Jesus answered and said, Suffer ye thus far. And he touched his ear, and healed him.

Acts 1:4 And, being assembled together with them, commanded them that they should not depart from Jerusalem, but wait for the promise of the Father, which, saith he, ye have heard of me. 5 For John truly baptized with water; but ye shall be baptized with the Holy Ghost not many days hence. 6 When they therefore were come together, they asked of him, saying, Lord, wilt thou at this time restore again the kingdom to Israel? 7 And he said unto them, It is not for you to know the times or the seasons, which the Father hath put in his own power. 8 But ye shall receive power (*ability*), after that the Holy Ghost is come upon you: and ye shall be witnesses unto me both in Jerusalem, and in all Judaea, and in Samaria, and unto the uttermost part of the earth.

Acts 2:14 But Peter … said… , 15 For these are not drunken, as ye suppose, seeing it is but the third hour of the day. 16 But this is that which was spoken by the prophet Joel; 17 And it shall come to pass in the last days, saith God, I will pour out of my Spirit upon all flesh: and your sons and your daughters shall prophesy, and your young men shall see visions, and your old men shall dream dreams: 18 and on my servants and on my handmaidens I will pour out in those days of my Spirit; and they shall prophesy: 19 and I will shew wonders in heaven above, and signs in the earth beneath; blood, and fire, and vapour of smoke: 20 the sun shall be turned into darkness, and the moon into blood, before that great and notable day of the Lord come: 21 and it shall come to pass, that whosoever shall call on the name of the Lord shall be *sozo*/saved. 22 Ye men of Israel, hear these words; Jesus of Nazareth, a man approved of God among you by miracles and wonders and signs, which God did by him in the midst of you, as ye yourselves also know: 23 him, being delivered by the determinate counsel and foreknowledge of God, ye have taken, and by wicked hands have crucified and slain: 24 whom God hath raised up, having loosed the pains of death: because it was not possible that he should be holden of it. 25 For David speaketh concerning him, I foresaw the Lord always before my face, for he is on my right hand, that I should not be moved: 26 therefore did my heart rejoice, and my tongue was glad; moreover also my flesh shall rest in hope: 27 because thou wilt not leave my soul in hell, neither wilt thou suffer thine Holy One to see corruption. ... 31 He seeing this before spake of the resurrection of Christ, that his soul was not left in hell, neither his flesh did see corruption. 32 This Jesus hath God raised up, whereof we all are witnesses. 33 Therefore being by the right hand of God exalted, and having received of the Father the promise of the Holy Ghost, he hath shed forth this, which ye now see and hear. 34 For David is not ascended into the heavens: but he saith himself, The LORD said unto my Lord, Sit thou on my right hand, 35 until I make thy foes thy footstool. 36 Therefore let all the house of Israel know assuredly, that God hath made that same Jesus, whom ye have crucified, both Lord and Christ. 37 Now when they heard this, they were pricked in their heart, and said unto Peter and to the rest of the apostles, Men and brethren, what shall we do? 38 Then Peter said unto them, Repent, and be baptized every one of you in the name of Jesus Christ for the remission of sins, and ye shall receive the gift of the Holy Ghost. 39 For the promise is unto you, and to your children, and to all that are afar off, even as many as the Lord our God shall call.

John 19:30 When Jesus therefore had received the vinegar, he said, It is finished: and he bowed his head, and gave up the ghost. ... 34 But one of the soldiers with a spear pierced his (*Jesus'*) side, and forthwith came there out blood and water. 35 And he that saw it bare record, and his record is true: and he knoweth that he saith true, that ye might believe. 36 For these things were done, that the scripture should be fulfilled, A bone of him shall not be broken. 37 And again another scripture saith, They shall look on him whom they pierced. 38 And after this Joseph of Arimathaea, being a disciple of Jesus, but secretly for fear of the Jews, besought Pilate that he might take away the body of Jesus: and Pilate gave him leave. He came therefore, and took the body of Jesus. 39 And there came also Nicodemus, which at the first came to Jesus by night, and brought a mixture of myrrh and aloes, about an hundred pound weight. 40 Then took they the body of Jesus, and wound it in linen clothes with the spices, as the manner of the Jews is to bury. 41 Now in the place where he was crucified there was a garden; and in the garden a new sepulchre, wherein was never man yet laid.

1 John 2:12 I write unto you, little children, because your sins are forgiven you for his (*Jesus'*) name's sake.

1 John 4:16 And we have known and believed the *agape*/love that God hath to us. God is *agape*/love; and he that dwelleth in *agape*/love dwelleth in God, and God

in him. 17 Herein is our *agape*/love made perfect, that we may have boldness in the day of judgment: because as he is, so are we in this world. 18 There is no fear in *agape*/love; but perfect *agape*/love casteth out fear: because fear hath torment. He that feareth is not made perfect in *agape*/love.

Heb 13:8 Jesus Christ the same yesterday, and to day, and for ever.

Mal 3:6 For I am the Lord, I change not; therefore ye sons of Jacob are not consumed.

Ps 118:17 I shall not die, but live, and declare the works of the LORD.

Isa 38:1 In those days was Hezekiah sick unto death. And Isaiah the prophet the son of Amoz came unto him, and said unto him, Thus saith the Lord, Set thine house in order: for thou shalt die, and not live. 2 Then Hezekiah turned his face toward the wall, and prayed unto the Lord, 3 and said, Remember now, O Lord, I beseech thee, how I have walked before thee in truth and with a perfect heart, and have done that which is good in thy sight. And Hezekiah wept sore. 4 Then came the word of the Lord to Isaiah, saying, 5 Go, and say to Hezekiah, Thus saith the Lord, the God of David thy father, I have heard thy prayer, I have seen thy tears: behold, I will add unto thy days fifteen years.

Isa 33:21 But there the glorious Lord will be unto us a place of broad rivers and streams; wherein shall go no galley with oars, neither shall gallant ship pass thereby. 22 For the Lord is our judge, the Lord is our lawgiver, the Lord is our king; he will save us. 23 Thy tacklings are loosed; they could not well strengthen their mast, they could not spread the sail: then is the prey of a great spoil divided; the lame take the prey. 24 And the inhabitant shall not say, I am sick: the people that dwell therein shall be forgiven their iniquity.

Deut 33:25 Thy shoes shall be iron and brass (*in warrior strength*); and as thy days, so shall thy strength be. 26 There is none like unto the God of Jeshurun, who rideth upon the heaven in thy help, and in his excellency on the sky. 27 The eternal God is thy refuge, and underneath are the everlasting arms: and he shall thrust out the enemy from before thee; and shall say, Destroy them. 28 Israel then shall dwell in safety alone: the fountain of Jacob shall be upon a land of corn and wine; also his heavens shall drop down dew. 29 Happy art thou, O Israel: who is like unto thee, O people saved by the Lord, the shield of thy help, and who is the sword of thy excellency! and thine enemies shall be found liars unto thee; and thou shalt tread upon their high places.

BATTLE PRAYER FOR DIVINE HEALING: FIELD MANUAL 2

Father, in the name of Jesus, I make this, my confession: Psalm 91:1 He that dwelleth in the secret place of the most High shall abide under the shadow of the Almighty. 2 I will say of the LORD, He is my refuge and my fortress: my God; in him will I trust. 3 Surely he shall deliver *me* from the snare of the fowler, and from the noisome pestilence. 4 He shall cover *me* with his feathers, and under his wings *I do* trust: his truth *is my* shield and buckler. 5 *I shall* not be afraid for the terror by night; nor for the arrow that flieth by day; 6 nor for the pestilence that walketh in darkness; nor for the destruction that wasteth at noonday. 7 A thousand shall fall at *my* side, and ten thousand at *my* right hand; but it shall not come nigh *me*. 8 Only with *my* eyes *shall I* behold and see the reward of the wicked. 9 Because *I make* the LORD, which is my refuge, even the most High, *my* habitation; 10 there shall no evil befall *me*, neither shall any plague come nigh *my* dwelling. 11 For he shall give his angels charge over *me*, to keep *me* in all *my* ways. 12 They shall bear *me* up in their hands, lest *I* dash *my* foot against a stone. 13 *I do* tread upon the lion and adder: the young lion and the dragon *I do* trample under feet. 14 *Therefore God says to me:* "Because he hath set his love upon me, therefore will I deliver him: I will set him on high, because he hath known my name. 15 He shall call upon me, and I will answer him: I will be with him in trouble; I will deliver him, and honour him. 16 With long life will I satisfy him, and shew him my salvation.

Mal 4:2 But unto you that fear my name shall the Sun of righteousness arise with healing in his wings; and ye shall go forth, and grow up as calves of the stall. 3 And ye shall tread down the wicked; for they shall be ashes under the soles of your feet in the day that I shall do this, saith the LORD of hosts.

Isa 49:8 Thus saith the LORD, In an acceptable time have I heard thee, and in a day of salvation have I helped thee: and I will preserve thee, and give thee for a covenant of the people, to establish the earth, to cause to inherit the desolate heritages; 9 that thou mayest say to the prisoners, Go forth; to them that are in darkness, Shew yourselves. They shall feed in the ways, and their pastures shall be in all high places.

2 Cor 6:1 We then, as workers together with him, beseech you also that ye receive not the grace of God in vain. 2 (For he saith, I have heard thee in a time accepted, and in the day of *soteria*/salvation have I succoured thee: behold, now is the accepted time; behold, now is the day of *soteria*/salvation.)

Isa 61:1 The Spirit of the Lord GOD is upon me; because the LORD hath anointed me to preach good tidings unto the meek; he hath sent me to bind up the brokenhearted, to proclaim liberty to the captives, and the opening of the prison to them that are bound; 2 to proclaim the acceptable year of the Lord, and the day of vengeance of our God; to comfort all that mourn.

Luke 4:14 And Jesus returned in the power of the Spirit into Galilee: and there went out a fame of him through all the region round about. 15 And he taught in their synagogues, being glorified of all. 16 And he came to Nazareth, where he had been brought up: and, as his custom was, he went into the synagogue on the sabbath day, and stood up for to read. 17 And there was delivered unto him the book of the prophet Esaias. And when he had opened the book, he found the place where it was written, 18 The Spirit of the Lord is upon me, because he hath anointed me to preach the gospel to the poor; he hath sent me to heal the brokenhearted, to preach deliverance to the captives, and recovering of sight to the blind, to set at liberty them that are bruised, 19 to preach the acceptable year of the Lord. 20 And he closed the book, and he gave it again to the minister, and sat down. And the eyes of all them that were in the synagogue were fastened on him. 21 And he began to say unto them, This day is this scripture fulfilled in your ears.

John 12:31 Now is the judgment of this world: now shall the prince of this world be cast out.

John 16:11 Of judgment, because the prince of this world is judged.

Luke 10:18 And he said unto them, I beheld Satan as lightning fall from heaven. 19 Behold (*make this change your life*), I give unto you power (*authority, commission, the resources of Heaven*) to tread on serpents and scorpions, and over all the power of the enemy: and nothing shall by any means hurt you. 20 Notwithstanding in this rejoice not, that the spirits are subject unto you; but rather rejoice, because your names are written in heaven.

James 4:6 But he giveth more grace. Wherefore he saith, God resisteth the proud, but giveth grace unto the humble. 7 Submit yourselves therefore to God. Resist the devil, and he will flee from you. 8 Draw nigh to God, and he will draw nigh to you. Cleanse your hands, ye sinners; and purify your hearts, ye double minded.

Acts 8:5 Then Philip went down to the city of Samaria, and preached Christ unto them. 6 And the people with one accord gave heed unto those things which Philip spake, hearing and seeing the miracles which he did. 7 For unclean spirits, crying with loud voice, came out of many that were possessed with them: and many taken with palsies, and that were lame, were healed. 8 And there was great joy in that city.

Acts 5:16 There came also a multitude out of the cities round about unto Jerusalem, bringing sick folks, and them which were vexed with unclean spirits: and they were healed every one.

Acts 16:16 And it came to pass, as we went to prayer, a certain damsel possessed with a spirit of divination met us, which brought her masters much gain by soothsaying: 17 the same followed Paul and us, and cried, saying, These men are the servants of the most high God, which shew unto us the way of salvation. 18 And this did she many days. But Paul, being grieved, turned and said to the spirit, I command thee in the name of Jesus Christ to come out of her. And he came out the same hour.

Acts 16:31 And they said, Believe on the Lord Jesus Christ, and thou shalt be *sozo*/saved, and thy house.

Acts 14:3 Long time therefore abode they speaking boldly in the Lord, which gave testimony unto the word of his grace, and granted signs and wonders to be done by their hands.

Acts 19:4 Then said Paul, John verily baptized with the baptism of repentance, saying unto the people, that they should believe on him which should come after him, that is, on Christ Jesus. 5 When they heard this, they were baptized in the name of the Lord Jesus. 6 And when Paul had laid his hands upon them, the Holy Ghost came on them; and they spake with tongues, and prophesied.

Acts 19:11 And God wrought special miracles by the hands of Paul: 12 so that from his body were brought unto the sick handkerchiefs or aprons, and the diseases departed from them, and the evil spirits went out of them.

Acts 9:33 And there he found a certain man named Aeneas, which had kept his bed eight years, and was sick of the palsy. 34 And Peter said unto him, Aeneas, Jesus Christ maketh thee whole: arise, and make thy bed. And he arose immediately.

Acts 28:3 And when Paul had gathered a bundle of sticks, and laid them on the fire, there came a viper out of the heat, and fastened on his hand. 4 And when the barbarians saw the venomous beast hang on his hand, they said among themselves, No doubt this man is a murderer, whom, though he hath escaped the sea, yet vengeance suffereth not to live. 5 And he shook off the beast into the fire, and felt no harm. 6 Howbeit they looked when he should have swollen, or fallen down dead suddenly: but after they had looked a great while, and saw no harm come to him, they changed their minds, and said that he was a god. 7 In the same quarters were possessions of the chief man of the island, whose name was Publius; who received us, and lodged us three days courteously. 8 And it came to pass, that the father of Publius lay sick of a fever and of a bloody flux: to whom Paul entered in, and prayed, and laid his hands on him, and healed him. 9 So when this was done, others also, which had diseases in the island, came, and were healed.

Acts 4:9 If we this day be examined of the good deed done to the impotent man, by what means he is made whole; 10 be it known unto you all, and to all the people of Israel, that by the name of Jesus Christ of Nazareth, whom ye crucified, whom God raised from the dead, even by him doth this man stand here before you whole. 11 This is the stone which was set at nought of you builders, which is become the head of the corner. 12 Neither is there *soteria*/salvation in any other: for there is none other name under heaven given among men, whereby we must be *sozo*/saved (*healed, made whole*).

Acts 10:34 Then Peter opened his mouth, and said, Of a truth I perceive that God is no respecter of persons: 35 but in every nation he that feareth him, and worketh righteousness (*such as believing God in* aiteo *commands to heal the sick*), is accepted with him. 36 The word which God sent unto the children of Israel, preaching peace by Jesus Christ: (he is Lord of all:) 37 that word, I say, ye know, which was published throughout all Judaea, and began from Galilee, after the baptism which John preached; 38 how God anointed Jesus of Nazareth with the Holy Ghost and with power: who went about doing good, and healing all that were oppressed (*under the active rule, reign and lordship*) of the devil; for God was with him. 39 And we are witnesses of all things which he did both in the land of the Jews, and in Jerusalem; whom they slew and hanged on a tree: 40 him God raised up the third day, and shewed him openly; 41 not to all the people, but unto witnesses chosen before of God, even to us, who did eat and drink with him after he rose from the dead. 42 And he commanded us to preach unto the people, and to testify that it is he which was ordained of God to be the Judge of quick and dead. 43 To him give all the prophets witness, that through his name whosoever believeth in him shall receive remission (*removal, washing, purging, obliteration and putting away*) of sins. 44 While Peter yet spake these words, the Holy Ghost fell on all them which heard the word.

Ps 103:1 Bless the LORD, O my soul: and all that is within me, bless his holy name. 2 Bless the LORD, O my soul, and forget not all his benefits: 3 who forgiveth all thine iniquities; who healeth all thy diseases; 4 who redeemeth thy life from destruction; who crowneth thee with *chesed*/lovingkindness and *racham*/tender mercies; 5 who satisfieth thy mouth with good things; so that thy youth is renewed like the eagle's. 6 The LORD executeth righteousness and judgment for all that are oppressed [*through us, the believers in Jesus Christ.*].

Rom 16:20 And the God of peace shall bruise (*crush in healing the works of*) Satan under your feet shortly (*as shattered glass*). The grace of our Lord Jesus Christ be with you [*to think, know, be and do this*]. Amen.

Luke 10:19 Behold, I (*Jesus*) give unto you power (*authority, commission and the resources of Heaven*) to tread (*under your feet*) on serpents and scorpions, and over all the power (*ability, rule, lordship and oppression*) of the enemy: and nothing shall by any means hurt you. 20 Notwithstanding in this rejoice not, that the spirits are subject unto you; but rather rejoice, because your names are written in heaven.

And I am made, by Father's grace, to be just like my elder brother Jesus to preach Acts 10:36 the word which God sent unto the children of Israel, preaching peace by Jesus Christ: (he is Lord of all:) ... 38 *for Father* God *has* anointed *me in* Jesus of Nazareth with the Holy Ghost and with power: *and I go* about doing good, and healing all that *are* oppressed (*under the active rule and lordship*) of the devil (*in judgment against the devil*); for *Father* God *is* with *me, for I am brought nigh by the blood of Jesus.* Acts 13:37 For Jesus, whom God raised again, saw no corruption. 38 *For I make* it known ... that through this man, *Jesus,* is preached unto *all* the forgiveness (*remission, purging, putting away and obliteration*) of sins: 39 and by him all that believe are justified from all things, from which *we* could not be justified by the law of Moses. Mark 16:15 And *I* go into all the world, and preach the gospel to every creature. 16 He that believeth and is baptized shall be *sozo*/saved; but he that believeth not shall be damned. 17 And these signs *follow me who believes; in the* name *of* Jesus *I* cast out devils; *I* speak with new tongues; 18 *I* take up serpents; and if *I* drink any deadly thing, it shall not hurt *me; I* lay hands on the sick, and they ... recover totally. Because 19 ... the Lord Jesus ... has been received up into heaven, and *sits* on the right hand of God, *I do even greater works than Jesus and I* 20 *go* forth, and *I preach* everywhere, *in word and good deeds,* the Lord working with *me,* and confirming the word with signs following. Amen, *just as Father God wants for all His sons. For* 1 John 4:4 *I am* of God, *one of His* little children, *a son of God*, and have overcome *the lie of the devil*: because greater is he that is in *me*, than he that is in the world. *Praise You, Lord Jesus for Your great work of salvation and that Your Spirit dwells in me to complete Your work in healing the sick. Thank You!*

~ 2 ~
WHY JESUS CAME SCRIPTURES

Father, in the name of Jesus Christ, teach me Your ways concerning Jesus and what He came to do and accomplish. Give me, those I pray for, and all those given me Your Spirit of wisdom and revelation in the knowledge of You, with the eyes of our understanding being enlightened unto repentance, conversion, healing, strengthening the brethren and zealously doing good works, by faith, in *agape/* love, to Your glory. Eph 3:16 ... grant us, according to the riches of *Your* glory, to be strengthened with might by *Your* Spirit in the inner man; 17 that Christ may dwell in *our* hearts by faith; that *we*, being rooted and grounded in *agape/*love, 18 may be able to comprehend with all saints what is the breadth, and length, and depth, and height; 19 and to know the *agape/*love of Christ, which passeth knowledge, that *we* might be filled with all the fulness of *You, Father* God. 20 Now unto *You* that is able to do exceeding abundantly above all that we *aiteo/*ask or think, according to the *dunamis/*power that worketh in us, 21 unto *You, Father God*, be glory in the church by Christ Jesus throughout all ages, world without end. Amen.

Col 1:9 ... *Fill us* with the knowledge of *Your* will in all wisdom and spiritual understanding; 10 that *we* might walk worthy of the Lord unto all pleasing, being fruitful in every good work, and increasing in the knowledge of *You, Father* God; 11 strengthened with all might, according to *Your* glorious power, unto all patience and longsuffering with joyfulness; *so that we are* 12 giving thanks (*continuously*) unto *You*, the Father, which hath made us meet (*qualified and enabled by grace*) to be partakers of the inheritance of the saints in light: 13 who hath delivered us from the power of darkness, and hath translated us into the kingdom of *Your agape/*dear Son:

14 in whom we have redemption through his blood, even the forgiveness (*remission, purging, putting away and obliteration*) of sins: 15 who is the image of *You, Father*, the invisible God, the firstborn of every creature: 16 for by him were all things created, that are in heaven, and that are in earth, visible and invisible, whether they be thrones, or dominions, or principalities, or powers: all things were created by him, and for him: 17 and he is before all things, and by him all things consist. 18 And he is the head of the body, the church: who is the beginning, the firstborn from the dead; that in all things he might have the preeminence. 19 For it pleased *You*, the Father, that in him should all fulness dwell; 20 and, having made peace through the blood of his cross, by him to reconcile all things unto *Yourself*; by him, I say, whether they be things in earth, or things in heaven. 1 John 5:11 And this is the record, that God hath given to us eternal *zoe*/life, and this *zoe*/life is in his Son. 12 He that hath the Son hath *zoe*/life; and he that hath not the Son of God hath not *zoe*/life. *Thank You Father! In the name of Jesus, thank You!*

Gen 1:26 And God said, Let us make man in our image, after our likeness: and let them have dominion over the fish of the sea, and over the fowl of the air, and over the cattle, and over all the earth, and over every creeping thing that creepeth upon the earth. 27 So God created man in his own image, in the image of God created he him; male and female created he them. 28 And God blessed them, and God said unto them, Be fruitful, and multiply, and replenish the earth, and subdue it: and have dominion over the fish of the sea, and over the fowl of the air, and over every living thing that moveth upon the earth. 29 And God said, Behold, I have given you every herb bearing seed, which is upon the face of all the earth, and every tree, in the which is the fruit of a tree yielding seed; to you it shall be for meat. 30 And to every beast of the earth, and to every fowl of the air, and to every thing that creepeth upon the earth, wherein there is life, I have given every green herb for meat: and it was so. 31 And God saw every thing that he had made, and, behold, it was very good. And the evening and the morning were the sixth day.

Gen 2:7 And the LORD God formed man of the dust of the ground, and breathed into his nostrils the breath of life; and man became a living soul. 8 And the LORD God planted a garden eastward in Eden; and there he put the man whom he had formed. 9 And out of the ground made the LORD God to grow every tree that is pleasant to the sight, and good for food; the tree of life also in the midst of the garden, and the tree of knowledge of good and evil. 10 And a river went out of Eden to water the garden; and from thence it was parted, and became into four heads. 11 The name of the first is Pison: that is it which compasseth the whole land of Havilah, where there is gold; 12 and the gold of that land is good: there is bdellium and the onyx stone. 13 And the name of the second river is Gihon: the same is it that compasseth the whole land of Ethiopia. 14 And the name of the third river is Hiddekel: that is it which goeth toward the east of Assyria. And the fourth river is Euphrates. 15 And the LORD God took the man, and put him into the garden of Eden to dress it and to keep it. 16 And the LORD God commanded the man, saying, Of every tree of the garden thou mayest freely eat: 17 but of the tree of the knowledge of good and evil, thou shalt not eat of it: for in the day that thou eatest thereof thou shalt surely die. 18 And the LORD God said, It is not good that the man should be alone; I will make him an help meet for him. 19 And out of the ground the LORD God formed every beast of the field, and every fowl of the air; and brought them unto Adam to see what he would call them: and whatsoever Adam called every living creature, that was the name thereof. 20 And Adam gave names to all cattle, and to the fowl of the air, and to every beast of the field; but for Adam there was not found an help meet for him. 21 And the LORD God caused a deep sleep to fall upon Adam and he slept: and he took one of his ribs, and closed up the flesh instead thereof; 22 and the rib, which the LORD God had taken from man, made he a woman, and brought her unto the man. 23 And Adam said, This is now bone of my bones, and flesh of my flesh: she shall be called Woman, because she was taken out of Man. 24 Therefore shall a man leave his father and his mother, and shall cleave unto his wife: and they shall be one flesh. 25 And they were both naked, the man and his wife, and were not ashamed.

Gen 3:13 And the LORD God said unto the woman, What is this that thou hast done? And the woman said, The serpent beguiled me, and I did eat. 14 And the LORD God said unto the serpent, Because thou hast done this, thou art cursed above all cattle, and above every beast of the field; upon thy belly shalt thou go, and dust shalt thou eat all the days of thy life: 15 and I will put enmity between thee and the woman, and between thy seed and her seed; it shall bruise (*crush*) thy head, and thou shalt bruise (*crush*) his heel. 16 Unto the woman he said, I will greatly multiply thy sorrow and thy conception; in sorrow thou shalt bring forth children; and thy desire shall be to thy husband, and he shall rule over thee.

Luke 4:5 And the devil, taking him up into an high mountain, shewed unto him all the kingdoms of the world in a moment of time. 6 And the devil said unto him, All this power will I give thee, and the glory of them: for that is delivered unto me; and to whomsoever I will I give it. 7 If thou therefore wilt worship me, all shall be thine. 8 And Jesus answered and said unto him, Get thee behind me, Satan: for it is written, Thou shalt worship the Lord thy God, and him only shalt thou serve.

John 16:7 Nevertheless I tell you the truth; It is expedient for you that I go away: for if I go not away, the Comforter will not come unto you; but if I depart, I will send him unto you. 8 And when he is come, he will reprove the world of sin, and of righteousness, and of judgment: 9 of sin, because they believe not on me; 10 of righteousness, because I go to my Father, and ye see me no more; 11 of judgment, because the prince of this world (*Satan*) is judged. 12 I have yet many things to say unto you, but ye cannot bear them now. 13 Howbeit when he, the Spirit of truth, is come, he will guide you into all truth: for he shall not speak of himself; but whatsoever he shall hear, that shall he speak: and he will shew you things to come. 14 He shall glorify me: for he shall receive of mine, and shall shew it unto you. 15 All things that the Father hath are mine: therefore said I, that he shall take of mine, and shall shew it unto you. 16 A little while, and ye shall not see me: and again, a little while, and ye shall see me, because I go to the Father.

Matt 18:11 For the Son of man is come to *sozo*/save that which was lost.

1 John 3:8 He that committeth sin is of the devil; for the devil sinneth from the beginning. For this purpose the Son of God was manifested, that he might destroy the works of the devil.

Rom 5:12 Wherefore, as by one man sin entered into the world, and death by sin; and so death passed upon all men, for that all have sinned: 13 (for until the law sin was in the world: but sin is not imputed when there is no law. 14 Nevertheless death reigned from Adam to Moses, even over them that had not sinned after the similitude of Adam's transgression, who is the figure of him that was to come. 15 But not as the offence, so also is the free gift. For if through the offence of one many be dead, much more the grace of God, and the gift by grace, which is by one man, Jesus Christ, hath abounded unto many. 16 And not as it was by one that sinned, so is the gift: for the judgment was by one to condemnation, but the free gift is of many offences unto justification. 17 For if by one man's offence death reigned (*as king*) by one; much more they which (*continually*) *lambano*/receive abundance of grace and of the gift of righteousness shall reign (*as kings*) in *zoe*/life by one, Jesus Christ.) 18 Therefore as by the offence of one judgment came upon all men to condemnation; even so by the righteousness of one the free gift came upon all men unto justification of *zoe*/life. 19 For as by one man's disobedience many were made sinners, so by the obedience of one shall many be made righteous. 20 Moreover the law entered, that the offence might abound. But where sin abounded, grace did much more abound: 21 that as sin hath reigned (*as king*) unto death, even so might grace reign (*as king*) through righteousness unto eternal *zoe*/life by Jesus Christ our Lord.

Eph 4:7 But unto every one of us is given grace according to the measure of the gift of Christ. 8 Wherefore he saith, When he ascended up on high, he led captivity captive, and gave gifts unto men. 9 (Now that he ascended, what is it but that he also descended first into the lower parts of the earth? 10 He that descended is the same also that ascended up far above all heavens, that he might fill all things.) 11 And he gave some, apostles; and some, prophets; and some, evangelists; and some, pastors and teachers; 12 for the perfecting of the saints, for the work of the ministry, for the edifying of the body of Christ: 13 till we all come in the unity of the faith, and of the knowledge of the Son of God, unto a perfect man, unto the measure of the stature of the fulness of Christ: 14 that we henceforth be no more children, tossed to and fro, and carried about with every wind of doctrine, by the sleight of men, and cunning craftiness, whereby they lie in wait to deceive; 15 but speaking the truth in *agape*/love, may grow up into him in all things, which is the head, even Christ.

1 Pet 5:6 Humble yourselves therefore under the mighty hand of God, that he may exalt you in due time: 7 casting all your care upon him; for he careth for you. 8 Be sober, be vigilant; because your adversary the devil, as a roaring lion, walketh about, seeking whom he may devour: 9 whom resist stedfast in the faith, knowing that the same afflictions are accomplished in your brethren that are in the world. 10 But the God of all grace, who hath called us unto his eternal glory by Christ Jesus, after that ye have suffered a while, make you perfect, stablish, strengthen, settle you. 11 To him be glory and dominion for ever and ever. Amen.

Rev 1:5 And from Jesus Christ, who is the faithful witness, and the first begotten of the dead, and the prince of the kings of the earth. Unto him that *agape*/loved us, and washed us from our sins in his own blood, 6 and hath made us kings and priests unto God and his Father; to him be glory and dominion for ever and ever. Amen.

Titus 1:1 Paul, a servant of God, and an apostle of Jesus Christ, according to the faith of God's elect, and the acknowledging of the truth which is after godliness; 2 in hope of eternal *zoe*/life, which God, that cannot lie, promised before the world began; 3 but hath in due times manifested his word through preaching, which is committed unto me according to the commandment of God our Saviour.

Rev 13:8 ... of the Lamb slain from the foundation of the world.

Rom 16:25 Now to him that is of power to stablish you according to my gospel, and the preaching of Jesus Christ, according to the revelation of the mystery, which was kept secret since the world began, 26 but now is made manifest, and by the scriptures of the prophets, according to the commandment of the everlasting God, made known to all nations for the obedience of faith: 27 to God only wise, be glory through Jesus Christ for ever. Amen.

John 12:46 I (*Jesus*) am come a light into the world, that whosoever believeth on me should not abide in darkness. 47 And if any man hear my words, and believe not, I judge him not: for I came not to judge the world, but to *sozo*/save the world.

John 12:27 Now is my soul troubled; and what shall I say? Father, *sozo*/save me from this hour: but for this cause came I unto this hour. 28 Father, glorify thy name. Then came there a voice from heaven, saying, I have both glorified it, and will glorify it again. 29 The people therefore, that stood by, and heard it, said that it thundered: others said, An angel spake to him. 30 Jesus answered and said, This voice came not because of me, but for your sakes. 31 Now is the judgment of this world: now shall the prince of this world be cast out. 32 And I, if I be lifted up from the earth, will draw all men unto me. 33 This he said, signifying what death he should die.

John 18:37 Pilate therefore said unto him, Art thou a king then? Jesus answered, Thou sayest that I am a king. To this end was I born, and for this cause came I into the world, that I should bear witness unto the truth. Every one that is of the truth heareth my voice.

2 Tim 1:1 Paul, an apostle of Jesus Christ by the will of God, according to the promise of *zoe*/life which is in Christ Jesus ... 15 This is a faithful saying, and worthy of all acceptation, that Christ Jesus came into the world to *sozo*/save sinners; of whom I am chief.

Matt 18:11 For the Son of Man has come to *sozo*/save that which was lost. NKJV

Matt 20:28 Just as the Son of Man did not come to be served, but to serve, and to give His *psuche*/life (*soul*) a ransom for many. NKJV

Acts 3:26 To you first, God, having raised up His Servant Jesus, sent Him to bless you, in turning away every one of you from your iniquities. NKJV

Titus 2:14 Who gave himself for us, that he might redeem us from all iniquity, and purify unto himself a peculiar people, zealous of good works.

1 John 3:5 And ye know that he was manifested to take away our sins; and in him is no sin.

Why Jesus Came Scriptures

1 John 1:2 (For the *zoe*/life was manifested, and we have seen it, and bear witness, and shew unto you that eternal *zoe*/life, which was with the Father, and was manifested unto us.)

1 John 4:9 In this was manifested the *agape*/love of God toward us, because that God sent his only begotten Son into the world, that we might *zao*/live through him. 10 Herein is *agape*/love, not that we *agape*/loved God, but that he *agape*/loved us, and sent his Son to be the propitiation for our sins. 11 *Agape*/beloved, if God so *agape*/loved us, we ought also to *agape*/love one another. 12 No man hath seen God at any time. If we *agape*/love one another, God dwelleth in us, and his *agape*/love is perfected in us. 13 Hereby know we that we dwell in him, and he in us, because he hath given us of his Spirit. 14 And we have seen and do testify that the Father sent the Son to be the Saviour of the world.

John 1:31 And I knew him (*Jesus*) not: but that he should be made manifest to Israel, therefore am I come baptizing with water. 32 And John bare record, saying, I saw the Spirit descending from heaven like a dove, and it abode upon him. 33 And I knew him not: but he that sent me to baptize with water, the same said unto me, Upon whom thou shalt see the Spirit descending, and remaining on him, the same is he which baptizeth with the Holy Ghost. 34 And I saw, and bare record that this is the Son of God.

1 Tim 1:15 This is a faithful saying, and worthy of all acceptation, that Christ Jesus came into the world to *sozo*/save sinners; of whom I am chief. 16 Howbeit for this cause I obtained mercy, that in me first Jesus Christ might shew forth all longsuffering, for a pattern to them which should hereafter believe on him to *zoe*/life everlasting.

1 Tim 3:16 And without controversy great is the mystery of godliness: God was manifest in the flesh, justified in the Spirit, seen of angels, preached unto the Gentiles, believed on in the world, received up into glory.

Rom 4:24 But for us also, to whom it shall be imputed, if we believe on him that raised up Jesus our Lord from the dead; 25 who was delivered for our offences, and was raised again for our justification.

Luke 1:46 And Mary said, My soul doth magnify the Lord, 47 and my spirit hath rejoiced in God my Saviour. 48 For he hath regarded the low estate of his handmaiden: for, behold, from henceforth all generations shall call me blessed. 49 For he that is mighty hath done to me great things; and holy is his name. 50 And his mercy is on them that fear him from generation to generation. 51 He hath shewed strength with his arm; he hath scattered the proud in the imagination of their hearts. 52 He hath put down the mighty from their seats, and exalted them of low degree. 53 He hath filled the hungry with good things; and the rich he hath sent empty away. 54 He hath holpen his servant Israel, in remembrance of his mercy; 55 as he spake to our fathers, to Abraham, and to his seed for ever.

Luke 1:67 And his (*John the Baptist's*) father Zacharias was filled with the Holy Ghost, and prophesied, saying, 68 Blessed be the Lord God of Israel; for he hath visited and redeemed his people, 69 and hath raised up an horn of *soteria*/salvation for us in the house of his servant David; 70 as he spake by the mouth of his holy prophets, which have been since the world began: 71 that we should be *sozo*/saved from our enemies, and from the hand of all that hate us; 72 to perform the mercy promised to our fathers, and to remember his holy covenant; 73 the oath which he sware to our father Abraham, 74 that he would grant unto us, that we being delivered out of the hand of our enemies might serve him without fear, 75 in holiness and righteousness before him, all the days of our life. 76 And thou, child, shalt be called the prophet of the Highest: for thou shalt go before the face of the Lord to prepare his ways; 77 to give knowledge of *soteria*/salvation unto his people by the remission of their sins, 78 through the tender mercy of our God; whereby the dayspring from on high hath visited us, 79 to give light to them that sit in darkness and in the shadow of death, to guide our feet into the way of peace.

Luke 2:8 And there were in the same country shepherds abiding in the field, keeping watch over their flock by night. 9 And, lo, the angel of the Lord came upon them, and the glory of the Lord shone round about them: and they were sore afraid. 10 And the angel said unto them, Fear not: for, behold, I bring you good tidings of great joy, which shall be to all people. 11 For unto you is born this day in the city of David a Saviour, which is Christ the Lord. 12 And this shall be a sign unto you; Ye shall find the babe wrapped in swaddling clothes, lying in a manger. 13 And suddenly there was with the angel a multitude of the heavenly host praising God, and saying, 14 Glory to God in the highest, and on earth peace, good will toward men.

Matt 1:21 And she shall bring forth a son, and thou shalt call his name JESUS: for he shall *sozo*/save his people from their sins.

Luke 2:49 And he (*Jesus*) said unto them (*Joseph and Mary*), How is it that ye sought me? Wist ye not that I must be about my Father's business?

Why Jesus Came Scriptures

Matt 4:13 And leaving Nazareth, he came and dwelt in Capernaum, which is upon the sea coast, in the borders of Zabulon and Nephthalim: 14 that it might be fulfilled which was spoken by Esaias the prophet, saying, 15 The land of Zabulon, and the land of Nephthalim, by the way of the sea, beyond Jordan, Galilee of the Gentiles; 16 the people which sat in darkness saw great light; and to them which sat in the region and shadow of death light is sprung up. 17 From that time Jesus began to preach, and to say, Repent: for the kingdom of heaven is at hand.

Luke 4:17 And there was delivered unto him the book of the prophet Esaias. And when he had opened the book, he found the place where it was written, 18 The Spirit of the Lord is upon me, because he hath anointed me to preach the gospel to the poor; he hath sent me to heal the brokenhearted, to preach deliverance to the captives, and recovering of sight to the blind, to set at liberty them that are bruised, 19 to preach the acceptable year of the Lord. 20 And he closed the book, and he gave it again to the minister, and sat down. And the eyes of all them that were in the synagogue were fastened on him. 21 And he began to say unto them, This day is this scripture fulfilled in your ears.

Mark 1:14 Now after that John was put in prison, Jesus came into Galilee, preaching the gospel of the kingdom of God, 15 and saying, The time is fulfilled, and the kingdom of God is at hand: repent ye, and believe the gospel.

Luke 7:20 When the men were come unto him (*Jesus*), they said, John Baptist hath sent us unto thee, saying, Art thou he that should come? or look we for another? 21 And in that same hour he cured many of their infirmities and plagues, and of evil spirits; and unto many that were blind he gave sight. 22 Then Jesus answering said unto them, Go your way, and tell John what things ye have seen and heard; how that the blind see, the lame walk, the lepers are cleansed, the deaf hear, the dead are raised, to the poor the gospel is preached. 23 And blessed is he, whosoever shall not be offended in me.

Matt 26:42 He (*Jesus*) went away again the second time, and prayed, saying, O my Father, if this cup may not pass away from me, except I drink it, thy will be done. 43 And he came and found them asleep again: for their eyes were heavy. 44 And he left them, and went away again, and prayed the third time, saying the same words.

Mark 15:2 And Pilate asked him, Art thou the King of the Jews? And he answering said unto him, Thou sayest it.

Luke 23:2 And they began to accuse him, saying, We found this fellow perverting the nation, and forbidding to give tribute to Caesar, saying that he himself is Christ a King. 3 And Pilate asked him, saying, Art thou the King of the Jews? And he answered him and said, Thou sayest it.

John 18:33 Then Pilate entered into the judgment hall again, and called Jesus, and said unto him, Art thou the King of the Jews? 34 Jesus answered him, Sayest thou this thing of thyself, or did others tell it thee of me? 35 Pilate answered, Am I a Jew? Thine own nation and the chief priests have delivered thee unto me: what hast thou done? 36 Jesus answered, My kingdom is not of this world: if my kingdom were of this world, then would my servants fight, that I should not be delivered to the Jews: but now is my kingdom not from hence. 37 Pilate therefore said unto him, Art thou a king then? Jesus answered, Thou sayest that I am a king. To this end was I born, and for this cause came I into the world, that I should bear witness unto the truth. Every one that is of the truth heareth my voice.

John 1:49 Nathanael answered and saith unto him, Rabbi, thou art the Son of God; thou art the King of Israel. 50 Jesus answered and said unto him, Because I said unto thee, I saw thee under the fig tree, believest thou? thou shalt see greater things than these. 51 And he saith unto him, Verily, verily, I say unto you, Hereafter ye shall see heaven open, and the angels of God ascending and descending upon the Son of man.

Luke 22:66 And as soon as it was day, the elders of the people and the chief priests and the scribes came together, and led him into their council, saying, 67 Art thou the Christ? tell us. And he said unto them, If I tell you, ye will not believe: 68 and if I also ask you, ye will not answer me, nor let me go. 69 Hereafter shall the Son of man sit on the right hand of the power of God. 70 Then said they all, Art thou then the Son of God? And he said unto them, Ye say that I am.

Mark 14:61 But he held his peace, and answered nothing. Again the high priest asked him, and said unto him, Art thou the Christ, the Son of the Blessed? 62 And Jesus said, I am: and ye shall see the Son of man sitting on the right hand of power, and coming in the clouds of heaven.

1 Pet 1:18 Forasmuch as ye know that ye were not redeemed with corruptible things, as silver and gold, from your vain conversation received by tradition from your fathers; 19 but with the precious blood of Christ, as of a lamb without blemish and without spot: 20 who verily was foreordained before the foundation of the

world, but was manifest in these last times for you, 21 who by him do believe in God, that raised him up from the dead, and gave him glory; that your faith and hope might be in God.

1 John 1:7 But if we walk in the light, as he is in the light, we have fellowship one with another, and the blood of Jesus Christ his Son cleanseth us from all sin.

Hos 14:2 Take with you words, and turn to the LORD: say unto him, Take away all iniquity, and receive us graciously: so will we render the calves of our lips.

John 1:29 The next day John seeth Jesus coming unto him, and saith, Behold the Lamb of God, which taketh away the sin of the world.

Rom 3:24 Being justified freely by his grace through the redemption that is in Christ Jesus: 25 whom God hath set forth to be a propitiation through faith in his blood, to declare his righteousness for the remission of sins that are past, through the forbearance of God; 26 to declare, I say, at this time his righteousness: that he might be just, and the justifier of him which believeth in Jesus.

Eph 5:25 Husbands, *agape*/love your wives, even as Christ also *agape*/loved the church, and gave himself for it; 26 that he might sanctify and cleanse it with the washing of water by the word, 27 that he might present it to himself a glorious church, not having spot, or wrinkle, or any such thing; but that it should be holy and without blemish.

1 Tim 1:15 This is a faithful saying, and worthy of all acceptation, that Christ Jesus came into the world to *sozo*/save sinners; of whom I am chief.

Heb 1:1 God, who at sundry times and in divers manners spake in time past unto the fathers by the prophets, 2 hath in these last days spoken unto us by his Son, whom he hath appointed heir of all things, by whom also he made the worlds; 3 who being the brightness of his glory, and the express image of his person, and upholding all things by the word of his power, when he had by himself purged our sins, sat down on the right hand of the Majesty on high.

Heb 9:26 For then must he often have suffered since the foundation of the world: but now once in the end of the world hath he appeared to put away sin by the sacrifice of himself. ... 28 So Christ was once offered to bear the sins of many; and unto them that look for him shall he appear the second time without sin unto *soteria*/salvation.

1 Pet 2:24 Who his own self bare our sins in his own body on the tree, that we, being dead to sins, should *zao*/live unto righteousness: by whose stripes ye were healed.

Rev 1:5 And from Jesus Christ, who is the faithful witness, and the first begotten of the dead, and the prince of the kings of the earth. Unto him that *agape*/loved us, and washed us from our sins in his own blood.

1 John 2:1 My little children, these things write I unto you, that ye sin not. And if any man sin, we have an advocate with the Father, Jesus Christ the righteous.

2 Cor 5:21 For he hath made him to be sin for us, who knew no sin; that we might be made the righteousness of God in him.

Heb 4:15 For we have not an high priest which cannot be touched with the feeling of our infirmities; but was in all points tempted like as we are, yet without sin.

Heb 7:26 For such an high priest became us, who is holy, harmless, undefiled, separate from sinners, and made higher than the heavens.

1 Pet 3:18 For Christ also hath once suffered for sins, the just for the unjust, that he might bring us to God, being put to death in the flesh, but quickened by the Spirit.

Gal 3:8 And the scripture, foreseeing that God would justify the heathen through faith, preached before the gospel unto Abraham, saying, In thee shall all nations be blessed. 9 So then they which be of faith are blessed with faithful Abraham. 10 For as many as are of the works of the law are under the curse: for it is written, Cursed is every one that continueth not in all things which are written in the book of the law to do them. 11 But that no man is justified by the law in the sight of God, it is evident: for, The just shall *zao*/live by faith. 12 And the law is not of faith: but, The man that doeth them shall *zao*/live in them. 13 Christ hath redeemed us from the curse of the law, being made a curse for us: for it is written, Cursed is every one that hangeth on a tree: 14 that the blessing of Abraham might come on the Gentiles through Jesus Christ; that we might receive the promise of the Spirit through faith. 15 Brethren, I speak after the manner of men; Though it be but a man's covenant, yet if it be confirmed, no man disannulleth, or addeth thereto. 16 Now to Abraham and his seed were the promises made. He saith not, And to seeds, as of many; but as of one, And to thy seed, which is Christ. ... 22 But the scripture hath concluded all under sin, that the promise by faith of Jesus Christ might be given to them that believe.

Why Jesus Came Scriptures

Gal 3:26 For you are all sons of God through faith in Christ Jesus. 27 For as many of you as were baptized into Christ have put on Christ. 28 There is neither Jew nor Greek, there is neither slave nor free, there is neither male nor female; for you are all one in Christ Jesus. 29 And if you are Christ's, then you are Abraham's seed, and heirs according to the promise. NKJV (Note: son is a title, like general or officer.)

Gal 4:1 Now I say, That the heir, as long as he is a child, differeth nothing from a servant, though he be lord of all; 2 but is under tutors and governors until the time appointed of the father. 3 Even so we, when we were children, were in bondage under the elements of the world: 4 but when the fulness of the time was come, God sent forth his Son, made of a woman, made under the law, 5 to redeem them that were under the law, that we might receive the adoption of sons. 6 And because ye are sons, God hath sent forth the Spirit of his Son into your hearts, crying, Abba (*Daddy*), Father. 7 Wherefore thou art no more a servant, but a son; and if a son, then an heir of God through Christ.

Gal 2:16 Knowing that a man is not justified by the works of the law, but by the faith of Jesus Christ, even we have believed in Jesus Christ, that we might be justified by the faith of Christ, and not by the works of the law: for by the works of the law shall no flesh be justified. ... 19 For I through the law am dead to the law, that I might *zao*/live unto God. 20 I am crucified with Christ: nevertheless I *zao*/live; yet not I, but Christ *zao*/liveth in me: and the life which I now *zao*/live in the flesh I *zao*/live by the faith of the Son of God, who *agape*/loved me, and gave himself for me. 21 I do not frustrate the grace of God: for if righteousness come by the law, then Christ is dead in vain.

Gen 49:8 Judah, thou art he whom thy brethren shall praise: thy hand shall be in the neck of thine enemies; thy father's children shall bow down before thee. 9 Judah is a lion's whelp: from the prey, my son, thou art gone up: he stooped down, he couched as a lion, and as an old lion; who shall rouse him up? 10 The sceptre shall not depart from Judah, nor a lawgiver from between his feet, until Shiloh come; and unto him shall the gathering of the people be. 11 Binding his foal unto the vine, and his ass's colt unto the choice vine; he washed his garments in wine, and his clothes in the blood of grapes: 12 his eyes shall be red with wine, and his teeth white with milk.

Deut 18:17 And the Lord said unto me, They have well spoken that which they have spoken. 18 I will raise them up a Prophet from among their brethren, like unto thee, and will put my words in his mouth; and he shall speak unto them all that I shall command him. 19 And it shall come to pass, that whosoever will not hearken unto my words which he shall speak in my name, I will require it of him.

Dan 7:13 I saw in the night visions, and, behold, one like the Son of man came with the clouds of heaven, and came to the Ancient of days, and they brought him near before him. 14 And there was given him dominion, and glory, and a kingdom, that all people, nations, and languages, should serve him: his dominion is an everlasting dominion, which shall not pass away, and his kingdom that which shall not be destroyed.

Dan 9:23 At the beginning of thy supplications the commandment came forth, and I am come to shew thee; for thou art greatly beloved: therefore understand the matter, and consider the vision. 24 Seventy weeks are determined upon thy people and upon thy holy city, to finish the transgression, and to make an end of sins, and to make reconciliation for iniquity, and to bring in everlasting righteousness, and to seal up the vision and prophecy, and to anoint the most Holy. 25 Know therefore and understand, that from the going forth of the commandment to restore and to build Jerusalem unto the Messiah the Prince shall be seven weeks, and threescore and two weeks: the street shall be built again, and the wall, even in troublous times. 26 And after threescore and two weeks shall Messiah be cut off, but not for himself: and the people of the prince that shall come shall destroy the city and the sanctuary; and the end thereof shall be with a flood, and unto the end of the war desolations are determined. 27 And he shall confirm the covenant with many for one week: and in the midst of the week he shall cause the sacrifice and the oblation to cease, and for the overspreading of abominations he shall make it desolate, even until the consummation, and that determined shall be poured upon the desolate.

Mal 3:1 Behold, I will send my messenger, and he shall prepare the way before me: and the Lord, whom ye seek, shall suddenly come to his temple, even the messenger of the covenant, whom ye delight in: behold, he shall come, saith the LORD of hosts. 2 But who may abide the day of his coming? and who shall stand when he appeareth? for he is like a refiner's fire, and like fullers' soap: 3 and he shall sit as a refiner and purifier of silver: and he shall purify the sons of Levi, and purge them as gold and silver, that they may offer unto the LORD an offering in righteousness. 4 Then shall the offering of Judah and Jerusalem be pleasant unto the LORD, as in the days of old, and as in former years.

Isa 5:19 That say, Let him make speed, and hasten his work, that we may see it: and let the counsel of the Holy One of Israel draw nigh and come, that we may know it! 20 Woe unto them that call evil good, and good evil; that put darkness for light, and light for darkness; that put bitter for sweet, and sweet for bitter! 21 Woe unto them that are wise in their own eyes, and prudent in their own sight! 22 Woe unto them that are mighty to drink wine, and men of strength to mingle strong drink: 23 which justify the wicked for reward, and take away the righteousness of the righteous from him! 24 Therefore as the fire devoureth the stubble, and the flame consumeth the chaff, so their root shall be as rottenness, and their blossom shall go up as dust: because they have cast away the law of the LORD of hosts, and despised the word of the Holy One of Israel. 25 Therefore is the anger of the LORD kindled against his people, and he hath stretched forth his hand against them, and hath smitten them: and the hills did tremble, and their carcases were torn in the midst of the streets. For all this his anger is not turned away, but his hand is stretched out still. 26 And he will lift up an ensign to the nations from far, and will hiss unto them from the end of the earth: and, behold, they shall come with speed swiftly.

Matt 3:9 And think not to say within yourselves, We have Abraham to our father: for I say unto you, that God is able of these stones to raise up children unto Abraham. 10 And now also the axe is laid unto the root of the trees: therefore every tree which bringeth not forth good fruit is hewn down, and cast into the fire. 11 I indeed baptize you with water unto repentance: but he that cometh after me is mightier than I, whose shoes I am not worthy to bear: he shall baptize you with the Holy Ghost, and with fire: 12 whose fan is in his hand, and he will throughly purge his floor, and gather his wheat into the garner; but he will burn up the chaff with unquenchable fire. 13 Then cometh Jesus from Galilee to Jordan unto John, to be baptized of him.

Luke 3:15 And as the people were in expectation, and all men mused in their hearts of John, whether he were the Christ, or not; 16 John answered, saying unto them all, I indeed baptize you with water; but one mightier than I cometh, the latchet of whose shoes I am not worthy to unloose: he shall baptize you with the Holy Ghost and with fire: 17 whose fan is in his hand, and he will throughly purge his floor, and will gather the wheat into his garner; but the chaff he will burn with fire unquenchable. 18 And many other things in his exhortation preached he unto the people.

1 Cor 3:10 According to the grace of God which is given unto me, as a wise masterbuilder, I have laid the foundation, and another buildeth thereon. But let every man take heed how he buildeth thereupon. 11 For other foundation can no man lay than that is laid, which is Jesus Christ. 12 Now if any man build upon this foundation gold, silver, precious stones, wood, hay, stubble; 13 every man's work

shall be made manifest: for the day shall declare it, because it shall be revealed by fire; and the fire shall try every man's work of what sort it is. 14 If any man's work abide which he hath built thereupon, he shall receive a reward. 15 If any man's work shall be burned, he shall suffer loss: but he himself shall be *sozo*/saved; yet so as by fire. 16 Know ye not that ye are the temple of God, and that the Spirit of God dwelleth in you?

2 Cor 13:5 Examine yourselves, whether ye be in the faith; prove your own selves. Know ye not your own selves, how that Jesus Christ is in you, except ye be reprobates (*useless, impotent, suitable only for burning as chaff or stubble*)?

Acts 17:22 Then Paul stood in the midst of Mars' hill, and said, Ye men of Athens, I perceive that in all things ye are too superstitious. 23 For as I passed by, and beheld your devotions, I found an altar with this inscription, TO THE UNKNOWN GOD. Whom therefore ye ignorantly worship, him declare I unto you. 24 God that made the world and all things therein, seeing that he is Lord of heaven and earth, dwelleth not in temples made with hands; 25 neither is worshipped with men's hands, as though he needed any thing, seeing he giveth to all *zoe*/life, and breath, and all things; 26 and hath made of one blood all nations of men for to dwell on all the face of the earth, and hath determined the times before appointed, and the bounds of their habitation; 27 that they should seek the Lord, if haply they might feel after him, and find him, though he be not far from every one of us: 28 for in him we *zao*/live, and move, and have our being; as certain also of your own poets have said, For we are also his offspring. 29 Forasmuch then as we are the offspring of God, we ought not to think that the Godhead is like unto gold, or silver, or stone, graven by art and man's device. 30 And the times of this ignorance God winked at; but now commandeth all men every where to repent: 31 because he hath appointed a day, in the which he will judge the world in righteousness by that man whom he hath ordained; whereof he hath given assurance unto all men, in that he hath raised him from the dead. 32 And when they heard of the resurrection of the dead, some mocked: and others said, We will hear thee again of this matter. 33 So Paul departed from among them.

Luke 7:19 And John calling unto him two of his disciples sent them to Jesus, saying, Art thou he that should come? or look we for another? 20 When the men were come unto him, they said, John Baptist hath sent us unto thee, saying, Art thou he that should come? or look we for another? 21 And in that same hour he cured many of their infirmities and plagues, and of evil spirits; and unto many that were blind he gave sight. 22 Then Jesus answering said unto them, Go your way, and tell John what things ye have seen and heard; how that the blind see, the lame walk, the lepers are cleansed, the deaf hear, the dead are raised, to the poor the gospel is preached. 23 And blessed is he, whosoever shall not be offended in me. 24 And when the messengers of John were departed, he began to speak unto the people concerning John, What went ye out into the wilderness for to see? A reed shaken with the wind? 25 But what went ye out for to see? A man clothed in soft raiment? Behold, they which are gorgeously apparelled, and live delicately, are in kings' courts. 26 But what went ye out for to see? A prophet? Yea, I say unto you, and much more than a prophet. 27 This is he, of whom it is written, Behold, I send my messenger before thy face, which shall prepare thy way before thee. 28 For I say unto you, Among those that are born of women there is not a greater prophet than John the Baptist: but he that is least in the kingdom of God is greater than he. 29 And all the people that heard him, and the publicans, justified God, being baptized with the baptism of John. 30 But the Pharisees and lawyers rejected the counsel of God against themselves, being not baptized of him.

Mark 1:14 Now after that John was put in prison, Jesus came into Galilee, preaching the gospel of the kingdom of God, 15 and saying, The time is fulfilled, and the kingdom of God is at hand: repent ye, and believe the gospel.

Eph 1:3 Blessed be the God and Father of our Lord Jesus Christ, who hath blessed us with all spiritual blessings in heavenly places in Christ: 4 according as he hath chosen us in him before the foundation of the world, that we should be holy and without blame before him in *agape*/love: 5 having predestinated us unto the adoption of children by Jesus Christ to himself, according to the good pleasure of his will, 6 to the praise of the glory of his grace, wherein he hath made us accepted in the *agape*/beloved. 7 In whom we have redemption through his blood, the forgiveness (*remission, purging, putting away and obliteration*) of sins, according to the riches of his grace; 8 wherein he hath abounded toward us in all wisdom and prudence; 9 having made known unto us the mystery of his will, according to his good pleasure which he hath purposed in himself: 10 that in the dispensation of the fulness of times he might gather together in one all things in Christ, both which are in heaven, and which are on earth; even in him: 11 in whom also we have obtained an inheritance, being predestinated according to the purpose of him who worketh all things after the counsel of his own will: 12 that we should be to the praise of his glory, who first trusted in Christ. 13 In whom ye also trusted, after that ye heard the word of truth, the gospel of your *soteria*/salvation: in whom also after that ye believed, ye were sealed with that holy Spirit of promise, 14 which is the earnest of our inheritance until the redemption of the purchased possession, unto the praise of his glory.

Heb 2:1 Therefore we ought to give the more earnest heed to the things which we have heard, lest at any time we should let them slip. 2 For if the word spoken by angels was stedfast, and every transgression and disobedience received a just recompence of reward; 3 how shall we escape, if we neglect so great *soteria*/salvation; which at the first began to be spoken by the Lord, and was confirmed unto us by them that heard him; 4 God also bearing them witness, both with signs and wonders, and with divers miracles, and gifts of the Holy Ghost, according to his own will?

Heb 9:6 Now when these things were thus ordained, the priests went always into the first tabernacle, accomplishing the service of God. 7 But into the second went the high priest alone once every year, not without blood, which he offered for himself, and for the errors of the people: 8 the Holy Ghost this signifying, that the way into the holiest of all was not yet made manifest, while as the first tabernacle was yet standing: 9 which was a figure for the time then present, in which were offered both gifts and sacrifices, that could not make him that did the service perfect, as pertaining to the conscience; 10 which stood only in meats and drinks, and divers washings, and carnal ordinances, imposed on them until the time of reformation. 11 But Christ being come an high priest of good things to come, by a greater and more perfect tabernacle, not made with hands, that is to say, not of this building; 12 neither by the blood of goats and calves, but by his own blood he entered in once into the holy place, having obtained eternal redemption for us.

1 John 3:8 He that committeth sin is of the devil; for the devil sinneth from the beginning. For this purpose the Son of God was manifested, that he might destroy the works of the devil.

Gen 3:15 And I will put enmity between thee and the woman, and between thy seed and her seed; it shall bruise thy head, and thou shalt bruise his heel.

1 John 3:5 And ye know that he was manifested to take away our sins; and in him is no sin.

2 Cor 1:19 For the Son of God, Jesus Christ, who was preached among you by us, even by me and Silvanus and Timotheus, was not yea and nay, but in him was yea. 20 For all the promises of God in him are yea, and in him Amen, unto the glory of God by us. 21 Now he which stablisheth us with you in Christ, and hath anointed us, is God; 22 who hath also sealed us, and given the earnest of the Spirit in our hearts.

Why Jesus Came Scriptures

Isa 49:8 Thus saith the Lord, In an acceptable time have I heard thee, and in a day of salvation have I helped thee: and I will preserve thee, and give thee for a covenant of the people, to establish the earth, to cause to inherit the desolate heritages; 9 that thou mayest say to the prisoners, Go forth; to them that are in darkness, Shew yourselves. They shall feed in the ways, and their pastures shall be in all high places. 10 They shall not hunger nor thirst; neither shall the heat nor sun smite them: for he that hath *racham*/mercy on them shall lead them, even by the springs of water shall he guide them. 11 And I will make all my mountains a way, and my highways shall be exalted. 12 Behold, these shall come from far: and, lo, these from the north and from the west; and these from the land of Sinim. 13 Sing, O heavens; and be joyful, O earth; and break forth into singing, O mountains: for the Lord hath comforted his people, and will have *racham*/mercy upon his afflicted. 14 But Zion said, The Lord hath forsaken me, and my Lord hath forgotten me. 15 Can a woman forget her sucking child, that she should not have compassion on the son of her womb? yea, they may forget, yet will I not forget thee. 16 Behold, I have graven thee upon the palms of my hands; thy walls are continually before me. 17 Thy children shall make haste; thy destroyers and they that made thee waste shall go forth of thee. 18 Lift up thine eyes round about, and behold: all these gather themselves together, and come to thee. As I live, saith the Lord, thou shalt surely clothe thee with them all, as with an ornament, and bind them on thee, as a bride doeth. 19 For thy waste and thy desolate places, and the land of thy destruction, shall even now be too narrow by reason of the inhabitants, and they that swallowed thee up shall be far away. 20 The children which thou shalt have, after thou hast lost the other, shall say again in thine ears, The place is too strait for me: give place to me that I may dwell. 21 Then shalt thou say in thine heart, Who hath begotten me these, seeing I have lost my children, and am desolate, a captive, and removing to and fro? and who hath brought up these? Behold, I was left alone; these, where had they been? 22 Thus saith the Lord God, Behold, I will lift up mine hand to the Gentiles, and set up my standard to the people: and they shall bring thy sons in their arms, and thy daughters shall be carried upon their shoulders. 23 And kings shall be thy nursing fathers, and their queens thy nursing mothers: they shall bow down to thee with their face toward the earth, and lick up the dust of thy feet; and thou shalt know that I am the Lord: for they shall not be ashamed that wait for me (*entwine God into every part of life*). 24 Shall the prey be taken from the mighty, or the lawful captive delivered? 25 But thus saith the Lord, Even the captives of the mighty shall be taken away, and the prey of the terrible shall be delivered: for I will contend with him that contendeth with thee, and I will save thy children. 26 And I will feed them that oppress thee with their own flesh; and they shall be drunken with their own blood, as with sweet wine: and all flesh shall know that I the Lord am thy Saviour and thy Redeemer, the mighty One of Jacob.

BATTLE PRAYER FOR DIVINE HEALING: FIELD MANUAL 2

<u>2 Cor 6:1</u> We then, as workers together with him, beseech you also that ye receive not the grace of God in vain. 2 (For he saith, I have heard thee in a time accepted, and in the day of *soteria*/salvation have I succoured thee: behold, now is the accepted time; behold, now is the day of *soteria*/salvation.)

<u>Luke 4:16</u> And he came to Nazareth, where he had been brought up: and, as his custom was, he went into the synagogue on the sabbath day, and stood up for to read. 17 And there was delivered unto him the book of the prophet Esaias. And when he had opened the book, he found the place where it was written, 18 The Spirit of the Lord is upon me, because he hath anointed me to preach the gospel to the poor; he hath sent me to heal the brokenhearted, to preach deliverance to the captives, and recovering of sight to the blind, to set at liberty them that are bruised, 19 to preach the acceptable year of the Lord. 20 And he closed the book, and he gave it again to the minister, and sat down. And the eyes of all them that were in the synagogue were fastened on him. 21 And he began to say unto them, This day is this scripture fulfilled in your ears.

<u>Isa 61:1</u> The Spirit of the Lord God is upon me; because the Lord hath anointed me to preach good tidings unto the meek; he hath sent me to bind up the brokenhearted, to proclaim liberty to the captives, and the opening of the prison to them that are bound; 2 to proclaim the acceptable year of the Lord, and the day of vengeance of our God; to comfort all that mourn; 3 to appoint unto them that mourn in Zion, to give unto them beauty for ashes, the oil of joy for mourning, the garment of praise for the spirit of heaviness; that they might be called trees of righteousness, the planting of the Lord, that he might be glorified.

You write truth on your heart with repetition and emotional intensity. Say these scriptures with excitement, praise and thanks until you are operating in spiritual excitement, prase and thanks. Do the right actions in faith; feelings may come later.

<u>Isa 27:1</u> In that day the Lord with his sore and great and strong sword shall punish leviathan the piercing serpent, even leviathan that crooked serpent; and he shall slay the dragon that is in the sea.

<u>Matt 8:14</u> And when Jesus was come into Peter's house, he saw his wife's mother laid, and sick of a fever. 15 And he touched her hand, and the fever left her: and she arose, and ministered unto them. 16 When the even was come, they brought unto him many that were possessed with devils: and he cast out the spirits with his word, and healed all that were sick: 17 that it might be fulfilled which was

spoken by Esaias the prophet, saying, Himself *lambano*/took our infirmities, and bare (*completely*) our sicknesses.

Mark 1:24 Saying, Let us alone; what have we to do with thee, thou Jesus of Nazareth? art thou come to destroy us? I know thee who thou art, the Holy One of God.

Luke 4:34 Saying, Let us alone; what have we to do with thee, thou Jesus of Nazareth? art thou come to destroy us? I know thee who thou art; the Holy One of God.

Luke 10:18 And he said unto them, I beheld Satan as lightning fall from heaven.

John 12:31 Now is the judgment of this world: now shall the prince of this world be cast out.

John 16:11 Of judgment, because the prince of this world is judged.

Rom 16:20 And the God of peace shall bruise Satan under your feet *like glass shattered into dust*. The grace of our Lord Jesus Christ be with you [*to know, be and do as Jesus would*]. Amen.

Mark 12:36 For David himself said by the Holy Ghost, The Lord said to my Lord, Sit thou on my right hand, till I make thine enemies thy footstool.

Ps 110:1 The LORD said unto my Lord, Sit thou at my right hand, until I make thine enemies thy footstool. 2 The LORD shall send the rod of thy strength out of Zion: rule thou in the midst of thine enemies.

1 Cor 15:24 Then cometh the end, when he shall have delivered up the kingdom to God, even the Father; when he shall have put down all rule and all authority and power. 25 For he must reign, till he hath put all enemies under his feet. 26 The last enemy that shall be destroyed is death. 27 For he hath put all things under his feet. But when he saith, all things are put under him, it is manifest that he is excepted, which did put all things under him. 28 And when all things shall be subdued unto him, then shall the Son also himself be subject unto him that put all things under him, that God may be all in all.

Heb 1:13 But to which of the angels said he at any time, Sit on my right hand, until I make thine enemies thy footstool?

Heb 10:12 But this man, after he had offered one sacrifice for sins for ever, sat down on the right hand of God; 13 from henceforth expecting till his enemies be made his footstool. 14 For by one offering he hath perfected for ever them that are sanctified. 15 Whereof the Holy Ghost also is a witness to us: for after that he had said before, 16 This is the covenant that I will make with them after those days, saith the Lord, I will put my laws into their hearts, and in their minds will I write them; 17 and their sins and iniquities will I remember no more. 18 Now where remission (*purging, removal, putting away*) of these is, there is no more offering for sin. 19 Having therefore, brethren, boldness to enter into the holiest by the blood of Jesus, 20 by a new and *zao*/living way, which he hath consecrated for us, through the veil, that is to say, his flesh; 21 and having an high priest over the house of God; 22 let us draw near with a true heart in full assurance of faith, having our hearts sprinkled from an evil conscience, and our bodies washed with pure water. 23 Let us hold fast the profession of our faith without wavering; (for he is faithful that promised;) 24 and let us consider one another to provoke unto *agape*/love and to good works: 25 not forsaking the assembling of ourselves together, as the manner of some is; but exhorting one another: and so much the more, as ye see the day approaching. 26 For if we sin wilfully after that we have received the knowledge of the truth, there remaineth no more sacrifice for sins, 27 but a certain fearful looking for of judgment and fiery indignation, which shall devour the adversaries.

2 Thes 2:8 And then shall that Wicked be revealed, whom the Lord shall consume with the spirit of his mouth, and shall destroy with the brightness of his coming.

Col 2:15 And having spoiled principalities and powers, he made a shew of them openly, triumphing over them in it.

Heb 2:14 Forasmuch then as the children are partakers of flesh and blood, he also himself likewise took part of the same; that through death he might destroy him that had the power of death, that is, the devil.

Luke 9:56 For the Son of man is not come to destroy men's lives, but to *sozo*/save them. And they went to another village.

John 10:10 The thief cometh not, but for to steal, and to kill, and to destroy: I am come that they might have *zoe*/life, and that they might have it more abundantly.

Luke 19:10 For the Son of man is come to seek and to *sozo*/save that which was lost.

Why Jesus Came Scriptures

Matt 18:11 For the Son of man is come to *sozo*/save that which was lost.

Matt 20:28 Even as the Son of man came not to be ministered unto, but to minister, and to give his *psuche*/life (*soul*) a ransom for many.

John 3:17 For God sent not his Son into the world to condemn the world; but that the world through him might be *sozo*/saved.

John 12:7 And if any man hear my words, and believe not, I judge him not: for I came not to judge the world, but to *sozo*/save the world.

John 14:3 And if I go and prepare a place for you, I will come again, and receive you unto myself; that where I am, there ye may be also.

Acts 1:10 And while they looked stedfastly toward heaven as he went up, behold, two men stood by them in white apparel; 11 which also said, Ye men of Galilee, why stand ye gazing up into heaven? this same Jesus, which is taken up from you into heaven, shall so come in like manner as ye have seen him go into heaven.

Rom 2:16 In the day when God shall judge the secrets of men by Jesus Christ according to my gospel.

Luke 23:34 Then said Jesus, Father, forgive them; for they know not what they do. And they parted his raiment, and cast lots.

Rom 3:24 being justified freely by His grace through the redemption that is in Christ Jesus, 25 whom God set forth as a propitiation by His blood, through faith, to demonstrate His righteousness, because in His forbearance God had passed over the sins that were previously committed, 26 to demonstrate at the present time His righteousness, that He might be just and the justifier of the one who has faith in Jesus. NKJV

Rom 5:6 For when we were still without strength, in due time Christ died for the ungodly. 7 For scarcely for a righteous man will one die; yet perhaps for a good man someone would even dare to die. 8 But God demonstrates His own *agape*/love toward us, in that while we were still sinners, Christ died for us. 9 Much more then, having now been justified by His blood, we shall be *sozo*/saved from wrath through Him. 10 For if when we were enemies we were reconciled to God through the death of His Son, much more, having been reconciled, we shall be *sozo*/saved by

His *zoe*/life. 11 And not only that, but we also rejoice in God through our Lord Jesus Christ, through whom we have now received the reconciliation. NKJV

John 17:17 Sanctify them through thy truth: thy word is truth. 18 As thou hast sent me into the world, even so have I also sent them into the world. 19 And for their sakes I sanctify myself, that they also might be sanctified through the truth. 20 Neither pray I for these alone, but for them also which shall believe on me through their word.

John 18:37 Pilate therefore said unto him, Art thou a king then? Jesus answered, Thou sayest that I am a king. To this end was I born, and for this cause came I into the world, that I should bear witness unto the truth. Every one that is of the truth heareth my voice.

Eph 1:13 In whom ye also trusted, after that ye heard the word of truth, the gospel of your *soteria*/salvation: in whom also after that ye believed, ye were sealed with that holy Spirit of promise, 14 which is the earnest of our inheritance until the redemption of the purchased possession, unto the praise of his glory.

Matt 22:29 Jesus answered and said unto them, Ye do err, not knowing the scriptures, nor the power of God.

Mark 12:24 And Jesus answering said unto them, Do ye not therefore err, because ye know not the scriptures, neither the power of God? 25 For when they shall rise from the dead, they neither marry, nor are given in marriage; but are as the angels which are in heaven. 26 And as touching the dead, that they rise: have ye not read in the book of Moses, how in the bush God spake unto him, saying, I am the God of Abraham, and the God of Isaac, and the God of Jacob? 27 He is not the God of the dead, but the God of the *zao*/living: ye therefore do greatly err.

Rev 1:17 And when I saw him, I fell at his feet as dead. And he laid his right hand upon me, saying unto me, Fear not; I am the first and the last: 18 I am he that *zao*/liveth, and was dead; and, behold, I am *zao*/alive for evermore, Amen; and have the keys of hell and of death 19 write the things which thou hast seen, and the things which are, and the things which shall be hereafter.

John 10:10 The thief cometh not, but for to steal, and to kill, and to destroy: I am come that they might have *zoe*/life, and that they might have it more abundantly.

John 3:17 For God sent not his Son into the world to condemn the world; but that the world through him might be *sozo*/saved.

John 6:33 For the bread of God is he which cometh down from heaven, and giveth *zoe*/life unto the world.

Matt 4:4 But he (*Jesus*) answered and said, It is written, Man shall not *zao*/live by bread alone, but by (*doing*) every word that proceedeth out of the mouth of God.

Gal 3:11 But that no man is justified by the law in the sight of God, it is evident: for, The just shall *zao*/live by faith. 12 And the law is not of faith: but, The man that doeth them shall *zao*/live in them. 13 Christ hath redeemed us from the curse of the law, being made a curse for us: for it is written, Cursed is every one that hangeth on a tree: 14 that the blessing of Abraham might come on the Gentiles through Jesus Christ; that we might receive the promise of the Spirit through faith.

Gen 12:3 ... all the families of the earth be blessed.

Acts 10:37 The same message which was proclaimed throughout all Judea, starting from Galilee after the baptism preached by John— 38 How God anointed and consecrated Jesus of Nazareth with the [Holy] Spirit and with strength and ability and power; how He went about doing good and, in particular, curing all who were harassed and oppressed by [the power, *reign and lordship* of] the devil, for God was with Him. AMP

John 8:29 And he that sent me is with me: the Father hath not left me alone; for I do always those things that please him.

1 John 3:8 [But] he who commits sin [who practices evildoing] is of the devil [takes his character from the evil one], for the devil has sinned (violated the divine law) from the beginning. The reason the Son of God was made manifest (visible) was to undo (destroy, loosen, and dissolve) the works the devil [has done]. 9 No one born (begotten) of God [deliberately, knowingly, and habitually] practices sin, for God's nature abides in him [His principle of life, the divine sperm, remains permanently within him]; and he cannot practice sinning because he is born (begotten) of God. AMP

Titus 2:11 For the grace of God that bringeth *soteria*/salvation hath appeared to all men, 12 teaching us that, denying ungodliness and worldly lusts, we should *zao*/live soberly, righteously, and godly, in this present world; 13 looking for that blessed hope, and the glorious appearing of the great God and our Saviour Jesus Christ; 14 who gave himself for us, that he might redeem us from all iniquity, and purify unto himself a peculiar people, zealous of good works. 15 These things speak, and exhort, and rebuke with all authority. Let no man despise thee.

Titus 3:3 For we ourselves also were sometimes foolish, disobedient, deceived, serving divers lusts and pleasures, living in malice and envy, hateful, and hating one another. 4 But after that the kindness and *agape*/love of God our Saviour toward man appeared, 5 not by works of righteousness which we have done, but according to his mercy he *sozo*/saved us, by the washing of regeneration, and renewing of the Holy Ghost; 6 which he shed on us abundantly through Jesus Christ our Saviour; 7 that being justified by his grace, we should be made heirs according to the hope of eternal *zoe*/life.

1 Tim 1:14 And the grace of our Lord was exceeding abundant with faith and *agape*/love which is in Christ Jesus. 15 This is a faithful saying, and worthy of all acceptation, that Christ Jesus came into the world to *sozo*/save sinners; of whom I am chief. 16 Howbeit for this cause I obtained mercy, that in me first Jesus Christ might shew forth all longsuffering, for a pattern to them which should hereafter believe on him to *zoe*/life everlasting. 17 Now unto the King eternal, immortal, invisible, the only wise God, be honour and glory for ever and ever. Amen.

1 Tim 2:3 For this is good and acceptable in the sight of God our Saviour; 4 who will have all men to be *sozo*/saved, and to come unto the knowledge of the truth. 5 For there is one God, and one mediator between God and men, the man Christ Jesus; 6 who gave himself a ransom for all, to be testified in due time.

1 Tim 3:16 And without controversy great is the mystery of godliness: God was manifest in the flesh, justified in the Spirit, seen of angels, preached unto the Gentiles, believed on in the world, received up into glory.

Rom 4:25 (*Jesus Christ*) Who was delivered for our offences, and was raised again for our justification (*and when we were justified*).

2 Tim 1:1 Paul, an apostle of Jesus Christ by the will of God, according to the promise of *zoe*/life which is in Christ Jesus.

2 Tim 1:8 Be not thou therefore ashamed of the testimony of our Lord, nor of me his prisoner: but be thou partaker of the afflictions of the gospel according to the power of God; 9 who hath *sozo*/saved us, and called us with an holy calling,

not according to our works, but according to his own purpose and grace, which was given us in Christ Jesus before the world began, 10 but is now made manifest by the appearing of our Saviour Jesus Christ, who hath abolished death, and hath brought *zoe*/life and immortality to light through the gospel: 11 whereunto I am appointed a preacher, and an apostle, and a teacher of the Gentiles. 12 For the which cause I also suffer these things: nevertheless I am not ashamed: for I know whom I have believed, and am persuaded that he is able to keep that which I have committed unto him against that day. 13 Hold fast the form of sound words, which thou hast heard of me, in faith and *agape*/love which is in Christ Jesus. 14 That good thing which was committed unto thee keep by the Holy Ghost which dwelleth in us.

Rev 20:10 And the devil that deceived them was cast into the lake of fire and brimstone, where the beast and the false prophet are, and shall be tormented day and night for ever and ever.

Heb 2:3 How shall we escape [appropriate retribution] if we neglect and refuse to pay attention to such a great *soteria*/salvation [as is now offered to us, letting it drift past us forever]? For it was declared at first by the Lord [Himself], and it was confirmed to us and proved to be real and genuine by those who personally heard [Him speak]. 4 [Besides this evidence] it was also established and plainly endorsed by God, Who showed His approval of it by signs and wonders and various miraculous manifestations of [His] power and by imparting the gifts of the Holy Spirit [to the believers] according to His own will. ... 14 Since, therefore, [these His] children share in flesh and blood [in the physical nature of human beings], He [Himself] in a similar manner partook of the same [nature], that by [going through] death He might bring to nought and make of no effect him who had the power of death—that is, the devil— 15 and also that He might deliver and completely set free all those who through the [haunting] fear of death (*ignorance, sickness, disease, lack, weakness*) were held in bondage throughout the whole course of their *zao*/lives. AMP

John 8:31 Then said Jesus to those Jews which believed on him, If ye continue in my word, then are ye my disciples indeed; 32 and ye shall know the truth, and the truth shall make you free.

John 10:25 Jesus answered them, I told you, and ye believed not: the works that I do in my Father's name, they bear witness of me ... . 32 Jesus answered them, Many good works have I shewed you from my Father; for which of those works do ye stone me?

Battle Prayer for Divine Healing: Field Manual 2

John 10:37 If I do not the works of my Father, believe me not. 38 But if I do, though ye believe not me, believe the works: that ye may know, and believe, that the Father is in me, and I in him.

John 14:10 Believest thou not that I am in the Father, and the Father in me? the words that I speak unto you I speak not of myself: but the Father that dwelleth in me, he doeth the works. 11 Believe me that I am in the Father, and the Father in me: or else believe me for the very works' sake. 12 Verily, verily, I say unto you, He that believeth on me, the works that I do shall he do also; and greater works than these shall he do; because I go unto my Father. 13 And whatsoever ye shall *aiteo/* ask in my name, that will I do, that the Father may be glorified in the Son. 14 If ye shall *aiteo*/ask (*require, demand and expect as due by covenant promise*) any thing in my name, I will do it.

Rev 1:12 And I turned to see the voice that spake with me. And being turned, I saw seven golden candlesticks; 13 and in the midst of the seven candlesticks one like unto the Son of man, clothed with a garment down to the foot, and girt about the paps with a golden girdle. 14 His head and his hairs were white like wool, as white as snow; and his eyes were as a flame of fire; 15 and his feet like unto fine brass, as if they burned in a furnace; and his voice as the sound of many waters. 16 And he had in his right hand seven stars: and out of his mouth went a sharp twoedged sword: and his countenance was as the sun shineth in his strength. 17 And when I saw him, I fell at his feet as dead. And he laid his right hand upon me, saying unto me, Fear not; I am the first and the last: 18 I am he that *zao/*liveth, and was dead; and, behold (*make this change your life*), I am *zao*/alive for evermore, Amen; and have the keys of hell and of death.

Acts 10:38 How God anointed Jesus of Nazareth with the Holy Ghost and with power: who went about doing good, and healing [*in judgment against the devil*] all that were oppressed (*under the active dominion, reign or lordship*) of the devil; for God was with him.

Ps 9:9 The LORD also will be a refuge for the oppressed, a refuge in times of trouble. 10 And they that know thy name will put their trust in thee: for thou, LORD, hast not forsaken them that seek thee.

Ps 103:1 Bless the LORD, O my soul: and all that is within me, bless his holy name. 2 Bless the LORD, O my soul, and forget not all his benefits: 3 who forgiveth all thine iniquities; who healeth all thy diseases; 4 who redeemeth thy life from destruction; who crowneth thee with *chesed*/lovingkindness and *racham*/tender mercies; 5 who satisfieth thy mouth with good things; so that thy youth is renewed like the eagle's. 6 The Lord executeth righteousness and judgment for all that are oppressed.

John 5:26 For as the Father hath *zoe*/life in himself; so hath he given to the Son to have *zoe*/life in himself; 27 and hath given him authority to execute judgment also, because he is the Son of man.

Luke 11:17 But he, knowing their thoughts, said unto them, Every kingdom divided against itself is brought to desolation; and a house divided against a house falleth. 18 If Satan also be divided against himself, how shall his kingdom stand? because ye say that I cast out devils through Beelzebub. 19 And if I by Beelzebub cast out devils, by whom do your sons cast them out? therefore shall they be your judges. 20 But if I with the finger of God cast out devils, no doubt the kingdom of God is come upon you. 21 When a strong man armed keepeth his palace, his goods are in peace: 22 But when a stronger than he shall come upon him, and overcome him, he taketh from him all his armour wherein he trusted, and divideth his spoils. 23 He that is not with me is against me: and he that gathereth not with me scattereth.

Matt 12:24 But when the Pharisees heard it, they said, This fellow doth not cast out devils, but by Beelzebub the prince of the devils. 25 And Jesus knew their thoughts, and said unto them, Every kingdom divided against itself is brought to desolation; and every city or house divided against itself shall not stand: 26 and if Satan cast out Satan, he is divided against himself; how shall then his kingdom stand? 27 And if I by Beelzebub cast out devils, by whom do your children cast them out? therefore they shall be your judges. 28 But if I cast out devils by the Spirit of God, then the kingdom of God is come unto you. 29 Or else how can one enter into a strong man's house, and spoil his goods, except he first bind the strong man? and then he will spoil his house.

Ps 146:5 Happy is he that hath the God of Jacob for his help, whose hope is in the Lord his God: 6 which made heaven, and earth, the sea, and all that therein is: which keepeth truth for ever: 7 which executeth judgment for the oppressed: which giveth food to the hungry. The Lord looseth the prisoners: 8 the Lord openeth the eyes of the blind: the Lord raiseth them that are bowed down: the Lord loveth the righteous: 9 the Lord preserveth the strangers; he relieveth the fatherless and widow: but the way of the wicked he turneth upside down. 10 The Lord shall reign for ever, even thy God, O Zion, unto all generations. Praise ye the Lord.

Rom 8:1 There is therefore now no condemnation to them which are in Christ Jesus, who walk not after the flesh, but after the Spirit. 2 For the law of the Spirit of *zoe*/life in Christ Jesus hath made me free from the law of sin and death. 3 For what the law could not do, in that it was weak through the flesh, God sending his own Son in the likeness of sinful flesh, and for sin, condemned sin in the flesh: 4 that the righteousness of the law might be fulfilled in us, who walk not after the flesh, but after the Spirit [*in the word of Christ in us*].

1 Cor 15:45 And so it is written, The first man Adam was made a living soul; the last Adam was made a quickening spirit.

Rom 5:12 Wherefore, as by one man sin entered into the world, and death by sin; and so death passed upon all men, for that all have sinned: 13 (for until the law sin was in the world: but sin is not imputed when there is no law. 14 Nevertheless death reigned from Adam to Moses, even over them that had not sinned after the similitude of Adam's transgression, who is the figure of him that was to come. 15 But not as the offence, so also is the free gift. For if through the offence of one many be dead, much more the grace of God, and the gift by grace, which is by one man, Jesus Christ, hath abounded unto many.

2 Pet 3:9 The Lord is not slack concerning his promise, as some men count slackness; but is longsuffering to us-ward, not willing that any should perish, but that all should come to repentance. 10 But the day of the Lord will come as a thief in the night; in the which the heavens shall pass away with a great noise, and the elements shall melt with fervent heat, the earth also and the works that are therein shall be burned up.

Rev 22:20 He which testifieth these things saith, Surely I come quickly. Amen. Even so, come, Lord Jesus. 21 The grace of our Lord Jesus Christ be with you all. Amen.

Rev 5:6 And I beheld, and, lo, in the midst of the throne and of the four beasts, and in the midst of the elders, stood a Lamb as it had been slain, having seven horns and seven eyes, which are the seven Spirits of God sent forth into all the earth. 7 And he came and took the book out of the right hand of him that sat upon the throne. 8 And when he had taken the book, the four beasts and four and twenty elders fell down before the Lamb, having every one of them harps, and golden vials full of odours, which are the prayers of saints. 9 And they sung a new song, saying, Thou art worthy to take the book, and to open the seals thereof: for thou wast slain, and hast redeemed us to God by thy blood out of every kindred, and tongue, and people, and nation; 10 and hast made us unto our God kings and priests: and we shall reign on the earth. 11 And I beheld, and I heard the voice of many angels round about the throne and the beasts and the elders: and the number of them was ten thousand times ten thousand, and thousands of thousands; 12 saying with a loud voice, Worthy is the Lamb that was slain to receive power, and riches, and wisdom, and strength, and honour, and glory, and blessing. 13 And every creature which is in heaven, and on the earth, and under the earth, and such as are in the sea, and all that are in them, heard I saying, Blessing, and honour, and glory, and power, be unto him that sitteth upon the throne, and unto the Lamb for ever and ever. 14 And the four beasts said, Amen. And the four and twenty elders fell down and worshipped him that *zao*/liveth for ever and ever.

<u>Heb 4:4</u> For we which have believed do enter into rest, as he said, As I have sworn in my wrath, if they shall enter into my rest: although the works were finished from the foundation of the world.

<u>1 Pet 1:18</u> Forasmuch as ye know that ye were not redeemed with corruptible things, as silver and gold, from your vain conversation received by tradition from your fathers; 19 but with the precious blood of Christ, as of a lamb without blemish and without spot: 20 who verily was foreordained before the foundation of the world, but was manifest in these last times for you, 21 who by him do believe in God, that raised him up from the dead, and gave him glory; that your faith and hope might be in God.

<u>2 Cor 5:14</u> For the *agape*/love of Christ constraineth us; because we thus judge, that if one died for all, then were all dead: 15 and that he died for all, that they which *zao*/live should not henceforth *zao*/live unto themselves, but unto him which died for them, and rose again. 16 Wherefore henceforth know we no man after the flesh: yea, though we have known Christ after the flesh, yet now henceforth know we him no more. 17 Therefore if any man be in Christ, he is a new creature: old things are passed away; behold, all things are become new. 18 And all things are of God, who hath reconciled us to himself by Jesus Christ, and hath given to us the ministry of reconciliation; 19 to wit, that God was in Christ, reconciling the world unto himself, not imputing their trespasses unto them; and hath committed unto us the word of reconciliation. 20 Now then we are ambassadors for Christ, as though God did beseech you by us: we pray you in Christ's stead, be ye reconciled to God. 21 For he hath made him to be sin for us, who knew no sin; that we might be made the righteousness of God in him. 6:1 We then, as workers together with him, beseech you also that ye receive not the grace of God in vain. 2 (For he saith, I have heard thee in a time accepted, and in the day of *soteria*/salvation have I suc-

coured thee: behold (*make this change your life*), now is the accepted time; behold, now is the day of *soteria*/salvation.)

Rev 13:8 And all that dwell upon the earth shall worship him, whose names are not written in the book of *zoe*/life of the Lamb slain from the foundation of the world.

Acts 2:22 Ye men of Israel, hear these words; Jesus of Nazareth, a man approved of God among you by miracles and wonders and signs, which God did by him in the midst of you, as ye yourselves also know: 23 him, being delivered by the determinate counsel and foreknowledge of God, ye have taken, and by wicked hands have crucified and slain: 24 whom God hath raised up, having loosed the pains of death: because it was not possible that he should be holden of it.

Acts 10:34 Then Peter opened his mouth, and said, Of a truth I perceive that God is no respecter of persons: 35 but in every nation he that feareth him, and worketh righteousness, is accepted with him. 36 The word which God sent unto the children of Israel, preaching peace by Jesus Christ: (he is Lord of all:) 37 that word, I say, ye know, which was published throughout all Judaea, and began from Galilee, after the baptism which John preached; 38 how God anointed Jesus of Nazareth with the Holy Ghost and with power: who went about doing good, and healing all that were oppressed (*under the active dominion, reign or lordship*) of the devil; for God was with him.

Rom 16:20 And the God of peace shall bruise (*crush*) Satan under your feet shortly (*as shattered glass*). The grace of our Lord Jesus Christ be with you [*to know, be and do this like Jesus would*]. Amen.

John 9:4 I (*Jesus*) must work the works of him that sent me, while it is day: the night cometh, when no man can work.

Heb 2:1 Therefore we ought to give the more earnest heed to the things which we have heard, lest at any time we should let them slip. 2 For if the word spoken by angels was stedfast, and every transgression and disobedience received a just recompence of reward; 3 how shall we escape, if we neglect so great *soteria*/salvation; which at the first began to be spoken by the Lord, and was confirmed unto us by them that heard him; 4 God also bearing them witness, both with signs and wonders, and with divers miracles, and gifts of the Holy Ghost, according to his own will?

WHY JESUS CAME SCRIPTURES

Gal 3:17 And this I say, that the covenant, that was confirmed before of God in Christ, the law, which was four hundred and thirty years after, cannot disannul, that it should make the promise of none effect. 18 For if the inheritance be of the law, it is no more of promise: but God gave it to Abraham by promise. 19 Wherefore then serveth the law? It was added because of transgressions, till the seed should come to whom the promise was made; and it was ordained by angels in the hand of a mediator. 20 Now a mediator is not a mediator of one, but God is one. 21 Is the law then against the promises of God? God forbid: for if there had been a law given which could have given *zoe*/life, verily righteousness should have been by the law. 22 But the scripture hath concluded all under sin, that the promise by faith of Jesus Christ might be given to them that believe. 23 But before faith came, we were kept under the law, shut up unto the faith which should afterwards be revealed. 24 Wherefore the law was our schoolmaster to bring us unto Christ, that we might be justified by faith. 25 But after that faith is come, we are no longer under a schoolmaster. 26 For ye are all the children (*sons*) of God by faith in Christ Jesus. 27 For as many of you as have been baptized into Christ have put on Christ. 28 There is neither Jew nor Greek, there is neither bond nor free, there is neither male nor female: for ye are all one in Christ Jesus. 29 And if ye be Christ's, then are ye Abraham's seed, and heirs according to the promise. 4:1 Now I say, That the heir, as long as he is a child, differeth nothing from a servant, though he be lord of all; 2 but is under tutors and governors until the time appointed of the father. 3 Even so we, when we were children, were in bondage under the elements of the world: 4 but when the fulness of the time was come, God sent forth his Son, made of a woman, made under the law, 5 to redeem them that were under the law, that we might receive the adoption of sons. 6 And because ye are sons, God hath sent forth the Spirit of his Son into your hearts, crying, Abba (*Daddy*), Father. 7 Wherefore thou art no more a servant, but a son; and if a son, then an heir of God through Christ.

2 Pet 1:17 For he received from God the Father honour and glory, when there came such a voice to him from the excellent glory, This is my *agape*/beloved Son, in whom I am well pleased. 18 And this voice which came from heaven we heard, when we were with him in the holy mount. 19 We have also a more sure word of prophecy; whereunto ye do well that ye take heed, as unto a light that shineth in a dark place, until the day dawn, and the day star arise in your hearts: 20 knowing this first, that no prophecy of the scripture is of any private interpretation. 21 For the prophecy came not in old time by the will of man: but holy men of God spake as they were moved by the Holy Ghost.

Rom 1:1 Paul, a servant of Jesus Christ, called to be an apostle, separated unto the gospel of God, 2 (which he had promised afore by his prophets in the holy scriptures,) 3 concerning his Son Jesus Christ our Lord, which was made of the seed of David according to the flesh; 4 and declared to be the Son of God with power, according to the spirit of holiness, by the resurrection from the dead: 5 by whom we have received grace and apostleship, for obedience to the faith among all nations, for his name: 6 among whom are ye also the called of Jesus Christ: 7 to all that be in Rome, *agape*/beloved of God, called to be saints: Grace to you and peace from God our Father, and the Lord Jesus Christ.

Gen 49:10 The sceptre shall not depart from Judah, nor a lawgiver from between his feet, until Shiloh come; and unto him shall the gathering of the people be.

Mark 1:14 Now after that John was put in prison, Jesus came into Galilee, preaching the gospel of the kingdom of God, 15 and saying, The time is fulfilled, and the kingdom of God is at hand: repent ye, and believe the gospel.

Heb 9:8 The Holy Ghost this signifying, that the way into the holiest of all was not yet made manifest, while as the first tabernacle was yet standing: 9 which was a figure for the time then present, in which were offered both gifts and sacrifices, that could not make him that did the service perfect, as pertaining to the conscience; 10 which stood only in meats and drinks, and divers washings, and carnal ordinances, imposed on them until the time of reformation. 11 But Christ being come an high priest of good things to come, by a greater and more perfect tabernacle, not made with hands, that is to say, not of this building; 12 neither by the blood of goats and calves, but by his own blood he entered in once into the holy place, having obtained eternal redemption for us.

1 John 3:1 Behold (*make this change your life*), what manner of *agape*/love the Father hath bestowed upon us, that we should be called the sons of God: therefore the world knoweth us not, because it knew him not. 2 *Agape*/beloved, now are we the sons of God, and it doth not yet appear what we shall be: but we know that, when he shall appear, we shall be like him; for we shall see him as he is. 3 And every man that hath this hope in him purifieth himself, even as he is pure.

Acts 13:26 Men and brethren, children of the stock of Abraham, and whosoever among you feareth God, to you is the word of this *soteria*/salvation sent. ... 37 But he, whom God raised again, saw no corruption. 38 Be it known unto you therefore, men and brethren, that through this man is preached unto you the forgiveness (*remission, purging, putting away and obliteration*) of sins: 39 and by him all that believe are justified from all things, from which ye could not be justified by the law of Moses.

Why Jesus Came Scriptures

Rom 10:2 For I bear them record that they have a zeal of God, but not according to knowledge. 3 For they being ignorant of God's righteousness, and going about to establish their own righteousness, have not submitted themselves unto the righteousness of God. 4 For Christ is the end of the law for righteousness to every one that believeth. 5 For Moses describeth the righteousness which is of the law, That the man which doeth those things shall *zao*/live by them. 6 But the righteousness which is of faith speaketh on this wise, Say not in thine heart, Who shall ascend into heaven? (that is, to bring Christ down from above:) 7 Or, Who shall descend into the deep? (that is, to bring up Christ again from the dead.) 8 But what saith it? The word is nigh thee, even in thy mouth, and in thy heart: that is, the word of faith, which we preach; 9 that if thou shalt confess with thy mouth the Lord Jesus, and shalt believe in thine heart that God hath raised him from the dead, thou shalt be *sozo*/saved. 10 For with the heart man believeth unto righteousness; and with the mouth confession is made unto *soteria*/salvation. 11 For the scripture saith, Whosoever believeth on him shall not be ashamed. 12 For there is no difference between the Jew and the Greek: for the same Lord over all is rich unto all that call upon him. 13 For whosoever shall call upon the name of the Lord shall be *sozo*/saved.

Rom 8:3 For what the law could not do, in that it was weak through the flesh, God sending his own Son in the likeness of sinful flesh, and for sin, condemned sin in the flesh: 4 that the righteousness of the law might be fulfilled in us, who walk not after the flesh, but after the Spirit. 5 For they that are after the flesh do mind the things of the flesh; but they that are after the Spirit the things of the Spirit. 6 For to be carnally minded is death; but to be spiritually minded is *zoe*/life and peace. 7 Because the carnal mind is enmity against God: for it is not subject to the law of God, neither indeed can be. 8 So then they that are in the flesh cannot please God. 9 But ye are not in the flesh, but in the Spirit, if so be that the Spirit of God dwell in you. Now if any man have not the Spirit of Christ, he is none of his. 10 And if Christ be in you, the body is dead because of sin; but the Spirit is *zoe*/life because of righteousness.

1 Cor 1:30 But of him are ye in Christ Jesus, who of God is made unto us wisdom, and righteousness, and sanctification, and redemption: 31 that, according as it is written, He that glorieth, let him glory in the Lord.

Ps 68:16 Why leap ye, ye high hills? this is the hill which God desireth to dwell in; yea, the LORD will dwell in it for ever. 17 The chariots of God are twenty thousand, even thousands of angels: the Lord is among them, as in Sinai, in the holy place. 18 Thou hast ascended on high, thou hast led captivity captive: thou hast received gifts for men; yea, for the rebellious also, that the LORD God might dwell among them. 19 Blessed be the Lord, who daily loadeth us with benefits, even the God of our salvation. Selah. 20 He that is our God is the God of salvation; and unto God the Lord belong the issues from death. 21 But God shall wound the head of his enemies, and the hairy scalp of such an one as goeth on still in his trespasses.

Eph 4:7 But unto every one of us is given grace according to the measure of the gift of Christ. 8 Wherefore he saith, When he ascended up on high, he led captivity captive, and gave gifts unto men. 9 (Now that he ascended, what is it but that he also descended first into the lower parts of the earth? 10 He that descended is the same also that ascended up far above all heavens, that he might fill all things.) 11 And he gave some, apostles; and some, prophets; and some, evangelists; and some, pastors and teachers; 12 for the perfecting of the saints, for the work of the ministry, for the edifying of the body of Christ: 13 till we all come in the unity of the faith, and of the knowledge of the Son of God, unto a perfect man, unto the measure of the stature of the fulness of Christ: 14 that we henceforth be no more children, tossed to and fro, and carried about with every wind of doctrine, by the sleight of men, and cunning craftiness, whereby they lie in wait to deceive; 15 but speaking the truth in *agape*/love, may grow up into him in all things, which is the head, even Christ.

Gal 2:16 Knowing that a man is not justified by the works of the law, but by the faith of Jesus Christ, even we have believed in Jesus Christ, that we might be justified by the faith of Christ, and not by the works of the law: for by the works of the law shall no flesh be justified. ... 19 For I through the law am dead to the law, that I might *zao*/live unto God. 20 I am crucified with Christ: nevertheless I *zao*/live; yet not I, but Christ *zao*/liveth in me: and the life which I now *zao*/live in the flesh I *zao*/live by the faith of the Son of God, who *agape*/loved me, and gave himself for me. 21 I do not frustrate the grace of God: for if righteousness come by the law, then Christ is dead in vain.

John 17:55 And now, O Father, glorify thou me with thine own self with the glory which I had with thee before the world was. 6 I have manifested thy name unto the men which thou gavest me out of the world: thine they were, and thou gavest them me; and they have kept thy word. 7 Now they have known that all things whatsoever thou hast given me are of thee. 8 For I have given unto them the words which thou gavest me; and they have received them, and have known surely that I came out from thee, and they have believed that thou didst send me.

Rom 3:21 But now the righteousness of God without the law is manifested, being witnessed by the law and the prophets; 22 even the righteousness of God which is by faith of Jesus Christ unto all and upon all them that believe: for there is no difference.

Heb 1:1 God, who at sundry times and in divers manners spake in time past unto the fathers by the prophets, 2 hath in these last days spoken unto us by his Son, whom he hath appointed heir of all things, by whom also he made the worlds; 3 who being the brightness of his glory, and the express image of his person, and upholding all things by the word of his power, when he had by himself purged our sins, sat down on the right hand of the Majesty on high; 4 being made so much better than the angels, as he hath by inheritance obtained a more excellent name than they. 5 For unto which of the angels said he at any time, Thou art my Son, this day have I begotten thee? And again, I will be to him a Father, and he shall be to me a Son? 6 And again, when he bringeth in the firstbegotten into the world, he saith, And let all the angels of God worship him. 7 And of the angels he saith, Who maketh his angels spirits, and his ministers a flame of fire.

8 But unto the Son he saith, Thy throne, O God, is for ever and ever: a sceptre of righteousness is the sceptre of thy kingdom. 9 Thou hast *agape*/loved righteousness, and hated iniquity; therefore God, even thy God, hath anointed thee with the oil of gladness above thy fellows. 10 And, Thou, Lord, in the beginning hast laid the foundation of the earth; and the heavens are the works of thine hands: 11 they shall perish; but thou remainest; and they all shall wax old as doth a garment; 12 and as a vesture shalt thou fold them up, and they shall be changed: but thou art the same, and thy years shall not fail. 13 But to which of the angels said he at any time, Sit on my right hand, until I make thine enemies thy footstool? 14 Are they not all ministering spirits, sent forth to minister for them who shall be heirs of *soteria*/salvation?

Heb 2:1 Therefore we ought to give the more earnest heed to the things which we have heard, lest at any time we should let them slip. 2 For if the word spoken by angels was stedfast, and every transgression and disobedience received a just recompence of reward; 3 how shall we escape, if we neglect so great *soteria*/salvation; which at the first began to be spoken by the Lord, and was confirmed unto us by them that heard him; 4 God also bearing them witness, both with signs and wonders, and with divers miracles, and gifts of the Holy Ghost, according to his own will? 5 For unto the angels hath he not put in subjection the world to come, whereof we speak.

6 But one in a certain place testified, saying, What is man, that thou art mindful of him? or the son of man, that thou visitest him? 7 Thou madest him a little lower

than the angels; thou crownedst him with glory and honour, and didst set him over the works of thy hands: 8 thou hast put all things in subjection under his feet. For in that he put all in subjection under him, he left nothing that is not put under him. But now we see not yet all things put under him.

9 But we see Jesus, who was made a little lower than the angels for the suffering of death, crowned with glory and honour; that he by the grace of God should taste death for every man. 10 For it became him, for whom are all things, and by whom are all things, in bringing many sons unto glory, to make the captain of their *soteria*/salvation perfect through sufferings. 11 For both he that sanctifieth and they who are sanctified are all of one: for which cause he is not ashamed to call them brethren, 12 saying, I will declare thy name unto my brethren, in the midst of the church will I sing praise unto thee. 13 And again, I will put my trust in him. And again, Behold I and the children which God hath given me.

14 Forasmuch then as the children are partakers of flesh and blood, he also himself likewise took part of the same; that through death he might destroy him that had the power of death, that is, the devil; 15 and deliver them who through fear of death were all their lifetime subject to bondage. 16 For verily he took not on him the nature of angels; but he took on him the seed of Abraham. 17 Wherefore in all things it behoved him to be made like unto his brethren, that he might be a merciful and faithful high priest in things pertaining to God, to make reconciliation for the sins of the people. 18 For in that he himself hath suffered being tempted, he is able to succour them that are tempted.

Heb 4:11 Let us labour therefore to enter into that rest, lest any man fall after the same example of unbelief. 12 For the word of God is quick, and powerful, and sharper than any twoedged sword, piercing even to the dividing asunder of soul and spirit, and of the joints and marrow, and is a discerner of the thoughts and intents of the heart. 13 Neither is there any creature that is not manifest in his sight: but all things are naked and opened unto the eyes of him with whom we have to do. 14 Seeing then that we have a great high priest, that is passed into the heavens, Jesus the Son of God, let us hold fast our profession (*confession*). 15 For we have not an high priest which cannot be touched with the feeling of our infirmities; but was in all points tempted like as we are, yet without sin. 16 Let us therefore come boldly unto the throne of grace, that we may *lambano*/obtain mercy, and find (*perceive*) grace to help in time of need.

Heb 5:1 For every high priest taken from among men is ordained for men in things pertaining to God, that he may offer both gifts and sacrifices for sins: 2 who can have compassion on the ignorant, and on them that are out of the way; for that he himself also is compassed with infirmity. 3 And by reason hereof he ought, as for the people, so also for himself, to offer for sins. 4 And no man taketh this honour unto himself, but he that is called of God, as was Aaron. 5 So also Christ glorified not himself to be made an high priest; but he that said unto him, Thou art my Son, to day have I begotten thee. 6 As he saith also in another place, Thou art a priest for ever after the order of Melchisedec. 7 Who in the days of his flesh, when he had offered up prayers and supplications with strong crying and tears unto him that was able to *sozo*/save him from death, and was heard in that he feared; 8 though he were a Son, yet learned he obedience by the things which he suffered; 9 and being made perfect, he became the author of eternal *soteria*/salvation unto all them that obey him; 10 called of God an high priest after the order of Melchisedec.

Heb 6:12 That ye be not slothful, but followers of them who through faith and patience inherit the promises. 13 For when God made promise to Abraham, because he could swear by no greater, he sware by himself, 14 saying, Surely blessing I will bless thee, and multiplying I will multiply thee. 15 And so, after he had patiently endured, he obtained the promise. 16 For men verily swear by the greater: and an oath for confirmation is to them an end of all strife. 17 Wherein God, willing more abundantly to shew unto the heirs of promise the immutability of his counsel, confirmed it by an oath: 18 that by two immutable things, in which it was impossible for God to lie, we might have a strong consolation, who have fled for refuge to lay hold upon the hope set before us: 19 which hope we have as an anchor of the soul, both sure and stedfast, and which entereth into that within the veil; 20 whither the forerunner is for us entered, even Jesus, made an high priest for ever after the order of Melchisedec.

Heb 7:14 For it is evident that our Lord sprang out of Juda; of which tribe Moses spake nothing concerning priesthood. 15 And it is yet far more evident: for that after the similitude of Melchisedec there ariseth another priest, 16 who is made, not after the law of a carnal commandment, but after the power of an endless *zoe*/life. 17 For he testifieth, Thou art a priest for ever after the order of Melchisedec. 18 For there is verily a disannulling of the commandment going before for the weakness and unprofitableness thereof. 19 For the law made nothing perfect, but the bringing in of a better hope did; by the which we draw nigh unto God. 20 And inasmuch as not without an oath he was made priest: 21(for those priests were made without an oath; but this with an oath by him that said unto him, The Lord sware and will not repent, Thou art a priest for ever after the order of Melchisedec.)

22 By so much was Jesus made a surety of a better testament. 23 And they truly were many priests, because they were not suffered to continue by reason of death: 24 but this man, because he continueth ever, hath an unchangeable priesthood. 25 Wherefore he is able also to *sozo*/save them to the uttermost that come unto God

by him, seeing he ever *zao*/liveth to make intercession for them. 26 For such an high priest became us, who is holy, harmless, undefiled, separate from sinners, and made higher than the heavens; 27 who needeth not daily, as those high priests, to offer up sacrifice, first for his own sins, and then for the people's: for this he did once, when he offered up himself. 28 For the law maketh men high priests which have infirmity; but the word of the oath, which was since the law, maketh the Son, who is consecrated for evermore.

Heb 8:6 But now hath he obtained a more excellent ministry, by how much also he is the mediator of a better covenant, which was established upon better promises. 7 For if that first covenant had been faultless, then should no place have been sought for the second. 8 For finding fault with them, he saith, Behold, the days come, saith the Lord, when I will make a new covenant with the house of Israel and with the house of Judah: 9 not according to the covenant that I made with their fathers in the day when I took them by the hand to lead them out of the land of Egypt; because they continued not in my covenant, and I regarded them not, saith the Lord. 10 For this is the covenant that I will make with the house of Israel after those days, saith the Lord; I will put my laws into their mind, and write them in their hearts: and I will be to them a God, and they shall be to me a people: 11 and they shall not teach every man his neighbour, and every man his brother, saying, Know the Lord: for all shall know me, from the least to the greatest. 12 For I will be merciful to their unrighteousness, and their sins and their iniquities will I remember no more. 13 In that he saith, A new covenant, he hath made the first old. Now that which decayeth and waxeth old is ready to vanish away.

Acts 13:26 Men and brethren, children of the stock of Abraham, and whosoever among you feareth God, to you is the word of this *soteria*/salvation sent. ... 32 And we declare unto you glad tidings, how that the promise which was made unto the fathers, 33 God hath fulfilled the same unto us their children, in that he hath raised up Jesus again; as it is also written in the second psalm, Thou art my Son, this day have I begotten thee. 34 And as concerning that he raised him up from the dead, now no more to return to corruption, he said on this wise, I will give you the sure mercies of David. 35 Wherefore he saith also in another psalm, Thou shalt not suffer thine Holy One to see corruption. 36 For David, after he had served his own generation by the will of God, fell on sleep, and was laid unto his fathers, and saw corruption: 37 but he, whom God raised again, saw no corruption. 38 Be it known unto you therefore, men and brethren, that through this man is preached unto you the forgiveness (*remission, purging, putting away and obliteration*) of sins: 39 and by him all that believe are justified from all things, from which ye could not be justified by the law of Moses.

Heb 9:11 But Christ being come an high priest of good things to come, by a greater and more perfect tabernacle, not made with hands, that is to say, not of this building; 12 neither by the blood of goats and calves, but by his own blood he entered in once into the holy place, having obtained eternal redemption for us. 13 For if the blood of bulls and of goats, and the ashes of an heifer sprinkling the unclean, sanctifieth to the purifying of the flesh: 14 how much more shall the blood of Christ, who through the eternal Spirit offered himself without spot to God, purge your conscience from dead works to serve the *zao*/living God? 15 And for this cause he is the mediator of the new testament, that by means of death, for the redemption of the transgressions that were under the first testament, they which are called might receive the promise of eternal inheritance.

16 For where a testament is, there must also of necessity be the death of the testator. 17 For a testament is of force after men are dead: otherwise it is of no strength at all while the testator *zao*/liveth. 18 Whereupon neither the first testament was dedicated without blood. 19 For when Moses had spoken every precept to all the people according to the law, he took the blood of calves and of goats, with water, and scarlet wool, and hyssop, and sprinkled both the book, and all the people, 20 saying, This is the blood of the testament which God hath enjoined unto you. 21 Moreover he sprinkled with blood both the tabernacle, and all the vessels of the ministry. 22 And almost all things are by the law purged with blood; and without shedding of blood is no remission (*removal, purging, washing, obliteration and putting away of sins*). 23 It was therefore necessary that the patterns of things in the heavens should be purified with these; but the heavenly things themselves with better sacrifices than these.

24 For Christ is not entered into the holy places made with hands, which are the figures of the true; but into heaven itself, now to appear in the presence of God for us: 25 nor yet that he should offer himself often, as the high priest entereth into the holy place every year with blood of others; 26 for then must he often have suffered since the foundation of the world: but now once in the end of the world hath he appeared to put away sin by the sacrifice of himself. 27 And as it is appointed unto men once to die, but after this the judgment: 28 so Christ was once offered to bear the sins of many; and unto them that look for him shall he appear the second time without sin unto *soteria*/salvation.

Heb 10:4 For it is not possible that the blood of bulls and of goats should take away sins. 5 Wherefore when he cometh into the world, he saith, Sacrifice and offering thou wouldest not, but a body hast thou prepared me: 6 in burnt offerings and sacrifices for sin thou hast had no pleasure. 7 Then said I, Lo, I come (in the volume of the book it is written of me,) to do thy will, O God. 8 Above when he said, Sacrifice and offering and burnt offerings and offering for sin thou wouldest not, neither hadst pleasure therein; which are offered by the law; 9 then said he, Lo, I come to do thy will, O God. He taketh away the first, that he may establish the second. 10 By the which will we are sanctified through the offering of the body of Jesus Christ once for all. 11 And every priest standeth daily ministering and offering oftentimes the same sacrifices, which can never take away sins: 12 but this man, after he had offered one sacrifice for sins for ever, sat down on the right hand of God; 13 from henceforth expecting till his enemies be made his footstool. 14 For by one offering he hath perfected for ever them that are sanctified.

15 Whereof the Holy Ghost also is a witness to us: for after that he had said before, 16 This is the covenant that I will make with them after those days, saith the Lord, I will put my laws into their hearts, and in their minds will I write them; 17 and their sins and iniquities will I remember no more. 18 Now where remission (*obliteration, removal, purging*) of these (*sins and iniquities*) is, there is no more offering for sin. 19 Having therefore, brethren, boldness to enter into the holiest by the blood of Jesus, 20 by a new and *zao*/living way, which he hath consecrated for us, through the veil, that is to say, his flesh; 21 and having an high priest over the house of God.

Heb 13:8 Jesus Christ the same yesterday, and to day, and for ever.

1 Thes 5:9 For God hath not appointed us to wrath, but to obtain *soteria*/salvation by our Lord Jesus Christ, 10 who died for us, that, whether we wake or sleep, we should *zao*/live together with him.

Rom 7:24 O wretched man that I am! who shall deliver me from the body of this death? 25 I thank God through Jesus Christ our Lord. So then with the mind I myself serve the law of God; but with the flesh the law of sin. 8:1 There is therefore now no condemnation to them which are in Christ Jesus, who walk not after the flesh, but after the Spirit. 2 For the law of the Spirit of *zoe*/life in Christ Jesus hath made me free from the law of sin and death. 3 For what the law could not do, in that it was weak through the flesh, God sending his own Son in the likeness of sinful flesh, and for sin, condemned sin in the flesh: 4 that the righteousness of the law might be fulfilled in us, who walk not after the flesh, but after the Spirit. 5 For they that are after the flesh do mind the things of the flesh; but they that are after the Spirit the things of the Spirit. 6 For to be carnally minded is death; but to be spiritually minded is *zoe*/life and peace. 7 Because the carnal mind is enmity against God: for it is not subject to the law of God, neither indeed can be. 8 So then they that are in the flesh cannot please God. 9 But ye are not in the flesh, but in the Spirit, if so be that the Spirit of God dwell in you. Now if any man have not the Spirit of Christ, he is none of his. 10 And if Christ be in you, the body is dead because of sin; but the Spirit is *zoe*/life because of righteousness. 11 But if the Spirit of him that raised up Jesus from the dead dwell in you, he that raised up Christ from the dead shall also quicken your (*current*) mortal bodies by his Spirit that dwelleth in you. 12 Therefore, brethren, we are debtors, not to the flesh, to *zao*/live after the flesh. 13 For if ye *zao*/live after the flesh, ye shall die: but if ye through the Spirit do mortify the deeds of the body, ye shall *zao*/live. 14 For as many as are led by the Spirit of God, they are the sons of God. 15 For ye have not received the spirit of bondage again to fear; but ye have received the Spirit of adoption, whereby we cry, Abba (*Daddy*), Father. 16 The Spirit itself beareth witness with our spirit, that we are the children (*sons*) of God: 17 and if children (*sons*), then heirs; heirs of God, and joint-heirs with Christ; if so be that we suffer with him, that we may be also glorified together. 18 For I reckon that the sufferings of this present time are not worthy to be compared with the glory which shall be revealed in us. 19 For the earnest expectation of the creature waiteth for the manifestation of the (*mature*) sons of God. 20 For the creature was made subject to vanity, not willingly, but by reason of him who hath subjected the same in hope, 21 because the creature itself also shall be delivered from the bondage of corruption into the glorious liberty of the children (*sons*) of God. 22 For we know that the whole creation groaneth and travaileth in pain together until now. 23 And not only they, but ourselves also, which have the firstfruits of the Spirit, even we ourselves groan within ourselves, waiting for the adoption, to wit, the redemption of our body. 24 For we are *sozo*/saved by hope: but hope that is seen is not hope: for what a man seeth, why doth he yet hope for? 25 But if we hope for that we see not, then do we with patience wait for it. 26 Likewise the Spirit also helpeth our infirmities: for we know not what we should pray for as we ought: but the Spirit itself maketh intercession for us with groanings which cannot be uttered. 27 And he that searcheth the hearts knoweth what is the mind of the Spirit, because he maketh intercession for the saints according to the will of God, 28 and we know that all things work together for good to them that *agape*/love God, to them who are the called according to his purpose. 29 For whom he did foreknow, he also did predestinate to be conformed to the image of his Son, that he might be the firstborn among many brethren.

Heb 2:11 ... he (*Jesus*) is not ashamed to call them (*us*) brethren.

1 Cor 1:1 Paul, called to be an apostle of Jesus Christ through the will of God, and Sosthenes our brother, 2 unto the church of God which is at Corinth, to them that are sanctified in Christ Jesus, called to be saints, with all that in every place call upon the name of Jesus Christ our Lord, both theirs and ours: 3 grace be unto you, and peace, from God our Father, and from the Lord Jesus Christ. 4 I thank my God always on your behalf, for the grace of God which is given you by Jesus Christ; 5 that in every thing ye are enriched by him, in all utterance, and in all knowledge; 6

even as the testimony of Christ was confirmed in you: 7 so that ye come behind in no gift; waiting for the coming of our Lord Jesus Christ: 8 who shall also confirm you unto the end, that ye may be blameless in the day of our Lord Jesus Christ. 9 God is faithful, by whom ye were called unto the fellowship of his Son Jesus Christ our Lord.

Rom 5:6 For when we were yet without strength, in due time Christ died for the ungodly. 7 For scarcely for a righteous man will one die: yet peradventure for a good man some would even dare to die. 8 But God commendeth his *agape*/love toward us, in that, while we were yet sinners, Christ died for us. 9 Much more then, being now justified by his blood, we shall be *sozo*/saved from wrath through him. 10 For if, when we were enemies, we were reconciled to God by the death of his Son, much more, being reconciled, we shall be *sozo*/saved by his *zoe*/life. 11 And not only so, but we also joy in God through our Lord Jesus Christ, by whom we have now received the atonement (*reconciliation*). 12 Wherefore, as by one man sin entered into the world, and death by sin; and so death passed upon all men, for that all have sinned: 13 (for until the law sin was in the world: but sin is not imputed when there is no law. 14 Nevertheless death reigned from Adam to Moses, even over them that had not sinned after the similitude of Adam's transgression, who is the figure of him that was to come. 15 But not as the offence, so also is the free gift. For if through the offence of one many be dead, much more the grace of God, and the gift by grace, which is by one man, Jesus Christ, hath abounded unto many. 16 And not as it was by one that sinned, so is the gift: for the judgment was by one to condemnation, but the free gift is of many offences unto justification. 17 For if by one man's offence death reigned by one; much more they which (*continually*) *lambano*/receive abundance of grace and of the gift of righteousness shall reign in *zoe*/life by one, Jesus Christ.) 18 Therefore as by the offence of one judgment came upon all men to condemnation; even so by the righteousness of one the free gift came upon all men unto justification of *zoe*/life. 18 Therefore as by the offence of one judgment came upon all men to condemnation; even so by the righteousness of one the free gift came upon all men unto justification of *zoe*/life. 19 For as by one man's disobedience many were made sinners, so by the obedience of one shall many be made righteous. 20 Moreover the law entered, that the offence might abound. But where sin abounded, grace did much more abound: 21 that as sin hath reigned unto death, even so might grace reign through righteousness unto eternal *zoe*/life by Jesus Christ our Lord.

Gal 3:9 So then they which be of faith are blessed with faithful Abraham. 10 For as many as are of the works of the law are under the curse: for it is written, Cursed is every one that continueth not in all things which are written in the book of the law to do them. 11 But that no man is justified by the law in the sight of God, it is evident: for, The just shall *zao*/live by faith. 12 And the law is not of faith: but, The man that doeth them shall *zao*/live in them. 13 Christ hath redeemed us from the curse of the law (*every sickness, disease, limitation and lack on Earth*), being made a curse for us: for it is written, Cursed is every one that hangeth on a tree: 14 that the blessing of Abraham might come on the Gentiles through Jesus Christ; that we might receive the promise of the Spirit through faith.

Gal 1:1 Paul, an apostle, (not of men, neither by man, but by Jesus Christ, and God the Father, who raised him from the dead;) 2 and all the brethren which are with me, unto the churches of Galatia: 3 grace be to you and peace from God the Father, and from our Lord Jesus Christ, 4 who gave himself for our sins, that he might deliver us from this present evil world (*system*), according to the will of God and our Father: 5 to whom be glory for ever and ever. Amen.

John 20:30 And many other signs truly did Jesus in the presence of his disciples, which are not written in this book: 31 but these are written, that ye might believe that Jesus is the Christ, the Son of God; and that believing ye might have *zoe*/life through his name.

Luke 24:25 Then he said unto them, O fools, and slow of heart to believe all that the prophets have spoken: 26 ought not Christ to have suffered these things, and to enter into his glory? 27 And beginning at Moses and all the prophets, he expounded unto them in all the scriptures the things concerning himself.

Luke 24:42 And they gave him (*Jesus*) a piece of a broiled fish, and of an honeycomb. 43 And he took it, and did eat before them. 44 And he said unto them, These are the words which I spake unto you, while I was yet with you, that all things must be fulfilled, which were written in the law of Moses, and in the prophets, and in the psalms, concerning me. 45 Then opened he their understanding, that they might understand the scriptures, 46 And said unto them, Thus it is written, and thus it behoved Christ to suffer, and to rise from the dead the third day: 47 and that repentance and remission (*removal, purging, obliteration, washing and putting away*) of sins should be preached in his name among all nations, beginning at Jerusalem. 48 And ye are witnesses of these things. 49 And, behold, I send the promise of my Father upon you: but tarry ye in the city of Jerusalem, until ye be endued with *dunamis*/power from on high.

Acts 1:1 The former treatise have I made, O Theophilus, of all that Jesus began both to do and teach, 2 Until the day in which he was taken up, after that he through the Holy Ghost had given commandments unto the apostles whom he had chosen: 3 to whom also he shewed himself alive after his passion by many infallible proofs, being seen of them forty days, and speaking of the things pertaining to the kingdom of God: 4 and, being assembled together with them, commanded them that they should not depart from Jerusalem, but wait for the promise of the Father, which, saith he, ye have heard of me. 5 For John truly baptized with water; but ye shall be baptized with the Holy Ghost not many days hence. 6 When they therefore were come together, they asked of him, saying, Lord, wilt thou at this time restore again the kingdom to Israel? 7 And he said unto them, It is not for you to know the times or the seasons, which the Father hath put in his own power. 8 But ye shall receive *dunamis*/power, after that the Holy Ghost is come upon you: and ye shall be witnesses unto me both in Jerusalem, and in all Judaea, and in Samaria, and unto the uttermost part of the earth. 9 And when he had spoken these things, while they beheld, he was taken up; and a cloud received him out of their sight. 10 And while they looked stedfastly toward heaven as he went up, behold, two men stood by them in white apparel; 11 which also said, Ye men of Galilee, why stand ye gazing up into heaven? this same Jesus, which is taken up from you into heaven, shall so come in like manner as ye have seen him go into heaven.

John 1:12 But as many as *lambano*/received him, to them gave he power to become (*and act as*) the sons of God, even to them that believe on his name: 13 which were born, not of blood, nor of the will of the flesh, nor of the will of man, but of God. 14 And the Word was made flesh, and dwelt among us, (and we beheld his glory, the glory as of the only begotten of the Father,) full of grace and truth.

Acts 13:23 Of this man's seed hath God according to his promise raised unto Israel a Saviour, Jesus: 24 when John had first preached before his coming the baptism of repentance to all the people of Israel. 25 And as John fulfilled his course, he said, Whom think ye that I am? I am not he. But, behold, there cometh one after me, whose shoes of his feet I am not worthy to loose. 26 Men and brethren, children of the stock of Abraham, and whosoever among you feareth God, to you is the word of this *soteria*/salvation sent. 27 For they that dwell at Jerusalem, and their rulers, because they knew him not, nor yet the voices of the prophets which are read every sabbath day, they have fulfilled them in condemning him. 28 And though they found no cause of death in him, yet desired they Pilate that he should be slain. 29 And when they had fulfilled all that was written of him, they took him down from the tree, and laid him in a sepulchre. 30 But God raised him from the dead: 31 and he was seen many days of them which came up with him from Galilee to Jerusalem, who are his witnesses unto the people. 32 And we declare unto you glad tidings, how that the promise which was made unto the fathers, 33 God hath fulfilled the same unto us their children, in that he hath raised up Jesus again; as it is also written in the second psalm, Thou art my Son, this day have I begotten thee. 34 And as concerning that he raised him up from the dead, now no more to return to corruption, he said on this wise, I will give you the sure mercies (*chesed, grace and lovingkindness*) of David. 35 Wherefore he saith also in another psalm, Thou shalt not suffer thine Holy One to see corruption. 36 For David, after he had served his own generation by the will of God, fell on sleep, and was laid unto his fathers, and saw corruption: 37 but he, whom God raised again, saw no corruption. 38 Be it known unto you therefore, men and brethren, that through this man is preached unto you the forgiveness (*remission, removal, purging, obliteration, washing and putting away*) of sins: 39 and by him all that believe are justified from all things, from which ye could not be justified by the law of Moses.

Acts 10:34 Then Peter opened his mouth, and said, Of a truth I perceive that God is no respecter of persons: 35 but in every nation he that feareth him, and worketh righteousness (*in believing God for the work He did in Jesus to bring the Kingdom of God to Earth in ministering healing by* aiteo *commands, in the name of Jesus, per His promise*) is accepted with him. 36 The word which God sent unto the children of Israel, preaching peace by Jesus Christ: (he is Lord of all:) 37 that word, I say, ye know, which was published throughout all Judaea, and began from Galilee, after the baptism which John preached; 38 how God anointed Jesus of Nazareth with the Holy Ghost and with power: who went about doing good, and healing all that were oppressed (*in the active rule, reign and lordship*) of the devil; for God was with him. 39 And we are witnesses of all things which he did both in the land of the Jews, and in Jerusalem; whom they slew and hanged on a tree: 40 him God raised up the third day, and shewed him openly; 41 not to all the people, but unto witnesses chosen before of God, even to us, who did eat and drink with him after he rose from the dead. 42 And he commanded us to preach unto the people, and to testify that it is he which was ordained of God to be the Judge of quick and dead. 43 To him give all the prophets witness, that through his name whosoever believeth in him shall receive remission (*removal, purging, obliteration and putting away*) of sins.

John 14:12 Verily, verily, I say unto you, He that believeth on me, the works that I do shall he do also; and greater works than these shall he do; because I go unto my Father. 13 And whatsoever ye shall *aiteo*/ask (*require, demand and expect as due by covenant promise*) in my name, that will I do, that the Father may be glorified in the Son. 14 If ye shall *aiteo*/ask (*require, demand and expect as due by covenant promise*) any thing in my name, I will do it. 15 If ye *agape*/love me, keep my commandments.

BATTLE PRAYER FOR DIVINE HEALING: FIELD MANUAL 2

Father, Thank You for the strength of Your work in Jesus: Eph 1:3 Blessed be *You*, the God and Father of our Lord Jesus Christ, who hath blessed us with all spiritual blessings in heavenly places in Christ: 4 according as *You* have chosen us in him before the foundation of the world, that we should be holy and without blame before *You* in *agape*/love: 5 having predestinated us unto the adoption of children by Jesus Christ to *Yourself*, according to the good pleasure of *Your* will, 6 to the praise of the glory of *Your* grace, wherein *You have* made us accepted in the *agape*/beloved. 7 In whom (*Jesus*) we have redemption through his blood, the forgiveness (*remission, purging, putting away and obliteration*) of sins, according to the riches of *Your* grace; 8 wherein *You, Father God, have* abounded toward us in all wisdom and prudence; 9 having made known unto us the mystery of *Your* will, according to *Your* good pleasure which *You have* purposed in *Yourself*: 10 that in the dispensation of the fulness of times *You* might gather together in one all things in Christ, both which are in heaven, and which are on earth; even in him: 11 in whom also we have obtained an inheritance, being predestinated according to the purpose of *You* who *works* all things after the counsel of *Your* own will: 12 that we should be to the praise of *Your* glory, who ... trusted in Christ. 1 John 3:1 Behold (*ponder in awe and make this change the way you live your life and your self-identity*) what manner of *agape*/love the Father hath bestowed upon us, that we should be called the sons of God: therefore the world knoweth us not, because it knew him not. 2 *Agape*/beloved, now are we the sons of God, and it doth not yet appear what we shall be: but we know that, when he shall appear, we shall be like him; for we shall see him as he is. *We praise and thank You, Father, in the name of Jesus, for Your mighty work! We are redeemed by the blood of the Lamb in that Great Work of Jesus, the Mighty Arm of God! In You, Lord Jesus, we have wisdom, sanctification, righteousness, redemption, adoption and Holy Spirit. Glory to You, Father, for your goodness, in Jesus' Name. Amen! Hallelujah to the Lamb of God. You got the job done! Hallelujah!*

~ 3 ~

THE BLOOD OF JESUS SCRIPTURES

L̲o̲r̲d̲ **Father, in the name of Jesus**, who purged us from our sins with His own blood, give us Your Spirit of wisdom and revelation in the knowledge of You and Your ways in the blood of Jesus that we walk not in the spirit of fear, but in Your Spirit of power, *agape*/love and a sound mind, unto the measure of the stature of the fullness of Christ.

Rev 19:11 And I saw heaven opened, and behold a white horse; and he that sat upon him was called Faithful and True, and in righteousness he doth judge and make war. 12 His eyes were as a flame of fire, and on his head were many crowns; and he had a name written, that no man knew, but he himself. 13 And he was clothed with a vesture dipped in blood: and his name is called The Word of God. 14 And the armies which were in heaven followed him upon white horses, clothed in fine linen, white and clean. 15 And out of his mouth goeth a sharp sword, that with it he should smite the nations: and he shall rule them with a rod of iron: and he treadeth the winepress of the fierceness and wrath of Almighty God. 16 And he hath on his vesture and on his thigh a name written, KING OF KINGS, AND LORD OF LORDS.

Matt 26:26 And as they were eating, Jesus took bread, and blessed it, and brake it, and gave it to the disciples, and said, Take, eat; this is my body. 27 And he took the cup, and gave thanks, and gave it to them, saying, Drink ye all of it; 28 for this is my blood of the new testament, which is shed for many for the remission of sins. 29 But I say unto you, I will not drink henceforth of this fruit of the vine, until that day when I drink it new with you in my Father's kingdom. 30 And when they had sung an hymn, they went out into the mount of Olives.

Matt 27:26 Then released he Barabbas unto them: and when he had scourged Jesus, he delivered him to be crucified. 27 Then the soldiers of the governor took Jesus into the common hall, and gathered unto him the whole band of soldiers. 28 And they stripped him, and put on him a scarlet robe. 29 And when they had platted a crown of thorns, they put it upon his head, and a reed in his right hand: and they bowed the knee before him, and mocked him, saying, Hail, King of the Jews! 30 And they spit upon him, and took the reed, and smote him on the head. 31 And after that they had mocked him, they took the robe off from him, and put his own raiment on him, and led him away to crucify him. 32 And as they came out, they found a man of Cyrene, Simon by name: him they compelled to bear his cross. 33 And when they were come unto a place called Golgotha, that is to say, a place of a skull, 34 they gave him vinegar to drink mingled with gall: and when he had tasted thereof, he would not drink. 35 And they crucified him, and parted his garments, casting lots: that it might be fulfilled which was spoken by the prophet, They parted my garments among them, and upon my vesture did they cast lots.

Mark 14:22 And as they did eat, Jesus took bread, and blessed, and brake it, and gave to them, and said, Take, eat: this is my body. 23 And he took the cup, and when he had given thanks, he gave it to them: and they all drank of it. 24 And he said unto them, This is my blood of the new testament, which is shed for many. 25 Verily I say unto you, I will drink no more of the fruit of the vine, until that day that I drink it new in the kingdom of God. 26 And when they had sung an hymn, they went out into the mount of Olives.

Luke 22:15 And he said unto them, With desire I have desired to eat this passover with you before I suffer: 16 for I say unto you, I will not any more eat thereof, until it be fulfilled in the kingdom of God. 17 And he took the cup, and gave thanks, and said, Take this, and divide it among yourselves: 18 for I say unto you, I will not drink of the fruit of the vine, until the kingdom of God shall come. 19 And he took bread, and gave thanks, and brake it, and gave unto them, saying, This is my body which is given for you: this do in remembrance of me. 20 Likewise also the cup after supper, saying, This cup is the new testament in my blood, which is shed for you.

Luke 22:42 Saying [*the second time*], Father, if thou be willing, remove this cup from me: nevertheless not my will, but thine, be done. 43 And there appeared an angel unto him from heaven, strengthening him. 44 And being in an agony he prayed more earnestly: and his sweat was as it were great drops of blood falling down to the ground. 45 And when he rose up from prayer, and was come to his disciples, he found them sleeping for sorrow, 46 and said unto them, Why sleep ye? rise and pray, lest ye enter into temptation.

John 6:44 No man can come to me, except the Father which hath sent me draw him: and I will raise him up at the last day. 45 It is written in the prophets, And they shall be all taught of God. Every man therefore that hath heard, and hath learned of the Father, cometh unto me. 46 Not that any man hath seen the Father, save he which is of God, he hath seen the Father. 47 Verily, verily, I say unto you, He that believeth on me hath everlasting *zoe*/life. 48 I am that bread of *zoe*/life. 49 Your fathers did eat manna in the wilderness, and are dead. 50 This is the bread which cometh down from heaven, that a man may eat thereof, and not die. 51 I am the *zao*/living bread which came down from heaven: if any man eat of this bread, he shall *zao*/live for ever: and the bread that I will give is my flesh, which I will give for the *zoe*/life of the world. 52 The Jews therefore strove among themselves, saying, How can this man give us his flesh to eat? 53 Then Jesus said unto them, Verily, verily, I say unto you, Except ye eat the flesh of the Son of man, and drink his blood, ye have no *zoe*/life in you. 54 Whoso eateth my flesh, and drinketh my blood, hath eternal *zoe*/life; and I will raise him up at the last day. 55 For my flesh is meat indeed, and my blood is drink indeed. 56 He that eateth my flesh, and drinketh my blood, dwelleth in me, and I in him. 57 As the *zao*/living Father hath sent me, and I *zao*/live by the Father: so he that eateth me, even he shall *zao*/live by me. 58 This is that bread which came down from heaven: not as your fathers did eat manna, and are dead: he that eateth of this bread shall *zao*/live for ever.

John 19:33 But when they came to Jesus, and saw that he was dead already, they brake not his legs: 34 but one of the soldiers with a spear pierced his side, and forthwith came there out blood and water.

Acts 20:28 Take heed therefore unto yourselves, and to all the flock, over the which the Holy Ghost hath made you overseers, to feed the church of God, which he hath purchased with his own blood.

Rom 3:23 For all have sinned, and come short of the glory of God; 24 being justified freely by his grace through the redemption that is in Christ Jesus: 25 whom God hath set forth to be a propitiation through faith in his blood, to declare his righteousness for the remission of sins that are past, through the forbearance of God; 26 to declare, I say, at this time his righteousness: that he might be just, and the justifier of him which believeth in Jesus.

Battle Prayer for Divine Healing: Field Manual 2

Rom 5:8 But God commendeth his *agape*/love toward us, in that, while we were yet sinners, Christ died for us. 9 Much more then, being now justified by his blood, we shall be *sozo*/saved from wrath through him. 10 For if, when we were enemies, we were reconciled to God by the death of his Son, much more, being reconciled, we shall be *sozo*/saved by his *zoe*/life.

1 Cor 10:16 The cup of blessing which we bless, is it not the communion of the blood of Christ? The bread which we break, is it not the communion of the body of Christ? 17 For we being many are one bread, and one body: for we are all partakers of that one bread.

1 Cor 11:23 For I have received of the Lord that which also I delivered unto you, That the Lord Jesus the same night in which he was betrayed took bread: 24 and when he had given thanks, he brake it, and said, Take, eat: this is my body, which is broken for you: this do in remembrance of me. 25 After the same manner also he took the cup, when he had supped, saying, This cup is the new testament in my blood: this do ye, as oft as ye drink it, in remembrance of me. 26 For as often as ye eat this bread, and drink this cup, ye do shew the Lord's death till he come. 27 Wherefore whosoever shall eat this bread, and drink this cup of the Lord, unworthily, shall be guilty of the body and blood of the Lord. 28 But let a man examine himself, and so let him eat of that bread, and drink of that cup. 29 For he that eateth and drinketh unworthily, eateth and drinketh damnation to himself, not discerning the Lord's body. 30 For this cause many are weak (*impotent, ineffective in the faith*) and sickly (*physically and spiritually weak/impotent*) among you, and many sleep (*die before their time/asleep in sin, idolatry and indifferent to God*). 31 For if we would judge ourselves, we should not be judged. 32 But when we are judged, we are chastened of the Lord (*by the law of sowing sin and reaping death, until you exert active faith in the body and blood of Jesus*), that we should not be condemned with the world.

Eph 1:5 Having predestinated us unto the adoption of children by Jesus Christ to himself, according to the good pleasure of his will, 6 to the praise of the glory of his grace, wherein he hath made us accepted in the *agape*/beloved. 7 In whom we have redemption through his blood, the forgiveness (*remission, purging, putting away and obliteration*) of sins, according to the riches of his grace; 8 wherein he hath abounded toward us in all wisdom and prudence; 9 having made known unto us the mystery of his will, according to his good pleasure which he hath purposed in himself.

Eph 2:12 That at that time ye were without Christ, being aliens from the commonwealth of Israel, and strangers from the covenants of promise, having no hope, and without God in the world: 13 but now in Christ Jesus ye who sometimes were far off are made nigh by the blood of Christ. 14 For he is our peace, who hath made both one, and hath broken down the middle wall of partition between us; 15 having abolished in his flesh the enmity, even the law of commandments contained in ordinances; for to make in himself of twain one new man, so making peace; 16 and that he might reconcile both unto God in one body by the cross, having slain the enmity thereby: 17 and came and preached peace to you which were afar off, and to them that were nigh.

Col 1:12 Giving thanks (*continually*) unto the Father, which hath made us meet (*qualified and enabled by grace*) to be partakers of the inheritance of the saints in light: 13 who hath delivered us from the power of darkness, and hath translated us into the kingdom of his *agape*/dear Son: 14 in whom we have redemption through his blood, even the forgiveness (*remission, purging, putting away and obliteration*) of sins: 15 who is the image of the invisible God, the firstborn of every creature: 16 for by him were all things created, that are in heaven, and that are in earth, visible and invisible, whether they be thrones, or dominions, or principalities, or powers: all things were created by him, and for him: 17 and he is before all things, and by him all things consist. 18 And he is the head of the body, the church: who is the beginning, the firstborn from the dead; that in all things he might have the preeminence. 19 For it pleased the Father that in him should all fulness dwell; 20 and, having made peace through the blood of his cross, by him to reconcile all things unto himself; by him, I say, whether they be things in earth, or things in heaven. 21 And you, that were sometime alienated and enemies in your mind by wicked works, yet now hath he reconciled 22 in the body of his flesh through death, to present you holy and unblameable and unreproveable in his sight.

Col 2:1 For I would that ye knew what great conflict I have for you, and for them at Laodicea, and for as many as have not seen my face in the flesh; 2 that their hearts might be comforted, being knit together in *agape*/love, and unto all riches of the full assurance of understanding, to the acknowledgement of the mystery of God, and of the Father, and of Christ; 3 in whom are hid all the treasures of wisdom and knowledge. 4 And this I say, lest any man should beguile you with enticing words. 5 For though I be absent in the flesh, yet am I with you in the spirit, joying and beholding your order, and the stedfastness of your faith in Christ. 6 As ye have therefore received Christ Jesus the Lord, so walk ye in him: 7 rooted and built up in him, and stablished in the faith, as ye have been taught, abounding therein with thanksgiving. 8 Beware lest any man spoil you through philosophy and vain deceit, after the tradition of men, after the rudiments of the world, and not after Christ. 9 For in him dwelleth all the fulness of the Godhead bodily. 10 And ye are complete in him, which is the head of all principality and power.

Heb 2:14 Forasmuch then as the children are partakers of flesh and blood, he also himself likewise took part of the same; that through death he might destroy him that had the power of death, that is, the devil; 15 and deliver them who through fear of death were all their lifetime subject to bondage. 16 For verily he took not on him the nature of angels; but he took on him the seed of Abraham. 17 Wherefore in all things it behoved him to be made like unto his brethren, that he might be a merciful and faithful high priest in things pertaining to God, to make reconciliation for the sins of the people. 18 For in that he himself hath suffered being tempted, he is able to succour them that are tempted.

Heb 9:7 But into the second went the high priest alone once every year, not without blood, which he offered for himself, and for the errors of the people: 8 the Holy Ghost this signifying, that the way into the holiest of all was not yet made manifest, while as the first tabernacle was yet standing: 9 which was a figure for the time then present, in which were offered both gifts and sacrifices, that could not make him that did the service perfect, as pertaining to the conscience; 10 which stood only in meats and drinks, and divers washings, and carnal ordinances, imposed on them until the time of reformation. 11 But Christ being come an high priest of good things to come, by a greater and more perfect tabernacle, not made with hands, that is to say, not of this building; 12 neither by the blood of goats and calves, but by his own blood he entered in once into the holy place, having obtained eternal redemption for us. 13 For if the blood of bulls and of goats, and the ashes of an heifer sprinkling the unclean, sanctifieth to the purifying of the flesh: 14 how much more shall the blood of Christ, who through the eternal Spirit offered himself without spot to God, purge your conscience from dead works to serve the *zao*/living God? 15 And for this cause he is the mediator of the new testament, that by means of death, for the redemption of the transgressions that were under the first testament, they which are called might receive the promise of eternal inheritance. 16 For where a testament is, there must also of necessity be the death of the testator. 17 For a testament is of force after men are dead: otherwise it is of no strength at all while the testator *zao*/liveth. 18 Whereupon neither the first testament was dedicated without blood. 19 For when Moses had spoken every precept to all the people according to the law, he took the blood of calves and of goats, with water, and scarlet wool, and hyssop, and sprinkled both the book, and all the people, 20 saying, This is the blood of the testament which God hath enjoined unto you. 21 Moreover he sprinkled with blood both the tabernacle, and all the vessels of the ministry. 22 And almost all things are by the law purged with blood; and without shedding of blood is no remission. 23 It was therefore necessary that the patterns of things in the heavens should be purified with these; but the heavenly things themselves with better sacrifices than these. 24 For Christ is not entered into the holy places made with hands, which are the figures of the true; but into heaven itself, now to appear in the presence of God for us: 25 nor yet that he should offer himself often, as the high priest entereth into the holy place every year with blood of others; 26 for then must he often have suffered since the foundation of the world: but now once in the end of the world hath he appeared to put away sin by the sacrifice of himself. 27 And as it is appointed unto men once to die, but after this the judgment: 28 so Christ was once offered to bear the sins of many; and unto them that look for him shall he appear the second time without sin unto *soteria*/salvation.

<u>Heb 10:4</u> For it is not possible that the blood of bulls and of goats should take away sins. 5 Wherefore when he cometh into the world, he saith, Sacrifice and offering thou wouldest not, but a body hast thou prepared me: 6 in burnt offerings and sacrifices for sin thou hast had no pleasure. 7 Then said I, Lo, I come (in the volume of the book it is written of me,) to do thy will, O God. 8 Above when he said, Sacrifice and offering and burnt offerings and offering for sin thou wouldest not, neither hadst pleasure therein; which are offered by the law; 9 then said he, Lo, I come to do thy will, O God. He taketh away the first, that he may establish the second. 10 By the which will we are sanctified through the offering of the body of Jesus Christ once for all.

<u>Heb 12:1</u> Wherefore seeing we also are compassed about with so great a cloud of witnesses, let us lay aside every weight, and the sin which doth so easily beset us, and let us run with patience the race that is set before us, 2 looking unto Jesus the author and finisher of our faith; who for the joy that was set before him endured the cross, despising the shame, and is set down at the right hand of the throne of God. 3 For consider him that endured such contradiction of sinners against himself, lest ye be wearied and faint in your minds. 4 Ye have not yet resisted unto blood, striving against sin.

<u>Heb 12:24</u> And to Jesus the mediator of the new covenant, and to the blood of sprinkling, that speaketh better things than that of Abel. 25 See that ye refuse not him that speaketh. For if they escaped not who refused him that spake on earth, much more shall not we escape, if we turn away from him that speaketh from heaven.

<u>Heb 13:20</u> Now the God of peace, that brought again from the dead our Lord Jesus, that great shepherd of the sheep, through the blood of the everlasting cov-

enant, 21 make you perfect in every good work to do his will, working in you that which is wellpleasing in his sight, through Jesus Christ; to whom be glory for ever and ever. Amen.

1 Pet 1:1 Peter, an apostle of Jesus Christ, to the strangers scattered throughout Pontus, Galatia, Cappadocia, Asia, and Bithynia, 2 elect according to the foreknowledge of God the Father, through sanctification of the Spirit, unto obedience and sprinkling of the blood of Jesus Christ: Grace unto you, and peace, be multiplied. 3 Blessed be the God and Father of our Lord Jesus Christ, which according to his abundant mercy hath begotten us again unto a *zao*/lively hope by the resurrection of Jesus Christ from the dead.

1 Pet 1:18 Forasmuch as ye know that ye were not redeemed with corruptible things, as silver and gold, from your vain conversation received by tradition from your fathers; 19 but with the precious blood of Christ, as of a lamb without blemish and without spot: 20 who verily was foreordained before the foundation of the world, but was manifest in these last times for you, 21 who by him do believe in God, that raised him up from the dead, and gave him glory; that your faith and hope might be in God.

1 John 1:5 This then is the message which we have heard of him, and declare unto you, that God is light, and in him is no darkness at all. 6 If we say that we have fellowship with him, and walk in darkness, we lie, and do not the truth: 7 but if we walk in the light, as he is in the light, we have fellowship one with another, and the blood of Jesus Christ his Son cleanseth us from all sin. 8 If we say that we have no sin, we deceive ourselves, and the truth is not in us. 9 If we confess our sins, he is faithful and just to forgive us our sins, and to cleanse us from all unrighteousness. 10 If we say that we have not sinned, we make him a liar, and his word is not in us.

1 John 5:4 For whatsoever is born of God overcometh the world: and this is the victory that overcometh the world, even our faith. 5 Who is he that overcometh the world, but he that believeth that Jesus is the Son of God? 6 This is he that came by water and blood, even Jesus Christ; not by water only, but by water and blood. And it is the Spirit that beareth witness, because the Spirit is truth. 7 For there are three that bear record in heaven, the Father, the Word, and the Holy Ghost: and these three are one. 8 And there are three that bear witness in earth, the spirit, and the water, and the blood: and these three agree in one. 9 If we receive the witness of men, the witness of God is greater: for this is the witness of God which he hath testified of his Son. 10 He that believeth on the Son of God hath the witness in himself: he that believeth not God hath made him a liar; because he believeth not the

record that God gave of his Son. 11 And this is the record, that God hath given to us eternal *zoe*/life, and this *zoe*/life is in his Son.

Rev 1:5 And from Jesus Christ, who is the faithful witness, and the first begotten of the dead, and the prince of the kings of the earth. Unto him that *agape*/loved us, and washed us from our sins in his own blood, 6 and hath made us kings and priests unto God and his Father; to him be glory and dominion for ever and ever. Amen.

Rev 7:13 And one of the elders answered, saying unto me, What are these which are arrayed in white robes? and whence came they? 14 And I said unto him, Sir, thou knowest. And he said to me, These are they which came out of great tribulation, and have washed their robes, and made them white in the blood of the Lamb. 15 Therefore are they before the throne of God, and serve him day and night in his temple: and he that sitteth on the throne shall dwell among them. 16 They shall hunger no more, neither thirst any more; neither shall the sun light on them, nor any heat. 17 For the Lamb which is in the midst of the throne shall feed them, and shall lead them unto *zao*/living fountains of waters: and God shall wipe away all tears from their eyes.

Rev 12:10 And I heard a loud voice saying in heaven, Now is come *soteria*/salvation, and strength, and the kingdom of our God, and the power of his Christ: for the accuser of our brethren is cast down, which accused them before our God day and night. 11 And they overcame him by the blood of the Lamb, and by the word of their testimony; and they *agape*/loved not their *psuche*/lives (*souls*) unto the death.

Rev 19:11 And I saw heaven opened, and behold a white horse; and he that sat upon him was called Faithful and True, and in righteousness he doth judge and make war. 12 His eyes were as a flame of fire, and on his head were many crowns; and he had a name written, that no man knew, but he himself. 13 And he was clothed with a vesture dipped in blood: and his name is called The Word of God. 14 And the armies which were in heaven followed him upon white horses, clothed in fine linen, white and clean. 15 And out of his mouth goeth a sharp sword, that with it he should smite the nations: and he shall rule them with a rod of iron: and he treadeth the winepress of the fierceness and wrath of Almighty God. 16 And he hath on his vesture and on his thigh a name written, KING OF KINGS, AND LORD OF LORDS.

Praise You, Father God, in the name of Jesus, the Lamb of God, who was slain before the foundation of the world was laid, who will come again as the Lion of the Tribe of Judah, the Word of God. Thank You that You accomplished all You wanted in Jesus when He came. 1 Pet 2:24 Who his own self bare our sins in his own body on the tree, that we, being dead to sins, should *zao*/live unto righteousness: by whose stripes *we* were healed. Rev 1:5 ... Jesus Christ, who is the faithful witness, and the first begotten of the dead, and the prince of the kings of the earth. Unto him that *agape*/loved us, and washed us from our sins in his own blood, 6 and hath made us kings and priests unto God and his Father; to him be glory and dominion for ever and ever. Amen. Acts 10:38 How *You, Father* God, anointed Jesus of Nazareth with the Holy Ghost and with power: who went about doing good, and healing (*in judgment against of the devil*) all that were oppressed (*under the active dominion, reign or lordship*) of the devil; for *You, Father* God, were with him. Heb 5:9 And being made perfect, he became the author of eternal *soteria*/salvation unto all them that obey him. Acts 2:33 Therefore being by the right hand of *You, Father* God, exalted, and having received of *You,* the Father, the promise of the Holy Ghost, he hath shed forth... Gal 4:6 And because *we* are sons, *You, Father* God, *have* sent forth the Spirit of *Your* Son into *our* hearts, crying, Abba (*Daddy*), Father. Rom 3:24 Being justified freely by his grace through the redemption that is in Christ Jesus: 25 whom *You, Father* God, hath set forth to be a propitiation through faith in his blood, to declare his righteousness for the remission of sins that are past, through the forbearance of God. *By Your grace in us, we continuously are* Col 1:12 giving thanks (*continually*) unto *You,* the Father, which hath made us meet (*qualified and enabled by grace*) to be partakers of the inheritance of the saints in light: 13 who *have* delivered us from the power of darkness, and *have* translated us into the kingdom of *Your agape*/dear Son: 14 in whom we have redemption through his blood, even the forgiveness (*remission, purging, putting away and obliteration*) of sins: 15 who is the image of *You, Father,* the invisible God, the firstborn of every creature: 16 for by him were all things created, that are in heaven, and that are in earth, visible and invisible, whether they be thrones, or dominions, or principalities, or powers: all things were created by him, and for him: 17 and he is before all things, and by him all things consist. 18 And he is the head of the body, the church: who is the beginning, the firstborn from the dead; that in all things he might have the preeminence. 19 For it pleased *You,* the Father, that in him should all fulness dwell; 20 and, having made peace through the blood of his cross, by him to reconcile all things unto *Yourself;* by him, I say, whether they be things in earth, or things in heaven. 21 And *we,* that were sometime alienated and enemies in *our* mind by wicked works, yet now *have You, Father God,* reconciled 22 in the body of his (*Jesus'*) flesh through death, to present *us* holy and unblameable and unreproveable in *Your* sight: 1 Pet 1:18 Forasmuch as *we* know that *we* were not redeemed with corruptible things, as silver and gold, from *our* vain conversation received by tradition from *our* fathers; 19 but with the precious blood of Christ, as of a lamb without blemish and without

The Blood of Jesus Scriptures

spot: 20 who verily was foreordained before the foundation of the world, but was manifest in these last times for *us*, 21 who by him do believe in *You, Father* God, that raised him up from the dead, and gave him glory; that *our* faith and hope might be in *You, Father* God. *This blood of Jesus shed 2000 years ago in the garden, in the beatings, at the whipping post, in the putting on of the crown of thorns, in the slog to the cross and on the cross, and celebrated in the communion cup that it made the New Testament, redeemed us with the remission of sins, fully propitiated the sins of the entire world, remitted, purged, brought all men near to God, reconciled all things in Earth and Heaven, justified and made us holy and unblameable in Father God's sight, totally forgave us, and gave us zoe/life. This eternal blood of Jesus is devil overcoming and devil work destroying, righteousness creating, zoe/life giving, healing and sin purging, remitting, taking away, washing and totally cleansing. All has been settled and made sozo/whole by the blood of Jesus. Praise You for Your work in Jesus Christ 2000 years ago.*

Thank You, Lord Jesus: Heb 1:3 Who being the brightness of *the Father's* glory, and the express image of the *Father's* person, and upholding all things by the word of *Your* power, when *You* had by *Yourself* purged our sins, sat down on the right hand of the Majesty on high. Heb 2:10 For it became him, for whom are all things, and by whom are all things, in bringing many sons unto glory, to make *You*, the captain of *our soteria*/salvation perfect through sufferings. 11 For both he that sanctifieth and they who are sanctified are all of one: for which cause *You, Lord Jesus, are* not ashamed to call *us* brethren. Gal 3:26 For *we* are all sons of God through faith in Christ Jesus. 27 For as many of *us* as were baptized into Christ have put on Christ. NKJV Rev 12:11 *I overcome Satan* by the blood of the Lamb, and by the word of *my* testimony; and *I agape/love* not *my psuche*/life (soul) unto the death. 1 Cor 6:1 ... *My body is* for the Lord; and the Lord for *my* body. 1 Cor 6:17 *For* he that is joined unto the Lord is one spirit. Eph 2:13 But now in Christ Jesus *we* who sometimes were far off are made nigh by the blood of Christ. 14 For he is our peace, who hath made both one, and hath broken down the middle wall of partition between us; 15 having abolished in his flesh the enmity, even the law of commandments contained in ordinances; for to make in himself of twain one new man, so making peace; 16 and that he might reconcile both unto God in one body by the cross, having slain the enmity thereby: 17 and came and preached peace to *us* which were afar off, and to them that were nigh. 18 For through him we both have access by one Spirit unto the Father. 19 Now therefore ye are no more strangers and foreigners, but fellowcitizens with the saints, and of the household of God; 20 and are built upon the foundation of the apostles and prophets, Jesus Christ himself being the chief corner stone; 21 in whom all the building fitly framed together groweth unto an holy temple in the Lord: 22 in whom *we* also are builded together for an habitation of God through the Spirit. Heb 13:20 Now the God of peace, that brought again from the dead our Lord Jesus, that great shepherd of the sheep, through the blood of the everlasting covenant, 21 make *me* perfect in every good work to do his will, working in *me* that which is wellpleasing in his sight, through Jesus Christ; to whom be glory for ever and ever. Amen. *Praise You, Father, You have put me in your agape/ beloved, made me one with You in Christ, and included me in the redeeming, cleansing, purging and overcoming blood of Jesus. Thank You Father. In the name of Jesus, thank You!*

Isa 11:9 ... For the earth shall be full of the knowledge of the Lord, as the waters cover the sea.

Part V

The Minister's Confession

And Jesus looking upon them saith, With men it is impossible, but not with God: for with God all things are possible. (Mark 10:27)

Prayers and Confessions of Preparation

A KEY TO POWER IN GOD: Reprogram your heart by speaking the Minister Confession daily. The more you do, the faster the results. Diligence, repetition and intensity are the keys. Remember, the purpose is to obey: Philem 1:6 "That the communication (*the outworking in word and deed*) of thy faith may become effectual (*in manifesting the glory of God*) by the *epignosis*/acknowledging (*by knowing and walking in as a master craftsman like Jesus*) of every good thing which is in you in Christ Jesus." Strong faith means strong knowing, not in the head (conscious mind), but in the heart (subconscious), knowing unto doing. This is how it is done. Ps 45:1 "My heart is inditing a good matter: I speak of the things which I have made touching the king: my tongue is the pen of a ready writer." Vary the speed of speaking this to improve results.

This may be difficult, and you may be tempted to only read through a few of these. But do not get sidetracked. Read them all out loud and faithfully. Every scripture is a window to God, so there is no limit to what God can reveal in any one scripture, much less all of them. So don't let the depth and power of His applied Word confuse you.

Rather than you understanding it all, trust God to get you to understand these confessions. Trust His Word to work on you. So read and use it like a medicine you may not understand, but trust. These confessions are almost pure Scripture. Let God's Word work on you by faith. Your mind will get renewed and your understanding will grow. These one or two hours per day will become one of the best you ever spent.

Prov 4:20 "My son, attend to my words; incline thine ear unto my sayings. 21 Let them not depart from thine eyes; keep them in the midst of thine heart. 22 For they are life unto those that find them, and health to all their flesh. 23 Keep thy heart with all diligence (*faithfully and when not easy*); for out of it are the issues of life."

A. **Father, in the name of Jesus, use these confessions** and affirmations to help me understand and walk in You and Your great work in Jesus better. I am Your son/daughter. Jesus is my Lord. Jesus uses me to save myself and others. He uses my hands, my mouth, my mind, even my entire life to bring His salvation to the Earth. Thank You, Lord Jesus, for working in me and through me. The same Holy Spirit who dwells in Jesus dwells in me. Any doubt, lie, fear, sin or unbelief in me I command to hear and obey the voice of the Word of God through me and **to go now**, in the name **of Jesus Christ of Nazareth**, my Lord, and to be replaced with truth, faith, hope, power, *agape*/love and a sound mind. Mind, you operate in the mind of Christ. Heart, receive only God's truth. Mind of the flesh, you are dead in Christ and have no authority over me. Body, you are whole and right in every way, so do your job. I put on Jesus Christ, I put on His righteousness, I put on His holiness and I put on His salvation. I have everything He has when He was raised from the dead. I am totally healed—spirit, soul and body, mind, heart, will and emotions—into His image. The chastisement of my peace was upon Jesus, the Christ of God and my only Lord, so I freely preach the Gospel, heal the sick, cleanse the lepers, raise the dead, cast out devils, handle poisons or snakes, and walk in blessing and prosperity in every part of life. I am Col 1:12 "giving thanks (*continually*) unto the Father, which hath made *me* meet to be *a partaker* of the inheritance of the saints in light: 13 who hath delivered *me* from the power of darkness, and hath translated *me* into the kingdom of his *agape*/dear Son: 14 in whom *I* have redemption through his blood, even the forgiveness (*remission, removal, purging, obliteration and putting away*) of sins: 15 who is the image of the invisible God, the firstborn of every creature." For greater is Jesus Christ who is in me than he who is in the world. I do all things through Jesus Christ who strengthens me, and Father God meets all my needs, *aiteo*, requirements and demands according to His covenant promises and according to His riches in glory by Christ Jesus, for I am made the righteousness of Father God in Christ Jesus, as a permanent gift, by grace and through faith in His blood. Rom 11:29 "For the gifts and calling of God are without repentance." The *agape*/love of God shed by Holy Spirit in my heart directs me to good works and healing all who are oppressed (*under the active rule and lordship*) of the devil, for God is in me and with me in all I do. I delight to do God's will in all ways. I believe Father God, for He and His Word are one. Therefore all things of God's Word are possible to me. As Jesus is, so am I in the world right now. Jesus Christ is in me, so the works of my hands are blessed, for I lay hands on the sick, and they recover totally right then, by Holy Spirit power. Whatever good I do prospers to the goodness of the Lord. I do greater works than Jesus, for He has gone to the Father and has obtained Holy Spirit for me. Jesus speaks through me as I speak rightly, and works healings, miracles, blessings and answers to prayer by me. All things of God are possible to me, for I believe God, who cannot lie in His promises. Thank You, Lord Jesus!

B. **You, Father God, have made me a son**, and because I am a son, You have sent forth the Spirit of Your Son, Jesus Christ, into my heart, crying, Abba, Daddy, Father to You. Right now, by You, Father God, empowering my word, I am pulling down every evil stronghold, casting out every vain imagination and every high thing in me that exalts itself against the knowledge of You, Father God, and bringing into captivity my every thought into the obedience of Christ, and walking in glad agreement with Holy Spirit. Eph 1:17 ... The God of my Lord Jesus Christ, the Father of glory, *has given me His* spirit of wisdom and revelation in the knowledge of him: 18 the eyes of *my* understanding *continuously* being enlightened; *and I continually grow in knowing* what is the hope of his calling, and what the riches of the glory of his inheritance in the saints, 19 and what is the exceeding greatness of his power *to me who believes*, according to the working of his mighty power, 20 which he wrought in Christ, when he raised him from the dead, and set him at his own right hand in the heavenly places, 21 far above all principality, and power, and might, and dominion, and every name that is named, not only in this world, but also in that which is to come: 22 and hath put all things under his feet, and gave him to be the head over all things to the church *of which I am a part*, 23 which is his body, the fulness of him that filleth all in all. *My heart is filled with the triumph of Christ in the call of God in my life!*

C. **God gives me His Spirit** without measure, for He gives me His words, and I speak them by faith, in *agape*/love, and the Lord confirms these words with signs abundantly following. Every day, in every way, I am getting better and better, for I continually grow in the knowledge of God in godliness and *zoe*/life. 1 Tim 2:3 For this is good and acceptable in the sight of God our Saviour; 4 who will have all men to be *sozo*/saved, and to come unto the knowledge of the truth [*and to receive the* agape/*love of the truth unto salvation*]. 5 For there is one God, and one mediator between God and men, the man Christ Jesus; 6 who gave himself a ransom for all, to be testified in due time. 7 Whereunto I am ordained a preacher, and an apostle, (I speak the truth in Christ, and lie not;) a teacher ... in faith and verity (*truth*). Heb 10:12 ...This man, *Jesus*

Christ, after he had offered one sacrifice for sins for ever, sat down on the right hand of God; Heb 9:26 ... now once in the end of the world hath he appeared to put away sin by the sacrifice of himself. 27 And as it is appointed unto men once to die, but after this the judgment: 28 so Christ was once offered to bear the sins of many; and unto them that look for him shall he appear the second time without sin unto *soteria*/salvation. Heb 1:3 Who being the brightness of *Father God's* glory, and the express image of his person, and upholding all things by the word of his power, when he had by himself purged our sins, sat down on the right hand of the Majesty on high; 1 John 3:5 and *I* know that he was manifested to take away our sins; and in him is no sin. Rev 1:5 ... Jesus Christ, who is the faithful witness, and the first begotten of the dead, and the prince of the kings of the earth. Unto him that *agape*/loved us, and washed (*dissolved, put off and destroyed from us*) our sins in his own blood, 6 and hath made us kings and priests unto God and his Father; to him be glory and dominion for ever and ever. Amen. Eph 4:20 *For I* have ...so learned Christ; 21 ... *I* have heard him, and have been taught by him, as the truth is in Jesus: 22 that *I* put off concerning the former conversation the old man, which is corrupt according to the deceitful lusts; 23 and *am* renewed in the spirit of *my* mind; 24 and that *I continuously* put on the new man, which after *Father* God is created in righteousness and true holiness. 25 Wherefore putting away lying, *I* speak *to* every man truth *as my* neighbour: for we are members one of another. *I may* 26 be angry, and sin not: *I* let not the sun go down upon *my* wrath: 27 neither give *I* place to the devil. *Knowing that Father has said that* 28 let him that stole steal no more: but rather let him labour, working with his hands the thing which is good, that he may have to give to him that needeth. *Therefore I* 29 let no corrupt communication proceed out of *my* mouth, but that which is good to the use of edifying, that it may minister grace unto the hearers. 30 And grieve not the Holy Spirit of God, whereby *I am* sealed unto the day of redemption. *I* 31 let all bitterness, and wrath, and anger, and clamour, and evil speaking, be put away from *me*, with all malice: 32 and *I am* kind to *others*, tenderhearted, forgiving *others*, even as God for Christ's sake hath forgiven *me*. 5:1 ... Therefore *I labor by the grace of God to be a follower (imitator)* of God, as *an agape*/dear *child*; 2 and walk in *agape*/love, as Christ also hath *agape*/loved us, and hath given himself for us an offering and a sacrifice to God for a sweetsmelling savour. *Father God* agape/*loves me, just like He loves Jesus. Praise You, Father, for the wonderful* agape/love *You have for me in Jesus. Thank You!*

D. Father, You are causing me to trust You with all my heart. You are uniting my heart to fear Your name. By You working in me, I do not lean on my own understanding, but I acknowledge You in all my ways, and You are directing my paths to Your glory. Right now You are filling me with Your words of peace, salvation, reconciliation, forgiveness, redemption, adoption, mercy, grace, truth and help, for I open my mouth, and You fill my lips, and I speak Your words in *agape*/love to Your glory. You, Holy Spirit, are my Helper. I am a co-worker with God for good. Eph 4:13 *As* we all come in the unity of the faith, and of the knowledge of the Son of God, unto a perfect man, unto the measure of the stature of the fulness of Christ. 2 Cor 10:4 For *this weapon of confession is* mighty through *You, Father* God, to the pulling down of strong holds; 5 casting down imaginations, and every high thing that exalteth itself against the knowledge of *You, Father* God, *in me*, and bringing into captivity *my* every thought to the obedience of Christ. *Thank You, Father, for the wonderful work You are doing. In the name of Jesus, thank You. Lord, be magnified. Thy kingdom come. Thy will be done on Earth as it is in Heaven. Thank You, Father. In Jesus' name, thank You.*

E. **I have power in the name of Jesus for** Gal 4:4 ... when the fulness of the time was come, God sent forth his Son, made of a woman, made under the law, 5 to redeem them that were under the law, that we might receive the adoption of sons. 6 And because *we* are sons, God hath sent forth the Spirit of his Son into *our* hearts, crying, Abba (*Daddy*), Father. 7 Wherefore *I am* no more a servant, but a son; and if a son, then an heir of God through Christ, *and a joint heir with Jesus as* Rom 8:17 ... children/*sons*, then heirs; heirs of God, and joint-heirs with Christ ... *Jesus is my King, and I am made a king for Him.* Eccl 8:4 Where the word of a king is, there is power .... *When I speak in the name of Jesus, there is God's power.* Rom 5:17 For if by one man's offence death reigned *as king* by one; much more *I* which *lambano*/receive abundance of grace and of the gift of righteousness ... *reign as a king* in *zoe*/life by one, Jesus Christ, Rev 1:5 ... who is the faithful witness, and the first begotten of the dead, and the prince of the kings of the earth. Unto him that *agape*/loved us, and washed us from our sins in his own blood, 6 and hath made *me a king and a priest* unto God and his Father; to him be glory and dominion for ever and ever. Amen. *All praise to* 1 Tim 6:14 ... our Lord Jesus Christ: 15 ... who is the blessed and only Potentate, the King of kings, and Lord of lords; 2 Cor 1:19 for the Son of God, Jesus Christ, ... was not yea and nay, but in him was yea. 20 For all the promises of God in him are yea, and in him Amen, unto the glory of God by us. 21 Now he which stablisheth us *together* in Christ, and hath anointed *me*, is *Father* God; 22 who hath also sealed *me*, and given the earnest of the Spirit in *me to fulfill my part in this promise*: Isa 49:24 Shall the prey be taken from the mighty, or the lawful captive delivered? 25 But thus saith the Lord, Even the captives of the mighty shall be taken away, and the prey of the terrible shall be delivered: for I will contend with him that contendeth with thee, and I will save thy children. *So I speak* Acts 14:3 … boldly in the Lord, which *gives* testimony unto the word of his grace, and *grants* signs and wonders to be done by *my* hands. *As it is with Jesus, so it is with me, for* Luke 4:18 the Spirit of the Lord is *also* upon me, because he hath anointed (*called, qualified and enabled*) me to preach the gospel to the poor; he hath sent me to heal the brokenhearted, to preach deliverance to the captives, and recovering of sight to the blind, to set at liberty them that are bruised, 19 to preach the acceptable year of the Lord. … *For* 21 … this *is the* day *of salvation in which* this scripture *is* fulfilled … . 2 Cor 5:14 For the *agape*/love of Christ constraineth *me*; because *I* thus judge, that if one died for all, then were all dead: 15 and that he died for all, that they which *zao*/live should not henceforth *zao*/live unto themselves, but unto him which died for them, and rose again. 16 Wherefore henceforth know *I* no man after the flesh: yea, though *I* have known Christ after the flesh, yet now henceforth know *I* him no more. 17 Therefore if any man be in Christ, he is a new creature: old things are passed away; behold, all things are become new. 18 And all things are of God, who hath reconciled us to himself by Jesus Christ, and hath given to *me* the ministry of reconciliation; 19 to wit, that God was in Christ, reconciling the world unto himself, not imputing their trespasses unto them; and hath committed unto *me* the word of reconciliation. 20 Now then *I am an ambassador* for Christ, as though God did beseech *all men* by *me*: I pray *for each one* in Christ's stead, *all men be* reconciled to God. 21 For *You, Father, have* made *Jesus* to be sin for us, who knew no sin; that we might be made the righteousness of *You, Father* God, in him. 6:1 *I* then, as *worker* together with him, beseech *all men* also that *they* receive not the grace of God in vain. 2 (For he saith, I have heard thee in a time accepted, and in the day of *soteria*/salvation have I succoured thee: behold, now is the accepted time; behold, now is the day of *soteria*/salvation.) 2 Cor 3:5 Not that *I am* sufficient of *myself* to think any thing as of *myself*; but *my* sufficiency is of God; 6 who also hath made *me an* able *minister* of the new testament; not of the letter, but of the spirit: for the letter killeth, but the spirit giveth *zoe*/life. *For by grace I* 1 Cor 3:16 know *that I am a* temple of God, and that the Spirit of God dwelleth in *me*. Rom 5:1 Therefore being justified by faith, *I* have peace with God through our Lord Jesus Christ: 2 by whom also *I* have access by faith into this grace wherein *I* stand, and rejoice in hope of the glory of God. 3 And not only so, but *I* glory in tribulations also: knowing that tribulation worketh patience; 4 and patience, experience; and experience, hope (*joyful expectation of coming good*): 5 and hope maketh not ashamed; because the *agape*/love of God is shed abroad in *my heart* by the Holy Ghost which is given unto *me*. 6 For when we were yet without strength, in due time Christ died for the ungodly. *By the grace of God* <u>1 Cor 2:16</u> ... *I* have the mind of Christ. <u>1 Cor 1:30</u> For *of Father God am I* in Christ Jesus, who of God is made unto *me* wisdom, and righteousness, and sanctification, and redemption: 31 that, according as it is written, He that glorieth, let him glory in the Lord. *I therefore continually* <u>2 Cor 13:5</u> examine *myself*, whether *I* be in the faith; *proving myself. Knowing myself*, how that Jesus Christ is in *me*, except *I* be *reprobate (useless and ineffective in my faith, worthy to be cast away). So my spirit thinks like Jesus* <u>2 Tim 1:7</u> for God hath not given *me* the spirit of fear; but of power, and of *agape*/love, and of a sound mind. 8 *So I am not* ashamed of the testimony of our Lord, nor *any of* his *prisoners*: but *am a* partaker of the afflictions of the gospel according to the power of God; 9 who hath *sozo*/saved *me*, and called *me* with an holy calling, not according to *my* works, but according to his own purpose and grace, which was given *me* in Christ Jesus before the world began, 10 but is now made manifest by the appearing of our Saviour Jesus Christ, who hath abolished death, and hath brought *zoe*/life and immortality to light through the gospel. <u>2 Cor 4:6</u> For God, who commanded the light to shine out of darkness, hath shined in *my heart*, to give the light of the knowledge of the glory of God in the face of Jesus Christ. 7 *And I* have this treasure in *an* earthen *vessel*, that the excellency of the power may be of God, and not of *me. So, like Jesus, God's power is in me to exercise the triumph of Jesus. Praise You, Lord Jesus, for Your triumphant victory!*

F. For Jesus is my one and only Lord <u>Rom 3:25</u> whom *Father* God hath set forth to be a propitiation through faith in his blood, to declare his righteousness for the remission of sins that are past, through the forbearance of *Father* God; 26 to declare, I say, at this time his righteousness: that *Father God* might be just, and the justifier of him which believeth in Jesus. <u>1 John 2:2</u> And he is the propitiation (*the satisfaction and payment in full*) for *my* sins: and not for *mine* only, but also for the sins of the whole world. *Father God is building in me the revelation unto my walking in* agape/love that <u>Rom 4:5</u> for to him that worketh not, but believeth on him that justifieth the ungodly, his faith is counted for righteousness. 6 Even as David also describeth the blessedness of the man, unto whom God imputeth righteousness without works, 7 saying, Blessed are they whose iniquities are forgiven, and whose sins are covered. 8 Blessed is the man to whom the Lord will not impute sin. *Therefore as I am in Jesus, Father God does not count my sins against me,* <u>Gal 3:8</u> and the scripture, foreseeing that God would justify the heathen through faith, preached before the gospel unto Abraham, saying, In thee shall all nations be blessed. 9 So then they which be of faith are blessed with faithful Abraham. *I am of faith and blessed with faithful Abraham in Jesus.* <u>Rom 5:17</u> For if by one man's offence death reigned *as king* by one; much more they which (*continually*) *lambano*/receive abundance of grace and of the gift of [*permanent*] righteousness shall reign *as kings* in *zoe*/life by one, Jesus Christ. Eph 2:4 *For Father* God, who is rich in mercy, for his great *agape*/love wherewith he *agape*/loved us, 5 even when we were dead in sins, hath quickened us together with Christ, (by grace *am I sozo*/saved;) 6 and hath raised *me* up together, and made *me* sit together in heavenly places in Christ Jesus: 7 that in the ages to come he might shew the exceeding riches of his grace in his kindness toward *me* through Christ Jesus. 8 For by grace *am I sozo*/saved through faith; and that not of *myself*: it is the gift of *Father* God: 9 not of works, lest any man should boast. 10 For *I am Father God's* workmanship, created in Christ Jesus unto good works, which *Father* God hath before ordained that *I* should walk in them. 11 Wherefore *by grace I* remember, that *I*, being in time past *a Gentile* in the flesh, who *is* called Uncircumcision by that which is called the Circumcision in the flesh made by hands; 12 that at that time we were without Christ, being aliens from the commonwealth of Israel, and strangers from the covenants of promise, having no hope, and without *Father* God in the world: 13 but now in Christ Jesus *we* who sometimes were far off are made nigh by the blood of Christ. 14 For he is our peace, who hath made both one, and hath broken down the middle wall of partition between us; 15 having abolished in his flesh the enmity, even the law of commandments contained in ordinances; for to make in himself of twain one new man, so making peace; 16 and that he might reconcile both unto *Father* God in one body by the cross, having slain the enmity thereby: 17 and came and preached peace to *us* which were afar off, and to them that were nigh. 18 For through him we both have access by one Spirit unto the Father. *Therefore I am blessed and highly favored of God to bless and be a blessing. Good things happen to me, and I make good things happen for others. And I am made, by Father's grace, to be just like my elder brother Jesus, to preach* Acts 10:36 the word which God sent unto the children of Israel, preaching peace by Jesus Christ: (he is Lord of all:) ... , 38 *for Father* God *has* anointed *me in* Jesus of Nazareth with the Holy Ghost and with power: *and I* go about doing good, and healing all that *are* oppressed (*under the active rule and lordship*) of the devil; for *Father* God *is* with *me, for I am brought nigh by the blood of Jesus.* Acts 13:37 For *Jesus*, whom God raised again, saw no corruption. 38 *For I make* it known ... that through this man, *Jesus*, is preached unto *all* the forgiveness (*remission, purging, putting away and obliteration*) of sins: 39 and by him all that believe are justified from all things, from which *we* could not be justified by the law of Moses. Mark 16:15 And *I* go into all the world, and *I* preach the gospel to every creature. 16 He that believeth and is baptized shall be *sozo*/saved; but he that believeth not shall be damned. 17 And these signs *follow me* that *believes*;

The Minister's Confession

in *the* name *of Jesus I* cast out devils; *I* speak with new tongues; 18 *I* take up serpents; and if *I* drink any deadly thing, it shall not hurt *me*; *I* lay hands on the sick, and they ... recover *totally. Because* 19 *...* the Lord *Jesus ... has been received* up into heaven, and *sits* on the right hand of God, *I do even greater works than Jesus and I* 20 go forth, and *I preach* everywhere, *in word and good deeds,* the Lord working with *me,* and confirming the word with signs following, *just as Father God wants all His sons.* Amen. *For* 1 John 4:4 *I am* of God, *one of His* little children, *a son of God,* and have overcome *the lie of the devil*: because greater is he that is in *me,* than he that is in the world. *For by Father God's spirit of wisdom and revelation I* 1 Cor 3:16 know ... *I am a* temple of *Father* God, and that the Spirit of God dwelleth in *me.* 1 John 3:20 For if *my un-renewed* heart *condemns me [due to my sins or sense of unworthiness, or sin consciousness and forgetting that my sins were purged, washed, destroyed, dissolved and purified two thousand years ago by Jesus through the cross]*, God is greater than *my* heart, and knoweth all things *that my sins are purged, washed, destroyed, dissolved and purified. By grace, knowing that I am* 21 *agape*/beloved, if *my* heart condemn *me* not, *or I remember my former purging, washing, destruction, dissolution and purification of all sins,* then have *I* confidence toward *Father* God. 22 And whatsoever *I aiteo*/ask (*by demanding as due by covenant promise*), I receive of him, because I keep his commandments, and do those things that are pleasing in his sight. 23 And this is his commandment, That *I* should believe on the name of his Son Jesus Christ, and *agape*/love one another, as he gave us commandment. 24 And he that keepeth his commandments dwelleth in him, and he in him. And hereby *I* know that he abideth in *me,* by the Spirit which he hath given *me. Knowing* Acts 3:12 ... *while men may* marvel *at the confirming signs and wonders the Lord does at my word or touch* or why look *they* so earnestly on *me,* as though by *my* own power or holiness *I* had made ... *healing miracles or wonders, knowing that it is the name of Jesus* Acts 3:16 ... through faith in his name *that* hath made *any sign and wonder, and not my holiness or power. For* Eph 1:7 in *Jesus I* have redemption through his blood, the forgiveness (*remission, purging, putting away and obliteration*) of sins, according to the riches of *Father God's* grace; Eph 1:13 in whom *I* also trusted, after that *I* heard the word of truth, the gospel of our *soteria*/salvation: in whom also after that *I* believed, *I was* sealed with that holy Spirit of promise, 14 which is the earnest of our inheritance until the redemption of the purchased possession, unto the praise of *Father's* glory. Phil 4:19 *And* my *Father* God shall supply all *my* need, *aiteo,* according to his riches in glory by Christ Jesus, *and perfect that which concerneth me and mine.* 20 Now unto God and our Father be glory for ever and ever. Amen.

Who lets us direct Him by our thoughts, words, hands and deeds. Thank You, Father! In the name of Jesus of Nazareth, the Christ, thank You! Almighty God, thank You! In the name of Jesus, thank You!

G. **For by the grace of God I proclaim the grace of God,** Acts 20:32 and ... commend *everyone* to God, and to the word of his grace, which is able to build *us* up, and to give *us* an inheritance among all them which are sanctified (*purified and made holy*). John 1:12 *For* as many as *lambano*/received (*hold on to, cling to and stand in*) him, to them gave he power to become the sons of God, even to them that believe on his name: 13 which were born, not of blood, nor of the will of the flesh, nor of the will of man, but of God. 14 And the Word was made flesh, and dwelt among *the first believers,* (and *they*) beheld his glory, the glory as of the only begotten of the Father,) full of grace and truth. ... 17 For the law was given by Moses, but grace and truth came by Jesus Christ. Rom 5:15 *For* not as the offence, so also is the free gift. For if through the offence of one many be dead, much more the grace of God, and the gift by grace, which is by one man, Jesus Christ, hath abounded unto many. 16 And not as it was by one that sinned, so is the gift: for the judgment was by one to condemnation, but the free gift is of many offences unto justification. 17 For if by one man's offence death reigned (*as king*) by one; much more *I, as one* which *lambano/ receives* abundance of grace and of the gift of [*permanent*] righteousness ... *reigns as a king for my Lord Jesus Christ* in *zoe*/life by one, Jesus Christ [*to bring the Kingdom of God to Earth as it is in Heaven, just as Jesus did.*] 18 Therefore as by the offence of one judgment came upon all men to condemnation; even so by the righteousness of one the free gift came upon all men unto justification of *zoe*/life. 19 For as by one man's disobedience many were made sinners, so by the obedience of one shall many be made [*new creatures that are permanently*] righteous. 20 Moreover the law entered, that the offence might abound. But where sin abounded, grace did much more abound: 21 that as sin hath reigned *as king* unto death, even so might grace reign *as a king in me* through *the gift of* righteousness unto eternal *zoe*/life by Jesus Christ our Lord. *I therefore* Rom 15:19 through mighty signs and wonders, by the power of the Spirit of God; so that from *home,* and round about unto *all the world*, I ... fully *preach* the gospel of Christ. *For* Rom 16:20 ... the God of peace *bruises* Satan under *my* feet *as shattered glass.* The grace of our Lord Jesus Christ *is* with *me* [*to know, be and do this*]. Amen. Acts 15:12 ... declaring what miracles and wonders God *has* wrought among *all men* by *me.* Acts 19:11 And God *does* special miracles by *my hands*: 12 so that from *my body are* brought unto the sick handkerchiefs or aprons, and the diseases *depart* from them, and the evil spirits *go* out of them, 2 Cor 12:12 ... in signs, and wonders, and mighty deeds [*because God's grace*

The Minister's Confession

reigns through me]. Knowing that Gal 3:5 he therefore that ministereth to *us* the Spirit, and worketh miracles among *us*, doeth he it *not* by the works of the law, *but* by the hearing of faith [*that no man is justified by the works of the law but by the faith of Jesus Christ*]. *As Holy Spirit has said*: Acts 13:38 Be it known unto you therefore, men and brethren, that through this man (*Jesus of Nazareth, the Christ*), is preached unto you the forgiveness (*remission, purging, obliteration and putting away*) of sins: 39 and by him all that believe are justified from all things, from which *we* could not be justified by the law of Moses. Acts 10:43 To him give all the prophets witness, that through his name whosoever believeth in him shall receive remission (*purging, removal, obliteration and putting away*) of sins. Ps 143:2 … For in thy sight shall no man living be justified. Rom 8:3 For what the law could not do, in that it was weak through the flesh, God sending his own Son in the likeness of sinful flesh, and for sin, condemned sin in the flesh: 4 that the righteousness of the law might be fulfilled in us, who walk not after the flesh, but after the Spirit. *As the Word of God says*: Rom 10:4 For Christ is the end of the law for righteousness to every one that believeth. 5 For Moses describeth the righteousness which is of the law, That the man which doeth those things shall *zao*/live by them. 6 But the righteousness which is of faith speaketh on this wise, Say not in thine heart, Who shall ascend into heaven? (that is, to bring Christ down from above:) 7 or, Who shall descend into the deep? (That is, to bring up Christ again from the dead.) 8 But what saith it? The word is nigh thee, even in thy mouth, and in thy heart: that is, the word of faith, which we preach; 9 that if thou shalt confess with thy mouth the Lord Jesus, and shalt believe in thine heart that God hath raised him from the dead, thou shalt be *sozo*/saved. 10 For with the heart man believeth unto righteousness; and with the mouth confession is made unto *soteria*/salvation. 11 For the scripture saith, Whosoever believeth on him shall not be ashamed. 12 For there is no difference between the Jew and the Greek: for the same Lord over all is rich unto all that call upon him. 13 For whosoever shall call upon the name of the Lord shall be *sozo*/saved. *As Philip preached Jesus to the eunuch, starting with Isaiah 53,* Acts 8:37 and Philip said, If thou believest with all thine heart, thou mayest. And *the eunuch* answered and said, I believe that Jesus Christ is the Son of God. 1 John 4:14 And we have seen and do testify that the Father sent the Son to be the Saviour of the world. 15 Whosoever shall confess that Jesus is the Son of God, God dwelleth in him, and he in God. 1 John 5:4 For whatsoever is born of God overcometh the world: and this is the victory that overcometh the world, even our faith. 5 Who is he that overcometh the world, but he that believeth that Jesus is the Son of God? 1 John 5:11 And this is the record, that God hath given to us eternal *zoe*/life, and this *zoe*/life is in his Son. 12 He that hath the Son hath *zoe*/life; and he that hath not the Son of

God hath not *zoe*/life. 13 These things *did John write* unto *us* that believe on the name of the Son of God; that *we* may know that *we* have eternal *zoe*/life, and that *we* may believe on the name of the Son of God. *Jesus, You are the Son of God. I have eternal* zoe/*life in You. Almighty God dwells in me and moves, in the name of Jesus, by me. Thank You, Father!*

H. For I preach the Heb 2:3 ... great *soteria*/salvation; which at the first began to be spoken by the Lord, and was confirmed unto *those* that heard him; 4 God also bearing *me* witness, both with signs and wonders, and with divers miracles, and gifts of the Holy Ghost, according to his own will. Gal 2:16 Knowing that a man is not justified by the works of the law, but by the faith of Jesus Christ, even *I* have believed in Jesus Christ, that *I* might be justified by the faith of Christ, and not by the works of the law: for by the works of the law shall no flesh be justified. ... 19 For I through the law am dead to the law, that I might *zao*/live unto God. 20 I am (*have been*) crucified with Christ: nevertheless I *zao*/live; yet not I, but Christ *zao*/liveth in me: and the life which I now *zao*/live in the flesh I *zao*/live by the faith of the Son of God, who *agape*/loved me, and gave himself for me. 21 I do not frustrate the grace of God: for if righteousness come by the law, then Christ is dead in vain. *By this justification, the* zoe/*life of Jesus is in me, to will and to do of the Father's good pleasure, including raising the dead.* Acts 26:18 To open *the* eyes *of Jew and Gentile,* and to turn them from darkness to light, and from the power (*authority, jurisdiction or force*) of Satan unto God, that they may receive forgiveness (*deliverance, remission, pardon and liberty*) of sins, and inheritance among them which are sanctified (*purified and made holy*) by faith that is in *Jesus.* 1 Cor 15:1 ... I declare ... the gospel which I *preach* unto *all*, which also *we* have *lambano*/received, and wherein *we* stand; 2 by which also *we* are (*continually being*) *sozo*/saved, *as we* keep in memory what I *preach* unto *all*, unless *we* have believed in vain. 3 ... How that Christ died for our sins according to the scriptures; 4 and that he was buried, and that he rose again the third day according to the scriptures: 5 and that he was seen of Cephas, then of the twelve: 6 after that, he was seen of above five hundred brethren at once .... 7 After that, he was seen of James; then of all the apostles. ... 17 And if Christ be not raised, *our* faith is vain; *we* are yet in *our* sins. 18 Then they also which are fallen asleep in Christ are perished. 19 If in this *zoe*/life only we have hope in Christ, we are of all men most miserable. 20 But now is Christ risen from the dead, and become the firstfruits of them that slept. 21 For since by man came death, by man came also the resurrection of the dead. 22 For as in Adam all die, even so in Christ shall all be made alive. Rom 4:24 But for us also, to whom it shall be imputed *for righteousness*, if we believe on him that raised up Jesus our Lord from the dead; 25 who was delivered for our offences, and was raised again for our justification. Rom 6:22 But now being made free from sin, and become servants to God, *we* have *our* fruit unto holiness, and the end everlasting *zoe*/life. 23 For the wages of sin is death; but the gift of God is eternal *zoe*/life through Jesus Christ our Lord. Luke 24:46 And *Jesus* said unto them, Thus it is written, and thus it behoved Christ to suffer, and to rise from the dead the third day: 47 and that repentance and remission of sins should be preached in his name among all nations, beginning at Jerusalem. … 49 And, behold, I (*Jesus*) send the promise of my Father upon you: but tarry ye in the city of Jerusalem, until ye be endued with *dunamis*/power (*ability*) from on high. *Holy Spirit now dwells in me in power.* Acts 17:30 And the times of this ignorance God winked at; but now commandeth all men every where to repent: 31 because he hath appointed a day, in the which he will judge the world in righteousness by that man whom he hath ordained; whereof he hath given assurance unto all men, in that he hath raised him from the dead. *That is* Rom 2:16 in the day when God shall judge the secrets of men by Jesus Christ according to *the* gospel. *Praise You, Lord Jesus!*

I. 1 Cor 3:6 I *plant, and water, others plant and water*; but God *gives* the increase. 7 So then neither is he that planteth any thing, neither he that watereth; but God that giveth the increase. 8 Now he that planteth and he that watereth are one: and every man shall receive his own reward according to his own labour. 9 For *I am a laborer* together with God: *they* are God's husbandry, *they* are God's building. 10 According to the grace of God which is given unto me, as a wise masterbuilder, I *continue* the foundation, and *build* thereon. But *I* take heed how *I build* thereupon. 11 For other foundation can no man lay than that is laid, which is Jesus Christ. 12 Now if any man build upon this foundation gold, silver, precious stones, wood, hay, stubble; 13 every man's work shall be made manifest: for the day shall declare it, because it shall be revealed by fire; and the fire shall try every man's work of what sort it is. 14 If any man's work abide which he hath built thereupon, he shall receive a reward. 15 If any man's work shall be burned, he shall suffer loss: but he himself shall be *sozo*/saved; yet so as by fire. *For I* 16 know … that *I am* the temple of God, and that the Spirit of God dwelleth in *me*. 2 Cor 5:9 Wherefore *I* labour, that, whether present or absent, *I* may be accepted of him. 10 For we must all appear before the judgment seat of Christ; that every one may receive the things done in his body, according to that he hath done, whether it be good or bad. 11 Knowing therefore the terror of the Lord, *I* persuade men; but *I am* made manifest unto God; and I trust also are made manifest in *the* consciences *of those who hear and see me.* Gal 4:4 But when the fulness of the time was come, *Father* God sent forth his Son, made of a woman, made under the law, 5 to redeem them that were under the law, that we might receive the adoption of sons. 6 And because *we* are sons, God hath sent forth the Spirit of his Son into *our* hearts, crying, Abba (*Daddy*), Father. 7 Wherefore *I am* no more a servant, but a son; and if a son, then an heir of God through Christ. *I am agape/loved and liked by God, who sent His Son to die for me. I am loved by God!*

J. <u>Gal 3:8</u> **And the scripture**, foreseeing that God would justify the heathen through faith, preached before the gospel unto Abraham, saying, In thee shall all nations be blessed. 9 So then they which be of faith are blessed with faithful Abraham. *Therefore I am blessed with Abraham.* 10 For as many as are of the works of the law are under the curse: for it is written, Cursed is every one that continueth not in all things which are written in the book of the law to do them. 11 But that no man is justified by the law in the sight of God, it is evident: for, The just shall *zao*/live by faith. 12 And the law is not of faith: but, The man that doeth them shall *zao*/live in them. 13 Christ hath redeemed us from the curse of the law, being made a curse for us: for it is written, Cursed is every one that hangeth on a tree: 14 that the blessing of Abraham might come on the Gentiles through Jesus Christ; that we might receive the promise of the Spirit through faith. *Therefore I have Holy Spirit of God as a gift by Jesus Christ. For I* <u>Rom 6:3</u> **know** … that so many of us as were baptized into Jesus Christ were baptized into his death. 4 Therefore we are buried with him by baptism into death: that like as Christ was raised up from the dead by the glory of the Father, even so we also should walk in newness of *zoe*/life (*now*). 5 For if we have been planted together in the likeness of his death, we shall be also in the likeness of his resurrection: 6 **knowing** this, that our old man is crucified with him, that the body of sin might be destroyed, that henceforth we should not serve sin. 7 For he that is dead is freed from sin. 8 Now if we be dead with Christ, we believe that we shall also *zao*/live with him: 9 **knowing** that Christ being raised from the dead dieth no more; death hath no more dominion over him. 10 For in that he died, he died unto sin once: but in that he *zao*/liveth, he *zao*/liveth unto God. 11 **Likewise I reckon** *myself to be dead indeed unto sin, but zao/alive unto God through Jesus Christ our Lord. Knowing, by the grace of Father God, that* <u>Rom 13:10</u> *agape*/love worketh no ill to his neighbour: therefore *agape*/love is the fulfilling of the law. 11 And that, knowing the time, that now it is high time to awake out of sleep: for now is *my soteria*/salvation nearer than when *I* believed. 12 The night is far spent, the day is at hand: *I* therefore cast off the works of darkness, and *I* put on the armour of light. 13 *I, by the grace of God working in me,* walk honestly, as in the day; not in rioting and drunkenness, not in chambering and wan-

The Minister's Confession

tonness, not in strife and envying. 14 *And I put* on the Lord Jesus Christ, and make not provision for the flesh, to fulfil the lusts thereof. Eph 4:22 *I put* off concerning the former conversation the old man, which is corrupt according to the deceitful lusts; 23 and *am* renewed in the spirit of *my* mind; 24 and that *I* put on the new man *in the attitude of my heart that I am a new creation in Jesus*, which after God is created in righteousness and true holiness [*and no longer a mere human, but my new nature is just like Jesus'*]. 25 Wherefore putting away lying, *I* speak ... truth with *my* neighbour: for we are members one of another. ... 29 *I* let no corrupt communication proceed out of *my* mouth, but that which is good to the use of edifying, that it may minister grace unto the hearers. 30 And grieve not the Holy Spirit of God, whereby *I am* sealed unto the day of redemption. *Therefore I do acts of* agape/*love by obeying Him*. Matt 10:7 And as *I* go, *I* preach, saying, The kingdom of heaven is at hand. *I* 8 heal the sick, cleanse the lepers, raise the dead, cast out devils: freely *I* have *lambano/ received*, freely *I* give. *For not with my holiness, but by the name of Jesus and faith in the name of Jesus, I deliver Father God to do the works He has longed to do by His Spirit, who dwells in me and is greater than he who is in the world, and by which I zao/live to Father's glory as the king and priest Jesus has made me to be. Thank You, Father, in Jesus' name! Thank You! Thank You! Thank You!*

K. **2 Thes 1:11** Wherefore *I pray that You, Father* God, *in the name of Jesus*, would count *me* worthy of this calling, and fulfil all the good pleasure of *Your* goodness, and the work of faith with power 12 that the name of our Lord Jesus Christ may be glorified in *me*, and *me* in him, according to the grace of our God and the Lord Jesus Christ. Phil 1:9 And this I pray, that *my agape*/love may abound yet more and more in knowledge and in all judgment; 10 that *I* may approve things that are excellent; that *I* may be sincere and without offence till the day of Christ; 11 being filled with the fruits of righteousness, which are by Jesus Christ, unto the glory and praise of *You, Father* God. Col 1:9 ... That *I, Father, in the name of Jesus*, might be filled with the knowledge of *Your* will in all wisdom and spiritual understanding; 10 that *I* might walk worthy of the Lord unto all pleasing, being fruitful in every good work, and increasing in the knowledge of *You, Father* God; 11 strengthened with all might, according to *Your* glorious power, unto all patience and longsuffering with joyfulness; 12 giving thanks (*continuously*) unto *You, the Father*, which hath made us meet to be partakers of the inheritance of the saints in light: 13 who hath delivered us from the power of darkness, and hath translated us into the kingdom of *Your agape*/dear Son: 14 in whom we have redemption through his blood, even the forgiveness (*remission, purging, obliteration and putting away*) of sins: 15 who is the image of *You, Father*, the invisible God, the firstborn of every creature: 16 for by *Jesus* were all things created, that are in heaven, and that are in earth, visible and invisible, whether they be thrones, or dominions, or principalities, or powers: all things were created by *Jesus*, and for *Jesus*: 17 and *Jesus* is before all things, and by *Jesus* all things consist. 18 And *Jesus* is the head of the body, the church: who is the beginning, the firstborn from the dead; that in all things *Jesus* might have the preeminence. 19 For it pleased *You*, the Father, that in *Jesus* should all fulness dwell; 20 and, having made peace through the blood of *Jesus'* cross, by *Jesus* to reconcile all things unto *Yourself;* by *Jesus*, I say, whether they be things in earth, or things in heaven. *Thank You, Father God! Thank You! In the name of Jesus, thank You!*

L. <u>Eph 3:14</u> **For this cause** I bow my knees unto *You*, the Father of our Lord Jesus Christ, 15 of whom the whole family in heaven and earth is named, 16 that *You, Father,* would grant *me*, according to the riches of *Your* glory, to be strengthened with might by *Your* Spirit in *my* inner man; 17 that Christ may dwell in *my heart* by faith; that *I*, being rooted and grounded in *agape*/love, 18 may be able to comprehend with all saints what is the breadth, and length, and depth, and height; 19 and to know the *agape*/love of Christ, which passeth knowledge, that *I* might be filled with all the fulness of *You, Father* God. 20 Now unto *You, Father*, that *are* able to do exceeding abundantly above all that *I aiteo*/ask *(by demanding as due by covenant promise)* or think, according to the power that worketh in *me*, 21 unto *You* be glory in the church by Christ Jesus throughout all ages, world without end. Amen. <u>Eph 4:4</u> There is one body, and one Spirit, even as *we* are called in one hope of *our* calling; 5 one Lord, one faith, one baptism, 6 one God and Father of all, who is above all, and through all, and in *us* all. 7 But unto every one of us is given grace according to the measure of the gift of Christ. *I, therefore,* <u>Col 1:12</u> *give* thanks *(continually)* unto *You*, the Father, *through the name of Jesus Christ, my Lord,* which hath made *me* meet *(qualified and able)* to be *a partaker* of the inheritance of the saints in light: *for it is You, Father,* 13 who hath delivered *me* from the power of darkness, and hath translated *me* into the kingdom of *Your agape*/dear Son: 14 in whom *I* have redemption through his blood, even the forgiveness *(remission, purging, obliteration and putting away)* of sins: 15 who is the image of *You*, the invisible God, the firstborn of every creature: 16 for by *Jesus* were all things created, that are in heaven, and that are in earth, visible and invisible, whether they be thrones, or dominions, or principalities, or powers: all things were created by *Jesus*, and for *Jesus*: 17 and *Jesus* is before all things, and by *Jesus* all things consist. 18 And *Jesus* is the head of the body, the church: who is the beginning, the firstborn from the dead; that in all things *Jesus* might have the preeminence. 19 For it pleased *You*, the Father, that in *Jesus* should all fulness

The Minister's Confession

dwell; 20 and, having made peace through the blood of *Jesus'* cross, by *Jesus* to reconcile all things unto *Yourself*; by *Jesus*, I say, whether they be things in earth, or things in heaven. 21 And *I, that was* sometime alienated and *an enemy* in *my* mind by wicked works, yet now hath *Jesus* reconciled *me to You, Father God*, 22 in the body of his flesh through death, to present *me* holy and unblameable and unreproveable in *Your* sight: 23 *so I* continue in the faith grounded and settled, and *I am* not moved away from the hope of the gospel *(of Christ in me the hope of Your glory in me and through me)*, which *I* have heard, and … *I* am made a minister. 2 Cor 5:7 For *I* walk by faith, not by sight: *I gladly call those things that be not yet of His promises as if they are until I see God do them. Thank you, Father! In the name of Jesus, thank You! Thank You, Lord Jesus, for Your mighty work! Thank You for Your* agape/love! *Glory!*

M. Just like Jesus, wherever I am I deliver the reconciliation of Father God; I heal the sick, cleanse the lepers, raise the dead, cast out demons, to proclaim the sovereignty of God in action. God heals as I lay hands or speak words of *zoe*/life. God does special miracles through me. I do greater works than Jesus because He has gone to the Father. I am sent as Jesus was sent to speak God's words in fullness. John 3:34 For he whom God hath sent speaketh the words of God: for God giveth not the Spirit by measure unto *me*. *So no disease, infirmity, death, lack, terror or destruction is able to stand before me, in the name of Jesus. God gives me His Spirit without measure, to speak His words of reconciliation through the blood of Jesus Christ.* 2 Cor 5:21 For he hath made *Jesus* to be sin for us who knew no sin; that we might be made the righteousness of God in him. Luke 4:18 The Spirit of the Lord is upon me, because he hath anointed me to preach the gospel to the poor; he hath sent me to heal the brokenhearted, to preach deliverance to the captives, and recovering of sight to the blind, to set at liberty them that are bruised, 19 to preach the acceptable year of the Lord, *now*. 2 Cor 4:6 For God, who commanded the light to shine out of darkness, hath shined in *my heart*, to give the light of the knowledge of the glory of God in the face of Jesus Christ. 7 *And I* have this treasure in *an* earthen *vessel*, that the excellency of the power may be of God, and not of *me*. 8 *As a warrior of Holy Spirit, to bring Heaven to Earth, I am* troubled on every side, yet not distressed; *I am* perplexed, but not in despair; 9 persecuted, but not forsaken; cast down, but not destroyed; 10 always bearing about in the body the dying of the Lord Jesus, that the *zoe*/life also of Jesus might be made manifest in *my* body. 2 Cor 3:17 Now the Lord is that Spirit: and where the Spirit of the Lord is, there is liberty *(to be all God wants me to be by Holy Spirit in me)*. 18 But we all, with open face beholding as in a glass *(mirror)* the glory of the Lord *(within us)*, are changed into the same image from glory to glory, even as by the Spirit of the

Lord. <u>Col 1:27</u> To whom God *makes* known *through me* what is the riches of the glory of this mystery… , which is Christ in *us*, the hope of glory: 28 whom *I* preach, warning every man, and teaching every man in all wisdom; that we may present every man perfect (*mature*) in Christ Jesus. <u>2 Cor 1:3</u> Blessed be God, even the Father of our Lord Jesus Christ, the Father of mercies, and the God of all comfort; 4 who comforteth *me* in all *my* tribulation, that *I* may be able to comfort them which are in any trouble, by the comfort wherewith *I myself am* comforted of God. 5 For as the sufferings of Christ abound in *me*, so *my* consolation also aboundeth by Christ. *For* <u>Ps 31:23</u> *I* love the Lord, *as one of* his saints: for the Lord preserveth the faithful, and plentifully rewardeth the proud doer. 24 *I am* of good courage, and he shall strengthen *my* heart, *as I* hope in the Lord (*who raises the dead*). *Knowing* <u>Ps 27:13</u> I had fainted, unless I had believed to see the goodness of the Lord in the land of the living. *But no matter what, I do see the goodness of the Lord in the land of the living. I therefore* 14 wait on the Lord (*by entwining Him into every part of my life continually*): *so I am* of good courage, and he *strengthens my* heart: wait (*entwine*), I say, on the Lord. *For* <u>Eph 6:10</u> finally … *I am* strong in the Lord, and in the power of his might. 11 *I* put on the whole armour of God, that *I* may be able to stand against the wiles of the devil. 12 For *I* wrestle not against flesh and blood, but against principalities, against powers, against the rulers of the darkness of this world, against spiritual wickedness in high places. 13 Wherefore *I* take unto *myself* the whole armour of God, that *I* may be able to withstand in the evil day, and having done all, to stand. 14 *I* stand therefore, having *my* loins girt about with truth, and having on the breastplate of righteousness; 15 and *my* feet shod with the preparation of the gospel of peace; 16 above all, *I continually take* the shield of faith, wherewith *I* shall be able to quench all the fiery darts of the wicked. 17 And *I* take the helmet of salvation, and the sword of the Spirit, which is the word of God: 18 *I am* praying always with all prayer and supplication in the Spirit, and watching thereunto with all perseverance and supplication for all saints; 19 and for (*myself and other Gospel preachers*), that utterance may be given unto *us*, that *we* may open *our mouths* boldly, to make known the mystery of the gospel, 20 … that therein *we* may speak boldly, as *we* ought to speak. *Knowing* <u>Acts 10:38</u> how *You, Father God, have* anointed *me in* Jesus of Nazareth with the Holy Ghost and with power: *so I* go about doing good, and healing all that *are* oppressed (*under the active rule and lordship*) of the devil; for *You, Father* God, *are* with *me*. <u>Rom 15:19</u> Through mighty signs and wonders, by the power of the Spirit of God; so that from *home* and round about *all the world*, I … fully *preach* the gospel of Christ. <u>Matt 10:7</u> And as *I* go, *I* preach, saying, The kingdom of heaven is at hand. 8 *With Jesus beside the Father, I* heal the sick, cleanse the lepers, raise the dead, cast out devils: freely *I* have *lambano*/received, freely *I give, in every city or place, in the name of Jesus Christ.* Mark 16:15 *As* Jesus said, *by Jesus through Holy Spirit, I go into all the world, and by Jesus through Holy Spirit, I preach the gospel to every creature.* 16 He that believeth and is baptized shall be *sozo*/saved, *by Jesus through Holy Spirit*; but he that believeth not shall be damned. 17 And, *by Jesus through Holy Spirit, to the glory of Father God,* these signs follow *me* that *believes*; in *the* name *of Jesus I* cast out devils, *by Jesus through Holy Spirit; I* speak with new tongues, *by Jesus through Holy Spirit*; 18. *I* take up serpents, *by Jesus through Holy Spirit*; and if *I* drink any deadly thing, it shall not hurt *me, by Jesus through Holy Spirit; I* lay hands on the sick, and they ... recover *totally, by Jesus through Holy Spirit.* 19 ... The Lord *Jesus* ... was received up into heaven, and *sits* on the right hand of God. 20 *I go* forth, and *I preach* everywhere, *by Jesus through Holy Spirit,* the Lord *Jesus* working with *me,* and confirming the word with signs following, *by Jesus through Holy Spirit, to the glory of Father God.* Amen! *Lord Jesus, You accomplished Your great work! You have obtained Holy Spirit for us. You, Lord Jesus, are the Administrator of Holy Spirit, and we, Your Body, administer Holy Spirit on the Earth for and with You. Thank You for this calling. Thank You for Your great work. Thank You, Lord Jesus, thank You! Hallelujah! Hallelujah! Hallelujah!*

N. **Father, in the name of Jesus**, give me Your spirit of wisdom and revelation in the knowledge of You, with the eyes of my understanding being enlightened so that I walk to Your glory by Jesus Christ, knowing that 2 Pet 1:2 grace and peace *are* multiplied unto *us* through the knowledge of *You, Father* God, and of Jesus our Lord, 3 according as, *in Jesus, Your* divine power hath given unto us all things that pertain unto *zoe*/life and godliness, through the knowledge of *You, Father,* that have called us to glory and virtue: 4 whereby are given unto us, *in Jesus,* exceeding great and precious promises: that by these *we* might be partakers of the divine nature, *in Jesus,* having escaped the corruption that is in the world through lust. 5 And beside this, *I, by Your Spirit, give* all diligence, *that I* add to *my* faith virtue; and to virtue knowledge; 6 and to knowledge temperance; and to temperance patience; and to patience godliness; 7 and to godliness brotherly kindness; and to brotherly kindness *agape*/charity. *So that* 8 ... these things *are in me,* and abound, *so that* they make *me* that *I* shall neither be barren nor unfruitful in the knowledge of our Lord Jesus Christ. *Knowing, unto being zealous for good works, by faith in* agape/love*, that* 9 ... he that lacketh these things is blind, and cannot see afar off, and hath forgotten that he was purged from his old sins. *So, Father, open my eyes, cause me to see afar off and keep me in remembrance that I have been purged from my old sins by the blood of Jesus.* 10 Wherefore the rather, *Father, build in me the knowing, so that I give* diligence to make *my* calling and election sure, *in abounding in the manifestation of Your divine nature through me, to the knowing that, as I do* these things, *I* shall never fall: 11 for so an entrance shall be ministered unto *me* abundantly into the everlasting kingdom of our Lord and Saviour Jesus Christ, *to the praise of Your glory. Father, keep me in right remembrance of these things, unto glad obedience in* agape/love. *Thank You, Father! In the name of Jesus, thank You!* 12 Wherefore I will not be negligent to put *myself and others* always in remembrance of these things, though *we* know them, and be established in the present truth [*in this Day of Salvation in the remission of sins through the blood of Jesus Christ.*] *So that I soften my heart, so I hear You in Your Word and know the greatness of Your power, so that I* <u>Matt 13:15</u> ... should see with *my* eyes, and hear with *my* ears, and should understand with *my* heart, and should be converted, and *You* should heal *me in any area* <u>2 Pet 1:9</u> *that I lack in the* things (*of Your divine nature or godliness, so I am no longer*) blind, and cannot see afar off, *or forget* that *I* was purged from *my* old sins [*in Your mighty work in Jesus*]. *So I am one that believes and to whom You have revealed the greatness of the power of Your Arm, for*: <u>**Isa 53:1**</u> Who hath believed our report? and to whom is the arm of the Lord revealed? 2 For he shall grow up before him as a tender plant, and as a root out of a dry ground: he hath no form nor comeliness; and when we shall see him, there is no beauty that we should desire him. 3 He is despised and rejected of men; a man of sorrows, and acquainted with grief: and we hid as it were our faces from him; he was despised, and we esteemed him not. 4 Surely he hath *cabal*/borne our griefs *and infirmities*, and *nasa*/carried our sorrows *and sicknesses*: yet we did esteem him stricken, smitten of God, and afflicted. 5 But he was wounded for our transgressions, he was bruised for our iniquities: the chastisement of our peace was upon him; and with his stripes we are healed. 6 All we like sheep have gone astray; we have turned every one to his own way; and the Lord hath laid on him the iniquity of us all. 7 He was oppressed, and he was afflicted, yet he opened not his mouth: he is brought as a lamb to the slaughter, and as a sheep before her shearers is dumb, so he openeth not his mouth. 8 He was taken from prison and from judgment: and who shall declare his generation? for he was cut off out of the land of the living: for the transgression of my people was he stricken. 9 And he made his grave with the wicked, and with the rich in his death; because he had done no violence, neither was any deceit in his mouth. 10 Yet it pleased the Lord to bruise him; he hath put him to grief (*and sickness*): when thou shalt make his soul an offering for sin, he shall see his seed, he shall prolong his days, and the pleasure of the Lord shall prosper in his hand. 11 He shall see of the travail of his soul, and shall be satisfied: by his knowledge shall my righteous servant justify many; for he shall *cabal*/bear their iniquities. 12 Therefore will I divide

The Minister's Confession

him a portion with the great, and he shall divide the spoil with the strong; because he hath poured out his soul unto death: and he was numbered with the transgressors; and he *nasa*/bare the sin of many, and made intercession for the transgressors. *So I say continually:* **Ps 103:1** Bless the Lord, O my soul: and all that is within me, bless his holy name. 2 Bless the Lord, O my soul, and forget not all his benefits: 3 who forgiveth all thine iniquities; who healeth all thy diseases; 4 who redeemeth thy life from destruction; who crowneth thee with *chesed*/lovingkindness and *racham*/tender mercies; 5 who satisfieth thy mouth with good things; so that thy youth is renewed like the eagle's. 6 The Lord executeth righteousness and judgment for all that are oppressed. 7 He made known his ways unto Moses, his acts unto the children of Israel. 8 The Lord is merciful and gracious, slow to anger, and plenteous in *chesed*/mercy. 9 He will not always chide: neither will he keep his anger for ever. 10 He hath not dealt with us after our sins; nor rewarded us according to our iniquities. 11 For as the heaven is high above the earth, so great is his *chesed*/mercy toward them that fear him. 12 As far as the east is from the west, so far hath he removed our transgressions from us. 13 Like as a father pitieth his children, so the Lord pitieth them that fear him. 14 For he knoweth our frame; he remembereth that we are dust. 15 As for man, his days are as grass: as a flower of the field, so he flourisheth. 16 For the wind passeth over it, and it is gone; and the place thereof shall know it no more. 17 But the *chesed*/mercy of the Lord is from everlasting to everlasting upon them that fear him, and his righteousness unto children's children; 18 to such as keep his covenant, and to those that remember his commandments to do them. 19 The Lord hath prepared his throne in the heavens; and his kingdom ruleth over all. 20 Bless the Lord, ye his angels, that excel in strength, that do his commandments, hearkening unto the voice of his word. 21 Bless ye the Lord, all ye his hosts; ye ministers of his, that do his pleasure. 22 Bless the Lord, all his works in all places of his dominion: bless the Lord, O my soul. *Bless You, O loving Father, in the name of Jesus! Bless You, O Lord Jesus! Hallelujah! Hallelujah! Hallelujah!*

O. By the grace of God, knowing that Jesus, <u>1 Pet 2:24</u> who his own self bare our sins in his own body on the tree, that we, being dead to sins, should *zao*/live unto righteousness: by whose stripes *we* were healed. 25 For *we* were as sheep going astray; but now *I have* returned unto the Shepherd and Bishop of *our* souls. <u>Eph 1:12</u> That we should be to the praise of his glory, *by trusting* in Christ, 13 ... after that *I* heard the word of truth, the gospel of *our soteria*/salvation: in whom also after that *I* believed, *I was* sealed with that holy Spirit of promise, 14 which is the earnest of our inheritance until the redemption of the purchased possession, unto the praise of his glory. *That by me, Father*

Col 1:27 ... God would make known what is the riches of the glory of this mystery among *all peoples*; which is Christ in you, the hope of glory. Rom 15:19 Through mighty signs and wonders, by the power of the Spirit of God; so that from *home* unto *the world* I fully *preach* the gospel of Christ. Rom 1:16 For I am not ashamed of the gospel of Christ: for it is the power of God unto *soteria*/salvation to every one that believeth; to the Jew first, and also to the Greek. 17 For therein is the righteousness of God revealed from faith to faith: as it is written, The just shall *zao*/live by faith. 1 John 3:8 ... For this purpose the Son of God was manifested *in me*, that he might destroy the works of the devil [*though me*]. Rom 16:20 And the God of peace *bruises* Satan under *my* feet *as shattered glass*. The grace of our Lord Jesus Christ *is* with *me* [*to know, be and do this*]. Amen. Heb 3:1 Wherefore, *as one of the* holy brethren, partakers of the heavenly calling, *I* consider the Apostle and High Priest of *my* profession (*confession*), Christ Jesus; ... 8 *and I* harden not *my heart*, as in the provocation, in the day of temptation in the wilderness (*when many times things looked bad, as if the Word and love of God were going to fail*): ... *so I enter in by believing God to perform and confirm His Word, no matter what the circumstances, knowing that* Ps 23:1 the Lord is my shepherd; I shall not want, 2 he maketh me to lie down in green pastures: he leadeth me beside the still waters. 3 He restoreth my soul: he leadeth me in the paths of righteousness for his name's sake. 4 Yea, though I walk through the valley of the shadow of death, I will fear no evil: for thou art with me; thy rod and thy staff they comfort me. 5 Thou preparest a table before me in the presence of mine enemies: thou anointest my head with oil; my cup runneth over. 6 Surely goodness and *chesed*/mercy shall follow (*pursue and overtake*), me all the days of my life: and I will dwell in the house of the LORD for ever. *For* 1 John 4:4 *I am* of God, *one of His* little children (*a full adopted son of God*), and have overcome *the devil and all his works*: because greater is he that is in *me*, than he that is in the world. Heb 10:35 *I* cast not away therefore *my* confidence, which hath great recompence of reward. 36 For *I* have need of patience, that, after *I* have done the will of God, *I* might receive the promise. 37 For yet a little while, and he that shall come will come, and will not tarry. *Knowing that* 38 now the just shall *zao*/live by faith: but if any man draw back, my soul shall have no pleasure in him. 39 But *I am* not of them who draw back unto perdition; but of them that believe to the *sozo*/saving of the soul. Heb 11:1 Now faith *in Father God, in His Word,* is the substance *and the strength* of things hoped for (*the joyful expectation of coming good*), the evidence of things not seen. 2 For by it *I obtain* a good report. 2 Cor 4:13 *And I,* having the same spirit of faith, according as it is written, I believed and therefore have I spoken; *I* also believe, and therefore speak [*God's Word of salvation, knowing He will perform it*]. 1 Cor 15:10 *For* by the grace of God I am what I am [*born again of God*]: and his grace which was bestowed upon me was not in vain; but I labour more abundantly than they all: yet not I, but the grace of God which *is* with me. *Knowing,* Gal 2:19 for I through the law am dead to the law, that I might *zao/live* unto God. 20 I am (*have been*) crucified with Christ: nevertheless I *zao*/live; yet not I, but Christ *zao*/liveth in me: and the life which I now *zao*/live in the flesh I *zao*/live by the faith of the Son of God, who *agape*/loved me, and gave himself for me. 21 I do not frustrate the grace of God: for if righteousness come by the law, then Christ is dead in vain. John 14:12 Verily, verily, *Jesus has said* unto *me, that continually believe,* The works that *He did* shall *I* do also; and greater works than these shall *I* do; because *Jesus has gone unto* Father. 13 And whatsoever *I* shall *aiteo*/ask (*by demanding, expecting as due by covenant promise*) in *His* name, that will *Jesus* do, that the Father may be glorified in the Son. *For He said:* 14 If ye shall *aiteo*/ask (*by demanding, expecting as due by covenant promise*) any thing in my name, I will do it. *And not my holiness, but the name of Jesus and faith in the name of Jesus makes people and situations whole, to the glory of You, Father God.* 2 Thes 1:11 Wherefore *I* pray that *You, Father,* our God, would count *me* worthy of this calling, and fulfil all the good pleasure of *Your* goodness, and the work of faith with power: 12 that the name of our Lord Jesus Christ may be glorified in *me,* and *me* in him, according to the grace of our God and the Lord Jesus Christ. Heb 13:20 Now *You, Father,* the God of peace, that brought again from the dead our Lord Jesus, that great shepherd of the sheep, through the blood of the everlasting covenant, 21 make *me* perfect in every good work to do *Your* will, working in *me* that which is wellpleasing in *Your* sight, through Jesus Christ; to whom be glory for ever and ever. Amen. *Thank You, Father! You are working in and for me to my good! You agape/love me! You call me valuable to You! Thank You for the value You set on me, Jesus! Thank You, Jesus, for ransoming me by Your blood! Thank You!*

P. Father, by You I preach Your Word that You reign through us. Acts 10:36 The word which *You* sent unto the children of Israel, preaching peace by Jesus Christ: (he is Lord of all:) ... 38 how *You* anointed Jesus of Nazareth with the Holy Ghost and with power: who went about doing good, and healing all that were oppressed (*under the active rule and lordship*) of the devil; for *You were* with him. 1 Pet 2:24 Who his own self bare our sins in his own body on the tree, that we, being dead to sins, should *zao*/live unto righteousness: by whose stripes *we* were healed. Ps 18:27 For thou wilt save the afflicted people; but wilt bring down high looks. 28 For thou wilt light my candle: the Lord my God will enlighten my darkness. 29 For by thee I ... run through a troop; and by my God I *leap* over a wall. 30 As for God, his way is perfect: the word of the Lord is tried: he is a buckler to all those that trust in him. 31 For who is

BATTLE PRAYER FOR DIVINE HEALING: FIELD MANUAL 2

God save the LORD? Or who is a rock save our God? 32 It is God that girdeth me with strength, and maketh my way perfect. 33 He maketh my feet like hinds' feet, and setteth me upon my high places. 34 He teacheth my hands to war, so that a bow of steel is broken by mine arms. 35 Thou hast also given me the shield of thy salvation: and thy right hand hath holden me up, and thy gentleness hath made me great. 36 Thou hast enlarged my steps under me, that my feet *do* not slip. *By Your warrior heart in me,* 37 *I pursue* mine enemies, and *overtake* them: neither *do* I turn again till they *are* consumed. 38 I *wound* them that they *are* not able to rise: they *fall* under my feet, *in Jesus' name.* 39 For thou hast girded me with strength unto the battle: thou hast subdued under me *all the work of the enemy* that *rises* up against me. 40 Thou hast also given me the necks of mine enemies [*the devil and his works*]; that I might destroy them that hate me. 41 They *cry,* but there *is* none to save them: even unto the LORD, but *You answer* them not. 42 ... I beat them small as the dust before the wind: I ... cast them out as the dirt in the streets. Rom 15:13 Now *You, Father,* the God of hope fill *me* with all joy and peace in believing, that *I* may abound in hope, through the power of the Holy Ghost. 2 Tim 2:3 *I* therefore endure hardness, as a good soldier of Jesus Christ. 1 Tim 1:18 ... That *I, by the prophecies and promises of God, might* war a good warfare; 19 holding faith, and a good conscience .... *For I use the shield of faith to quench the fiery darts and fears of the enemy, knowing*: Ps 27:1 The LORD is my light and my salvation; whom shall I fear? The LORD is the strength of my life; of whom shall I be afraid? Ps 42:11 Why art thou cast down, O my soul? and why art thou disquieted within me? hope thou in God: for I shall yet praise him, who is the health of my countenance, and my God. *I proclaim, in the name of Jesus, I am strong in the Lord and in the power of His might and that* Phil 4:13 I can do all things through Christ which strengtheneth me. *For You said*: Joel 3:10 ... Let the weak say, I am strong. *I am strong in the Lord, for this is my true born-again nature, just like my elder brother, Jesus, in the power of Holy Spirit.* Ps 112:7 *I* shall not be afraid of evil tidings: *my* heart is fixed, trusting in the LORD. 8 *My* heart is established, *I* shall not be afraid, until *I* see *my* desire upon *my* enemies. *For* Ps 46:1 God is our refuge and strength, a very present help in trouble. 2 Therefore will not we fear, though the earth be removed, and though the mountains be carried into the midst of the sea; 3 though the waters thereof roar and be troubled, though the mountains shake with the swelling thereof. Selah. Phil 4:13 I can do all things through Christ which strengtheneth me. Ps 27:13 I had fainted, unless I had believed to see the goodness of the LORD in the land of the living. *I say* 14 wait on the LORD (*entwine Him into every part of your life*): be of good courage, and he shall strengthen thine heart: wait (*entwine, trust*) I say, on the LORD. *Therefore I do not faint, but am strong in His strength in me, proclaiming in absolute certainty that He will perform His Word, I will see the goodness of the Lord in the land of the living, and I am in joyful thanksgiving, knowing He confirms His Word of grace through me.* Phil 1:6 Being confident of this very thing, that he which hath begun a good work in *me* will perform it until the day of Jesus Christ. *For You, Father* Heb 1:1 God, who at sundry times and in divers manners spake in time past unto the fathers by the prophets, 2 *have* in these last days spoken unto us by *Your* Son, whom *You have* appointed heir of all things, by whom also *You* made the worlds; 3 who being the brightness of *Your* glory, and the express image of *Your* person, and upholding all things by the word of his power, when he had by himself purged our sins, sat down on the right hand of *You,* the Majesty on high; ... 13 *for* to which of the angels said *You* at any time, Sit on my right hand, until I make thine enemies thy footstool? *With Jesus at Your right hand,* Rom 16:20 ... *You, Father,* the God of peace, shall bruise Satan under *my* feet *as shattered glass, as I preach Your Kingdom, heal the sick, cleanse the lepers, raise the dead and cast out devils.* The grace of our Lord Jesus Christ is with *me* [*to know, be and do this*]. Amen. ... 25 Now to *You, Father,* that is of power to stablish *me* according to *Your* gospel, and the preaching of Jesus Christ, according to the revelation of the mystery, which was kept secret since the world began, 26 but now is made manifest, and by the scriptures of the prophets, according to the commandment of *You,* the everlasting God, made known to all nations for the obedience of faith: 27 to *You, Father* God, only wise, be glory through Jesus Christ for ever. Amen. *Hallelujah! Hallelujah! Hallelujah! Hallelujah! Hallelujah!*

Q. **I am sent of God to do the works of Jesus.** As a believer: Mark 16:17 And these signs shall follow them that believe; in *Jesus'* name *I, as a believer,* cast out devils; *I, as a believer,* speak with new tongues; 18. *I, as a believer,* take up serpents; and if *I, as a believer,* drink any deadly thing, it shall not hurt *me; I, as a believer,* lay hands on the sick, and they shall recover *totally. For I constantly walk in the absolute certainty and* Luke 10:19 behold *that I have* power (*authority, commission and the resources of Heaven*) to tread on serpents and scorpions, and over all the power of the enemy: and nothing shall by any means hurt *me.* 20 Notwithstanding in this *I* rejoice not, that the spirits are subject unto *me;* but rather *I* rejoice, because *my name is* written in heaven. *I am equipped and commanded to walk as Jesus walked.* 1 John 2:5 But whoso keepeth his word, in him verily is the *agape*/love of God perfected: hereby know we that we are in him. 6 He that saith he abideth in him ought himself also so to walk, even as he walked. *I am to follow or imitate God as Jesus did.* Eph 5:1 Be ye therefore followers (*imitators*) of God, as *agape*/dear (*loved*) children; 2 and walk in *agape*/love, as Christ also hath *agape*/loved us, and hath given himself for us an offering and a sacrifice to God for a sweetsmelling savour. 1Cor 2:4 And my speech and my preaching *are* not with enticing words of man's wisdom, but in demonstration of the Spirit and of power: 5 that *our* faith should not stand in the wisdom of men, but in the power of God. ... 12 Now *I* have received, not the spirit of the world, but the spirit which is of God; that *I* might know the things that are freely given to us of God. *I am made for and get* zoe*/life for anyone in any sin or any effect of sin, including sickness or disease, for* 1 John 5:16 if any man see his brother sin a sin which is not unto death, he shall *aiteo*/ask (*by demanding as due by covenant promise*), and *therefore Father God* shall give me zoe/life for them ... . *By the grace of God, I do not let sin, sickness or disease rule in me or others.* Rom 6:14 For sin shall not have dominion over you: for ye are not under the law, but under grace. *I am to* zao/*live for God to serve others.* Rom 8:2 For the law of the Spirit of *zoe*/life in Christ Jesus hath made me free from the law of sin and death. 2 Cor 5:15 And that he died for all, that they which *zao*/live should not henceforth *zao*/live unto themselves, but unto him which died for them, and rose again, *and do greater works than Jesus, as Jesus said:* John 14:12 Verily, verily, I say unto you, He that believeth on me, the works that I do shall he do also; and greater works than these shall he do; because I go unto my Father. 13 And whatsoever ye shall *aiteo*/ask (*by requiring, demanding and expecting as due by covenant promise*) in my name, that will I do, that the Father may be glorified in the Son. 14 If ye shall *aiteo*/ask (*by requiring, demanding and expecting as due by covenant promise*) any thing in my name, I will do it. *I obey Jesus to see answered* aiteo/*asking, requiring, demanding and expecting as due by covenant promise.* John 16:23 ... Verily, verily, I (*Jesus*) say unto you, Whatsoever ye shall *aiteo*/ask (*by requiring, demanding and expecting as due by covenant promise*) the Father in my name, he will give it you. So I 24 ... *aiteo*/ask (*by requiring, demanding and expecting as due by covenant promise, in Jesus' name*), and *I* receive, that *my* joy may be full. *God's very nature is to heal the sick, so it is my new-creation nature also.* Ps 103:2 Bless the LORD ... 3 who forgiveth all *my* iniquities; who healeth all *my* diseases; 4 who redeemeth *my* life from destruction; who crowneth *me* with *chesed*/lovingkindness and *racham*/tender mercies; 5 who satisfieth *my* mouth with good things; so that *my* youth is renewed like the eagle's. 6 The LORD executeth righteousness and judgment *through me* for all that are oppressed. *As a part of Jesus' Body, I do what Jesus would do in proclaiming and demonstrating* Acts 10:36 the word which God sent unto the children of Israel, preaching peace by Jesus Christ: (he is Lord of all:) 38 how God anointed Jesus of Nazareth with the Holy Ghost and with power: who went about doing good, and healing all that were oppressed (*by the active reign, lordship and power*) of the devil; for God was with him. 39 And we *believe the* witnesses of all things which he (*Jesus*) did both

The Minister's Confession

in the land of the Jews, and in Jerusalem; whom they slew and hanged on a tree: 40 him God raised up the third day, and shewed him openly; 41 not to all the people, but unto witnesses chosen before of God, even to *the early disciples*, who did eat and drink with him after he rose from the dead. 42 And he commanded us, *by them*, to preach unto the people, and to testify that it is he which was ordained of God to be the Judge of quick and dead. 43 To him give all the prophets witness, that through his name whosoever believeth in him shall receive remission (*purging, obliteration, removal and putting away*) of sins. 2 Cor 1:21 Now he which stablisheth us, *including me*, in Christ, and hath anointed *me*, is God; 22 who hath also sealed us, and given the earnest of the Spirit in our hearts. *Therefore my new spirit thinks like Jesus*: Gal 4:6 And because ye are sons, God hath sent forth the Spirit of his Son into *my heart*, crying, Abba (*Daddy*), Father. 2 Tim 1:7 For God hath not given *me* the spirit of fear; but of *dunamis*/power (*ability*), and of *agape*/love, and of a sound mind *to walk in* agape *love, just as Jesus did*. Rom 13:14 So I put on the Lord Jesus Christ, and make not provision for the flesh, to fulfil the lusts thereof. *I am called by Father God to agape/love Him, and others for Him with all kinds of good works, just like Jesus did, so Father's agape/love can be seen in the Earth.* 1 John 4:17 Herein is our *agape*/love made perfect, that we may have boldness in the day of judgment: because as he is, so are we in this world. 18 There is no fear in *agape*/love; but perfect *agape*/love casteth out fear: because fear hath torment. He that feareth is not made perfect in *agape*/love. *Therefore I always focus on the* agape/love *the Father has for me and through me for others, knowing all the requirements have been met in Jesus.* Isa 53:4 Surely he hath *cabal*/borne our griefs *and infirmities*, and *nasa*/carried our sorrows *and sicknesses*: yet we did esteem him stricken, smitten of God, and afflicted. 5 But he was wounded for our transgressions, he was bruised for our iniquities: the chastisement of our peace was upon him; and with his stripes we are healed. 6 All we like sheep have gone astray; we have turned every one to his own way; and the Lord hath laid on him the iniquity of us all. ... 10 Yet it pleased the Lord to bruise him; he hath put him to grief (*and sickness*): when thou shalt make his soul an offering for sin, he shall see his seed, he shall prolong his days, and the pleasure of the Lord shall prosper in his hand. 11 He shall see of the travail of his soul, and shall be satisfied: by his knowledge shall my righteous servant justify many; for he shall *cabal*/ bear their iniquities. *Praise God! I am justified by faith in the mighty work of Jesus! He is making me to know and understand this, so I walk in Him and His triumph more and more every day! Praise You, Lord Jesus Christ, King of Kings and Lords of Lords! Praise Your great work in the cross! Praise You! Thank You, Father! In the name of Jesus, thank You for Your great work in Jesus! Hallelujah!*

R. **Just like Jesus, *I am* given the Spirit of Jesus** to be just like Jesus, a vessel of God's love to man. Gal 4:6 And because ye are sons, God hath sent forth the Spirit of his Son into *our* hearts, crying, Abba (*Daddy*), Father. Gal 3:26 For ye are all the children, *sons* of God by faith in Christ Jesus. Gal 2:20 I am (*have been*) crucified with Christ: nevertheless I *zao*/live *the zoe/life of Jesus*; yet not I, but Christ *zao*/liveth in me *to walk like He walked*: and the life which I now *zao*/live *of Jesus' agape in the flesh I zao/*live [*of walking like Jesus in power, agape/ love, sound mind, grace and truth, doing good, and healing those oppressed of the devil by, for, through and with Father God, by and in His Spirit, because of the terrible sacrifice and mighty work in the soul-life, body and blood of Jesus, His Firstborn,* Agape/Beloved Son, *and I* zao/live this] by the faith of the Son of God, who *agape*/loved me, and gave himself for me. 21 I do not frustrate the grace of God: for if righteousness come by the law, then Christ is dead in vain. Rom 8:26 Likewise the Spirit also helpeth (*me to stand for God, against*) *my* infirmities (*weaknesses*): for *when I* know not what *I* should pray for as *I* ought: the Spirit itself maketh intercession for *me* with groanings which cannot be uttered. 27 And he that searcheth the hearts knoweth what is the mind of the Spirit, because he maketh intercession for the saints according to the will of God. 28 And *by grace I* know that all things work together for good to them that *agape*/love God, to them who are the called according to his purpose. 29 For whom he did foreknow, he also did predestinate to be conformed to the image of his Son, that he might be the firstborn among many brethren. 30 Moreover whom he did predestinate, them he also called: and whom he called, them he also justified: and whom he justified, them he also glorified. 31 What shall *I* then say to these things? If God be for *me*, who can be against *me*? 32 He that spared not his own Son, but delivered him up for us all, how shall he not with him also freely give us all things? 33 Who shall lay any thing to the charge of God's elect? It is God that justifieth. 34 Who is he that condemneth? It is Christ that died, yea rather, that is risen again, who is even at the right hand of God, who also maketh intercession for *me*. Rom 5:1 Therefore being justified by faith, *I* have peace with God through our Lord Jesus Christ: 2 by whom also *I* have access by faith into this grace wherein *I* stand, and rejoice in hope of the glory of God. 2 Cor 5:21 For *Father God* hath made *Jesus* to be sin for us, who knew no sin; that we might be made the righteousness of *Father* God in *Jesus*. 2 Cor 1:19 For the Son of God, Jesus Christ, who was preached ... by *Paul* ... was not yea and nay, but in him was yea. 20 For all the promises of God in *Jesus* are yea, and in him Amen, unto the glory of God by us. 21 Now he which stablisheth *me* in Christ, and hath anointed *me*, is God; 22 who hath also sealed *me*, and given the earnest of the Spirit in *my* heart. Thus Isa 11:2 ... *the spirit of the* Lord *rests upon me in Jesus, the spirit of*

The Minister's Confession

wisdom and understanding, the spirit of counsel and might, the spirit of knowledge and of the fear of the LORD; 3 and *makes me* of quick understanding in the fear of the LORD: and *I do* not judge after the sight of *my* eyes, neither reprove after the hearing of *my* ears: 4 but with righteousness *I* judge the poor, and reprove with equity for the meek of the earth: and *I* smite the earth with the rod of *my* mouth, and with the breath of *my* lips *I* slay the wicked. 5 And righteousness shall be the girdle of *my* loins, and faithfulness the girdle of *my* reins. Luke 4:18 The Spirit of the Lord is upon me, because he hath anointed me to preach the gospel to the poor; he hath sent me to heal the brokenhearted, to preach deliverance to the captives, and recovering of sight to the blind, to set at liberty them that are bruised, 19 to preach the acceptable year of the Lord. Acts 10:38 ... God *has* anointed *me in* Jesus of Nazareth with the Holy Ghost and with power: *so I go* about doing good, and healing all that *are* oppressed *(under the active rule and lordship)* of the devil; for God *is* with *me*. ... 40 God raised up *Jesus* the third day, and shewed him openly; 41 not to all the people, but unto witnesses chosen before of God, even to *those disciples*, who did eat and drink with him after he rose from the dead. 42 And he commanded us to preach unto the people, and to testify that it is *Jesus* which was ordained of God to be the Judge of quick and dead. 43 To him give all the prophets witness, that through his name whosoever believeth in him shall receive remission *(purging, obliteration and putting away)* of sins. Acts 26:18 To open *the* eyes *of all mankind*, and to turn them from darkness to light, and from the power *(authority)* of Satan unto God, that they may receive forgiveness *(remission, purging, obliteration and putting away)* of sins, and inheritance among them which are sanctified by faith that is in *Jesus*. Gal 3:27 For as many of *us* as have been baptized into Christ have put on Christ. *I continuously renew my mind by putting on Jesus to glorify God.* Eph 4:21 ... As the truth is in Jesus: 22 *I* put off concerning the former conversation the old man, which is corrupt according to the deceitful lusts; 23 and *am* renewed in the spirit of *my* mind; 24 *by putting* on the new man, which after God is created in righteousness and true holiness. *My true, born-again nature is to walk just like Jesus, knowing* Rom 13:10 agape/love worketh no ill to his neighbour: therefore *agape*/love is the fulfilling of the law. 11 And that, knowing the time, that now it is high time to awake out of sleep: for now is *my soteria*/salvation nearer than when *I* believed. 12 The night is far spent, the day is at hand: *I* therefore *continuously* cast off the works of darkness, and ... *I continuously* put on the armour of light. 13 *I continuously walk* honestly, as in the day; not in rioting and drunkenness, not in chambering and wantonness, not in strife and envying. 14 *I continuously* put on the Lord Jesus Christ, and make not provision for the flesh, to fulfil the lusts thereof. *I continuously strive to walk in Holy Spirit, for* 2 Cor 3:17 now the Lord is that Spirit: and where the Spirit of the Lord is, there is liberty *to be all I am in God.* 18 *So I,* with open face beholding as in a glass *(mirror), seeing myself filled with* the glory of the Lord, *I am* changed into the same image from glory to glory, even as by the Spirit of the Lord. *I* Col 3:9 lie *to no one,* seeing that I have put off the old man with his deeds; 10 and have put on the new man, which is renewed in knowledge after the image of *Father God* that created *me anew in Jesus*: 11 where there is neither Greek nor Jew, circumcision nor uncircumcision, Barbarian, Scythian, bond nor free: but Christ is all, and in all. *I* 12 put on therefore, as the elect of God, holy and *agape*/beloved, bowels of mercies, kindness, humbleness of mind, meekness, longsuffering; 13 forbearing one another, and forgiving one another, if any man have a quarrel against any: even as Christ forgave *me*, so also do *I*. 14 And above all these things *I put* on *agape*/charity, which is the bond of perfectness. 15 And *I let* the peace of God rule in *my heart*, to the which also *I am* called in one body; and *I am* thankful. 16 *I* let the word of Christ dwell in *me* richly in all wisdom; teaching and admonishing *myself and* one another in psalms and hymns and spiritual songs, singing with grace in *my heart* to the Lord. 17 And, *by the grace of God working in me,* whatsoever *I* do in word or deed, *I* do all in the name of the Lord Jesus, giving thanks to God and the Father by him. 1 Cor 15:10 For by the grace of God I am what I am: and his grace which was bestowed upon me was not in vain; but I *labor* more abundantly than they all: yet not I, but the grace of God which *is* with me. *Thank You, Father God, Father of Lights, Father of Love and Truth! Thank You, in the name of Jesus! Thank You! Glory to Your goodness to me in Jesus!*

S. **By the grace of God working in me** I Phil 2:3 let nothing be done through strife or vainglory; but in lowliness of mind *I esteem others* better than *myself*. 4 *I* look … on *mine* own things, but … also on the things of others. 5 *I* let this mind be in *me* which was also in Christ Jesus: 6 who, being in the form of God, thought it not robbery to be equal with God: 7 but made himself of no reputation, and took upon him the form of a servant, and was made in the likeness of men: 8 and being found in fashion as a man, he humbled himself, and became obedient unto death, even the death of the cross. … 12 Wherefore, *as one of the agape*/beloved, as *I* always *obey, I* work out *my* own *soteria*/salvation with fear and trembling. 13 For it is God which worketh in *me* both to will and to do of his good pleasure. 14 *I* do all things without murmurings and disputings: 15 that *I* may be blameless and harmless, *a son* of God, without rebuke, in the midst of a crooked and perverse nation, among whom *I* shine as *a light* in the world; 16 holding forth the word of *zoe*/life; that I may rejoice in the day of Christ, that I have not run in vain, neither laboured in

The Minister's Confession

vain. Phil 3:8 Yea ... I count all things *of this world* but loss for the excellency of the knowledge of Christ Jesus my Lord: ... that I may win Christ, 9 and be found in him, not having mine own righteousness, which is of the law *or works*, but that which is through the faith of Christ, the righteousness which is of God by faith: [*and not by the holiness which I walk in more of every day*]. 10 That I may know him, and the power of his resurrection, and the fellowship of his sufferings, being made conformable unto his death; 11 if by any means I might attain unto the resurrection of the dead. 12 Not as though I had already attained, either were already perfect: but I follow after, if that I may apprehend that for which also I am apprehended of Christ Jesus. 13 ... I count not myself to have apprehended: but this one thing I do, forgetting those things which are behind, and reaching forth unto those things which are before, 14 I press toward the mark for the prize of the high calling of God in Christ Jesus. *I delight to do Your will, O God! Praise to You! I am* agape/*loved by You forever!*

T. 1 Pet 1:13 **Wherefore,** *in cooperation with Holy Spirit,* **I gird** up the loins of *my* mind, *am* sober, and hope to the end for the grace that is to be brought unto *me* at the revelation of Jesus Christ; 14 as *an* obedient *child*, not fashioning *myself* according to the former lusts in *my* ignorance: 15 but as he which hath called *me* is holy, so *I am* holy in all manner of conversation; 16 because it is written, Be ye holy; for I am holy. *And, Father, in the name of Jesus, keep me* Eph 6:10 ... strong in *You*, and in the power of *Your* might. *To* 11 *continuously keep* on *Your* whole armour, *Father* God, that *I* may be able to stand against the wiles of the devil. 12 For *I* wrestle not against flesh and blood, but against principalities, against powers, against the rulers of the darkness of this world, against spiritual wickedness in high places. 13 Wherefore *I keep* unto *myself* the whole armour of *You, Father* God, that *I* may be able to withstand in the evil day, and having done all, to stand. 14 *I* stand therefore, *keeping my* loins girt about with truth, and *keeping* on the breastplate of righteousness; 15 and *keeping my* feet shod with the preparation of the gospel of peace; 16 above all, *keeping* the shield of faith, wherewith *I* shall be able to quench all the fiery darts of the wicked. 17 And *keeping* the helmet of *soteria*/salvation, and the sword of the Spirit, which is the word of God: 18 praying always with all prayer and supplication in the Spirit, and watching thereunto with all perseverance and supplication for all saints; 19 and *I pray, Father, in the name of Jesus, that* utterance may be given unto me, that I may open my mouth boldly, to make known the mystery of the gospel, 20 ... that therein I may speak boldly, as I ought to speak. 2 Cor 10:3 For though we walk in the flesh, we do not war after the flesh: 4 (for the weapons of our warfare are not carnal, but mighty through *You, Father* God, to the pulling down of strong holds;) 5 casting down imaginations, and every high thing that exalteth itself against the knowledge of *You, Father* God, *and* bringing into captivity every thought to the obedience of Christ; 6 and having in a readiness to revenge all disobedience, when *my* obedience is fulfilled. 2 Tim 1:2 ... Grace, mercy, and peace, from God the Father and Christ Jesus our Lord *to me*. ... 6 Wherefore I put *myself* in *continual* remembrance that *I* stir up the gift of God, which is in *me* ... . 7 For God hath not given *me* the spirit of fear; but of *dunamis*/power *(ability),* and of *agape*/love, and of a sound mind, *to think and do as Jesus would*. ... 12 for I know whom I have believed, and am persuaded that he is able to keep that which I have committed unto him against that day. *I therefore* 13 hold fast the form of sound words, which *I have* heard of [*the Gospel*], in faith and *agape*/love which is in Christ Jesus. *For Jesus commanded*: Luke 10:19 Behold, I give unto you power *(authority, commission and the resources of Heaven)* to tread on serpents and scorpions, and over all the power of the enemy: and nothing shall by any means hurt you. 20 Notwithstanding in this rejoice not, that the spirits are subject unto you; but rather rejoice, because your names are written in heaven. 2 Tim 2:14 Of these things *I* put *(myself and those that hear me)* in remembrance, charging *all of us* before the Lord that *we* strive not about words to no profit, but to the subverting of the hearers. *I* 15 study *(in thoughtful and diligent labor)* to shew *myself* approved unto God, a workman that needeth not to be ashamed [*by grace in Holy Spirit of wisdom and revelation in the knowledge of Him, with the eyes of my understanding being enlightened to*] rightly dividing the word of truth. ... 23 But foolish and unlearned questions *I* avoid, knowing that they do gender strifes. 24 And, *I, as a* servant of the Lord, *do* not strive; but *am* gentle unto all men, apt to teach, patient, 25 in meekness instructing those that oppose themselves; if God peradventure will give them repentance to the acknowledging of the truth; 26 and that they may recover themselves out of the snare of the devil, who are taken captive by him at his will. John 8:31 *For I believe on Jesus, and I continue in His* Word, *so I am one of His* disciples indeed; 32 and *I, by Spirit of Truth,* shall know the truth, and the truth shall make *me* free, *to be and do all that Father has for me*. *For* 2 Tim 3:16 all scripture is given by inspiration of God, and is profitable for doctrine, for reproof, for correction, for instruction in righteousness: 17 that *I, as a* man/woman of God, may be perfect, throughly furnished unto all good works. 1 John 5:11 *I believe the witness of God in His Son Jesus and no longer call God a liar but only true in all things,* ... that God hath given to us eternal *zoe*/life, and this *zoe*/life is in his Son. 13 ... *I* know that *I* have eternal *zoe*/life, and that *I* may believe on the name of the Son of God. *So, Father, keep me in Your Spirit of wisdom and understanding in You so that if none go with me, I know that* 2 Tim 4:17 notwithstanding the Lord *stands* with me, and *strengthens*

The Minister's Confession

me; that by me the preaching might be fully known, and that all *men* might hear [*unto glad obedience the glorious gospel of Christ in us the hope of glory*]: and *I am* delivered out of the mouth of the lion. 18 And the Lord shall deliver me from every evil work, and will preserve me unto his heavenly kingdom: to whom be glory for ever and ever. Amen. Rom 15:17 I ... glory through Jesus Christ in those things which pertain to God. 18 ... To make *all men* obedient, by word and deed, 19 through mighty signs and wonders, by the power of the Spirit of God; so that from *home and into all the world I* fully *preach* the gospel of Christ, Mark 16:20 ... the Lord working with *me*, and confirming the word [*of His grace*] with signs following. Amen. 1 Tim 1:17 Now unto the King eternal, immortal, invisible, the only wise God, be honour and glory for ever and ever. Amen. Jude 24 Now unto him that is able to keep *me and is keeping me* from falling, and to present *me* faultless before the presence of his glory with exceeding joy, 25 to the only wise God our Saviour, be glory and majesty, dominion and power, both now and ever. Amen. *Yahoo! Jesus, You are in me. Hallelujah! Thank You, Father God, in the name of Jesus, Thank You!*

U. **For I know** Eph 5:8 *I was* sometimes darkness, but now *by the new creation, I am* light in the Lord: *by the grace of God ever with me, I* walk as *a child* of light: 9 *and continually grow* the fruit of the Spirit ... in all goodness and righteousness and truth. [Gal 5:22 For the fruit of the Spirit is *agape*/love, joy, peace, longsuffering, gentleness, goodness, faith, 23 meekness, temperance: against such there is no law. 24 And, *because I am* Christ's, I have crucified the flesh with the affections and lusts. 25 *So I ever grow in living* in the Spirit, *so I also* walk in the Spirit. 26 *I am* not desirous of vain glory, *I do not* provoke one another *to evil but to do* agape/love, *I do not* envy *others*.] *Instead, I walk in* agape/*love and am continually* 10 proving *and demonstrating* what is acceptable unto the Lord. 11 And *I* have no fellowship with the unfruitful works of darkness, but rather *I* reprove them. 12 For it is a shame even to speak of those things which are done of them in secret. 13 *For I know* all things that are reproved are made manifest by the light: for whatsoever doth make manifest is light. 14 Wherefore he saith, Awake thou that sleepest, and arise from the dead, and Christ shall give thee light. *So I readily acknowledge my sins as purged in Jesus, make any right restitutions or reconciliations, give grace to others and receive my healing given two thousand (2000) years ago.* 15 *So I* walk circumspectly, not as *a rebel or a fool*, but as wise *unto God, knowing the wisdom of God is greater than silver or jewels; so I grow continually in wisdom, knowledge and understanding, and am constantly* 16 redeeming the time, because the days are evil. 17 Wherefore *I am* not unwise, but understanding what the will of the Lord is. 18 And *I do* not *get* drunk with wine, wherein is excess; but *I am continually being* filled with the Spirit; 19 speaking to *myself and others* in psalms and hymns and spiritual songs, singing and making melody in *my* heart to the Lord; 20 giving thanks always for all things unto God and the Father in the name of our Lord Jesus Christ; 21 submitting *myself*; one to another in the fear of God. Eph 4:20 For *I have so* learned Christ; 21 ... as the truth is in Jesus: 22 that *I continually* put off concerning the former conversation the old man, which is corrupt according to the deceitful lusts; 23 and *am continually* renewed in the spirit of *my* mind *in the Word of Christ and my new creation*; 24 and *I continually* put on, *and stay in* the new *creation* man, which after God is created in righteousness and true holiness. 25 Wherefore putting away lying, *I* speak ... truth with *my every* neighbour: for we are members one of another. *And I work and live zealously in doing good works, in faith working by* agape/love, *to the glory of God the Father, through Jesus, my Lord, by His Spirit. Whenever fear, doubt or unbelief comes on me I am* Phil 4:6 ... careful for nothing (*I do not tolerate fear or anxiety in anything, even though they seem logical and real*); but in every thing by prayer and supplication with thanksgiving *I* let *my* aiteo/requests be made known unto God [*by proclaiming His promises and* aiteo/*asking, by requiring, demanding and expecting as due by covenant promise His answer unto joyful thanksgiving, for I* lambano/*receive it, knowing I will possess it*]. 7 And the peace of God, which passeth all understanding, *keeps my heart and mind* through Christ Jesus. 8 Finally, *and above all else* ... , whatsoever things are **true**, whatsoever things are **honest**, whatsoever things are **just**, whatsoever things are **pure**, whatsoever things are **lovely**, whatsoever things are of **good report**; if there be any **virtue**, and if there be any **praise**, *I* think on these things *constantly*. *Grace and peace to victory is in me from God my Father,* Rev 1:5 and from Jesus Christ, who is the faithful witness, and the first begotten of the dead, and the prince of the kings of the earth. Unto him that *agape*/loved us, and washed us from our sins in his own blood, 6 and hath made us kings and priests unto God and his Father; to him be glory and dominion for ever and ever. Amen. Rev 5:9 And they sung a new song, saying, Thou art worthy to take the book, and to open the seals thereof: for thou wast slain, and hast redeemed us to God by thy blood out of every kindred, and tongue, and people, and nation; 10 and hast made us unto our God kings and priests: and we shall reign on the earth. (Rom 5:17 ... *For I hold on to, cling to and will not let go, I lambano/ receive abundance of grace and of the [permanent] gift of righteousness ...*) ... 12 Saying with a loud voice, Worthy is the Lamb that was slain to receive power, and riches, and wisdom, and strength, and honour, and glory, and blessing. *Thank You, Father! Lord, be magnified! Blessed be the name of the Lord! Praise to You, Lord Jesus Christ, and Your mighty work, for You got the job done, to the glory of God our Father! Hallelujah!*

The Minister's Confession

V. Father, I thank You that You are getting me to rest in You and believe that as I *aiteo*, I do trust that You hear me, Jesus hears me and Holy Spirit hears me, and I believe You because You said whatever I *aiteo*/ask in the name of Jesus, Jesus will do. I do not just try, but I do trust You to honor Your Word. I will have what I *aiteo* in the name of Jesus because You *agape*/love people and cannot lie. I speak to the mountains and You do move them in Your covenant promises. I do rest in You to fulfill Your Word on my lips and in my heart. Thank You! Oh, God of truth and without iniquity, thank You!

W. I know and give thanks in the wonder that I am given the Spirit of Jesus to be just like Jesus, a vessel of God's love to man. Gal 4:6 And because ye are sons, God hath sent forth the Spirit of his Son into our hearts, crying, Abba (*Daddy*), Father. Gal 3:26 For ye are all the children (*sons*) of God by faith in Christ Jesus. Gal 2:20 I am (*have been*) crucified with Christ: nevertheless I *zao*/live *the* zoe/*life of Jesus*; yet not I, but Christ *zao*/liveth in me *to walk like He walked*: and the life which I now *zao*/live *of Jesus'* agape in the flesh I *zao*/live *the nature of Jesus* by the faith of the Son of God, who *agape*/loved me, and gave himself for me. 21 I do not frustrate the grace of God: for if righteousness come by the law, then Christ is dead in vain. Rom 5:1 Therefore being justified by faith, *I* have peace with God through our Lord Jesus Christ: 2 by whom also *I* have access by faith into this grace wherein *I* stand, and rejoice in hope of the glory of God. 2 Cor 5:21 For *Father God* hath made *Jesus* to be sin for us, who knew no sin; that we might be made the righteousness of God in him. 2 Cor 1:19 For the Son of God, Jesus Christ, who was preached ... by Paul ... was not yea and nay, but in him was yea. 20 For all the promises of God in him are yea, and in him Amen, unto the glory of God by us. 21 Now he which stablisheth *me* in Christ, and hath anointed *me*, is God; 22 who hath also sealed me, and given the earnest of the Spirit in *my heart*. Thus Isa 11:2 ... the spirit of the Lord *rests* upon *me in Jesus*, the spirit of wisdom and understanding, the spirit of counsel and might, the spirit of knowledge and of the fear of the Lord; 3 and *makes me* of quick understanding in the fear of the Lord: and *I do* not judge after the sight of *my* eyes, neither reprove after the hearing of *my* ears: 4 but with righteousness *I* judge the poor, and reprove with equity for the meek of the earth: and *I* smite the earth with the rod of *my* mouth, and with the breath of *my* lips *I* slay the wicked. 5 And righteousness shall be the girdle of *my* loins, and faithfulness the girdle of *my* reins. Luke 4:18 The Spirit of the Lord is upon me, because he hath anointed me to preach the gospel to the poor; he hath sent me to heal the brokenhearted, to preach deliverance to the captives, and recovering of sight to the blind, to set at liberty them that are bruised, 19 to preach the acceptable year of the Lord. *I preach that*: Acts 13:38 Be it known unto you therefore, men and brethren, that through this man (*Jesus*) is preached unto you the forgiveness (*remission, purging, obliteration and putting away*) of sins: 39 and by him all that believe are justified from all things, from which ye could not be justified by the law of Moses. Acts 10:38 … God *has* anointed *me in* Jesus of Nazareth with the Holy Ghost and with power: so *I* go about doing good, and healing all that are oppressed (*under the active rule and lordship*) of the devil; for God is with *me*. Acts 10:43 To him (*Jesus*) give all the prophets witness, that through his name whosoever believeth in him shall receive remission (*purging, obliteration and putting away*) of sins. *And God is with me* Acts 26:18 to open *the* eyes *of all mankind*, and to turn them from darkness to light, and from the power of Satan unto God, that they may receive forgiveness (*remission, purging, obliteration and putting away*) of sins, and inheritance among them which are sanctified by faith that is in *Jesus*. Gal 3:27 For as many of us as have been baptized into Christ have put on Christ. *I renew my mind by putting on Jesus to glorify God*. Eph 4:21 … As the truth is in Jesus: 22 *I* put off concerning the former conversation the old man, which is corrupt according to the deceitful lusts; 23 and *am* renewed in the spirit of *my* mind; 24 by putting on the new man, which after God is created in righteousness and true holiness. *Knowing* Rom 13:10 *agape*/love worketh no ill to his neighbour: therefore *agape*/love is the fulfilling of the law. 11 And that, knowing the time, that now it is high time to awake out of sleep: for now is *my soteria*/salvation nearer than when *I* believed. 12 The night is far spent, the day is at hand: *I* therefore cast off the works of darkness, and … put on the armour of light. 13 *I* walk honestly, as in the day; not in rioting and drunkenness, not in chambering and wantonness, not in strife and envying. 14 *I* put on the Lord Jesus Christ (*in my self-concept*), and make not provision for the flesh, to fulfil the lusts thereof. Col 3:9 *I* lie to *no one*, seeing [*in the new birth*], that *I* have put off the old man with his deeds; 10 and have put on the new man, which is renewed in knowledge after the image of him that created him: 11 where there is neither Greek nor Jew, circumcision nor uncircumcision, Barbarian, Scythian, bond nor free: but Christ is all, and in all. 12 *I* put on (*in my mind and attitude*) therefore, as the elect of God, holy and *agape*/beloved, bowels of mercies, kindness, humbleness of mind, meekness, longsuffering; 13 forbearing one another, and forgiving one another, if any man have a quarrel against any: even as Christ forgave *me*, so also do *I*. 14 And above all these things *I* put on *agape*/charity, which is the bond of perfectness. 15 And *I* let the peace of God rule in *my heart*, to the which also *I am* called in one body; and *I am* thankful. 16 *I* let the word of Christ dwell in *me* richly in all wisdom; teaching and admonishing *myself and* one another in psalms and hymns and spiritual songs, singing with grace in *my heart* to the Lord. 17 And [*by the grace of God working in me*] whatsoever *I* do in word or deed, *I* do all in the name of the Lord Jesus, giving thanks to God and the Father by him. Phil 3:8 Yea … I count all things of this world but loss for the excellency of the knowledge of Christ Jesus my Lord: … that I may win Christ, 9 and be found in him, not having mine own righteousness, which is of the law *or works*, but that which is through the faith of Christ, the righteousness which is of God by faith: 10 that I may know him, and the power of his resurrection, and the fellowship of his sufferings, being made conformable unto his death; 11 if by any means I might attain unto the resurrection of the dead. 12 Not as though I had already attained, either were already perfect: but I follow after, if that I may apprehend that for which also I am apprehended of Christ Jesus. 13 … I count not myself to have apprehended: but this one thing I do, forgetting those things which are behind, and reaching forth unto those things which are before, 14 I press toward the mark for the prize of the high calling of God in Christ Jesus. Jude 24 Now unto him that is able to keep *me* from falling, and to present *me* faultless before the presence of his glory with exceeding joy, 25 to the only wise God our Saviour, be glory and majesty, dominion and power, both now and ever. Amen. *Lord, glorify Your name through me! Thank You, Father, in the name of Jesus, thank You!*

X. **Father, in the name of Jesus, the Baptizer** with Holy Spirit and fire, give abundant manifestations of Your Spirit, including words of wisdom, knowledge, faith, healings, working of miracles, prophecy, discerning of spirits, diverse kinds of tongues, interpretation of tongues, dead raising, creative restorations, wholeness and special miracles and works. Stir me that I 1 Cor 12:31 … covet earnestly *unto effective faith* the best gifts: *and walk by Your Spirit in the* more excellent way *of* agape/love. So that I 1 Cor 14:1 follow after *agape/*charity, and desire spiritual gifts, but rather that *I* may prophesy *to the edification of the church. And devote myself to prayer and the ministry of the Word, in the unity of the Spirit, in the bond of peace. Father, teach me to walk in the glad assurance that I have the same Spirit You gave Jesus, so that I gladly confess,* 2 Cor 13:5 *knowing* …that Jesus Christ is in *me, as by Your grace I am not reprobate* (*useless in my faith in You, Father God*), *but I am proclaiming*: Luke 4:18 The Spirit of the Lord is upon me, because he hath anointed me to preach the gospel to the poor; he hath sent me to heal the brokenhearted, to preach deliverance to the captives, and recovering of sight to the blind, to set at liberty them that are bruised, 19 to preach the acceptable year of the Lord. 2 Cor 6:2 (For he saith, I have heard thee in a time accepted, and in the day of *soteria*/salvation have I succoured thee: behold, now is the accepted time; behold, now is the day of *soteria*/salvation.) Acts 10:38 How *that You, Father* God, *anoint us in* Jesus of Nazareth with the Holy Ghost and with power: *so we go* about doing good, and healing all that *are* oppressed (*under the active reign and lordship*) of the devil; for *You, Father* God *are* with *us in Jesus just like You are with Jesus.* 1 John 4:17 Herein is our *agape*/love made perfect, that we may have boldness in the day of judgment: because as he is, so are we in this world. *For* 1 John 4:4 ye are of God, little children, and have overcome them: because greater is he that is in you, than he that is in the world. *And, Father, get me to know that* Gal 4:3 even so we, when we were children, were in bondage under the elements of the world: 4 but when the fulness of the time was come, *You, Father* God, sent forth *Your* Son, made of a woman, made under the law, 5 to redeem them that were under the law, that we might receive the adoption of sons. 6 And because *we* are sons, *You, Father* God, *have* sent forth the Spirit of *Your* Son into *our* hearts, crying, Abba, (*Daddy*) Father. 7 Wherefore *I am* no more a servant, but a son; and if a son, then an heir of *You, Father* God, through Christ. *Father, reveal the glory of Your inheritance in us that* Phil 3:14 *we* press toward the mark for the prize of the high calling of *You, Father* God, in Christ Jesus, *so that we walk in Your total and complete remission in Jesus, that we might* agape/love *You totally. For Jesus said*: John 17:22 And the glory which thou gavest me I have given them; that they may be one, even as we are one: 23 I in them, and thou in me, that they may be made perfect in one; and that the world may know that thou hast sent me, and hast *agape*/loved them, as thou hast *agape*/loved me. Rom 15:6 That *we* may with one mind and one mouth glorify God, even *You*, the Father of our Lord Jesus Christ. 7 Wherefore receive *we* one another, as Christ also received us to the glory of God. 1 Cor 10:31 Whether therefore *we* eat, or drink, or whatsoever *we* do, *we* do all to the glory of God. *Father, give us Your Spirit of wisdom and revelation in the knowledge of You, that we might behold Your glory in the face of Jesus in us, that we might be changed.* 2 Cor 3:17 Now the Lord is that Spirit: and where the Spirit of the Lord is, there is liberty. 18 But we all, with open face beholding as in a glass (*mirror*) the glory of the Lord, are changed into the same image from glory to glory, even as by the Spirit of the Lord. *And, Father, keep us so that we* 2 Cor 4:5 …preach not ourselves, but Christ Jesus the Lord; and ourselves *as* servants for Jesus' sake. 6 For God, who commanded the light to shine out of darkness, hath shined in our hearts, to give the light of the knowledge of the glory of God in the face of Jesus Christ. 7 But we have this treasure in earthen vessels, that the excellency of the power may be of God, and not of us. *Father, in the name of Jesus, give me Your Spirit of wisdom and revelation in the knowledge of You, with the eyes of my understanding being enlightened, so that I,* Eph 6:10 finally, *as one of the* brethren, *am* strong in *You,* and in the power of *Your* might, *that I* 11 put

The Minister's Confession

on the whole armour of God, that *I* may be able to stand against the wiles of the devil, *knowing* 12 *that* we wrestle not against flesh and blood, but against principalities, against powers, against the rulers of the darkness of this world, against spiritual wickedness in high places. 13 Wherefore *I* take unto *myself* the whole armour of God, that *I* may be able to withstand in the evil day, and having done all, to stand. *So I resist the devil, knowing he will flee from me as I* 14 stand therefore, having *my* loins girt about with truth, and having on the breastplate of righteousness; 15 and *my* feet shod with the preparation of the gospel of peace; 16 above all, taking the shield of faith, wherewith *I* shall be able to quench all the fiery darts of the wicked. 17 And *continually taking* the helmet of *soteria*/salvation, and the sword of the Spirit, which is the word of God: *so that I am* 18 praying always with all prayer and supplication in the Spirit, and watching thereunto with all perseverance and supplication for all saints; 19 and for *all preachers*, that utterance may be given unto *us*, that *we* may open *our mouths* boldly, to make known the mystery of the gospel, 20 … that therein *we* may speak boldly, as *we* ought to speak. <u>2 Thes 1:11</u> Wherefore *I pray* that *You, Father*, our God, would count *me* worthy of this calling, and fulfil all the good pleasure of *Your* goodness, and the work of faith with power: 12 that the name of our Lord Jesus Christ may be glorified in *me*, and *me* in him, according to the grace of our God and the Lord Jesus Christ. *Thank You, Father, in the name of Jesus Christ, thank You! Hallelujah! Jesus is Lord!*

Y. **Father, You have shown Yourself as He who raises the dead.** When the widow's son died, Your prophet Elijah called on You: <u>1 Kings 17:20</u> "And he cried unto the LORD, and said, O LORD my God, hast thou also brought evil upon the widow with whom I sojourn, by slaying her son?" And Your resounding answer was NO! And then You commanded one who thought like You to pray until that boy was raised. Father, in the name of Jesus, You know where I am, what I have done, what You can do through me, and that You have made me one of Your own through Jesus Christ my Lord. Make me one who You can think and fight through to heal the sick, raise the dead, cleanse the lepers, cast out devils and proclaim and deliver freedom to the lawful and unlawful prisoners of any kind. I want to be one whom You can work with and through. Be my strength, my courage, my help, my wisdom and my *agape*/love in Your work. Just as when the man of God, Elijah, demanded the last water and food of the widow You had commanded to house and feed him, and she faced her fears and put her eyes on You and Your supply. She gave Elijah her last, and they were all fed, as You promised, for a whole year. In the same way, teach me to face my fears of lack and not enough so that I look to You rather than the situation. And when I start to sink, as I look at circumstances, just as Peter did, as he walked on the water with Jesus, send me Your living Word that picks me up and gets me back on and in You. I proclaim my testimony is: Ps 107:20 "He sent his word, and healed them, and delivered them from their destructions. 21 Oh ... *and I* praise the LORD for his *chesed*/goodness, and for his wonderful works to the children of men! 22 And *I* sacrifice the sacrifices of thanksgiving, and declare his works with rejoicing." Heb 13:15 "By *Jesus Christ I* therefore ... offer the sacrifice of praise to *You, Father* God, continually, that is, the fruit of *my* lips, giving thanks to *Your* name. 16 *And I* do good and *do* communicate *in good and generous works and deliver Your salvation to all those in need, especially those in need of healing, I* forget not: for with such sacrifices *I know You, Father* God, *are* well pleased." Father, Your anointing abides on me and teaches me to walk like Jesus. For 1 John 2:27 "... the anointing which *I* have received of *You, Father,* abideth in *me,* and *I* need not that any man teach *me, so I look to You, teaching me through Your Word and Your teachers for me*: but as the same anointing teacheth *me* of all things, and is truth, and is no lie, and even as it hath taught *me to renew my mind, I* shall abide in *You, as I walk in You, knowing*: 1 Cor 1:21 "Now he, which stablisheth us ... in Christ, and hath anointed us, is *You, Father* God; 22 who hath also sealed us, and given the earnest of the Spirit in our hearts." And I 1 John 3:1 "behold, what manner of *agape*/love *You,* the Father, *have* bestowed upon us, that we should be called the sons of *You, Father* God: therefore the world knoweth us not, because it knew *Jesus* not. *As the* 2 *agape*/beloved, now are we the sons of *You, Father* God, and it doth not yet appear what we shall be: but we know that, when *Jesus* shall appear, we shall be like him; for we shall see him as he is. 3 And every man that hath this hope in him purifieth himself, even as he is pure." So, Father, as I work out my own salvation in fear and trembling, to purify myself by Your grace, I know, Gal 2:19 "for I through the law am dead to the law, that I might *zao*/live unto *You, Father* God, *just as Jesus did for*: 20 I am *(have been)* crucified with Christ: nevertheless I *zao*/live; yet not I, but Christ *zao*/liveth in me: and the life which I now *zao*/live in the flesh I *zao*/live by the faith of the Son of God, who *agape*/loved me, and gave himself for me. 21 I do not frustrate the grace of *You, Father* God: for if righteousness come by the law, then Christ is dead in vain." Father, in the name of Jesus, Deut 31:6 "*I am* strong (*in Your strength for me*) and of a good courage (*in my heart*), *I* fear not (*by considering only failure*), nor *am I* afraid (*or allow myself to be harassed by the evil power*) of *any evil situation or people*: for *You, Father,* the LORD *my* God, *You* it is that *do* go with *me, You* will not fail *me,* nor forsake *me.*" In the name of Jesus, I take authority over and command all evil fear to leave me now, and I command my inner man to rise up and think the thoughts of God and His goodness toward me. Father, by Your grace, 2 Cor

The Minister's Confession

<u>10:3</u> "for though *I* walk in the flesh, *I* do not war after the flesh: 4 (for the weapons of *my* warfare are not carnal, but mighty through *You, Father* God, to the pulling down of strong holds;) 5 casting down imaginations, and every high thing that exalteth itself against the knowledge of *You, Father* God, and bringing into captivity *my* every thought to the obedience of Christ," to stop all evil thoughts and only allow myself to <u>Phil 4:4</u> "rejoice in the Lord alway: and again I say, Rejoice. 5 *I let my* moderation be known unto all men. *For I am continually knowing the* Lord is at hand (*in power and authority*). 6 *I am* careful for nothing; but in every thing by prayer and supplication with thanksgiving *I* let *my aiteo*/requests be made known unto God. 7 And the peace of God, which passeth all understanding, shall keep *my heart* and *mind* through Christ Jesus. 8 Finally, *as one of the* brethren *in the Lord*, whatsoever things are **true**, whatsoever things are **honest**, whatsoever things are **just**, whatsoever things are **pure**, whatsoever things are **lovely**, whatsoever things are of **good report**; if there be any **virtue**, and if there be any **praise**, *I only* think on these things. 9 Those things, which *I* have both learned, and received, and heard, and seen in *Jesus and of God's goodness in the Scriptures*, *I* do: and the God of peace *to victory over any oppression, reign or lordship of the devil* shall be with *and operate in me*." And You are released by me, as I control my mind to think like You, my Father God. So when I am harassed with dreadful fear, I fill my mind with confidence in You, Father, and Your goodness toward me. For I am saved by Your grace, Father God, through faith, and I am made Your righteousness in Jesus, to be an imitator of You in Jesus. Praise You, Father, that You get me to cooperate more and more with Holy Spirit to *zao*/live the *zoe*/life of Jesus in me to Your good pleasure. Thank You, Father, in the Name of Jesus, thank You! Hallelujah! Jesus is Lord! Jesus, You are mighty, awesome and wonderful! Glory to You! Jesus, You are Lord! Yahoo!

Z. **I am born again** after the image of Father God in Christ Jesus, and I delight to do the will of God. Anything in me that resists the will of God is not of me, and Father, in the name of Jesus, build in me to <u>Rom 6:3</u> **know** … that so many of us as were baptized into Jesus Christ were baptized into his death. 4 Therefore we are buried with him by baptism into death: that like as Christ was raised up from the dead by the glory of *You, the Father*, even so we also should walk in newness of *zoe*/life *now*. 5 For if we have been planted together in the likeness of his death, we shall be also in the likeness of his resurrection: *Father, build in me the* 6 **knowing** this, that our old man is crucified with him, that the body of sin might be destroyed, that henceforth we should not serve sin. 7 For he that is dead is freed from sin. 8 Now if we be dead with Christ, we believe that we shall also *zao*/live with him. *Build in me the* 9 **knowing** that Christ being raised from the dead dieth no more; death hath no more dominion over him. 10 For in that he died, he died unto sin once: but in that he *zao*/liveth, he *zao*/liveth unto *You, Father* God. 11 Likewise *I* **reckon** *myself* to be dead indeed unto sin, but *zao*/alive unto *You, Father* God, through Jesus Christ *my* Lord. 12 *I* let not sin therefore reign in my mortal body. *Rather, by the grace of You, Father God, I acknowledge my sins and all works of the devil in me, and I therefore* Rom 13:12 … cast off the works and lies of darkness, and put on the armour of light. 13 *I* walk honestly, as in the day; not in rioting and drunkenness, not in chambering and wantonness, not in strife and envying. 14 But *I* put on the Lord Jesus Christ, and make not provision for the flesh, to fulfil the lusts thereof, *and I put on Jesus Christ now. Father God is conforming me to the image of His Son, Jesus Christ, for I renew the spirit of my mind. I delight to do His will in all ways,* Phil 2:15 that *I* may be blameless and harmless, *a son* of God, without rebuke, in the midst of a crooked and perverse nation, among whom *I* shine as a light in the world; 16 holding forth the word of *zoe*/life … . Eph 2:4 *For Father* God, who is rich in mercy, for his great *agape*/love wherewith he *agape*/loved us, 5 even when we were dead in sins, hath quickened us together with Christ, (by grace *am I sozo*/saved;) 6 and hath raised me up together, and made me sit together in heavenly places in Christ Jesus. *So I walk in Father God's righteousness in Christ Jesus, to bring Heaven to Earth in righteousness, peace and joy by* dunamis *power,* agape *love and operate in the mind of Christ, to think, speak and do as Jesus would, no matter where I am.* Col 3:1 "For *I am* risen with Christ, and *I do* seek those things which are above, where Christ sitteth on the right hand of God. 2 *I* set *my* affection on things above, not on things on the earth. 3 For *I am* dead, and *my zoe*/life is hid with Christ in God. Col 2:9 For in Jesus dwelleth all the fulness of the Godhead bodily. 10 And we are complete in him, which is the head of all principality and power: 11 in whom also we are circumcised with the circumcision made without hands, in putting off the body of the sins of the flesh by the circumcision of Christ: 12 buried with him in baptism, wherein also ye are risen with him through the faith of the operation of God, who hath raised him from the dead. *I fear not, and I am not afraid.* Deut 31:6 *I am* strong (*in the Lord's strength for me*) and of a good courage (*in my heart*), *I* fear not (*by considering only failure*), nor *am I* afraid (*or allow myself to be harassed by the evil power*) of the *devil and his agents*: for *You, Father,* the Lord *my* God, *You, O God,* it is *You, Father,* that *do* go with *me; You, Father God,* will not fail *me*, nor forsake *me. By Your grace I* 1 Pet 1:18 … know that *I* was not redeemed with corruptible things, as silver and gold, from *my* vain conversation received by tradition from *my* fathers; 19 but with the precious blood of Christ, as of a lamb without blemish and without spot: 20 who verily was foreordained before the foundation of the world, but was manifest in these last times for *me*, 21 who by him *do* believe in God, that raised him up from the dead, and gave him glory; that *my* faith and hope might be in God. 22 Seeing, *by Your grace, I continually* purify *my soul* in obeying the truth through the Spirit unto unfeigned *phileo*/love of the brethren, *I* see that *I agape*/love one another with a pure heart fervently: 23 being born again, not of corruptible seed, but of incorruptible, by the word of God, which *zao*/liveth and abideth for ever, *knowing* 24 for all flesh is as grass, and all the glory of man as the flower of grass. The grass withereth, and the flower thereof falleth away: 25 but the word of the Lord endureth for ever. *And this is the Word which by the Gospel is preached unto me, and so that I* 2 Pet 3:18 ... grow in grace, and in the knowledge of our Lord and Saviour Jesus Christ. To him be glory both now and for ever. Amen, *and that* Jude 20 ... *I, as agape*/beloved, therefore, *by His Spirit, am continually* building up *myself* on our most holy faith, praying in the Holy Ghost, 21 keeping *myself* in the *agape*/love of *You, Father* God, looking for the mercy of our Lord Jesus Christ unto eternal *zoe*/life: 22 and of some *I* have compassion, making a difference: 23 and others *I sozo*/save with fear, pulling them out of the fire; hating even the garment spotted by the flesh. 24 Now unto him that is able to keep *me* from falling, and to present *me* faultless before the presence of his glory with exceeding joy, 25 to the only wise God our Saviour, be glory and majesty, dominion and power, both now and ever. Amen.

Thank You, Father God, that You set my value as worth the spirit, soul, body and blood of Jesus to redeem me and make me Yours. You *agape*/love me! I am loved! I am *agape*/loved! I am known, chosen, adopted and still *agape*/loved. Thank You, Father! In the name of Jesus, thank You!

Hallelujah! Jesus is Lord! Jesus, You are mighty, awesome and wonderful! Glory to You, Lord Jesus! Hallelujah! *Hallelujah! Hallelujah!*

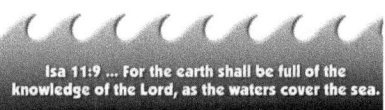
Isa 11:9 ... For the earth shall be full of the knowledge of the Lord, as the waters cover the sea.

Part VI

The Battle Prayer

He sent his word, and healed them, and delivered them from their destructions. 21 Oh that men would praise the Lord for his chesed/goodness, and for his wonderful works to the children of men! (Ps 107:20-21)

~ 1 ~

BEGINNING THE BATTLE PRAYER

Jesus came to do the Father's will, and that included indiscriminate healing of all who had need. John 6:38 "For I (*Jesus*) came down from heaven, not to do mine own will, but the will of him that sent me." Acts 10:38 "How God anointed Jesus of Nazareth with the Holy Ghost and with power: who went about doing good, and healing (*in judgment against the devil*) all that were oppressed (*under the active dominion, reign or lordship*) of the devil; for God was with him." Luke 9:11 "And the people, when they knew it, followed him: and he received them, and spake unto them of the kingdom of God, and healed them that had need of healing."

You can pray or declare the entire Battle Prayer or any portion of it that seems to fit the needs of the situation. The louder or firmer your attitude and voice, especially if from your gut or spirit, the better, as this keeps you focused.

We have been given authority to tread, crush and rule over all the ability of the devil, to destroy all his works, as Jesus decreed: Luke 10:19 "Behold, I give unto you power (*authority, commission and the resources of Heaven*) to tread on serpents and scorpions, and over **all the power (*ability*) of the enemy**: and nothing shall by any means hurt you. 20 Notwithstanding in this rejoice not, that the spirits are subject unto you; but rather rejoice, because your names are written in heaven." Verse 20 makes it clear that even poison in snakes and spiders has a spirit component.

As Jesus demonstrated, command or dominion ministry is effective for healing, casting out demons, providing finances, multiplying food, controlling the weather, moving mountains and even making trees grow in salt water. We do not have authority over people; for that we intercede to the Father. Look at the prayers of Esther or Ezra or that of Paul in Ephesians 1 and 3 and Colossians 1

BATTLE PRAYER FOR DIVINE HEALING: FIELD MANUAL 2

for guidance on intercession for people. Intercession prayers are included in the Battle Prayer.

Here are several ways to use this manual (which from beginning to end takes about 25 hours to read aloud). The Battle Prayer itself takes an hour and a half to 3 hours to read straight through out loud:

a) As a ready reference on how to start praying when in a critical situation and you need a starting place. Go right to the Battle Prayer and start reading and commanding the Battle Prayer out loud. Go through to the end, and then start again if necessary.
b) Use the whole manual as a way to stir yourself up in God.
c) Read the Minister Confessions daily and proclaim them for yourself. Do the same with the other confessions and prayers.
d) Pick specific sections that encourage you and use them as a starting place for proclamation, prayer, mediation or study.
e) For longer periods of prayer, read, command, and pray the entire book out loud, whether at the bedside of a sick person or at a distance. Then repeat as necessary.
f) Use the various prayers as training tools for shorter battles. For example, within the Battle Prayer, prayer No. 1 is a favorite.
g) Use the various sections of the book for encouragement, teaching and preaching on healing, the work of the cross, salvation or prayer.
h) Keep a few short prayers memorized and use them often. You will find yourself getting many healed without the book in hand.
i) Some battles may require someone on continuous faith vigil. Many have reported, in critical cases, especially in emergency or operating room situations, that continuous prayer was necessary until vital signs stabilized or various healing stages occurred. Let the vital sign reports help guide you in how to use this book. Remember: God is your Helper, the devil your enemy, and your weapons include thanksgiving in advance, praise for a victory you do not yet see, the name of Jesus and the Word of God. Keep commanding the various vital signs and healing steps to get better as needed with the attitude that this evil will go and God will be glorified, now.
j) Look for skin color changes as you minister. As the sick person looks better, your ministry is working, and often you are at least half way there. As Jesus said (Matt 26:41) "Watch and pray." Keep at it determined this evil work will go in the name of Jesus, and God will be glorified.
k) For multi-day battles, consider mixing and matching portions of the manual. For example: Read the Minister Confessions, then the Battle Prayer, then pages of the Scriptures, then the Battle Prayer again, and end with a time of thanksgiving and praise. Repeat this until victory comes.
l) Use any 5- to 15-minute portion of the manual as a daily devotional on salvation (healing, finances, prosperity, peace, wholeness in every way).

BEGINNING THE BATTLE PRAYER

m) You will notice in the Battle Prayer that certain words are capitalized, such as JESUS, FREEDOM, NOW, IN THE NAME OF JESUS, etc. This is to help you to focus on shouting that word or at least saying it with great intensity and determination, compared to the other words in the *aiteo* prayer. You want to have the attitude "this must happen and must happen now, so, devil, go and healing be." Before you say this capitalized word or words, you may want to stop and reaffirm in your heart what you are doing. Fill yourself with the hatred of the evil the devil has done, the compassion to set a suffering one free, and the *agape*/love of God that Jesus suffered in intense agony to pay for this healing by His stripes, His bondage in Hell and then His defeat of the devil, when God raised Him from the dead. Say the word from your gut, not casually or with mild interest, but as if you were telling a mean dog to go away by looking it straight in the eye and commanding, "GO!" Speak with authority, determination and intensity, from your spirit. You can even do this silently, by just mouthing the words, but it takes more effort to keep focused. Remember, Jesus healed with His Word as well as with His touch. Matt 8:15 "When the even was come, they brought unto him many that were possessed with devils: and he cast out the spirits with **his word**, and healed all that were sick." This is the same kind of "word" or shout a man makes when he swings an axe to split a log, or a soldier when he swings his sword to cut through the armor and overcome the strength of an enemy. As you learn to do this properly, here is what you will look like in the spirit in this description given of Jesus: Rev 1:13 "And in the midst of the seven candlesticks one like unto the Son of man, clothed with a garment down to the foot, and girt about the paps with a golden girdle. 14 His head and his hairs were white like wool, as white as snow; **and his eyes were as a flame of fire.**" This is the passion of the fire of God in His heart, and you are made after this very same image. Remember, your true condition as a Christian: 1 John 4:17 "Herein is our *agape*/love made perfect, that we may have boldness in the day of judgment: because as he is, so are we in this world." So shout (loudly or softly) with intensity, determination, and compassion. Then, if you can, touch the sick person briefly to a few moments to allow the *zoe*/life flow into them, or, again, utter the command, "LIFE!"

n) If you are not near the person(s) you are ministering to, you can command several times. For example, just as Elijah prayed, praised and affirmed 3 times to raise a dead boy and 8 times to bring the rain, command, "LIFE!" or "LIFE in the name of JESUS!" 8 times. This is just a guideline; the exact number is up to you. Command each "LIFE" with intensity from your gut and not just the top of your lungs or chest. Issue each command as if it were the only command you were to make, and you are totally committed to that command for immediate obedience and full healing.

o) If you are not near the person, keep praying until you are able to confirm what results you are getting. If you barely know the person(s), you can still call them or write and ask how they are doing. Tell them, "I have been praying for you and wanted to see how you were doing. I will keep at it until you are completely healed." Keep checking back once a week, keep asking God to fill you with His love and compassion for them, and keep praying until victory comes.

Faith is deciding God is not a liar and praising Him for His truth.

CONFESSION: Just like Jesus, *I am* given the Spirit of Jesus, to be just like Jesus, a vessel of God's love to mankind: Gal 4:6 And because ye are sons, God hath sent forth the Spirit of his Son into *our* hearts, crying, Abba (*Daddy*), Father. Gal 3:26 For ye are all the children (*sons*) of God by faith in Christ Jesus. Gal 2:20 I am crucified with Christ: nevertheless I *zao*/live *the life of Jesus*; yet not I, but Christ *zao*/liveth in me, *to walk like He walked*: and the life which I now *zao*/live *of Jesus' agape* in the flesh I *zao*/live *the nature of Jesus* by the faith of the Son of God, who *agape*/loved me, and gave himself for me. 21 I do not frustrate the grace of God: for if righteousness come by the law, then Christ is dead in vain. Rom 5:1 Therefore being justified by faith, *I* have peace with God through our Lord Jesus Christ: 2 by whom also *I* have access by faith into this grace wherein *I* stand, and rejoice in hope of the glory of God. 2 Cor 5:21 For *Father God* hath made *Jesus* to be sin for us, who knew no sin; that we might be made the righteousness of God in him. 2 Cor 1:19 For the Son of God, Jesus Christ, who was preached ... by *Paul* ... was not yea and nay, but in him was yea. 20 For all the promises of God in him are yea, and in him Amen, unto the glory of God by us. 21 Now he which stablisheth *me* in Christ, and hath anointed *me*, is God; 22 who hath also sealed *me*, and given the earnest of the Spirit in *my heart. Thus* Isa 11:2 ... the spirit of the LORD *rests upon me in Jesus*, the spirit of wisdom and understanding, the spirit of counsel and might, the spirit of knowledge and of the fear of the LORD; 3 and *makes me* of quick understanding in the fear of the LORD: and *I do* not judge after the sight of *my* eyes, neither reprove after the hearing of *my* ears: 4 but with righteousness *I* judge the poor, and reprove with equity for the meek of the earth: and *I* smite the earth with the rod of *my* mouth, and with the breath of *my* lips *I* slay the wicked. 5 And righteousness shall be the girdle of *my* loins, and faithfulness the girdle of *my* reins. Luke 4:18 The Spirit of the Lord is upon me, because he hath anointed me to preach the gospel to the poor; he hath sent me to heal the brokenhearted, to preach deliverance to the captives, and recovering of sight to the blind, to set at liberty them that are bruised, 19 to preach the acceptable year of the Lord. Acts 13:38 Be it known unto you therefore, men and brethren, that through this man (*Jesus*) is preached unto you the forgiveness (*remission, purging, putting away and obliteration*) of sins: 39 and by him all that believe are justified from all things, from which ye could not be justified by the law of Moses. Acts 10:38 ... God *has* anointed *me in* Jesus of Nazareth with the Holy Ghost and with power: *so I go* about doing good, and healing all that *are* oppressed (*under the active rule and lordship*) of the devil; for God *is* with *me*. Acts 26:18 To open *the* eyes *of all mankind*, and to turn them from darkness to light, and from the power of Satan unto God, that they may receive forgiveness (*remission, purging, putting away and obliteration*) of sins, and inheritance among them which are sanctified by faith that is in *Jesus*. Gal 3:27 For as many of *us* as have been baptized into Christ have put on Christ. *I renew my mind by putting on Jesus to glorify God.* Eph 4:21 ... As the truth is in Jesus: 22 *I* put off concerning the former conversation the old man, which is corrupt according to the deceitful lusts; 23 and *am* renewed in the spirit of *my* mind; 24 *by putting* on the new man, which after God is created in righteousness and true holiness. *Knowing* Rom 13:10 *agape*/love worketh no ill to his neighbour: therefore *agape*/love is the fulfilling of the law. 11 And that, knowing the time, that now it is high time to awake out of sleep: for now is *my soteria*/salvation nearer than when *I* believed. 12 The night is far spent, the day is at hand: *I* therefore cast off the works of darkness, and ... *I* put on the armour of light. 13 *I walk* honestly, as in the day; not in rioting and drunkenness, not in chambering and wantonness, not in strife and envying. 14 *I* put on the Lord Jesus Christ *in my self-concept*, and *I* make not provision for the flesh, to fulfil the lusts thereof. Col 3:9 *I* lie *to no one*, seeing *in the new birth* that I have put off the old man with his deeds; 10 and have put on the new man, which is renewed in knowledge after the image of him that created him: 11 where there is neither Greek nor Jew, circumcision nor uncircumcision, Barbarian, Scythian, bond nor free: but Christ is all, and in all. 12 *I* put on, *in my mind and attitude* therefore, as the elect of God, holy and *agape*/beloved, bowels of mercies, kindness, humbleness of mind, meekness, longsuffering; 13 forbearing one another, and forgiving one another, if any man have a quarrel against any: even as Christ forgave *me*, so also do *I*. 14 And above all these things *I put* on *agape*/charity, which is the bond of perfectness. 15 And *I let* the peace of God rule in *my heart*, to the which also *I am* called in one body; and *I am* thankful. 16 *I* let the word of Christ dwell in *me* richly in all wisdom; teaching and admonishing *myself and* one another in psalms and hymns and spiritual songs, singing with grace in *my heart* to the Lord. 17 And *by the grace of God working in me* whatsoever *I* do in word or deed, *I* do all in the name of the Lord Jesus, giving thanks to God and the Father by him. Phil 3:8 Yea ... I count all things *of this world* but loss for the excellency of the knowledge of Christ Jesus my Lord: ... that I may win Christ, 9 and be found in him, not having mine own righteousness, which is of the law *or works*, but that which is through the faith of Christ, the righteousness which is of God by faith: 10 that I may know him, and the power of his resurrection, and the fellowship of his sufferings, being made conformable unto his death; 11 if by any means I might attain unto the resurrection of the dead. 12 Not as though I had already attained, either were already perfect: but I follow after, if that I may apprehend that for which also I am apprehended of Christ Jesus. 13 ... I count not myself to have apprehended: but this one thing I do, forgetting those things which are behind, and reaching forth unto those things which are before, 14 I press toward the mark for the prize of the high calling of God in Christ Jesus. Jude 24 Now unto him that is able to keep *me* from falling, and to present *me* faultless before the presence of his glory with exceeding joy, 25 to the only wise God our Saviour, be glory and majesty, dominion and power, both now and ever. Amen! *Lord, glorify Your name through me! Thank You, Father! In the name of Jesus, thank You!*

I am born again after the image of Father God in Christ Jesus, and I delight to do the will of God. Anything in me that resists the will of God is not of me, so, Father, in the name of Jesus, build in me to Rom 6:3 **know** ... that so many of us as were baptized into Jesus Christ were baptized into his death. 4 Therefore we are buried with him by baptism into death: that like as Christ was raised up from the dead by the glory of *You*, the Father, even so we also should walk in newness of zoe/life *now*. 5 For if we have been planted together in the likeness of his death, we shall be also in the likeness of his resurrection: *Father, build in me the* 6 **knowing** this, that our old man is crucified with him, that the body of sin might be destroyed, that henceforth we should not serve sin. 7 For he that is dead is freed from sin. 8 Now if we be dead with Christ, we believe that we shall also zao/live with him: *Build in me the* 9 **knowing** that Christ being raised from the dead dieth no more; death hath no more dominion over him. 10 For in that he died, he died unto sin once: but in that he zao/liveth, he zao/liveth unto *You, Father* God. 11 **Likewise *I* reckon** *myself* to be dead indeed unto sin, but zao/alive unto *You, Father* God, through Jesus Christ *my* Lord. 12 *I* let not sin therefore reign in *my* mortal body. *Rather, by Your grace, Father God, I acknowledge my sins and all works of the devil in me, and I therefore* Rom 13:12 ... cast off the works *and lies* of darkness, and put on the armour of light. 13 *Walking* honestly, as in the day; not in rioting and drunkenness, not in chambering and wantonness, not in strife and envying. 14 But *I* put on the Lord Jesus Christ, and make not provision for the flesh, to fulfil the lusts thereof, *and I put on Jesus Christ now. Father God is conforming me to the image of His Son, Jesus Christ, for I renew the spirit of my mind. I delight to do His will in all ways,* Phil 2:15 that *I* may be blameless and harmless, *a* son of God, without rebuke, in the midst of a crooked and perverse nation, among whom *I* shine as *a* light in the world; 16 holding forth the word of zoe/life ... . Col 2:9 For in *Jesus* dwelleth all the fulness of the Godhead bodily. 10 And *we* are complete in him, which is the head of all

Beginning the Battle Prayer

principality and power: 11 in whom also *we* are circumcised with the circumcision made without hands, in putting off the body of the sins of the flesh by the circumcision of Christ: 12 buried with him in baptism, wherein also ye are risen with him through the faith of the operation of God, who hath raised him from the dead. *By Your grace, so I* 1 Pet 1:18 … know that *I was* not redeemed with corruptible things, as silver and gold, from *my* vain conversation received by tradition from *my* fathers; 19 but with the precious blood of Christ, as of a lamb without blemish and without spot: 20 who verily was foreordained before the foundation of the world, but was manifest in these last times for *me*, 21 who by him do believe in God, that raised him up from the dead, and gave him glory; that *my* faith and hope might be in God. 22 Seeing, *by Your grace, I continually purify my soul* in obeying the truth through the Spirit unto unfeigned *phileo*/love of the brethren, *I* see that *I agape*/love one another with a pure heart fervently: 23 being born again, not of corruptible seed, but of incorruptible, by the word of God, which *zao*/liveth and abideth for ever. *Knowing* 24 for all flesh is as grass, and all the glory of man as the flower of grass. The grass withereth, and the flower thereof falleth away: 25 but the word of the Lord endureth for ever. And this is the word which by the gospel is preached unto *me*. *And so that I* 2 Pet 3:18 … grow in grace, and in the knowledge of our Lord and Saviour Jesus Christ. To him be glory both now and for ever. Amen. *And that* Jude 20 … *I, as agape*/beloved, *therefore, by His Spirit, am continually* building up *myself* on *my* most holy faith, praying in the Holy Ghost, 21 *keeping myself* in the *agape*/love of *You, Father* God, looking for the mercy of our Lord Jesus Christ unto eternal *zoe*/life. 22 And of some *I* have compassion, making a difference: 23 and others *I sozo*/save with fear, pulling them out of the fire; hating even the garment spotted by the flesh. 24 Now unto him that is able to keep *me* from falling, and to present *me* faultless before the presence of his glory with exceeding joy, 25 to the only wise God our Saviour, be glory and majesty, dominion and power, both now and ever. Amen.

~ 2 ~

THE BATTLE PRAYER

The exact words of the ministry are not as important as your attitude and intent. This is not about formulas. Besides the name of Jesus and faith in His name by His finished work on the cross, the words simply help adjust your attitude and focus your intent, while the Scriptures help you stay reliant on Father God in His Word. Believe that God will heal the sick you are ministering to totally as you minister healing on His behalf because He *agape*/loves all people, and He paid the awful and total price of sacrificing Jesus for their healing. Jesus gave His body to heal us by His stripes.

Father, in the name of Jesus, have Holy Spirit pray through me now, and fill me with Your dominion, love and compassion for this situation to victory. Thank You, Father! In the name of Jesus, thank You! (This is a place to pray in tongues.)

STIR YOURSELF UP! Speak in tongues loud, fast and strong. Shout (either out loud or under your breath) the Scriptures and commands, as you read the Battle Prayer. Cheer yourself, clap your hands, dance around, speak or sing a favorite psalm or scripture verses. Get strong in your faith and confidence in God that He is the one who heals us and raises the dead and has made you His righteousness in Christ Jesus. (Aim for about 45 minutes or as Holy Spirit leads. Let the peace of God in your heart guide you). Then spend time thanking and praising God for His power in the name of Jesus.

<u>Acts 4:10</u> Be it known unto you [*that not by our holiness, but*] by the name of Jesus Christ of Nazareth [*and faith in that name*], whom ye crucified, whom God

raised from the dead, even by him doth this man stand here before you whole. 11 This is the stone which was set at nought of you builders, which is become the head of the corner. 12 Neither is there *soteria*/salvation in any other: for there is none other name under heaven given among men, whereby we must be *sozo*/saved (*made whole*).

Your battle is not against the person but the source of the disease or sickness. Anything that stands between you and the health of the person (or any promise of God) is a devil. You are not getting the healing, that was accomplished in Jesus by His stripes 2000 years ago, and Holy Spirit is helping you to enforce and deliver that healing already obtained. Our job is to: Eph 6:10 Finally, my brethren, be strong in the Lord, and in the power of his might. 11 Put on the whole armour of God, that ye may be able to stand against the wiles of the devil. 12 For we wrestle not against flesh and blood, but against principalities, against powers, against the rulers of the darkness of this world, against spiritual wickedness in high places. 13 Wherefore take unto you the whole armour of God, that ye may be able to withstand in the evil day, and having done all, to stand.

Acts 3:12 And when Peter saw it, he answered unto the people, Ye men of Israel, why marvel ye at this? or why look ye so earnestly on us, as though by our own power or holiness we had made this man to walk? 13 The God of Abraham, and of Isaac, and of Jacob, the God of our fathers, hath glorified his Son Jesus; whom ye delivered up, and denied him in the presence of Pilate, when he was determined to let him go. 14 But ye denied the Holy One and the Just, and desired a murderer to be granted unto you; 15 and killed the Prince of *zoe*/life, whom God hath raised from the dead; whereof we are witnesses. 16 And his name through faith in his name hath made this man strong, whom ye see and know: yea, the faith which is by him hath given him this perfect soundness in the presence of you all. Ps 149:5 Let the saints be joyful in glory: let them sing aloud upon their beds. 6 Let the high praises of God be in their mouth, and a twoedged sword in their hand; 7 to execute vengeance upon the heathen, and punishments upon the people; 8 to bind their kings with chains, and their nobles with fetters of iron; 9 to execute upon them the judgment written: this honour have all his saints. Praise ye the LORD. Isa 60:18 Violence shall no more be heard in thy land, wasting nor destruction within thy borders; but thou shalt call thy walls Salvation, and thy gates Praise. Isa 49:24 Shall the prey be taken from the mighty, or the lawful captive delivered? 25 But thus saith the LORD, Even the captives of the mighty shall be taken away, and the prey of the terrible shall be delivered: for I will contend with him that contendeth with thee, and I will save thy children. *Glory! We are redeemed from the curse by the blood of Jesus. Praise the power of that blood!*

Father, heal, as I command in the name of Jesus. Bring Your salvation! Father, Jesus has risen and sits at Your right hand. Thy will be done on Earth as it is in Heaven! Amen; and so be it!

THE BATTLE PRAYER

You can act your way into believing quicker than you can believe your way into acting. Do first, and you may then feel it.

1. Father, in the name of Jesus, I/we thank You this is already done. And, Father, in the name of Jesus, right now, for (*Person's Name*), I speak to you, devil, and take authority over you and bind you to obey me, in the name of Jesus. I speak to this (*Problem*), and I speak to your body, (*Person's Name*), and I say, in the name of Jesus Christ of Nazareth, the Lord of Heaven and Earth, that RIGHT NOW all works of (*Problem*) will GO, (*Any Infection and Disease Will Die*), none of this will ever return. Any pain, I break you, and command you to go and never return. In the name of Jesus, fear of this (*Disease, Problem and/or Pain*) will leave and not ever return RIGHT NOW, in the name of JESUS; and, (*Person's Name*), you will be absolutely healed and normal; you and your body will operate normally, and you will do all things well and normally; and you will be a testimony to God. In the name of Jesus, so be it! RECEIVE NOW, in the name of Jesus of Nazareth, by His blood and His stripes. Amen; and So Be It!

2. Father, in the name of Jesus, I take authority over the devil working in (*person's name*) right now, by the redeeming blood and healing stripes of Jesus, and, in the name of Jesus, just as if Jesus were here right now, I command you, devil, to hear and obey the voice of the Word of God through me and go NOW. Take all your works, IN THE NAME OF JESUS, and GO NOW, and do not come back. Go NOW, in the name of JESUS! (*Problem*), in the name of Jesus, you hear and obey the voice of the Word of God through me, and you go now. In the name of Jesus, all symptoms, causes, effects and damage, you go NOW, and do not come back. I command, in the name of Jesus, for (*person's name*)'s body to be made whole. Body, you hear and obey, and be whole, in the name of Jesus. Pain, fear of pain, and fear of this (*problem*), in the name of Jesus, you GO NOW. I bless the entire (*person's family name*) family, all relatives, generations, relationships and their right worship and finances, now, in the name of Jesus Christ. Furthermore, in the name of Jesus, devil, all income, property and peace you have destroyed, I command you to repay to (*person's*) family, seven times to each one it was taken from, per Proverbs 6:31. So, devil, pay and pay NOW, in the name of JESUS. Thank You, Father, in the name of Jesus, for Your Word and Your *agape*/love. Thank You!

3. Father, in the name of Jesus, bring Your kingdom, Your will be done now, on Earth as it is in Heaven. Give deliverance and wholeness as promised, blast the devil out with all his works and manifest your salvation in (*Situation*). Ps 68:1 Let God arise, let his enemies be scattered: let them also that hate him flee before him. 2 As smoke is driven away, so drive them away: as wax melteth before the fire, so let the wicked perish at the presence of God. *For You said:* Ps 21:8 Thine hand shall find out all thine enemies: thy right hand shall find out those that hate thee. 9 Thou shalt make them as a fiery oven in the time of thine anger: the LORD shall swallow them up in his wrath, and the fire shall devour them. Ps 68:35 O God, thou art terrible out of thy holy places: the God of Israel *is You* that gives strength and power unto his people. Blessed be God. Ps 60:12 Through *You, Father* God, we shall do valiantly: for *You* it is that shall tread down our enemies. Ps 44:4 Thou art my King, O God: command deliverances for Jacob. 5 Through thee will we push down our enemies: through thy name will we tread them under that rise up against us. *Praise You, Father God, for it is You* Ps 103:3 who forgiveth all *our* iniquities; who healeth all *our* diseases; 4 who redeemeth *our* life from destruction; who crowneth *us* with *chesed*/lovingkindness and *racham*/tender mercies; 5 who satisfieth *our* mouth with good things; so that *our* youth is renewed like the eagle's. 6 The LORD executeth righteousness and judgment for all that are oppressed. Ps 72:4 He shall judge the poor of the people, he shall save the children of the needy, and shall break in pieces the oppressor. Ps 109:31 For he shall stand at the right hand of the poor, to save him from those that condemn his soul. Ps 146:5 Happy *am I* that *have* the God of Jacob for *my* help, whose hope is in the LORD his God: 6 which made heaven, and earth, the sea, and all that therein is: which keepeth truth for ever: 7 which executeth judgment for the oppressed: which giveth food to the hungry. The LORD looseth the prisoners: 8 the LORD openeth the eyes of the blind: the LORD raiseth them that are bowed down: the LORD loveth the righteous: 9 the LORD preserveth the strangers; he relieveth the fatherless and widow: but the way of the wicked he turneth upside down. *Father, turn the devil and His works upside down, now, in the name of Jesus.* 1 John 4:13 Hereby know we that we dwell in him, and he in us, because he hath given us of his Spirit. *So I also say:* Luke 4:18 The Spirit of the Lord is upon me, because he hath anointed me to preach the gospel to the poor; he hath sent me to heal the brokenhearted, to preach deliverance to the captives, and recovering of sight to the blind, to set at liberty them that are bruised, 19 to preach the acceptable year of the Lord. *As Jesus said:* Matt 28:18 ... All power is given unto me in heaven and in earth. Luke 10:19 Behold, I give unto you power to tread on serpents and scorpions, and over all the power of the enemy: and nothing shall by any means hurt you. *Praise You, Father God, that You are using me to destroy the works of the devil on Your behalf.* Rom 16:20 ... the God of peace, shall bruise Satan under *my* feet *(as a glass shattered)*. The grace of our Lord Jesus Christ be with *me* [*to know, be and do this*]. Amen. *Jesus has given us* Matt 10:1 ... power against unclean spirits, to cast them out,

THE BATTLE PRAYER

and to heal all manner of sickness and all manner of disease. *That I may obey 7 ... as I go,* preach, saying, The kingdom of heaven is at hand. *And* 8 heal the sick, cleanse the lepers, raise the dead, cast out devils: freely *I* have received, *I* freely give. Mark 16:15 *As Jesus said ...* 17 And these signs shall follow them that believe; In my name shall they cast out devils; they shall speak with new tongues; 18 they shall take up serpents; and if they drink any deadly thing, it shall not hurt them; they shall lay hands on the sick, and they shall recover. ... 20 And *I now go* forth, and *preach to this* (P<small>ROBLEM</small>), the Lord working with *me*, and confirming the word with signs following. Amen. Acts 10:38 How God anointed *me as a member of the Body of* Jesus of Nazareth with the Holy Ghost and with power: *so that I go* about doing good, and healing (*in judgment against the devil*) all that *are* oppressed (*under the active rule, lordship and power*) of the devil; for God *is* with *me because* 1 Cor 3:16 ... the Spirit of God dwelleth in *me. That by my words and* Acts 5:12 ... hands *are* many signs and wonders ... . Gal 4:6 And because *we* are sons, *You, Father* God, *have* sent forth the Spirit of *Your* Son into *our* hearts, crying, Abba (*Daddy*), Father. For Gal 3:13 Christ hath redeemed us from the curse of the law, being made a curse for us: for it is written, Cursed is every one that hangeth on a tree: 14 that the blessing of Abraham might come on the Gentiles through Jesus Christ; that we might receive the promise of the Spirit through faith. *Thank You, Father! In the name of Jesus, thank You that You have given me the same Holy Spirit that You gave Jesus. Thank You! So I say again:* Luke 4:18 The Spirit of the Lord is upon me, because he hath anointed me to preach the gospel to the poor; he hath sent me to heal the brokenhearted, to preach deliverance to the captives, and recovering of sight to the blind, to set at liberty them that are bruised, 19 to preach the acceptable year of the Lord. *Thank You, Father! In the name of Jesus, thank You that through me You will bring this salvation!*

In the name of Jesus, for (P<small>ROBLEM</small>), devil, I take authority over you, and, in Jesus' name, I command you to listen, obey and go NOW, in the name of Jesus. (P<small>ERSON'S</small>) body, I command you to be whole, free of pain and healthy now, in the name of Jesus. I proclaim FREEDOM, in the name of JESUS! Amen; so be it!

4. Lord Jesus, come and save, restore and prosper, per Your Word. John 14:13 "And whatsoever ye shall *aiteo*/ask *by demanding as due by covenant promise of the Father* in my name, that will I do, that the Father may be glorified in the Son. 14 If ye shall *aiteo*/ask *by demanding as due by covenant promise* any thing in my name, I will do it." Father, in the name of Jesus Christ, I demand and expect as due by Your Word, heal and make whole (P<small>ERSON'S</small> N<small>AME</small>). Be whole! In the name of JESUS! Thank You, Father God, in the name of Jesus! Thank You, Lord Jesus! And thank You, Holy Spirit.

In the name of Jesus, for (_Person's Name_) in this (_Problem_), devil, I take authority over you, and, in Jesus' name, I command you to listen, obey and go NOW, in the name of Jesus. (_Person's_) body, I command you to be whole and healthy, now, in the name of Jesus. I proclaim FREEDOM, in the name of JESUS! Amen; so be it!

5. In Jesus' name, I proclaim Jesus is Lord, Redeemer and Healer over (_Person's Name_)'s entire life, that they were included in the finished work of Jesus Christ, and forgive every sin and break every curse, snare, trap, net, cord, lie and evil yoke and reverse to blessing every curse over and in (_Person_)'s life. I bless (_Person's Name_), (_his/her_) entire family, their enemies and any who have ever hurt them in any way. I ask You, Father God, to manifest healing of all infirmities and pain and its causes in this (_Problem: Infirmity/Oppression of the Devil_), and to manifest the salvation Jesus purchased when You raised Jesus from the dead. Give Your peace and make whole (_Person_)'s body from the top of the head to the bottom of (_his/her_) feet, all in Jesus' name. So, in the name of Jesus, (_Person's Name_), be WHOLE. (_Problem_), GO, in the name of Jesus. All pain, GO in the name of Jesus. (_Person's Name_), YOU will live and be perfectly normal, NOW, in the name of Jesus. Amen, so be it!

6. In the name of Jesus Christ, Son of the _Zao_/Living God, who 1 John 2:2 "... is the propitiation for our sins: and not for ours only, but also for the sins of the whole world." So there is no legal curse for (_Person's Name_), (_his/her_) family and all those given them. I forgive every sin, break and reverse every curse to blessing, break every evil covenant, curse, snare, trap, net, cord and evil yoke, bind every strongman to hear and obey, at the name of Jesus Christ of Nazareth through me, pull down all strongholds of this (_Situation/Infirmity_), loose and command to go every form, tie and manifestation of Satan's works behind this (_Situation/Infirmity_), bind all evil strongmen and every helper demon from further work, and render each of you powerless. Now loose and let (_Person's Name_) go NOW, in the name of JESUS Christ. In the name of Jesus, all pain, fear of pain, and fear of this (_Situation/Infirmity_), GO now, in the name of Jesus! Praise You, Jesus, that You have made captivity captive! (Eph 4:8, Ps 68:16)

In the name of Jesus, I loose Holy Spirit and God's angels to bring total salvation, including this healing, right now, IN THE NAME OF JESUS CHRIST. Be whole, NOW, in the name of Jesus! I proclaim that the blood of Jesus shed 2000 years ago has redeemed (_Person's Name_) from the curse. For (_Person's Name_), all (_his/her_) families and their possessions, I take authority over the devil and his works. I command them to hear and obey me, now, in the name of

THE BATTLE PRAYER

Jesus. I break the devil's power, that all may be saved and protected. GO now, in the name of Jesus. Life, truth, and grace, come NOW, in the name of Jesus. Praise God! Praise You, Father God, in the name of Jesus, praise You!

7. Father, I thank You that You sent Jesus to die for me so that He might redeem me from the authority of Satan and You might be glorified by my life. Thank You that You call me worthy of the suffering and horrible death of Jesus, so that Holy Spirit might dwell in me. Thank You for sealing Holy Spirit to me. Eph 1:12 "That *I* should be to the praise of *Your* glory, who *have* trusted in Christ. 13 In whom *I* also trusted, after that *I* heard the word of truth, the gospel of *my soteria*/salvation: in whom also after that *I* believed, *I was* sealed with that holy Spirit of promise, 14 which is the earnest of our inheritance until the redemption of the purchased possession, unto the praise of *Your* glory." Gal 3:13 "Christ hath redeemed us from the curse of the law, being made a curse for us: for it is written, Cursed is every one that hangeth on a tree: 14 that the blessing of Abraham might come on the Gentiles through Jesus Christ; that we might receive the promise of the Spirit through faith." Thank You, Father, for Your *agape*/love for me and also for this one I am ministering Your *zoe*/life to. Thank You that You *agape*/love them. Thank You that You want them free and to know Your goodness more than I can *aiteo*, think or imagine. I place myself beside You, at Your throne, and proclaim this evil thing has violated Your law and must go because of the resurrection, blood and the stripes of Jesus. This disorder is nothing to Your strength and power. You are able and willing to set them free. Thank You for empowering my word for them to receive what You, Holy Spirit and Jesus already paid for. Thank You, in the name of Jesus! Thank You!

In Jesus' name, in His place and for Him, I command any and all demons involved in (PERSON'S NAME) in this (PROBLEM/INFIRMITY) to not talk, to be bound from further work, for all help to these demons to be cut off and for them to go now, in Jesus' name, and not relocate in (PERSON)'s body, but go to the pit and stay there and not return. I command, in Jesus Christ's name, that pain, discomfort, destruction and damage come out, leave, go to the pit and stay there and not return, NOW. In the name of Jesus!

(INFIRMITY), in the name of Jesus Christ of Nazareth, I take authority over you and declare, decree and establish the death sentence upon you! Therefore, in Jesus' name, (INFIRMITY AND ALL YOUR WORKS), die at the roots, dry up and come out of (PERSON)'s body and life, now. Go to the pit and stay there, and do not return! Now! In the name of Jesus, I cut off and kill the sources of (INFIRMITY), pain and fear, and command it all to come out and go to the pit, now, and not return, in the name of Jesus, Lord of Heaven and Earth!

In the name of Jesus, in His place and for Him, I declare, decree and establish healing in (PERSON)'s life, from the top of (HIS/HER) head to the bottom of (HIS/HER) feet. Therefore, in Jesus' name, I speak words of life. (PERSON'S NAME), BE HEALED and MADE WHOLE, now! Thank You, Father, in the name of Jesus. It is done. Thank You!

Thank You, Father, that Your Word is alive and quick, Your anointing is on Your Word to perform it, and by Jesus' stripes we were healed. Praise You for Your *agape*/love and mercy, in Jesus my Lord. Praise the name of Jesus. <u>1 Pet 2:24</u> Who his own self bare our sins in his own body on the tree, that we, being dead to sins, should *zao*/live unto righteousness: by whose stripes *we* were healed. *For:* <u>Isa 53:4</u> Surely he hath borne our griefs (*infirmities*), and carried our sorrows (*sicknesses*): yet we did esteem him stricken, smitten of God, and afflicted. 5 But he was wounded for our transgressions, he was bruised for our iniquities: the chastisement of our peace was upon him; and with his stripes we are healed. *Thank You for the total good work of Jesus!*

(REPEAT THE ENTIRE PRAYER AS NECESSARY)
<u>The first one that quits loses</u>. It is like a wrestling match. So don't quit. Hit hard and continuously. The Bible compares the name of Jesus to a sword, a machete and a sledgehammer. Keep on slashing, and keep on hammering away with the Word of God until you win over the devil and his work.

Father, in the name of Jesus, I thank You and trust in You. I come to You for (PERSON'S NAME) concerning (PROBLEM) for You to manifest the finished work of Jesus Christ in (PERSON'S NAME) body. Father God, get Holy Spirit to lead and guide me in this battle to extend Your Kingdom. I submit myself to You and proclaim Jesus is Lord over this situation, so I am saying: <u>Luke 11:2</u> "And he said unto them, When ye pray, say, Our Father which art in heaven, Hallowed be thy name. Thy kingdom come. Thy will be done, as in heaven, so in earth." Father, perform Your Word of salvation, in the name of Jesus, as I command deliverance, in Jesus' name. I command *Zoe*/LIFE in (PERSON'S NAME). Father, praise Your salvation in Jesus Christ, my Lord.

Praise You, Father God, in the name of Jesus, the Prince of Life, my Redeemer, the Word of God and King of kings and Lord of Lords, my only Lord, the Captain of the Army of the Lord of Hosts. You have revealed Yourself as the Man of War, Mighty Warrior, the Lord of Hosts, the Lord of the Armies of God. Rise to do battle for this need: <u>Ps 18:6</u> In my distress I called upon the LORD, and cried unto my God: he heard my voice out of his temple, and my cry came before him, even into his ears. 7 Then the earth shook and trembled; the

THE BATTLE PRAYER

foundations also of the hills moved and were shaken, because he was wroth. 8 There went up a smoke out of his nostrils, and fire out of his mouth devoured: coals were kindled by it. 9 He bowed the heavens also, and came down: and darkness was under his feet. 10 And he rode upon a cherub, and did fly: yea, he did fly upon the wings of the wind. 11 He made darkness his secret place; his pavilion round about him were dark waters and thick clouds of the skies. 12 At the brightness that was before him his thick clouds passed, hail stones and coals of fire. 13 The LORD also thundered in the heavens, and the Highest gave his voice; hail stones and coals of fire. 14 Yea, he sent out his arrows, and scattered them; and he shot out lightnings, and discomfited them (*defeated them in battle*). 15 Then the channels of waters were seen, and the foundations of the world were discovered at thy rebuke, O LORD, at the blast of the breath of thy nostrils. 16 He sent from above, he took me, he drew me out of many waters. 17 He delivered me from my strong enemy, and from them which hated me: for they were too strong for me. Job 4:9 By the blast of God they perish, and by the breath of his nostrils are they consumed. 10 The roaring of the lion, and the voice of the fierce lion, and the teeth of the young lions, are broken. *Glory to God, who is greater than any evil. Hallelujah! Glory!*

In the name of Jesus, in (PERSON'S NAME) for this (PROBLEM), devil, I take authority over you, and, in Jesus' name, I command you to listen, obey and go NOW, in the name of Jesus. (PERSON)'s body, I command you to be whole and healthy, now, in the name of Jesus. All pain, fear of pain and fear of (PROBLEM), I command you to GO now. I proclaim FREEDOM, IN THE NAME OF JESUS! Amen; so be it!

8. <u>Laying on of Hands</u>: Father, God Almighty, in the name of Jesus Christ, my Lord, restore (PERSON'S NAME) of this (INFIRMITY). Kill every cause, blast this curse of Hell and burn it up by Your power. Send Your redeeming and destroying lightning. Let Holy Spirit live in (HIM/HER); let Him move as I place my hands, per Your Word, Mark 16:16 "… they shall lay hands on the sick and they shall recover," to being made fully well. In the name of Jesus, (INFIRMITY), GO; (PERSON'S NAME), be whole; life, come into this body now. Every part, do your job, in the name of JESUS, the Christ. Thank You, Father! In Jesus' name, thank You! (*Now touch the person gently and shout:*) "RECEIVE, in the name of Jesus!"

9. <u>At a Distance</u>: Father, God Almighty, in the name of Jesus Christ, my Lord, restore (PERSON'S NAME) of this (INFIRMITY). Kill every cause, blast this curse of Hell and burn it up by Your power. Send Your redeeming and destroying lightning and fire. Let Holy Spirit live in (_HIM/HER_); let Him move, per Your word: Ps 107:20 "He sent his word, and healed them, and delivered [them] from their destructions," to being made fully well. In the name of Jesus, (_IN-FIRMITY_), GO; (_PERSON'S NAME_), be whole; life, come into this body, now. Every part, do your job, in the name of JESUS, the Christ. Thank You, Father! In Jesus' name, thank You.

Continue, whether praying at a distance or laying your hands on the sick until they are fully healed. Keep at it, whether it happens in steps or at once.

10. Father God, Mighty Man of War, in the name of Jesus, My Redeemer, stir Yourself and me to destroy Your enemies with Your lightning and arrows through my words. Fill my soul with Your compassion. Fill my soul with courage and strength in You. Thank You, Father, for You delight in bringing Your Kingdom to Earth. In the name of Jesus, I proclaim: it is over, devil. I bring the Kingdom of God upon you, now for (_PERSON'S NAME_) for (_PROBLEM_). Satan, in the name of Jesus, the name above every name that is named, including you and yours, above all rulers, authorities, principalities and powers, including yours, the name at which every knee must bow and every tongue confess that Jesus Christ is Lord, to the glory of God the Father. ... Devil, you give God glory now, and bow your knee, and you confess Jesus as your Lord. And, in the name of Jesus, Your Lord, leave. Take all your evil works and go, NOW. That name has been given to us, for there in no other name under Heaven by which we must be saved, healed, delivered, and made whole and prosperous. In Jesus' name, Father, thank You for empowering Your Word, for You are my strength. Thank You! The great work of the cross is sufficient. Praise Jesus!

Praise You, Father God, for Col 2:10 ... *I am* complete in *Jesus*, which is the head of all principality and power, *including every* Eph 6:12 ... *evil* principalities, ... powers, ... the rulers of the darkness of this world, *and* spiritual wickedness in high places. Col 2:11 In whom also *I am* circumcised with the circumcision made without hands, in putting off the body of the sins of the flesh by the circumcision of Christ: 12 buried with him in baptism, wherein also *I am* risen with *Jesus Christ* through the faith of the operation of *You, Father* God, who *have* raised him from the dead. 13 And *me*, being dead in *my* sins and the uncircumcision of *my* flesh, *You, Father, have* quickened *me* together with *Jesus*, having forgiven *me* all trespasses; 14 blotting out the handwriting of ordinances that was against *me*, which was contrary to *me*, and took it out of the way, nailing it to his cross; 15 and having spoiled principalities and powers, *Jesus* made a shew of them openly, triumphing over them in it. Eph 1:20 Which *You, Father God*, wrought in Christ, when *You* raised *Jesus* from the dead, and set

THE BATTLE PRAYER

him at *Your* own right hand in the heavenly places, 21 far above all principality, and power, and might, and dominion, and every name that is named, not only in this world, but also in that which is to come: 22 and have put all things under his feet, and gave him to be the head over all things to the church, 23 which is his body, the fulness of him that filleth all in all, *of which I am a part*. Eph 3:10 To the intent that now unto the principalities and powers in heavenly places might be known by the church the manifold wisdom of *You, Father* God. *As Jesus said:* Luke 10:19 Behold, I give unto you power (*authority, commission, and ability*) to tread on serpents and scorpions, and over all the power (*ability and works*) of the enemy: and nothing shall by any means hurt you.

So Satan, in the name of Jesus, your Lord, know the authority given me, one of the blood-bought in Jesus Christ. Go out of (<u>Person's Name</u>) in (<u>Problem</u>), now. In the name of Jesus Christ of Nazareth, by the blood of the eternal covenant, GO NOW! (<u>Person</u>)'s body, I command you to be whole and healthy now, in the name of Jesus. I proclaim FREEDOM, IN THE NAME OF JESUS! Amen; so be it! Thank You, Father, for empowering me to deliverance, to wholeness. In the name of Jesus, thank You. Praise You for Your work in the cross! Praise You for Your *agape*/love.

11. Father, I come in the name of Jesus Christ, my only Lord, for (<u>Person's Name</u>). Father, You say: Isa 55:11 So shall my word be that goeth forth out of my mouth: it shall not return unto me void, but it shall accomplish that which I please, and it shall prosper in the thing whereto I sent it. *And:* Isa 45:11 thus saith the Lord, the Holy One of Israel, and his Maker, Ask me of things to come concerning my sons, and concerning the work of my hands command ye me. *So, Father, in the name of Jesus, as I proclaim Your Word, perform Your Word, to extend Your Kingdom on Earth, with these words in my mouth.* Rom 16:20 And You, Father, the God of peace *in wholeness, healing, prosperity, and encouragement* … bruise (*crush*) Satan under *my* feet *quickly as shattered glass*. The grace of our Lord Jesus Christ be with *me and those I pray for* (*to know, be and do this*). Amen. *Confirm Your Word* 2 Cor 1:9 … that we should not trust in ourselves, but in *You, Father* God, which raiseth the dead: 1 Cor 2:5 that *my* faith should not stand in the wisdom of men, but in the *dunamis*/power of *You, Father* God. *And that You, Father* Heb 2:4 God also bearing *me* witness, both with signs and wonders, and with divers miracles, and gifts of the Holy Ghost, according to *Your* own will. *You,* Eph 1:11 … who worketh all things after the counsel of *Your* own will. 1 John 5:14 And this is the confidence that *I* have in *You, Father God*, that, if *I aiteo/ask by demanding as due by covenant promise* any thing according to *Your* will, *You hear me*: 15 and if *I* know that *You* hear *me*, whatsoever *I aiteo/*ask *by demanding* *as due by covenant promise, I* know that *I* have the *aiteo*/petitions that *I* desired of *You, Father God, Jehovah Rapha, the God Who Heals. Father, as I pray this prayer, renew my mind with Your Word, that I may* Eph 4:23 ... be renewed in the spirit of *my* mind; 24 and ... put on *and walk in* the new man, which after *You, Father God,* is created in righteousness and true holiness. *Praise You, Father, in the name of Jesus Christ of Nazareth, my Lord. Let the Lord be magnified who takes pleasure in the prosperity of His servants, and I am a son/daughter who is His servant. Hallelujah!*

In the name of Jesus, for (<u>Problem</u>), devil, I take authority over you, and, in Jesus' name, I command you to listen, obey and go NOW, in the name of Jesus. (<u>Person</u>)'s body, I command you to be whole and healthy now, in the name of Jesus. All pain, fear of pain and fear of (<u>Problem</u>), I command you to GO now. I proclaim FREEDOM, IN THE NAME OF JESUS! Amen; so be it!

12. And I pray, Father, in the name of Jesus, Eph 1:17 that *You*, the God of our Lord Jesus Christ, the Father of glory, may give unto *me and those I pray for* the spirit of wisdom and revelation in the knowledge of *You*: 18 the eyes of *our* understanding being enlightened; that *we* may know what is the hope of *Your* calling, and what the riches of the glory of *Your* inheritance in the saints, 19 and what is the exceeding greatness of *Your* power to us-ward who believe, according to the working of *Your* mighty power, 20 which *You* wrought in Christ, when *You* raised him from the dead, and set him at *Your* own right hand in the heavenly places, 21 far above all principality, and power, and might, and dominion, and every name that is named, not only in this world, but also in that which is to come: 22 and hath put all things under his feet, and gave him to be the head over all things to the church, *of which I am a partaker,* 23 which is his body, the fulness of him that filleth all in all. Eph 3:16 That *You* would grant *us,* according to the riches of *Your* glory, to be strengthened with might by *Your* Spirit in the inner man; 17 that Christ may dwell in *our* hearts by faith; that *we*, being rooted and grounded in *agape*/love, 18 may be able to comprehend with all saints what is the breadth, and length, and depth, and height; 19 and to know the *agape*/love of Christ, which passeth knowledge, that *we* might be filled with all the fulness of *You, Father* God. 20 Now unto *You, Father,* that is able to do exceeding abundantly above all that we *aiteo*/ask *by demanding as due by covenant promise* or think, according to the power that worketh in us, 21 unto *You* be glory in the church by Christ Jesus throughout all ages, world without end. Amen. *Worthy is the Lamb that was slain! And great is Your mighty work! Jesus, YOU got it done! Thank You! Thank You, Father God, for Jesus! Thank You!*

THE BATTLE PRAYER

Father, in the name of Jesus, that You would fill us <u>Col 1:9</u> ... with the knowledge of *Your* will in all wisdom and spiritual understanding; 10 that *we* might walk worthy of the Lord unto all pleasing, being fruitful in every good work, and increasing in the knowledge of *You, Father* God; 11 strengthened with all might, according to *Your* glorious power, unto all patience and longsuffering with joyfulness; *to* 12 giving thanks (*continually*) unto *You*, the Father, which hath made us meet (*qualified and enabled by grace*) to be partakers of the inheritance of the saints in light: 13 who hath delivered us from the power of darkness, and hath translated us into the kingdom of *Your agape*/dear Son: 14 in whom we have redemption through his blood, even the forgiveness (*pardon*) of sins: 15 who is the image of *You, Father*, the invisible God, the firstborn of every creature: 16 for by him were all things created, that are in heaven, and that are in earth, visible and invisible, whether they be thrones, or dominions, or principalities, or powers: all things, *including me*, were created by him, and for him: 17 and he is before all things, and by him all things consist. 18 And *Jesus* is the head of the body, the church: who is the beginning, the firstborn from the dead; that in all things he might have the preeminence. 19 For it pleased *You, O God*, the Father, that in him should all fulness dwell; 20 and, having made peace through the blood of his cross, by him to reconcile all things unto *Yourself*; by him, I say, whether they be things in earth, or things in heaven. 21 And *we*, that were sometime alienated and enemies in *our* mind by wicked works, yet now *have You, Father,* reconciled 22 in the body of his (*Jesus'*) flesh through death, to present *us* holy and unblameable and unreproveable in *Your* sight. *Father, this is Your Mighty Work! Thank You that it is done! Thank You!*

Father, work in us so that we <u>Phil 2:12</u> ... always *obey, independent of authorities that we*, work out *our* own *soteria*/salvation with fear and trembling. 13 For it is *You, Father* God, which worketh in *us* both to will and to do of *Your* good pleasure. *So that* <u>2 Thes 1:3</u> ... *our* faith groweth exceedingly, and the *agape*/charity of every one of *us* all toward each other aboundeth; *and that* <u>2 Thes 1:11</u> ... *You, Father, our* God, would count *us* worthy of this calling, and fulfil all the good pleasure of *Your* goodness, and the work of faith with power: 12 that the name of our Lord Jesus Christ may be glorified in *us*, and *we* in him, according to the grace of *You*, our God, and the Lord Jesus Christ. *Father, work in us so that we* <u>1 Thes 2:13</u> ... *receive* the word of God ... not as the word of men, but as it is in truth, the word of *You, Father* God, which effectually worketh also in *us* that believe. <u>Phil 1:9</u> And this I pray, that *our chesed/agape*/love may abound yet more and more in knowledge and in all judgment; 10 that *we* may approve things that are excellent; that *we* may be sincere and without offence till the day of Christ; 11 being filled with the fruits of righteousness, which are by Jesus

Christ, unto the glory and praise of *You, our Father* God. *Thank You, Father! In the name of Jesus Christ, my Lord, thank You for allowing me to be a co-laborer with You, to bring Your will on Earth as it is in Heaven, where there is no sickness, want or tears. Thank You, Father! In Jesus' name, thank You!*

Father, the God who calls things that are not as if they are and they become, thank You that Jesus carried for me and all mankind our griefs, infirmities, sicknesses, sorrows and pains. These were punishments we deserved, but Jesus took them. He took our punishment upon His body and redeemed us by His blood, and we do not have to carry those just punishments of griefs, infirmities, sicknesses, sorrows and pains in whatever form they might come. Isa 53:4 "Surely he hath borne our griefs (*infirmities*), and carried our sorrows (*sicknesses*): yet we did esteem him stricken, smitten of *You, Father* God, and afflicted. Gal 3:13 "Christ hath redeemed us *by His body and blood* from the curse of the law, being made a curse for us: for it is written, Cursed is every one that hangeth on a tree: 14 that the blessing of Abraham might come on the Gentiles through Jesus Christ; that we might receive the promise of the Spirit through faith." Thank You, Lord Jesus Christ, for bearing our curse, so we do not have to bear the curses due us for our sins or the sins of others. Thank You that You did it by the cross once, forever!

In the name of Jesus, for (PERSON'S NAME) in this (PROBLEM), devil, I take authority over you, and, in Jesus' name, I command you to listen, obey and go NOW, never to return, in the name of Jesus. (PERSON)'s body, I command you to be whole and healthy now, in the name of Jesus. All damages, symptoms, pain, fear of pain and fear of (PROBLEM), I command to GO now, never to return. I proclaim FREEDOM, IN THE NAME OF JESUS! Amen; so be it!

13. My Lord Jesus Christ, You bore my curses so I do not have to bear them. I receive my redemption for every curse working in my life right now, in the name of Jesus Christ. By this mighty work You qualified and empowered me to be Your agent, as a saint of light, a redeemed human being, to set this person free in and with the name of Jesus. 1 Pet 3:18 "For Christ also hath once suffered for sins, the just for the unjust, that he might bring us to God, being put to death in the flesh, but quickened by the Spirit." In particular, I proclaim redemption unto *zoe*/life to (PERSON'S NAME) in this (PROBLEM), in the name of Jesus Christ of Nazareth. FREEDOM, in the name of Jesus! Thank You, for Your *zoe*/life in me and (PERSON'S NAME) is setting us free from every curse and work of sin and death now, unto perfect working order, just as Father God designed it. Satan, in the name of Jesus Christ of Nazareth, you hear and obey me NOW, and take this curse working in (PERSON'S NAME). Take it and go now,

THE BATTLE PRAYER

IN JESUS' NAME. Thank You, Father God, for Holy Spirit dwelling in me now and empowering these words now to establish Your Kingdom in us NOW. For 1 John 4:9 "in this was manifested the *agape*/love of *You, Father* God, toward us, because that *You, Father* God, sent *Your* only begotten Son into the world, that we might *zoe*/live through him. 10 Herein is *agape*/love, not that we *agape*/loved *You, Father* God, but that *You agape*/loved us, and sent *Your* Son to be the propitiation for our sins." In Jesus' name, I proclaim, (PERSON'S NAME), BE WHOLE NOW, in the name of Jesus! Thank You, Father! In Jesus' name, thank You! It is done, Jesus is risen, and by His stripes we were healed. Amen! Thank You!

Thank You, Father God, for You are the God Ps 103:3 "who forgiveth all *our* iniquities; who healeth all *our* diseases; 4 who redeemeth *our* life from destruction; who crowneth *us* with *chesed*/lovingkindness and *racham*/tender mercies; 5 who satisfieth *our* mouth with good things; so that *our* youth is renewed like the eagle's. *Bless You, O* LORD *God, You are:* 6 the LORD *who* executeth righteousness and judgment for all that are oppressed." *By Holy Spirit within me,* Acts 10:38 "… healing *and restoring to Your peace* all that *are* oppressed (*under the active rule and lordship*) of the devil; for *You, Father* God *are with me as I am in Jesus."* 1 John 4:17 "Herein is *my agape*/love made perfect, that *I* may have boldness in *this* day of judgment *against the works of the devil in* (PERSON'S NAME): because as *Jesus* is, so *am I* in this world." I break every work, and command you, devil, and your works, to hear and obey me and to go NOW, and never return, in the name of Jesus. Thank You, Father God! In the name of Jesus, thank You! Praise You for Your *agape*/love in Jesus! Thank You! You set our value as worth the life of Jesus. Thank You!

Phil 2:13 "For it is God which worketh in *us*, *those I pray for and myself,* both to will and to do of his good pleasure," as I read and speak out loud His Word, the Spirit of *zoe*/life is working in us. As I intercede for others, His *zoe*/life is flowing in me and to them. As I take communion, Father God's *zoe*/life is flowing in me and to them, and Phil 1:6 "*I am* confident of this very thing, that *Father God,* which hath begun a good work in *us,* will perform it until the day of Jesus Christ." Thank You, Father! In the name of Jesus, thank You! Amen; so be it!

14. Father, I come to You, in the name of the Lord Jesus Christ, as a member of His earthly Body, against this work of the devil in (PERSON'S NAME), as You have said: Isa 1:18 Come now, and let us reason together, saith the LORD … . *And:* Isa 43:26 Put me in remembrance: let us plead together: declare thou, that thou mayest be justified (*acquitted*). Rom 5:1 Therefore being justified (*made just as if I had never sinned*) by faith (*in the promise of God through Jesus Christ*), *I* have peace (*no enmity, everything working well, with aggressive goodness from God to me*) with *You, Father* God, through *my* Lord Jesus Christ: *For You have told us, by Holy Spirit, that* 2 *by the Lord Jesus Christ* also we have access by faith into this grace wherein we stand, and rejoice in hope of the glory of *You, Father* God. ... 6 For when we were yet without strength, in due time Christ died for the ungodly. 8 But *You, Father* God, *commended Your agape*/love toward us, in that, while we were yet sinners, Christ died for us. 9 Much more then, being now justified (*made just as if I had never sinned or will ever sin, in Heaven and legally on Earth*) by his blood, we shall be *sozo*/saved from wrath through him. 10 For if, when we were enemies, we were reconciled to *You, Father* God, *with no enmity and only aggressive blessing and goodness in every way, spirit, soul, body, place and family*, by the death of *Your* Son, much more, being reconciled, we shall be *sozo*/saved (*restored, healed, made prosperous now and for eternity*) by his *zoe*/life.

Rom 5:11 And not only so, but *by Your Spirit working in me to will and to do of Your good pleasure* I also joy in You, Father God, through our Lord Jesus Christ, by whom I have now received the atonement (*the reconciliation, exchange, payment, cleansing of all sin, past, present and future, with deliverance of all effects of the curse justly due for my sins*). 12 Wherefore, as by one man sin entered into the world, and death by sin; and so death passed upon all men, for that all have sinned: 13 (for until the law sin was in the world: but sin is not imputed when there is no law. 14 Nevertheless death reigned from Adam to Moses, even over them that had not sinned after the similitude of Adam's transgression, who is the figure of him that was to come. 15 But not as the offence, so also is the free gift. For if through the offence of one many be dead, much more the grace of *You, Father* God, and the gift by grace, which is by one man, Jesus Christ, hath abounded unto many. 16 And not as it was by one that sinned, so is the gift: for the judgment was by one to condemnation, but the free gift is of many offences unto justification (*legally declared to be just as if I had never sinned or ever will sin*). Rom 3:22 Even the righteousness of You, Father God which is by faith of Jesus Christ unto all and upon all them that believe: for there is no difference. 2 Cor 5:21 For You, Father God, *have* made Jesus to be sin for *me*, who knew no sin; that *I* might be made the righteousness of *You, Father* God, in him. *For to be as righteous as You, Father God, means:* John 14:30 Hereafter I, Jesus, will not talk much with you: for the prince of this world cometh, and hath nothing in me. *Therefore Satan has no legal grounds to my (or any person's) spirit, soul or body, my place, my family or the work of my hands. I may still sin, but even then, Satan has no legal grounds to put any curse on me or mine in any way, for the blood of Jesus continually cleanses me of sin. Praise You, Father, for the wonderful redeeming, reconciling, bringing near, justifying, overcoming and sin-purging blood of Jesus, my Lord. Praise You, Father God, for the name of Jesus, my Lord!*

THE BATTLE PRAYER

<u>Rom 5:17</u> For if by one man's offence death reigned by one; much more they which (*continually*) *lambano*/receive abundance of grace and of the gift of righteousness shall reign *for Jesus* in/*through zoe*/life by one, Jesus Christ.) <u>Rev 1:5</u> *For* Jesus Christ, who is the faithful witness, and the first begotten of the dead, and the prince of the kings of the. Unto him that *agape*/loved us, and washed us from our sins in his own blood, 6 and hath made us kings and priests unto *You, O,* God and his Father; to *Jesus* be glory and dominion for ever and ever. Amen. <u>2 Cor 5:18</u> And all things are of *You, Father* God, who hath reconciled us to *Yourself* by Jesus Christ, and hath given to us the ministry of reconciliation. *So that we could be the contact agents for You, Father God, on the Earth, to bring Your promised peace* (*total healing, restoration, prosperity, nothing broken, nothing missing, devil-destroying, to the glory of the Lord, filling all in all, on Earth as it is in Heaven, to all men*) *that You obtained in Jesus.* <u>Rev 5:9</u> And they sung a new song, saying, Thou, *Jesus,* art worthy to take the book, and to open the seals thereof: for thou wast slain, and hast redeemed us to God by thy blood out of every kindred, and tongue, and people, and nation; 10 and hast made us unto our God kings and priests: and we shall reign on the earth *for You, in the ministry of reconciliation, in the Word of righteousness, proclaiming that the righteous judgments of You, Father God, were placed on Jesus, that we might have* zoe/*life in Him.* <u>Rom 3:22</u> Even the righteousness of *You, Father* God, which is by faith of Jesus Christ unto all and upon all them that believe: for there is no difference: 23 for all have sinned, and come short of the glory of *You, Father* God; 24 being justified (*made just as if I had never or will ever sin*) freely by *Your* grace through the redemption that is in Christ Jesus: 25 whom *You, Father* God, *have* set forth to be a propitiation through faith in his blood, to declare his righteousness for the remission of sins that are past, through the forbearance of *You, Father* God; 26 to declare, I say, at this time *Your* righteousness: that *You, Father,* might be just (*righteous judge, calling for the just penalty of sin, which is death*), and the justifier (*making me just as if I had never sinned or ever will sin*) of *me* which believeth in Jesus. <u>Rom 6:23</u> For the wages of sin is death; but the gift of *You, Father* God, is eternal *zoe*/life through Jesus Christ our Lord. *Praise You, Father,* <u>Rom 8:2</u> for the law of the Spirit of *zoe*/life in Christ Jesus hath made me free from the law of sin and death. <u>Acts 13:37</u> But he, whom God raised again, saw no corruption. 38 Be it known unto you therefore, men and brethren, that through this man is preached unto you the forgiveness *and remission* of sins: 39 and by him all that believe are justified from all things, from which ye could not be justified by the law of Moses. <u>Gal 2:20</u> I *have been* crucified with Christ: nevertheless I *zao*/live; yet not I, but Christ *zao*/liveth in me: and the life which I now *zao*/live in the flesh I *zao*/live by the faith of the Son of God, who *agape*/loved me, and gave himself for me. 21 I do not frustrate the grace of God: for if righteousness come by the law, then Christ is dead in vain. <u>Gal 5:4</u> Christ is become of no effect unto you,

whosoever of you are justified by the law; ye are fallen from grace. Rom 10:4 For Christ is the end of the law for righteousness to every one that believeth. Rom 3:23 For all have sinned, and come short of the glory of God; 24 being justified freely by his grace through the redemption that is in Christ Jesus: 25 whom God hath set forth to be a propitiation through faith in his blood, to declare his righteousness for the remission of sins that are past, through the forbearance of God; 26 to declare, I say, at this time his righteousness: that he might be just, and the justifier of him which believeth in Jesus. Acts 26:18 To open their eyes, and to turn them from darkness to light, and from the power of Satan unto God, that they may receive forgiveness (*remission, purging, removal and obliteration*) of sins, and inheritance among them which are sanctified by faith that is in *Jesus*.

Praise You, Abba Father, God of Peace, in the name of Jesus, the Prince of Peace, for Titus 2:13 ... our Saviour Jesus Christ; 14 who gave himself for us, that he might redeem us from all iniquity, and purify unto himself a peculiar people, zealous of good works. *The kind of works Jesus said:* John 14:11 Believe me that I am in the Father, and the Father in me: or else believe me for the very works' sake. Eph 2:10 For we are *Your* workmanship, created in Christ Jesus unto good works, which *You, Father God, have* before ordained that we should walk in them. *As Jesus said:* John 5:36 But I, *Jesus*, have greater witness than that of John: for the works which the Father hath given me to finish, the same works that I do, bear witness of me, that the Father hath sent me. John 14:10 Believest thou not that I am in the Father, and the Father in me? the words that I speak unto you I speak not of myself: but the Father that dwelleth in me, he doeth the works. ... 12 Verily, verily, I say unto you, He that believeth on me, the works that I do shall he do also; and greater works than these shall he do; because I go unto my Father. Acts 10:38 How *You, Father* God, anointed Jesus of Nazareth with the Holy Ghost and with power: who went about doing good, and healing all that were oppressed (*under the active dominion, reign or lordship*) of the devil; for *You, Father* God, *were* with him. Mal 3:6 For I am the LORD, I change not .... *Praise You, Father, as You have always revealed Yourself as a healing God, beginning with Abraham (Gen 20:17) and working through Jesus and the early believers, and, You, who change not, are still working today.* Acts 8:6 And the people with one accord gave heed unto those things which Philip spake, hearing and seeing the miracles which he did. 7 For unclean spirits, crying with loud voice, came out of many that were possessed with them: and many taken with palsies, and that were lame, were healed. Rom 15:9 Through mighty signs and wonders, by the power of the Spirit of God; so that from Jerusalem, and round about unto Illyricum, I (*Paul*) have fully preached the gospel of Christ. *For You, righteous Father, have made us* 1 Pet 2:9 ... a chosen generation, a royal priesthood, an holy nation, a peculiar people;

THE BATTLE PRAYER

that *we* should shew forth the praises of *You, Father God,* who hath called *us* out of darkness into *Your* marvellous light. Rom 5:18 Therefore as by the offence of one judgment came upon all men to condemnation; even so by the righteousness of one the free gift came upon all men unto justification (*just as if I never had or ever will sin*) of *zoe*/life. 19 For as by one man's disobedience many were made sinners, so by the obedience of one shall many be made righteous (*just like You, Father, in Jesus*). 20 Moreover the law entered, that the offence might abound. But where sin abounded, grace did much more abound: 21 that as sin hath reigned unto death, even so might grace reign *starting now* through righteousness (*of Yourself, Father*) unto eternal *zoe*/life by Jesus Christ our Lord. *So, Father, in the name of Jesus, use me as one of Your royal priesthood to bring Your Kingdom in* agape/*love to those I pray for. Thank You that I am called forth to show Your praises, not the praises of what men can do, but what You, Father, can and delight to do. Thank You, Father, who raises the dead. Thank You, Father! In the name of Jesus, thank You!*

Praise You, Father, in the name of Jesus. Thank You that You want us to know beyond any doubt that 1 John 5:13 these things have I written unto you that believe on the name of the Son of God; that ye may know that ye have, *right now, not later, but right now,* eternal *zoe*/life, and that ye may believe on the name of the Son of God *to release this zoe/life as needed.* 1 John 3:8 ... For this purpose the Son of God was manifested, that he might destroy the works of the devil. *You, Father* Acts 10:38 ... God, anointed Jesus of Nazareth with the Holy Ghost and with power: who went about doing good, and healing all that were oppressed (*under the active dominion, reign or lordship*) of the devil; for *You, Father* God, *were* with him. *You have told us that:* Ps 9:9 the LORD also will be a refuge for the oppressed, a refuge in times of trouble. *That You want us* Ps 10:18 to judge ... *for* the oppressed, that the man of the earth, *Satan and his helpers,* may no more oppress. *For You, Father, have called us to walk like Jesus, to preach peace like Jesus preached and have anointed us in Jesus with Holy Spirit and power, to go around doing good, healing all those oppressed of the devil, for You, Father God, are with us as You are with Jesus.*

Father, You have told us of Your awesome and enduring *agape*/love in Jesus: Col 2:9 for in *Jesus* dwelleth all the fulness of the Godhead bodily. And *I am* complete in him, which is the head of all principality and power. Eph 6:12 For we wrestle not against flesh and blood, but against (*satanic beings without bodies but working through people and nature*) principalities, against powers, against the rulers of the darkness of this world, against spiritual wickedness in high places. Phil 2:9 Wherefore *You, Father* God, *also have* highly exalted *Jesus,* and given him a name which is above every name: 10 that at the name of Jesus every knee should bow, of things in heaven, and things in earth, and things under the earth; 11 and that every tongue should confess that Jesus Christ is Lord, to the glory of *You, O* God, the Father. *For*: Luke 10:19 Behold, I, *Jesus*, give unto you power (*authority, commission and ability*) to tread on serpents and scorpions, and over all the power (*ability*) of the enemy: and nothing shall by any means hurt you. Luke 11:20 But if I (*Jesus*) with the finger of God (*the Holy Spirit*) cast out devils, no doubt the kingdom of God is come upon you. *As the Lord Jesus commanded us to go to every city,* Luke 10:9 and heal the sick that are therein, and say unto them, The kingdom of God is come nigh unto you. *Father, praise You, that You have given me Your Holy Spirit to bring Your Kingdom to Earth as it is in Heaven: that same Holy Spirit promised through Abraham and whom, You said, You are more eager to give Holy Spirit than a parent would give food to a crying child.* Luke 11:13 If ye then, being evil, know how to give good gifts unto your children: how much more shall your heavenly Father give the Holy Spirit to them that *aiteo*/ask him *by requiring, demanding and expecting as due by covenant promise?*

In the name of Jesus, for (*Person's Name*) in this (*Problem*), devil, I take authority over you, and, in Jesus' name, I command you to listen, obey and go NOW, never to return, in the name of Jesus. (*Person*)'s body, I command you to be whole and healthy now, in the name of Jesus. All pain, fear of pain and fear of (*Problem*), I command you to GO now. I proclaim FREEDOM, IN THE NAME OF JESUS! Amen; so be it!

1 Thes 4:8 He therefore that despiseth, despiseth not man, but God, who hath also given unto us his holy Spirit.

Acts 2:33 Therefore being by the right hand of God exalted, and having received of the Father the promise of the Holy Ghost, he, *Jesus*, hath shed forth this, which ye now see and hear (*of them speaking of the wonderful works of God in other tongues, and being excited, as if happily drunk on the Day of Pentecost*).

Gal 3:14 That the blessing of Abraham might come on the Gentiles through Jesus Christ; that we might receive the promise of the Spirit through faith.

Gal 4:6 And because ye are sons, God hath sent forth the Spirit of his Son into your hearts, crying, Abba (*Daddy*), Father. *Praise You, Father, for giving the same Holy Spirit who is ever ready to heal and bless as He did through Jesus, the apostles and other believers through all time.*

2 Cor 5:5 Now he that hath wrought us for the selfsame thing is God, who also hath given unto us the earnest of the Spirit.

2 Cor 1:22 Who hath also sealed us, and given the earnest of the Spirit in our hearts.

2 Cor 13:5 Examine yourselves, whether ye be in the faith; prove your own selves. Know ye not your own selves, how that Jesus Christ is in you, except ye be reprobates (*useless in your Christian walk*)? *Praise You, Father God, that Je-*

THE BATTLE PRAYER

sus Christ dwells in me and I in Him by Your grace. Thank You! In the name of Jesus Christ of Nazareth, my Lord, thank You!

<u>1 John 4:4</u> Ye are of God, little children, and have overcome them: because greater is he that is in you, than he that is in the world.

<u>Rom 5:5</u> And hope maketh not ashamed; because the *agape*/love of God is shed abroad in our hearts by the Holy Ghost which is given unto us.

<u>2 Tim 1:14</u> That good thing which was committed unto thee keep by the Holy Ghost which dwelleth in us.

<u>1 Cor 3:16</u> Know ye not that ye are the temple of God, and that the Spirit of God dwelleth in you?

<u>Heb 13:5</u> … *You, Father God, have* said, I will never leave thee, nor forsake thee. 6 So that *I* may boldly say, The Lord is my helper, and I will not fear … . <u>Phil 4:13</u> I can do all things through Christ which strengtheneth me. … 19 But *You, Father,* my God, shall supply all *my* need (*aiteo*) according to *Your* riches in glory by Christ Jesus. 20 Now unto *You,* God and our Father, be glory for ever and ever. Amen. *Having the same Holy Spirit as Jesus, I can boldly say,* <u>1 John 4:17</u> … As *Jesus* is, so *am I* in this world, *and I can also confess:* <u>Isa 61:1</u> The Spirit of the Lord God is upon me; because the Lord hath anointed me to preach good tidings unto the meek; he hath sent me to bind up the brokenhearted, to proclaim liberty to the captives, and the opening of the prison to them that are bound; *knowing by Your Spirit in me that You sent Jesus to show that Your desire and will is always to heal, make whole and prosper. Jesus proclaimed Your mission for Him, and as I am in Jesus, I may also say:* <u>Luke 4:18</u> The Spirit of the Lord is upon me, because he hath anointed me to preach the gospel to the poor; he hath sent me to heal the brokenhearted, to preach deliverance to the captives, and recovering of sight to the blind, to set at liberty them that are bruised, 19 to preach the acceptable year of the Lord. *Father God, Your works for us are to continue to execute the victory against the devil and all his works, in the name, authority and power of Jesus Christ of Nazareth, my only Lord.*

<u>Matt 8:16</u> When evening came, they brought to Him many who were under the power of demons, and He drove out the spirits with a word and restored to health all who were sick. 17 And thus He fulfilled what was spoken by the prophet Isaiah, He Himself *lambano*/took [in order to carry away] our weaknesses and infirmities and bore away our diseases. [Isa 53:4.] AMP *And Jesus heals today.* <u>2 Cor 1:20</u> For all the promises of *You, Father* God, in *Jesus* are yea, and in him Amen, unto the glory of *You, Father* God … . <u>2 Cor 6:2</u> (For *You, Father, say,* I have heard thee in a time accepted, and in the day of *soteria*/salvation have I succoured thee: behold, now is the accepted time; behold, now is the day of *soteria*/salvation.) *And that the day of salvation is*

a day of judgment against the devil that includes us bringing Your deliverance to any and all prisoners and the oppressed of the devil for 1 John 4:17 *herein is our agape/love made perfect, that we may have boldness in the day of judgment, and in every day of prayer against the works of the devil*: because as Jesus is, so are we in this world. *Father, empower my words with Your Spirit of zoe/life in Christ Jesus. Let them be Your words, the words of Jesus, my Lord, spoken in His stead, as His proxy on Earth, now, for those to whom I minister.* Matt 6:9 After this manner therefore pray ye: Our Father which art in heaven, Hallowed be thy name. 10 Thy kingdom come. Thy will be done in earth, as it is in heaven. *For You, Father, are* Ps 103:6 the Lord, *who* executeth righteousness and judgment [*through me*] for all that are oppressed. Ps. 74:21 O let not the oppressed return ashamed: let the poor and needy praise thy name. 2 Tim 2:1 I therefore, *as Your son/daughter, by You working in me, I am* strong in the grace that is in Christ Jesus.

Father God, You are my God, for Ps 146:5 happy is he that hath the God of Jacob for his help, whose hope is in the Lord his God: 6 which made heaven, and earth, the sea, and all that therein is: which keepeth truth for ever: 7 which executeth judgment for the oppressed: which giveth food to the hungry. The Lord looseth the prisoners: 8 the Lord openeth the eyes of the blind: the Lord raiseth them that are bowed down: the Lord loveth the righteous: 9 the Lord preserveth the strangers; he relieveth the fatherless and widow: but the way of the wicked he turneth upside down (*including the devil and all his works*). 10 The Lord shall reign for ever, even thy God, O Zion, unto all generations. Praise ye the Lord. Ps 103:1 Bless the Lord, O my soul: and all that is within me, bless his holy name. 2 Bless *You, O* Lord, O my soul, and forget not all his benefits: *for it is Father God* 3 who forgiveth all *our* iniquities; who healeth all *our* diseases; 4 who redeemeth *our* life from destruction; who crowneth *us* with *chesed*/lovingkindness and *racham*/tender mercies; 5 who satisfieth *our* mouth with good things; so that *our* youth is renewed like the eagle's. 6 The Lord executeth righteousness and judgment [*through us*] for all that are oppressed. *Praise You, Lord, who is ever our Healer, our overwhelming strength against the devil!*

Praise You, Father, that Jesus suffered for us all, for You said: 1 Pet 2:24 Who his own self bare our sins in his own body on the tree, that we, being dead to sins, should *zao*/live unto righteousness: by whose stripes ye were healed. *Repeating again the prophecy:* Isa 53:4 Surely he hath *cabal*/borne our griefs (*infirmities*), and *nasa*/carried our sorrows (*sicknesses and pain*): yet we did esteem him stricken, smitten of God, and afflicted. 5 But he was wounded for our transgressions, he was bruised for our iniquities: the chastisement of our peace was upon him; and with his stripes we are healed. 6 All we like sheep have

THE BATTLE PRAYER

gone astray; we have turned every one to his own way; and the LORD hath laid on him the iniquity of us all. 7 He was oppressed, and he was afflicted, yet he opened not his mouth: he is brought as a lamb to the slaughter, and as a sheep before her shearers is dumb, so he openeth not his mouth. Isa 53:10 Yet it was the will of the Lord to bruise Him; He has put Him to grief and made Him sick. When You and He make His life an offering for sin [and He has risen from the dead, in time to come], He shall see His [spiritual] offspring, He shall prolong His days, and the will and pleasure of the Lord shall prosper in His hand. 11 He shall see [the fruit] of the travail of His soul and be satisfied; by His knowledge of Himself [which He possesses and imparts to others] shall My [uncompromisingly] righteous One, My Servant, justify many and make many righteous (upright and in right standing with God), for He shall bear their iniquities and their guilt [with the consequences, says the Lord]. AMP *Praise Jesus, this work is fully done. Finished!*

You tell us Father: Isa 57:19 I create the fruit of the lips; Peace, peace to him that is far off, and to him that is near, saith the LORD; and I will heal him. Eph 2:13 But now in Christ Jesus *we Gentiles* who sometimes were far off are made nigh by the blood of Christ. Rom 10:6 *So that* the righteousness which is of faith speaketh on this wise, Say not in thine heart, Who shall ascend into heaven? (that is, to bring Christ down from above:) 7 or, Who shall descend into the deep? (that is, to bring up Christ again from the dead.) 8 But what saith it? The word is nigh thee, even in thy mouth, and in thy heart: that is, the word of faith, which we preach; 9 that if thou shalt confess with thy mouth the Lord Jesus, and shalt believe in thine heart that God hath raised him from the dead, thou shalt be *sozo*/saved (*healed, made whole, nothing missing, nothing broken, no shortage, no lack, prosperous in every area of life, now and eternally with the* agape/ *love of God freely flowing in me by Holy Spirit*). 10 For with the heart man believeth unto righteousness (*perfect right standing with God, the same as Jesus*); and with the mouth confession is made unto *soteria*/salvation (*bringing to Earth wholeness, now and eternally, the will of God on Earth as it is in Heaven*). 11 For the scripture saith, Whosoever believeth on him shall not be ashamed. 12 For there is no difference between the Jew and the Greek: for the same Lord over all is rich unto all that call upon him. 13 For whosoever shall call upon the name of the Lord shall be *sozo*/saved (*healed, made whole, nothing missing, nothing broken, no shortage, no lack, prosperous in every area of life, now and eternally*).

14 How then shall they call on him in whom they have not believed? and how shall they believe in him of whom they have not heard? and how shall they hear without a preacher? 15 And how shall they preach, except they be sent? as it is written, How beautiful are the feet of them that preach the gospel

of peace (*the absolute assurance of things unseen, specific expectations, and the joyful expectation of coming good based on God's Word that all the blessings of God are now ours in Christ Jesus, now and eternally*), and bring glad tidings of good things! (Isa 52:7 *That our God reigns through men.*) 16 But they have not all obeyed the gospel. For Esaias saith, Lord, who hath believed our report? (Isa 53:1) 17 So then faith cometh by hearing, and hearing by the word of God (*in Christ*). *So, Father, reveal and keep fresh in me Your Word of salvation through Jesus Christ. Thank You, Father! In the name of Jesus, thank You! Yahoo! Hallelujah! Glory to You, Father God! This work is already done. Thank You, Father, thank You! Glory!*

Holy Father, You told us, after You raised Jesus from the dead and proclaimed Him both Lord and Messiah/Christ: Matt 28:18 And Jesus came and spake unto them, saying, All power (*authority*) is given unto me in heaven and in earth. Go ye therefore, and teach all nations, baptizing them in the name of the Father, and of the Son, and of the Holy Ghost: 20 teaching them to observe all things whatsoever I have commanded you: and, lo, I am with you always, even unto the end of the world. Amen. *And Your commands include:* Matt 10:7 And as ye go, preach, saying, The kingdom of heaven is at hand. 8 Heal the sick, cleanse the lepers, raise the dead, cast out devils: freely ye have received, freely give. John 1:12 But as many as received him, to them gave he power (*authority*) to become (*and operate as*) the sons of God, even to them that believe on his name: 13 which were born, not of blood, nor of the will of the flesh, nor of the will of man, but of God.

John 14:12 Verily, verily, I, *Jesus*, say unto you, He that believeth on me, the works that I do shall he do also; and greater works than these shall he do; because I go unto my Father. 13 And whatsoever ye shall *aiteo*/ask (*by demanding, expecting as due by covenant promise*) in my name, that will I do, that the Father may be glorified in the Son. 14 If ye shall *aiteo*/ask (*by demanding as due by covenant promise*) any thing in my name, I will do it. John 16:23 And in that day ye shall *aiteo*/ask (*by demanding as due by covenant promise*) me nothing. Verily, verily, I say unto you, Whatsoever ye shall *aiteo*/ask (*by demanding as due by covenant promise*) the Father in my name, he will give it you. 24 Hitherto have ye *aiteo*/asked (*by demanding as due by covenant promise*) nothing in my name: *aiteo*/ask (*by demanding as due by covenant promise*) and ye shall receive, that your joy may be full. 25 These things have I spoken unto you in proverbs: but the time cometh, when I shall no more speak unto you in proverbs, but I shall shew you plainly of the Father. 26 At that day ye shall *aiteo*/ask (*by demanding as due by covenant promise*) in my name: and I say not unto you, that I will pray the Father for you: 27 for the Father himself *agape*/loveth you, because ye have *agape*/loved me, and have believed that I came out from God. 1 John 3:23 And this is his commandment, That we should believe on the name of his Son Jesus

THE BATTLE PRAYER

Christ, and *agape*/love one another, as he gave us commandment. *Praise You, Father! You have commanded us through Jesus to* aiteo/*ask by demanding as due by covenant promise, so that our joy may be full and that You may be glorified. Thank You for making us co-workers with You, to bring Your will to Earth as it is in Heaven by* aiteo/*asking, by demanding as due by covenant promise, in the name of Jesus, for You to perform Your promises. Thank You! Thank You that I am born again of You, by Your choice! You* agape/*love me and are for me to win this battle with You!*

Father, in the name of Jesus Christ, the Good Shepherd, I demand as due by covenant promise that You, the Acts 4:24 ... Lord, *who* thou art God, which hast made heaven, and earth, and the sea, and all that in them is: 25 who by the mouth of thy servant David hast said, Why did the heathen rage, and the people imagine vain things? 26 The kings of the earth stood up, and the rulers were gathered together against the Lord, and against his Christ. 27 For of a truth against thy holy child Jesus, whom thou hast anointed, both Herod, and Pontius Pilate, with the Gentiles, and the people of Israel, were gathered together, 28 for to do whatsoever thy hand and thy counsel determined before to be done. 29 And now, Lord, behold *the* threatenings *of evil reports in sickness, disease, infirmities, sins, bondages and any doctor's diagnosis*: in this (PROBLEM) and grant unto *me, thy son/daughter who is a Jesus-born-again son that serves You,* that with all boldness *I* may speak thy word, 30 by stretching forth thine hand to heal; and that signs and wonders may be done by the name of thy holy child Jesus. *Fill me* with the Holy Ghost, and *give me courage, wisdom, discernment and opportunity to speak Your* word ... with boldness *as I ought to speak in spirit, grace, truth, faith and* agape/*love, so that Your glory may be extended upon the Earth. For You said:* Num 14:21 But as truly as I live, all the earth shall be filled with the glory of the LORD.

In the name of Jesus, for (PERSON'S NAME) in this (PROBLEM), devil, I take authority over you, and, in Jesus' name, I command you to listen, obey and go NOW, in the name of Jesus. (PERSON)'s body, I command you to be whole and healthy now, in the name of Jesus. All pain, fear of pain and fear of (PROBLEM), I command you to GO now. I proclaim FREEDOM, IN THE NAME OF JESUS! Amen; so be it!

FOR REPEATS: Lord, I am coming again to intercede for (PERSON'S NAME), per Luke 18:1 And he spake a parable unto them to this end, that men ought always to pray, and not to faint.

15. So Father, in the name of Jesus, I thank You in advance that You hear me, per Your Word, I come boldly to Your throne, to obtain mercy and to find grace for this need (PROBLEM) in (PERSON'S NAME). Where Ps 106:42 *the Satanic* enemies also oppressed (HIM/HER), and (HE/SHE) *was* brought into subjection under their hand through this (SICKNESS, DISEASE, INFIRMITY OR PROBLEM). *I obey by Your Holy Spirit of Agape in me:* Jude 20 But ye, *agape/*beloved, building up yourselves on your most holy faith, praying in the Holy Ghost, 21 keep yourselves in the *agape/*love of God, looking for the mercy of our Lord Jesus Christ unto eternal *zoe/*life. 22 And of some have compassion, making a difference: 23 and others *sozo/save (heal totally, nothing broken, nothing missing, prosperous in all parts of life, now and eternally)* with fear *(phobos)*, pulling them out of the fire; hating even the garment spotted by the flesh. *Father, thank You for working in me to will and to do this, as You blast the work of the devil out of (*PERSON'S NAME*). Thank You! In the name of Jesus, thank You!*

In the name of Jesus, for (PERSON'S NAME) in this (PROBLEM), devil, listen, obey and go NOW, in the name of Jesus, never to return! All fear and pain go now, in the name of Jesus! (PERSON)'s body, I command you to be whole and healthy now, in the name of Jesus. All symptoms, pain, fear of pain and fear of (PROBLEM) I command to GO now, never to return. I proclaim FREEDOM, IN THE NAME OF JESUS! Amen; so be it!

If you speak in tongues: Father, in the name of Jesus, have Holy Spirit pray through me now for this situation to victory. Help me stir myself up into Your Spirit to victory. Thank You, Father! In the name of Jesus, thank You! (Aim for 15 to 45 minutes or as Holy Spirit leads, letting the peace of God in your heart guide you. Also see 1 John 4:1-3) and/or preach to yourself with intensity one of the Healing Teachings.

Father, You have said in Your Word that: Isa 64:7 And there is none that calleth upon thy name, that stirreth up himself to take hold of thee: for thou hast hid thy face from us, and hast consumed us, because of our iniquities. *So, Father, I take hold of the name You have given, that name of Jesus Christ, for* Acts 4:12 neither is there *soteria/*salvation *(healing, wholeness)* in any other: for there is none other name under heaven given among men, whereby we must be *sozo/* saved *(healed, wholeness, nothing missing, nothing broken, fully prosperous in this life and forever, God's will on Earth as it is in Heaven)*. Isa 59:16 And he saw that there was no man, and wondered that there was no intercessor: therefore his arm brought salvation unto him; and his righteousness, it sustained him. *Father, thank You that Your salvation is Jesus, my Lord! Help me to walk in Jesus. Amen!*

16. Father, I now come before You as (PERSON'S NAME)'s intercessor. I now come before You to stand in the gap for (PERSON'S Name). I now come boldly before You to take hold of You, in order to help deliver (PERSON'S NAME) out of the oppression of the devil. Destroy every bit of this evil work of the enemy, in the name of Jesus. You have told us: Heb 4:16 Let us therefore come boldly unto the throne of grace, that we may obtain mercy, and find grace to help in

THE BATTLE PRAYER

time of need. *So, Father, I come in the name of Jesus Christ, my Lord. I forgive the sins of myself and (*Person's Name*), and proclaim total salvation in every part of (*Person's Name*)'s life now, in the name of Jesus Christ, who already paid for it. So be it! Thank You, Father!*

By Your grace, I am not afraid, for, Father, Your Word tells us that: Luke 18:27 And he (*Jesus*) said, The things which are impossible with men are possible with God. Luke 1:37 For with God nothing is ever impossible and no word from God shall be without power or impossible of fulfillment. AMP *Father, Thy Kingdom come! Thy will be done on Earth now, as it is in Heaven, in the name of Jesus!*

Again, Your Word tells us that: Ps 86:15 But thou, O Lord, art a God full of compassion, and gracious, longsuffering, and plenteous in *chesed*/mercy and truth. Ps 100:5 For the Lord is good; his *chesed*/mercy is everlasting; and his truth endureth to all generations. Ps 103:17 But the *chesed*/mercy of the Lord is from everlasting to everlasting upon them that fear him, and his righteousness unto children's children. Ps 119:142 Thy righteousness is an everlasting righteousness, and thy law is the truth. Ps 119:144 The righteousness of thy testimonies is everlasting. John 1:14 And the Word was made flesh (*Jesus of Nazareth*), and dwelt among us, (and we beheld his glory, the glory as of the only begotten of the Father,) full of grace (*chesed*) and truth. ... 17 For the law was given by Moses, ... grace (*chesed*) and truth came by Jesus Christ.

Father, in the name of Jesus, give (*Person's Name*) understanding, and he/she shall live free from this disease. In the name of Jesus Christ, I command the blindness to the Gospel to go and the light of the Gospel to shine on me and those for whom I pray. 2 Cor 4:6 For *You, Father* God, who commanded the light to shine out of darkness, hath shined in our hearts, to give the light of the knowledge of the glory of *You, Father* God, in the face of Jesus Christ. *I command myself and those I pray for to hear and see the Word of God and His hand, unto understanding, repentance, conversion and healing, unto strengthening the brethren and good works by faith in* agape/love, *to Your glory, by Jesus Christ. Thank You, Father, for Your love. Thank You! Thank You, Lord Jesus, by Your stripes we were healed!*

Thank You, Mighty Warrior, Father God, in the name of Jesus, for telling us so that we might have hope that: Mal 3:6 For I am the Lord, I change not; therefore ye sons of Jacob are not consumed. *That the God of the Old Testament is the same God of the New Testament who sent Jesus to show grace (chesed) and truth, that He heals all who come, anytime, anywhere, and that, as no man could save himself, so You, Father, sent Jesus to destroy the works of the devil and thereby save and reconcile us to You. And*: Heb 13:8 Jesus Christ the same yesterday, and to day, and for ever. *Praise You, Lord Jesus, that You are the same in the Old Testament and in the New.* Acts 10:34 ... God is no respecter of persons. Rom 2:11 For there is no respect of persons with *You, Father* God. *Your will was to heal through Jesus, and it is still Your will to heal through His Body on Earth, of which I am part. So, Lord, heal through me, in the name of the Lord Jesus Christ, my Intercessor and my Elder Brother. Thy salvation will be done on Earth now, as it already is in Heaven. Thank You, Abba, Father God, in Jesus' name.*

In the name of Jesus, for (<u>PERSON'S NAME</u>) *in this* (<u>PROBLEM</u>), devil, listen, obey and go NOW, in the name of Jesus, never to return. All fear and pain, go now, in the name of Jesus! (<u>PERSON</u>)'s body, I command you to be whole and healthy now, in the name of Jesus. All symptoms, damages, pain, fear of pain and fear of (<u>PROBLEM</u>) I command to GO now, never to return. I proclaim FREEDOM, IN THE NAME OF JESUS! Amen; so be it!

17. Bless You Father, in the name of Jesus Christ, 2 Cor 5:21 for *You have made Jesus to be sin for us, who knew no sin; that we might be made the righteousness of You, Father God in him. Therefore by the strength of Your Word that* John 20:23 *whose soever sins I remit, they are remitted unto them; and whose soever sins I retain, they are retained. I forgive all* (<u>PERSON</u>)'s *sins, and because* Gal 3:13 *Christ hath redeemed us from the curse of the law, being made a curse for us: for it is written, Cursed is every one that hangeth on a tree, and You,* Ps 129:4 *the* LORD *are righteous: You have cut asunder the cords of the wicked, for You justly decreed that:* Prov 5:22 *His own iniquities shall take the wicked himself, and he shall be holden with the cords of his sins. In the name of Jesus Christ of Nazareth, I bless* (<u>PERSON'S NAME</u>) *and break every curse in* (<u>PERSON</u>)'s *life and reverse it to blessing, break every snare, trap, net and cord, bind the strong man and all the helper demons, loose and command them to go now, and say, "Destroy" to every evil stronghold. And, in the name of Jesus, I command:* Ps 35:4 *Let them be confounded and put to shame that seek after* (<u>PERSON</u>)'s *soul: let them be turned back and brought to confusion that devise* (<u>PERSON</u>)'s *hurt and cut off all associated with the work of the devil in* (<u>PERSON'S NAME</u>). *For, Father, You said:* James 5:15 *And the prayer of faith shall sozo/save (heal, make whole and prosperous) the sick, and the Lord shall raise him up; and if he have committed sins, they shall be forgiven him. I proclaim they are HEALED NOW! Devil, go! Zoe/life come, NOW! All in the name of Jesus! Thank You, Father, it is already done. Amen and so be it!*

18. Isa 45:11 Thus saith the LORD, *the Holy One of Israel, and his Maker, Ask me of things to come concerning my sons, and concerning the work of my hands command ye me. Father, in the name of Jesus Christ, heal* (<u>PERSON'S NAME</u>)

THE BATTLE PRAYER

and fill (HIM/HER) with agape/love *for You and Your Word. Give (HIM/HER) eyes to see, ears to hear, a heart that hears and understands, to conversion, repentance, healing, strengthening the brethren and good works by faith in* agape/love *to Your glory. For You said:* Matt 7:11 If ye then, being evil, know how to give good gifts unto your children, how much more shall your Father which is in heaven give good things to them that *aiteo/ask (by demanding as due by covenant promise of)* him? *Father, heal totally spirit, soul and body, destroy the enemy oppressing him/her and pour out Your Spirit on (PERSON'S NAME), to walk gladly in all Your ways. Do Your salvation will now! Thank You, Father! In the name of Jesus Christ, my Lord, thank You!*

Father, You have told us You are the God 1 Tim 2:4 who will have all men to be *sozo*/saved (*healed, made perfectly whole and prosperous, spirit, soul and body, now and eternally*), and to come unto the *experiential* knowledge of the truth, *So I receive (PERSON'S NAME)'s full healing from this horrible enemy which has attacked his/her body, soul and spirit. As You have said this is Your will, I proclaim that the answer of wholeness is mine, as Jesus said:* Mark 11:24 Therefore I say unto you, What things soever ye *aiteo*/desire, *require, demand and expect as due by covenant promise, knowing all requirements have been met in Jesus,* when ye pray, believe that ye receive them, and ye shall have them. *Therefore, thank You, Father, in the name of Jesus, for healing (PERSON'S NAME).*

In the name of Jesus, for (PERSON'S NAME) in this (PROBLEM), devil, listen, obey and go NOW, in the name of Jesus, never to return. All fear and pain, go now, in the name of Jesus! (PERSON'S) body, I command you to be whole and healthy now, in the name of Jesus. I proclaim FREEDOM, IN THE NAME OF JESUS! Amen; so be it! Thanks be to God! Bless God and His power, in Jesus' name! Amen!

19. Father, You say in Your Word that James 5:16 ... the effective, fervent prayer of a righteous man avails much. *I am now going to take this (PROBLEM) head on, operating under Your authority, Father, Your power and Your anointing.* 2 Cor 5:21 For *You, Father, have* made *Jesus* to be sin for us, who knew no sin; that we might be made the righteousness of *You, Father* God, in him. 6:1 We then, as workers together with him ... receive not the grace of *Father* God in vain. 2 (*For You said,* I have heard thee in a time accepted, and in the day of *soteria*/salvation have I succoured thee: behold, now is the accepted time; behold, now is the day of *soteria*/salvation.) *Praise You, Farther, that this Day of Salvation means judgment against the devil and his works, just like Jesus did.* 2 Cor 1:19 For the Son of God, Jesus Christ, who was preached ... by *Holy Spirit through Paul,* was not yea and nay, but in him was yea. 20 For all the promises of God in him are yea, and in him Amen, unto the glory of God by us. 21 Now he which stablisheth us ... in

Christ, and hath anointed us, is *You, Father* God. Col 2:6 As ye have therefore received Christ Jesus the Lord, so walk ye in him. 1 John 2:2 And he is the propitiation for our sins: and not for ours only, but also for the sins of the whole world. 3 And hereby we do know that we know him, if we keep his commandments. 4 He that saith, I know him, and keepeth not his commandments, is a liar, and the truth is not in him. 5 But whoso keepeth his word, in him verily is the *agape*/love of God perfected: hereby know we that we are in him. 6 He that saith he abideth in him ought himself also so to walk, even as he walked. 1 John 5:2 By this we know that we *agape*/love the children of God, when we *agape*/love God, and keep his commandments. 3 For this is the *agape*/love of God, that we keep his commandments: and his commandments are not grievous. 4 For whatsoever is born of God overcometh the world: and this is the victory that overcometh the world, even our faith. 1 John 5:12 He that hath the Son hath *zoe*/life; and he that hath not the Son of God hath not *zoe*/life. 13 These things have I written unto you that believe on the name of the Son of God; that ye may know that ye have eternal *zoe*/life, and that ye may believe on the name of the Son of God. 1 Tim 6:12 Fight the good fight of faith, lay hold on eternal *zoe*/life, whereunto thou art also called … . Eph 2:4 But God, who is rich in mercy, for his great *agape*/love wherewith he *agape*/loved us, 5 even when we were dead in sins, hath quickened us together with Christ, (by grace ye are *sozo*/saved;) 6 and hath raised us up together, and made us sit together in heavenly places in Christ Jesus: 7 that in the ages to come he might shew the exceeding riches of his grace in his kindness toward us through Christ Jesus. 8 For by grace are ye *sozo*/saved through faith; and that not of yourselves: it is the gift of God: 9 not of works, lest any man should boast. 10 For we are his workmanship, created in Christ Jesus unto good works, which God hath before ordained that we should walk in them. John 6:29 Jesus answered and said unto them, This is the work of God, that ye believe on him whom he hath sent. John 8:31 Then said Jesus to those Jews which believed on him, If ye continue in my word, then are ye my disciples indeed; 32 and ye shall know the truth, and the truth shall make you free (*to set yourself and others free of all rule of the devil*). Mark 16:15 And he (*Jesus*) said unto them, Go ye into all the world, and preach the gospel to every creature. 16 He that believeth and is baptized shall be *sozo*/saved; but he that believeth not shall be damned. 17 And these signs shall follow them that believe; In my name shall they cast out devils; they shall speak with new tongues; 18 they shall take up serpents; and if they drink any deadly thing, it shall not hurt them; they shall lay hands on the sick, and they shall recover. 19 So then after the Lord had spoken unto them, he was received up into heaven, and sat on the right hand of God. 20 And they went forth, and preached everywhere,

THE BATTLE PRAYER

the Lord working with them, and confirming the word with signs following. Amen. 3 John 2 *Agape*/beloved, I wish (*pray*) above all things that thou mayest prosper and be in health, even as thy soul prospereth.

Father, You have also told us in Your Word that we have Your anointing: 1 John 2:20 But ye have an unction from the Holy One, and ye know all things. 1 John 2:27 But the anointing which ye have received of him abideth in you, and ye need not that any man teach you: but as the same anointing teacheth you of all things, and is truth, and is no lie, and even as it hath taught you, ye shall abide in him. So *that we can boldly say:* Luke 4:18 The Spirit of the Lord is upon me, because he hath anointed me to preach the gospel to the poor; he hath sent me to heal the brokenhearted, to preach deliverance to the captives, and recovering of sight to the blind, to set at liberty them that are bruised, 19 to preach the acceptable year of the Lord. *Jesus has given us the power to heal all kinds of diseases, and we are to lay hands on the sick and they will recover. You said:* Luke 10:19 Behold, I give unto you power (*authority, commission and ability*) to tread on (*totally crush*) serpents and scorpions, and over all the power (*ability*) of the enemy: and nothing shall by any means hurt you.

This (*PROBLEM*) that has attacked (*PERSON'S NAME*) is (*HIS/HER*) enemy and is using this (*PROBLEM*) to rob, kill and to destroy (*HIM/HER/THEM*), and as such, I am now going to war directly against it, in the name of Jesus Christ of Nazareth, my Lord. Father, as You have said in Your Word: Isa 57:19 I create the fruit of the lips; Peace, peace to him that is far off, and to him that is near, saith the LORD; and I will heal him. *So, Father, in the name of Jesus, create the fruit of my lips to heal* (*PERSON'S NAME*). Heb 3:1 Wherefore, holy brethren, partakers of the heavenly calling, consider the Apostle and High Priest of our profession, Christ Jesus. *So, Lord Jesus, take these words of my intercession, proclamation, thanksgiving and commands and produce fruit, that the Father may be glorified. So I put on Your strength:* Eph 6:10 Finally, my brethren, be strong in the Lord, and in the power of his might. Zec 4:6 ... Not by might, nor by power, but by my spirit, saith the LORD of hosts. *According to* Eph 1:19 ... the exceeding greatness of *Your* power to us-ward who believe, according to the working of *Your* mighty power, 20 which *You* wrought in Christ, when *You* raised *Jesus* from the dead, and set him at *Your* own right hand in the heavenly places, 21 far above all principality, and power, and might, and dominion, and every name that is named, not only in this world, but also in that which is to come: 22 and hath put all things under his feet, and gave him to be the head over all things to the church, *of which I am a part*, 23 which is his body, the fulness of him that filleth all in all. 1 Cor 12:27 Now ye are the body of Christ, and members in particular. *So, by Your grace, I will* 1 Sam 12:16 now therefore stand and see this great thing, which the LORD will do before *my* eyes. *For You said:* Jer 30:17 For I will restore health unto thee, and I will heal thee of thy wounds, saith the LORD … , *and* Ps 34:17 the righteous cry, and the LORD heareth, and delivereth them out of all their troubles … . 19 Many are the afflictions of the righteous: but the LORD delivereth him out of them all … . *As I intercede, I say:* 1 John 1:10 If we say that we have not sinned, we make *You, Father God,* a liar, and *Your* word is not in us. *Therefore* Ps 106:6 we have sinned with our fathers, we have committed iniquity, we have done wickedly. *And* Dan 9:5 we have sinned, and have committed iniquity, and have done wickedly, and have rebelled, even by departing from thy precepts and from thy judgments. Isa 37:20 Now therefore, O LORD our God, save us from *the hand of the enemy*, that all the kingdoms of the earth may know that thou art the LORD, even thou only.

Father, as You said: Isa 45:11 "… Concerning the work of my hands command (*require*) ye me." **So, in the name of Jesus**, for (*PERSON'S NAME*) in this or any (*PROBLEM*), devil and all works, listen, obey and go, NOW, in the name of Jesus, never to return. All fear and pain, go now, in the name of Jesus! Do not ever return. (*PERSON*)'s body, I command you to be whole and healthy, now, in the name of Jesus. All pain, fear of pain and fear of (*PROBLEM*) I command to GO, now. I proclaim FREEDOM, IN JESUS' NAME! Amen; so be it!

20. Father, God of All Comfort, in the name of Jesus, I thank You that both Jesus and Holy Spirit help and intercede for me. John 14:26 *For* the Comforter, which is the Holy Ghost, whom the Father *hath sent* in my name, he shall teach you all things, and bring all things to your remembrance, whatsoever I have said unto you. John 16:13 Howbeit when he, the Spirit of truth, is come, he will guide you into all truth: for he shall not speak of himself; but whatsoever he shall hear, that shall he speak: and he will shew you things to come. 14 He shall glorify me: for he shall receive of mine, and shall shew it unto you. 15 All things that the Father hath are mine: therefore said I, that he shall take of mine, and shall shew it unto you. Rom 8:26 Likewise the Spirit also helpeth (*us to stand against*) our (*or others'*) infirmities: for we know not what we should pray for as we ought: but the Spirit itself maketh intercession for us with groanings which cannot be uttered. 27 And he that searcheth the hearts knoweth what is the mind of the Spirit, because he maketh intercession for the saints according to the will of God. Heb 7:25 Wherefore he (*Jesus*) is able also to *sozo*/save (*heal, restore, make whole and prosperous, with no lack, now and eternally*) them to the uttermost that come unto You, *Father* God, by him, seeing he ever *zao*/liveth to make intercession for them.

So, Father I trust that as I pray, You will lead me in the battle for this victory to see Your Kingdom extended and that You, Father, Son and Holy Ghost,

THE BATTLE PRAYER

help me, as I intercede for (*Person's Name*). Father, I ask You to go before me to take this (*Problem*), to take it fully out of (*Person's Name*)'s body and to restore (*his/her*) physical body to perfect physical health. Let Your miracle and healing power flow through me as (*his/her*) intercessor to fully heal (*him/her*), in the name of Your Son, Jesus Christ. Let Your saving will be done on Earth now! Give this daily bread of deliverance. Empower my word with Your love.

Father, as You said, Isa 45:11 "… Concerning the work of my hands command (*require*) ye me." **So, in the name of Jesus,** for (*Person's Name*) in this or any (*Problem*), devil and all works, listen, obey and go, NOW, in the name of Jesus, never to return. All fear and pain, go now, in the name of Jesus! Do not ever return. (*Person*)'s body, I command you to be free, whole and healthy, now, in the name of Jesus. All pain, fear of pain and fear of (*Problem*) I command to GO, now. I proclaim FREEDOM, IN JESUS' NAME! Amen; so be it!

If the sick person dies, change the command to this: Ps 118:17 "(*Person's Name*) shall not die, but live, and declare the works of the Lord." Lord, keep me in this fight until Your glory is manifested! Don't let me faint just because it appears the devil is winning.

If you need to, turn you head or close your eyes and look to Jesus as Lord and Conqueror and not the situation/person. Jesus is Lord!

21. Father, in the name of Jesus, the Living Word of God, give me and (*Person's Name*) Your Spirit of wisdom and revelation in the knowledge of You, with the eyes of our understanding being enlightened to You in Your Word unto Your Warrior's heart against our enemy, the devil, and all his works:

John 17:17 Sanctify *my heart* through thy truth: thy word is truth. *Perform Your Word, as You tell us that:* Ex 15:3 The Lord is a man of war: the Lord is his name. … 6 Thy right hand, O Lord, is become glorious in power: thy right hand, O Lord, hath dashed in pieces the enemy.

Isa 42:13 The Lord shall go forth as a mighty man, he shall stir up jealousy like a man of war: he shall cry, yea, roar; he shall prevail against his enemies.

Deut 9:3 Understand therefore this day, that the Lord thy God is he which goeth over before thee; as a consuming fire he shall destroy them, and he shall bring them down before thy face: so shalt thou drive them out, and destroy them quickly, as the Lord hath said unto thee.

Isa 45:2 I will go before thee, and make the crooked places straight: I will break in pieces the gates of brass, and cut in sunder the bars of iron.

Isa 59:19 So shall they fear the name of the Lord from the west, and his glory from the rising of the sun. When the enemy shall come in like a flood, the Spirit of the Lord shall lift up a standard against him.

Isa 54:17 No weapon that is formed against thee shall prosper; and every tongue that shall rise against thee in judgment thou shalt condemn. This is the heritage of the servants of the Lord, and their righteousness is of me, saith the Lord.

Ps 105:37 He brought them forth also with silver and gold: and there was not one feeble person among their tribes.

2 Tim 4:18 And the Lord shall deliver me from every evil work, and will preserve me unto his heavenly kingdom: to whom be glory for ever and ever. Amen.

Ps 18:2 The Lord is my rock, and my fortress, and my deliverer; my God, my strength, in whom I will trust; my buckler, and the horn of my salvation, and my high tower. 3 I will call upon the Lord, who is worthy to be praised: so shall I be saved from mine enemies.

Ps 37:9 For evildoers shall be cut off: but those that wait upon the Lord, they shall inherit the earth. ... 39 But the salvation of the righteous is of the Lord: he is their strength in the time of trouble. 40 And the Lord shall help them and deliver them: he shall deliver them from the wicked, and save them, because they trust in him.

Ex 14:14 The Lord shall fight for you, and ye shall hold your peace.

2 Chron 32:7 Be strong and courageous, be not afraid nor dismayed ... for there be more with us than with him: 8 with him is an arm of flesh; but with us is the Lord our God to help us, and to fight our battles. And the people rested themselves upon the words of Hezekiah king of Judah.

Deut 33:26 There is none like unto the God of Jeshurun, who rideth upon the heaven in thy help, and in his excellency on the sky. 27 The eternal God is thy refuge, and underneath are the everlasting arms: and he shall thrust out the enemy from before thee; and shall say, Destroy them.

Rom 8:33 Who shall lay any thing to the charge of God's elect? It is God that justifieth. 34 Who is he that condemneth? It is Christ that died, yea rather, that is risen again, who is even at the right hand of God, who also maketh intercession for us.

Rom 6:6 **Knowing** this, that our old man is crucified with him, that the body of sin might be destroyed, that henceforth we should not serve sin. 7 For he that is dead is freed from sin. 8 Now if we be dead with Christ, we believe that we shall also *zao*/live with him: 9 **knowing** that Christ being raised from the dead dieth no more; death hath no more dominion over him. 10 For in that he died, he died unto sin once: but in that he *zao*/liveth, he *zao*/liveth unto God. 11 **Likewise reckon** ye also yourselves to be dead indeed unto sin, but *zao*/alive unto God through Jesus Christ our Lord.

THE BATTLE PRAYER

Rom 6:17 But God be thanked, that ye were the servants (*slaves*) of sin, but ye have obeyed from the heart that form of doctrine which was delivered you. 18 Being then made free from sin, ye became the servants (*slaves*) of righteousness.

Rom 5:19 For as by one man's disobedience many were made sinners, so by the obedience of one shall many be made righteous. 20 Moreover the law entered, that the offence might abound. But where sin abounded, grace did much more abound: 21 that as sin hath reigned unto death, even so might grace reign through righteousness unto eternal *zoe*/life by Jesus Christ our Lord.

2 Cor 4:13 We having the same spirit of faith, according as it is written, I believed, and therefore have I spoken; we also believe, and therefore speak … . 18 While we look not at the things which are seen, but at the things which are not seen: for the things which are seen are temporal; but the things which are not seen are eternal.

2 Cor 5:18 And all things are of God, who hath reconciled us to himself by Jesus Christ, and hath given to us the ministry of reconciliation; 19 to wit, that God was in Christ, reconciling the world unto himself, not imputing their trespasses unto them; and hath committed unto us the word of reconciliation. 20 Now then we are ambassadors for Christ, as though God did beseech you by us: we pray you in Christ's stead, be ye reconciled to God. 21 For he hath made him to be sin for us, who knew no sin; that we might be made the righteousness of God in him. *Praise You, Father, in the name of Jesus, for You have judged and healed all the sins of the human race in one action of Jesus on the cross, so that Jesus never need die again. Praise Your eternal salvation in the blood of Jesus, our High Priest.*

Heb 5:9 And being made perfect, he (*Jesus*) became the author of eternal *soteria*/salvation unto all them that obey him.

Isa 49:6 And he said, It is a light thing that thou shouldest be my servant to raise up the tribes of Jacob, and to restore the preserved of Israel: I will also give thee for a light to the Gentiles, that thou mayest be my salvation unto the end of the earth.

Heb 9:12 Neither by the blood of goats and calves, but by his own blood he entered in once into the holy place, having obtained eternal redemption for us. 13 For if the blood of bulls and of goats, and the ashes of an heifer sprinkling the unclean, sanctifieth to the purifying of the flesh: 14 how much more shall the blood of Christ, who through the eternal Spirit offered himself without spot to God, purge your conscience from dead works to serve the *zao*/living God? 15 And for this cause he is the mediator of the new testament, that by means of death, for the redemption of the transgressions that were under the first testament, they which are called might receive the promise of eternal inheritance.

Heb 9:26 For then must he (*Jesus*) often have suffered since the foundation of the world: but now once in the end of the world hath he appeared to put away sin by the sacrifice of himself. 27 And as it is appointed unto men once to die, but after this the judgment: 28 so Christ was once offered to bear the sins of many; and unto them that look for him shall he appear the second time without sin unto *soteria*/salvation.

Heb 10:10 By the which will we are sanctified through the offering of the body of Jesus Christ once for all. ... 12 But this man, after he had offered one sacrifice for sins for ever, sat down on the right hand of God; 13 from henceforth expecting till his enemies be made his footstool. 14 For by one offering he hath perfected for ever them that are sanctified.

Rom 6:10 For in that he died, he died unto sin once: but in that he *zao*/liveth, he *zao*/liveth unto God.

Heb 7:26 For such an high priest became us, who is holy, harmless, undefiled, separate from sinners, and made higher than the heavens; 27 who needeth not daily, as those high priests, to offer up sacrifice, first for his own sins, and then for the people's: for this he did once, when he offered up himself. 28 For the law maketh men high priests which have infirmity; but the word of the oath, which was since the law, maketh the Son, who is consecrated for evermore.

Acts 28:26 Go to this people and say to them, You will indeed hear and hear with your ears but will not understand, and you will indeed look and look with your eyes but will not see [not perceive, have knowledge of or become acquainted with what you look at, at all]. 27 For the heart (the understanding, the soul) of this people has grown dull (stupid, hardened, and calloused), and their ears are heavy and hard of hearing and they have shut tight their eyes, so that they may not perceive and have knowledge and become acquainted with their eyes and hear with their ears and understand with their souls and turn [to Me and be converted], that I may heal them. 28 So let it be understood by you then that [this message of] the *soteria*/salvation of God has been sent to the Gentiles, and they will listen [to it]! AMP

Acts 28:26 Saying, Go unto this people, and say, Hearing ye shall hear, and shall not understand; and seeing ye shall see, and not perceive: 27 for the heart of this people is waxed gross, and their ears are dull of hearing, and their eyes have they closed; lest they should see with their eyes, and hear with their ears, and understand with their heart, and should be converted, and I should heal them. 28 Be it known therefore unto you, that the *soteria*/salvation of God is sent unto the Gentiles, and that they will hear it. [*This is repeated in Isa 6:9-10, Ezek 12:2, Matt 13:14-15, Mark 4:12, John 12:38, Rom 11:8-10, Deut 29:4, Jer 5:21, and then explained in 2 Cor 4:4.*]

THE BATTLE PRAYER

<u>2 Cor 4:3</u> But if our gospel be hid, it is hid to them that are lost (*perish, have death working in them in any and every way*): 4 in whom the god of this world hath blinded the minds of them which believe not, lest the light of the glorious gospel of Christ, who is the image of God, should shine unto them. 5 For we preach not ourselves, but Christ Jesus the Lord; and ourselves your servants for Jesus' sake. 6 For God, who commanded the light to shine out of darkness, hath shined in our hearts, to give the light of the knowledge of the glory of God in the face of Jesus Christ. 7 But we have this treasure in earthen vessels, that the excellency of the power may be of God, and not of us.

<u>Heb 4:12</u> For the word of God is quick, and powerful, and sharper than any twoedged sword, piercing even to the dividing asunder of soul and spirit, and of the joints and marrow, and is a discerner of the thoughts and intents of the heart. 13 Neither is there any creature that is not manifest in his sight: but all things are naked and opened unto the eyes of him with whom we have to do.

<u>Matt 7:7</u> Keep on *aiteo*/asking (*by demanding, expecting as due by covenant promise*) and it will be given you; keep on seeking and you will find; keep on knocking [reverently] and [the door] will be opened to you. 8 For everyone who keeps on *aiteo*/asking (*by demanding, expecting as due by covenant promise*) receives; and he who keeps on seeking finds; and to him who keeps on knocking, [the door] will be opened. AMP

<u>Eph 2:4</u> But God, who is rich in mercy, for his great *agape*/love wherewith he *agape*/loved us, 5 even when we were dead in sins, hath quickened us together with Christ, (by grace ye are *sozo*/saved;) 6 and hath raised us up together, and made us sit together in heavenly places in Christ Jesus: 7 that in the ages to come he might shew the exceeding riches of his grace in his kindness toward us through Christ Jesus. 8 For by grace are ye *sozo*/saved through faith; and that not of yourselves: it is the gift of God: 9 not of works, lest any man should boast. 10 For we are his workmanship, created in Christ Jesus unto good works, which God hath before ordained that we should walk in them.

Father, as You said, <u>Isa 45:11</u> "… Concerning the work of my hands command (*require*) ye me." **So, in the name of Jesus**, for (<u>Person's Name</u>) in this (<u>Problem</u>), the devil and all his works, listen, obey and go, NOW, in the name of Jesus, never to return. All fear and pain, go now, in the name of Jesus! Do not ever return. (<u>Person's Name</u>)'s body, I command you to be free, whole and healthy, now, in the name of Jesus. All pain, fear of pain and fear of (<u>Problem</u>) I command to GO, now. I proclaim FREEDOM, IN JESUS' NAME! Amen; so be it!

<u>Rom 8:11</u> But if the Spirit of him that raised up Jesus from the dead dwell in you, he that raised up Christ from the dead shall also quicken your mortal

(current, subject to die) bodies by his Spirit that dwelleth in you. [*Note: this is the body you have right now, not the immortal, free-from-death one you will get later.*]

Mark 11:23 For verily I say unto you, That whosoever shall say unto this mountain, Be thou removed, and be thou cast into the sea; and shall not doubt in his heart, but shall believe that those things which he saith shall come to pass; he shall have whatsoever he saith. 24 Therefore I say unto you, What things soever ye *aiteo*/desire, *demand as due by covenant promise, knowing all requirements have been met in Jesus*, when ye pray, believe that ye receive them, and ye shall have them.

Mal 4:2 But unto you that fear my name shall the Sun of righteousness arise with healing in his wings; and ye shall go forth, and grow up as calves of the stall. 3 And ye shall tread down the wicked; for they shall be ashes under the soles of your feet in the day that I shall do this, saith the LORD of hosts.

Ps 61:4 I will abide in thy tabernacle for ever: I will trust in the covert of thy wings. Selah. 5 For thou, O God, hast heard my vows: thou hast given me the heritage of those that fear thy name.

John 10:38 But if I *(Jesus)* do, though ye believe not me, believe the works: that ye may know, and believe, that the Father is in me, and I in him.

Ex 14:15 And the LORD said unto Moses, Wherefore criest thou unto me? speak unto the children of Israel, that they go forward: 16 but lift thou up thy rod, and stretch out thine hand over the sea, and divide it: and the children of Israel shall go on dry ground through the midst of the sea.

Ex 15:1 Then sang Moses and the children of Israel this song unto the LORD, and spake, saying, I will sing unto the LORD, for he hath triumphed gloriously: the horse and his rider hath he thrown into the sea. 2 The LORD is my strength and song, and he is become my salvation: he is my God, and I will prepare him an habitation; my father's God, and I will exalt him. 3 The LORD is a man of war: the LORD is his name.

Eph 5:1 Be ye therefore followers *(imitators, copycats)* of God, as *agape*/dear children [*and develop that attitude, like He has, of an* agape/*love warrior against the devil and his works, for the blessing of mankind, using the authority and the name of Jesus, in the power of Holy Spirit, as did Jesus*]; 2 and walk in *agape*/love, as Christ also hath *agape*/loved us, and hath given himself for us an offering and a sacrifice to God for a sweetsmelling savour.

Col 2:8 Beware lest any man spoil you through philosophy and vain deceit, after the tradition of men, after the rudiments of the world, and not after Christ. 9 For in him dwelleth all the fulness of the Godhead bodily. 10 And ye are complete in him, which is the head of all principality and power: 11 in whom also ye are circumcised with the circumcision made without hands,

THE BATTLE PRAYER

in putting off the body of the sins of the flesh by the circumcision of Christ: 12 buried with him in baptism, wherein also ye are risen with him through the faith of the operation of God, who hath raised him from the dead. 13 And you, being dead in your sins and the uncircumcision of your flesh, hath he quickened together with him, having forgiven you all trespasses; 14 blotting out the handwriting of ordinances that was against us, which was contrary to us, and took it out of the way, nailing it to his cross; 15 and having spoiled principalities and powers, he made a shew of them openly, triumphing over them in it [*the suffering and stripes, being made sin, death for all men, being made alive in spirit and then in body of resurrection, and then glorification, to sending back Holy Spirit*].

1 Pet 3:21 … by the resurrection of Jesus Christ: 22 who is gone into heaven, and is on the right hand of God; angels and authorities and powers being made subject unto him.

John 16:8 And when he (*Holy Spirit*) is come, he will reprove the world of sin, and of righteousness, and of judgment: 9 of sin, because they believe not on me; 10 of righteousness, because I go to my Father, and ye see me no more; 11 of judgment, because the prince of this world is judged.

Heb 2:14 Forasmuch then as the children are partakers of flesh and blood, he also himself likewise took part of the same; that through death he might destroy him that had the power of death, that is, the devil; 15 and deliver them who through fear of death were all their lifetime subject to bondage.

1 John 3:8 He that committeth sin is of the devil; for the devil sinneth from the beginning. For this purpose the Son of God was manifested, that he might destroy the works of the devil.

James 4:7 Submit yourselves therefore to God. Resist (*fight with the name of Jesus*) the devil, and he (*the devil*) will flee from you [*for our battle is not against flesh and blood, but against the devil and his works*]. 8 Draw nigh to God, and he will draw nigh to you. Cleanse your hands, ye sinners; and purify your hearts, ye double minded. 9 Be afflicted, and mourn, and weep: let your laughter be turned to mourning, and your joy to heaviness. 10 Humble yourselves in the sight of the Lord [*to do it His way, by faith in the authority and name of Jesus*], and he shall lift you up.

1 Pet 5:6 Humble yourselves therefore under the mighty hand of God, that he may exalt you in due time: 7 casting all your care upon him; for he careth for you. 8 Be sober, be vigilant; because your adversary the devil, as a roaring lion, walketh about, seeking whom he may devour: 9 whom resist (*fight with the name and authority of Jesus*) stedfast in the faith, knowing that the same afflictions are accomplished in your brethren that are in the world.

Rom 16:20 And the God of peace shall bruise (*crush*) Satan under your feet shortly (*as shattered glass*). The grace of our Lord Jesus Christ be with you [*to think, know, be and do this*]. Amen.

Acts 10:38 How God anointed Jesus of Nazareth with the Holy Ghost and with power: who went about doing good, and healing all that were oppressed (*under the active rule and lordship*) of the devil (*in sickness, disease, leprosy, having demons, maiming, early death, poverty, lack of knowing God and His power by the Scriptures, and religious lies and deceptions*); for God was with him.

Ps 27:13 I had fainted, unless I had believed to see the goodness of the LORD in the land of the living.

3 John 2 *Agape*/beloved, I wish above all things that thou mayest prosper and be in health, even as thy soul prospereth.

1 John 5:4 For whatsoever is born of God overcometh the world: and this is the victory that overcometh the world, even our faith.

1 Cor 15:57 But thanks be to God, which giveth us the victory through our Lord Jesus Christ. 58 Therefore, my *agape*/beloved brethren, be ye stedfast, unmoveable, always abounding in the work of the Lord, forasmuch as ye know that your labour is not in vain in the Lord.

Ps 24:8 Who is this King of glory? The LORD strong and mighty, the LORD mighty in battle.

Ps 45:3 Gird thy sword upon thy thigh, O most mighty, with thy glory and thy majesty.

Rev 19:11 And I saw heaven opened, and behold a white horse; and he that sat upon him was called Faithful and True, and in righteousness he doth judge and make war. 12 His eyes were as a flame of fire, and on his head were many crowns; and he had a name written, that no man knew, but he himself. 13 And he was clothed with a vesture dipped in blood: and his name is called The Word of God.

Rev 1:18 I (*Jesus*) am he that *zao*/liveth, and was dead; and, behold, I am *zao*/alive for evermore, Amen; and have the keys of hell and of death.

Matt 12:20 A bruised reed shall he not break, and smoking flax shall he not quench, till he send forth judgment [*against the devil and his works to sozo/save that which was lost and put under the devil's rule*] unto victory. 21 And in his name shall the Gentiles trust.

Father, You, who do the works by Your Spirit, in the name of Jesus, I now ask that you stir Yourself up like a Man of War; You proceed to go before me like a mighty Warrior King; You proceed to go before me as a consuming fire to make this crooked path straight. Show Your salvation though me now.

THE BATTLE PRAYER

Father, I thank You this is already done and, as You said: Isa 45:11 "… Concerning the work of my hands command (*require*) ye me." **So, in the name of Jesus,** for (P<small>ERSON'S</small> N<small>AME</small>) in this or any (P<small>ROBLEM</small>), devil and all your works, in the name of Jesus, I take authority over you and command you to listen, obey and go, NOW, in the name of Jesus, never to return. All fear and pain, go now, in the name of Jesus! Do not ever return. (P<small>ERSON</small>)'s body, I command you to be free, whole and healthy now, in the name of Jesus. All damages, symptoms, pain, fear of pain and fear of (P<small>ROBLEM</small>) I command to GO now, never to return. I proclaim FREEDOM, IN JESUS' NAME! Amen; so be it! Thanks be to You, Father God! In the name of Jesus, thank You!

22. Father, I now ask that You deliver (P<small>ERSON'S</small> N<small>AME</small>) from this (P<small>ROBLEM</small>). I now ask that You fight for (P<small>ERSON'S</small> N<small>AME</small>), per Your covenant promises: Ex 14:14 The L<small>ORD</small> shall fight for *us*, and *we* shall hold *our* peace. Deut 1:30 The L<small>ORD</small> your God which goeth before you, he shall fight for you, according to all that he did for you in Egypt before your eyes. Deut 3:22 Ye shall not fear them: for the L<small>ORD</small> your God he shall fight for you. Deut 20:4 For the L<small>ORD</small> your God is he that goeth with you, to fight for you against your enemies, to save you. Ps 2:9 Thou shalt break *Satan's works* with a rod of iron; thou shalt dash them in pieces like a potter's vessel. *And that You dash this enemy into pieces, that You cut this cord of wickedness that has bound (*<small>HIM/HER</small>*) up, that You thrust this enemy out quickly and that You completely destroy every single (*P<small>ROBLEM</small>*) that has invaded (*<small>HIS/HER</small>*) body, now, in the name of the Lord Jesus Christ of Nazareth! Now, body, be whole, fully restored and functioning wonderfully, as Father God designed it, now, in the name of Jesus Christ!*

Father, release and empower Your angels to win this battle: Heb 1:14 Are they not all ministering spirits, sent forth to minister for them who shall be heirs of *soteria*/salvation (*saved from the penalty, wages, curse, power, presence, sickness, disease, infirmity, limits, bondage, restlessness, poverty, future and pleasure of sin*)? *Father, in the name of Jesus, destroy this enemy for:* Job 4:9 By the blast of God they perish, and by the breath of his nostrils are they consumed. Ps 144:6 Cast forth lightning, and scatter them: shoot out thine arrows, and destroy them. *Thank you, Father, in the name of Jesus, it is already done. Amen and so be it! Praise the name of Jesus! God's salvation has come. Praise the power of the name of Jesus, praise the name of Jesus! Praise You, Lord Jesus, praise You for Your mighty work! Glory!*

Father, as You said: Isa 45:11 "… Concerning the work of my hands command (*require*) ye me." **So, in the name of Jesus,** for (P<small>ERSON'S</small> N<small>AME</small>) in this or any (P<small>ROBLEM</small>), the devil and all his works, listen, obey and go, NOW, in the name of Jesus, never to return. All fear and pain, go now, in the name of Jesus! Do not ever return. (P<small>ERSON</small>)'s body, I command you to be whole and healthy, now, in the name of Jesus. All pain, fear of pain and fear of (PROBLEM) I command to GO, now. I proclaim FREEDOM, IN JESUS' NAME! Amen; so be it!

Be sensitive, as Holy Spirit may want you to repeat any of these sections several times. Dig in and fight with trust. Faint not!

FOR REPEATS: *Lord, I am coming again to intercede for (PERSON'S NAME), per* Luke 18:1 And he spake a parable unto them to this end, that men ought always to pray, and not to faint, a*nd* Ps 18:42 Then did I beat them small as the dust before the wind: I did cast them out as the dirt in the streets.

23. Father, Mighty Man of War, thank You this is already done, in the name of Jesus. Stir Yourself and destroy Your enemies with Your lightning and arrows through my words. It's over, devil! I bring the Kingdom of God near now to (PERSON'S NAME) through me, and in my thoughts and words. In the name of Jesus, the name above every name that is named, including you and yours devil, above all rulers, authorities, principalities and powers, the name at which every knee must bow and every tongue confess that Jesus is Lord. Satan, you bow and you confess Jesus as your Lord right now, and in the name of Jesus, your Lord, leave, take all your evil works, and go from (PERSON'S NAME), now, never to return, in the name of Jesus! So be it! Amen!

Father of lights, in the name of Jesus, send this healing word by Your ministering spirits to (PERSON'S NAME), per: Ps 107:20 He sent his word, and healed them, and delivered them from their destructions. *And:* Heb 1:14 Are they (*God's angels*) not all ministering spirits, sent forth to minister for them who shall be heirs of *soteria*/salvation (*including healing and prosperity*)? *And:* Ps 103:20 Bless the LORD, ye his angels, that excel in strength, that do his commandments, hearkening unto the voice of his word. 21 Bless ye the LORD, all ye his hosts; ye ministers of his, that do his pleasure. *And:* Ps 91:11 For he shall give his angels charge over thee, to keep thee in all thy ways.

Father, in the name of Jesus, I now put the redeeming, cleansing and devil-work-destroying, sanctifying, way-making, reconciling, overcoming, peace-making and unifying blood of Jesus Christ against every single source and type of pain and against every single cell, virus, fungus, agent, damage and spirit that is operating in (PERSON)'s body. **_Against specific symptoms:_** I now put the blood and stripes of my Lord and Savior Jesus Christ on and against every single (PROBLEM) that is operating in (HIS/HER) life. I now put the blood of Jesus on and against every single (PROBLEM) that is running or working in (HIS/HER) life. All pain, fear of pain and fear of (PROBLEM) I command to GO, now. I command every evil living thing to obey my voice and to die, and the

THE BATTLE PRAYER

devil and all evil works to GO, NOW, never to return, in the name of JESUS Christ of Nazareth, Lord of lords and King of kings! Freedom, in Jesus! Thank You, Father!

In the name of Jesus, I now put the redeeming blood of Jesus Christ and the stripes of Jesus on and against every single source and type of pain and discomfort that is running through (<u>HIS/HER</u>) body and life. In the name of Jesus Christ of Nazareth, I command every demon associated with these and any other activity in (<u>HIM/HER</u>) to be bound, confounded, destroyed, broken, cut off, loosened, and to go now, in the name of Jesus Christ, and total righteous wholeness to come to (<u>PERSON'S NAME</u>)'s body and life. BE WHOLE, in the name of Jesus! Thank You, Father God!

Father, in the name of Jesus, I thank You that in the face of this work of Satan, 1 John 4:4 *I am of You, Father God, one of Your little children whom Satan fears, and have overcome Satan and all his works by the redeeming, sanctifying and cleansing blood of Jesus*: because greater *are You* that is in *me* than he that is in the world. 1 John 5:4 For whatsoever is born of God overcometh the world: and this is the victory that overcometh the world, even our faith. 5 Who is he that overcometh the world, but he that believeth that Jesus is the Son of God? *And I believe that Jesus is the Son of God, and by His Word I do have eternal* zoe/life *and operate in His authority against this work of the devil, to destroy it, now, in the name of Jesus.* 2 Cor 5:21 For *You, Father God, have* made *Jesus* to be sin for *me*, who knew no sin; that *I* might be made the righteousness of *You, Father* God, in *Jesus*. Rom 3:24 Being justified freely by *Your* grace through the redemption that is in Christ Jesus. 1 John 4:17 Herein *is my agape*/love made perfect, that *I* may have boldness in *this* Day of Judgment *against Satan and his works*: because as *Jesus Christ, my Lord* is, so am *I* [*His agent of* agape/love] in this world [*and in this situation right now*]. *And, Lord, You are my strength, the courage, the rod of iron in my back. Help, as I* Matt 10:7 ... preach, *I say*, the kingdom of heaven is at hand *here and now for this situation. By You in me, I* 8 heal the sick, cleanse the lepers, raise the dead, cast out devils: freely *I* have received, freely *I* give. *As:* Luke 10:19 ... *Jesus has given* unto *me* power (*authority, commission and the resources of Heaven*) to tread on serpents and scorpions, and over all the power (*ability and works*) of the enemy: and nothing shall by any means hurt *me*.

Thank You and praise You, Father, in the name of Jesus. We call this victory won; (<u>PERSON'S NAME</u>) is whole. It is done, in the name of Jesus of Nazareth! Thank You, Father! Thank You!

Remember, if success seems slow: Phil 4:6 Be careful for nothing; but in every thing by prayer and supplication with thanksgiving let your requests (*aiteo*) be made known unto God. 7 And the peace of God, which passeth all understanding, shall keep your hearts and minds through Christ Jesus. *You can act your way* into believing by doing quicker than you can believe your way into action. *So stop and pray about any concern, and then give much thanks to God that you have the answer. Thanksgiving is not a mild word, but more like an intense explosion or a bubbling fountain. Make your* aiteo/*request and thank God loudly and intensely until you feel grateful, thankful and full of praise. Then you have prayed and performed* aiteo *with thanksgiving. Do it until you feel it. If it takes 10 years to feel it, get started now! The feelings will come and go as you obey in* agape/*love, and the knowing, as you do, will build truth into your heart by repetition and passion.*

24. Thank You, Father God, You who delights in judgment to set the oppressed free, this is already done. In the name of Jesus, judge against the enemy, as I judge this evil work to be destroyed and command all damage healed and restored, in the name of Jesus Christ of Nazareth. Father, make the devil and all his works dust as I now hammer the enemy:

1. In the name of Jesus Christ, all demons in this (PROBLEM), hear me and go, now, and, (PERSON'S NAME), be made whole, now, in Jesus' name;

2. In the name of Jesus Christ, all demons in this (PROBLEM), hear me and go, now, and, (PERSON'S NAME), be made whole, now, in Jesus' name;

3. In the name of Jesus Christ, all demons in this (PROBLEM), hear me and go, now, and, (PERSON'S NAME), be made whole, now, in Jesus' name;

4. In the name of Jesus Christ, all demons in this (PROBLEM), hear me and go, now, and, (PERSON'S NAME), be made whole, now, in Jesus' name;

5. In the name of Jesus Christ, all demons in this (PROBLEM), hear me and go, now, and, (PERSON'S NAME), be made whole, now, in Jesus' name;

6. In the name of Jesus Christ, all demons in this (PROBLEM), hear me and go, now, and, (PERSON'S NAME), be made whole, now, in Jesus' name;

7. In the name of Jesus Christ, all demons in this (PROBLEM), hear me and go, now, and, (PERSON'S NAME), be made whole, now, in Jesus' name.

8. In the name of Jesus Christ, all demons in this (PROBLEM), hear me and go, now, and, (PERSON'S NAME), be made whole, now, in Jesus' name.

Isa 52:7 How beautiful upon the mountains are the feet of him that bringeth good tidings, that publisheth peace; that bringeth good tidings of good, that publisheth salvation; that saith unto Zion, Thy God reigneth! *Thank You, Lord Jesus, for how You told us to reign for You:* Luke 10:9 And heal the sick that are therein, and say unto them, The kingdom of God is come nigh unto you.

Thank You for Your deliverance and wholeness, Father, for You are the one who empowers these words. Thank You! Matt 12:28 ... I cast out devils by the Spirit of God, *and* the kingdom of God is come unto (PERSON'S NAME).

For any and all demons causing this (PROBLEM) in or around (PERSON)'s body or life, I now command you to leave (HIM/HER), now, in the name of Jesus

THE BATTLE PRAYER

Christ, and never return. By the stripes of Jesus, I have now petitioned for (*Person*)'s life before God the Father, and you, agents of the devil, have no legal right to torment (*him/her*) any further. Devil, go, now! GO! NOW! In the name of JESUS! And do not come back. For I proclaim: Luke 11:20 *For if I with the finger of God cast out devils, no doubt the kingdom of God is come upon* (*Person's Name*). *In the name of Jesus, I proclaim:* Acts 3:16 And *the name of Jesus* through faith in his name hath made this *person* strong, … yea, the faith which is by *Jesus* hath given (*him/her*) this perfect soundness in the presence of you all.

I now proclaim the sin-cleansing, devil-work destroying, redeeming and devil-overcoming blood of Jesus Christ on and against every single demon that has any hold on (*Person's Name*) in any way. Heb 10:19 Having therefore, brethren, boldness to enter into the holiest by the blood of Jesus, a*nd I* Col 1:12 *give* thanks (*continually*) *unto You,* the Father, which hath made us meet (*qualified and enabled by grace*) to be partakers of the inheritance of the saints in light [*so by You, Father, I am qualified by Your work in Jesus, to be an agent of Your deliverance for this situation now. Thank You, Father*]: 13 who hath delivered us from the power of darkness, and hath translated us into the kingdom *Your agape*/dear Son: 14 in whom we have redemption through his blood, even the forgiveness *and remission* of sins: 15 who is the image of *You, Father,* the invisible God, the firstborn of every creature: 16 for by him were all things created, that are in heaven, and that are in earth, visible and invisible, whether they be thrones, or dominions, or principalities, or powers: all things were created by him, and for him: 17 and he is before all things, and by him all things consist. *Praise to You, Father, for Your Son Jesus, my Elder Brother! JESUS IS LORD!*

This restoration to wholeness will come not through (*my/our*) Acts 3:12 … own power or holiness 16 *but by* his name, *the name of Jesus*, through faith in his name *will make this one* strong … yea, the faith which is by *Jesus Christ* hath given *this one* this perfect soundness … . Acts 4:12 Neither is there *soteria*/salvation (*God's wholeness*) in any other *name than the name of Jesus Christ*: for there is none other name under heaven given among men, whereby we must be *sozo*/saved (*healed, made whole*). Per: 1 John 3:23 … *Father God's* commandment, That we should believe on the name of his Son Jesus Christ, and *agape*/love one another, as he gave us commandment. *I believe in the name of Jesus, and in the name of Jesus Christ of Nazareth, I command all you demons and evil works to leave* (*Person's Name*), *now, and you are to never ever come back on* (*him/her*) *again. Go now, in the name of Jesus Christ! You must obey, as:* Phil 2:10 That at the name of Jesus every knee should bow, of things in heaven, and things in earth, and things under the earth; 11 and that every tongue should confess that Jesus Christ is Lord, to the glory of God the Father. *Therefore, in the name of Jesus Christ of Nazareth, your Lord and Master, devil,* *go now and do not return or counter-attack in any way for "no harm shall come" to me or (P˜ERSON'S N˜AME) as I minister to (H˜IM/H˜ER).*

If there are any other things that may be causing this (P˜ROBLEM) that I may not be aware of, I now come against whatever they may be. In the name of Jesus, I now put the blood of my Lord, my King, my Savior, and my Shepherd, Jesus Christ, against whatever else may be causing this (P˜ROBLEM) to attack (P˜ERSON)'s body/life. I command you, Satan, to hear, obey and loose your grip on (H˜IM/H˜ER) now, and to go, now, and never return, in the name of Jesus Christ!

Devil, your hold has now been broken and destroyed by the body, stripes, resurrection and blood of Jesus. In the name of Jesus Christ, I command the cause of this (P˜ROBLEM) to be completely destroyed under the full healing power of God the Father and His Son Jesus Christ, by the power of Holy Spirit. Thank You, Father, in the name of Jesus! Thank You! Amen!

Father, as You said: Isa 45:11 "… Concerning the work of my hands command *(require)* ye me." **So, in the name of Jesus,** for (P˜ERSON'S NAME) in this or any (P˜ROBLEM), *the* devil and all his works, listen, obey and go, NOW, in the name of Jesus, never to return. All fear and pain, go now, in the name of Jesus! Do not ever return. (P˜ERSON)'s body, I command you to be whole and healthy, now, in the name of **JESUS**. All pain, fear of pain and fear of (P˜ROBLEM) I command to GO, now. I proclaim FREEDOM, IN JESUS' NAME! Amen; so be it!

25. Father, in the name of Jesus Christ, let Your miracle and healing power now flow through the shed blood and stripes of Your Son, Jesus Christ, against every single evil power that has invaded (P˜ERSON'S N˜AME)'s body and life. Let Your saving power flow through me as your anointed vessel, as (P˜ERSON)'s intercessor. Let Your miracle and healing power flood into (P˜ERSON)'s body from head to foot, completely saturating every single cell and fiber of (P˜ERSON)'s body. **Father, let Your restoring power, Your** *zoe***/life now flow** into every single cell of (P˜ERSON)'s body that has been invaded by this disease, infirmity or sickness. Father, completely destroy this (P˜ROBLEM) now, from (H˜IS/H˜ER) head to (H˜IS/H˜ER) feet, in the name of Jesus! In the name of Jesus, (P˜ERSON'S N˜AME), be FREE! Amen! Father, You already paid for this healing with Jesus. So be it! Praise the *agape*/love and name of Jesus! Amen! Thank You, Father! In the name of Jesus!

Heb 13:15 "By *Jesus* therefore let us offer the sacrifice of praise to God continually, that is, the fruit of our lips giving thanks to his name."

26. Father, in the name of Jesus, help me to STIR MYSELF **up into You and Your Love, to defeating this enemy.** Ps 47:1 O clap your hands, all ye people; shout unto God with the voice of triumph. 2 For the L˜ORD most high is terrible;

THE BATTLE PRAYER

he is a great King over all the earth. 3 He shall subdue the people under us, and the nations under our feet. 4 He shall choose our inheritance for us, the excellency of Jacob whom he loved. Selah. 5 God is gone up with a shout, the LORD with the sound of a trumpet. 6 Sing praises to God, sing praises: sing praises unto our King, sing praises. 7 For God is the King of all the earth: sing ye praises with understanding. 8 God reigneth over the heathen: God sitteth upon the throne of his holiness. 9 The princes of the people are gathered together, even the people of the God of Abraham: for the shields of the earth belong unto God: he is greatly exalted. Ps 82:8 Arise, O God, judge the earth: for thou shalt inherit all nations. Ps 88:10 Wilt thou shew wonders to the dead? shall the dead arise and praise thee? Selah. 11 Shall thy *chesed*/lovingkindness be declared in the grave? or thy faithfulness in destruction? 12 Shall thy wonders be known in the dark? and thy righteousness in the land of forgetfulness? 13 But unto thee have I cried, O LORD … . Ps 52:1 Why boastest thou thyself in mischief, O mighty man (*of death*)? the *chesed*/goodness of God endureth continually. 2 Thy tongue deviseth mischiefs; like a sharp razor, working deceitfully. 3 Thou lovest evil more than good; and lying rather than to speak righteousness. Selah. 4 Thou lovest all devouring words, O thou deceitful tongue (*of death and fear*). 5 God shall likewise destroy thee for ever, he shall take thee away, and pluck thee out of thy dwelling place, and root thee out of the land of the living. Selah. 6 The righteous also shall see, and fear, and shall laugh at him: 7 Lo, this is the man (*death or the devil*) that made not God his strength; but trusted in the abundance of his riches, and strengthened himself in his wickedness. 8 But I am like a green olive tree in the house of God: I trust in the *chesed*/mercy of God for ever and ever. 9 I will praise thee for ever, because thou hast done it: and I will wait on thy name; for it is good before thy saints. Ps 103:1 Bless the LORD, O my soul: and all that is within me, bless his holy name. 2 Bless the LORD, O my soul, and forget not all his benefits: 3 who forgiveth all thine iniquities; who healeth all thy diseases; 4 who redeemeth thy life from destruction; who crowneth thee with *chesed*/lovingkindness and *racham*/tender mercies; 5 who satisfieth thy mouth with good things; so that thy youth is renewed like the eagle's. 6 The LORD executeth righteousness and judgment for all that are oppressed. Ps 54:1 Save me, O God, by thy name, and judge me by thy strength. 2 Hear my prayer, O God; give ear to the words of my mouth. Ps 48:8 As we have heard, so have we seen in the city of the LORD of hosts, in the city of our God: God will establish it for ever. Selah. 9 We have thought of thy *chesed*/lovingkindness, O God, in the midst of thy temple. 10 According to thy name, O God, so is thy praise unto the ends of the earth: thy right hand is full of righteousness. Prov 23:11 For their redeemer is mighty; he shall plead their cause with thee. Isa 49:24 Shall the prey be taken from the mighty, or the lawful captive delivered?

25 But thus saith the LORD, Even the captives of the mighty shall be taken away, and the prey of the terrible shall be delivered: for I will contend with him that contendeth with thee, and I will save thy children. Ps 108:5 Be thou exalted, O God, above the heavens: and thy glory above all the earth; 6 That thy beloved may be delivered: save with thy right hand, and answer me. *In the name of Jesus*, 1 Pet 2:24 who his own self bare our sins in his own body on the tree, that we, being dead to sins, should *zao*/live unto righteousness: by whose stripes ye were healed. 25 For *we* were as sheep going astray; but are now returned unto the Shepherd and Bishop of *our* souls. Luke 11:2 ... Our Father which art in heaven, Hallowed be thy name. Thy kingdom come. Thy will be done, as in heaven, so in earth. 3 Give us day by day our daily bread (*in healing, deliverance, strength, wisdom and prosperity*). Ps 68:1 Let God arise, let his enemies be scattered: let them also that hate him flee before him. 2 As smoke is driven away, so drive them away: as wax melteth before the fire, so let the wicked perish at the presence of God. 3 But let the righteous be glad; let them rejoice before God: yea, let them exceedingly rejoice. Ps 18:14 Yea, *Lord, send* out *Your* arrows, and *scatter* them *that hold* (PERSON'S NAME) *in wickedness; and shoot* out *lightnings, and discomfort* them *and remove this wickedness, this evil rule of the devil, not by my holiness,* but *by the name of Jesus and faith in that name!* Acts 2:36 Therefore let all ... know assuredly, that *You, Father* God, *have* made that same Jesus, whom *they* have crucified, both Lord and Christ. Heb 1:3 Who being the brightness of *Your* glory, and the express image of *Your* person, and upholding all things by the word of his power, when he had by himself purged (*washed, dissolved, destroyed and removed*) our sins, sat down on the right hand of *You, Father,* the Majesty on high. Heb 10:12 But this man, after he had offered one sacrifice for sins for ever, sat down on the right hand of God; 13 from henceforth expecting till his enemies be made his footstool. Rom 16:20 *So, Father,* the God of peace, ... bruise Satan under *my* feet *as shattered glass.* The grace of our Lord Jesus Christ be with *me* [*to know, be and do this*]. Amen. Mark 16:20 And ... *confirm* the word with signs following. Amen.

Father, as You said: Isa 45:11 "... Concerning the work of my hands command (*require*) ye me." **So, in the name of Jesus**, for (PERSON'S NAME) in this or any (PROBLEM), devil, and all your works, listen, obey and go, NOW, in the name of Jesus, never to return! All fear and pain, go, now, in the name of Jesus! Do not ever return. (PERSON)'s body, I command you to be whole and healthy, now, in the name of Jesus. All pain, fear of pain and fear of (PROBLEM) I command to GO now. I proclaim FREEDOM, IN JESUS' NAME! Amen; so be it!

27. Father, in the name of Jesus, for (PERSON'S NAME) **I ask that you destroy** this (PROBLEM) quickly! I ask that you spare (PERSON'S NAME) any more suffering

THE BATTLE PRAYER

from this enemy from the devil, and no longer let the devil rule and be glorified against You and Your will in this situation. Manifest Your *agape*/love in healing. Let freedom come now, in the name of Jesus!

Father, Almighty God, in the name of Jesus, let (<u>PERSON'S NAME</u>) be fully made whole now! Be whole, in the name of Jesus! Father, destroy fully every single one of these evil powers, now, so that they never ever come back on (<u>HIM/ HER</u>) again. Every part of (<u>HIS/HER</u>) body that is not now operating totally well and normal, including: _____, _____, _____, and _____, I command Holy Spirit life to come now and flow into (<u>PERSON</u>)'s body to heal and restore them to wholeness, in Jesus' name! Thank You, Father! Thank You!

Thank You, Father, in the name of Jesus: 1 John 5:14 And this is the confidence that *I have in You, that, if I aiteo/ask by demanding as due by covenant promise any thing according to Your will, You hear me*: 15 And if *I know that You hear me, whatsoever I aiteo/ask by demanding as due by covenant promise, I know that I have the petitions that I aiteo/desired of You. Father* Jer 1:12 ... hasten *Your word to perform it. Thank You, Father, in the name of Jesus! Thank You!* 1 Cor 15:57 But thanks be to *You, Father* God, *who gives* us the victory through our Lord Jesus Christ.

2 Cor 2:14 Now thanks be unto *You, Father* God, which always *causes* us to triumph in Christ, and *makes* manifest the savour of *Your* knowledge by us in every place. *Thank You, Father God, Jesus Christ, My Lord, and Holy Spirit for Your* racham, chesed, *grace, mercy and* agape/love *flowing in* (<u>PERSON'S NAME</u>) *right now and answering this prayer. Thank You, O, Mighty God, in the name of Jesus! Thank You! Praise Your holy name! Thank You for Your Word of Grace in Jesus!*

Rom 15:8 Now I say that Jesus Christ was a minister of the circumcision for the truth of God, to confirm the promises made unto the fathers: 9 and that the Gentiles might glorify God for his mercy; as it is written, For this cause I will confess to thee among the Gentiles, and sing unto thy name. 10 And again he saith, Rejoice, ye Gentiles, with his people. 11 And again, Praise the Lord, all ye Gentiles; and laud him, all ye people. 12 And again, Esaias saith, There shall be a root of Jesse, and he that shall rise to reign over the Gentiles; in him shall the Gentiles trust. *Thank You, Father, that as I have prayed, You have written Your Word into my mind and heart; You have renewed my mind and the spirit of my mind. Thank You, Father, for* Ps 107:20 he sent his word, and healed them, and delivered them from their destructions. *Thank You for eyes to see, ears to hear, hearts that understand to repentance, healing, conversion unto strengthening the brethren and good works by faith in* agape/love, *to Your glory. Thank You Father! In the name of Jesus, thank You!*

Father, as You said, Isa 45:11 "... Concerning the work of my hands command (*require*) ye me." **So, in the name of Jesus,** for (<u>PERSON'S NAME</u>) in this or any (<u>PROBLEM</u>), devil, and all your works, listen, obey and go, NOW, in the name of Jesus, never to return! All fear and pain, go, now, in the name of Jesus! Do not ever return. (*Person's Name*)'s body, I command you to be whole and healthy, now, in the name of Jesus! I proclaim FREEDOM, IN JESUS' NAME! Amen; so be it! Glory to God for Jesus! Amen!

28. Thank You, Father, in the name of Jesus, that I have taken Your word and applied it to this need, and Your *zoe*/life is now flowing to restore totally (*Person's Name*). Heb 4:12 For the word of God is quick, and powerful, and sharper than any twoedged sword, piercing even to the dividing asunder of soul and spirit, and of the joints and marrow, and is a discerner of the thoughts and intents of the heart. 13 Neither is there any creature that is not manifest in his sight: but all things are naked and opened unto the eyes of him with whom we have to do. *For by Your Spirit in me* Isa 49:2 … *You have* made my mouth like a sharp sword; in the shadow of *Your* hand *have You* hid me, and made me a polished shaft; in *Your* quiver *have You* hid me; 3 and said unto me, Thou art my servant, O Israel, in whom I will be glorified. *For* Luke 8:11 … the seed is the word of God. *And You are making it to grow to fruits of righteousness in* (*Person's Name*). *As You have said:* Isa 55:11 So shall *Your* word be that goeth forth out of my mouth: it shall not return unto *You* void, but it shall accomplish that which *You* please, and it shall prosper in the thing whereto *You* sent it. 12 For *I* shall go out with joy, and be led forth with peace: the mountains and the hills shall break forth before *me* into singing, and all the trees of the field shall clap their hands. Ps 119:50 This is (*Person's Name*)'s comfort in (*his/her*) affliction; for *Your* Word hath quickened (*Person's Name*).

Praise You, Father, in the name of Jesus Christ, my Lord, the Bread of Life, the Word of God, for You have said concerning Your Word in my mouth: Jer 23:29 Is not my word like as a fire? saith the Lord; and like a hammer that breaketh the rock in pieces? *So thank You, Father, that Your Word is burning out and smashing into pieces this work and oppression of the devil. For I am* 1 Pet 1:23 … born again, not of corruptible seed, but of incorruptible, by the word of *You, Father* God, which *zao*/liveth and abideth for ever. *And I have used* Eph 6:17 … the sword of the Spirit, which is the word of *You, Father* God: *and Your* zoe/ *life is now flowing to restore everything in* (*Person's Name*)'s *life for* Matt 4:4 … it is written, Man shall not *zao*/live by bread alone, but by every word that proceedeth out of the mouth of *You,* O God. *Thank You, Father, for Your* zoe/life *in Jesus Christ, the life of salvation, Your quickening Spirit. Thank You, Father! In Jesus' name, thank You!*

Heb 13:20 Now *You, Father God,* the God of peace, that brought again from the dead our Lord Jesus, that great shepherd of the sheep, through the blood of the everlasting covenant, 21 make (*Person's Name*) perfect in every good work

THE BATTLE PRAYER

to do *Your* will, working in (Person's Name) that which is wellpleasing in *Your* sight, *Father God*, through Jesus Christ; to whom be glory for ever and ever. Amen!

Eph 1:3 Blessed be *You*, the God and Father of our Lord Jesus Christ, who hath blessed us with all spiritual blessings in heavenly places in Christ: 4 according as *You have* chosen us in him before the foundation of the world, that we should be holy and without blame before *You* in *agape*/love: 5 having predestinated us unto the adoption of children by Jesus Christ to *Yourself*, according to the good pleasure of *Your* will, 6 to the praise of the glory of *Your* grace, wherein *You have* made us accepted in the *agape*/beloved. 7 In whom we have redemption through his blood, the forgiveness *and remission* of sins, according to the riches of *Your* grace; 8 wherein *You have* abounded toward us in all wisdom and prudence; 9 having made known unto us the mystery of *Your* will, according to *Your* good pleasure which *You have* purposed in *Yourself*: 10 that in the dispensation of the fulness of times *You, Father God,* might gather together in one all things in Christ, both which are in heaven, and which are on earth; even in him: 11 in whom also we have obtained an inheritance, being predestinated according to the purpose of *You* who worketh all things after the counsel of *Your* own will: 12 that we should be to the praise of *Your* glory, who *have* trusted in Christ. Jude 24 Now unto *You, Father God,* that is able to keep *us* from falling, and to present *us* faultless before the presence of *Your* glory with exceeding joy, 25 to *You,* the only wise God our Saviour, be glory and majesty, dominion and power, both now and ever. Amen.

Isa 53:3 He is despised and rejected of men; a man of sorrows, and acquainted with grief: and we hid as it were our faces from him; he was despised, and we esteemed him not. 4 Surely he hath *cabal*/borne our griefs *and infirmities*, and *nasa*/carried our sorrows *and sicknesses*: yet we did esteem him stricken, smitten of God, and afflicted. 5 But he was wounded for our transgressions, he was bruised for our iniquities: the chastisement of our peace was upon him; and with his stripes we are healed. 6 All we like sheep have gone astray; we have turned every one to his own way; and the Lord hath laid on him the iniquity of us all.

Ps 40:16 Let all those that seek thee rejoice and be glad in thee: let such as love thy salvation say continually, The Lord be magnified.

So I say, Lord, be magnified, Rev 7:20 … saying, *soteria*/salvation to *You,* our God, which sitteth upon the throne, and unto the Lamb. 12 Saying, Amen: Blessing, and glory, and wisdom, and thanksgiving, and honour, and power, and might, be unto *You,* our God, for ever and ever. Amen.

Rom 15:13 Now *You, Father,* the God of hope, fill *us* with all joy and peace in believing, that *we* may abound in hope, through the power of the

Battle Prayer for Divine Healing: Field Manual 2

Holy Ghost. Rom 16:24 The grace of our Lord Jesus Christ be with *us* all. Amen. 25 Now to *you, Father,* that is of power to stablish *us* according to *the* gospel, and the preaching of Jesus Christ, according to the revelation of the mystery, which was kept secret since the world began, 26 but now is made manifest, and by the scriptures of the prophets, according to the commandment of *You, Father,* the everlasting God, made known to all nations for the obedience of faith: 27 to *You, Father* God only wise, be glory through Jesus Christ for ever. Amen. Rev 4:8 Holy, holy, holy, LORD God Almighty, which was, and is, and is to come. 11 Thou art worthy, O Lord, to receive glory and honour and power: for thou hast created all things, and for thy pleasure they are and were created. 1 Tim 1:17 Now unto the King eternal, immortal, invisible, the only wise God, be honour and glory for ever and ever. Amen. Rev 22:20 ... Amen. Even so, come, Lord Jesus. 21 The grace of our Lord Jesus Christ be with *us* all. Amen. *Thank You, Father God! I do see Your goodness in the land of the living. In the name of Jesus, thank You! Glory to our Father God, for Jesus! So be it!*

Father, as You said, Isa 45:11 "... Concerning the work of my hands command (*require*) ye me." **So, in the name of Jesus**, for (PERSON'S NAME) in this or any (PROBLEM), devil and all your works, listen, obey and go, NOW, in the name of Jesus, never to return! All fear and pain, go, now, in the name of Jesus! Do not ever return. (PERSON)'s body, I command you to be free, whole and healthy, now, in the name of Jesus! All damage, symptoms, pain, fear of pain and fear of (PROBLEM) I command to GO, now, never to return! I proclaim FREEDOM, IN JESUS' NAME! Amen; so be it!

If you speak in tongues: Father, in the name of Jesus, have Holy Spirit pray through me now and fill me with Your dominion, love and compassion for this situation to victory. Thank You, Father! In the name of Jesus, thank You!

(Aim for about 15 to 45 minutes of tongues or as Holy Spirit leads. Let the peace of God in your heart guide you. Two or more hours is also fine. Keep it loud and hard, and aimed at the situation to victory. Challenge any fear in your mind with *agape*/love of His truth. And then obey Phil 4:6 and attack again.)

If you do not speak in tongues, rejoice in the Lord, singing to yourself in psalms, hymns and spiritual songs, making melody in your heart to the Lord, letting the wonder of Christ in you, the Word of Christ, the hope of glory, overwhelm you. Preach to yourself any part/s of this manual, and do it with intensity. And pray: **Father, in the name of Jesus**, have Holy Spirit pray through me now and fill me with Your dominion, love and compassion for this situation to victory. Thank You, Father! In the name of Jesus, thank You!

THE BATTLE PRAYER

Lord, I thank You that this is not about praying better words in prayer but knowing You in Your dominion, in the great victory Jesus won by the cross and Your desire for all men and women to be free of anything and everything that is not of You. By Your grace, I will keep at it, as does a hammer on a rock or a sword in battle. Your Word is more than sufficient, the blood of Jesus is more than sufficient, and Holy Spirit is more than sufficient. I will be Your voice and Your agent to proclaim Your deliverance already paid for in Jesus until the sick are free. Thank You that Your angels minister, as I voice Your Word! Thank You!

Repeat all or parts of the Minister Confessions with passion, thanksgiving and intensity. What you are doing is immersing yourself in God's truth.

As you have time, for every scripture in the Minister Confession, go back to your Bible and read two chapters above it, the entire chapter where it appears and the two chapters following it to see if how we have used it fits with the context of the passage. Yes, this will take lots of time as you read and study 5 chapters for every scripture, but we are the issue, not God. It is our soul's lack of agreement with God that limits Him from moving through us.

God's will is clear: Mark 1:40 "And there came a leper to him, beseeching him, and kneeling down to him, and saying unto him, If thou wilt, thou canst make me clean. 41 And Jesus, moved with compassion, put forth his hand, and touched him, and saith unto him, I will; be thou clean." When Jesus said "I will," in the Greek it meant, "Yes, I will with delight, for this is what I am, what I do, and I always delight to heal." Heb 13:8 "Jesus Christ the same yesterday, and to day, and for ever."

So go back and validate every scripture in this manual with two chapters above and below it in the Bible and persuade yourself that healing is God's will. As you read the healing scriptures, do so as if you are reading them to the devil and saying: "Remember this one, devil, how you were defeated?" Or, "See, devil, this is a promise of God where you and your works are to be defeated. This proves just how much of an enemy of God this sickness or problem is. Praise God, He destroys His enemies through me!"

Keep yourself stirred up in God. If you have to, go outside to shout. Ps 47:1 "O clap your hands, all ye people; shout unto God with the voice of triumph. 2 For the LORD most high is terrible; he is a great King over all the earth." Shout and clap until you know life inside. Make or let your spirit, in Jesus, arise!

Also consider praying the Psalms All 150 take about 4 to 6 hours if prayed out loud. Use them to stir yourself up. Find one or more you like and keep repeating it or them with passion and intensity over the situation or in praises to God.

Faint not, stay in the battle until you see Jesus win through you, as a co-laborer. The devil will pressure you with the circumstances to keep you down. He fears your stirred-up spirit, you and Christ together! Remember, you can act yourself into believing quicker than you can believe yourself into acting. If your spirit is not moving, move your spirit anyway. Jesus lives in you! Praise God! Jesus is Lord though us. Jesus is Lord!

1 John 4:4 "Ye are of God, little children, and have overcome *the devil and his lies*: because greater is he that is in you, than he that is in the world." Faint not! Fight with the Word of God until you win! As you keep speaking to that mountain, keep believing God's power is moving, and God will do it. Cut with His Word, His sword, until victory comes!

It is not the formula of the words, but, rather, who is speaking them. You are speaking for God as one of His. You are speaking directly to the wicked devil and commanding him and his works to go, in the name Jesus. Agree with God that this work of the devil must go, in the name of Jesus. Act into believing! You are trusting Father God, by Holy Spirit, to do it, in the name of Jesus! As you speak that name, know His *zoe*/life is released and moving. Like a mustard seed, it will do its job!

You have the *zoe*/life of God. John 20:31 "But these are written, that ye might believe that Jesus is the Christ, the Son of God; and that believing ye might have *zoe*/life through his name."

If you are in Christ, you have His *zoe*/life and you are to use His name to deliver that *zoe*/life to the world. 1 John 5:10 "He that believeth on the Son of God hath the witness in himself: he that believeth not God hath made him a liar; because he believeth not the record that God gave of his Son. 11 And this is the record, that God hath given to us eternal *zoe*/life, and this *zoe*/life is in his Son. 12 He that hath the Son hath *zoe*/life; and he that hath not the Son of God hath not *zoe*/life. 13 These things have I written unto you that believe on the name of the Son of God; that ye may know that ye have eternal *zoe*/life, and that ye may believe on the name of the Son of God."

Persuade yourself (which is the purpose of this manual) that you have that same *zoe*/life as Jesus and that God wants to use you to heal others, as His agent. The only requirement is that you see a need. 1 John 5:14 "And this is the confidence that we have in him, that, if we *aiteo*/ask (*require, demand and expect as due by covenant promise*) any thing according to his will, he heareth us: 15 and if we know that he hear us, whatsoever we *aiteo*/ask (*require, demand and expect*

THE BATTLE PRAYER

as due by covenant promise), we know that we have the petitions that we *aiteo/ desired (required, demanded and expected as due by covenant promise*) of him."

We confess and shout the Scriptures, to get to believe them, and then we confess the Scriptures, because we believe them. The Scriptures go from being our hope to being our meat, to keep us going in God, to our measure for controlling our thoughts, to our sword of power against the devil. John 4:33 "Therefore said the disciples one to another, Hath any man brought him ought to eat? 34 Jesus saith unto them, My meat is to do the will of him that sent me, and to finish his work." John 9:4 "I (*Jesus*) must work the works of him that sent me ... . 5 ... I (*Jesus*) am the light of the world (*of how God really is*)." Eph 6:17 "And take the helmet of *soteria/ salvation*, and the sword of the Spirit, which is the word of God."

Father, in the name of Jesus, teach me how to abide in Jesus and to make His words abide in me. John 15:7 "If ye abide in me, and my words abide in you, ye shall *aiteo/*ask (*require, demand and expect as due by covenant promise*) what ye will, and it shall be done unto you. 8 Herein is my Father glorified, that ye bear much fruit; so shall ye be my disciples." John 8:31 "Then said Jesus to those Jews which believed on him, If ye continue in my word, then are ye my disciples indeed; 32 and ye shall know the truth, and the truth shall make you free." Praise You, Lord Jesus, for sending us Your Spirit of Truth. Keep us in Your truth. John 14:16 "And I (*Jesus*) will pray the Father, and he shall give you another Comforter, that he may abide with you for ever; 17 even the Spirit of truth; whom the world cannot receive, because it seeth him not, neither knoweth him: but ye know him; for he dwelleth with you, and shall be in you." Praise God, by Jesus we are part of the God who cannot lie, and His truth endures forever!

~ 3 ~

REPEATING THE BATTLE PRAYER

The Battle Prayer contains 28 healing prayers mixed with scriptures, intercessory prayers, praise and thanksgiving. So just ministering the Battle Prayer one time through is repeated prayer. There is no limit on how many times you can pray the Battle Prayer or the whole manual. The only limit is what it takes to get the job done. The Bible teaches repeated prayer, Jesus specifically taught and used (in the Garden) repeated prayer, and Dr. Lake discovered how to use in for predictable healing.

Our key scriptures for repetition are as follows: Jer 23:29 "Is not my word like as a fire? saith the Lord; and like a hammer that breaketh the rock in pieces?" Eph 6:17 "And take the helmet of *soteria*/salvation, and the sword of the Spirit, which is the word of God." Fire, hammers and swords usually require more than one action. Even a fire has multiple flames to do the job. Sure, we all prefer the one-stoke release, and as we grow in the truth, we will be more effective. Until then, keep the heat on and keep swinging with the Word of God, fully expecting Him to bring glory with every stroke.

For repetition, you can add: "Lord, I am coming again to intercede in battle for (PERSON'S NAME), per: Luke 18:1 "And he spake a parable unto them to this end, that men ought always to pray, and not to faint. ... 7 And shall not God avenge his own elect, which cry day and night unto him, though he bear long with them?" Acts 12:5 "Peter therefore was kept in prison: but prayer was made without ceasing of the church unto God for him." 1 Thes 5:17 "Pray without ceasing. 18 In every thing give thanks: for this is the will of God in Christ Jesus concerning you. 19 Quench not the Spirit." Eph 6:18 "Praying always with all prayer and supplication in the Spirit, and watching thereunto with all perseverance and supplication for all saints."

Battle Prayer for Divine Healing: Field Manual 2

We are told to pray like Elijah, using him as a standard. James 5:16 "Confess your faults one to another, and pray one for another, that ye may be healed. The effectual fervent prayer of a righteous man availeth much. 17 Elias was a man subject to like passions as we are, and he prayed earnestly that it might not rain: and it rained not on the earth by the space of three years and six months. 18 And he prayed again (*8 times*), and the heaven gave rain, and the earth brought forth her fruit." Verse eighteen says "he prayed again," and yet, per 1 Kings 18:42-44, it appears he prayed 8 times (1+7), and each time he sent his servant to look for signs of the answer. Each time he prayed it was as if it was the last time, and he prayed until he got the desired results. In 1 Kings 17:21, Elijah appears to pray 3 times to raise the dead boy. In each case, if he did not see the answer completed, he prayed or ministered again until he got the answer. To pray like Elijah means to keep at it until you win against the devil unto *zoe*/life, and the answer manifested. This is *aiteo* praying until the job is done.

In this rain case, we are not told the exact words Elijah prayed, but based on his other prayers, we can say that his prayers were to God. And in this case, he prayed 8 times, that is, until he got the answer, or prayed, affirmed, praised and/or expected each additional time. In no way does the scripture infer that there was some special benefit in the number 8 (or 3). It was just that Elijah prayed until he got what he knew to be the clear will of God to send rain. In the case of the dead boy, Elijah appears to have understood the clear will of God, as God only heals by His will, and God was able to raise the boy from the dead as Elijah kept at it.

Jesus, on the other hand, did not pray to God in direct prayer when He ministered. Instead, He gave thanks and then commanded what needed to be, to come into existence. Jesus is our example. When we are commanding the devil in that mountain to leave and a situation to get right, we are not praying to God as much as we are commanding the devil and his works to go, the situation to get right, and we are believing God to enforce our words. Once you have spoken to the Lord, keep speaking to the problem or that mountain. Mark 11:23 "For verily I say unto you, That whosoever shall say unto this mountain, Be thou removed, and be thou cast into the sea; and shall not doubt in his heart, but shall believe that those things which he saith shall come to pass; he shall have whatsoever he saith. 24 Therefore I say unto you, What things soever ye *aiteo*/desire, when ye pray, believe that ye *lambano*/receive them, and ye shall have them."

God does the healing; we do the commanding. So, like Elijah, we may pray 3 or 8 times (or 800 times or more) to provide the path for God to move a situation. We are the ones who make the path from Heaven to Earth with our right and effective faith. That is our job in this, the Day of Salvation. Repeated prayer *aiteo* is also against the devil and not against God, as if God were responsible for the delay in some sort of super-spiritual education process for the victim. Jesus never told anyone, "I cannot heal you until you or they learn the lesson." No, He healed them all.

Repeating the Battle Prayer

As Jesus and the early disciples demonstrated, answered prayer for healing is all about us, not God's resistance, especially in the case of His covenant promises concerning healing. So, for healing, deliverance from demons, missing and maimed body part restoration, control of storms and food multiplication, the answers were all rather quick. The more our minds and hearts get like Jesus' and the apostles', in confidence in God, the more we will see quicker responses like they got.

Otherwise the clear message of scripture is to pray like Elijah (and Dr. Lake) until you get the answer. 1 John 5:13 "These things have I written unto you that believe on the name of the Son of God; that ye may know that ye have eternal *zoe*/life, and that ye may believe on the name of the Son of God. 14 And this is the confidence that we have in him, that, if we *aiteo*/ask any thing according to his will, he heareth us: 15 and if we know that he hear us, whatsoever we *aiteo*/ask, we know that we have the petitions (aiteo *requirements, demands and expectations*) that we *aiteo* / desired of him."

All of this is included in the definition of *lambano*, where you will hold on to and not let go of God's promise of healing, no matter what the devil does to resist you. As you *aiteo*/command again and again, you are making that word your testimony, and the devil will be overcome. Rev 12:11 "And they overcame him (*Satan*) by the blood of the Lamb, and by the word of their testimony; and they *agape*/loved not their *psuche*/lives (*souls*) unto the death."

Remember, the issue is how much *zoe*, as *dunamis* power, we release each time we minister healing. As "no labor in the Lord is in vain," we always release some *zoe*. If we need more results, keep at it. 1 Cor 15:57 "But thanks be to God, which giveth us the victory through our Lord Jesus Christ. 58 Therefore, my *agape*/beloved brethren, be ye stedfast (*keep at it until you win*), unmoveable (*unshaken by any apparent delay or failure*), always abounding in the work of the Lord, forasmuch as ye know that your labour is not in vain in the Lord." Faint not!

We repeat: the exact words of the ministry are not as important as your attitude and intent. This is not about formulas. Besides the name of Jesus and faith in that name by the work of the cross, the words simply help adjust your attitude and focus your intent, while the Scriptures help you keep reliant upon Father God. To be strong in the strength of the Lord, who made Heaven and Earth, includes being strong in His *agape*/love for all men, where He had Jesus pay for the healing of all. Strong firmness in voice and attitude stirs you to boldness and confidence in God.

Our confession is that "by His stripes we were healed." Isa 53:3 "He is despised and rejected of men; a man of sorrows, and acquainted with grief: and we hid as it were our faces from him; he was despised, and we esteemed him not. 4 Surely he hath *cabal*/borne our griefs (*infirmities*), and *nasa*/carried our sorrows (*sicknesses*): yet we did esteem him stricken, smitten of God, and afflicted. 5 But he was wounded for our transgressions, he was bruised for our iniquities: the chastisement of our peace was upon him; and with his stripes we are healed. 6 All we like sheep have gone astray; we have turned every one to his own way; and the LORD hath laid on him the iniquity (*evil thoughts that lead to evil actions/omissions*) of us all."

We confess God's Word is greater than the evil circumstances, and we bring the Kingdom of God, by obeying Father God and speaking His Word to the evil circumstances and casting off all works of darkness, including any oppressions of the devil. We keep speaking God's Word to that sickness, disease, infirmity, weakness, rebellion, anything of the curse, using God's Word like a hammer and a sword, in the name of Jesus, and telling it to go, and to go NOW!

We humble ourselves before God by not giving up or being defeated by the devil's resistance to or in us, but keeping ourselves encouraged in God, keeping our mind renewed, and striking until the healing and victory is complete. We obey: James 4:7 "Submit yourselves therefore to God (*by believing and speaking His Word to the evil circumstances*). Resist the devil, and he (*the devil and his works*) will flee from you." 1 Pet 5:8 "Be sober, be vigilant; because your adversary the devil, as a roaring lion, walketh about, seeking whom he may devour: 9 whom resist stedfast in the faith, knowing that the same afflictions are accomplished in your brethren that are in the world." 1 Tim 6:12 "Fight the good fight of faith, lay hold on eternal *zoe*/life ... ." Fight implies many hits.

We must be steadfast in our confession and speaking God's Word to the evil oppression until we have victory, for he (Satan's rule) will have to flee! We exercise the authority given by Jesus and command that oppression to go and healing to come. We obey God, by demanding that His covenant promises be fulfilled: Isa 45:11 "Thus saith the LORD, the Holy One of Israel, and his Maker, Ask (*require*) me of things to come concerning my sons, and concerning the work of my hands command ye me." Require of God to build you into an effective warrior. Require of God to release the mind of Christ, as you submit to His Word. The more the Word and attitude of God, as seen in Jesus, are seen in you, the more power in your *aiteo* commands. The process is amazing: the more you require of the Lord, the stronger you become in Him and against the devil, and the more you see of God's glory manifested in the Earth. The Battle Prayer is designed to do all this at once, so you can grow as you fight!

We have a battle, and it is not against flesh and blood: 2 Cor 10:3 "For though we walk in the flesh, we do not war after the flesh: 4 (for the weapons of our warfare are not carnal, but mighty through God to the pulling down of strong holds;) 5 casting down imaginations, and every high thing that exalteth itself against the knowledge of God, and bringing into captivity every thought to the obedience of Christ." In spite of science (praise God for medicine, else many would be dead), the Scriptures proclaim that sickness, evils in nature, etc. are caused by the devil, and the ultimate cure is in Jesus.

Every devil that resists the work of the cross is exalting itself against the knowledge of God. Our job is to enforce the work of Jesus, in His name, as if He were there, knowing He is in you to do just this. This is what the Father wants us to be doing NOW: Rom 16:20 "And the God of peace shall **bruise Satan under your feet** (*as shattered glass*). The grace of our Lord Jesus Christ be with you [*to know, be and do this as sons like Jesus*]. Amen." (Note: son is a title like general or officer.) We believe the report of God, that Jesus got the job done.

Because our battle is not against God or people, we obey: Eph 6:10 "Finally, my brethren, be strong in the Lord, and in the power of his might. 11 Put on the whole armour of God, that ye may be able to stand against the wiles of the devil. 12 For we wrestle not against flesh and blood, but against principalities, against powers, against the rulers of the darkness of this world, against spiritual wickedness in high places. 13 Wherefore take unto you the whole armour of God, that ye may be able to withstand in the evil day, and having done all, to stand. 14 Stand therefore, having your loins girt about with truth, and having on the breastplate of righteousness; 15 and your feet shod with the preparation of the gospel of peace; 16 above all, taking the shield of faith, wherewith ye shall be able to quench all the fiery darts of the wicked. 17 And take the helmet of *soteria*/salvation, and the sword of the Spirit, which is the word of God: 18 praying always with all prayer and supplication in the Spirit, and watching thereunto with all perseverance and supplication for all saints; 19 and for me, that utterance may be given unto me, that I may open my mouth boldly, to make known the mystery of the gospel, 20 for which I am an ambassador in bonds: that therein I may speak boldly, as I ought to speak."

How often to pray the Battle Prayer? Consider: Ps 55:16 "As for me, I will call upon God; and the LORD shall save me. 17 Evening, and morning, and at noon, will I pray, and cry aloud: and he shall hear my voice."

Listen to this promise: Isa 62:1 "For Zion's sake will I not hold my peace, and for Jerusalem's sake I will not rest, until the righteousness thereof go forth as brightness, and the salvation thereof as a lamp that burneth." And how will He do this? Is 61:6 "I have set watchmen upon thy walls, O Jerusalem, which shall never hold their peace day nor night: ye that make mention of the LORD, keep not silence, 7 and give him no rest, till he establish, and till he make Jerusalem a praise in the earth." Here is a clear command to not stop until the job is done.

Notice the amount of prayer, "day and night," in verse 6 is just like the widow in the parable of Luke 18 on why we are to keep praying and faint not. One of God's answers to delivering His goodness on the Earth is people who will pray until the job is done. This is included in why we are to pray the "Our Father" often. Keep at it until you see the deliverance complete: 1 Tim 5:5 "… continueth in supplications and prayers night and day." 1 Thes 5:17 "Pray without ceasing."

This is consistent with the Greek present continuous tense which means to keep *aiteo*/asking, but is not always translated that way. Here are some examples translated properly: Matt 7:7 "Keep on *aiteo*/asking and it will be given you; keep on seeking and you will find; keep on knocking [reverently] and [the door] will be opened to you. 8 For everyone who keeps on *aiteo*/asking receives; and he who keeps on seeking finds; and to him who keeps on knocking, [the door] will be opened. AMP (Also see the same in Luke 11:9-10 below.)

John 16:24 "Up to this time you have not *aiteo*/asked a [single] thing in My Name [as presenting all that I AM]; but now *aiteo*/ask and keep on *aiteo*/asking (*by requiring, demanding and expecting as due by covenant promise, knowing all the requirements have been met in Jesus*) and you will receive, so that your joy (gladness, delight) may be full and complete." AMP

1 John 5:13 "These things I write to you in order that you may know with an absolute knowledge that *zoe*/life you are having, eternal *zoe*/life, to you who believe on the Name of the Son of God. And this is the assurance which we are having toward Him, that if we keep on *aiteo*/asking anything for ourselves, [which is] according to His will, He hears us. And if we know with an absolute knowledge that He hears us, whatever we are *aiteo*/asking for ourselves, we know with an absolute knowledge that we have the *aiteo*/things which we have *aiteo*/asked from Him." KSW

So we are to keep on *aiteo*/asking until the answer comes, knowing that Father God wants us to, and Holy Spirit is encouraging us. The proper attitude includes insistence in our repeated *aiteo*/asking. Luke 11:5 "And he (*Jesus*) said unto them, Which of you shall have a friend, and shall go unto him at midnight, and say unto him, Friend, lend me three loaves; 6 for a friend of mine in his journey is come to me, and I have nothing to set before him? 7 And he from within shall answer and say, Trouble me not: the door is now shut, and my children are with me in bed; I cannot rise and give thee. 8 I say unto you, Though he will not rise and give him, because he is his friend, yet because of his importunity he will rise and give him as many as he needeth. 9 And I say unto you, *Aiteo*/ask *and keep on asking (by requiring, demanding and expecting as due by covenant promise*), and it shall be given you; seek *and keep on seeking*, and ye shall find; knock, and it shall be opened unto you. 10 For every one that *aiteo*/asketh *and keeps on aiteo/asking (by requiring, demanding and expecting as due by covenant promise*) receiveth; and he that seeketh findeth; and to him that knocketh it shall be opened." So, as in the parable in Luke 18, where we are told to fight the unjust judge night and day, faint not!

In any part of life, God makes His wisdom available to us, as He always has through study of the Scriptures and seeking Him. Notice again the present continuous tense for *aiteo* here. James 1:5 "If any of you lack wisdom, let him *aiteo*/ask (*keep on asking by requiring, demanding and expecting as due by covenant promise*) of God, that giveth to all men liberally, and upbraideth not; and it shall be given him. 6 But let him *aiteo*/ask in faith, nothing wavering. For he that wavereth is like a wave of the sea driven with the wind and tossed. 7 For let not that man think that he shall receive any thing of the Lord. 8 A double minded man is unstable in all his ways." So part of this *aiteo* process is to make a decision that you will not heed the harassing fears and dread of the devil's rule in the situation, but, instead, trust in the name of Jesus to set people free, by *aiteo*ing until you get the answer, whether it be for wisdom or healing (or any Bible covenant promise of God).

God has no sickness in Him, and He sent Jesus to heal us. James 1:13 "Let no man say when he is tempted (*which includes any unhappy situation, sickness, disease, infirmity, poverty, sorrow and grief*), I am tempted of God: for God cannot be tempted with evil, neither tempteth he any man: 14 but every man is tempted, when he is drawn away of his own lust [*or evil fear-induced lust/worry/terror*], and enticed. 15 Then when lust hath conceived, it bringeth forth sin: and sin, when it is finished, bringeth forth death. 16 Do not err, my *agape*/beloved brethren. 17 Every good gift and every perfect gift [*including divine healing*] is from above, and cometh down from the Father of lights, with whom is no variableness, neither shadow of turning. [*So God has no sickness in Him, and He tempts no man with sickness. It is a work of the devil and not of God.*] 18 Of his own will begat he us with the word of truth [*the Gospel of our salvation, with the stripes of Jesus and when God raised Jesus from the dead and declared Him both Lord and Christ, and redeeming us from sin and the curse of death in any form, fast or slow*], that we should be a kind of firstfruits of his creatures."

A word on medicine: Unless you have specific information to the contrary, do not fight it; use it, according to your faith. Praise God for the benefits of modern Western medicine. Millions would be dead and no longer able to hear the Gospel today without it. Is it perfect? No. As reasonable, you should include the doctors, nurses, machines, medicines, treatments and therapies in your prayers. Our faith weapon is total: Luke 10:19 "Behold, I give unto you power (*authority, commission and the resources of Heaven*) to tread on serpents and scorpions, and over **all the power (*ability*) of the enemy**: and **nothing shall by any means hurt you**."

A Summary Exhortation: 2 Cor 1:19 For the Son of God, Jesus Christ, who was preached among you ... even by me and *the apostles*, was not yea and nay, but in him was yea. 20 For all the promises of God in him are yea, and in him Amen (*so be it*), unto the glory of God by *all of* us. Study the 2 Tim 3:15 ... holy scriptures, which are able to make thee wise unto *soteria*/salvation through faith which is in Christ Jesus. 16 All scripture is given by inspiration of God, and is profitable for doctrine, for reproof, for correction, for instruction in righteousness: 17 that the man *or woman* of God may be perfect, throughly furnished unto all good works. 2 Tim 2:24 And the servant of the Lord must not strive; but be gentle unto all men, apt to teach, patient, 25 in meekness instructing those that oppose themselves; if God peradventure will give them repentance to the acknowledging of the truth; 26 and that they may recover themselves out of the snare of the devil, who are taken captive by him at his will. John 8:31 Then said Jesus to those Jews which believed on him, If ye continue

BATTLE PRAYER FOR DIVINE HEALING: FIELD MANUAL 2

in my word, then are ye my disciples indeed; 32 and ye shall know the truth, and the truth shall make you *and others* free. John 15:7 If ye abide in me, and my words abide in you, ye shall *aiteo*/ask *(by requiring, demanding and expecting as due by covenant promise)* what ye will, and it shall be done unto you. 8 Herein is my Father glorified, that ye bear much fruit; so shall ye be my disciples. 9 As the Father hath *agape*/loved me, so have I *agape*/loved you: continue ye in my *agape*/love. John 3:33 He that hath received his *(Jesus')* testimony hath set to his seal that God is true. 34 For he whom God hath sent speaketh the words of God: for God giveth not the Spirit by measure unto him. *(And we have grace to the measure of Christ in us.)* 35 The Father *agape*/loveth the Son, and hath given all things into his hand. 36 He that believeth on the Son hath everlasting *zoe*/life … . John 20:31 But these are written, that ye might believe that Jesus is the Christ, the Son of God; and that believing ye might have *zoe*/life through his name. 1 John 5:10 He that believeth on the Son of God hath the witness in himself: he that believeth not God hath made him a liar; because he believeth not the record that God gave of his Son. 11 And this is the record, that God hath given to us eternal *zoe*/life, and this *zoe*/life is in his Son. 12 He that hath the Son hath *zoe*/life; and he that hath not the Son of God hath not *zoe*/life. 13 These things have I written unto you that believe on the name of the Son of God; **that ye may know that ye have eternal zoe/life**, and that ye **may believe on the name of the Son of God**. 14 And this is the confidence that we have in him, that, if we *aiteo*/ask *(demand)* any thing according to his will, he heareth us: 15 and if we know that he hear us, whatsoever we *aiteo*/ask *(by keeping on requiring, demanding and expecting as due by covenant promise)*, we know that we have the *aiteo*/petitions that we *aiteo*/desired *(required, demanded and expected as due by covenant promise)* of him. Gal 6:7 Be not deceived; God is not mocked: for whatsoever a man soweth, that shall he also reap. 8 For he that soweth to his flesh shall of the flesh reap corruption; but he that soweth to the Spirit shall of the Spirit reap *zoe*/life everlasting. 9 And let us not be weary in well doing: for in due season we shall reap, if we faint not. 1 Thes 5:17 Pray without ceasing. 18 In every thing give thanks: for this is the will of God in Christ Jesus concerning you. Rom 16:20 And the God of peace shall bruise *(crush)* Satan under your feet *(as shattered glass)*. The grace of our Lord Jesus Christ be with you *(to know, be and do this)*. Amen *(so be it)*.

If you do not yet see the full manifestation of the victory in the situation, speak this entire book and the Battle Prayer until you do.

Remember: good works do not make you righteous; faith in the blood of Jesus does that; but the righteous do good works. Praying often does not make you righteous; believing that God raised Jesus from the dead does that; but the righteous pray often. Going to church does not make you righteous; believing that Jesus is the Son of God does that; but the righteous go to church. Phil 3:8 "Yea doubtless, and I count all things but loss for the excellency of the knowledge of Christ Jesus my Lord:

for whom I have suffered the loss of all things, and do count them but dung, that I may win Christ, 9 and be found in him, not having mine own righteousness, which is of the law (*doing what God requires*), but that which is through the faith of Christ, the righteousness (*perfect right standing, just like Jesus*) which is of God by faith." Get the mind of Christ in you by His Word.

In general, your soul is housed in two parts, your conscious mind (2-4% of your brain) and the unconscious mind (96-98% of your brain mass). Truth in just the conscious mind is mental assent and, by itself, of little power. With intensity and focus, over the course of a few days, you can fill your cognitive mind with truth, "cramming as a student does," and then attack the devil with power.

But the effect of confidence in God from this "cramming" will only last for 3 to 5 days unless you maintain your efforts to renew your subconscious also. We are not talking about the healing, dead raising or improvement in the situation; we are talking about your heart confidence in God, so you can deliver more healing to others. Or, if you do not get the full result, keep at it until you do. There is no limit to how long you can "cram" to adjust your mind and stir yourself up, so you can win for God. God *agape*/loves with an intensity we cannot comprehend. He paid the great price of Jesus by the cross. Jesus paid that price so no curse could ever again reside on or afflict any human — ever again. The issue is for us to build a path of effective faith that allows Him to manifest that *agape*/love in healing and other good works through us. This manual is designed to help you in such "cramming" so that you can build that path and win the battle at hand.

Long-term results come as you imprint into your heart, your unconscious mind, your soul, with repetition and emotional intensity, not feelings. Your subconscious mind cannot tell if you are faking joy or really feeling joy. But joy, thanksgiving and praise are high emotion and activity words in the true meaning. They are not gentle or passive, like polite manners. So with intensity and emotion, you can overwrite fear and lies in your heart with love, faith, hope, grace and truth. Phil 4:6 "Be careful for nothing; but in every thing by prayer and supplication with thanksgiving let your requests (*aiteo*) be made known unto God. 7 And the peace of God, which passeth all understanding, shall keep your hearts and minds through Christ Jesus." As you apply strong, excited, faking-it-if-need-be/happy or game-face thanksgiving with your prayer, you write over fear and unbelief with trust in God and His goodness, unto confidence and certainty. Healing is more about agreeing with God in truth in your mind and heart. This manual is also designed to help reprogram your heart for the long term.

Praise, thanks, and joy actions are not emotions, but actions that can lead to emotions. Obey with gladness and intensity, and you write those praises, thanks and joys into your subconscious (heart, inner man), to release the love of God. The mind of Christ within you longs, with intensity, to release that love into the Earth.

The mind of Christ within you gladly does the right behaviors of confession, praise, thanks and joy, independent of emotion or with forced glad emotion (sometimes called fake emotion or putting on your game or happy face) both to train your soul, subconscious mind, and to release more *zoe* through you now. James 4:5 "Do ye think that the scripture saith in vain, The spirit that dwelleth in us lusteth to envy?" That is strong emotion and motivation against anything in our life that is not Jesus working freely in your totally-renewed soul to manifest the Kingdom of God through you.

As you read a truth such as Phil 4:13 "I can do all things through Christ which strengtheneth me," don't read fast. Instead, stop and dwell a while on it. Repeat this with joy, praise and thanksgiving, to drive or write it onto your heart and overwrite the fears that keep you in bondage. Encourage yourself daily in this way. In a critical battle, you may need to encourage yourself every five minutes, and at every negative report, so you don't give up.

Phil 4:6-7 is telling us to identify our fears, pray to God about the fear to fix whatever the concern, then give Him deep, strong and loud thanks (which is all in the meaning of thanksgiving). Then the Peacemaker, the one who makes peace by destroying the works of the devil, will rule in your heart (subconscious mind) and your conscious mind to think like Jesus. The more you think like Jesus on healing, the more you will see of God's healing power. Faint not!

When doubts start to assail you and temp you to stop, speak the Minister Confession and the Scriptures: for Healing, Why Jesus Came, and the Blood of Jesus, and do it over and over with joy, faking it if need be, until you are ready again. Also pray in tongues for a time, loud, hard and fast, and aim these prayers at the situation. Then swing that sword of reconciliation and blast that devil out in the mighty name of Jesus.

The problem is not the truth of God in Jesus; the problem and call of God for every believer is the enforcement by the believer in the Spirit with God's Word, to use that Word like fuller's soap, and scrub with *aiteo*/commands until the answer comes. Or plant the seed of God's Word and water it with *aiteo*/commands until it bears fruit. In either case, the victory will come. Faint not!

Father, in the name of Jesus, have Holy Spirit pray through me now and fill me with Your dominion, love and compassion for this situation to victory. Thank You, Father! In the name of Jesus, thank You! Yahoo!

Isa 11:9 ... For the earth shall be full of the knowledge of the Lord, as the waters cover the sea.

Part VII

A Summary

And there he found a certain man named Aeneas, which had kept his bed eight years, and was sick of the palsy. And Peter said unto him, Aeneas, Jesus Christ maketh thee whole: arise, and make thy bed. And he arose immediately. (Acts 9:33-34)

SOME CONCLUSIONS

The milk of the Word is in the teaching; the meat of the Word is in the doing. Right thinking in God's zoe gets us to right doing.

John 4:34 Jesus saith unto them, My meat is to do the will of him that sent me, and to finish his work.

John 6:38 For I came down from heaven, not to do mine own will, but the will of him that sent me.

Luke 10:19 Behold (*appreciate, understand and make this change your life*), I (*Jesus*) give unto you power (*authority, commission and ability*) to tread on serpents and scorpions, and over all the power (*ability*) of the enemy: and nothing shall by any means hurt you. 20 Notwithstanding in this rejoice not, that the spirits are subject unto you; but rather rejoice, because your names are written in heaven.

James 2:26 For as the body without the spirit is dead, so faith without works is dead also.

1 Cor 8:1 ... We know that we all have knowledge. Knowledge puffeth up, but *agape*/charity edifieth. 2 And if any man think that he knoweth anything, he knoweth nothing yet as he ought to know. 3 But if any man *agape*/love God, the same is known of him.

James 1:12 Blessed is the man that endureth temptation (*to give up trusting God to fulfill His Word*): for when he is tried (*in the face of continued delay while* lambano-ing *the grace of God, the gift of righteousness and the promises of God*), he shall receive the crown of *zoe*/life, which the Lord hath promised to them that *agape*/love him.

1 John 5:2 By this we know that we *agape*/love the children of God, when we *agape*/love God, and keep his commandments. 3 For this is the *agape*/love of God, that we keep his commandments: and his commandments are not grievous. 4 For whatsoever is born of God overcometh the world: and this is the victory that over-

cometh the world, even our faith. 5 Who is he that overcometh the world, but he that believeth that Jesus is the Son of God?

1 Thes 5:5 Ye are all the children of light, and the children of the day: we are not of the night, nor of darkness. 6 Therefore let us not sleep, as do others; but let us watch and be sober. 7 For they that sleep sleep in the night; and they that be drunken are drunken in the night. 8 But let us, who are of the day, be sober, putting on the breastplate of faith and *agape*/love; and for an helmet, the hope of *soteria*/salvation. 9 For God hath not appointed us to wrath, but to obtain *soteria*/salvation by our Lord Jesus Christ, 10 who died for us, that, whether we wake or sleep, we should *zao*/live together with him.

Eph 5:8 For ye were sometimes darkness, but now are ye light in the Lord: walk as children of light:

Under Dr. Lake's ministry a man prayed in English and tongues for about 20 hours every day to break a killing plague. At the end of about 3 to 4 weeks suddenly all the sick were quickly made well in the whole region (Liardon, *John G. Lake*, p 607). More recently a group of 3 men stopped a plague in Mexico by praying in tongues for 3 days and then laying hands on the sick in Jesus' name, per Mark 16:18. (Hogan, *Recordings*) Faint not! Jesus is Lord through us! Stay in the battle!

One man took 8 hours of constant healing confession to break the flu in his own body, and another time it took him only 10 seconds. One took six 6 weeks of thanksgiving to remove a tumor, another 30 seconds. One straightened club feet in 3 minutes, while, in another case it took 2 full days of constant commanding battle. The problem was not the work of the devil, nor the power of God. It was the attitude of the warrior. In all cases, victory went to those who would not give up, but stayed in the dominion of Jesus until freedom came.

Our problem is not God. He is our Helper, but we are the ones who have to do the doing. "Anything between you and a promise of God and its fulfillment is an enemy, for you to grasp, to beat and to defeat" (Blake, *The Official Teachings*, p 204). The problem is a devil, in either some lies we believe and/or in active resistance to healing or salvation. Get rid of the lies in you with truth and the devils with commands in the name of Jesus, and you will see godly results. Agree with God that the devil has had his way long enough, and exercise the authority Jesus has given you to set people free, in enforcing the judgment against the devil. While you fight, pray, "Father, fix me!"

Pray as long as it takes. "The only excuse for not getting a healing of God is that you believe there is one" (Blake, *The Voice of Healing*, Episode 2). So keep at it. God is not the problem. He paid for it all!

You will never do enough to be worthy or to deserve to be used by God; it is by grace, not works. But do the right things, and you will see right results. A large part of believing is in doing. What you do is what you really believe. It is a law of the

A Summary

human spirit that you can act yourself into believing quicker than you can believe yourself into acting. Act with the attitude of Jesus' victory to see His results.

One way to describe healing or any activity that releases the *zoe*/life of God into a situation is to imagine an irrigation pump. First, there is a source of water, the healing *zoe* in the Word of God and in your spirit, with Holy Spirit. Faith is both the hose and the pump. The valve for water to flow is your heart, single-minded on healing, in compassion and/or judgment against the devil. Put the hose to the water, turn on the pump, open the valve and pump life. We are the hose, the pump and the valve is our soul. The *zoe* travels by faith through your soul to the one in need. Soul agreement with God, in compassion, righteousness and judgment, is the pump pressure. Co-laborers, man and God, heal people of the devil's oppressions with God's *zoe*/life. Together we crush the devil's works.

1 Cor 3:9 For we are labourers together with God: ye are God's husbandry, ye are God's building.

2 Cor 6:1 We then, as workers together with him, beseech you also that ye receive not the grace of God in vain. 2 (For he saith, I have heard thee in a time accepted, and in the day of *soteria*/salvation have I succoured thee: behold, now is the accepted time; behold, now is the day of *soteria*/salvation.)

James 4:6 But he giveth more grace. Wherefore he saith, God resisteth the proud, but giveth grace unto the humble. 7 Submit yourselves therefore to God. Resist the devil, and he (*the devil and his works*) will flee from you.

Eph 5:14 Wherefore he saith, Awake thou that sleepest, and arise from the dead, and Christ shall give thee light. 15 See then that ye walk circumspectly, not as fools, but as wise, 16 redeeming the time, because the days are evil. 17 Wherefore be ye not unwise, but understanding what the will of the Lord is.

Rom 5:17 For if by one man's offence death reigned by one; much more they which (*continually*) *lambano*/receive abundance of grace and of the gift of righteousness shall reign (*as kings for Jesus, like Jesus*) in *zoe*/life by one, Jesus Christ.) 18 Therefore as by the offence of one judgment came upon all men to condemnation; even so by the righteousness of one the free gift came upon all men unto justification of *zoe*/life. 19 For as by one man's disobedience many were made sinners, so by the obedience of one shall many be made righteous. 20 Moreover the law entered, that the offence might abound. But where sin abounded, grace did much more abound: 21 that as sin hath reigned unto death, even so might grace reign (*as a king for Jesus, like Jesus*) through righteousness unto eternal *zoe*/life by Jesus Christ our Lord.

1 Pet 2:24 Who his own self bare our sins in his own body on the tree, that we, being dead to sins, should *zao*/live unto righteousness: by whose stripes ye were healed. 25 For ye were as sheep going astray; but are now returned unto the Shepherd and Bishop of your souls.

Battle Prayer for Divine Healing: Field Manual 2

Jesus said: Luke 10:19 "Behold (*make this change the way you operate in this world*), I give unto you power (*authority, commission and the resources of Heaven*) to tread on serpents and scorpions, and over all the power (*ability*) of the enemy: and nothing shall by any means hurt you." Like a policeman, you do not have to feel the power, but you do have to exercise the authority you have been given. Authority commands and directs.

He did not promise the disciples power first, but authority first; and as they used the authority, the power would be manifest and the results would follow. ["These signs follow them that believe."]

"Faith steps out to act with the authority of God's Word, seeing no sign of the promised power, but believing and acting as if it were real. As it speaks the word of authority and command [*to creation, the devil and his works*], and puts its foot without fear upon the head of its conquered foes, lo, their power is disarmed, and all the forces of the heavenly world are there to make the victory complete." (A.B. Simpson, *The Alliance Weekly*, "The Authority of Faith," p 263)

Jesus gave us *dunamis*/power, ability, on the Day of Pentecost. Acts 1:8 "But ye shall receive *dunamis*/power, after that the Holy Ghost is come upon you: and ye shall be witnesses unto me both in Jerusalem, and in all Judaea, and in Samaria, and unto the uttermost part of the earth." The ability comes as you exercise the authority as Jesus would, the same way Jesus did, by faith. John 11:41 "Then they took away the stone from the place where the dead was laid. And Jesus lifted up his eyes, and said, Father, I thank thee that thou hast heard me. 42 And I knew that thou hearest me always: but because of the people which stand by I said it, that they may believe that thou hast sent me." Raising the untimely dead is Father's will. There are no limits!

Hear the description of the disciples, as Jesus fought to get them to believe after His resurrection. Luke 24:41 "And while they yet believed not for (*soul and not spirit*) joy, and wondered, he said unto them, Have ye here any meat?" Notice the definition of belief, unto the spirit joy Jesus had promised in John 16:24. This was so they could get this promise, so they could walk in the joy of that day. That day is when they believed unto true spirit joy that He was from Father God, His works were from Father God, He was raised from the dead by Father God, He went back to Father God for their benefit as members of His Kingdom on Earth, He sent Holy Spirit by and from Father God, and Father God will work through them as He did through Jesus. John 16:23 "And **in that day** ye shall *aiteo*/ask me nothing. Verily, verily, I say unto you, Whatsoever ye shall *aiteo*/ ask the Father in my name, he will give it you. 24 Hitherto have ye *aiteo*/asked nothing in my name: *aiteo*/ask, and ye shall receive, that your joy may be full." That is the goal of the affirmations in the Minister Confessions and the rest of this manual.

Unbelief fears, obeys and honors that God will not do His Word, and the devil's or the world's predictions will be what becomes true. So unbelief does not pray

A Summary

in authority, and, instead, uses words like, "if it be thy will." This is a clear case of "My people are destroyed for lack of knowledge" (Hos 4:6) for Jesus said: <u>Matt 8:7</u> "And Jesus saith unto him, I will come and heal him." <u>Mark 1:40</u> "And there came a leper to him, beseeching him, and kneeling down to him, and saying unto him, If thou wilt, thou canst make me clean. 41 And Jesus, moved with compassion, put forth his hand, and touched him, and saith unto him, I will (*because this is what I am made for, I delight to do, and I will always do*); be thou clean. 42 And as soon as he had spoken, immediately the leprosy departed from him, and he was cleansed." <u>Heb 13:8</u> "Jesus Christ the same yesterday, and to day, and for ever."

Courage or faith will be plagued and harassed with fears and dread, but keep *aiteo*ing in authority anyway. Faith believes God will do His Word in spite of what the current evidence looks like, while you keep an attitude of thanksgiving, praise and joy over what is coming of His Word, per your *aiteo*/prayer, by demanding, requiring and expecting as due by covenant promise of God. Judge and replace each fear thought with a promise from God, and decide that is what you will do.

Do not ignore the physical problems present. They are real but illegal in Jesus. Handle them to your ability, and then, or while you handle the physical symptoms present, in *agape*/love, attack the root with *aiteo* demands, in the name of Jesus.

This *aiteo* includes demanding and commanding that the devil, with his works and oppressions, will go, and for blessing to come like Heaven on Earth. The more you practice *aiteo* in the face of fear, the more it will become part of your life, no longer bold courage in the face of fear, but what and who you are, an officer of the Kingdom of God, doing your job of enforcing the judgment written against a cruel and defeated foe, who continues to torment, in cruel oppression, God's redeemed race. Jesus has bound the strongman; let us go and spoil his goods!

Be just like Abraham, who exercised faith with joy, in spite of the physical evidence before him, and, instead, believed God's Word and acted in joy until he got what he was believing God for. <u>Rom 4:18</u> "Who against hope believed in hope, that he might become the father of many nations; according to that which was spoken, So shall thy seed be. 19 And being not weak in faith, he considered not his own body now dead, when he was about an hundred years old, neither yet the deadness of Sara's womb: 20 he staggered not at the promise of God through unbelief; but was strong in faith, giving glory (*loud thanks, praise and joy*) to God; 21 and being fully persuaded that, what he had promised, he was able also to perform. 22 And therefore it was imputed to him for righteousness. 23 Now it was not written for his sake alone, that it was imputed to him; 24 but for us also, to whom it shall be imputed, if we believe on him that raised up Jesus our Lord from the dead; 25 who was delivered for our offences, and was raised again for our justification." Per verse 24, this is how we show we believe God, just as Abraham did. Acting in joy and constant rehearsal of God's truth is what it takes to "fully persuade yourself" in God's grace, mercy, truth, power and *agape*/love.

Strong faith believes His promise such that you start giving Him much thanks and praise that it is already done, even as you continue *aiteo*/asking Him to do His Word, His covenant promises, by commanding the devil and his works to obey, in the name of Jesus. Deal with the symptoms as needed and keep in *aiteo*.

To be an effective gateway for God into the Earth He requires that we keep proclaiming His Word, expecting Him to do it over any situation, until it is done, by Holy Spirit, through Jesus and you, from the Father. Remember, what makes you a Christian is God dwelling in a human. Your cooperation with Him in spirit, grace and truth makes you a gateway for Him to deliver His *agape*/love to men.

One way to tell your own troubled or doubting heart you do believe, you intend to believe, and you will believe, and to stir it up to power in God, is to start the behaviors of affirmation, declaration, command, thanksgiving, gladness, praise, joy and *aiteo* in God anyway. Write *agape*/love onto your heart with much repetition of Bible truth and right behaviors of *agape*/love, *aiteo*, thanks, praise and joy.

In some 1,500 Bible commands to fear not, give thanks, be glad, praise or rejoice, our God never says that we must feel like it first, but, rather, to do it till we feel it. Or discover the issue in your heart preventing you from feeling, usually unforgiveness of some kind, and clean it out. The secret is to obey in gladness, and if you don't feel it, put words of Scripture into your mouth that match and support the desired emotion and actions of gladness, and do this until you do feel it and/or expose and deal with the reasons you cannot.

If you don't feel it, you can do the right behaviors until you do feel it. At the same time, you are renewing your mind so your heart is cleansed into agreeing with God on that topic. Then, right emotions will come. It is not that we don't have fears and fear attacks; it is how we handle them when they come that matters. Stir yourself up into God's love and faithfulness. Faint not in your faith actions!

Hopefully you are now beginning to know, or have re-affirmed, that healing is always God's will. All the requirements have been met in Jesus, so we can *aiteo*/demand, require and expect Father God to fulfill all His covenant promises, including healing, because Jesus has risen from the dead and sits at the Father's right hand. Let your heart touch His love and dominion. Our job is to fight the good fight of faith, by taking the authority given to us by Jesus to resist the devil, so that healing can come, all in the name of Jesus, the Risen Lord and our Redeemer.

All the requirements have been met in Jesus. 1 Pet 2:24 "Who his own self bare our sins in his own body on the tree, that we, being dead to sins, should *zao*/live unto righteousness: by whose stripes ye were healed." 2 Cor 1:19 "For the Son of God, Jesus Christ, who was preached … was not yea and nay, but in him was yea. 20 For all the promises of God in him are yea, and in him Amen, unto the glory of

A Summary

God by us. 21 Now he which stablisheth us with you in Christ, and hath anointed us, is God; 22 who hath also sealed us, and given the earnest of the Spirit in our hearts." The Day of Father God's Salvation is now! Jesus took the stripes for our healing! Jesus is risen, glorified and has sent His Spirit!

The chastisement of the Lord is not His active hand in hurting you, as He has no pain in Him. His chastisement has always been: Gal 6:7 "Be not deceived; God is not mocked: for whatsoever a man soweth, that shall he also reap. 8 For he that soweth to his flesh shall of the flesh reap corruption; but he that soweth to the Spirit shall of the Spirit reap *zoe*/life everlasting. 9 And let us not be weary in well doing: for in due season we shall reap, if we faint not."

Thus we are both warned and promised in hope: 1 Cor 11:28 "But let a man examine himself, and so let him eat of that bread, and drink of that cup. 29 For he that eateth and drinketh unworthily, eateth and drinketh damnation to himself, not discerning the Lord's body. 30 For this cause many are weak and sickly among you, and many sleep. 31 For if we would judge ourselves, we should not be judged. 32 But when we are judged, we are chastened of the Lord, that we should not be condemned with the world." Heb 12:11 "Now no chastening for the present seemeth to be joyous, but grievous: nevertheless afterward it yieldeth the peaceable fruit of righteousness unto them which are exercised thereby (*to be a healing believer*). 12 Wherefore lift up the hands which hang down, and the feeble knees; 13 and make straight paths for your feet, lest that which is lame be turned out of the way; but let it rather be *iaomai*/healed (*physically*)."

This is exactly per the age-old promise of God for those who will work with Him to deliver His healing: **Isa 35:1** "The wilderness and the solitary place shall be glad for them; and the desert shall rejoice, and blossom as the rose. 2 It shall blossom abundantly, and rejoice even with joy and singing: the glory of Lebanon shall be given unto it, the excellency of Carmel and Sharon, they shall see the glory of the LORD, and the excellency of our God. **3 Strengthen ye the weak hands, and confirm the feeble knees.** 4 Say to them that are of a fearful heart, Be strong, fear not: behold, your God will come with vengeance, even God with a recompence; **he will come and save (*heal*) you.** 5 Then the eyes of the blind shall be opened, and the ears of the deaf shall be unstopped. 6 Then shall the lame man leap as an hart, and the tongue of the dumb sing: for in the wilderness shall waters break out, and streams in the desert. 7 And the parched ground shall become a pool, and the thirsty land springs of water: in the habitation of dragons, where each lay, shall be grass with reeds and rushes. 8 And an highway shall be there, and a way, and it shall be called The way of holiness; the unclean shall not pass over it; but it shall be for those: the wayfaring men, though fools, shall not err therein. 9 No lion shall be there, nor any ravenous beast shall go up thereon, it shall not be found there; but the redeemed shall walk there: 10 and the ransomed of the LORD shall return, and come to Zion with songs and everlasting joy upon their heads: they shall obtain joy and gladness, and sorrow and sighing shall flee away."

Jesus never told anyone that He could not heal them because God needed to take them home through a disease, that they needed to learn some lesson, they had to accept Him first, or that they could not be healed because of some sin. The only sin issue we need to focus on is our giving up disbelief, unpersuadableness, fainting and lack of courage in believing God to do it the way He said to do it. "Lord, give us light until we do Your will in thankful joy." The battle is ours to win, in the name of Jesus. Do not let the devil snare you with thoughts that you or the victim needs to learn some lesson in this delay or failure.

If Jesus were the one ministering, you know the sick you are ministering to would be healed, either instantly, within an hour or at the very least, within a few days. You know that if Jesus did not heal completely on the first ministry, He would minster again and keep doing so until the person was healed. You must not accept a lesser standard. The only lesson you need to learn is that the devil is a liar and the father of lies, and, for you, this is about the gift of righteousness and the abundance of grace, because of the holiness of Jesus that is given to us. The life of Jesus is the abundant spotlight of God's will and how God really is concerning healing and His desire to bruise, crush and destroy the works of the devil, including sickness, disease and early death, through you, with the *zoe*/life in you, by Holy Spirit dwelling in you.

You will see God's healing hand as you work the power that is in you! Jesus as Victor is enforced through us! Faint not in faith actions! Keep at it until you overcome the devil in the situation.

Hear the great lament of Jesus. Matt 13:14 "And in them is fulfilled the prophecy of Esaias, which saith, By hearing ye shall hear, and shall not understand; and seeing ye shall see, and shall not perceive: 15 for this people's heart is waxed gross, and their ears are dull of hearing, and their eyes they have closed; lest at any time they should see with their eyes, and hear with their ears, and should understand with their heart, and should be converted, and I should *iaomai* (*physically*) heal [*and prosper*] them."

3 John 2 "*Agape*/beloved, I wish (*pray*) above all things that thou mayest prosper and be in health, even as thy soul prospereth."

The more we focus on the Mighty Arm of God, Jesus, and the work He accomplished through the stripes, cross, resurrection and glorification of Jesus, to where we are seated with Him beside the Father, the smaller the issues of this life become. This is God's Good News in Jesus Christ.

Curry Blake: "The weakest Christian is stronger than the strongest devil, for greater is He that is in you than he that is in the world." (Blake, *The Voice of Healing*,

A Summary

Episode 2) We already have the power; clean out your soul so God can do what He wants through you.

In his powerful follow-on ministry of John G. Lake, Rev. Blake states: "The only hindrance to healing is that if the Christian thinks there is a hindrance to healing." (Blake, *The Official Teachings*, p 10.)

Many worry if the person being ministered to has faith or not. Prepare your mind for every ministry, as if you are raising the dead. The only person recorded who clearly had faith for his own resurrection was Jesus. When Jesus raised the dead boy in Nain, no one had faith. When He raised Lazarus from the dead, if his sisters had had faith, then the graves of the world would be empty. Those ladies may have loved Jesus, but they did not have faith. When the men tossed the dead body onto the bones of Elisha, in 2 Kings 13:21, neither the dead man, nor his friends had faith. Jesus commended faith when He found it, for He wanted all to have faith in God through Him, but if faith was not there, He still healed. Ps 103:6 "The LORD executeth righteousness and judgment for all that are oppressed." So in ministry you treat everyone as if you were raising the dead. If they have some faith, then fine. If not, you exercise faith for them. If they had enough faith, they would already be healed. So plan on doing it yourself, and have the attitude that every case is a resurrection, and you will see the results of Jesus, and avoid a whole lot of less-than-perfect theology.

Do not get caught up in the trap of trying to build up the faith of the sick person. Instead, focus on getting them healed, and then building their faith will be much easier. If you are ministering to those who are in a hospital or under caregivers, most of those caregivers are spending all day reinforcing their sick condition and destroying the patient's faith. They are not doing this maliciously, but in the normal course of doing their jobs. You cannot counter "blow for blow," trying to build the patient's faith. In the presence of the patient, you may only have 5 minutes to a few hours, while the caregivers have all the rest of 24-hours, and every day they pump death into their patients, with worldly facts and, at best, worldly hope. While many may be good hearted, few minister in God's *agape*/love, power, grace and truth.

Instead, you know that: 1 John 4:4 "Ye are of God, little children, and have overcome them: because greater is he that is in you, than he that is in the world." What professional healthcare providers have is worldly facts. What you have and enforce, in God's Spirit of *dunamis*/power, *agape*/love and a sound mind, God's Word, *zoe*/life and the name of Jesus. Instead, know that, as you minister that *zoe*/life with godly thoughts, words and actions, it is a seed that will grow in that person and overcome what others are planting in them. The sick are simply the battleground for you to blast the devil out of, and healing will come.

You *aiteo*, knowing God will do the healing and overcome anything that is harming the sick you minister to because Jesus said in the Bible: John 14:12 "Verily, verily, I say unto you, He that believeth on me, the works that I do shall he do also; and greater works than these shall he do; because I go unto my Father. 13 And whatsoever ye shall *aiteo*/ask (*require, demand and expect as due by covenant promise*) in my name, that will I do, that the Father may be glorified in the Son. 14 If ye shall *aiteo*/ask (*require, demand and expect as due by covenant promise*) any thing in my name, I will do it. 15 If ye *agape*/love me, keep my commandments." Those commandments are to *agape*/love one another and believe on the name of Jesus, to crush the kingdom of darkness and enforce the Kingdom of God, just as Jesus would.

Encourage and stir yourself up by magnifying the Lord in your heart, by giving thanks and praising Jesus and invoking the power of His name. *Aiteo* in confidence, knowing, as you do your work of believing, God will do His work of signs and wonders. Acts 14:3 "Long time therefore abode they speaking boldly in the Lord, which gave testimony unto the word of his grace, and granted signs and wonders to be done by their hands." That *"boldly"* includes *aiteo* commands.

If you do have time to teach and share scripture, use the Scriptures in this manual as well as the teachings. Keep it simple and direct. Often it is best to have the sick use or read the Battle Prayer with you. You don't have to answer all questions. Avoid all debate, and just keep the conversation on the Scriptures.

God got the job done in Jesus 2000 years ago. Jesus never told anyone they could not be healed because of sin, or that they had to wait until they learned some "lesson." He did not need their faith; He had His own. To know God, look at Jesus. He is the light of who and what God is like. John 1:1 "In the beginning was the Word, and the Word was with God, and the Word was God. 2 The same was in the beginning with God. 3 All things were made by him; and without him was not any thing made that was made. 4 In him was *zoe*/life; and the *zoe*/life was the light of men. 5 And the light shineth in darkness; and the darkness comprehended it not."

1 John 1:1 "That which was from the beginning, which we have heard, which we have seen with our eyes, which we have looked upon, and our hands have handled, of the Word of *zoe*/life; 2 (for the *zoe*/life was manifested, and we have seen it, and bear witness, and shew unto you that eternal *zoe*/life, which was with the Father, and was manifested unto us;) 3 that which we have seen and heard declare we unto you, that ye also may have fellowship with us: and truly our fellowship is with the Father, and with his Son Jesus Christ. 4 And these things write we unto you, that your joy may be full. 5 This then is the message which we have heard of him, and declare unto you, that God is light, and in him is no darkness at all." Any and all infirmity, sickness, death or lack is darkness and a work of the devil and not of God.

A Summary

Heb 1:1 "God, who at sundry times and in divers manners spake in time past unto the fathers by the prophets, 2 hath in these last days spoken unto us by his Son, whom he hath appointed heir of all things, by whom also he made the worlds; 3 who being the brightness of his glory, and the express image of his person, and upholding all things by the word of his power, when he had by himself purged our sins, sat down on the right hand of the Majesty on high; 4 being made so much better than the angels, as he hath by inheritance obtained a more excellent name than they."

Use this manual, the Psalms and the Gospels as prayer tools to develop an ear that can hear to glad obedience and physical healing!

As you have time, other authors to study include: Curry Blake, Jay Snell, John G. Lake, E.W. Kenyon, Francis McNutt, Roger Sapp, Dan Mohler, Todd White, David Hogan, T.L. Osborn, Kenneth Copeland, Jesse Duplantis and Creflo Dollar. When you find anything that does not fit the weight of Scripture, drop that for now and go with God's Word in Christ.

Your goal is to become a peacemaker, just like Jesus was: Acts 10:36 "The word which God sent unto the children of Israel, preaching peace by Jesus Christ: (he is Lord of all:) ... 38 How God anointed Jesus of Nazareth with the Holy Ghost and with power: who went about doing good, and healing all that were oppressed (*under the active rule, reign and lordship*) of the devil; for God was with him. 39 And we are witnesses of all things which he did both in the land of the Jews, and in Jerusalem; whom they slew and hanged on a tree: 40 him God raised up the third day, and shewed him openly; 41 not to all the people, but unto witnesses chosen before of God, even to us, who did eat and drink with him after he rose from the dead. 42 And he commanded us to preach unto the people, and to testify that it is he which was ordained of God to be the Judge of quick and dead. 43 To him give all the prophets witness, that through his name whosoever believeth in him shall receive remission (*purging, removal, obliteration and putting away*) of sins."

Make this your regular prayer: Col 1:9 "For this cause *I* ... do not cease to pray ... , and to *aiteo*/desire that *I* might be filled with the knowledge of *Your* will, Father, in all wisdom and spiritual understanding; 10 that *I* might walk worthy of the Lord unto all pleasing, being fruitful in every good work, and increasing in the knowledge of *You, Father* God; 11 strengthened with all might, according to *Your* glorious *dunamis*/power, unto all patience and longsuffering with joyfulness; 12 giving thanks (*continually*) unto *You*, the Father, which hath made *me* meet, *by Your grace in Jesus*, to be *a partaker* of the inheritance of the saints in light: 13 who hath delivered us from the power of darkness, and hath translated us into the kingdom of his *agape*/dear Son: 14 in whom we have redemption through his blood, even the *aphesis*/forgiveness (*remission to the putting away*) of sins:

God will answer your prayer for faith, power, growth and anything else, by sending you to the Scriptures to learn of Him in His Word. Failure to see God in the Scriptures is to miss the message. Matt 22:29 "Jesus answered and said unto them, Ye do err, not knowing the scriptures, nor the *dumanis*/power of God." 2 Pet 1:9 "But he that lacketh these things (*of becoming more like Jesus*) is blind, and cannot see afar off, and hath forgotten that he was purged from his old sins [*the remission of sin in our redemption*]." Jesus is the message of what God is really like.

If you are born again and have been baptized by Holy Spirit, you already have Holy Spirit within you. The issue is working with Holy Spirit and the Scriptures until that Word of the Gospel of Christ in us, the hope of glory (Col 1:27), that we are made and qualified to be the hope of Heaven by the work of Jesus, is engrafted into you. James 1:21 "Wherefore lay apart all filthiness and superfluity of naughtiness, and receive with meekness the engrafted word, which is able to *sozo*/save your souls. 22 But be ye doers of the word, and not hearers only, deceiving your own selves."

As we learn to abide in Jesus and let His words abide in us, answers to prayer of any kind will be less and less of a problem. John 15:7 "If ye abide in me, and my words abide in you, ye shall *aiteo*/ask (*require, demand and expect as due by covenant promise*) what ye will, and it shall be done unto you. 8 Herein is my Father glorified, that ye bear much fruit; so shall ye be my disciples."

For any blindness to the Gospel, command that lying demon of blindness to go, ask Holy Spirit to help, and then go study the Scriptures. 2 Cor 4:3 "But if our gospel be hid, it is hid to them that are lost (*perishing in lies and death working in them*): 4 in whom the god of this world (*Satan*) hath blinded the minds of them which believe not, lest the light of the glorious gospel of Christ, who is the image of God, should shine unto them."

Holy Spirit will emphasize the eternal and all-powerful truth of the great and mighty work of the Mighty Arm of God. Jesus has redeemed mankind from sin and the curse of sin. The sting of death has been removed. Let us go and enforce His great salvation on a hurting world, like Jesus did. 1 Cor 15:55 "O death, where is your victory? O death, where is your sting? [Hos 13:14.] 56 Now sin is the sting of death, and sin exercises its power [upon the soul] through [the abuse of] the Law. 57 But thanks be to God, Who gives us the victory [making us conquerors] through our Lord Jesus Christ. 58 Therefore, my *agape*/beloved brethren, be firm (steadfast), immovable, always abounding in the work of the Lord [always being superior, excelling, doing more than enough in the service of the Lord], knowing and being continually aware that your labor in the Lord is not futile [it is never wasted or to no purpose]." AMP

Prov 4:20 My *child*, attend [*lambano*/*hold on to, keep by continual repetition and study, to release God's* zoe/*life, to do greater works than Jesus*] to my words [*as seen in*

A Summary

this manual]; incline thine ear unto *the Lord's* sayings. 21 Let them not depart from thine eyes; keep them [*continually as in the Minister Confessions*] in the midst of thine heart. 22 For they are life unto those that find them, and health to all their flesh. 23 Keep thy heart with all diligence; for out of it are the issues of life. 24 Put away from thee a froward mouth, and perverse lips put far from thee [*in fault finding, murmuring and complaining; instead, be anxious for nothing and make your* aiteo *requests known unto God in prayer, supplication and thanksgiving*].

1 Tim 6:12 Fight the good fight of faith, *lambano*/lay hold on eternal *zoe*/life, whereunto thou art also called, and hast professed a good profession before many witnesses. 13 I give thee charge in the sight of God, who quickeneth all things, and before Christ Jesus, who before Pontius Pilate witnessed a good confession; 14 that thou keep this commandment without spot, unrebukeable, until the appearing of our Lord Jesus Christ.

James 4:6 *For God* giveth more grace. Wherefore he saith, God resisteth the proud, but giveth grace unto the humble. 7 Submit yourselves therefore to God. Resist the devil, and he will flee from you. 8 Draw nigh to God, and he will draw nigh to you. Cleanse your hands, ye sinners; and purify your hearts, ye double minded.

Gal 5:1 Stand fast therefore in the liberty wherewith Christ hath made us free, and be not entangled again with the yoke of bondage [*of self-righteousness in lies, fear and ignorance of the Word of Christ*].

1 John 5:13 These things have I written unto you that believe on the name of the Son of God; that ye may know that ye have eternal *zoe*/life, and that ye may believe on the name of the Son of God."

1 Cor 16:13 Watch ye, stand fast in the faith, quit you like men, be strong [*in the name of Jesus*]. 14 Let all your things be done with *agape*/charity.

1 Cor 15:57 But thanks be to God, which giveth us the victory through our Lord Jesus Christ. 58 Therefore, my *agape*/beloved brethren, be ye stedfast, unmoveable, always abounding in the work of the Lord, forasmuch as ye know that your labour is not in vain in the Lord.

The Lord is near and in you. He will empower your righteous good works. Faint not!

Ob 1:21 And saviours shall come up on mount Zion to judge (*rule and remove*) the mount of Esau (*the devil and all his works*); and the kingdom shall be the LORD's.

Titus 2:11 For the grace of God that bringeth *soteria*/salvation hath appeared to all men, 12 teaching us that, denying ungodliness and worldly lusts, we should *zao*/live soberly, righteously, and godly, in this present world; 13 looking for that blessed hope, and the glorious appearing of the great God and our Saviour Jesus Christ; 14 who gave himself for us, that he might redeem us from all iniquity, and purify unto himself a peculiar people, zealous of good works [*like the Father did through Jesus, and even greater works of God's power and wisdom, because Jesus now sits at the right hand of the Father*]. 15 These things speak, and exhort (*excite, urge, advise, warn, encourage and stir up*), and rebuke (*tell them where they are wrong and to get right with appropriate action*) with all authority. Let no man [*or woman*] despise thee.

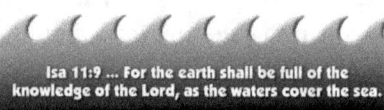

APPENDICES

RECOMMENDED READING

There are many books on Christian healing in the name of Jesus. The first half is usually a wonderful discussion and testimonies of this divine truth. Then often the second half goes to explain why healing is delayed and then deviate from what the Scripture says to explain the situation. The effect is often to send the serious inquirer into deep soul searching and sin consciousness, and not in glorifying what God did in our redemption by the blood of Jesus Christ. It is holding onto the gift of righteousness and the abundance of grace that releases the Kingdom, not just confession of sin. We must put on the new man in the spirit of our mind to grow in Jesus. We should define our situations and experience only from Scripture, and not use our failed or unique experiences to explain Scripture.

While much of his teaching is solid truth, Dr. Lake believed that un-confessed sin hindered healing. Jesus never told anyone that their healing was delayed or would not come due to sin. While pastoral concerns for clean living are valid, Jesus is our example for healing, not anyone else. As Jesus demonstrated, the only hindrance to healing is you believing that there are valid hindrances to healing. "As your faith, so be it unto you."

God heals through those who do not have perfect theology, but if your theology hinders you, you will see healing hindrances that are not from or by God. Instead recognize that any hindrance to healing is a devil in either lies we believe, or an active demon resisting you. Get rid of lies by renewing your mind with Scripture, and demons with *aiteo* commands in the name of Jesus.

I recommend all the writings of Curry Blake and:

Copeland, Kenneth. Compiler and editor, *John G. Lake: His Life, His Sermons, His Boldness of Faith*, (Kenneth Copeland Publications, Fort Worth, Texas: 1994)

Lindsay, Gordon. Editor, *The John G. Lake Sermons on Dominion Over Demons, Disease and Death*, (Voice of Healing Publishing Co., Dallas, Texas: 1949)

Sapp, Roger. *Performing Miracles and Healing*, (All Nations Publications, Southlake, TX 76092: 2000)

GLOSSARY CONTENTS

Agape 512
Aiteo 512
Aphesis 513
Bios 513
Cabal 513
Chesed 513
Dianoia 514
Diasozo 514
Dunamis 514
Epignosis 514
Exousia 516
Fear of God, The 516
Glory 524
Grace 526
Ginosko 527
Hugies 527
Iaomai 527
Iniquity 527
Ischus 529
Justified/Justification 529
Kardia 530
Lambano 530
Leb/Lebab 528
Logos 530
Meod 531
Mercy 531
Nasa 531
Nephesh 531
Peace 531
Phileo 534
Phobos 534
Pneuma 534
Psuche 535
Propitiation 535
Racham 536
Redeem/Ransom 536
Remission/Forgiveness 537
Rhema 539
Righteousness 542
Sin/Transgressions 548
Sozo/Soteria 549
Spirit/Soul/Body 550
The Wrath of God 556
Zao/Zoe 571

A GLOSSARY OF OFT-MISUNDERSTOOD BIBLICAL WORDS

These are definitions for everyday use in effective ministry. For more academic definitions, I suggest you start with *Strong's Exhaustive Concordance*. Also our books, *The Prayer Cards* and *OK, God, Now What*, have extensive discussions and Scripture references.

AGAPE

Agape (*Strong's* NT 25, pronounced: ag-ah'pay) is a Greek word (*agape*, the noun form, *agapao*, the verb form, *Strong's* NT 24) which, in the KJV, is translated as love and charity, i.e. caring in action, and has within its meaning an aggressive working for another's benefit, total good at your own expense, with no expectation of recognition, appreciation, reciprocation or honor and a desire to always be with the one loved. The definition of *charity*, love (*agape*) in 1 Corinthians 13 describes the basic nature of God and the true nature of Christians, as born-again ones, what Holy Spirit fills our hearts with, and what we are to walk in. *Agape* always is ever-ready and seeking a way to help or do the one loved good. Because *agape* has an emotional content, it is much like the best of a perfect father's and/or a perfect mother's love. John 3:16 "For God so *agape*/loved the world, that he gave his only begotten Son, that whosoever believeth in him should not perish, but have everlasting *zoe*/life. 17 For God sent not his Son into the world to condemn the world; but that the world through him might be *sozo*/saved." *Agape* means not without trouble, but one with you in all trouble. *Agape* is related to the Hebrew word *racham*. In this book, *agape* is used when other forms are the actual word to show the root.

AITEO

Aiteo (*Strong's* NT 154, pronounced: ahee-teh'-o) is the Greek word translated ask or desire in many New Testament scriptures related to prayer. It means to ask or demand of one in authority because that one made a promise based on requirements, and now the requirements have been met, so the one who promised is now to give what has been promised and desired by the one asking. It also includes the sense that you have intensity or focus in your desire to see the request fulfilled. For example: you are working on a task, and you promised your little daughter that you would take her for an ice cream cone or some other treat when you were done. You are now done and your daughter *aiteo*/demands, by saying, "You are finished. You said you would take me when you were done. You are done; please take me now." Or, in a legal sense, such as in a situation where you fell behind in your property taxes and, as authorities come to kick you out, you get the money and pay the taxes. Then you wave your paid-up receipt and *aiteo*/say, "I paid my taxes; now take your people and go!" Or you pawned an item, and now you have the money to redeem it. You *aiteo*/say, as you wave the pawn ticket, "Here is the money; give it back, now!" Even if the pawnshop owner had a better offer for that item, he must give it back to you. *Aiteo* is not a quiet or polite word in this sense. There is another sense in which you follow all the procedures, and the appropriate results will come. If you go to a bank and have the proper verification, checks, signatures and sufficient balance, you can cash a check. This is also included in the meaning of *aiteo*. (See also pages 29-34)

APHESIS

Aphesis (*Strong's* NT, 859, pronounced: af'-es-is) means remitted and paid for in such a way that there is no evidence of the debt ever existing, which is stronger and more complete than forgiveness, which removes the curse of sin, but not the sin.

BIOS

Bios (*Strong's* NT, 979, pronounced: bee'-os) means period of life, natural life and not just human life.

CABAL

Cabal (*Strong's* OT, 5445, pronounced: saw-bal') means to totally carry a burden that is heavy or massive so nothing is left out, strong labor, complete removal and delivery.

CHESED

Chesed (*Strong's* OT 2617, pronounced: keh'-sed) is an Old Testament word often translated in the KJV as mercy, kindness, lovingkindness, goodness or favor. It is only defined by covenant, which is stronger than a contract or modern marriage agreement, and can never be broken. It is the absolute commitment to fulfill the legal covenant conditions, even at the expense of your life, as demonstrated by what you actually do or cause to happen. It is to do good as promised, no matter what. It is only defined by action, not thoughts. The modern world has lost much of this concept, so it is hard to understand in today's Western world-view. 1 Samuel 18 shows David and Jonathan cutting a covenant, 2 Samuel 9 shows how *chesed* is implemented. In vs. 3, it is called the "*chesed*/kindness of God." It is similar to New Testament grace in concept, as grace has a legal and royal meaning.

DIANOIA

Dianoia (*Strong's* NT 1271, pronounced: dee-an'-oy-ah) means deep thought, mind, understanding, visualization, imagination or the faculty of using the mind.

DIASOZO

Diasozo (*Strong's* NT, 1295, pronounced: dee-as-odze'-o) means saved, rescued, made whole, or healed totally or throughout, to cure, preserve or rescue; limitations removed totally.

DUNAMIS

Dunamis (*Strong's* NT, 1411, pronounced: doo'-nam-is) means strong capacity, continuous power, ability, miracles or acts of great power and effectiveness.

EPIGNOSIS

Epignosis (*Strong's* NT, 1922, pronounced: ep-ig'-no-sis) means full knowing and discernment so you are an expert at doing it, more than just book learning or awareness, but deep experience and superior performance, knowing completely with nothing else to learn about it or to do it in a superior manner with ease and confidence. This would be a master chef whereas *ginosko* means a chef or even one who knows about cooking, but may not cook.

The New Testament Greek root word is *ginosko* (*Strong's* NT 1097), meaning knowledge by experience and observation, experiential knowledge or full and complete knowledge or understanding. *Epignosis* (*Strong's* NT 1922) is even a deeper knowing, a knowledge that perfectly unites the person with the subject at all levels. This is the knowledge from expert, reliable and repeatable doing, not just study or a few practice efforts.

Many swim, but few are Olympic swimmers, and even fewer have gold medals. Many can read the instructions on how to make a cake. Make a few acceptable cakes, and you begin to *ginosko* cake making. It takes a master bakery chef with years of experience to make a repeatable and proper cake. This is *epignosis* (or *epiginosko*). In modern times, with our classroom and few laboratory sessions, head or basic familiarization is talked about as knowing, even to an "A" or 100% grade on a test, but it does not meet the meaning of the word *ginosko*, much less *epignosis*.

In the Bible sense, it is a knowing that unites with the *zoe*/life of God and produces "God-results" in the Earth. So whether it is a godly businessman, Samson ripping off gates to a city, or raising the dead, the knowing is only effective if God's life mixes with man's life and produces results on a repeatable or "at will" basis. So this is not the typical education process, where students can remember a few facts or get all the questions right in Sunday School, or pass a driver's classroom test. Even to get a vehicle driver's license, a practical demonstration of basic skills and judgment are required. Just reading the Bible may give you familiarization, but not a personal knowledge of God.

In our modern world, where many have seen or heard about a subject and, thus, become an expert, to the Hebrew or Greek mind, mere mental recognition was of little performance value. Seeing a master musician or ballerina does not make one an expert in either. You may be an expert watcher or listener, but you are not an expert performer. So, in Christianity, until you can do at will a command or demonstrate reliably a desirable characteristic, you are not yet in the realm of *gnosis*, much less *epignosis*. For example, praying for the sick is much different than getting the sick healed by prayer.

The concept is seen in this scripture: Gen 4:1 "And Adam knew Eve his wife; and she conceived, and bare Cain, and said, I have gotten a man from the LORD." Adam and Eve probably had sex many times, but when their union produced a child it was also called "knowing." One level of knowing comes with sex, *ginosko*, but there is a deeper level of knowing when a man and woman create a child together. The first is experiential; the second produces life in union with God.

The Greek word *epignosis* is such a deep knowing, a full knowing. Eph 4:13 "Till we all come in the unity of the faith, and of the *epignosis*/knowledge of the Son of God, unto a perfect man, unto the measure of the stature of the fulness of Christ." Here this knowledge is not talking about what it takes to be born again. That is a relatively low level of agreement with God. As miraculous as it is, it is but a basic beginning. What this scripture is referring to is a "knowledge" that, when complete, you cannot tell the person as different from Jesus in their behavior or their operation in the full power of God. This is Bible "*epignosis*/knowing" and God's goal for each of us.

Here are these two concepts in the same scripture: 1 Cor 13:12 "For now we see through a glass, darkly; but then face to face: now I *gnosis*/know in part; but then shall I *epignosis*/know even as also I am *epignosis*/known." We may start at some level of *ginosko*, but the goal is to *epignosis* God. Eph 4:15 "But speaking the truth in *agape*/love, may grow up into him in all things, which is the head, even Christ." 2 Pet 1:2 "Grace and peace be multiplied unto you through the *epignosis*/knowledge of God, and of Jesus our Lord, 3 according as his divine power hath given unto us all things that pertain unto *zoe*/life and godliness, through the *epignosis*/knowledge of him that hath called us to glory and virtue."

If this seems like splitting hairs, which would you rather have do a critical brain surgery on you—a medical school student, who read about it in a book, a resident brain surgeon, who has just learned the process, or a fine practicing doctor, who has done the procedure hundreds or thousands of times without failure? The medical student has familiarization, the resident perhaps *ginosko*; and the fine practitioner has *epignosis* of the procedure and is a master craftsman.

EXOUSIA

Exousia (*Strong's* NT 1849, pronounced: ex-oo-see'-ah) means authority, right or freedom to act, commission, force, and capacity; competency to act, jurisdiction, power and strength to operate.

FEAR OF GOD, THE

The fear of God is designed to keep us from sinning (in which case the devil can try and enforce the law of sin and death, the curses, the wrath of the Law) and for men to want to do righteousness so that God's *agape*/love can fill the Earth. Job 28:28 "And unto man he said, Behold, the fear of the LORD, that is wisdom; and to depart from evil is understanding." Ps 111:7 "The works of his (*the LORD's*) hands are verity and judgment; all his commandments are sure. 8 They stand fast for ever and ever, and are done in truth and uprightness. 9 He sent redemption unto his people: he hath commanded his covenant for ever: holy and reverend is his name. 10 The fear of the LORD is the beginning of wisdom: a good understanding have all they that do his commandments: his praise endureth for ever." Prov 9:9 "Give instruction to a wise man, and he will be yet wiser: teach a just man, and he will increase in learning. 10 The fear of the LORD is the beginning of wisdom: and the knowledge of the holy is understanding. 11 For by me thy days shall be multiplied, and the years of thy life shall be increased."

Thus, the fear of God is to not sin but do the ways of God, so the healing and prospering life of God can fill the Earth. The first level attitude is to fear and avoid violating God's ways, knowing the consequences are death and destruction, but the real secret of fearing God is to do what He wants so His *zoe*/life can fill and prosper all you think, say and do, and, thus, bring Heaven to Earth. Operate in this kind of fear, and you will walk in joy and gladness because of the goodness of the Lord.

For those who think the fear of the Lord is not to be without intensity and control your every thought, word and action: Phil 2:10 "That at the name of Jesus every knee should bow, of things in heaven, and things in earth, and things under the earth; 11 and that every tongue should confess that Jesus Christ is Lord, to the glory of God the Father. 12 Wherefore, my *agape*/beloved, as ye have always obeyed, not as in my presence only, but now much more in my absence, work out your own *soteria*/salvation with fear and trembling. 13 For it is God which worketh in you both to will and to do of his good pleasure. 14 Do all things without murmurings and disputings: 15 that ye may be blameless and harmless, the sons of

APPENDICES

God, without rebuke, in the midst of a crooked and perverse nation, among whom ye shine as lights in the world; 16 holding forth the word of *zoe*/life; that I may rejoice in the day of Christ, that I have not run in vain, neither laboured in vain."

Thus every sin committed in either commission or omission is a failure to fear the Lord effectively, like Jesus did, and every sin has consequences. To know the consequences is one of the ways to keep from sinning.

The fear of the Lord is that which causes you to seek and hear God and to obey His Word in gladness. This is described on four levels. All are the territory of a humble (*I repent that I exalted myself against God and did it my way*) and contrite (*I know what I deserve, and I know I will reap evil if I do not fix it with God*) heart.

1) The absolute assurance that all sin, every evil work, will be destroyed and that we will reap whatever evil we sow that we do not confess, agree Jesus died for, make whatever restitution on Earth is required, receive total healing, and put on Jesus Christ over it. This is "knee-knocking" self-preservation, avoid-all-loss fear, and the one most mentioned in the Bible. (Deut 28 has an impressive list of blessing and what to fear for disobedience, 2 Cor 5:10 and Phil 2:12 show the "knee-knocking attitude a Christian is to have.)
2) Awesome reverence that God is great and to be obeyed, for it is to our benefit. This fear is still a form of self-protection. (2 Cor 7:1, Deut 10:20)
3) God is a loving Father, and our sins hurt Him, by cutting off His love in that area. This is a loving fear, where we are more concerned that God does not get all He wants, and we are the reason. This is a loving fear that does not want to offend Him. (Rev 14:7, Heb 12:28)
4) This is walking in *agape*/love, where you are an active agent of God, delivering His *agape*/love in every part of life and, therefore, do not sin and only do righteousness. This is where Jesus and mature Christians walk, as *agape*/love slaves to God, delighting to only please Him in holding on to His Word in trouble and setting others free. (1 John 4:16-19)

Whatever level of fear keeps you from sin and keeps you doing righteousness is the place to start. There are many scriptures showing each aspect; here are a few describing these different aspects of the fear of God. 2 Cor 5:10 "For we must all appear before the judgment seat of Christ; that every one may receive the things done in his body, according to that he hath done, whether it be good or bad. 11 Knowing therefore the terror of the Lord, we persuade men; but we are made manifest unto God; and I trust also are made manifest in your consciences." Phil 2:12 "Wherefore, my beloved, as ye have always obeyed, not as in my presence only, but now much more in my absence, work out your own *soteria*/salvation with fear and trembling." 2 Cor 7:1 "Having therefore these promises, dearly *agape*/beloved, let us cleanse ourselves from all filthiness of the flesh and spirit, perfecting holiness in the fear of God." Deut 10:20 "Thou shalt fear the Lord thy God; him shalt thou serve, and to him shalt thou cleave, and swear by his name. 21 He is thy praise, and he is thy God, that hath done for thee these great and terrible things, which thine eyes have seen. 22 Thy fathers went down into Egypt with threescore and ten persons; and now the LORD thy God hath made thee as the stars of heaven for multitude." Rev 14:7 "Saying with a loud voice, Fear God, and give glory to him; for the hour of his judgment is come: and worship him that made heaven, and earth, and the sea, and the fountains of waters." Heb 12:28 "Wherefore we receiving a kingdom which cannot be moved, let us have grace, whereby we may serve God acceptably with reverence and godly fear: 29 for our God is a consuming fire." 1 John 4:16 "And we have known and believed the *agape*/love that God hath to us. God is *agape*/love; and he that dwelleth in *agape*/love dwelleth in God, and God in him. 17 Herein is our *agape*/love made perfect, that we may have boldness in the day of judgment: because as he is, so are we in this world. 18 There is no fear in *agape*/love; but perfect *agape*/love casteth out fear: because fear hath torment. He that feareth is not made perfect in *agape*/love. 19 We *agape*/love him, because he first *agape*/loved us."

God does not have to actively judge wrath on us in this life. The laws that He made when He created the Earth and pronounced good do that. Rom 2:11 "For there is no respect of persons with God." Gal 6:7 "Be not deceived; God is not mocked: for whatsoever a man soweth, that shall he also reap. 8 For he that soweth to his flesh shall of the flesh reap corruption; but he that soweth to the Spirit shall of the Spirit reap *zoe*/life everlasting."

These two scriptures tell us a fundamental truth. It does not matter who you are; if you plant and nurture good seed, you will reap good fruit; if you plant and nurture bad seed, you will reap bad fruit. This applies to anyone on the Earth, everyone, and everywhere. This is a basic law of the universe that God has put in place. Like gravity, God does not have to do anything to enforce the law of sowing and reaping. So reaping what we sow, good or bad, is not a direct judgment from God, just the normal process of His existing laws in operation.

In contrast, every healing of Jesus was an example of God actively judging the works of the devil and the application of His wrath against the devil to set people free from either devil attacks, accidents or evil reaping. He gave us that job to continue. Luke 10:19 "Behold (*make this change your life*), I give unto you power (*authority, commission and the resources of Heaven*) to tread on serpents and scorpions, and over all *dunamis*/power (*ability*) of the enemy: and nothing shall by any means hurt you." As Jesus is the exact representation of God, we can know He delights in judging the devil to freedom for the oppressed through men–you and me.

Many people think that the God of the Old Testament is a God of wrath and the God of the New Testament one of *agape*/love. Well, He is the same God in both and has always been and always will be the same. He is also a God of forgiveness. Hear the cry of God to the people of the Old Testament, who had sown and nurtured bad seed: Hos 10:12 "Sow to yourselves in righteousness, reap in *chesed/* mercy; break up your fallow ground: for it is time to seek the LORD, till he come and rain righteousness upon you. 13 Ye have plowed wickedness, ye have reaped iniquity; ye have eaten the fruit of lies: because thou didst trust in thy way, in the multitude of thy mighty men [*rather than in God*]."

Look at the example of Job. In Job 1 and 2, we see a throne- or courtroom scene where Satan, the god of this world, accuses God and Job. God does not stop the devil, because the devil is working within God's laws; but God does limit what Satan can do. First, God limits Satan to not touching Job's life; and then, second, God limits him to not killing Job.

Then we see God go to work. First, in Job 32 He sends Elihu to adjust Job's thinking and help him to quit finding fault with God. Job did well in holding on to God for goodness, no matter what, but he still sinned in accusing God of evil or making a mistake. After Elihu had worked a little humility into Job, God appeared and Job repented.

Here is what God did. First, He got Job to pray as an intercessor for his friends who did not repent. Now Job was thinking like God. Then God blessed. Job got twice as much wealth and a new set of children, and he lived 140 years longer. This was God at work!

In God's history with Israel, they continually would not cooperate with Him, to allow Him to bless them, and, thus, their actions produced the curse and not the blessing. He continually sent prophets, just as He did to Job, to turn men from their sins and get life from Him; but they did not. In spite of this, He mitigated the situation, reducing as much as He could, to save them. Mal 3:6 "For I am the LORD, I change not; therefore ye sons of Jacob are not consumed." It is as if our unresolved sin builds up, and even though God's hand is around us as a wall, the sin overflows the wall, and we reap the judgment of Satan due. God's ultimate triumph is that He can bless the "saved" in Heaven, in spite of our Earth life, because of the right actions of Jesus.

We see this in the numerous times Israel sinned and yet God showed them a way to stop the curse or judgment. In Numbers 12, Miriam contracted leprosy for sinning, but then Moses prayed, and she was healed. In the process, Moses had to forgive Miriam for speaking against his wife. This same series of events happened repeatedly in the Bible. God has always looked for one who will deal with Him so He can heal. Ps 103:3 "Who forgiveth all thine iniquities; who healeth all thy diseases;" When He could find no man, He sent Jesus: Isa 59:16 "And he saw that there was no man, and wondered that there was no intercessor: therefore his arm brought salvation unto him; and his righteousness, it sustained him. 17 For he put on righteousness as a breastplate, and an helmet of salvation upon his head; and he put on the garments of vengeance for clothing, and was clad with zeal as a cloak."

BATTLE PRAYER FOR DIVINE HEALING: FIELD MANUAL 2

Here is God's attitude toward death in any form–from a small headache or scrape, to loss of all limbs, to untimely death, to famine and war: Hos 13:14 "I will ransom them from the power of the grave; I will redeem them from death: O death, I will be thy plagues; O grave, I will be thy destruction: repentance shall be hid from mine eyes." 1 Cor 15:26 "The last enemy that shall be destroyed is death." Rev 1:17 "And when I saw him (*Jesus*), I fell at his feet as dead. And he laid his right hand upon me, saying unto me, Fear not; I am the first and the last: 18 I am he that *zao*/liveth, and was dead; and, behold, I am *zao*/alive for evermore, Amen; and have the keys of hell and of death."

Bottom line: Anything anyone needs healed from is an enemy to God. Jesus cast out devils and healed people to show what God delights to do. Jesus made it clear sickness is God's enemy and is to be destroyed by any Christian at any time.

God has no desire for us to suffer any of His wraths. Jesus took all the wrath of God due us on Himself, per Isaiah 53.

Father God sent Jesus to demonstrate His true nature and to "destroy the works of the devil" (1 John 3:8). The word *destroy* could also mean "to exercise wrath." So this could be stated as "God sent Jesus to exercise His wrath and, thus, destroy what the devil has built on the Earth, so men could be saved and Heaven come to Earth."

Zoe/life is the opposite of the effects of sin and death. John 3:16 "For God so *agape*/loved the world, that he gave his only begotten Son, that whosoever believeth in him should not perish, but have everlasting *zoe*/life. 17 For God sent not his Son into the world to condemn the (*people of the*) world; but that the world through him might be *sozo*/saved." In these scriptures, we see God's attitude toward us and the devil; life for us, wrath for the devil and all his works. The problem is, if our hearts and minds are in love with the works of the devil, we will suffer the consequences of evil fruit and loss, along with the devil on that Day, per 1 Cor 3.

Consider: how did Adam and Eve turn this world over to the curse? By disobeying God's word, they gave this Earth to the consequences of sin and the rule of Satan. One of the meanings of the word *god* is source. When they believed Satan rather than God, they made the devil their source of life, releasing sin, Satan's anti-life force, death, into the world or their domain. Rom 5:14 "Nevertheless death reigned from Adam to Moses, even over them that had not sinned after the similitude of Adam's transgression, who is the figure of him that was to come." With Moses, God started to deal with death by giving a more direct and open source of life, until Jesus came.

Consider: 2 Cor 4:4 "In whom the god of this world hath blinded the minds of them which believe not, lest the light of the glorious gospel of Christ, who is the image of God, should shine unto them." Just as he did with Adam and Eve, Satan, the god of this world, is still blinding people's minds to the *agape*/love of God in Jesus Christ. The Bible tells us that in the end, Jesus will be established as the rightful ruler of this world, and Satan put fully in the Lake of Fire.

The wrath of God is that impartial force of *agape*/love that must clean up sin, all evil that would hurt or hinder His children. God is light, sin is darkness, and light must dispel darkness till darkness is no more. The darkness then feels the "wrath" of the light. The opposite is also true: if light is extinguished, it has felt the wrath of darkness. John 8:12 "Then spake Jesus again unto them, saying, I am the light of the world: he that followeth me (*as I followed and imitated Father God*) shall not walk in darkness, but shall have the light of *zoe*/life (*as seen in Me in your own life*)." Jesus, as seen in the gospels, is the true light of what God is and delights to do good when He finds one who will work with Him to do what He wants. True light is to see Jesus as how Father God really is.

Here is the true nature of the God of the Old Testament. Even when Adam and Eve sinned and, thus, unleashed the entire misery of all history upon the human race, God sought them out, gave them garments and even gave them the promise that one of the woman's seed would "crush Satan's head" (see Genesis 3). Father God could have destroyed Adam and Eve in a heartbeat, but He did not. Instead, He showed them how to live in the mess they had made with the promise of ultimate victory and restored fellowship with Him. In Genesis 3 Adam released the curse into the Earth. God mitigated it so that man could live, but by the sweat of his brow. Otherwise the devil would have killed Eve in childbirth and men in famine. So, even if God must exercise His wrath, His justice, His consequences for sin, He always made a way to bless in the end. He promised One who would "bruise" the devil's head. Because we all sin and fall short of the glory of God, He sent His Son John 3:17 "For God sent not his Son into the world to condemn the world; but that the world through him might be *sozo*/saved," thus "bruising" the devil's head.

Most of what men call judgments of God are simply this:
- Evil sowing and reaping: getting back what we have done to others, or reaping the evil bounty of our own sins
- Attacks of the devil
- Accidents in a world with sin
- Failure to walk effectively in Psalms 23 and 91.

In these cases, it is not God at work, but, rather, the devil.

Ps 34:21 "Evil shall slay the wicked … ." Ps 18:26 "With the pure thou wilt shew thyself pure; and with the froward thou wilt shew thyself froward." Ps 141:10 "Let the wicked fall into their own nets … ." Luke 6:37 "Judge not (*against*), and ye shall not be judged (*against*): condemn not, and ye shall not be condemned: forgive, and ye shall be forgiven: 38 give, and it shall be given unto you; good measure, pressed down, and shaken together, and running over, shall men give into your bosom. For with the same measure that ye mete withal it shall be measured to you again." Ezek 18:30 "Therefore I will judge you, O house of Israel, every one according to his ways, saith the Lord GOD. Repent, and turn yourselves from all your transgressions; so iniquity shall not be your ruin. 31 Cast away from you all your transgressions, whereby ye have transgressed; and make you a new heart and a new spirit: for why will ye die, O house of Israel? 32 For I have no pleasure in the death of him that dieth, saith the Lord GOD: wherefore turn yourselves, and live ye." (Notice that, per Heb 8:10 and Ezek 26:36, in the New Covenant of Jesus, God gives us this new heart and this new spirit. And again: Rom 8:15 "For ye have not received the spirit of bondage again to fear; but ye have received the Spirit of adoption, whereby we cry, Abba (*Daddy*), Father.")

God holds back His wrath to give us time to repent and to provide a way of escape, for, through it all, God is calling, "Turn to my Son and live!" It is amazing that people can have faith in God's wrath, but not His blessing. If we confess our sins to God, receive His forgiveness and remission, apply that forgiveness to the consequences of sin and the curse sin brings, and put on the new man in Jesus, with all our defects totally healed, we can destroy the consequences and the curse sin brings, just like Jesus did.

Every healing Jesus performed was an example of God's attitudes to evil that hurts men, when He has someone with His view on His goodness (see Ps 103). King David knew the truth: Ps 86:5 "For thou, Lord, art good, and ready to forgive; and plenteous in *chesed*/mercy unto all them that call upon thee. 6 Give ear, O LORD, unto my prayer; and attend to the voice of my supplications. 7 In the day of my trouble I will call upon thee: for thou wilt answer me."

As we agree with God, we will enforce the benefits of all the wrath due us falling on Jesus, and resist the devil in any of his works, until he flees. Acts 10:34 "Then Peter opened his mouth, and said, Of a truth I perceive that God is no respecter of persons: 35 but in every nation he that feareth him, and worketh righteousness, is accepted with him. 36 The word which God sent unto the children of Israel, preaching peace by Jesus Christ: (he is Lord of all:) 37 that word, I say, ye know, which was published throughout all Judaea, and began from Galilee, after the baptism which John preached; 38 how God anointed Jesus of Nazareth with the Holy Ghost and with power: who went about doing good, and healing (*in judgment against the devil*) all that were oppressed (*under the active dominion, reign or lordship*) of the devil; for God was with him." Notice, in verse 35, using the name of Jesus to get people healed is a work of righteousness. No matter how good or bad at it you are, this makes you acceptable to God. The more you reprogram your heart, the better you will be at using the name of Jesus to put the wrath of God on the devil and his works. God will deal with man and

APPENDICES

our works on the Day of Judgment, and God is dealing with Satan through the Church in this, the Day of Salvation.

We see, many times, in the Old Testament where men built an altar to make a sacrifice, and God sent fire and consumed it: Gideon (Judg 6:21), David (1 Chron 21:26) and Elijah (1 Kings 18:38). The sacrifice stood for the sin, and God destroyed it by fire. Then God started, through a man, to set things right. When God destroys something, it is all gone. The great flood destroyed all, as did the judgment on Sodom and Gomorrah. Rev 21 and 22 show the Earth fully cleaned and prepared for God to bring Heaven to Earth. Jesus destroyed, purged, and dissolved our sins once for all men 2000 years ago. The job was fully and completely done. God does not live in time, and this work of Jesus was timeless, eternal, once, for all time. This is what He means when Holy Spirit says: Heb 10:10 "By the which will we are sanctified through the offering of **the body of Jesus Christ once for all**. 11 And every priest standeth daily ministering and offering oftentimes the same sacrifices, which can never take away sins: 12 but this man, after he had offered **one sacrifice for sins for ever**, sat down on the right hand of God; 13 from henceforth expecting till his enemies be made his footstool [*by us, the Church*]. 14 For **by one offering he hath perfected for ever** them that are sanctified. 15 Whereof the Holy Ghost also is a witness to us: for after that he had said before, 16 This is the covenant that I will make with them after those days, saith the Lord, I will put my laws into their hearts, and in their minds will I write them; 17 and their **sins and iniquities will I remember no more**. 18 Now where remission of these is, **there is no more offering for sin**." The wrath due us fell on Jesus. It is done! Our job is to praise God for His work in Jesus, and now deliver the wrath of God on the devil and get people set free. Doing this is how we walk in the fear of God like Jesus did.

Jesus came to baptize with Holy Spirit and fire. That fire burns up all the chaff, the useless parts of the Earth, and chaff is a symbol of any work of the devil. Luke 3:16 "John answered, saying unto them all, I indeed baptize you with water; but one mightier than I cometh, the latchet of whose shoes I am not worthy to unloose: he shall baptize you with the Holy Ghost and with fire: 17 whose fan is in his hand, and he will throughly purge his floor, and will gather the wheat into his garner; but the chaff he will burn with fire unquenchable." The final day is the Day of Judgment. Until then we are to judge the devil by Holy Spirit fire, in setting people free of any oppression of the devil, in Jesus' name, in this, the Day of God's Salvation, in judgment against the devil and his works by the Church.

Jesus, by Holy Spirit, burns with fire the works of the devil in men and makes them whole; thus delivering the wrath of God to the devil and not to men. Acts 14:3 "Long time therefore abode they speaking boldly in the Lord, which gave testimony unto the word of his grace, and granted signs and wonders to be done by their hands." Mark

16:19 "So then after the Lord had spoken unto them, he was received up into heaven, and sat on the right hand of God. 20 And they went forth, and preached everywhere, the Lord working with them, and confirming the word with signs following. Amen."

And we are to continue that same word, in the same way, against the wrath of the devil by using the wrath of God to create peace like Jesus did. Acts 10:36 "The word which God sent unto the children of Israel, preaching peace by Jesus Christ: (he is Lord of all:) 37 that word, I say, ye know, which was published throughout all Judaea, and began from Galilee, after the baptism which John preached; 38 how God anointed Jesus of Nazareth with the Holy Ghost and with power: who went about doing good, and healing all that were oppressed (*under the active dominion, reign or lordship*) of the devil; for God was with him."

Let us go and do likewise, making peace in the name of Jesus, knowing: Isa 55:11 "So shall my word be that goeth forth out of my mouth (*through you*): it shall not return unto me void, but it shall accomplish that which I please, and it shall prosper in the thing whereto I sent it." Isa 49:24 "Shall the prey be taken from the mighty, or the lawful captive delivered? 25 But thus saith the Lord, Even the captives of the mighty shall be taken away, and the prey of the terrible shall be delivered: for I will contend with him that contendeth with thee, and I will save thy children. 26 And I will feed them that oppress thee with their own flesh; and they shall be drunken with their own blood, as with sweet wine: and all flesh shall know that I the Lord am thy Saviour and thy Redeemer, the mighty One of Jacob." Heb 13:8 "Jesus Christ the same yesterday, and to day, and for ever." He is ever the Healer.

So we see that the fear of the Lord is really two parts. First things not to do because that will be destroyed on the Last Day and as you do them you are sowing to the flesh and will reap corruption in this life. The second is that the fear of the Lord will cause you to go and do those things God requires so you can sow to the Spirit and reap *zoe*/life on the Day of Judgment as rewards of silver, gold and jewels, and the benefits of *zoe*/life in this life now.

GLORY

Means: honor, splendor, shiny, beauty, wealth, the best of, the strength of, or power of, radiance and light. An overall definition is that God's glory is released or dwells when Holy Spirit can freely do all God wants to on the Earth, of His goodness, through His people, i.e., in you. This includes the Shekinah glory filling a place of worship (Ex 40:34-35, 1 Kings 8:11), clouds/mist, or a light or glow on people, such as on Moses and Jesus: Luke 9:29 "And as he (*Jesus*) prayed, the fashion of his countenance was altered, and his raiment was white and glistering. 30 And, behold, there talked with him two men, which were Moses and Elias: 31 who appeared in glory, and spake of his decease which he should accomplish at

Jerusalem." The glory of God also includes raising the dead: Rom 6:4 "… as Christ was raised up from the dead by the glory of the Father …" Holy Spirit and God's manifested glory are tightly linked.

God defines His glory as (or it is released by) His goodness and His name: Ex 33:18 "And he (*Moses*) said, I beseech thee, shew me thy glory. 19 And he said, I will make all my goodness pass before thee, and I will proclaim the name of the Lord before thee; and will be gracious to whom I will be gracious, and will shew *racham*/mercy on whom I will shew *racham*/mercy. 20 And he said, Thou canst not see my face: for there shall no man see me, and live. 21 And the Lord said, Behold, there is a place by me, and thou shalt stand upon a rock: 22 and it shall come to pass, while my glory passeth by, that I will put thee in a clift of the rock, and will cover thee with my hand while I pass by: 23 and I will take away mine hand, and thou shalt see my back parts: but my face shall not be seen." Ex 34:5 "And the Lord descended in the cloud, and stood with him there, and proclaimed the name of the Lord. 6 And the Lord passed by before him, and proclaimed, The Lord, The Lord God, merciful and gracious, longsuffering, and abundant in *chesed*/goodness and truth, 7 keeping *chesed*/mercy for thousands, forgiving iniquity and transgression and sin, and that will by no means clear the guilty (*those who will not confess their sin to God for forgiveness*); visiting the iniquity of the fathers upon the children, and upon the children's children, unto the third and to the fourth generation (*clarified as not a generational curse of God in Ezek 18*). 8 And Moses made haste, and bowed his head toward the earth, and worshipped." This is God's definition of the glory that will fill the Earth.

There are two main aspects of glory revealed in the Scriptures: glory that comes from God in manifestations of Heaven on Earth, and glory that comes from man to God. The word *glory* has the root of heaviness or weighty, implying the true substance, that which lasts when other things pass away. Thus, all righteous works that survive the Day of Judgment, as silver, gold and jewels, are the result of the glory of the Lord (Holy Spirit) and you working together to produce those works. 1 Cor 3:9 "For we are **labourers together with God**: ye are God's husbandry, ye are God's building. 10 According to the grace of God which is given unto me, as a wise masterbuilder, I have laid the foundation, and another buildeth thereon. But let every man take heed how he buildeth thereupon. 11 For other foundation can no man lay than that is laid, which is Jesus Christ. 12 Now if any man build upon this foundation gold, silver, precious stones, wood, hay, stubble; 13 every man's work shall be made manifest: for the day shall declare it, because it shall be revealed by fire; and the fire shall try every man's work of what sort it is. 14 If any man's work abide which he hath built thereupon, he shall receive a reward. 15 If any man's work shall be burned, he shall suffer loss: but he himself shall be *sozo*/saved; yet so as by fire." Wood, hay and stubble are those things not of His glory.

The amazing thing is that this same word for glory applies to what man praises and exalts, i.e., gives glory to, be it God, nature or man. The combined effect of the glory of the Lord and the glory of man is found in our thanksgiving, praise, worship and obedience. Ps 149:4 "For the LORD taketh pleasure in his people: he will beautify the meek with salvation. 5 Let the saints be joyful in glory: let them sing aloud upon their beds" Even our mouths are described as our glory or the place where our glory is shown or released: Ps 30:12 "To the end that my glory may sing praise to thee, and not be silent. O LORD my God, I will give thanks unto thee for ever."

No wonder that, when we exalt God, Holy Spirit then inhabits our praise, as He (Holy Spirit) is the administrator of glory/manifestations of God's goodness in the Earth: Ps 22:3 "But thou art holy, O thou that inhabitest the praises of Israel." 1 Pet 2:9 "But ye are a chosen generation, a royal priesthood, an holy nation, a peculiar people; that ye should shew forth the praises of him who hath called you out of darkness into his marvellous light: 10 which in time past were not a people, but are now the people of God: which had not obtained mercy, but now have obtained mercy." Rom 6:4 "Therefore we are buried with him by baptism into death: that like as Christ was raised up from the dead by the glory of the Father, even so we also should walk in newness of *zoe*/life." Rom 8:11 "But if the Spirit of him that raised up Jesus from the dead dwell in you, he that raised up Christ from the dead shall also quicken your mortal bodies by his Spirit that dwelleth in you." 2 Cor 3:18 "But we all, with open face beholding as in a glass (*mirror*) the glory of the Lord, are changed into the same image from glory to glory, even as by the Spirit of the Lord." Related opposites of God's glory include darkness, sin, iniquity and death, none of which will survive the Day of Judgment.

GRACE

Grace is granted by one who has power/authority to one who does not, and is very similar to being blessed or given kindness/*chesed*, in that it is free, unmerited favor that is aggressively applied to you and does good for you. Grace is the free gift of God to be, think, act like and produce the results of Jesus in any situation, i.e., the will of Father God on Earth as it is in Heaven. Grace is always given, not earned, and is greater than ever could be earned. You don't have to seek it, although you are required to; it seeks you, to give you total goodness for any need. Grace is how you get the blessing benefit. It is God's free gift and attitude of favor to give you what you do not deserve, to walk into the blessings of God, to the fullness of Christ in you. As we are "*sozo*/saved by grace," grace is God's goodness empowered to produce blessing after the nature of God, and the result is more than you could ever come close to doing for yourself, but brings Heaven on Earth, both now and in the future. Eph 4:7 "But unto every one of us is given grace according to the measure of the gift of Christ." All of God's grace is available to us in gift, prayer and faith, per Heb 4:16. Grace has aspects of the Hebrew word *chesed*.

GINOSKO

Ginosko (*Strong's* NT, 1097, pronounced: ghin oce'-ko) means knowledge of, awareness, learned or book learned.

HUGIES

Hugies (*Strong's* NT, 5199, pronounced: hooge-ee-ace') means whole, sound, healed, or complete.

IAOMAI

Iaomai (*Strong's* NT, 2390, pronounced: ee-ah'-om-ahee) means physical healing or wholeness.

INIQUITY

Iniquity means every aspect of wrong thoughts and words that lead to sin, the sins themselves, their consequences and the punishment due for sin. It also can mean misfortunes that attack you. Iniquity specifically is those thoughts that are not of God and, therefore, lead you to sin in any act of commission, doing, or omission, not doing. This is called a propensity to sin or a wicked, adulterous heart, when you keep them in your mind. Keeping wicked thoughts in your mind is the start of doing evil, i.e., wickedness, evil, against God and His ways, violation of the covenant with God. Isa 59:7 "Their feet run to evil, and they make haste to shed innocent blood: their thoughts are thoughts of iniquity; wasting and destruction are in their paths. 8 The way of peace they know not; and there is no judgment in their goings: they have made them crooked paths: whosoever goeth therein shall not know peace." Ps 36:3 "The words of his mouth are iniquity and deceit: he hath left off to be wise, and to do good."

The Bible standard is to always control or rein in your thoughts and do not allow them to stray to wickedness or iniquity. 2 Cor 10:5 "Casting down imaginations, and every high thing that exalteth itself against the knowledge of God, and bringing into captivity every thought to the obedience of Christ." Ps 10:4 "The wicked, through the pride of his countenance, will not seek after God: God is not in all his thoughts." Prov 30:32 "If thou hast done foolishly in lifting up thyself, or if thou hast thought evil, lay thine hand upon thy mouth." James 1:14 "But every man is tempted, when he is drawn away of his own lust, and enticed. 15 Then when lust hath conceived, it bringeth forth sin: and sin, when it is finished, bringeth forth death." Another translation for iniquity is lawlessness: the refusal to obey God's known will in His Word and ways, i.e., disobedience, stubbornness, rebellion and accepting no one's rule but one's own, lawless.

God's remission, in the propitiation of Christ, completely forgives and removes the iniquities and sin and heals the punishment or curse due for them. Isa 53:5 "But he was wounded for our transgressions, he was bruised for our iniquities: the chastisement of our peace was upon him; and with his stripes we are healed. 6 All we like sheep have gone astray; we have turned every one to his own way; and the LORD hath laid on him the iniquity of us all. ... 11 He shall see of the travail of his soul, and shall be satisfied: by his knowledge shall my righteous servant justify many; for he shall *cabal*/bear their iniquities."

The propensity to sin is related to what is in our hearts and what we keep thinking on as acceptable. Matt 15:17 "Do not ye yet understand, that whatsoever entereth in at the mouth goeth into the belly, and is cast out into the draught? 18 But those things which proceed out of the mouth come forth from the heart; and they defile the man. 19 For out of the heart proceed evil thoughts, murders, adulteries, fornications, thefts, false witness, blasphemies: 20 these are the things which defile a man: but to eat with unwashen hands defileth not a man." A stingy man will not give even a penny and praises those who act likewise. This is how men reinforce iniquity among themselves. Prov 23:7 "For as he thinketh in his heart, so is he ... ." The opposite is true: think truth and you will do truth; think *agape*/love and you will do *agape*/love.

Iniquity is purged by knowing the *chesed*/grace of God that your sins were purged in Jesus, by the truth, His Word (pray Psalm 119 often), and an absolute assurance that every iniquity will be judged and destroyed on the Day of Judgment, and that while you sin on the Earth you are sowing to yourselves unrighteousness, with its sad and wicked fruit now and on that Day. Prov 16:6 "By *chesed*/mercy and truth iniquity is purged: and by the fear of the LORD men depart from evil." 2 Pet 1:9 "But he that lacketh these things (*of the fruits of abiding in Christ*) is blind, and cannot see afar off, and hath forgotten that he was purged from his old sins (*in the chesed, grace of the New Covenant in the blood of Jesus*)."

The cure to allowing iniquity to dwell in your heart is the ultimate positive attitude: Phil 4:4 "Rejoice in the Lord alway: and again I say, Rejoice. 5 Let your moderation be known unto all men. The Lord is at hand. 6 Be careful for nothing; but in every thing by prayer and supplication with thanksgiving let your *aiteo*/ requests be made known unto God. 7 And the peace of God, which passeth all understanding, shall keep your hearts and minds through Christ Jesus. 8 Finally, brethren, whatsoever things are true (*the Bible*), whatsoever things are honest, whatsoever things are just, whatsoever things are pure, whatsoever things are lovely, whatsoever things are of good report; if there be any virtue, and if there be any praise, think on these things. 9 Those things, which ye have both learned, and received, and heard, and seen in me, do: and the God of peace shall be with you."

Or, as God told Joshua: Josh 1:6 "Be strong and of a good courage: for unto this people shalt thou divide for an inheritance the land, which I sware unto their fathers to give them. 7 Only be thou strong and very courageous, that thou mayest observe to do according to all the law, which Moses my servant commanded thee: turn not from it to the right hand or to the left, that thou mayest prosper whithersoever thou goest. 8 This book of the law shall not depart out of thy mouth; but thou shalt meditate therein day and night, that thou mayest observe to do according to all that is written therein: for then thou shalt make thy way prosperous, and then thou shalt have good success. 9 Have not I commanded thee? Be strong and of a good courage; be not afraid, neither be thou dismayed: for the LORD thy God is with thee whithersoever thou goest."

A hard heart, steeped in iniquity, cannot see the goodness of the Lord. Rom 2:4 "Or despisest thou the riches of his goodness and forbearance and longsuffering; not knowing that the goodness of God leadeth thee to repentance? 5 But after thy hardness and impenitent heart treasurest up unto thyself wrath against the day of wrath and revelation of the righteous judgment of God." A Christian is to know, without doubt, that all iniquity and its fruits/works will be destroyed on the Day of Judgment. See Glossary entry "Wrath of God" for more detail.

ISCHUS

Ischus (*Strong's* NT, 2479, pronounced: is-khoos') means force, power, might, ability strength, money, armies, or intellect.

JUSTIFIED/JUSTIFICATION

This is the legal/governmental process of removing all elements of sin, enmity, loss, wrath and/or alienation, and making totally blessed, so good from God is forced upon one, i.e., the process by which one is made righteous. For a Christian, we are justified to be made the righteousness of God in Jesus in our spirit, by faith that God raised Him from the dead. Justification/justified has a very similar meaning to reconciliation, but is more legal in nature.

In Jesus we are justified to *zoe* life. Rom 5:15 "But not as the offence, so also is the free gift. For if through the offence of one (*Adam*) many be dead, much more the grace of God, and the gift by grace, which is by one man, Jesus Christ, hath abounded unto many. 16 And not as it was by one that sinned, so is the gift: for the judgment was by one to condemnation, but the free gift is of many offences unto justification. 17 For if by one man's offence death reigned by one; much more they which (*continually*) *lambano*/receive abundance of grace and of the gift of righteousness shall reign in *zoe*/life by one, Jesus Christ.) 18 Therefore as by the offence (*sin*) of one judgment came upon all men to condemnation; even so by the righteousness of one the free gift came upon all men unto justification of *zoe*/life." Justification with God through Jesus does not resolve any reconciliation or restitution you need to make with other humans on Earth. God will give you grace to resolve these earthly issues.

KARDIA

Kardia (*Strong's* NT 2588, pronounced: kar-dee'-ah) means both the physical heart and the center of being, the inner man, the center of feelings and mind. It is similar to the Hebrew *leb* in concept.

LAMBANO

Lambano (*Strong's* NT 2983, pronounced: lam-ban'-o) is a Greek word that means to hold on to like a man would hold on to a life preserver when overboard in a raging sea. It is often translated "receive" in the KJV. Here it means to "receive" as if you were a football player trying to catch a ball in the middle of a group of strong defenders. You catch it, and the defenders now try to knock and grab the ball from your hand, so you must defend and keep the ball in your hands, even as you run toward the goal. Another meaning is to carry a very heavy item, like a very heavy bucket and carry it no matter how far or difficult the ground, and deliver it full and on time.

LEB/LEBAB

Leb/Lebab (*Strong's* OT 3820/3823, pronounced: labe/law-babe') means heart, feelings or physical heart. Is a synonym with *lebab*.

LOGOS

Logos (*Strong's* NT 3056, pronounced: lo-gos') means all that something is, message, expression of the full thought, the message of God as God is one with His Word. We are commanded to do *logos* to produce the *zoe*/life of God. James 1:23 "For if any be a hearer of the *logos*/word, and not a doer, he is like unto a man beholding his natural face in a glass."

Matt 7:24 "Therefore whosoever heareth these *logos*/sayings of mine, and doeth them, I will liken him unto a wise man, which built his house upon a rock: 25 and the rain descended, and the floods came, and the winds blew, and beat upon that house; and it fell not: for it was founded upon a rock. 26 And every one that heareth these *logos*/sayings of mine, and doeth them not, shall be likened unto a foolish man, which built his house upon the sand: 27 and the rain descended, and the floods came, and the winds blew, and beat upon that house; and it fell: and great was the fall of it. 28 And it came to pass, when Jesus had ended these *logos*/sayings, the people were astonished at his doctrine."

When you hear a word to obey it, then that *logos*/word becomes *rhema*. In the military, this is very real. Failure to obey a *logos* and make it *rhema* puts you in danger of death because of dereliction of duty or mutiny. Obedience keeps you in the life of the organization. Greek and Roman slaves understood this very well, as has every soldier in all of history. The only thing that matters is what *logos* you do, not what you just study, memorize or quote.

MEOD

Meod (*Strong's* OT 3966, pronounced: meh-ode') means vehemence, strength, diligence, quick commitment, excited, positive, right attitude and enthusiasm, or eagerly with force and loudness.

MERCY

Mercy is ignoring/forgiving/exonerating all wrongs, so you do not get the full penalty, wrath or evil you deserve; and/or being given a great good you did not earn and are not worthy of. Lam 3:22 "It is of the LORD's *chesed*/mercies that we are not consumed, because his compassions fail not." 1 Pet 1:3 "Blessed be the God and Father of our Lord Jesus Christ, which according to his abundant mercy hath begotten us again unto a *zao*/lively hope by the resurrection of Jesus Christ from the dead, 4 to an inheritance incorruptible, and undefiled, and that fadeth not away, reserved in heaven for you, 5 who are kept by the power of God through faith unto *soteria*/salvation ready to be revealed in the last time."

NASA

Nasa (*Strong's* OT 5375, pronounced: naw-saw') means to lift, contain or carry so no more can be included and nothing is left out.

NEPHESH

Nephesh (*Strong's* OT 5315, pronounced: neh'-fesh) means soul, inner man, as exhibited by outward appearance, words and actions, feelings, appetite, greed, desire and behavior.

PEACE

The Bible word translated *peace* is based on the Hebrew word *shalom*, which means calm assurance and confidence in God because all things are working well and in order, with nothing missing, nothing broken and everything producing to the abundance of Heaven on Earth. This is not a passive state, similar to being drugged, but a calm assurance, no matter how bad it is, that God is making it right, because you have put in process and are continuing to do the things to allow/cause this to happen, i.e., thanksgiving, all kinds of prayer and supplication, praise, alms, legal justice, etc. Phil 4:4 "Rejoice in the Lord alway: and again I say, Rejoice. 5 Let your moderation be known unto all men. The Lord is at hand. 6 Be careful for nothing (*no anxiety*); but in every thing by prayer and supplication with thanksgiving let your *aiteo*/requests be made known unto God. 7 And the peace of God, which passeth all understanding (*because you have activated godly faith and will see the supernatural power of God, in answer to your prayers*), shall keep (*guard, be a fortress around*) your hearts and minds through Christ Jesus. 8 Finally, brethren, whatsoever things are true, whatsoever things are honest, whatsoever things are just, whatsoever things are pure, whatsoever things are lovely, whatsoever things are of good report; if there be any virtue, and if there be any praise, think on these things. 9 Those things, which ye have both learned, and received, and heard, and seen in me, do: and the God of peace shall be with you." Notice, this is actively managing your thoughts and behaviors. The best way to control thoughts is to go and do acts of *agape*/love. Controlling your thoughts is a learned skill.

The meaning of peace also includes the process by which this state is achieved, so it is very closely related to *soteria*/salvation, as a state or condition of being, and to *sozo*/saved, peacemaking on how it is achieved. Rom 16:20 "And the God of peace shall bruise Satan under your feet *as shattered glass*. The grace of our Lord Jesus Christ be with you [*to think, know, be and do this*]. Amen." So to give peace and grace means: all things working well to produce the blessing of Heaven on Earth, and you will destroy and shatter seven ways all your enemies, as you fight as Jesus would. Also, you will have in abundance all things you need to do this work well, in you and yours.

A more complete definition is that peace is: the blessing of God to make and enjoy the Kingdom of God, Heaven on Earth, in every aspect of life and to be doing all the right things to produce Heaven on Earth, now, including destroying all your enemies God's way. This process or warrior definition agrees with: John 14:26 "But the Comforter, which is the Holy Ghost, whom the Father will send in my name, he shall teach you all things, and bring all things to your remembrance, whatsoever I have said unto you (*so you can act as Jesus would*). 27 Peace (*the ability to fight and bring Heaven on Earth as I did*) I leave with you, my peace (*calm assurance and trust in God that you are doing all things, as Holy Spirit is helping you, to the glory of Father God, to bring the blessing of Heaven to Earth*) I give unto you: not as the world giveth, give I unto you. Let not your heart be troubled, neither let it be afraid." John 16:33 "These things I have spoken unto you, that in me ye might have peace (*calmness, knowing that Jesus has defeated all your enemies, for you to put them under your feet and bring Heaven on Earth, warring, fighting as Jesus taught us*). In the world ye shall have tribulation: but be of good cheer; I have overcome the world." 1 Cor 15:57 "But thanks be to God, which giveth us the victory through our Lord Jesus Christ. 58 Therefore, my *agape*/beloved brethren, be ye stedfast, unmoveable, always abounding in the work of the Lord, forasmuch as ye know that your labour is not in vain in the Lord." 2 Cor 2:14 "Now thanks be unto God, which always causeth us to triumph in Christ, and maketh manifest the savour of his knowledge by us in every place." And this knowledge includes everything from normal life (clean sheets and efficient garbage collection) to the Lord confirming His Word of grace in power (healing the sick, raising the dead, the blind seeing, the lame walking, etc.). So if you think peace is all about your comfort, so you can only enjoy the pleasures of this world, you have missed the Gospel of God in Jesus Christ.

Notice how this fits with the "peace," or "peacemaker" mission of Jesus: Acts 10:36 "The word which God sent unto the children of Israel, preaching peace by Jesus Christ: (he is Lord of all:) 37 that word, I say, ye know, which was published throughout all Judaea, and began from Galilee, after the baptism which John preached; 38 how God anointed Jesus of Nazareth with the Holy Ghost and with power: who went about doing good, and healing all that were oppressed (*under the active dominion, reign or lordship*) of the devil; for God was with him (*to make peace in this way*)." Luke 4:17 "And there was delivered unto him the book of the prophet Esaias. And when he (*Jesus*) had opened the book, he found the place where it was written, 18 The Spirit of the Lord is upon me, because he hath anointed me to preach the gospel to the poor; he hath sent me to heal the brokenhearted, to preach deliverance to the captives, and recovering of sight to the blind, to set at liberty them that are bruised, 19 to preach (*command, declare, proclaim and demonstrate*) the acceptable year of the Lord."

We have been given that same Spirit of power, *agape*/love and sound mind attitude of an *agape*/love warrior in Jesus: Gal 4:4 "But when the fulness of the time was come, God sent forth his Son, made of a woman, made under the law, 5 to redeem them that were under the law, that we might receive the adoption of sons. 6 And because ye are sons, God hath sent forth the Spirit of his Son into your hearts, crying, Abba (*Daddy*), Father."

Peace is knowing you have done and will continue doing those things that produce Heaven on Earth, to make nothing missing, nothing broken or twisted out of God's purpose, and all things, including your shattering the devil under your feet, are working well to abundance. This gives you a peace, an assurance that the world cannot give.

This also fits right in with the traditional definition of a policeman as a "peace officer," and therefore explains why we are to pray for the government, per 1 Tim 2 and Rom 13:1 "Let every soul be subject unto the higher powers (*government in all forms as they support the righteous work of God*). For there is no power but of God:

the powers that be are ordained of God. 2 Whosoever therefore resisteth the power, resisteth the ordinance of God: and they that resist shall receive to themselves damnation. 3 For rulers are not a terror to good works, but to the evil. Wilt thou then not be afraid of the power? do that which is good, and thou shalt have praise of the same: 4 for he is the minister of God to thee for good. But if thou do that which is evil, be afraid; for he beareth not the sword in vain: for he is the minister of God, a revenger to execute wrath upon him that doeth evil. 5 Wherefore ye must needs be subject, not only for wrath, but also for conscience sake. 6 For this cause pay ye tribute also: for they are God's ministers, attending continually upon this very thing. 7 Render therefore to all their dues: tribute to whom tribute is due; custom to whom custom; fear to whom fear; honour to whom honour. 8 Owe no man any thing, but to *agape/*love one another: for he that *agape/*loveth another hath fulfilled the law."

PHILEO

Phileo (*Strong's* NT, 5368, pronounced: fil-eh'-o) means brotherly love, friend, affection, love, kiss or feeling.

PHOBOS

Phobos (*Strong's* NT, 5401, pronounced: fob-os') means that which causes flight in dread or terror of an unpleasant thing, in intense attitude and quick action; exceedingly afraid. It is used in the New Testament to describe the fear of the Lord. This includes that absolute assurance that on the Day of Judgment every man's works will be tested by fire and that which does not survive will be a loss to that person. So we are continually admonished throughout the New Testament to live our lives, knowing they will be tested. If you are a Christian, you are *sozo/*saved (1 Cor 3:7-10), but your works, the fruit of your life, will be tested and that found wanting will be destroyed. See Glossary entry "Wrath of God" for more detail.

PNEUMA

Pneuma (*Strong's* NT, 4151, pronounced: pnyoo'mah) means air, breath, current and also spirit. Pneuma is used to describe the spirit of man and the Spirit of God. The spirit is that part of man that comes directly from God in Adam, and because the sin of Adam made the spirit dead and united with and under the authority of the devil by the law of sin and death, man must be recreated with God's *zoe/*life to be reunited with God, as was Jesus by the work of the cross and resurrection. When a person is born again, their spirit is recreated and justified unto *zoe/*life, the same as is in Jesus. This is a work God does in the new creation. (See Glossary entry "Spirit/Soul/Body" for more detail.)

APPENDICES

PSUCHE

Psuche (*Strong's* NT, 5590, pronounced: psoo-khay') means soul or life; that part of a person manifested through their body; a reflection of the inner man of the thoughts, intention, will and emotions exhibited or seen in how a person speaks and acts, not just animal or that the person is alive. The spirit and soul have similar characteristics and, thus, are hard to tell which is in operation, except by the Word of God (Heb 4:12), and, thus, easily confused. The soul is produced by the spirit of man inhabiting a body. The soul, which consists of the heart, mind, will and emotions, must be renewed by the believer with the Word of God, to mature the believer into the fullness of Christ, per Eph 4, Rom 12, Rom 13, Col 3 and many other scriptures. *Psuche* is also translated as life because what you actually say and do is a reflection of what is in your soul. In general, the spirit of man is limited to and must relate to the outside world through or with the soul.

PROPITIATION

When sin is propitiated all wrath is removed, and aggressive blessing is bestowed on the former sinner. If there were no sin, then aggressive blessing is now bestowed from a previous, less–blessed, passive or indifferent position. The Greek word is *hilasterion* (*Strong's* NT 2435), and means to conciliate or make propitious or to cause good things to come. *Random House Dictionary* defines propitiation as: that which propitiates or makes favorably inclined; appease; conciliate. And conciliate means: 1) To overcome the distrust or hostility of; placate; win over: to conciliate an angry competitor. 2) To win or gain (goodwill, regard, or favor). 3) To make compatible; reconcile.

The propitiation process removes all issues for disfavor, if any, and institutes or restores one to a favorable position of aggressive good and identification. This could be either to resolve a difficulty, to "bribe," or to give a token of love for favor. *Favorable* means now disposed to do well toward and wanting to do well toward. So the new position is not neutral or indifferent, but now is a position in which the one favorably inclined or conciliated is openly seeking to do well toward the one reconciled, as if to themselves. In the case of a king, the king does not now simply forgive any wrong or ignore you. Instead, he looks continually for ways to bless or prosper you in any way he can and takes great delight in the bestowment of these benefits. Of course, with this attitude in the king, when the person does come to him for help or a favor of any kind, the king will, gladly and with great cheer and joy, do whatever can be done. Rom 3:23 "For all have sinned, and come short of the glory of God; 24 being justified freely by his grace through the redemption that is in Christ Jesus: 25 whom God hath set forth to be a propitiation through faith in his blood, to declare his righteousness for the remission of sins that are past, through the forbearance of God; 26 to declare, I say, at this time his righteousness: that he might be just, and the justifier of him which believeth in Jesus." 1 John 2:1 "My little children, these things write I unto you, that ye sin not. And if any man sin, we have an advocate with the Father, Jesus Christ the righteous: 2 and he is the propitiation for our sins: and not for ours only, but also for the sins of the whole world." Eph 1:3 "Blessed be the God and Father of our Lord Jesus Christ, who hath blessed us with all spiritual blessings in heavenly places in Christ." Rom 5:1 "Therefore being justified by faith, we have peace with God through our Lord Jesus Christ." Our propitiation is complete in Christ. Thus, all enmity is reconciled and abundant blessing aggressively directed to man, general good and Holy Spirit in the Christian.

RACHAM

Racham (*Strong's* OT 7533, pronounced: raw-kham') is an Old Testament word often translated as mercy, tender mercies or compassion in the KJV. *Racham* is a deeper word than mercy, which in modern usage is more of a legal term. *Racham* means tender loving care, as a mother for a child, who can see no wrong in the child, no matter what it does; love that sees past our sins for our good. *Racham* has all the best of motherhood and fatherhood in its meaning, where love never stops, no matter what children do, and is similar to the New Testament *agape*/love/charity in concept.

REDEEM/RANSOM

Redeem or ransom is to pay the purchase price to take ownership and set under the control of the one who paid the price. Gal 3:13 "Christ **hath redeemed** us from the curse of the law, being made a curse for us: for it is written, Cursed is every one that hangeth on a tree: 14 that the blessing of Abraham might come on the Gentiles through Jesus Christ; that we might receive the promise of the Spirit through faith." 1 Pet 1:18 "Forasmuch as ye know that ye **were not redeemed** with corruptible things, as silver and gold, from your vain conversation received by tradition from your fathers; 19 but with the precious blood of Christ, as of a lamb without blemish and without spot." Rom 3:23 "For all have sinned, and come short of the glory of God; 24 being justified freely by his grace through the **redemption** that is in Christ Jesus: 25 whom God hath set forth to be a propitiation through faith in his blood, to declare his righteousness for the *aphesis*/remission (*removal, obliteration, cancellation and putting away*) of sins that are past, through the forbearance of God; 26 to declare, I say, at this time his righteousness: that he might be just, and the justifier of him which believeth in Jesus." Eph 1:7 "In whom **we have redemption** through his blood, the *aphesis*/forgiveness (*remission, obliteration, and putting away*) of sins, according to the riches of his grace." 1 Tim 2:5 "For there is one God, and one mediator between God and men, the man Christ Jesus; 6 who gave himself a ransom for all, to be testified in due time." Matt 20:28 "Even as the Son of man came not to be ministered unto, but to minister, and to **give his** *psuche/* **life (*soul*) a ransom** for many." (See Isa 53:11.)

To think your purpose in life is your own is an ultimate level of deception: 1 Cor 6:19 "What? know ye not that your body is the temple of the Holy Ghost which is in you, which ye have of God, and ye are not your own? 20 For ye are bought with a price (*the life, body and blood of Jesus*): therefore glorify God in your body, and in your spirit, which are God's." 1 Cor 7:23 "Ye are bought with a price; be not ye the servants of men." (Prov 29:25 "The fear of man bringeth a snare ... .") Eph 1:13 "In whom (*Jesus*) ye also trusted, after that ye heard the word of truth, the gospel of your *soteria*/salvation: in whom also after that ye believed, ye were sealed with that holy Spirit of promise, 14 which is the earnest of our inheritance until the redemption of the purchased possession, unto the praise of his glory." Peace is in those things that fulfill God's goals to produce Heaven on Earth in you and in the Earth through you.

As the redeemed, we are now called by God to fulfill His purpose of making Heaven on Earth through Jesus. We will face troubles, as the devil exalts himself against the knowledge of God, and as God sends us to set others free. Knowing you are bought, and not your own, but God's, is freedom.

REMISSION/FORGIVENESS

The same Greek noun-verb pair is translated in the KJV as remit or forgives. In Greek they have one meaning, in English forgive means to pardon, while remit means to pay in full to remove and pardon a debt or sin. *Aphiemi* (Strong's NT 863), the verb, has the primary meaning of "to send forth, as in to cry, forgive, forsake, lay aside, leave, let alone, allow, omit, put away, remit, suffer, or yield up." Throughout the New Testament *aphiemi* is translated as permit, allow, left , leave, let, send away, neglect, forsake, yield, lay aside, let go, let alone, cry, divorce, put away, and forgive. Thus it is a process or action word to remove and pay a debt or curse.

Aphesis (Strong's NT 859), the noun, means to be in the state or condition of freedom, with past bonds permanently broken and no record remaining. It has to do with the state or condition due to a past action or process of offense or debt dismissal, liberty and deliverance and a passing over of a just and due penalty, i.e., *aphiemi*. In the New Testament, we find *aphesis* translated variously as remission, forgiveness, and liberty. When looked at in context, its primary usage concerning sin is that of remission. As remission of sin, *aphesis* means to be in the state of abatement, alleviation, release, interruption, discharge, obliteration, purging, removal, or cancellation. So sin has no effect, debt or curse due. Both the sin, the record of the sin and the curse due are gone, no longer relevant to the case.

For example, when cancer goes into remission, it means that the symptoms disappear, or it is no longer actively working its destruction on the body, and all medical action stops. In the same way, when there is remission of sin, the symptoms of sin disappear, and sin no longer has power over an individual. The confusion comes as the translators use similar words or the same word (such as forgive and remit) for either Greek word and do not indicate the distinction between the English words. The Greek words are consistent, the English words forgive and remit are not.

The verb *aphiemi* is used one hundred and fifty-six times in the New Testament. When we look at the uses, from the various meanings of *aphiemi*, together with their context, we discover that they portray forgiveness as a judicial act of God, whereby He forgives or pardons us for our acts of transgression. It is basically a legal transaction which deals with our guilt and removes the penalty for our acts of sin. When we are convicted of our acts of sin, we confess our sins. God responds by judicially forgiving us of our sins, removing our guilt and rescinding the penalty from His side. We see this process in: Acts 8:22 "Repent therefore of this your wickedness, and pray God if perhaps the thought of your heart may be *aphiemi*/forgiven you"

The noun *aphesis* is used seventeen times in the New Testament. When we put these passages together and look at them, from the various meanings of *aphesis* together with their context, we discover that they portray a state of remission of sin, meaning sin has been removed, along with the defilement of that sin, a removal of all claims due based on a price paid. It results in a deliverance from sin, which, in turn, results in our liberty as the children of God. This remission of sin is usually associated, not with repentance, but, rather, with the baptism of the Holy Spirit, as described by John the Baptist (see Acts 2:38), to bring about our cleansing from sin. Hebrews tells us: Heb 9:22 "And according to the law almost all things are purified with blood, and without shedding of blood there is no *aphesis*/remission." Forgive (*aphiemi*) has to do with the process for remission, total purification of sins, while remission (*aphesis*), the noun, has to do with the permanent state of purification from sin and the sin nature into the new birth, by the blood of Christ. Luke 24:47 "And that repentance and **remission** of sins should be preached in His name to all nations, beginning at Jerusalem." Acts 5:31 "Him God has exalted to His right hand to be Prince and Savior, to give repentance to Israel and *aphesis*/**forgiveness** (*remission*) of sins." Notice, in both of these passages, that Jesus provides both forgiveness and purification, obliteration, removal or remission of sin. (The repentance is to manage your life, knowing that Jesus is the Son of God, Emmanuel and the Remover of sin.)

The confusion over forgiveness and remission is with us today, not the original Old or New Testament authors. In modern English, forgiveness is a decision to remove the offense and the curse of the offense, with no payment or redeeming price paid, while remission is the removal of the sin or offense based on full payment for the offense and the curse or penalty of the offense. In the Old Testament, the blood of the sacrifice covered the sin and removed the curse, or penalty, from operation on the Earth at that time. Thus, under atonement, the person then got healed, enemy armies were destroyed, crops grew, or some other form of prosperity or blessing came. But the sin was never removed until the work of Jesus by the cross. In the New Testament, Jesus has done that removal for all time, and the healing or prosperity is manifested by faith in the facts of the work of Jesus' stripes, cross, resurrection and glorification 2000 years ago.

Confusion comes when the English translation uses *forgive* rather than *remit* for *aphiemi* (verb), or *forgiveness* rather than *remission* for *aphesis* (noun). So relative to the blood sacrifices under Moses or the blood of Jesus, the English word *forgiveness* in not really appropriate. It appears that the translators were more concerned with the curse of the offense not being applied or being removed under atonement and, thus, they used *forgiveness*. Concerning the remission with the blood of Jesus, based on the full meaning of *forgiveness*, only *remission* should be used. You can rest assured that God always knows the work of the blood of Jesus, and Father God is never confused that Jesus paid the full price to remit our sin and remove the curse of sin.

The difference between forgiveness and remission is a key element between the covenant of Moses (the Old Testament) and the completed covenant of Abraham in Jesus (the New Testament). Under the law of Moses, sins were forgiven and healed, but sins could never be removed or remitted (*aphesis/aphiemi*). This is the meaning of the atonement or covering achieved once a year in Yom Kippur. Here all the sins of the nation were atoned, covered, but not removed. Heb 10:4 "For it is not possible that the blood of bulls and of goats should take away sins. … 12 But this man, after he had offered one sacrifice for sins for ever, sat down on the right hand of God; 13 from henceforth expecting till his enemies be made his footstool. 14 For by one offering he hath perfected for ever them that are sanctified (*separated from Satan back to God through Jesus, according to Col 1:13*). 15 Whereof the Holy Ghost also is a witness to us: for after that he had said before, 16 This is the covenant that I will make with them after those days, saith the Lord, I will put my laws into their hearts, and in their minds will I write them; 17 and their sins and iniquities will I remember no more. 18 Now where *aphesis*/remission of these is, there is no more offering for sin. 19 Having therefore, brethren, boldness to enter into the holiest by the blood of Jesus ..."

In Jesus, sins are not atoned for, but propitiated—removed—and the person is prepared for favorable, active and aggressive blessing from God in all ways. Rom 3:23 "For all have sinned, and come short of the glory of God; 24 being justified freely by his grace through the redemption that is in Christ Jesus: 25 whom God hath set forth to be a propitiation through faith in his blood, to declare his righteousness for the *aphesis*/remission of sins that are past, through the forbearance of God; 26 to declare, I say, at this time his righteousness: that he might be just, and the justifier of him which believeth in Jesus." 1 John 2:2 "And he (*Jesus*) is the propitiation for our sins: and not for ours only, but also for the sins of the whole world." God, thus, creates the new birth or new creation, making the believer the righteousness of God in Christ Jesus. This is only possible with the English word *remission*.

This is what God accomplished in Jesus for all mankind. We enter into it by faith (Rom 3), and we operate in it by faith. Rom 1:16 "For I am not ashamed of the gospel of Christ: for it is the power of God unto *soteria* / salvation to every one that believeth; to the Jew first, and also to the Greek. 17 For therein is the righteousness of God revealed from faith to faith: as it is written, The just shall *zao*/live by faith." 2 Cor 3:18 "But we all, with open face beholding as in a glass (*mirror*) the glory of the Lord *in ourselves, in spite of the mind of the flesh*, are changed into the same image from glory to glory, even as by the Spirit of the Lord."

Thus, remission is the legal removal of sin and consequences in Jesus two thousand years ago. We have now (present tense) remission. But we still sin in the present time, meaning our soul is not yet perfected or matured in Christ. When we acknowledge our sin and thank God for the blood of Jesus, then we implement the remission on that specific act in time. This is the *aphesis*/forgive referred in 1 John 1:9. Here we are to agree that we sinned (the meaning of confess) and thank God that we have remission. Thus, this *aphiemi*/forgiveness is more about present time soul cleansing, agreeing with God in truth and not the condition of your spirit. Failure to acknowledge that you have sown to the flesh means that you will reap corruption until you or someone else deals with the sin by the body and blood of Jesus or it will be dealt with as sin-works on the Day of Judgment (see Gal 6:1-10 and 1 Cor 3:1-15).

RHEMA

Rhema (*Strong's* NT, 4487, pronounced: hray'mah) means the message that leads to action or obedience; the word of God you do or obey. *Logos* becomes *rhema* as you do it. Hearing the *logos*/Word of God and not doing it is self-deception and produces no *zoe* life. Hearing the *logos*/Word of God and doing it produces *zoe* life. Matt 4:4 "But he (*Jesus*) answered and said, It is written, Man shall not *zao*/live by bread alone, but by every *rhema*/word that proceedeth out of the mouth of God (*that you do*)."

Jesus gave this parable to show it is about what you do, not what you have heard. Matt 21:28 "But what think ye? A certain man had two sons; and he came to the first, and said, Son, go work to day in my vineyard. 29 He answered and said, I will not: but afterward he repented, and went. 30 And he came to the second, and said likewise. And he answered and said, I go, sir: and went not. 31 Whether of them twain did the will of his father? They say unto him, The first. Jesus saith unto them, Verily I say unto you, That the publicans and the harlots go into the kingdom of God before you."

From *Vine's Expository Dictionary of Biblical Words*, copyright © 1985, Thomas Nelson Publishers: "The significance of *rhema* (as distinct from *logos*) is exemplified in the injunction to take 'the sword of the Spirit, which is the word of God,' Eph 6:17; here the reference is not to the whole Bible as such, but to the individual scripture which the Spirit brings to our remembrance for use in time of need, a prerequisite being the regular storing of the mind with scripture."

But this does not in any way imply that *rhema* is not just limited to Holy Spirit giving a special word, but rhema applies to any scripture that you use by repeating and commanding against the devil in any faith battle, for all the promises of God in Jesus are "yea and amen." The emphasis of Eph 6 is what you are to do independent of any special leading or word from Holy Spirit. The *logos* of the word of God becomes *rhema* as you do the *logos*. So even if you do get a special word from Holy Spirit, it is not *rhema* until you obey it to doing it to completion.

Rom 10:17 "So then faith cometh by hearing, and hearing by the *rhema*/word of God (*that you do*)." Hearing the message of salvation and not believing God raised Jesus from the dead will not make you righteous, and not confessing that Jesus is Lord with your mouth will not result in your salvation, per Rom 10:7-13. Conversely hearing that word of your salvation, that God raised Jesus from the dead, will get you made the righteousness of God in Christ Jesus, and confessing Jesus is Lord with your mouth will bring you salvation, according to God's riches.

In the military, *logos*/words of command that are obeyed become *rhema*/words that further the life of the military organization. If those words are not obeyed and remain simply *logos*, the military organization will not be furthered. Failure to know and obey the standing orders of the law, as in traffic signs, will put you on the wrong side of the law and under its wrath, if an accident occurs or if a police officer sees you disobeying the law. Ignorance of the *logos* law does not excuse you, if you disobey that *logos* law.

The message of the Scriptures is that if you do not do the *logos* that proceeds out of the mouth of God in the Scriptures and make it *rhema*, then the devil will enforce the law of sin and death, as the consequences for not doing it God's way. You can consider all of Scripture as a standing, written order to be fully obeyed. Disobedience to the written or spoken word of God is called rebellion or iniquity, and is "as the sin of witchcraft." 1 Sam 15:23 "For rebellion is as the sin of witchcraft, and stubbornness is as iniquity and idolatry. Because thou hast rejected the word (*logos*) of the Lord, he hath also rejected thee from being king."

Conversely, in the covenant in the blood of Jesus, your ability to operate as a king for Jesus and have your words produce the results of Jesus depends on how well you hold on to the redemption truths of being made the righteousness of God in Christ Jesus in the new birth and the abundance of God's grace in and through Jesus. Rom 5:17 "For if by one man's offence death reigned (*as king in enforcing the law of sin and death*) by one (*Adam in his sin in the garden*); much more they which (*continually*) *lambano*/receive abundance of grace and of the gift of righteousness shall reign (*as a king for Jesus, in enforcing the law of* agape/*love*) in *zoe*/life by one, Jesus Christ.)"

In the military, or in any home, there are standing orders, often written, such as: make your beds, take out the trash, do your homework or job on time and do it right, help your fellow soldier, stay on post or in the house until given permission to leave, etc. The New Testament has some 1,050 commands, and many are clearly standing orders, but they are of no effect until you do them. Here are just a few. 1 Thes 5:16 "Rejoice evermore. 17 Pray without ceasing. 18 In every thing give thanks: for this is the will of God in Christ Jesus concerning you. 19 Quench not the Spirit. 20 Despise not prophesyings. 21 Prove all things; hold fast that which is good. 22 Abstain from all appearance of evil." Phil 4:4 "Rejoice in the Lord alway: and again I say, Rejoice. 5 Let your moderation be known unto all men. The Lord is at hand. 6 Be careful for nothing; but in every thing by prayer and supplication with thanksgiving let your requests be made known unto God. 7 And the peace of God, which passeth all understanding, shall keep your hearts and minds through Christ Jesus. 8 Finally, brethren, whatsoever things are true, whatsoever things are honest, whatsoever things are just, whatsoever things are pure, whatsoever things are lovely, whatsoever things are of good report; if there be any virtue, and if there be any praise, think on these things. 9 Those things, which ye have both learned, and received, and heard, and seen in me, do: and the God of peace shall be with you."

Phil 4:7 and 9 make it clear you only get the desired results if you have obeyed, done, what is in the previous verses. These commands are all *logos* and only produce the *zoe*/life of God when you do them and, thus, make them *rhema* and receive the promise. (See also the definition of *logos*.)

RIGHTEOUSNESS

Biblical righteousness has three principle meanings:

1) Righteous acts or works are acts/results that God does through a person so they are perfectly right with God in every way and survive as gold, silver or jewels on the Day of Judgment. This is to obey and do all of God's commandments completely and gladly.
2) A legal state where the one is made as if they had never sinned or will never sin again. This is like being exonerated in a court of law, until you sin or break the law again. This righteousness is conditional, as it is lost when you sin or violate the law again, and you once again become a criminal or a "sinner," with a penalty due, as described in the Law of Moses. Then righteousness must be restored in some way by an action that exonerates, removes or hides the sin from further legal action or curse, and pays or forgives the penalties/curse due for the sin. This is to be legally forgiven of the sin, but your nature remains the same. If you sin again, it is as if you were never righteous, and the full penalty (death) again applies.
3) To be imputed/given the gift of righteousness, which means it is independent of your behavior. The one who is made righteous to this level can produce no alienation

or offence to the court or to the one granting righteousness, no matter what they do, and the one in authority aggressively pours all of the blessing and abundance on them (think spoiled, rich kid with a patient and just father). This righteousness of God does not depend upon your goodness, but Jesus', and is a permanent righteousness. Now your nature/spirit is new, and your sins obliterated once, forever, and you are reconciled to God forever, even if you sin again. You are now separated from your sins or evil works, but, until you apply the benefits of the work of Jesus to your current sins and problems, the devil will still try to apply the law of sin and death to you. This level of righteousness allows you to go to God at any time; you are never unclean before Him. God is in Heaven, you are on Earth. If you as a Christian sin, you are righteous with God before and after you sin, but you have to deal with the consequences of sin committed on Earth or God will deal with it under the New Covenant on the Day of Judgment.

Under the Law of Moses, sins were covered by the annual atonement, but they were never removed or fully paid for, pending the propitiation of Christ. The sins were forgiven, i.e. the penalty/curse/guilt of the law of sin and death removed, but the effect was the people were made the second type of righteousness, blessed, but conditional on right behavior. If you sinned again, you released death as the penalty for sin again. Jesus brought forgiveness and remission, the obliteration of sin, to make men the righteousness of God in Jesus and is made effective by faith in the work of Jesus by the cross.

In Christ we are made the third kind of righteousness before God. We died with Him, as our sins are paid in full by His suffering and death for us. Col 3:3 "For ye are dead, and your *zao*/life is hid with Christ in God." Rom 6:2 "God forbid. How shall we, that are dead to sin, *zao*/live any longer therein? 3 Know ye not, that so many of us as were baptized into Jesus Christ were baptized into his death?" Gal 2:19 "For I through the law am dead to the law, that I might *zao*/live unto God. 20 I am crucified with Christ: nevertheless I *zao*/live; yet not I, but Christ *zao*/liveth in me: and the life which I now *zao*/live in the flesh I *zao*/live by the faith of the Son of God, who *agape*/loved me, and gave himself for me. 21 I do not frustrate the grace of God: for if righteousness come by the law, then Christ is dead in vain." Rom 5:9 "Much more then, being now justified by his blood, we shall be *sozo*/saved from wrath through him. 10 For if, when we were enemies, we were reconciled to God by the death of his Son, much more, being reconciled, we shall be *sozo*/saved by his *zoe*/life." Luke 24:47 "And that repentance (*Jesus is Lord and Judge, and everyone will have to deal with Him now and later, and He is your Redeemer, Healer and Judge against the devil and every curse of sin*) and *aphesis*/remission (*removal, purging, washing and putting away*) of sins should be preached in his name among all nations, beginning at Jerusalem."

By this one act of Jesus, sin was remitted once, forever, and we enter into this remission and being made the righteousness of God in Jesus by faith. 2 Cor 5:20

"Now then we are ambassadors for Christ, as though God did beseech you by us: we pray you in Christ's stead, be ye reconciled to God. 21 For he hath made him to be sin for us, who knew no sin; that we might be made the righteousness of God in him." Rom 3:28 "Therefore we conclude that a man is justified by faith without the deeds of the law. 29 Is he the God of the Jews only? is he not also of the Gentiles? Yes, of the Gentiles also: 30 seeing it is one God, which shall justify the circumcision by faith, and uncircumcision through faith." Rom 4:5 "But to him that worketh not, but believeth on him that justifieth the ungodly, his faith is counted for righteousness." Rom 5:1 "Therefore being justified by faith, we have peace with God through our Lord Jesus Christ."

In 1 Cor 6 Paul upbraids the Corinthians for their sin, yet he still proclaims: 1 Cor 6:11 "And such [*functional sinners*] were some of you: but ye are washed, but ye are sanctified, but ye are justified in the name of the Lord Jesus, and by the Spirit of our God." In spite of their current sin, they still possessed the Type 3 righteousness obtained by the name of Jesus and the power of Holy Spirit.

Under the Law of Moses sin was forgiven and the annual atonement covered sin until Jesus came. This forgiveness (NT Greek – *aphiemi*) brought the peace and prosperity of Israel. *Remission* (NT Greek – *aphesis*) is the removal, purging, washing, obliteration, destruction and putting away of sin, with no evidence that it was ever there or will be again making us righteous, not just forgiven. Rom 3:25 "Whom God hath set forth to be a propitiation through faith in his blood, to declare his righteousness for the *aphesis*/remission (*removal, purging, washing, obliteration and putting away*) of sins that are past, through the forbearance of God; 26 to declare, I say, at this time his righteousness: that he might be just, and the justifier (*the one making righteous*) of him which believeth in Jesus." Heb 9:22 "And almost all things are by the law purged with blood; and without shedding of blood is no *aphesis*/remission." Acts 13:38 "Be it known unto you therefore, men and brethren, that through this man is preached unto you the *aphesis*/forgiveness (*remission, obliteration and putting away*) of sins: 39 and by him all that believe are justified from all things, from which ye could not be justified by the law of Moses." Type 3 includes Type 2 with God, but sin and the curse/guilt of sin must be reconciled on Earth.

In Jesus we see the fulfillment of God as our righteousness: Isa 45:24 "Surely, shall one say, in the LORD have I righteousness and strength: even to him shall men come; and all that are incensed against him shall be ashamed. 25 In the LORD shall all the seed of Israel be justified, and shall glory." Jer 23:6 "In his days Judah shall be saved, and Israel shall dwell safely: and this is his name whereby he shall be called, THE LORD OUR RIGHTEOUSNESS." Isa 53:11 "He shall see of the travail of his soul, and shall be satisfied: by his knowledge shall my righteous servant justify (*cleanse and make righteous unto holiness*) many; for he shall *cabal*/bear their iniquities."

Appendices

This is found in the New Covenant through the blood of Jesus. Heb 8:10 "For this is the covenant that I will make with the house of Israel after those days, saith the Lord; I will put my laws into their mind, and write them in their hearts: and I will be to them a God, and they shall be to me a people: 11 and they shall not teach every man his neighbour, and every man his brother, saying, Know the Lord: for all shall know me, from the least to the greatest. 12 For I will be merciful to their unrighteousness, and their sins and their iniquities will I remember no more." Heb 10:4 "For it is not possible that the blood of bulls and of goats should take away sins. … 16 This is the covenant that I will make with them after those days, saith the Lord, I will put my laws into their hearts, and in their minds will I write them; 17 and their sins and iniquities will I remember no more. 18 Now where *aphesis/*remission (*removal, purging, washing away, obliteration and putting away*) of these (*unrighteousness, sins and iniquities*) is, there is no more offering for sin. 19 Having therefore, brethren, boldness to enter into the holiest by the blood of Jesus…" To have your unrighteousness removed by faith means you are now righteous in spirit. As you confess your current sins, you give thanks for the forgiveness and remission already given 2000 years ago by faith in the work of Jesus by the cross.

And we get it the way it has always been given, by faith: Gen 15:6 "And he (*Abraham*) believed in the Lord; and he counted it to him for righteousness." To be righteous means there is now no wrath, only blessing. Rom 5:10 "For if, when we were enemies, we were reconciled to God by the death of his Son, much more, being reconciled, we shall be *sozo*/saved by his *zoe*/life. 11 And not only so, but we also joy in God through our Lord Jesus Christ, by whom we have now received the atonement (*reconciliation, propitiation*)." Eph 2:13 "But now in Christ Jesus ye who sometimes were far off are made nigh by the blood of Christ. 14 For he is our peace … ." Col 1:20 "And, having made peace through the blood of his cross, by him to reconcile all things unto himself; by him, I say, whether they be things in earth, or things in heaven. 21 And you, that were sometime alienated and enemies in your mind by wicked works, yet now hath he reconciled 22 in the body of his flesh through death, to present you holy and unblameable and unreproveable in his sight."

A key element is to understand that we, as Christians, are different than our works. We ourselves, our spirits, are *sozo*/saved, already judged dead, made righteous unto new *zoe*/life in Jesus by Holy Spirit. A Christian is one who has received that by faith. We are now dead to the Law, so the Law has no force over us, and we were made legally righteous, to the level of Jesus, before God, to walk in the experiential outworking of right acts (Type 1), even though our current walk is not perfect (until we walk just like Jesus). 2 Cor 5:21 "For he (*God*) hath made him (*Jesus*) to be sin for us, who knew no sin; that we might be made the righteousness of God in him (*Jesus*)."

Christian life works and behaviors will be judged for the Type 1 righteousness, per 1 Cor 3:15, by fire on the Day of Judgment. Yet the born-again, new man spirit is *sozo*/saved and survives that fire because of the third type of righteousness, which is by the faith of/in Christ and not our works (Rom 5:10, Rom 10:6-13). What survives that day you get to keep. 1 Cor 3:12 "Now if any man build upon this foundation gold, silver, precious stones, wood, hay, stubble; 13 every man's work shall be made manifest: for the day shall declare it, because it shall be revealed by fire; and the fire shall try every man's work of what sort it is. 14 If any man's work abide which he hath built thereupon, he shall receive a reward. 15 If any man's work shall be burned, he shall suffer loss: but he himself shall be *sozo*/saved; yet so as by fire." If you are a Christian, your sin-works may burn, but not you.

God's solution for us was to include us in the death and resurrection of Jesus. This saves our spirit. Yet we will still have our works or "soul fruit" judged: Matt 16:27 "For the Son of man shall come in the glory of his Father with his angels; and then he shall reward every man according to his works." Rom 2:5 "But after thy hardness and impenitent heart treasurest up unto thyself wrath against the day of wrath and revelation of the righteous judgment of God; 6 who will render to every man according to his deeds." 2 Cor 5:10 "For we must all appear before the judgment seat of Christ; that every one may receive the things done in his body, according to that he hath done, whether it be good or bad."

All the blessings of God go to the righteous: those who commit no sin in their Earth walk or who are now clean because they have had their sins forgiven (both the sin action and the curse consequence of sin). Type 2, conditional righteousness, depends on you, i.e., your holiness. Type 3 righteousness depends on Jesus' holiness and not yours. If you are a Christian, Type 2 righteousness no longer applies before God, as Type 3 has superseded it. Rom 5:1 "Therefore being justified by faith, we have peace with God through our Lord Jesus Christ." In peace, God only has favor toward us to produce Heaven on Earth. Eph 1:3 "Blessed be the God and Father of our Lord Jesus Christ, who hath blessed us with all spiritual blessings in heavenly places in Christ." 2 Pet 1:2 "Grace and peace be multiplied unto you through the knowledge of God, and of Jesus our Lord, 3 according as his divine power hath given unto us all things that pertain unto *zoe*/life and godliness, through the knowledge of him that hath called us to glory and virtue: 4 whereby are given unto us exceeding great and precious promises: that by these ye might be partakers of the divine nature, having escaped the corruption that is in the world through lust." We escaped that corruption when we were made the righteousness of God in Christ Jesus by faith. This righteousness depends on the holiness of Jesus and not our own.

If we sin, we have a choice. We can agree with what God says in His written Word, the Scriptures, or what Holy Spirit convicts us of. As we see that we sinned

Appendices

and call it sin, we are walking in the light. We are seeing clearly. If we do not call our sin as it is, we are walking in darkness and are still deceived in that sin. If we argue with God over what He calls sin, we put ourselves out of fellowship with Him. When we confess that it indeed was sin, that Jesus died for that sin, and that we already have remission for that sin, then this scripture applies. (Notice the first sign that you are out of fellowship, joyful agreement with God, is when your joy is lessened or gone.) 1 John 1:4 "And these things write we unto you, that your joy (*in God*) may be full. 5 This then is the message which we have heard of him, and declare unto you, that God is light, and in him is no darkness at all. 6 If we say that we have fellowship with him, and walk in darkness, we lie, and do not the truth: 7 but if we walk in the light, as he is in the light, we have fellowship one with another, and the blood of Jesus Christ his Son cleanseth us from all sin. 8 If we say that we have no sin, we deceive ourselves, and the truth is not in us. 9 If we confess our sins, he is faithful and just to *aphiemi*/forgive us our sins, and to cleanse us from all unrighteousness. 10 If we say that we have not sinned, we make him a liar, and his word is not in us. 2:1 My little children, these things write I unto you, that ye sin not. And if any man sin, we have an advocate with the Father, Jesus Christ the righteous: 2 and he is the propitiation for our sins: and not for ours only, but also for the sins of the whole world."

Removal of this lack of fellowship issue is called forgive *aphiemi* in the KJV, but *remit* is more accurate. The thing that dumbfounds the fleshly mind, that makes actions more important than the Word of God, is that even though you sin, you do not lose the righteousness of God in Christ that you are made in the new birth. The new birth is in your spirit, and perhaps in part of your heart, but not in the rest of your soul. Soul purity is your goal in the Christian life. For the Christian, or one in permanent covenant with God, *aphiemi* relates to your fellowship or agreement with God as you work out your own salvation in this life. When you receive that forgiveness given 2000 years ago for your present sin, you are then back in fellowship with God, and this is the *aphiemi* forgiveness. Thus, you control whether you walk in *aphiemi* forgiveness and blessing or not.

This is the realm of sowing and reaping. Gal 6:7 "Be not deceived; God is not mocked: for whatsoever a man soweth, that shall he also reap. 8 For he that soweth to his flesh shall of the flesh reap corruption; but he that soweth to the Spirit shall of the Spirit reap life everlasting." This is a clear warning to the sinning Christian. There are no free sins. All words and actions of the Christian constitute our works. The Christian has been separated from their sin works, but all works will be tried on the last Day.

You do not lose righteousness in your spirit for your present sin, but when you sin, you must deal with the devil and his application of the law of sin and death on the Earth. Likewise, you must also deal with God's law of sowing and reaping.

Because of lack of confession and lack of application of communion in the bread and wine in truth and faith, you will reap evil or corruption in your physical body and life, in spite of your spirit righteousness. Holy Spirit is sealed in the Christian unto the Day of Redemption, when God will reap in fullness what He has already paid for. Eph 1:13 "In whom ye also trusted, after that ye heard the word of truth, the gospel of your *soteria*/salvation: in whom also after that ye believed, ye were sealed with that holy Spirit of promise, 14 which is the earnest of our inheritance until the redemption of the purchased possession, unto the praise of his glory." So in spite of the Christian who is not just like Jesus in their walk (anything less is sin), Holy Spirit is not going anywhere. God will get what He paid for.

It is not until you apply the truth of the Gospel of Jesus Christ to your sins and/or the curses operating in your life that you will walk in soul-righteousness and blessing in this life. So this is a case of burn it by the fire of the Gospel now, or it will try to kill you in this life. The spirit-righteousness of God in Christ Jesus in your spirit ensures your final salvation after the Day of Judgment. The reality of your soul-righteousness will determine the quality of your testing on the Day of Judgment.

This explains how the Christian can be the righteousness of God and yet sin, or have sin works. The Christian is separated, sanctified from their sin works and unto God. The source of our sanctification is God, by Jesus, not our works. 1 Cor 1:30 "But of him (*God*) are ye in Christ Jesus, who of God is made unto us wisdom, and righteousness, and sanctification, and redemption." This is part of the Gospel, and is really good news! Rom 6:10 "For in that he (*Jesus*) died, he died unto sin once: but in that he *zao*/liveth, he *zao*/liveth unto God. 11 Likewise reckon ye also yourselves to be dead indeed unto sin, but *zao*/alive unto God through Jesus Christ our Lord."

Those works in your life that are not just like Jesus would do them will not survive the Day of Judgment, yet God, who cannot lie, says the Christian will. 1 Cor 3:12 "Now if any man build upon this foundation gold, silver, precious stones, wood, hay, stubble; 13 every man's work shall be made manifest: for the day shall declare it, because it shall be revealed by fire; and the fire shall try every man's work of what sort it is. 14 If any man's work abide which he hath built thereupon, he shall receive a reward. 15 If any man's work shall be burned, he shall suffer loss: but he himself shall be *sozo*/saved; yet so as by fire. 16 Know ye not that ye are the temple of God, and that the Spirit of God dwelleth in you?" Eternal salvation with indwelling Holy Spirit comes with being made the Type 3 righteousness of God in Christ Jesus. See Glossary "The Wrath of God" for more detail on this.

SIN/TRANSGRESSIONS

Sin is actually missing any mark or path God has set, whether by commission, by what we do, or by omission, by what we do not do. Transgressions or willful sins are those violations of God's law that are knowingly done, or you may have discovered after the fact that you sinned. Sin includes transgressions and those violations you did not know you committed. Ignorance of the law does not forgive violations of the law, thus sin is sin, whether you know you committed it or not, and, thus, requires levels of restitution or payment on Earth and in Heaven. Per Genesis 2:17, the law of sin and death is to do right and be blessed, or to sin and die. Rom 6:23 "For the wages of sin is death; but the gift of God is eternal *zoe*/life through Jesus Christ our Lord." Ezek 18:4 "Behold, all souls are mine; as the soul of the father, so also the soul of the son is mine: the soul that sinneth, it shall die." Rom 1:18 "For the wrath of God is revealed from heaven against all ungodliness and unrighteousness of men, who hold the truth in unrighteousness." Rom 2:9 "Tribulation and anguish, upon every soul of man that doeth evil, of the Jew first, and also of the Gentile…"

The penalty for sin is death through the curse/guilt of sin, which is death in a fast or a slow, or prolonged, form. Deut 28:14 "And thou shalt not go aside from any of the words which I command thee this day, to the right hand, or to the left, to go after other gods to serve them. 15 But it shall come to pass, if thou wilt not hearken unto the voice of the LORD thy God, to observe to do all his commandments and his statutes which I command thee this day; that all these curses shall come upon thee, and overtake thee. … 61 Also every sickness, and every plague, which is not written in the book of this law, them will the LORD bring upon thee, until thou be destroyed." Gal 3:10 "For as many as are of the works of the law are under the curse: for it is written, Cursed is every one that continueth not in all things which are written in the book of the law to do them."

Christ removed the curse from us to give us the ultimate blessing, God Himself, dwelling in us by His Spirit: Gal 3:13 "Christ hath redeemed us from the curse of the law, being made a curse for us: for it is written, Cursed is every one that hangeth on a tree: 14 that the blessing of Abraham might come on the Gentiles through Jesus Christ; that we might receive the promise of the Spirit through faith." There is now no legal curse upon the Earth for anyone.

Sozo/Soteria

For these Greek words, *sozo* (*Strong's*' NT 4892, pronounced: sode'-zo) is the verb, save, the process through which you become whole and blessed; *soteria* (*Strong's*' NT 4991, pronounced: so-tay-ree'-ah) is the noun, salvation, the state of being whole and blessed, like Heaven on Earth. *Sozo* is the process by which all of Earth and human life is made like Heaven on Earth in the fullness of the glory of God, i.e., that which produces the peace of God or the Kingdom of God, from now to eternity. Physical healing is just a small portion of the meaning. Salvation has an eternal aspect, eternal life with God. The present life aspect is producing Heaven on Earth in your life and in those you are responsible for. *Salvation* means to be made prosperous and successful to the level of God Himself in every way possible, with no limits. So nothing related to the full potential of human life in Christ is left out. The root word from which salvation is derived means open, freedom from restraint. Sickness, poverty, danger, lameness, infirmity, weakness, etc., are all restraints, limits and pressure points. Salvation or wholeness has no restraints, limits or pressure points, and has the full freedom of God's blessings in action to fill the Earth with His glory.

Spirit/Soul/Body

Man is a three-part being, made up of spirit (the real you), soul (heart, mind, will and emotions and how you interface or function with this world through your body), and body (what operates in this earth). From Genesis we see that the addition of the spirit to the body created a living soul. Gen 2:7 "And the LORD God formed man of the dust of the ground, and breathed into his nostrils the breath/ *spirit* of life; and man became a living soul."

Your heart is not your spirit, but the heart seems to be that combination of inner life that includes your mind and touches your spirit. 1 Thes 5:23 "And the very God of peace sanctify you wholly; and I pray God your whole **spirit and soul and body** be preserved blameless unto the coming of our Lord Jesus Christ." Heb 4:12 "For the word of God is quick, and powerful, and sharper than any twoedged sword, piercing even to the dividing asunder **of soul and spirit**, and of the joints and marrow, and is a discerner of the **thoughts and intents of the heart**." When you die, your spirit and soul leave your mortal body. James 2:26 "For as the body without the spirit is dead ..." Your heart is to be purified in this life, especially hardness of heart, to God and His Word, by doing the Word and expecting God to do His part (Rom 2:4-5, 1 Tim 1:5, Heb 3:10-12, Eph 4:16-18, James 1:6, 2 Pet 2:14).

We are made righteous by faith in Jesus in our spirits. This is how we are born again, made a new creature in Christ Jesus. We will get a new, immortal body at the resurrection. Our soul is unchanged. Notice all your memories remain the same, before and after being born again. We are made the righteousness of God in Jesus and given *zoe*/life in our spirits, as Holy Spirit comes to dwell in our spirit.

Our goal in life is to renew our mind, heart or soul to think without iniquity, i.e., just like Jesus. 2 Cor 10:5 "Casting down imaginations, and every high thing that exalteth itself against the knowledge of God, and bringing into captivity every thought to the obedience of Christ." This process is called "saving our souls," or "outworked sanctification," and is demonstrated by how much our walk is like Jesus. This renewing process of the soul comes as we grow in the true knowledge of Jesus, not mere mental facts, but actually working with God, so that the fruits of God are produced in the Earth through you.

APPENDICES

2 Pet 1:2 "Grace and peace be multiplied unto you through the *experiential* knowledge of God, and of Jesus our Lord, 3 according as his divine power hath given unto us all things that pertain unto *zoe*/life and godliness, through the *experiential* knowledge of him that hath called us to glory and virtue: 4 whereby are given unto us exceeding great and precious promises: that by these ye might be partakers of the divine nature, having escaped the corruption that is in the world through lust." Our mental learning is solidified as we go and do *agape*/love. As we believe, to releasing *zoe*/life, we do this.

The old man is the un-recreated spirit and way of thinking that produces sin, also called the carnal mind, or the mind of the flesh and lust. An immature Christian thinks like a "mere man" (1 Cor 3:1-3). The old man, the body of sin, is killed in Jesus and recreated into the new man. John 1:12 "But as many as received him, to them gave he power to become the sons of God, even to them that believe on his name: 13 which were born, not of blood, nor of the will of the flesh, nor of the will of man, but of God." Col 3:9 "… seeing that ye have put off the old man with his deeds; 10 and have put on the new man, which is renewed (*made effective*) in knowledge after the image of him that created him." The new birth removes the spirit of the old man, but does not necessarily totally change the old-man-trained soul.

While we are made new creations in the new birth, we have to retrain our minds and hearts so we can walk like Jesus in this earth. Eph 4:22 "That ye put off concerning the former conversation the old man, which is corrupt according to the deceitful lusts; 23 and be renewed in the spirit of your mind; 24 and that ye put on the new man, which after God is created in righteousness and true holiness."

And this new man delights to walk in all the ways of God in *agape*/love. 1 John 5:2 "By this we know that we *agape*/love the children of God, when we *agape*/love God, and keep his commandments. 3 For this is the *agape*/love of God, that we keep his commandments: and his commandments are not grievous." The new man does not have any resistance to God, and none of God's commands are grievous to him.

Psuche and bios: The other Greek words translated in the KJV as "life" include *psuche* and *bios*. *Psuche* is also translated as "soul," which has a different connotation than "life." As translated in the Scriptures, there is much confusion between these words. *Zoe* is used in reference to general life and the *life* of God, implying it is what God gives. *Bios* is a general form of life that all living creatures have. *Zoe* is in reference to that which God alone gives. So He gives life to all things, and then Jesus said He came to give *zoe*/life as opposed to all other kinds of life or life force. This is in opposition to whatever form of life force people were operating in at the time. So He either meant that He came to give a different life force or a great increase of the good life force people already operated in.

The meaning for *soul* is even more difficult, in that many do not recognize what is clearly revealed in the Scriptures as a difference between *soul* and *spirit*.

The Greek word *psuche* (Strong's NT 5590) is translated "soul" fifty-eight times, "life" forty times, "mind" three times and "heart" once. This shows a lack of understanding on the part of the translators, not on Holy Spirit's part.

From *Vine's* explanation of *psuche* we have the following:

"The language of Heb 4:12 suggests the extreme difficulty of distinguishing between the soul and the spirit, alike in their nature and in their activities. Generally speaking the spirit is the higher, the soul the lower element. The spirit may be recognized as the life principle bestowed on man by God, the soul as the resulting life constituted in the individual, the body being the material organism animated by soul and spirit … .

"Body and soul are the constituents of the man according to Matt 6:25; 10:28; Luke 12:20; Acts 20:10; body and spirit according to Luke 8:55; 1 Cor 5:3; 7:34; James 2:26. In Matt 26:38 the emotions are associated with the soul, in John 13:21 with the spirit; cf. also Ps 42:11 with 1 Kings 21:5. In Ps 35:9 the soul rejoices in God, in Luke 1:47 the spirit. (*This confusion between Ps 35 and Luke 1 is a good example in which the modern thinkers translating the KJV did not understand that the soul and spirit are different, yet have, what can be described as, similar features.*)

"Apparently, then, the relationships may be thus summed up 'Soma, body, and pneuma, spirit, may be separated, pneuma and psuche, soul, can only be distinguished' (Cremer)." (NT:5590 *Soul* from *Vine's Expository Dictionary of Biblical Words: Nashville, Tn.*, Thomas Nelson Publishers, 1985).

One way to distinguish the soul is that it is the mind, the heart, the will and the emotions of all men, and constitutes that which receives information directly from the senses of the body and also from the spirit. So, concerning our acceptable thoughts, intentions, motives, attitudes of the heart, the soul is the joining and deciding ground between the body and the spirit. Thus, Heb 4:12 takes the Word of God to determine where either the soul or the spirit ends and the other begins. The spirit of the born-again man will always be in harmony with the Word of God. The soul of the born-again or the natural man may or may not be in harmony, agreement and commitment with the Word of God. This latter is more a function of an individual's experiences, culture and training. What one actually does and says is the result of the status of truth in their soul and, thus, the word *psuche* is often translated as "life." What is in your soul or heart is displayed in the life you live.

So when a person is in the spirit, their soul is mostly controlled or in cooperation with the thoughts and attitudes of a spirit being. This is seen when a demon speaks through a person, or Holy Spirit, as in biblical prophecy (also see the meaning of *zoe*). The life force exhibited is a function of whatever unity the soul has with that particular spirit being (life or *zoe*). For example, when one uses the name of Jesus to raise the dead, this is an action in unity with Holy Spirit. When one accepts the death of a person, especially a young one, they are in unity with their body senses, and the person is buried and not raised. In both cases, the soul is the deciding ground of "whose report will you believe?" The resulting behavior is then called the "life " of that person, as seen in the action of either raising the dead or burying them.

This understanding of the difference is seen in both the Hebrew and Greek texts, but not in the KJV and most other modern translations. For example, look at the Hebrew and the Greek and then the English translations relating to these important scriptures. Isa 53:11 "He shall see of the travail of his **soul,** and shall be satisfied: by his knowledge shall my righteous servant justify many; for he shall bear their iniquities." Matt 20:28 "Even as the Son of man came not to be ministered unto, but to minister, and to give his *psuche*/life (*soul*) a ransom for many." John 10:15 "As the Father knoweth me, even so know I the Father: and I lay down my *psuche*/life (*soul*) for the sheep." According to the original Hebrew and Greek, the meaning is clear and consistent, but not in the English translation.

Also here are both Greek words in the same verse translated as life: John 12:25 "He that loveth his *psuche*/life shall lose it; and he that hateth his *psuche*/life in this world shall keep it unto *zoe*/life eternal." Since we know God does not want us to kill ourselves, the meaning is that if your soul is not just like Father God's, work until it is, and when you do, your soul will release the *zoe*/life of God from your born-again spirit. You work on it according to 2 Cor 3:17 "Now the Lord is that Spirit: and where the Spirit of the Lord is, there is liberty *to be all Father God made you to be in Jesus.* 18 But we all, with open face beholding as in a glass (*mirror, seeing Jesus manifest Himself in and through me*) the glory of the Lord, are changed into the same image from glory to glory, even as by the Spirit of the Lord." Eph 4:22 "That ye put off concerning the former conversation the old man, which is corrupt according to the deceitful lusts; 23 and be renewed in the spirit of your mind; 24 and that ye put on the new man, which after God is created in righteousness and true holiness." The transformation occurs as you continually see aspects of Jesus that you desire and, in faith, see yourself walking in, first unto thanksgiving and joy, and then Holy Spirit will transform your inner man according to your faith, and it will be seen in your outer man or walk. Rom 1:17 "For therein is the righteousness of God revealed from faith to faith: as it is written, The just shall *zao*/live by faith."

As the New Testament describes the heart of the Christian as possibly dead or resistant to God, we do not consider the heart the dwelling place of Holy Spirit. Rom 2:5 "But after thy hardness and impenitent heart treasurest up unto thyself wrath against the day of wrath and revelation of the righteous judgment of God." The heart seems to be better described as that place or part of your soul or subconscious mind that connects to your spirit, and near that place is also the conscience part of your soul (that internal governor that is always judging your actions based on your beliefs and the soul part of your heart). Rom 2:29 "But he is a Jew, which is one inwardly; and circumcision is that of the *kardia*/heart, in *or by* the *pneuma*/spirit, and not in the letter; whose praise is not of men, but of God." The heart and the spirit are different, but closely tied together. A heart fully indwelt by a right spirit is a right heart. Eph 3:17 "That Christ/*Holy Spirit* may dwell (*happily or fully*) in your hearts by faith; that ye, being rooted and grounded in *agape*/love ..."

According to modern science, the cognitive mind is the cerebral cortex, and the unconscious mind is a combination of the rest of the brain and the neural material throughout the body. The term *heart*, as a portion of the soul, implies the part of the soul different than the cognitive mind. The spirit is considered to reside near the physical heart and the solar plexus (behind the stomach).

For the born-again one, the heart can be corrupted, but the spirit cannot. We understand Holy Spirit to be in our spirits, so our spirit can now always be pure, but our heart is included in the process of renewing the mind and must continually be kept clean. The goal of the Christian life is for the spirit to once again rule your soul and body, though a right heart, and not the pre-born-again condition, in which the body and/or soul rule instead.

Notice the warning not to let your heart be corrupted by sin: Heb 3:12 "Take heed, brethren, lest there be in any of you an evil heart of unbelief, in departing from the *zao*/ living God. 13 But exhort one another daily, while it is called To day; lest any of you be hardened through the deceitfulness of sin." James 3:14 "But if ye have bitter envying and strife in your hearts, glory not, and lie not against the truth." James 4:8 "Draw nigh to God, and he will draw nigh to you. Cleanse your hands, ye sinners; and purify your hearts, ye double minded." 1 John 3:20 "For if our heart condemn us, God is greater than our heart, and knoweth all things." Thus the heart is in need of constant maintenance to stay in cooperation with Holy Spirit.

Your conscious mind seems to be that active part of the way you think and accesses your memory and the events in the physical world by your senses. Below is a model that shows the distinction between the spirit, soul and body for the new-creation, born-again person:

THE BORN-AGAIN CHRISTIAN

THE SPIRIT WORLD	THE MENTAL WORLD	THE PHYSICAL WORLD
Your Spirit-The Real You	Your Soul	Your Body
	Habits, Attitudes, Desires	Flesh
Hunger for God	Conscience, Memory, Intentions	Senses
Born Again: Bible, Word	Heart, Emotions, Will, Mind	Bible: Word of God
Righteousness-Life-Zoe	Imagination, Cognitive Mind	
Holy Spirit>Jesus>Father	Subconscious Mind	

What this table conveys is that the physical world has a boundary, the world of the spirit, and good portions of the soul do not, or are not of the same kind of "stuff" as the physical universe our bodies inhabit. Note also that automatic responses, such as attitudes, habits, emotions and memory, are highly linked to the physical body in structure and effect. Damage to the physical brain, for example, can have major impacts on these elements of the soul. To be amused means to be without thinking, so the mind is a deeper part of the person. This also indicates the reason the devil has such a strong focus in our modern world on keeping people amused, mindless and entertained. To open your mind in such amusement means that you are programming your subconscious without knowledge. As you are responsible for the shape or godliness of your soul, you are still accountable for the effects, whether you are aware of it or not.

Jesus is the living Word made flesh. In the diagram, the Word of God is seen under the spirit and the body, as this is the only physical link God has given man to the spiritual world, and all godly definitions of the spirit must be consistent with the Bible. Ps 138:2 "I will worship toward thy holy temple, and praise thy name for thy *chesed*/lovingkindness and for thy truth: for thou hast magnified thy word above all thy name." Ps 119:88 "Quicken me after thy *chesed*/lovingkindness; so shall I keep the testimony of thy mouth. 89 For ever, O LORD, thy word is settled in heaven. 90 Thy faithfulness is unto all generations: thou hast established the earth, and it abideth. 91 They continue this day according to thine ordinances: for all are thy servants." 1 Pet 1:23 "Being born again, not of corruptible seed, but of incorruptible, by the word of God, which *zao*/liveth and abideth for ever. 24 For all flesh is as grass, and all the glory of man as the flower of grass. The grass withereth, and the flower thereof falleth away: 25 but the word of the Lord endureth for ever. And this is the word which by the gospel is preached unto you."

In reality, the spirit world is actually more solid or real than the physical world, as is all that physically exists is made from spirit. As with everything God makes, the soul and probably the spirit, is, in structure and operation, far more detailed and complex than described here. But remember, that thing which we call the soul was made to house God and, with you, to operate the universe for and with Him, so it is really quite capable and marvelous. The more you operate in this "completeness" of the new birth, the more you and He actively cooperate to do His will in this universe. The new creation is an instantaneous event of God, by decree; the renewed mind takes time and human effort, in cooperation and effort with Holy Spirit in the Word of God. The Word of God is so important, as it is the only physical link (in its printed form) that we are given to the spirit world and God. To hear the voice of God all you have to do is speak the Scriptures. If it does not sound like God, the problem is you, not it.

So to be "filled" with the Spirit means to have your soul in agreement with Holy Spirit and your behavior or "life" reflecting that agreement. One way to describe this is that God fully possess your soul, or you are "full of" or "filled with" His Spirit. Here is both a command and a description of what that looks like. Eph 5:18 "And be not drunk with wine, wherein is excess; but be filled with the Spirit; 19 speaking to yourselves in psalms and hymns and spiritual songs, singing and making melody in your heart to the Lord; 20 giving thanks always for all things unto God and the Father in the name of our Lord Jesus Christ; 21 submitting yourselves one to another in the fear of God." See *zoe* for more detail on this.

THE WRATH OF GOD

There are two aspects of the so-called "wrath of God": One is of God, and the other is of the devil, the dethroned, but obviously still functioning, god of this world:
   a) The great God, Creator of all, is a consuming fire that destroys all not like or of Him. (Heb 12:29, 1 Cor 3:10-14, Matt 3:11-12, Luke 12:49)
   b) The devil, unleashed due to sin in the Earth, in the curse of sin. (Rom 5:12-14)

In general, for now we see very little of the first type; most of the evil seen in the world is of the second type.

For the first type, the wrath of God, when you see a prayer answered and some evil had to be removed, that is the wrath of God against that evil. When you see a miracle of healing by God, that is the wrath of God against a work of the devil, in setting that person free. When it is complete, the person has no trace of the disorder, and the person is back to the way God intended. Acts 10:36 "The word which God sent unto the children of Israel, preaching peace by Jesus Christ: (he is Lord of all:) 37 that word, I say, ye know, which was published throughout all Judaea, and began from Galilee, after the baptism which John preached; 38 how God anointed Jesus of Nazareth with the Holy Ghost and with power: who went about doing good, and healing all that were oppressed (*under the active dominion, reign and lordship*) of the devil; for God was with him."

Wrath as a word is an intense application of force to achieve an end result. God's wrath is the force that removes corruption and restores His righteousness on the Earth.

The restoration spoken of in the Book of Revelation, in which all evil is destroyed, Satan bound into the Lake of Fire, and God comes to dwell on the Earth, is a demonstration of His effective wrath. Notice that the intended end result is good; it is "Heaven on Earth."

The devil's wrath destroys all that is like God, in a manner to cause the most fear of the devil among men, the most misery for man, and a twisted view of God for men to distrust God and all that is good. (Job 1-3; John 10:10; 1 Pet 5:8; Rev 12-9-12)

There is a third aspect of God's wrath. The negative consequences of violating God's laws are also called His wrath. This is what most people consider His wrath to be. This kind of wrath is the consequences of violation of His laws or of following laws that produce evil consequences. What people tend to forget is that God knows we sin and has solutions for that sin.

The negative consequence is not as sure as the blessed consequences for rightly working with God's laws, as evil is overcome by good, else Jesus never could have healed anyone. James 2:13 "For he shall have judgment without mercy, that hath shewed no mercy; and mercy rejoiceth against judgment (*or mercy triumphs over judgment*)."

If you ignore gravity and jump off a high cliff, the consequences of gravity, the wrath of gravity, will be felt when you hit the ground. God is the one who made gravity and also the parachute, as seen in dandelion seeds and the "wings" of flying squirrels, to show us how to manage the force of gravity and avoid its wrath.

God also showed us the law of flight in birds, that with added energy and right activity, you can fly against the force of gravity. This is the same God and the same law of gravity. It is our choice how we deal with it. Just as with gravity, ignorance of God's law is not bliss. Hos 4:6 "My people are destroyed for lack of knowledge … ."

The problem is not God, but our not knowing, or ignorance, or misapplication of the facts of Redemption, Reconciliation, Righteousness, Salvation, Sanctification, and Adoption, and then secondarily, not applying them properly, which is Wisdom.

By biblical standards, knowledge that does not cause right behavior as a master craftsman is deception, and not true knowledge. One term for this is mental assent, where you agree it is true, but you do not use it to manifest the Kingdom of God by grace in a situation. You may use law, but you are to reign with grace, not law.

Rom 5:21 "That as sin hath reigned (*as king*) unto death, even so might grace reign (*as a greater king*) through righteousness unto eternal *zoe*/life by Jesus Christ our Lord."

So you are not expert, *epignosis*, knowing the Word of righteousness until you can reign as Jesus would in any situation you are either in or aware of.

In the Garden, when Adam sinned, instead of running to God, because sin had blinded him, he ran *from* God. God went and helped Adam anyway. Gen 3:6 "And when the woman saw that the tree was good for food, and that it was pleasant to the eyes, and a tree to be desired to make one wise, she took of the fruit thereof, and did eat, and gave also unto her husband with her; and he did eat. 7 And the eyes of them both were opened, and they knew that they were naked; and they sewed fig leaves together, and made themselves aprons. 8 And they heard the voice of the Lord God walking in the garden in the cool of the day: and Adam and his wife hid themselves from the presence of the Lord God amongst the trees of the garden. 9 And the Lord God called unto Adam, and said unto him, Where art thou? 10 And he said, I heard thy voice in the garden, and I was afraid, because I was naked; and

I hid myself. 11 And he said, who told thee that thou wast naked? Hast thou eaten of the tree, whereof I commanded thee that thou shouldest not eat?"

God knew exactly what happened, but Adam would not speak honestly with God. Adam had released death into the world through his sin. Rom 5:12 "Wherefore, as by one man (*Adam*) sin entered into the world, and death by sin; and so death passed upon all men, for that all have sinned (*having come from the loins of Adam*)."

Now God had to deal with the consequences to save His mankind. So the first thing God did was to limit what Satan could do and to promise that God would one day destroy what Satan had done. Gen 3:12 "And the man said, The woman whom thou gavest to be with me, she gave me of the tree, and I did eat. 13 And the LORD God said unto the woman, What is this that thou hast done? And the woman said, The serpent beguiled me, and I did eat. 14 And the LORD God said unto the serpent, Because thou hast done this, thou art cursed above all cattle, and above every beast of the field; upon thy belly shalt thou go, and dust shalt thou eat all the days of thy life: 15 and I will put enmity between thee and the woman, and between thy seed and her seed; it shall bruise (*crush*) thy head, and thou shalt bruise his heel. 16 Unto the woman he said, I will greatly multiply thy sorrow and thy conception; in sorrow thou shalt bring forth children; and thy desire shall be to thy husband, and he shall rule over thee. 17 And unto Adam he said, Because thou hast hearkened unto the voice of thy wife, and hast eaten of the tree, of which I commanded thee, saying, Thou shalt not eat of it: cursed is the ground for thy sake; in sorrow shalt thou eat of it all the days of thy life; 18 thorns also and thistles shall it bring forth to thee; and thou shalt eat the herb of the field; 19 in the sweat of thy face shalt thou eat bread, till thou return unto the ground; for out of it wast thou taken: for dust thou art, and unto dust shalt thou return."

The so called "curses of God" were actually limits on the devil, so the devil could not kill Adam and Eve as he wanted. First, God limited the devil to the Earth. Yes, childbirth would be hard, and yes, man would have to work the land, but, no, the devil could not kill them with starvation, or no children/lack of fertility/infertility, death in child bearing or miscarriage. Because God judged Satan, that means that anytime anyone exercised faith in God, any effect of the law of sin and death could be overcome, because that is what Satan operated on. This was the source of all the goodness and miracles God was able to do before, during and after Jesus was manifested on Earth.

God had promised that from the woman would come a Deliverer who would crush Satan. The devil knew if she lived that One would indeed come. God made sure that, on a cursed Earth, man could still live.

Next, we see the first blood shed in covering sin and establishing covenant relationship. Gen 3:21 "Unto Adam also and to his wife did the LORD God make coats of skins, and clothed them."

APPENDICES

But the tragedies managed by the devil had just begun. Eve had two children, Abel and Cain. Abel followed God's laws in covenant sacrifice, and Cain did not. Gen 4:2 "And she again bare his brother Abel. And Abel was a keeper of sheep, but Cain was a tiller of the ground. 3 And in process of time it came to pass, that Cain brought of the fruit of the ground an offering unto the LORD. 4 And Abel, he also brought of the firstlings of his flock and of the fat thereof. And the LORD had respect unto Abel and to his offering: 5 but unto Cain and to his offering he had not respect. And Cain was very wroth, and his countenance fell."

Cain was already into pride, insisting on doing things his own way (a definition of iniquity) and was offended that God did not accept his offering (an attitude of pride and unforgiveness). Yet, instead of rejecting Cain, God tried to help Cain and went to him. Gen 4:6 "And the LORD said unto Cain, Why art thou wroth? and why is thy countenance fallen (*as in a severe depression or temper tantrum*)? 7 If thou doest well, shalt thou not be accepted? and if thou doest not well, sin (*a croucher, demon, monster, hungry beast, guilt or devil*) lieth at the door. And unto thee shall be his desire, and thou shalt rule over him."

God warned Cain that he had sinned and that he could recover by doing right, per God's law. If Cain did not do right, correcting his error and reconciling the sin, then he would be subject to the devil whom his sin had attracted. That devil now desired to control Cain for more evil, and Cain must fight to win freedom from that control. If Cain did not win, the devil would rule or lord over or control Cain, causing him to commit more sin. Rom 6:16 "Know ye not, that to whom ye yield yourselves servants to obey, his servants ye are to whom ye obey; whether of sin unto death, or of obedience unto righteousness?"

Unfortunately Cain did not win the battle. Gen 4:8 "And Cain talked with Abel his brother: and it came to pass, when they were in the field, that Cain rose up against Abel his brother, and slew him. 9 And the LORD said unto Cain, Where is Abel thy brother? And he said, I know not: Am I my brother's keeper? 10 And he said, What hast thou done? the voice of thy brother's blood crieth unto me from the ground."

Notice that the devil won and tempted Cain to even more anger, resentment and, finally, murder of the one who had done right. Cain killed Abel. The consequence was that Cain received even more of the curse of sin. Gen 4:11 "And now art thou cursed from the earth, which hath opened her mouth to receive thy brother's blood from thy hand; 12 when thou tillest the ground, it shall not henceforth yield unto thee her strength; a fugitive and a vagabond shalt thou be in the earth. 13 And Cain said unto the LORD, My punishment is greater than I can bear. 14 Behold, thou hast driven me out this day from the face of the earth; and from thy face shall I be hid; and I shall be a fugitive and a vagabond in the earth; and it shall come to pass, that every one that findeth me shall slay me."

The first time I understood this I was astounded. Based on the teachings of my past, I thought for sure God would have killed Cain when he killed Abel. Instead, God was merciful to Cain and made it so that Cain would not be killed. Gen 4:15 "And the LORD said unto him, Therefore whosoever slayeth Cain, vengeance shall be taken on him sevenfold. And the LORD set a mark upon Cain, lest any finding him should kill him. 16 And Cain went out from the presence of the LORD, and dwelt in the land of Nod, on the east of Eden."

Look at how God responded to sin in this book of "First Things." First, He went to the aide of Adam and Eve, then He went to correct Cain, to avoid a demonic attack upon him, then He was merciful to Cain and made a way for him to live. So when someone tells you that God hates sin, agree, but respond with something like this: "Yes, God hates everything about sin and He made sure all that hate fell on Jesus, but God loves the sinner." Every miracle Jesus did was an example of God's true attitude toward man. If man could not fix it, God would send someone who could–Jesus, the Messiah, the Mighty Arm of God.

John 3:16 "For God so greatly *agape*/loved and dearly prized the world that He [even] gave up His only begotten (unique) Son, so that whoever believes in (trusts in, clings to, relies on) Him shall not perish (come to destruction, be lost) but have eternal (everlasting) *zoe*/life. 17 For God did not send the Son into the world in order to judge (to reject, to condemn, to pass sentence on) the world, but that the world might find *soteria*/salvation and be made safe and sound through Him. 18 He who believes in Him [who clings to, trusts in, relies on Him] is not judged [he who trusts in Him never comes up for judgment; for him there is no rejection, no condemnation—he incurs no damnation]; but he who does not believe (cleave to, rely on, trust in Him) is judged already [he has already been convicted and has already received his sentence] because he has not believed in and trusted in the name of the only begotten Son of God. [He is condemned for refusing to let his trust rest in Christ's name.]" AMP

So God's response is to remove sin, put it away as an issue with Him and, thus, remove the legal grounds for the curse of sin. God hates sin so much that He sent Jesus to suffer and die to resolve it by redemption for the remission, obliteration, purging and putting away of both sin and the curse of sin. Heb 9:26 "For then must he often have suffered since the foundation of the world: but now once in the end of the world hath he appeared to put away sin by the sacrifice of himself."

You cannot sin without the devil, and when you do sin, he is your life source. 1 John 3:8 "He that committeth sin is of the devil; for the devil sinneth from the beginning. For this purpose the Son of God was manifested, that he might destroy the works of the devil."

And just as God warned Cain: Gen 4:7 "If thou doest well, shalt thou not be accepted? and if thou doest not well, sin (*demon, monster, hungering beast, guilt or devil*) lieth at the door. And unto thee shall be his desire, and thou shalt rule over him (*to be free of him*)": that law is still in operation.

APPENDICES

Jesus delivered the wrath of God in everyone He healed. Acts 10:36 "The word which God sent unto the children of Israel, preaching peace by Jesus Christ: (he is Lord of all:) 37 that word, I say, ye know, which was published throughout all Judaea, and began from Galilee, after the baptism which John preached; 38 how God anointed Jesus of Nazareth with the Holy Ghost and with power: who went about doing good, and healing all that were oppressed of the devil; for God was with him." This "doing good" included the wrath of God on the rulership/oppression of the devil for everyone that God healed by Jesus.

In our great Redemption, He did the same thing. Acts 10:42 "And he (*Jesus*) commanded us to preach unto the people, and to testify that it is he which was ordained of God to be the Judge of quick and dead. 43 To him give all the prophets witness, that through his name whosoever believeth in him shall receive remission (*purging, removal, obliteration, putting away*) of sins."

When we are born again and our sins are purged in Jesus, that is also the wrath of God, and they are forever destroyed. This is included in what Jesus came to do, that had not been done before. Acts 13:34 "And as concerning that he raised him up from the dead, now no more to return to corruption, he said on this wise, I will give you the sure mercies of David. 35 Wherefore he saith also in another psalm, Thou shalt not suffer thine Holy One to see corruption. 36 For David, after he had served his own generation by the will of God, fell on sleep, and was laid unto his fathers, and saw corruption: 37 but he, whom God raised again, saw no corruption. 38 Be it known unto you therefore, men and brethren, that through this man is preached unto you the *aphesis*/forgiveness (*purging, removal, obliteration, putting away*) of sins: 39 and by him all that believe are justified from all things, from which ye could not be justified by the law of Moses."

In Rev 21 and 22 we see God come to Earth after the wrath destroys all the works of the devil. This Day of Judgment against the devil started with Jesus. This is seen when Jesus cast out a devil who thought it was not yet the time. Matt 8:28 "And when he (*Jesus*) was come to the other side into the country of the Gergesenes, there met him two possessed with devils, coming out of the tombs, exceeding fierce, so that no man might pass by that way. 29 And, behold, they cried out, saying, What have we to do with thee, Jesus, thou Son of God? art thou come hither to torment us before the time?"

The day of Judgment against the devil with the wrath of God, the finger of God, Holy Spirit, started 2000 years ago and ends in Rev 21 and 22. The wrath of God against the devil is the Kingdom or reign of God removing the reign and effects of the devil. Acts 10:38 "How God anointed Jesus of Nazareth with the Holy Ghost and with power: who went about doing good, and healing all that were oppressed (*under the lordship, rule or reign*) of the devil; for God was with him." Matt 12:28 "But if I cast out devils by the Spirit of God, then the kingdom of God is come unto you." See also Luke 11:20

In this Day of Salvation we are to major on the Grace of Reconciliation in Redemption and do what Jesus commanded. 2 Cor 5:20 "Now then we are ambassadors for Christ, as though God did beseech you by us: we pray you in Christ's stead, be ye reconciled to God. 21 For he (*Father God*) hath made him (*Jesus*) to be sin for us, who knew no sin; that we might be made the righteousness of God in him (*Jesus*). 6:1 We then, as workers together with him, beseech you also that ye receive not the grace of God in vain. 2 (For he saith, I have heard thee in a time accepted, and in the day of *soteria*/salvation have I succoured thee: behold, now is the accepted time; behold, now is the day of *soteria*/salvation.)"

This is the Day in which we, the Body of Christ, are to exercise the Wrath of God on the works of the devil and set people free into the truth of God. Luke 10:9 "And heal the sick that are therein, and say unto them, The kingdom of God is come nigh unto you." This is part of the "all things" in Matt 28:20 "Teaching them to observe all things whatsoever I have commanded you ...."

Therefore disciples are to train all others to do the same as Jesus commanded in delivering the wrath of God against the devil and his works. Luke 10:19 "Behold (*perceive and make this change your life*), I give unto you *exousia*/power (*responsibility, commission and the resources of Heaven*) to tread on (*crush, bruise, destroy, remove, heal*) serpents and scorpions, and over all the *dunamis*/power (*ability, works*) of the enemy: and nothing shall by any means hurt you."

And you can rest assured, that if you are not delivering the Wrath of God against the devil, the devil is putting his wrath on you. 1 Pet 5:8 "Be sober (*no longer drunk and apathetic in the ways of the world*), be vigilant; because your adversary the devil, as a roaring lion, walketh about, seeking whom he may devour: 9 whom resist (*fight, deliver the wrath of God onto*) stedfast in the faith, knowing that the same afflictions are accomplished in your brethren that are in the world." See also Ephesians 6.

1 Cor 2:4 "And my speech and my preaching was not with enticing words of man's wisdom, but in demonstration of the Spirit and of *dunamis*/power: 5 that your faith should not stand in the wisdom of men, but in the *dunamis*/power of God."

Facing Off Against the Devil: The pattern seen throughout the Bible is that when men sin, the devil is released to perform great evil and misery on men, by the law of sin and death. This law says: you sin, you die. So we get attacks from the devil when we sin. Rom 5:12 "Wherefore, as by one man sin entered into the world, and death by sin; and so death passed upon all men, for that all have sinned." Rom 5:21 "That as sin hath reigned (*as king*) unto death, even so might grace reign (*to deliver God's salvation to the Earth*) through righteousness unto eternal *zoe*/life by Jesus Christ our Lord." Rom 8:2 "For the law of the Spirit of *zoe*/life in Christ Jesus hath made me free from the law of sin and death." 1 Cor 15:56 "The sting of death is sin; and the strength of sin is the law." James 1:15 "Then when lust hath conceived, it bringeth forth sin: and sin, when it is finished, bringeth forth death." Rom 6:23 "For the wages of sin is death; but the gift of God is eternal *zoe*/life through Jesus Christ our Lord."

APPENDICES

So, when we sin, that demon is death coming to work death in our lives. We are sowing to the flesh in evil seeds, and we will reap corruption of the flesh as that evil seed matures.

Since the devil is the enforcer of death, he tempts us to sin so he can enforce the law of sin and death upon us.

Another attack comes when the devil, looking for whomever he can attack, chooses to attack you, whether you have sinned or not. 1 Pet 5:8 "Be sober, be vigilant; because your adversary the devil, as a roaring lion, walketh about, seeking whom he may devour."

So the devil can inflict his wrath, the destruction of anything that looks like God, when we sin and when we do not sin, as long as he is free in this world. So a fuller definition of the law of sin and death is that when you sin death comes in either a fast or slow form, and if you do not sin, because the devil is in the world, he will try to inflict the law of sin and death on you anyway. The less you know about the work of Jesus by the cross, the less you can resist the devil in either kind of attack or oppression.

Most every action we do is designed to bring us good, as we define it at the moment. Even a person committing suicide thinks they are better off dead than alive. Men in combat can be brave and resist the fear, based on a greater good they see at the moment. So almost every action we commit is driven by our perception of what is good right then.

Our minds can be filled with dread, fear of loss or unpleasantness, and what we do now, we think, will make that loss or unpleasantness lessen or go away. If you know the Scriptures, then, at that moment, the Scriptures may seem far away and the pressing need of the moment more important and urgent to act upon.

Remember, when you sin you are either sinning in ignorance or willfully. In either case, you have faith that the sin you commit will get you the good you want in life. So, to sin is to have faith in a lie that activates the law of sin and death, and you must deal with the consequences.

When you do righteous works, per the Word of God, if you have faith in God, you will expect to get:

a) The perceived good and any natural law good (giving alms to the poor helps the poor, and they may thank you = natural good) and

b) Good from God (for you are then operating in faith in God by His Word).

Most actions are:

a) Immediate based on what is already in your heart, so you are almost unaware you did them, or

b) Planned (at least to some level).

In both cases, you are subject to what truth (God's Word) already exists in your heart or what word you are in agreement enough with to do. Ps 119:10 "With my whole heart have I sought thee: O let me not wander from thy commandments. 11

Thy word have I hid in mine heart, that I might not sin against thee. 12 Blessed art thou, O Lord: teach me thy statutes. 13 With my lips have I declared all the judgments of thy mouth."

The point of this is that when you sin you are in faith, but your faith is placed in a lie that will produce death, whether you like it or not. Like Adam and Eve, you are choosing the word of the devil over the Word of God. Or, by your culture and ignorance of the Bible, you are doing what seems right to you, but is, in reality, against the laws of God. Murder is murder, whether you or your culture consider it to be murder or not.

In all cases, the Universe is so designed by God that: Gal 6:7 "Be not deceived; God is not mocked: for whatsoever a man soweth, that shall he also reap. 8 For he that soweth to his flesh shall of the flesh reap corruption; but he that soweth to the Spirit shall of the Spirit reap *zoe*/life everlasting. 9 And let us not be weary in well doing: for in due season we shall reap, if we faint not. 10 As we have therefore opportunity, let us do good unto all men, especially unto them who are of the household of faith."

One possible focus of life is the fact that God is good. He is the source of grace to be and act like Him, so He can bless, and His Word is truth that never changes, in spite of the many conflicting situations and messages of the devil. Ps 100:4 "Enter into his gates with thanksgiving, and into his courts with praise: be thankful unto him, and bless his name. 5 For the Lord is good; his *chesed*/mercy is everlasting; and his truth endureth to all generations."

If you are not in faith in God, by His Word, you are in sin, and that is the devil's territory. Jesus came to destroy the works of the devil. 1 John 3:7 "Little children, let no man deceive you: he that doeth righteousness is righteous, even as he (*Jesus*) is righteous. 8 He that committeth sin is of the devil; for the devil sinneth from the beginning. For this purpose the Son of God was manifested, that he might destroy the works of the devil." This means the wrath of God in raising Jesus from the dead was "destroying" the devil, as was every healing Jesus performed.

In Exodus 4, God gave Moses two signs to convince people he was from God. The first was to put his hand under his robe, and when he removed it, it had become leprous. Then he put it back again, and when he had removed it, it was clean. God does not have leprosy in Heaven, but the devil does have it in Hell. When Moses first put his hand in and removed it, this looked like a work of the devil. When Moses put it in the second time and it came out healed, that was Holy Spirit gladly healing him and destroying that apparent work of the devil.

So we see numerous times in the Bible where a plague came (God sent, or could not stop, it by His laws), and then God was able to heal the people. But God is not confused. Just as with Job, for whatever reason the devil was involved and produced death in some form, and then God was able to heal Job by someone's right action.

APPENDICES

Notice, in the case of John 9, the man born blind at birth, that neither the parents nor the man had sinned. This was either an attack of the devil or an accident in this world of sin. What is clear is that God did not make the man blind, else Jesus would not have healed him. Where would God get blindness in Heaven? In either case, here is what Jesus said: John 9:3 "Jesus answered, Neither hath this man sinned, nor his parents: **but that the works of God should be made manifest in him. 4 I must work the works of him that sent me,** while it is day: the night cometh, when no man can work. 5 As long as I am in the world, I am the light of the world *in showing what God is really like."*

Like every other healing, this was a judgment of the wrath of God on the devil's work, by a man knowing it was God's will to always heal. Ps 103:3 "Who forgiveth all thine iniquities; who healeth all thy diseases."

Acts 10:36 "The word which God sent unto the children of Israel, preaching peace by Jesus Christ: (he is Lord of all:) 37 that word, I say, ye know, which was published throughout all Judaea, and began from Galilee, after the baptism which John preached; 38 how God anointed Jesus of Nazareth with the Holy Ghost and with power: who went about doing good, and healing all that were oppressed (*under the active lordship and control in some way*) of the devil; for God was with him."

Luke 13:11 "And, behold, there was a woman which had a spirit of infirmity eighteen years, and was bowed together, and could in no wise lift up herself. 12 And when Jesus saw her, he called her to him, and said unto her, Woman, thou art loosed from thine infirmity. 13 And he laid his hands on her: and immediately she was made straight, and glorified God. 14 And the ruler of the synagogue answered with indignation, because that Jesus had healed on the sabbath day, and said unto the people, There are six days in which men ought to work: in them therefore come and be healed, and not on the sabbath day. 15 The Lord then answered him, and said, Thou hypocrite, doth not each one of you on the sabbath loose his ox or his ass from the stall, and lead him away to watering? 16 And ought not this woman, being a daughter of Abraham, whom Satan hath bound, lo, these eighteen years, be loosed from this bond on the sabbath day?"

We understand that the power of God is His *zoe* life. That life is the wrath of God against the devil and his works. We have this *zoe* life because Jesus took all the death due us.

Per Isaiah 53, Jesus took the full wrath of God for us in one action forever. Heb 10:12 "But this man, after he had offered **one sacrifice for sins for ever**, sat down on the right hand of God; 13 from henceforth expecting till his enemies be made his footstool."

Rom 3:24 "Being justified freely by his grace through the redemption that is in Christ Jesus: 25 whom God hath set forth to be a propitiation through faith in his blood, to declare his righteousness for the remission of sins that are past, through the forbearance of God; 26 to declare, I say, at this time his righteousness: that he might be just, and the justifier of him which believeth in Jesus." See also Rom 4:25.

Rom 8:2 "For the law of the Spirit of *zoe*/life in Christ Jesus hath made me free from the law of sin and (*the curse of sin,*) death."

So, before God, there are now no legal attacks from the devil, whether we sin or not. What is missing is our enforcing the law of the spirit of *zoe*/life in Christ Jesus on the works of the devil, as Jesus did.

Luke 10:19 "Behold, I give unto you power (*authority, commission and the resources of Heaven*) to tread on serpents and scorpions, and over all the power (*ability*) of the enemy: and nothing shall by any means hurt you."

Don't blame God for our failure to obey this command and to enforce this responsibility from Jesus. Hear God's answer to Moses, who was "lost in prayer." Moses had prayed the prayer part, so that was done; now God needed faith action, the "go-do part."

Ex 14:13 "And Moses said unto the people, Fear ye not, stand still, and see the salvation of the Lord, which he will shew to you to day: for the Egyptians whom ye have seen to day, ye shall see them again no more for ever. 14 The Lord shall fight for you, and ye shall hold your peace."

This was a great proclamation and prayer and vitally necessary, but God said there was more to do, exercise His Word in command.

Ex 14:15 "And the Lord said unto Moses, Wherefore criest thou unto me? speak unto the children of Israel, that they go forward: 16 but lift thou up thy rod, and stretch out thine hand over the sea, and divide it: and the children of Israel shall go on dry ground through the midst of the sea."

Jesus is the exact way God is, in all a man can be. Heb 1:3 "Who being the brightness of his glory, and the express image of his person, and upholding all things by the word of his power, when he had by himself purged our sins, sat down on the right hand of the Majesty on high."

Col 1:14 "In whom we have redemption through his blood, even the forgiveness of sins: 15 who is the image of the invisible God, the firstborn of every creature." In the Gospels, God, through the life of Jesus, is showing His true nature operating in a man. Every act of healing Jesus did was a judgment of God against the devil for enforcing or implementing the law of sin and death.

Acts 10:34 "Then Peter opened his mouth, and said, Of a truth I perceive that God is no respecter of persons: 35 but in every nation he that feareth him, and worketh righteousness, is accepted with him. 36 The word which God sent unto the children of Israel, preaching peace by Jesus Christ: (he is Lord of all:) 37 that word, I say, ye know, which was published throughout all Judaea, and began from Galilee, after the baptism which John preached; 38 how God anointed Jesus of Nazareth with the Holy Ghost and with power: who went about doing good, and healing all that were oppressed (*under the active dominion, reign or lordship*) of the devil; for God was with him."

Father God used Jesus to destroy the works of the devil. Healing in the name of Jesus is a right act. Destroying sickness, death and disease, in the power and name of Jesus, is the wrath of God against the devil.

When Adam sinned, he released sin and death into the world. Rom 5:14 "Nevertheless death reigned (*as king*) from Adam to Moses, even over them that had not sinned after the similitude of Adam's transgression, who is the figure of him that was to come." Notice, the Law of Moses stopped the free reign of the devil and gave men a way to get *zoe*/life, to counter the law of sin and death until Jesus came.

Acts 13:37 "But he, whom God raised again, saw no corruption. 38 Be it known unto you therefore, men and brethren, that through this man is preached unto you the *aphesis*/forgiveness (*remission, purging, washing, removal, obliteration and putting away*) of sins: 39 and by him all that believe are justified from all things, from which ye could not be justified by the law of Moses."

John 10:10 "The thief cometh not, but for to steal, and to kill, and to destroy: I am come that they might have *zoe*/life, and that they might have it more abundantly."

Rom 5:21 "That as sin hath reigned (*as king, inflicting the curse in fast and slow forms*) unto death, even so might grace reign (*as a conquering king, delivering the salvation of God*) through righteousness unto eternal *zoe*/life by Jesus Christ our Lord."

The devils Jesus cast out thought the Day of God's Judgment against them was far away. Jesus demonstrated that it started with His ministry, as the Day of Salvation, which we are now in.

Matt 8:29 "And, behold, they cried out, saying, What have we to do with thee, Jesus, thou Son of God? art thou come hither to torment (*judge against*) us before the time? 30 And there was a good way off from them an herd of many swine feeding. 31 So the devils besought him, saying, If thou cast us out, suffer us to go away into the herd of swine. 32 And he said unto them, Go. And when they were come out, they went into the herd of swine: and, behold, the whole herd of swine ran violently down a steep place into the sea, and perished in the waters."

By casting out the devils, Jesus judged against them. The judgment was not complete until they were gone and the situation healed, i.e., the judgment was enforced to the final result intended. Ranting at the devil, "You are judged," does no good; deliverance (casting out the devil by *aiteo*/commands to go in the name of Jesus) and healing enforced by faith in the name of Jesus does.

The word *judgment* means a judicial decree for or against someone. The word in Matt 8:29 translated *torment* means misery as a result of a judicial decree against. Jesus issued a judicial decree against the demons and in favor of or for the man controlled by the demons when Jesus said "Go," in verse 32. So, yes, the devils had the timing wrong, and now is the Day of Salvation, which also starts the Day of Judgment against the devil and his works.

2 Cor 6:1 "We then, as workers together with him, beseech you also that ye receive not the grace of God in vain. 2 (For he saith, I have heard thee in a time accepted, and in the day of *soteria*/salvation have I succoured thee: behold, now is the accepted time; behold, now is the day of *soteria*/salvation.)"

The Day of Salvation means you control whether the heavens are brass or not. God has already spoken; they are open to you in the name of Jesus. That name means "God's Salvation is now and in force." Spoken in faith, He inhabits His name to deliver His salvation.

John 5:27 "And hath given him authority to execute judgment also, because he is the Son of man. 28 Marvel not at this: for the hour is coming, in the which all that are in the graves shall hear his voice, 29 and shall come forth; they that have done good, unto the resurrection of *zoe*/life; and they that have done evil, unto the resurrection of damnation. 30 I can of mine own self do nothing: as I hear, I judge: and my judgment is just; because I seek not mine own will, but the will of the Father which hath sent me."

John 16:8 "And when he is come, he will reprove the world of sin, and of righteousness, and of judgment (*condemnation*): 9 of sin, because they believe not on me; 10 of righteousness, because I go to my Father, and ye see me no more; 11 of judgment, because the prince of this world is judged."

1 John 3:8 "He that committeth sin is of the devil; for the devil sinneth from the beginning. For this purpose the Son of God was manifested, that he might destroy (*execute or deliver or enforce the judgment of God against*) the works of the devil."

The full Day of Judgment will come when God finally cleans the Universe of all of Satan's works. We now, by faith in the power of the blood of Jesus, have salvation from the full wrath of God when He cleans the Universe.

1 Thes 5:8 "But let us, who are of the day, be sober, putting on the breastplate of faith and *agape*/love; and for an helmet, the hope of *soteria*/salvation. 9 For God hath not appointed us to wrath, but to obtain *soteria*/salvation by our Lord Jesus Christ, 10 who died for us, that, whether we wake or sleep, we should *zao*/live together with him."

Rom 5:9 "Much more then, being now justified by his blood, we shall be *sozo*/saved from wrath through him. 10 For if, when we were enemies, we were reconciled to God by the death of his Son, much more, being reconciled, we shall be *sozo*/saved by his *zoe*/life. 11 And not only so, but we also joy in God through our Lord Jesus Christ, by whom we have now received the atonement (*reconciliation*)."

Appendices

Even though we are "saved," to be in eternity with God, in being born-again, we do not have freedom from our works being judged by the wrath of God on that Day. God has decreed: Num 14:21 "But as truly as I live, all the earth shall be filled with the glory of the Lord." The Day of Judgment is the final cleansing to allow this to happen.

Rom 2:5 "But after thy hardness and impenitent heart treasurest up unto thyself wrath against the day of wrath and revelation of the righteous judgment of God; 6 who will render to every man according to his deeds."

1 Cor 3:12 "Now if any (*Christian*) man build upon this foundation gold, silver, precious stones, wood, hay, stubble; 13 every man's work shall be made manifest: for the day shall declare it, because it shall be revealed by fire; and the fire shall try every man's work of what sort it is. 14 If any man's work abide which he hath built thereupon, he shall receive a reward. 15 If any man's work shall be burned, he shall suffer loss: but he himself shall be *sozo*/saved; yet so as by fire."

Rom 2:16 "In the day when God shall judge the secrets of men by Jesus Christ according to my gospel." In that Day, the Wrath of God will finally destroy all the works of the devil. In the meantime we are to use the name of Jesus to destroy the works of the devil as Jesus did in Acts 10:38.

We are commanded to: Rom 8:13 "For if ye *zao*/live after the flesh, ye shall die: but if ye through the Spirit [*the word of the Gospel of Christ*] do mortify (*call or count as dead in Christ by the Word of God*) the deeds of the body, ye shall *zao*/live."

This is similar to these commands: Rom 6:11 "Likewise reckon ye also yourselves to be dead indeed unto sin, but [*reckon yourselves*] *zao*/alive unto God through Jesus Christ our Lord."

As you become what you look at, do not spend as much time looking at the evil of your sins as the greatness of our salvation in Jesus. 2 Cor 3:17 "Now the Lord is that Spirit: and where the Spirit of the Lord is, there is liberty [*to be all God made you in Jesus*]. 18 But we all, with open face beholding as in a glass (*mirror*) the glory of the Lord [*being manifested in you*], are changed into the same image from glory to glory, even as by the Spirit of the Lord."

Eph 4:20 "But ye have not so learned Christ; 21 if so be that ye have heard him, and have been taught by him, as the truth is in Jesus: 22 that ye put off [*in your self-image and actions*] concerning the former conversation the old man, which is corrupt according to the deceitful lusts; 23 and be renewed in the spirit of your mind [*in your self-identity, image and actions*]; 24 and that ye put on the new man, which after God is created in righteousness and true holiness [*so you think, desire, speak and do as Jesus would*]."

Burn-It-Now Process: Notice on the Day of Judgment is the all-consuming fire of God, wrath/judgment, for any work of the devil in anyone's life that is not already destroyed by this 10-step renewing process, based on Isa 53, 1 Pet 2:24, Matt 26:26-28, Rom 6:1-13, Rom 13:11-14, Eph 4:20-32, Eph 6:10-20 and Col 3:5-10:

BATTLE PRAYER FOR DIVINE HEALING: FIELD MANUAL 2

1. Confessing (agreeing with what Holy Spirit calls sin)
2. Agreeing Jesus died for it and you are forgiven by His blood in the New Covenant 2000 years ago, and, therefore, thanking Him and Father God for sending Jesus
3. Judging that sin and its consequence was put on Jesus' body and remitted, forgiven by His blood, and healed by His stripes and when He was raised from the dead
4. Casting out the devil in the situation or yourself
5. Making any necessary restitution or reconciliation
6. Putting on your mental self, the new man, made after the image of God in true righteousness and true holiness–the real, born-again, new-creation, you
7. Receiving/enforcing any healing needed in Jesus' name
8. Finding specific areas to stop sinning in, confessing that is not your real nature in Jesus and seeing yourself no longer doing that same sin, but, rather, acting like Jesus would
9. Thanking Father God that He is changing you into being more like Jesus every day (obey Phil 4:6-7 when you struggle with this)
10. Going and helping others get free in the same way. You must go and do acts of *agape*/love because that is what Jesus would do and you have "put on Jesus Christ," and should now act like Him.

This is keeping short accounts with God. A contrite heart knows the judgment is there and sure. The only acceptable way to be sorry for your sin is to acknowledge that the Mighty Arm of God, Jesus, bore it for you already, suffered intensely for it, paid for it already and was healed of it already, so that you thank Him for the healing and then expect to receive that healing, to walk more like Him.

Keeping your eye on that Day, while, at the same time, knowing your sins are forgiven is a key to Christian growth: 2 Pet 1:8 "For if these things [*of God's divine nature manifested in abundance in your life*] be in you, and abound, they make you that ye shall neither be barren nor unfruitful in the *epignosis*/knowledge of our Lord Jesus Christ. 9 But he that lacketh these things [*of God's divine nature manifested in abundance in your life*] is blind, and cannot see afar off, and hath forgotten that he was purged from his old sins."

The sins of the human race, the race of Adam, are fully purged in the Record Hall of the Supreme Court of Creation. The blood of Jesus is more than sufficient.

To keep this in continual biblical remembrance is the key.

Thus, Paul cried for the mature Christian:

Phil 3:7 "But what things were gain to me, those I counted loss for Christ. 8 Yea doubtless, and I count all things but loss for the excellency of the knowledge of Christ Jesus my Lord: for whom I have suffered the loss of all things, and do count them but dung, that I may win Christ, 9 and be found in him, not having mine own righteousness, which is of the law, but that which is through the faith of Christ, the righteousness which is of God by faith: 10 that I may know him, and the power of his resurrection, and the fellowship of his sufferings, being made conformable unto his death."

God's answer for you committing sin and for you having sin-consciousness is to change your self-identity and to use every opportunity when you sin or you find sin ruling in others to proclaim His great Redemption in Jesus. So you can apply the 10-step process to yourself or, in faith, apply and pray for that process in others in the ministry of reconciliation.

Rom 13:10 "*Agape*/love worketh no ill to his neighbour: therefore *agape*/love is the fulfilling of the law. 11 And that, knowing the time, that now is high time to awake out of sleep: for now is our *soteria*/salvation nearer than when we believed. 12 The night is far spent, the day is at hand: let us therefore cast off the works of darkness, and let us put on the armour of light. 13 Let us walk honestly, as in the day; not in rioting and drunkenness, not in chambering and wantonness, not in strife and envying. 14 But put ye on the Lord Jesus Christ (*as your new-creation self-identity, the new man, made in righteousness and true holiness*), and make not provision for the flesh, to fulfil the lusts thereof."

Phil 2:5 "Let this mind be in you, which was also in Christ Jesus: 6 who, being in the form of God, thought it not robbery to be equal with God: 7 but made himself of no reputation [*against the pull of the world system and the praise of men*], and took upon him the form of a servant, and was made in the likeness of men: 8 and being found in fashion as a man, he humbled himself, and became obedient unto death, even the death of the cross."

Col 3:8 "But now ye also put off all these; anger, wrath, malice, blasphemy, filthy communication out of your mouth. 9 Lie not one to another, seeing that ye have put off the old man with his deeds; 10 and have put on the new man, which is renewed in *epignosis*/knowledge (*learning, doing as a master craftsmen and teaching others to walk as master craftsmen*) after the image of him (*God*) that created him: 11 where there is neither Greek nor Jew, circumcision nor uncircumcision, Barbarian, Scythian, bond nor free: but Christ is all, and in all. 12 Put on therefore, as the elect of God, holy and *agape*/beloved, bowels (*attitudes, self-image, self-identity to doing like Jesus*) of mercies, kindness, humbleness of mind, meekness, longsuffering; 13 forbearing one another, and forgiving one another, if any man have a quarrel against any: even as Christ forgave you, so also do ye. 14 And above all these things put on *agape*/charity, which is the bond of perfectness."

Zao/Zoe

Zao (*Strong's* NT 2198, pronounced: dzah'-o) is the verb form, live; *zoe* (*Strong's* NT 2222, pronounced: dzo-ah') is the noun, life. In the Bible it generally means the life, power, enthusiasm, and attitude that only comes from the true *zao*/living God. Bringing *zoe* to men was the primary propose of Jesus and the proof that He was from God. All the actions of Jesus in demonstrating the *zoe*/life of God in a man in miracles, dying on the cross, the resurrection from the dead and sending Holy Spirit were so that we could be justified unto *zoe*/life, to provide a dwelling place for Holy Spirit within our spirits. This is so we can do our part in finishing the job of destroying the works of the devil. John 10:10 "The thief cometh not, but for to steal, and to kill, and to destroy: I am come that they might have *zoe*/life, and that they might have it more abundantly." 1 John 5:9 "If we receive the witness of men, the witness of God is greater: for this is the witness of God which he hath testified of his Son. 10 He that believeth on the Son of God hath the witness in himself: he that believeth not God hath made him a liar; because he believeth not the record that God gave of his Son. 11 And this is the record, that God hath given to us eternal *zoe*/life, and this *zoe*/life is in his Son. 12 He that hath the Son hath *zoe*/life; and he that hath not the Son of God hath not *zoe*/life." This is clear and precise: we need the *zoe* of God, and God paid the price of Jesus to get this *zoe* to us. This *zoe*/life in our spirit, with Holy Spirit's indwelling, is a main mark of what it is to be a Bible Christian.

God's answer for defeating every work of the devil and operating in the abundance of God's blessing is the *zoe*/life of God. Per John 10:10, we see the opposite of anything that steals, kills or destroys is the *zoe* of God. Jesus bears the title of the Prince of Zoe/Life: Acts 3:15 "And killed the Prince of *zoe*/life, whom God hath raised from the dead; whereof we are witnesses." Rom 8:2 "For the law of the Spirit of *zoe*/life in Christ Jesus hath made me free from the law of sin and death." Thus we see that every work of the devil, in death in any form, is overcome and destroyed by the *zoe*/life of God.

In the Greek understanding, a human operated in the *zoe* of a god or spirit when they thought and/or acted like that god or spirit. A Greek warrior wanted to operate in the full *zoe* of Ares, the god of war, to prosper in battle and vanquish his enemies. To do this, a warrior would fill his mind with thoughts and attitudes of war and train with weapons and physical exercise, to make himself excel in war. While not addressing a specific "god," we see similar actions and effects in a team locker room, where the coach inspires the team to get in agreement so the "in-spirit-dwells," to inspire or "pump up" the team/players before the game or at half time; or in a motivational speaker to any group. They are now filled with that spirit, inspired, thinking alike and excited, to gird up their minds for courage, strength, endurance and pain, to overcome and win. In fact, the word *enthusiasm* means "one with god," or to be in *zoe*.

This is the same concept for operating in the *zoe* of God. Holy Spirit is within us. Per Eph 4:17-18, it is how we think and then act that releases Him/*zoe* from our new-creation spirit into the world to do good. To sin is to operate in the devil's death/ darkness (i.e., the devil's anti-*zoe*). 1 John 3:8 "He that committeth sin is of the devil; for the devil sinneth from the beginning. For this purpose the Son of God was manifested, that he might destroy the works of the devil. ... 10 In this the children of God are manifest, and the children of the devil: whosoever doeth not righteousness is not of God [*in his word and actions*], neither he that *agape*/loveth not his brother." Rom 6:21 "What fruit had ye then in those things whereof ye are now ashamed? for the end of those things is death. 22 But now being made free from sin, and become servants to God, ye have your fruit unto holiness, and the end everlasting *zoe*/life. 23 For the wages of sin is death; but the gift of God is eternal *zoe*/life through Jesus Christ our Lord."

And, for our own motivation into the *zoe*/life of God: Eph 5:18 "And be not drunk with wine, wherein is excess; but be (*continually being*) filled with the Spirit; 19 speaking to yourselves in psalms and hymns and spiritual songs, singing and making melody in your heart to the Lord; 20 giving thanks always for all things unto God and the Father in the name of our Lord Jesus Christ; 21 submitting yourselves one to another in the fear of God." Col 3:14 "And above all these things put on *agape*/charity, which is the bond of perfectness. 15 And let the peace of God rule in your hearts, to the which also ye are called in one body; and be ye thankful. 16 Let the word of Christ dwell in you richly in all wisdom; teaching and admonishing one another in psalms and hymns and spiritual songs, singing with grace in your hearts to the Lord. 17 And whatsoever ye do in word or deed, do all in the name of the Lord Jesus, giving thanks to God and the Father by him." Notice that right speaking and singing are ways to keep us operating in and releasing God's *zoe*.

A similar Old Testament word (*sharat*, OT 8334) translated as both worship and serve carries the concept that in all of God-life, we breathe and move in Him, thus, echoing the Greek word *zoe*. Thus, every part of life is an act of worship to God or some other god. There is no action of a human that does not have a spiritual source of one kind or the other. There are only two choices, God or the devil. Doing business deals, planting seed, cooking dinner or raising children are all to be done in total unity with the true and *zao*/living God. So when we sin we are actually serving, worshiping or "in-breathing" sin. 1 John 3:8 "He that committeth sin is of the devil; for the devil sinneth from the beginning. For this purpose the Son of God was manifested, that he might destroy the works of the devil." This job of destroying the works of the devil is complete on the Day of Judgment thus destroying all that is not by or in the *zoe* of God.

To minister healing in the *zoe* of God includes "breathing in" the attitude of God's promises against the devil and his works and, for those who need the blessing, knowing: John 16:11 "... the ruler (evil genius, prince) of this world [Satan] is judged and condemned and sentence already is passed upon him." AMP Luke 10:19 "Behold (*get into the* zao *of God and make this change the way you view and operate in this life*), I give unto you power (*authority, commission and the resources of Heaven*) to tread on (*bruise, crush*) serpents and scorpions, and over all the power (*ability*) of the enemy: and nothing shall by any means hurt you."

So we are to be continually Col 1:12 "giving thanks (*continually*) unto the Father, which hath made us meet (*qualified and enabled by grace*) to be partakers of the inheritance of the saints in light: 13 who hath delivered us from the power of darkness, and hath translated us into the kingdom of his *agape*/dear Son: 14 in whom we have redemption through his blood, even the forgiveness (*remission, purging, putting away and obliteration*) of sins." Rev 1:5 "... Jesus Christ, who is the faithful witness, and the first begotten of the dead, and the prince of the kings of the earth. Unto him that *agape*/loved us, and washed us from our sins in his own blood, 6 and hath made us kings and priests unto God and his Father; to him be glory and dominion for ever and ever. Amen. ... 17 ... And he (*Jesus*) ... (*says to us*), Fear not; I am the first and the last: 18 I am he that *zao*/liveth, and was dead; and, behold, I am *zao*/alive for evermore, Amen; and have the keys of hell and of death." Rom 16:20 "And the God of peace shall bruise (*crush, tread*) Satan under your feet shortly (*as shattered glass*). The grace of our Lord Jesus Christ be with you [*to know, be and do this*]. Amen." Ps 103:6 "The LORD executeth righteousness and judgment for all that are oppressed [*giving deliverance through us*]." 1 Tim 6:12 "*So* fight the good fight of faith, lay hold on eternal *zoe*/life, whereunto thou art also called ... ." Eph 6:10 "... be strong in the Lord, and in the power of his might," preaching His Word of grace, for Mark 16:20 "... the Lord *is* working with *you*, and confirming the word with signs following. Amen."

So to *zao* this means to take these Bible truths and operate, like Jesus did, in the *zoe* of God. Phil 2:4 "Look not every man on his own things, but every man also on the things of others. 5 Let this mind be in you, which was also in Christ Jesus: ... 12 Wherefore, my *agape*/beloved, as ye have always obeyed, not as in my presence only, but now much more in my absence, work out your own *soteria*/salvation with fear and trembling. 13 For it is God which worketh in you both to will and to do of his good pleasure. 14 Do all things without murmurings and disputings: 15 that ye may be blameless and harmless, the sons of God, without rebuke, in the midst of a crooked and perverse nation, among whom ye shine as lights in the world; 16 holding forth the word of *zoe*/life; that I may rejoice in the day of Christ, that I have not run in vain, neither laboured in vain."

Or, as in another direct command to the Christian: 1 Tim 6:11 "But thou, O man of God, flee these things; and follow after righteousness, godliness, faith, *agape*/love, patience, meekness. 12 Fight the good fight of faith, *lambano*/lay hold on eternal *zoe*/life, whereunto thou art also called, and hast professed a good profession before many witnesses."

So, yes, while we are saved by grace, we are required to labor to get our minds to operate in the *zoe* of God, so God can be released into the Earth.

BIBLIOGRAPHY

1. Blake, Curry. Compiler and editor, *John G. Lake's Writings from Africa*, (Xulon Press, 2005)
   "Pray and pray and pray …yourself into unbelief," p 99
2. Blake, Curry. *The Official Teaching of the John G. Lake Healing Rooms*, (JGLM Publishing, Edgewater, CO 80214, Jan 2006)
   "The only hindrance to healing is that Christians believe there are hindrances to healing" p 10, VOH, Episode 1 and 2.
   "Anything between the promise of God and its fulfillment is an enemy for you to grasp, to beat and to defeat." p 204, Episode 2.
3. Blake, Curry. *The Voice of Healing* (KWHB Television Broadcast, Episodes 1 and 2, Tulsa OK, March 2007)
   Lake: "It is a law of the human mind that one can act themselves into believing quicker than they can believe themselves into acting." Episode 1 and 2
   Wigglesworth: "If the spirit is not moving, I move the spirit." Episode 2.
4. Hogan, David. Recorded teachings (circa: 2001-2006)
5. Liardon, Roberts. Compiler and editor, *John G. Lake: The Complete Collection of His Life Teachings*, (New Kensington, PA 15068, Whitaker House, 1999)
6. Liardon, Roberts. *God's Generals DVD Series, Vol. 9, Jack Coe*, (Roberts Liardon Ministries, 2005)
7. Simpson, A. B. "The Authority of Faith" (The Christian and Missionary Alliance, *The Alliance Weekly*, New York, New York, Apr. 23, 1938)
8. Vines, W. E., Unger, Merrill F, and White, William Jr., *Vines Complete Expository Dictionary of Old and New Testament Words* (Thomas Nelson, Nashville, Tennessee:1996)
9. Wuest, Kenneth, *The New Testament, An Expanded Translation*, (Grand Rapids, MI, Wm. B. Eerdmans Publishing Company, 1961)
10. Wyatt, Brett. Compiler and editor, *The Fire of God: Pillars of Faith, Book 1, John G. Lake in Spokane*, (Spokane, Washington, Riley Christian Media, 2002)

Ministry Page

You may contact Don Mann in any of the following ways:

Don Mann
3 Crossan Court
Landenberg, PA 19350

www.CovenantPeaceMinistries.com
eMail: Info@CovenantPeaceMinistries.com

Please share your testimonies with us.

Book Website: *www.BattlePrayerForDivineHealing.com*

FREE GIFT WITH YOUR PURCHASE:
Visit our Book Store at www.CovenantPeaceMinistries.com to redeem your gift

FREE NEWSLETTER:
Sign up for our free eNewsletter for tools to help you grow in Christ

Did You Borrow This Book? Want a Copy of Your Own?

Need a Great Gift for a Friend or Loved One?

ORDER LIST

☐ Yes I want to invest $29.99 in my future and have a personal copy of this book (in paperback). For simplicity, go to Amazon.com and find *Battle Prayer for Divine Healing, Field Manual* 2 by Donald C. Mann, or go to the book store at our website, www.CovenantPeaceMinistries.com and use the Amazon.com link there. A hardback version and several eBook versions are also available (Kindle, Nook, iBook and Adobe Digital Editions).

For the following items, please go to our book store at www.CovenantPeaceMinistries.com to complete your order.

☐ Yes, I want the audio books for *Battle Prayer for Divine Healing, Field Manual 2* as read by the author. Unabridged. *
- Vol 1, Healing Teachings and Scriptures
    - _____ 10 CD Set $49.95
    - _____ 1 MP3 $39.95
- Vol 2, Scriptures, Minister Confession, Battle Prayer and Glossary
    - _____ 10 CD Set $49.95
    - _____ 1 MP3 $39.95

☐ Yes, for my regular ministry use, I want a special durable edition of *Battle Prayer for Divine Healing, Field Manual 2* for $75.00. *

* Prices subject to change without notice; please see our website for current pricing.

Book Website: www.BattlePrayerForDivineHealing.com

QUANTITY ORDERS INVITED

For bulk discount prices for all items, please email us at: Info@CovenantPeaceMinistries.com

To request Don to Speak to Your Group, or for more Valuable and Powerful Ministry Tools, please go to www.CovenantPeaceMinistries.com.

Many been helped by our free materials and videos!

For encouragement and understanding, see: Blog.CovenantPeace.com

Get the Entire POWER TRILOGY
www.CovenantPeaceMinistries.com

OK, God, Now What?
Activating His Ancient Secrets for Success

How to renew your mind for more power with God.

This book shows the Bible principles that are changing top sports, sales, business and Christian leaders, and ordinary people to godly success in every part of life.

Gain peace of mind, clarity, purpose, health, wealth and a better life. In just 21, 40 or 90 days you will see dramatic results.

For the new Christian, get started right; for the mature Christian, get revelation, a new fire and peace like you've only dreamed of.

Discovering Our Redemption
How to Be Transformed By the 50 Days that Changed the Universe

Experience the confidence as you know what Jesus did in each step of the critical last 50 days of His ministry 2000 years ago.

Feel your faith rise as you take these historical facts and use them for the foundation for your faith, just like the apostles did.

This book shows what Jesus did from the Last Supper to the Day of Pentecost and how to apply these historical facts to greater growth in God.

Battle Prayer for Divine Healing, Field Manual 2
Releasing God's Healing Power When You Need It

This book is a step-by-step scriptural guide on how to pray so God can heal through you.

Use this book as a spiritual first-aid kit in times of trouble, as a tool for a more effective ministry, and as a study guide so you can grow in Christ and the power of Holy Spirit. For Christians at every level, *Battle Prayer for Divine Healing, Field Manual 2* is for you!

Where are the answers I need?
They are in the *Power Trilogy.*
Get the complete set today and experience the transformation of your life!

- **Faith-building facts** of our Redemption ➔ *Discovering Our Redemption*
- **How to renew your mind** for miracles and blessing in God ➔ *OK, GOD, Now What?*
- **How to release** your faith for healing miracles ➔ *Battle Prayer for Divine Healing-Field Manual 2*

Go to www.CovenantPeaceMinistries.com to get yours today.

FREE BONUS GIFT: please use the contact form at www.CovenantPeaceMinistries.com to request your FREE Top 10 List of Awesome and Powerful Bible Affirmations and Slogans to get you started renewing your mind and increasing your manifestation of God's great love plan and blessings for your life.

There are numerous ways to renew your mind, but the Minister Confessions in *Battle Prayer for Divine Healing: Field Manual 2* are the best and the fastest way for dynamic results. This Top 10 List is the fastest way to get started. And we want you to have it, FREE.

With this BONUS offer you will now have 10 of the most powerful slogan affirmations on the planet to jump-start to a higher level God's best for you.

They are the first Affirmation (A) in *Battle Prayer for Divine Healing: Field Manual 2* broken into 10 bite-sized pieces, and are just a taste of the complete set of 86 full-length Affirmations in *Battle Prayer for Divine Healing: Field Manual 2*.

To keep it handy all day, you can fold this FREE starter set for your purse or wallet.

FREE TELECLASS

Learn How to Build Confidence In God and Break Any Habit

It all started when Donald had to explain how he took a failing company and, with the same people, and in 6 years they produced $500 million in sales.

He not only saved hundreds of jobs, but he saved a whole town from economic ruin.

Donald took what he learned and put the process in *Battle Prayer for Divine Healing: Field Manual 2* so anyone can do the same mind-renewing process over any adversity and reach their best life possible, and that includes divine healing.

In this Teleclass, you will:
- Find out what your favorite Olympic champion and little David fighting Goliath have in common for extraordinary success.
- Find out how to save $1,800 or more per family.
- Find out how to make education go from breaking your back to helping you.
- Learn why all the advice and self-help books in the world have done so little good because of this missing ingredient.
- Learn 5 steps that can break every negative habit and fill your life with word-driven creativity, fearless joy, health and prosperity as God promised.

... All this and more.

You're gonna love it!

See the FREE TELECLASS page at www.CovenantPeaceMinistries.com

IN THE RIGHT HANDS, THIS BOOK WILL CHANGE LIVES!

Most of the people who need this message will not be looking for this book. To change their lives, you need to put a copy of this book in their hands.

Still other seeds fell on fertile soil, and they produced a crop that was thirty, sixty, and even a hundred times as much as had been planted!
Matthew 13:8, NLV

Our ministry is constantly seeking methods to find good ground, the people who need this anointed message to change their lives. Will you help us reach them?

Remember this—a farmer who plants only a few seeds will get a small crop. But the one who plants generously will get a generous crop.
2 Corinthians 9:6, NLV

EXTEND THIS MINISTRY
BY SOWING
3 BOOKS, 5 BOOKS, 10 BOOKS,
OR MORE TODAY
AND BECOME A LIFE CHANGER!

Thanking you in advance,

Harold McDougal, Founder
The Published Word
Since 2004

McDougal & Associates
www.ThePublishedWord.com

Servants of Christ and Stewards of the Mysteries of God
(Your On-Demand Book Publisher and Bookseller)

Visit our newly designed site
www.ThePublishedWord.com

Free Subscription to **M&A Newsletter**
Receive free articles by ThePublishedWord authors, exclusive discounts, and free downloads from our best and newest books

Visit www.ThePublishedWord.com to subscribe

Write to: McDougal & Associates
            18896 Greenwell Springs Road
            Greenwell Springs, LA 70739

Email: orders@thepublishedword.com

For a complete list of our titles or to place an order online, visit www.ThePublishedWord.com

www.ingramcontent.com/pod-product-compliance
Lightning Source LLC
Chambersburg PA
CBHW060502230426
43665CB00013B/1353